1988

Medical and Health Annual

Encyclopædia Britannica, Inc.

CHICAGO

AUCKLAND•GENEVA•LONDON•MANILA•PARIS•ROME•SEOUL•SYDNEY•TOKYO•TORONTO

1988 Medical and Health Annual

Editor	Ellen Bernstein
Senior Editor	Linda Tomchuck
Contributing Editor	Charles Cegielski
Editorial Assistant	Lavonne Nannenga
Medical Editor	Drummond Rennie, M.D. Chairman of Medicine, West Suburban Hospital Medical Center, Oak Park, Ill.; Professor of Medicine, Rush Medical College, Chicago; Senior Contributing Editor, *The Journal of the American Medical Association*
Art Director	Cynthia Peterson
Senior Picture Editor	Holly Harrington
Picture Editor	April A. Oswald
Layout Artist	Dale Horn
Illustrators	Anne H. Becker, John L. Draves, Curtis E. Hardy, Marta Lyall
Art Production	Richard A. Roiniotis
Art Staff	Daniel M. Delgado, Patricia A. Henle, Raul Rios
Director, Yearbook Production and Control	J. Thomas Beatty
Manager, Copy Department	Anita Wolff
Senior Copy Editor	Barbara Whitney
Copy Staff	Ellen Finkelstein, Anthony L. Green, Sally Jaskold, Patrick Joyce, Elizabeth Laskey
Manager, Production Control	Mary C. Srodon
Production Control Staff	Marilyn L. Barton, Timothy A. Phillips
Manager, Composition and Page Makeup	Melvin Stagner
Coordinator	Philip Rehmer
Composition Staff	Duangnetra Debhavalya, Morna Freund, John Krom, Jr., Thomas Mulligan, Gwen Rosenberg, Tammy Tsou
Page Makeup Staff	Michael Born, Jr., Griselda Cháidez, Arnell Reed, Danette Wetterer
Director, Editorial Computer Services	Michael J. Brandhorst
Computer Services Staff	Steven Bosco, Clark Elliott, Rick Frye, Daniel Johnsen, Vincent Star
Manager, Index Department	Frances E. Latham
Assistant Manager	Rosa E. Casas
Senior Index Editor	Carmen Hetrea
Index Staff	Rosaline Keys, Edward Paul Moragne
Librarian	Terry Miller
Associate Librarian	Shantha Uddin
Curator/Geography	David W. Foster
Assistant Librarian	Robert M. Lewis
Secretarial Staff	Dorothy Hagen, Kay Johnson

Editorial Administration

Philip W. Goetz, Editor in Chief
Michael Reed, Managing Editor
Karen M. Barch, Executive Director of Editorial Production
Nathan Taylor, Executive Director of Planning and Technology
Carl Holzman, Director of Budgets and Controller

Encyclopædia Britannica, Inc.
Robert P. Gwinn, Chairman of the Board
Peter B. Norton, President

Foreword

"The art of life is the art of avoiding pain." So said Thomas Jefferson. Human life has always been attended by pain. Over the centuries progress in understanding the nature of pain—what the revered physician Albert Schweitzer called "a more terrible lord of mankind than even death himself"—has proceeded, like most progress in medicine, slowly and haltingly. Perhaps the most significant recognition has been the important distinction between acute and chronic pain. Acute pain is the result of injury or disease and involves tissue damage of some sort. It is resolved when the damage heals. Most pain, however, is chronic. It may or may not involve tissue damage, and it does not resolve. Further, it is complicated by psychological symptoms, and the patient often drifts into a state of invalidism. Chronic pain, then, is a disease in its own right. It is the predicament of chronic pain that is examined in this *Annual*'s special section, "Unlocking the Secrets of Pain." Three Feature articles offer the most recent thinking on the science, the psychology, and the most enlightened approach to the relief of pain.

In 1986 Bellevue Hospital Center in New York City celebrated its 250th anniversary, making it the oldest public hospital in the United States. "The Spirit of Service" looks at this venerable institution's tradition of caring for sick people. A hospital that began as a six-bed almshouse infirmary today treats over 100,000 patients a year and, as always, no one is ever turned away. The tradition of service at Bellevue has included many "firsts." Bellevue had the first U.S. civilian ambulances—horse drawn, of course. It was the first U.S. teaching hospital, had the first trained nurses in the country, and established the first rehabilitation service (in a nonmilitary hospital) for veterans disabled in war. It is a great tribute to Bellevue that the highly respected physician-writer Lewis Thomas has said, "If I were to be taken sick with something serious or struck down on a New York street I would want to be taken there."

James Randi is one of the most unlikely individuals ever selected by the MacArthur Foundation for one of its "genius awards," awards that annually recognize and generously support the work of "outstandingly talented" individuals. Randi, a world famous conjurer (who calls himself a professional charlatan), in recent years has focused his attention on exposing clairvoyants, "psychic surgeons," and certain preachers of the electronic media who claim to be Christian faith healers. In "The Healing Touch: Gift or Gimmick?" Randi describes the sad history of sick and desperate people who succumb to bogus practitioners and support them with huge sums of cash. Randi reveals, as only a magician can, the trickery behind their deceptions. Says Randi, "I have witnessed the heartbreak and the disillusionment suffered by those who are betrayed, . . . and I have wept with those whose loved ones died because they discarded proper medical care—imperfect though it may be—in favor of magic."

Another contemporary enterprise that takes advantage of huge numbers of desperate people and bilks them of their money and their hopes is the billion-dollar weight-loss "industry." "The Business of Thinness" describes how this thriving industry sells virtually any scheme or product—no matter how worthless or dangerous—to a population forever fighting the battle of the bulge.

"Ailing Continent" focuses on the overwhelming medical needs of Africa, the continent that comprises 29 of the world's 36 poorest countries. A horrifying 98% of all deaths of children under the age of four occur in these countries. African life expectancy is the lowest in the world, and death rates there are the highest. Nevertheless, the continent receives only a negligible portion of world spending on health. This dire situation is finally being addressed by the international community. *Only* with the humanitarian help of advantaged nations is there hope that Africa's tragic situation will be rectified.

A special contribution to this volume is the article "Time Out for the Gift of Life" by U.S. Sen. Jake Garn. Garn took time out to write a very personal account of his recent donation of a kidney to his daughter Susan, who has diabetes and whose health had become a matter of grave concern after the birth of her child. In order to aid her, Garn cut short his November 1986 reelection campaign for a third senatorial term. His compelling story describes his own fears and apprehensions but, most importantly, it tells of the great reward that came of his act. "There is simply no other thing I have ever done that has given me greater satisfaction," he reports.

Since the successful operation in September 1986, Susan Garn Horne and her father have made a joint crusade of enlightening other people about the great need for organ donations. The *Annual*'s editors believe Garn's words will inspire others who have the opportunity to be living, related donors. As the senator himself stresses, however, what is needed most is for people to authorize the donation of their vital organs for transplantation after they die—a simple procedure. On Oct. 1, 1987, a federal law became effective that requires U.S. hospitals to offer next of kin the opportunity to donate the organs of relatives who have died. A majority of people probably *would* willingly donate organs if they were asked. There is great hope that the law—and efforts like those of the senator and his daughter—will significantly decrease the nationwide shortage of transplantable organs. Anyone who needs information about organ donation can contact the American Council on Transplantation, P.O. Box 1709, Dept. Britannica, Alexandria, VA 22313, 1-800-228-4483 or 1-800-ACT-GIVE.

The articles cited above are just a few of the Features in the 1988 *Medical and Health Annual,* articles that aim to convey the vitality and challenge in the broad fields of medicine and health. In addition, this yearbook includes a selection of germane reprints: an essay from *Webster's Medical Desk Dictionary,* a new reference volume published in 1986 by Merriam-Webster Inc., and two newly revised articles from the 1987 printing of *Encyclopædia Britannica;* the alphabetically organized World of Medicine, a roundup of newsworthy developments; Special Reports; and instructive articles about such common health-related concerns as contemporary health hazards, physical fitness, medical procedures, drugs, caring for children, specific diseases, and diet and nutrition (the Health Information Update).

The editors have attempted to prepare a volume that is timely, informative, and well illustrated—one that will help readers keep pace with the exciting developments in medicine and health today. We hope we have succeeded.

Ellen Bernstein
—Editor

Contents

WALKING:

Nothing Pedestrian About It

by James M. Rippe, M.D., Ann Ward, Ph.D., and Patty S. Freedson, Ph.D.

In 1909 Edward Payson Weston walked from San Francisco to New York City in 104 days, averaging more than 64 kilometers (40 miles) a day. He was 71 years old at the time. By the time the legendary walker died in 1929, at age 91, the "evening constitutional" was a part of American life.

Then, in the mid-1980s, walking seemed suddenly to burst into public consciousness again as if it were a newly discovered activity. A U.S. national park survey in 1983 estimated that 55 million citizens participated in walking as a form of exercise—more than twice the number of joggers. A 1985 survey conducted by the National Sporting Goods Manufacturing Association indicated that more than eight million people in North America had adopted walking as their major fitness activity in that year, making it the fastest growing participant sport. Certainly to those people who have been walking for health and fitness for many years, the sudden "discovery" of walking as a health-promoting activity must seem slightly ironic.

What is this phenomenon really all about? Is the walking craze merely a fad, the beginning of another "boom," to follow in the wake of the running boom of the late 1960s and 1970s and the aerobic dance boom of the late 1970s and early 1980s? Or does the growing enthusiasm for walking indicate some more fundamental change in society, both in the United States and elsewhere?

In many ways the sudden emergence of interest in walking in the mid-1980s represents the culmination of a number of trends that have been building since the 1940s, coupled with some dramatic events of more recent times. To a large extent walking itself has come to stand for activity, or an active life-style. By the mid-1980s mounting scientific and clinical evidence clearly had begun to support the idea that an active life-style is associated with improved health. Specifically, several important studies linked consistent physical activity with a decrease in the likelihood of developing cardiovascular disease—the number one cause of death in Western countries.

The active life: benefits seen round the world

The idea that physical activity promotes well-being has been espoused by many cultures. The ancient Greek and ancient Roman philosophies emphasized the links between a sound mind and a sound body, and later

James M. Rippe, M.D., is Director of the Exercise Physiology Laboratory and Assistant Professor of Medicine at the University of Massachusetts Medical School, Worcester, and Director of the Rockport Walking Institute, a not-for-profit research institution in Marlboro, Massachusetts.
Ann Ward, Ph.D., is Director of Research in Exercise Physiology and Associate Professor of Medicine at the University of Massachusetts Medical School, Worcester.
Patty S. Freedson, Ph.D., is Assistant Professor, Department of Exercise Science, at the University of Massachusetts at Amherst.

(Opposite page) "Spring: Man and Girl Hiking" by Norman Rockwell; © 1928 The Curtis Publishing Company

6

THE SATURDAY EVENING POST

Volume 200, Number 45

MAY 5, 1928

Fo... ...lin

5c. THE COPY
10c. in Canada

SPRING

Walking for sport and fitness has a long and distinguished history. A celebrated American walker of the 19th century was Edward Payson Weston, whose cross-country journeys drew enthusiastic followers and well-wishers (above). In the six-day race, one of the fiercest competitive events of the time, Weston regularly covered well over 644 kilometers (400 miles). The mental and physical benefits of exercise—and of walking in particular—have been appreciated for centuries, at least as far back as the ancient Greek and Roman civilizations. (Opposite page) In the 1st century BC the Roman statesman and philosopher Cicero (left) wrote, "Exercise and temperance can preserve something of our early strength even in old age." Samuel Johnson ("Dr. Johnson"), the 18th-century English essayist and lexicographer, was well known for his perambulations through the streets of London (center). An ardent proponent of walking in more recent times was U.S. Pres. Harry S. Truman (right), who made an institution of the "evening constitutional," setting a brisk pace for his Secret Service detail and, occasionally, a few breathless reporters.

European physicians and philosophers continued to emphasize the health benefits of exercise.

While the current interest in specific research linking physical activity to improved health may appear to be a relatively new development, it traces its roots to several studies performed in England in the 19th century. One of these, dating from 1864, showed a high mortality rate among sedentary London tailors, while another explored the health of Cambridge and Oxford oarsmen after their rowing careers were over.

However, no study systematically looked at physical activity and the likelihood of disease until 1939, when O. F. Hedley, comparing workingmen in Philadelphia, reported a higher incidence of coronary occlusion (blockage of arteries that supply the heart muscle) in professionals than in manual laborers. A spate of scientific support for the health benefits of regular activity began to appear in the 1950s. An initial study found that London bus drivers, with their sedentary jobs, had a significantly higher incidence of heart attacks than the more physically active conductors, who walked up and down the aisles collecting fares. Similar studies were then done comparing postal clerks with the more active mail-deliverers, railroad workers and longshoremen who engaged in different levels of physical activity, and Israeli kibbutz residents in active versus inactive jobs. While all of these studies were criticized as lacking in certain scientific qualifications—for example, no control groups were used—the seeds of a link between physical activity and improved health were planted, and that link would continue to be a focus of serious research.

Over the past 25 years more than 50 major scientific investigations have examined the association between exercise and health. Populations as diverse as the Masai herdsmen of Africa and Finnish lumberjacks have been examined. The findings have been surprisingly uniform—physical activity that is carried out consistently throughout a lifetime results in improved health. In Western cultures consistent physical activity results specifically in the decreased incidence of heart attack and sudden death—the major

8

manifestations of coronary heart disease (CHD). While most of these studies were conducted at work sites and assessed physical activity on the job, by the late 1970s some investigations of the health effects of leisure-time physical activity had also begun to appear.

Rx for longevity: take the stairs

One study that received considerable public attention was the landmark "Harvard Alumni Study" undertaken by Ralph Paffenbarger, Jr., and colleagues, published in 1986 in the *New England Journal of Medicine*. The investigation focused on the relationship between physical activity and longevity. The test subjects, more than 16,000 graduates of Harvard University who had enrolled in college between 1916 and 1950, were followed medically after graduation and monitored for exercise habits and the development of CHD or sudden death due to heart attack. The study characterized respondents' physical activity according to the number of city blocks walked each week, the number of stairs climbed, or the number of hours

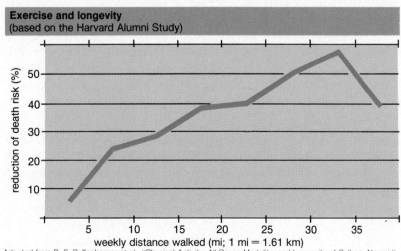

Exercise and longevity
(based on the Harvard Alumni Study)

reduction of death risk (%)

50
40
30
20
10

5   10   15   20   25   30   35

weekly distance walked (mi; 1 mi = 1.61 km)

Adapted from R. S. Paffenbarger *et al.*, "Physical Activity, All-Cause Mortality, and Longevity of College Alumni," *The New England Journal of Medicine*, vol. 314, no. 10 (March 6, 1986), pp. 605–613

"Walking makes for a long life," according to a Hindu proverb. Scientific support for this ancient saying was provided in 1986 when the results of an exhaustive long-term study of Harvard University alumni were published; some 16,000 Harvard graduates were followed medically and their daily exercise patterns monitored. The researchers concluded that physically active people can expect to live longer than their sedentary counterparts. Furthermore, up to a point, the risk of death appears to decrease in proportion to the expenditure of energy.

spent each week in "vigorous" sports play. The investigators found that men who expended between 500 and 3,500 kilocalories a week in physical activity were significantly less likely to suffer a heart attack than were their more sedentary counterparts. (In this study one hour of vigorous activity was defined as equal to 500 kilocalories; actual calories burned may vary considerably owing to differences in body weight and exercise intensity.) Individuals who walked 14.5 kilometers (nine miles) a week experienced a 21% decrease in the likelihood of heart attack compared with those who lived more sedentary lives.

The Paffenbarger study not only confirmed the findings of many earlier investigations of physical fitness but also lent strong support to the increasing number of people walking for health and fitness. Further, and perhaps even more important, this study answered the major question that previous research had not addressed: Does regular physical activity play a role in extending life-span? In other words, will regular exercise add to the quantity of life as well as to the quality? Paffenbarger reported in 1986 that regular physical activity *was* associated with a reduction in death due to cardiovascular and respiratory disease. In fact, by age 80 life-span was increased by one to two years for those who exercised regularly.

Message for the '80s: don't run—walk

By the mid-1980s a number of trends were converging to stimulate an interest in walking as a form of exercise and a health-promoting behavior. Certainly one factor was the aging of the population in most Western countries. Many older joggers found themselves ready to seek less stressful forms of exercise than running. The postwar "baby boomers," in particular, were beginning to enter their forties. Many were familiar with the pleasures of being physically fit, but some had also experienced injuries from higher impact activities such as jogging and racquet sports. To them, walking seemed like a reasonable, safer alternative and an activity that could be pursued with enjoyment for years to come.

Coupled with the aging of the population was an increased sophistication about health and life-style and a tremendous enthusiasm for information about these subjects. As reports from the medical literature filtered into the popular news media, it became increasingly apparent that in order for the most positive health benefits to be exerted, exercise needed to be combined with proper nutrition, reduction of cardiac risk factors, and other positive steps. Once exercise alone was no longer viewed as a panacea, running began to lose some of its popularity. Again, for many people, walking seemed to provide a reasonable alternative.

In the summer and fall of 1984, two events occurred that had major implications for the walking movement. In July author and marathoner Jim Fixx, whom many regarded as the "high priest" of the running movement, collapsed and died while running on a back road in Vermont. He was 52 years old. Fixx's tragic and untimely death underscored something doctors had been saying for many years—that exercise alone would not prevent heart disease. In September peripatetic lecturer and fitness expert Robert Sweetgall set off on a 50-week, 18,000-kilometer (11,200-mile) solo walk

through every state in the United States to carry the message that physical activity, proper nutrition, and avoiding cigarette smoking would improve the health of every American. Sweetgall's walk was covered by virtually every major publication and television station in the country and gave tremendous impetus to the "fitness walking" movement in the United States.

Fit "for life"?

While the Paffenbarger study showed that people who were physically active outlived their sedentary peers, there is still some question—and confusion—about the relationship between intensive physical conditioning and longevity and, in particular, the distinction between short-term training and long-term cardiovascular health. As people became increasingly active in aerobic conditioning sports such as fitness walking or jogging, knowledge of what exercise physiologists call "the training effect" began to spread. Simply stated, the training effect refers to the cluster of physiological changes that occur as the individual's body begins to adapt to the demands of aerobic conditioning. These changes include a lower resting heart rate, lower heart rate at submaximal levels of physical work, lower "perceived exertion" at any level of physical work, and greater maximum work capacity. This last concept is known as an increase in the maximum oxygen consumption or, in shorthand, increased VO_2 max.

In order to achieve these aerobic training benefits, it is necessary to progressively "overload" the cardiovascular system with activities that use the large muscle groups in a repetitive fashion. Sports such as fitness walking, jogging, aerobic dancing, swimming, and cycling are examples of aerobic training activities. The American College of Sports Medicine recommends that in order to achieve cardiovascular training effects, the individual should participate in an aerobic training activity three to five times a week for 20–60 minutes per session at an intensity sufficient to elevate the heart rate to 60–80% of predicted maximum. Since these guidelines have been widely accepted, millions of people have geared their exercise programs to fulfilling these criteria. Aerobic exercise confers a certain degree of physical

Race walking is an athletic event with its own specific rules, form, and strategies. Although the garb of the competitors at the U.S. Olympic trials in 1984 (above right) was slightly different from that of the men who competed in the "Great International Walking Match" of 1879 (above left), their expressions of fierce determination and total concentration were very much the same.

11

conditioning; it makes participants feel better, and it helps many to look better. But does it have any effect on long-term cardiovascular health? Of the large number of epidemiological studies that have linked physical activity to cardiovascular health, only a handful have correlated the level of conditioning with the likelihood of developing heart disease. And even in these few studies, the findings have been inconsistent and inconclusive.

The key finding that *has* emerged is that lifelong consistent exercise is important if the individual's goal is improved cardiovascular health. This is not to say that short-term training is unimportant. Improved cardiovascular conditioning gives the individual a feeling of greater vigor and improves the quality of life. Vigorous training also helps in maintaining proper body weight. Its long-term effects, however, remain a subject of speculation. Some scientists maintain that as further studies are conducted, links between the level of conditioning and cardiovascular health will become apparent. This remains to be seen.

What exercise can and cannot do

Another important concept to emerge from medical and scientific studies in the past 25 years is that exercise alone is only one part of an overall program for improving cardiovascular health and reducing the likelihood of heart disease. Numerous studies sponsored by such organizations as the U.S. National Institutes of Health and the American Heart Association have established that a number of predisposing, or "risk," factors are related to the likelihood that an individual will develop CHD.

Perhaps the most famous of these long-term epidemiological investigations of CHD is the Framingham Study. In this study more than 5,000 residents of the city of Framingham, Massachusetts, have been followed medically for over 25 years to determine whether certain factors are more important than others in assessing an individual's risk of developing coronary artery disease. As a result of the Framingham Study and other similar investigations, medical scientists have identified cigarette smoking, elevated cholesterol levels, and high blood pressure as major risk factors for CHD. Minor risk factors include obesity, family history of coronary artery disease, sedentary life-style, diabetes, and stress.

While a consistent exercise program deals directly only with the risk factor of a sedentary life-style, it may also exert an important impact on other

"Calvin and Hobbes" © 1986 Universal Press Syndicate; reprinted with permission; all rights reserved

When bus and subway workers went on strike in New York City in 1980, leaving some three million people without transportation, commuters rediscovered their feet. Today it is not at all uncommon to see sophisticated urbanites going to and from work on foot, fashionably garbed, sensibly shod.

factors. For example, studies have shown that individuals who exercise regularly are less likely to be obese, less likely to smoke cigarettes, and more likely to follow a low-cholesterol diet than are their sedentary counterparts. The major implication of the current understanding of risk factors, then, is that exercise, in order to be effective, must be accompanied by other good habits. These include avoiding smoking, keeping the intake of cholesterol low, and maintaining control over blood pressure.

Walking on a regular basis: the established health benefits

While the major benefit of a consistent walking program is improved cardiac health, a variety of other health benefits have been either demonstrated or suggested by scientific studies. A consistent walking program has been shown to have a positive effect on several aspects of health.

Weight loss. Regular exercise has been demonstrated to be a key component of successful weight-loss programs. It is becoming widely accepted that dieting—sharply and temporarily reducing caloric intake—does not help most overweight people to lose weight and, if current theories prove to be correct, may even aggravate the problem of obesity.

Osteoporosis. The progressive thinning of bones that accompanies aging, a particularly serious health threat for postmenopausal women, is affected by hormones, diet, and exercise. Regular weight-bearing exercise such as walking has been shown to slow the process of osteoporosis and may have a role as a preventive factor.

Mental outlook. A variety of mental benefits have been associated with many forms of regular physical activity, including walking. Among these benefits are a reduction in depression and anxiety and an enhanced sense of well being.

How far do they walk?		
distance covered daily by people in different jobs		
worker	kilometers	(miles)
dental hygienist	1.9	(1.2)
newspaper editor	2.4	(1.5)
law clerk	4.3	(2.7)
police officer	5.5	(3.4)
intern	5.6	(3.5)
homemaker	6.9	(4.3)
bank worker	7.2	(4.5)
nurse	8.7	(5.4)
commodities runner	10.8	(6.7)
factory worker	15.0	(9.3)
messenger	16.6	(10.3)

From "Health Facts," *The Good Health Magazine, The New York Times Magazine* part 2 (Sept. 28, 1986)

13

Musculoskeletal strength. With regular exercise, the muscles become stronger, muscular endurance improves, and the risk of musculoskeletal injury is reduced.

Walking as an aerobic activity

While walking is an ideal activity for a consistent, lifelong program of exercise, it also can provide all of the training benefits of aerobic conditioning. In the past many people underestimated walking as a short-term aerobic training activity. However, a number of studies have demonstrated that walking can serve as an excellent conditioner. In 1971 Michael L. Pollock and coinvestigators at Wake Forest University, Winston-Salem, North Carolina, showed that middle-aged men who engaged in a 20-week walking program derived an 18% increase in maximum oxygen consumption (VO_2 max) and significant decreases in body weight and fat. In a 1987 study investigators at the University of Massachusetts found that 67% of men and 91% of women achieved heart rates in the so-called target training zone when asked to walk a mile as briskly as possible.

In order to understand walking as an aerobic activity, it is essential to understand the underlying physiological concept of aerobic metabolism. The human body has two major pathways for generating the energy that is required for performing work: aerobic metabolism and anaerobic metabolism. The word aerobic literally means "in the presence of oxygen," and the aerobic pathway is by far the most efficient means available for energy production in the body.

A person sitting quietly requires a certain amount of energy for the maintenance of normal bodily processes and organ function. When an individual begins to exercise, however, the working muscles call for dramatic increases in energy. In both of these situations, resting and active, energy production is derived from aerobic processes—"combustion" in which oxygen is combined with fuel to produce energy. During activity, however, the rate of energy production increases over the rate at rest.

The oxygen in the human body is carried primarily in the red blood cells and at the muscle-cell level is used to metabolize glycogen to produce energy. As a person begins to train with an aerobic conditioning activity, the oxygen-delivery system becomes temporarily "overloaded," and some adaptations occur to make the system better able to meet the needs of exercise. First, the heart's ability to pump oxygenated blood (called the "cardiac output") improves. Second, the ability of the exercising muscles to extract oxygen from the blood ("peripheral extraction") improves. The improvements in cardiac output and peripheral extraction are the physiological processes underlying the common perception of "getting in shape," a feeling the individual experiences as a result of consistent aerobic exercise at the proper intensity.

It used to be a common belief among exercise physiologists that walking could not be performed at an intensity adequate for eliciting training benefits—particularly for young, previously active individuals. Now a number of studies from the laboratories at the University of Massachusetts Medical School at Worcester and the department of exercise science at

The walking tour, a favorite of active vacationers, may involve strolling the cobbled streets of a medieval city or "trekking" in Tibet. In foreign cities those who go on foot can discover hidden corners and byways, seeing sights at their own pace or selecting an off-the-beaten-track cafe once frequented by the local literati for lunch. (Opposite page) A couple exploring one of the oldest parts of Quebec City pass along the Rue St.-Louis, one of the district's most historic streets.

the University of Massachusetts at Amherst, as well as studies from other universities, have shown that a large majority of individuals can achieve an intensity from walking adequate for deriving aerobic training benefits.

In the walking research laboratories at Worcester, studies showed that the average individual needed to walk slightly faster than 6.4 kilometers (four miles) per hour to achieve a heart rate in the aerobic training range. To put this in perspective, one should consider that the average person walks at approximately 4.8 kilometers (three miles) per hour when going about daily activities such as walking to the store. Thus, to increase the intensity of walking enough to derive aerobic training benefits, the average individual must increase his or her walking speed by 25%. A number of terms are used for walking at this slightly increased speed; *e.g.,* "fast walking," "exercise walking," and "striding." The term fitness walking is used here—defined as walking at a speed fast enough to elevate the heart rate into the aerobic training zone. It should be emphasized that this type of walking is very similar in technique to regular walking and is quite different from so-called race-walking, which requires a fundamentally different technique and is used for the high speeds required in competition.

Initiating a fitness walking program

Oftentimes people are confused about how to start their own fitness walking program. Over the past decade a number of guidelines have emerged to make this process safer and more understandable.

Safety first: the preprogram evaluation. For any individual initiating a fitness walking program (or any kind of exercise program), it is very important to make certain that it is safe. Obtaining advice and clearance from one's personal physician is a wise first step. This is particularly important if an individual has been previously inactive, is significantly overweight, or has any other questions about the safety of a personal walking regimen. In

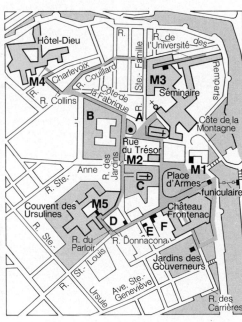

Quebec City
Place d'Armes and vicinity

A Basilica of Notre-Dame de Québec

B City Hall

C Holy Trinity Anglican Cathedral

D Maison Jacquet

E Maison Kent

F Maison Maillou

M1 museum of the fort

M2 wax museum

M3 museum of the seminary

M4 museum of the Hôtel-Dieu

M5 museum of the convent

many instances getting this information requires only a phone call. In other cases the physician may wish to perform a physical examination or even a graded exercise test.

The exercise tolerance test, also called exercise stress test, is an office procedure in which one exercises at progressively higher workloads usually on a treadmill apparatus while the physician monitors the individual's electrocardiogram. The American College of Sports Medicine recommends this test for any individual over the age of 45 who wishes to start a new exercise program. The test may also be advisable for younger people who have any history of heart disease or major risk factors for heart disease.

"Target" heart rate. All serious fitness walkers should know how to take their pulse to determine their heart rate. It is also important to understand the concept of "target" heart rate, or target training zone—the heart rate zone in which one achieves the greatest aerobic training benefits—and how to compute one's own target rate. The easiest way to determine heart rate is to feel the pulse of the artery on the thumb side of one wrist with the fingertips of the other hand. Once the pulse has been located, while standing or sitting still one counts the number of beats for 15 seconds and multiplies by four to determine resting heart rate in beats per minute. For example, if one counts 18 beats in 15 seconds, the resting heart rate is 72 (18×4) beats per minute.

The target training zone extends from 60 to 80% of predicted maximum heart rate. It is in this zone that the most important aerobic training benefits of exercise occur. To determine predicted maximum heart rate and target training zone, the following procedure is used. First, maximum heart rate is determined by subtracting age in years from 220. Then, to determine target training zone, the maximum heart rate is multiplied by 0.6 and by 0.8. For someone who is 45 years old this procedure would work as follows:

$$\begin{array}{r} \text{maximum heart rate} \quad 220 \\ -45 \\ \hline 175 \end{array}$$

$$\text{target training zone} \quad \begin{array}{l} 175 \times 0.6 = 105 \\ 175 \times 0.8 = 140 \end{array}$$

Determining target heart rate zone				
age	average maximum heart rate (beats/minute)	target training zone (beats/minute) 60%	80%	70% maximum heart rate (beats/minute)
20	200	120	160	140
25	195	117	156	137
30	190	114	152	133
35	185	111	148	130
40	180	108	144	126
45	175	105	140	123
50	170	102	136	119
55	165	99	132	116
60	160	96	128	112
65	155	93	124	109
70	150	90	120	105

The enclosed shopping mall, intended as a boon for buyers, has now also become a haven for fitness walkers. Climate controlled, its passages unimpeded by curbs or stoplights, the mall provides a perfect environment for those determined to put in their daily mileage, rain or shine, while eliminating many of the outdoor hazards that may deter older pedestrians. Some mall walkers, like the Galleria Mall GoGetters in Glendale, California (shown at left), have formed their own clubs. A few malls now issue special walking maps, while others will open on holidays, even when the stores are closed, just to accommodate the local ramblers.

Therefore, for a 45-year-old who wishes to initiate a fitness walking program, the heart rate for the target training zone is anywhere from 105 to 140 beats per minute.

Stretching. Most experts recommend stretching both before and after a fitness walking session—typically approximately five minutes of stretching prior to and following a walk, with the emphasis on the major muscle groups of the legs and the back. Several precautions will make the stretching session safer and more beneficial. First, one should never stretch to the point of actual pain but only gently until a mild "tugging" sensation is felt on the muscle and tendon that is being stretched. Pain is a warning signal, and if one actually begins to experience discomfort, one should not continue the stretch but should ease out of it instead. Second, one should not bounce up and down in a stretch. Rather, a steady, constant pressure should be maintained during the stretch.

Warm-up and cooldown. Several studies have shown that dramatic increases in heart rate and blood pressure can accompany the sudden initiation of vigorous exercise without a proper warm-up. Recent medical reports have also presented evidence that potentially dangerous disturbances in heart rhythm can occur following exercise in the absence of a proper cooldown.

The best warm-up and cooldown exercises involve the same activity that is performed during the exercise session itself. Therefore, for the fitness walker the warm-up period should consist of five minutes of walking with a gradual increase in intensity until the target heart rate zone has been reached. Similarly, following the fitness walking session, a five-minute period during which the speed is gradually reduced until the heart rate is back to within 15 beats of the resting heart rate is advisable.

Self-testing for fitness walking. Once an individual has obtained clearance from his or her physician to start a fitness walking program, the next step

17

is to determine current level of cardiovascular fitness. The purpose of this precaution is to make certain the person is not starting a program that is too difficult, thus risking the possibility of injury, or initiating a regimen that is too easy and therefore not deriving the greatest benefit.

What is the best way to assess cardiovascular fitness? In general, the test should involve the activity that is to be performed in the exercise program. Thus, a runner should employ a running test, the cyclist a cycling test, and so on. In the past this raised a problem for walkers since there was no validated test of cardiovascular fitness based on walking. In 1986, however, researchers published a test of cardiovascular fitness based on the physiological response to walking one mile (1.61 kilometers) at a brisk pace. The test is called the Rockport Fitness Walking Test. It was based on a two-year laboratory study of several hundred men and women between the ages of 20 and 79. The test was developed at the University of Massachusetts and was funded by the Rockport Co., a major manufacturer of walking shoes in the U.S. and an enthusiastic corporate participant in the fitness walking movement. It allows the individual to estimate cardiovascular fitness (VO_2 max) accurately on the basis of the response to walking one mile as briskly as possible. The test consists of three steps:

1. Walk one mile as briskly as possible. It is important to stretch and to do a warm-up and cooldown for five to ten minutes before and after the mile walk. Wear loose-fitting clothes and good walking shoes. Walk comfortably but briskly, maintaining a steady pace. Walk on a measured track or level course with no interruptions (*e.g.,* no traffic lights).

2. Record the time. Time should be recorded to the nearest second. Since most people walk between 3 and 6 miles per hour, an average time should be between 10 and 20 minutes for a single mile.

3. Record heart rate immediately at the end of the mile. Remember that heart rate is determined by counting the pulse for 15 seconds and

Walking has always been a favorite pastime in England, where it was enjoyed both as a hobby and as a health pursuit by the landed aristocracy of past centuries. The parklands surrounding their country homes—like this French estate with grounds in the "English style" (map, below)—were replete with meandering paths, quaint pavilions, and poetic vistas, designed as much to inspire the imagination as to stretch the legs. The hedge maze, an element in the more formal tradition of garden design, challenges the intellect as well as the feet. The maze at Hampton Court, the oldest extant maze in England (opposite page), was built in the 17th century and remains a popular attraction today.

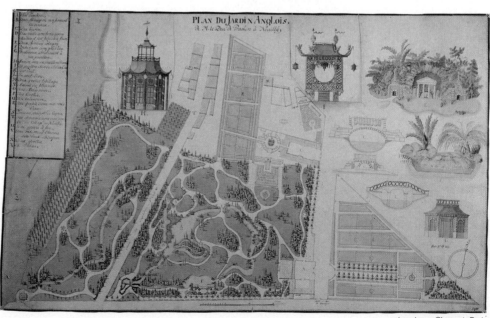

PLAN DU JARDIN ANGLOIS,

multiplying by four. This yields the exercise heart rate. It is important that the heart rate be checked as quickly as possible at the end of the one-mile walk since it begins to slow down almost immediately.

Having completed this process, one is able to estimate his or her cardio-vascular fitness by using the charts that show relative fitness levels rated according to age and sex (page 20). These relative fitness levels are based on standards established by the American Heart Association. Marking the point on the chart defined by one's walking time and heart rate at the end of the walk allows the individual to compare his or her relative fitness level with that of others in the same age and sex category.

A personalized exercise prescription

Once one has determined his or her relative fitness level, the next step is to identify the appropriate fitness walking program for that level (*see* page 20 again; colored bands indicate graded exercise programs). Once again, the coordinates used are the time it took to walk a mile and the heart rate at the end of the mile. Instructions for the individual exercise programs are given in the color-coded 20-week fitness walking programs (page 21). At the end of the first 20 weeks, retesting may be used to establish a new, more challenging program. (From blue or green one advances to yellow or orange. Once an individual has reached the end of the yellow, orange, or red 20-week walking programs, he or she may elect to enter one of the two maintenance programs.)

Answers to walkers' questions

Perhaps because walking is such a simple activity—after all, most people have been doing it since the first year of their lives—there is some skepti-cism about its legitimacy as a form of exercise. Many people have questions about its effectiveness in promoting fitness, contributing to weight loss,

Georg Gerster—Photo Researchers, Inc.

Creating a personal fitness walking program

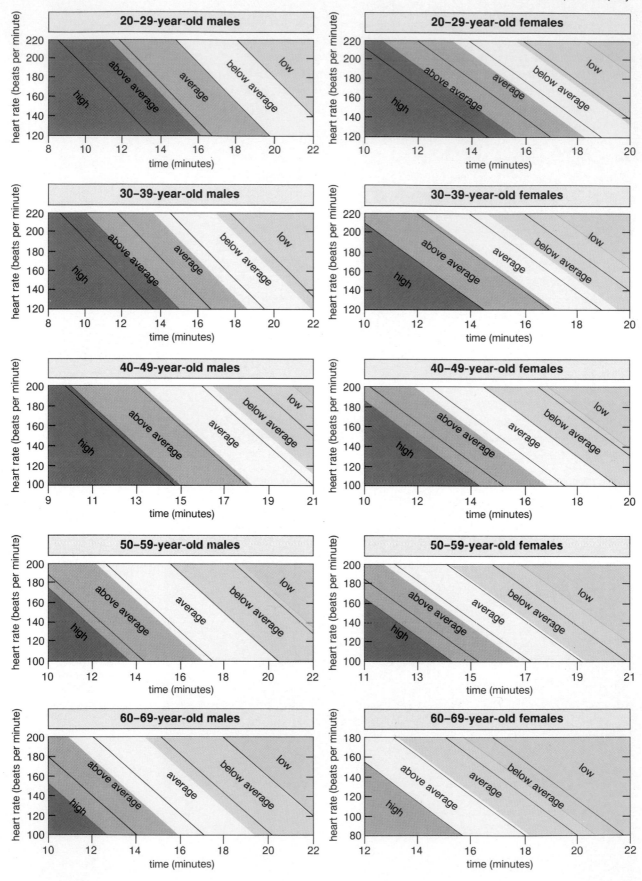

blue program*

week	mileage†	pace (mph)†	heart rate (% of maximum)
1	1.0	3.0	60
2	1.0	3.0	60
3	1.25	3.0	60
4	1.25	3.0	60
5	1.5	3.0	60
6	1.5	3.5	60–70
7	1.75	3.5	60–70
8	1.75	3.5	60–70
9	2.0	3.5	60–70
10	2.0	3.75	60–70
11	2.0	3.75	70
12	2.25	3.75	70
13	2.25	3.75	70
14	2.5	3.75	70
15	2.5	4.0	70
16	2.5	4.0	70
17	2.75	4.0	70–80
18	2.75	4.0	70–80
19	3.0	4.0	70–80
20‡	3.0	4.0	70–80

green program*

week	mileage†	pace (mph)†	heart rate (% of maximum)
1	1.5	3.0	60–70
2	1.5	3.0	60–70
3	1.75	3.0	60–70
4	1.75	3.0	60–70
5	2.0	3.0	60–70
6	2.0	3.0	60–70
7	2.0	3.5	70
8	2.25	3.5	70
9	2.25	3.5	70
10	2.5	3.5	70
11	2.5	3.5	70
12	2.5	3.5	70
13	2.75	3.5	70
14	2.75	4.0	70–80
15	3.0	4.0	70–80
16	3.0	4.0	70–80
17	3.25	4.0	70–80
18	3.25	4.0	70–80
19	3.5	4.0	70–80
20‡	3.5	4.0	70–80

yellow program*

week	mileage†	pace (mph)†	heart rate (% of maximum)
1	2.0	3.0	70
2	2.25	3.0	70
3	2.5	3.0	70
4	2.5	3.0	70
5	2.75	3.0	70
6	2.75	3.5	70
7	2.75	3.5	70
8	2.75	3.5	70
9	3.0	3.5	70
10	3.0	3.5	70
11	3.0	4.0	70–80
12	3.0	4.0	70–80
13	3.25	4.0	70–80
14	3.25	4.0	70–80
15	3.5	4.0	70–80
16	3.5	4.5	70–80
17	3.5	4.5	70–80
18	4.0	4.5	70–80
19	4.0	4.5	70–80
20§	4.0	4.5	70–80

orange program*

week	mileage†	pace (mph)†	incline/weight	heart rate (% of maximum)
1	2.5	3.5		70
2	2.75	3.5		70
3	3.0	3.5		70
4	3.0	3.5		70
5	3.25	3.5		70
6	3.25	4.0		70–80
7	3.5	4.0		70–80
8	3.75	4.0		70–80
9	4.0	4.0		70–80
10	4.0	4.0		70–80
11	4.0	4.5		70–80
12	4.0	4.5		70–80
13	4.0	4.5		70–80
14	4.0	4.5		70–80
15	4.0	4.5	+	70–80
16	4.0	4.5	+	70–80
17	4.0	4.5	+	70–80
18	4.0	4.5	+	70–80
19	4.0	4.5	+	70–80
20‖	4.0	4.5	+	70–80

red program*

week	mileage†	pace (mph)†	incline/weight	heart rate (% of maximum)
1	3.0	4.0		70
2	3.25	4.0		70
3	3.5	4.0		70
4	3.5	4.5		70–80
5	3.75	4.5		70–80
6	4.0	4.5		70–80
7	4.0	4.5	+	70–80
8	4.0	4.5	+	70–80
9	4.0	4.5	+	70–80
10	4.0	4.5	+	70–80
11	4.0	4.5	+	70–80
12	4.0	4.5	+	70–80
13	4.0	4.5	+	70–80
14	4.0	4.5	+	70–80
15	4.0	4.5	+	70–80
16	4.0	4.5	+	70–80
17	4.0	4.5	+	70–80
18	4.0	4.5	+	70–80
19	4.0	4.5	+	70–80
20‖	4.0	4.5	+	70–80

yellow maintenance program*

total time: 1 hour
aerobic workout:
    mileage: 4†
    pace: 4.5 miles† per hour
heart rate: 70 to 80% of maximum
frequency: 3 to 5 times per week
weekly mileage: 12 to 20 miles†

orange/red maintenance program*

total time: 1 hour
aerobic workout:
    mileage: 4†
    pace: 4.5 miles† per hour
    weight/incline: weights (to upper body) or incline (hill walking) may be added as needed to keep heart rate in target zone (70 to 80% of the predicted maximum)
heart rate: 70 to 80% of maximum
frequency: 3 to 5 times per week
weekly mileage: 12 to 20 miles†

Before starting a fitness walking program, a person must determine his or her heart rate during exercise. This is done by first walking one mile, briskly but at a steady pace, then measuring heart rate immediately at the end of the walk. By consulting the appropriate chart on the opposite page, a person can then determine his or her relative fitness level (compared with others of the same age and sex) and pick a suitable exercise program. This is done by locating the number that represents walking time (the time it took to walk the mile) and the number that represents heart rate at the end of the one-mile walk. The point that marks the coordinate of these two shows both fitness level (average, above or below average, etc.) and the color-coded exercise program to be followed for the first 20 weeks. At the end of that time, the individual may take the one-mile test again, reassess fitness level, and, depending on the results, move on to a new fitness walking program or repeat the original program. Eventually a lifetime maintenance program can be adopted, based on the charts on this page.

* each program includes a 5–7-minute period of warm-up and stretching and a similar cooldown; frequency is 5 times a week for the blue and green programs, decreasing to 3 times a week after week l4 of the orange program and week 6 of the red program
† 1 mile = 1.61 kilometers
‡ retest at the end of 20 weeks to establish new program
§ retest at the end of 20 weeks to establish new program or go directly to yellow maintenance program for a lifetime fitness walking plan
‖ at the end of 20 weeks go on to orange/red maintenance program for a lifetime fitness walking plan

helping in the rehabilitation of heart attack victims, and so forth. A few of the most commonly asked questions are addressed here.

Does the fitness walker need special equipment? As more and more people have turned to fitness walking as the cornerstone of their exercise program, more emphasis has been placed on equipment. This trend has become particularly apparent as increasingly younger, more fit individuals turn to walking as a major form of exercise. Manufacturers have responded by introducing technological innovations into walking equipment to make the sport safer, easier to perform, and more enjoyable.

By 1986 in the United States there were more than 60 different brands of walking shoes being sold. While different manufacturers stress different aspects of their shoes, there is general agreement that it is both desirable and possible to create a shoe designed to meet the demands of serious fitness walking. Much of the scientific data to support this notion comes from studies in the field of biomechanics. In this discipline high-speed filming and computer techniques are used to break movements down into small components. Biomechanical studies of the walking stride have helped scientists understand the forces and motions at work, facilitating the production of comfortable, safer, more effective shoes.

In a series of biomechanical studies of fitness walking and walking shoes performed at the University of Massachusetts in 1985 and 1986, a number of important findings emerged. First, these investigations confirmed that the forces applied to bones and joints during the "heel-strike" and "push-off" phases of the stride were significantly lower during walking than running. Second, the forces on the heel were significantly better cushioned by a shoe designed specifically for walking than by a shoe designed for running. The walking shoe also controlled pronation (the tendency of the ankle and foot to rotate inward during heel strike) better than the running shoe did. Such studies suggest that the biomechanics of walking and running are different and that different footwear should be worn for the two activities.

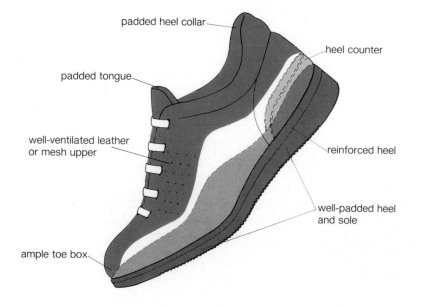

A general consensus has arisen that properly designed walking shoes should incorporate the following attributes: (1) a firm heel counter to "cup" the heel and help control pronation; (2) leather or leather-and-mesh construction to provide adequate support while allowing for proper ventilation; (3) overall light weight; (4) a roomy toe box to allow the toes to spread comfortably during the push-off phase of the walking stride; (5) a well-cushioned heel to counteract the major forces of the heel-strike portion of the stride; (6) a design that accommodates the unique biomechanics of the walking stride.

Appropriate footwear also includes socks. A number of different fabrics are used in walking socks, including 100% cotton and cotton/orlon blends. The major requirement of socks used for walking is that they keep the feet warm (or cool, depending on the climate) and dry. They should be absorbent and should not bunch up in such a way as to cause friction or irritation. These considerations are particularly important for individuals with diabetes or primary circulatory disorders, because they are more susceptible to infection should a blister develop on a foot or toe.

For the serious fitness walker, exercise suits made of nylon cut down on wind chill and provide some protection from the elements. A number of so-called breathable water-resistant fabrics have been introduced that provide further protection against inclement weather but at the same time allow perspiration vapor to escape. These garments feature some extra weatherproofing; for example, seams sealed against water leakage and zippers covered with storm flaps. For the person not ready to invest in an exercise suit, layered clothing—with absorbent cotton nearest the skin and a windbreaker on top—can be both comfortable and serviceable.

Depending on one's needs and the amount of money one wants to spend, many other accessories can be purchased that can add to the convenience, comfort, safety, and fun of the sport. In order to allow their arms to swing freely, serious walkers like to rid themselves of hand-held purses, shoulder bags, and even heavy key rings that make pockets bulky. The answer is a scaled-down version of the backpack that slips over a belt or straps around the waist on its own belt. These "fanny packs" have a zippered compartment big enough to hold a wallet, keys, a soft hat, and a few more small items. On longer walks, or when layered clothing might be removed en route, a standard daypack can be useful. A pedometer, a small pocketwatch-sized instrument that measures distance walked, is fun and adds to motivation by recording mileage in a visible way. When one is walking in unfamiliar territory or using a map, a compass is handy to have. People who walk at night along highways or city streets would do well to wear some sort of reflective gear—a belt or vest, for example—that will signal their presence to motorists.

Is walking less likely than other exercise to cause injury? In thinking about the safety of any exercise program, two considerations typically come to mind: the likelihood of developing a cardiac complication and the likelihood of developing a musculoskeletal injury. The publicity surrounding the untimely death of Jim Fixx sparked a lively debate over the safety of running, particularly for middle-aged men. For many critics of running,

23

Wonders of the world, both natural and man-made, attract the foot traveler. The English novelist Charles Dickens, touring Italy with his family in the summer of 1845, organized a climbing party to see the smoking crater of Vesuvius. The ascent, as depicted in the drawing at right, was arduous but, according to Dickens's notes, well worth the effort. Today visitors who scale the Great Wall of China (below) find the experience awe inspiring and unforgettable.

Fixx's death galvanized some sweeping and frequently made but largely unsubstantiated allegations about the dangers of physical exertion in general and jogging in particular. In fairness, some exercise enthusiasts had made equally outrageous claims for the benefits of extremely vigorous exercise. For example, in 1972 pathologist Thomas Bassler put forth the notion that marathon running provided absolute protection from death from coronary artery disease. Subsequent studies have clearly shown that the so-called Bassler hypothesis was incorrect. In one study that examined 18 runners who had died during or immediately after running, 13 were found to have significant coronary artery disease. Still, the exact danger to the heart of either running or walking is not known. The best advice remains to seek medical clearance before embarking on an exercise program, as already discussed, and to observe appropriate precautions and common sense about any worrisome symptoms that occur during or after exercise.

The incidence of musculoskeletal injuries incurred during walking is also unknown. Anecdotal reports suggest that in a given year 25 to 30% of runners suffer an injury serious enough to interrupt their training. It has been proposed that walking should carry a much lower injury rate. This belief is based on the premise that runners leave the ground with each stride and land with three to four times their body weight on each leg, while walkers always have one foot on the ground and land with only one to 1.25 times their body weight. While such observations make sense, the belief that walkers incur fewer musculoskeletal injuries than do joggers or, say, aerobic dancers lacks rigorous scientific proof.

Does walking burn calories effectively? One area of health where walking programs have proved particularly beneficial is weight loss. Obesity remains a major health problem in many developed countries. In the United States, for example, if one considers a total body weight 20% above desirable weight as an index of obesity, more than 16 million adult women and more than 8 million men would be judged as significantly overweight. Obesity has been associated with a variety of health hazards, among them high blood

24

pressure, elevated serum cholesterol, diabetes, and degenerative joint disease. Some cancers appear to be more common in overweight individuals, although obesity per se may not be the key risk factor.

A regular exercise program has repeatedly been demonstrated to be an important component of a successful weight-loss program. Walking is a particularly effective—and vastly underestimated—method of assisting in weight loss. When rated with other forms of exercise, walking compares favorably with other activities in terms of calories burned. Many people do not realize what a potent tool exercise can be for effective weight loss. For example, an average person, weighing 68 kilograms (150 pounds), who engages in fitness walking for 45 minutes a day four times a week throughout a year and does not increase food intake will lose 8 kilograms (18 pounds) over the course of the year. Perhaps even more important, however, is the fact that including a regular exercise regimen as part of a weight-loss program will help preserve lean body mass, while fat will be selectively lost. In dieting alone both muscle and fat are lost, and subsequent weight gain is likely to be entirely fat.

Can walking slow the aging process? As the populations of the developed countries have begun to grow older, a number of questions have arisen concerning the relationship between regular exercise and the aging process. There is no question that certain physiological processes slow down with age. A number of recent reports, however, have suggested that the rate of decline of cardiovascular endurance, musculoskeletal strength, and even certain mental processes may be dictated at least as much by life-style and habits as by physiological imperatives. Individuals who remain physically active throughout their lives appear to experience a much slower decline in cardiovascular endurance than do their more sedentary peers. Furthermore, it appears that it is possible for people to achieve cardiovascular training benefits from fitness walking programs even at fairly advanced ages. In one study in the exercise physiology laboratory at the University of Massachusetts, a group of individuals over the age of 70 (mean age, 74 years)

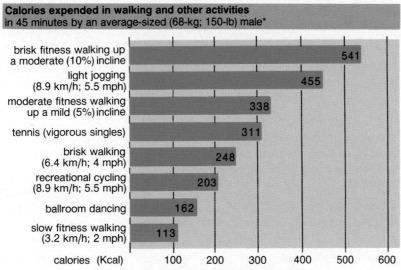

Calories expended in walking and other activities
in 45 minutes by an average-sized (68-kg; 150-lb) male*

Activity	Calories (Kcal)
brisk fitness walking up a moderate (10%) incline	541
light jogging (8.9 km/h; 5.5 mph)	455
moderate fitness walking up a mild (5%) incline	338
tennis (vigorous singles)	311
brisk walking (6.4 km/h; 4 mph)	248
recreational cycling (8.9 km/h; 5.5 mph)	203
ballroom dancing	162
slow fitness walking (3.2 km/h; 2 mph)	113

*average-sized female (56 kg; 124 lb) would burn 20% fewer calories
From R. Sweetgall et al., Rockport's © Fitness Walking (New York: The Putnam Publishing Group, 1985)

Some kind of exercise program is an integral part of nearly every heart patient's program of rehabilitation, and many cardiologists encourage fitness walking as a means of improving cardiac function and overall physical fitness. This was not always the case. At one time anyone who survived a heart attack could look forward to life as an invalid, avoiding all physical exertion. One man who was largely responsible for the change in therapeutic approach was U.S. cardiologist Paul Dudley White, shown below with his most famous patient, Pres. Dwight D. Eisenhower. A great believer in the salutary effects of the active life, White himself would walk rather than ride and climb stairs rather than use elevators; at the age of 85, he continued to mow his own lawn with a hand mower.

achieved an average gain in cardiovascular endurance of 10% following a 12-week supervised walking program.

Is walking a good form of exercise for heart patients? As already indicated, considerable interest has developed in the role of walking programs in the primary prevention of coronary artery disease. However, walking has also played a central part in the secondary prevention of recurrent manifestations of already established disease. In fact, supervised walking programs are central to virtually all cardiac rehabilitation programs around the world.

This was not always so. In fact, at one time many physicians believed that vigorous physical exercise might even contribute to the development of atherosclerosis. Survivors of heart attacks were advised to refrain from all physical exercise. A leading figure who helped change prevailing medical attitudes toward heart patients was U.S. physician Paul Dudley White, considered by many to be the "father" of American cardiology. White believed strongly in the value of regular physical exercise in both prevention and rehabilitation. An active man who always chose walking over riding and stairs instead of elevators, White wrote in 1927:

Exercise as an aid in maintaining good health is beneficial in heart disease providing there is cardiac reserve sufficient to permit it. . . . Walking is probably the best exercise because it is easy for anyone to accomplish and easy to grade from the slowest, shortest walks to the most rapid and longest.

Along with his Harvard University colleague Samuel Levine, White revolutionized the care of heart attack patients by encouraging early ambulation (*i.e.*, getting out of bed as soon as possible). Perhaps nowhere was White's influence more profoundly noted than in the treatment of his most famous patient, U.S. Pres. Dwight D. Eisenhower. Following President Eisenhower's heart attack in 1955, White assured an anxious nation that the president would be able to resume an active life and carry out his duties as chief executive. This event was an important landmark in the history of cardiac rehabilitation.

Since the 1950s a number of controlled trials have looked at regular exercise as a means of preventing recurrent heart attack. These studies suggest that for individuals with established coronary artery disease regular exercise is most effective when it is combined with a multifaceted program that also targets such other risk factors as cigarette smoking and high-cholesterol diets.

Motivation and persistence: keys to success

A major and often overlooked issue in the discussion of consistent lifelong exercise programs is the problem of adherence to the program. Many studies performed in a wide range of countries and cultures have shown one-year drop-out rates ranging from 50 to 80%. In other words, more than half of the people who start an exercise program will have stopped exercising on a regular basis one year later. And, of course, not everyone is interested in getting started to begin with. Among health professionals in the United States, there has been some concern that the current emphasis on exercise is largely a phenomenon of the well-educated, economically advantaged,

Health and longevity are almost certain rewards of a lifetime of walking.

white-collar portion of the population. The advertisements for many popular health clubs, to say nothing of their membership fees, attest to the fact that the appeal of exercise today is to the affluent professional. At any rate, it has been estimated that only 20% of the adult U.S. population exercise regularly enough to maintain cardiovascular fitness or to significantly reduce the likelihood of developing coronary artery disease. Another 40% exercise sporadically, and 40% are entirely sedentary. Therefore, there are two problems here—how to get people interested in exercising and how to motivate them to continue.

Certainly the facts that walking costs virtually nothing, does not require a partner or an advance reservation, and can be done nearly anywhere make it a uniquely accessible sport. It has been argued that because walking programs are more social and enjoyable and carry lower injury rates than most other types of exercise, they should achieve higher levels of adherence. This hypothesis, although attractive, remains to be supported in research studies.

The rage for walking: will it endure?

In some ways the apparently sudden increase of interest in walking during the mid-1980s represents a striking new development in exercise habits. In other ways, however, it can be seen as a natural step in the evolution of a number of trends that have been building since the early 1950s. People became interested in walking as part of a positive life-style, convinced by the prevailing medical, scientific, and social viewpoint that daily habits and choices exert a profound impact on the risks for certain chronic diseases. If someone from 1887 who believed in the health benefits of the "evening constitutional" were plunked down a century later, he or she could be forgiven for observing that for all the sophistication of the late 20th century, people are just now discovering a simple truth that was obvious to their grandparents.

27

The Spirit of Service
by Allan E. Dumont, M.D.

HAPPY
BIRTHDAY
Bellevue

*New York City's Bellevue Hospital had
its beginnings in colonial times and can
claim to be the oldest public hospital
in the United States. The original
almshouse—a six-bed infirmary—was a
single room on the top floor of this Public
Workhouse and House of Correction,
which also sheltered vagrants, alcoholics,
orphans, paupers, and the insane. The
almshouse was erected in 1736 on the
present site of City Hall Park.*

Allan E. Dumont, M.D., *is the Jules
Leonard Whitehill Professor of Surgery at
New York University School of Medicine
and an attending surgeon at Bellevue
Hospital Center, New York City.*

*(Overleaf) Original collage
by Bellevue's pediatric patients;
Children of Bellevue, Inc.*

I regard it still as I did when I first walked through the unhinged doors of the old building as the most distinguished hospital in the country, with the most devoted professional staff. If I were to be taken sick with something serious or struck down on a New York street I would want to be taken there.
—Lewis Thomas, *The Youngest Science,* 1983

In 1986 New York City's Bellevue Hospital, the institution referred to by Lewis Thomas, marked its 250th anniversary. One of the world's foremost general hospitals and the oldest existing hospital in the United States, Bellevue has always been a public hospital, one that functions primarily to serve the sick poor. Since hospitals in general, and public hospitals in particular, can be regarded as a measure of the progress of civilization, Bellevue's 250th is a significant milestone, an appropriate time to look back and attempt to place in some crude historical perspective how this institution came to be where and what it is.

Almshouse with a beautiful view

Bellevue can trace its origin to a six-bed infirmary on the upper floor of an almshouse located on what is now City Hall Park. New York City at the time was little more than a rather unhealthy settlement of some 8,000–9,000 persons, and its affairs were in the hands of a mayor and common council. In 1713 a people's petition was presented to the council asking for an almshouse, but the petition was rejected, and nothing further came of the idea until 1734, three years after a smallpox epidemic had devastated the colony. The council then agreed to establish an almshouse and to include in it a single room for the sick, specifically directing that "the upper room at the west end of the said house be suitably furnished for an infirmary and for no other use whatsoever." The infirmary's patients were placed under the care of John Van Beuren, a graduate of the renowned medical school at Leiden, The Netherlands.

After the almshouse opened, recurrent outbreaks of yellow fever led to an increasingly urgent public demand that fever patients be isolated in some remote corner of the city. Responding to this demand in 1794, the common council leased property that bordered the East River just north of what is now 23rd Street. This property had long been known as "Belle Vue" (beautiful view) and in 1794 was part of the Kip's Bay Farm. During the next few years as the epidemics recurred, yellow fever patients were housed on this property in what had formerly been the manor house; then in 1798 the house and property were actually purchased by the city.

In 1796 the almshouse and infirmary had been moved to larger and somewhat grander quarters directly behind the original structure. Three years later the first lying-in ward in New York was opened there. By 1811, with the city's population at almost 100,000, there was an obvious need for a larger facility. The city decided to build a new almshouse and hospital on an additional two and one-half hectares (six acres) of the Kip's Bay Farm. This was a charming pastoral setting famous for its beautiful flowers and fruit trees and well away from the center of the city's population. It is the site upon which Bellevue Hospital now stands. (Of course, this location in Manhattan is no longer remote.)

The cornerstone of the new almshouse on the Kip's Bay property was laid by Mayor DeWitt Clinton on July 20, 1811. Although construction was begun immediately, the outbreak of the War of 1812 caused the completion of the facility to be delayed until 1816. Within a year of its opening, there were 200 patients in the wards of the new institution under the care of two visiting and two house physicians. The "hospital" at Belle Vue, or the Establishment, as it was then known, comprised a central three-story building—the almshouse, with a pavilion of six large rooms on each side for the sick—and, in addition, a prison, a bake shop, a blacksmith shop, a soap factory, a chapel, a school, and a superintendent's house, all surrounded by a three-meter (ten-foot)-high stone wall. After still another outbreak of yellow fever in 1822, a "fever hospital" was then added to this complex at the southwest end of the property. By 1825 the epidemic had subsided, and the sick at the almshouse were moved to this newer structure, now officially named Bellevue Hospital. Prisoners, orphans, alcoholics, the insane, and the healthy poor, who had all been housed together, were gradually separated from the almshouse and quartered elsewhere, largely on Blackwell's (now Roosevelt) Island. The sick, along with the name Bellevue Hospital, were then transferred from the fever hospital back to the larger almshouse building. This was how Bellevue came to be.

First teaching hospital in the U.S.

Medical instruction had begun in the almshouse as early as 1750, when an executed criminal was dissected for the instruction of students. By 1787 the institution was in regular use for teaching purposes. The almshouse began to be used for clinical instruction by the faculty of Columbia University's College of Physicians and Surgeons in 1807 and by New York University in 1841. Teaching had all but stopped by 1846, however, when conditions at the hospital became truly desperate. This state of affairs arose because

In 1794, when New York was beset by recurring outbreaks of yellow fever, a new facility that isolated patients in a remote part of the city was built, set along the East River on property that was part of the Kip's Bay Farm. The bucolic setting on the river's edge accounted for the name, Belle Vue ("beautiful view"). The above list from the late summer of 1795 tells the fates of resident yellow fever patients, who ranged from servant girl to blacksmith to English officer. By 1811 New York City, with a population of some 100,000, was clearly in need of a larger facility; in 1816 an almshouse and hospital were completed just north of the yellow fever facility. The blue Staffordshire platter commemorating Bellevue's setting is part of the "Beauties of America" series produced by the English firm of Ridgway.

politicians at the time held Bellevue in a very tight grip, and the hospital and its grounds as well as appointments to the professional staff were all considered to be the means of distributing the spoils of office. In 1845 the city fathers (or "stepfathers" or "the gang of 40 thieves," as they were variously called) went so far as to sell at public auction—and to their own personal advantage—five hectares (12 acres) of the hospital's grounds.

In the history of institutions such as Bellevue, there are often brief periods that seem to determine the direction of a long future. For Bellevue the year 1847 was clearly such a time. Conditions in the hospital had never been worse. Responding once again to public outrage, to newspaper publicity, and to the persuasive arguments of James Rushmore Wood, the city authorities finally placed the affairs of the hospital into the hands of a permanent medical board, a small group of some of the most distinguished physicians in the country.

James Rushmore Wood, or Jimmy Wood, as he was affectionately called, was actually the visionary on this board who saw that Bellevue had the potential to be a great teaching hospital. From 1847 until his death in 1882, Wood, a surgeon, had a rather unusual role at Bellevue, where many of the staff compared him to God. According to Frederick Dennis, one of his younger surgical colleagues: "His great familiarity with . . . every department made him its recognized if unofficial head. From the visiting staff to the house staff, from the executive head to the most insignificant employee all conceded his right to dictate, his power to interfere and his influence to control."

Refusing to allow City Hall to rule over the hospital's affairs, Wood and other members of the board initiated a plan to build a large amphitheater where teaching could be conducted without charge to the students. They also divided the hospital into medical and surgical services, each under the direction of voluntary attending physicians or surgeons who had allegiances to either Columbia or New York University. In 1861 a third division was assigned to the newly established Bellevue Hospital Medical College, the first hospital-based medical school in the United States. In 1898 when New York University and the Bellevue Hospital Medical College merged, Cornell University assumed responsibility for one of these divisions. These medical school connections became pivotally important in 1882 when, in an action unprecedented anywhere, the medical board of that year gave to each school the exclusive right to nominate attending and house staff to serve at the hospital. As a result of this action, Bellevue, which had functioned essentially from its beginning as a "teaching hospital," was transformed in fact if not in name into a "university hospital."

Greatness realized

Beginning in 1850 Bellevue's fortunes began to change drastically, and it became one of the world's most renowned hospitals. The Carnegie Laboratory, a facility of the Bellevue Hospital Medical College, opened directly across the street from the hospital in 1885. It was the first laboratory in the United States established specifically for purposes of medical research. Made possible as the result of a gift from Andrew Carnegie, the

In its early days Bellevue acquired a patient population that was exemplary for learning purposes—patients drawn from the vast waves of immigrants entering New York, who were particularly prone to infectious diseases. By the 1780s Bellevue was being used regularly for clinical instruction in medicine. In 1807 Columbia University's College of Physicians and Surgeons became affiliated with Bellevue, as did the Cornell University and New York University schools of medicine in subsequent years. In 1861 the Bellevue Hospital Medical College, the first official hospital-based medical school in the U.S., was established. The famed Bellevue amphitheater (pictured c. 1890) served as a classroom for demonstrating medical and surgical procedures and was typically filled to capacity by students from New York's major medical schools. Bellevue has always flourished as a unique center for learning, and it continues to do so today. Some two centuries after its beginnings as a teaching institution, Bellevue was hailed by the New York Times *as "a glittering seat of learning with the unmistakeable air of intellectual excitement that has traditionally marked it as a great teaching hospital."*

laboratory was established as a U.S. counterpart to the best equipped European medical research laboratory of the day. The gift was the result of a personal appeal to Carnegie by Bellevue attending surgeon Frederick Dennis, who had stipulated that under the direct supervision of his old and close friend William Welch, studies in the new laboratory would focus on problems relating to the bacteriology of surgical wounds. Following their internship together at Bellevue, Welch had been appointed to the faculty of the Bellevue Hospital Medical College and had organized at Bellevue the first formal course in pathology ever offered at a U.S. medical school. By placing the Carnegie Laboratory at Welch's disposal, Dennis had hoped (in vain) to deter the latter from accepting the offer of a chair at the newly organized Johns Hopkins Medical School in Baltimore, Maryland.

Apart from an outpatient department, known as the Bureau of Medical and Surgical Relief of the Outdoor Poor, established in a building adjoining the hospital in 1867, the hospital itself had changed very little since its construction in 1816. Underfinanced and overburdened (as it also is now), the hospital was, nevertheless, exceptionally well endowed in several important respects.

First, owing to its strategic location in a city that was the port of entry for millions of immigrants, it acquired a patient population that was unsurpassed in providing opportunities for learning as well as for healing. By glancing through patients' names in the hospital's record books, one can easily identify the sequential tides of immigration: the Irish in the 1850s, then the Germans and Scandinavians, and in the 1880s the eastern and southern Europeans. With each new wave, Bellevue's doctors had to learn a bit of a new language—German, Yiddish, Italian, and even Chinese. Many of these immigrants bore their children at Bellevue, constituting an important part of the institution's heritage. Huddled together on New York City's Lower East Side in overcrowded, dirty, and decaying tenements that lacked proper

During the Civil War, when crude vehicles for moving wounded soldiers to medical sites were used, it became clear that fast transport meant that the chances of saving lives were vastly improved. After the war a Bellevue physician who had served in the Army of the Potomac's medical corps applied the quick-transport concept to civilian patients, establishing at Bellevue the first hospital-based ambulance system in the United States. The horse-drawn ambulance is shown leaving the Bellevue yard in 1896.

sanitation and ventilation, these new arrivals were particularly susceptible to the ravages of infectious disease and in particular to tuberculosis.

Second, the hospital had acquired an attending staff made up of some of the country's most distinguished physicians and surgeons. In surgery they included Valentine Mott, the best known U.S. surgeon of the day, with an impressive list of surgical "firsts" to his credit; James R. Wood, mentioned earlier, an extraordinarily skilled operator who could perform a mid-thigh amputation in nine seconds and who established at Bellevue in 1857 the first museum of pathological specimens in the United States; Stephen Smith (*see* below), who was one of the earliest advocates of the British surgeon Joseph Lister's advanced principles of antisepsis and wound care, which revolutionized modern surgery (Smith's own famous textbook, *The Principles and Practice of Operative Surgery,* was published in three editions); Frank H. Hamilton, the author of a textbook on fractures that was the first standard reference work on this subject published in the United States; and Lewis Sayre, the "father of American orthopedic surgery," who was the first U.S. surgeon to remove a hip joint and who developed the first successful nonsurgical treatment for tuberculosis of the spine.

Responsible for the care of patients on the medical services were physicians who were no less prominent, including Edward Janeway, a contemporary of William Osler at Johns Hopkins, who conducted the first systematic autopsies in New York City and was considered with Osler to be among the most preeminent physicians in the U.S., and Austin Flint, Sr., who introduced the stethoscope into general use in U.S. medicine. Luminaries in other specialties included William Hammond, author of the first U.S. textbook on disease of the nervous system, and Abraham Jacobi, the "father of American pediatrics," who became director of the children's ward at Bellevue in 1874. Also on this service was Job Smith, who was in

34

charge of the children's outpatient department and was the author of the standard text on infant feeding.

Third, because of these assets, the hospital was able to recruit an unusually capable and determined house staff. Several of these recruits—house officers between 1850 and the turn of the century—were men whose lives became an integral part of Bellevue's history, and they and their accomplishments are of more than usual interest.

Ferreting out filth and fever. Smith, a surgical house officer in 1852, took the unusual but important step of examining the Bellevue admissions records during an epidemic of typhus fever. He discovered that over 100 of these patients had come from a single nearby tenement. Visiting the place on his day off, he found what he later called a "veritable fever nest"—sewage on the floor, broken windows, and other unhealthful conditions. Smith's outrage at these conditions and the unwillingness of any city agency to act led him to seek help from William Cullen Bryant, the editor of New York City's *Evening Post*. With the threat of public exposure, the tenement's landlord was finally "brought to terms." Formation of city and state boards of health were direct outgrowths of this incident.

Smith's continued concern and involvement in matters of public health succeeded in establishing the tradition of public responsibility for the health of the urban poor and particularly the health of newly arrived immigrants. He subsequently served as the commissioner of health of both the city and the state and was appointed to a national health board by Pres. Rutherford B. Hayes. In 1872 Smith founded the American Public Health Association; he served as its president four times.

First hospital ambulances. Edward B. Dalton finished his service as a Bellevue house officer in medicine in 1859. Volunteering for active duty in the Civil War, he was assigned to the Army of the Potomac and placed in charge of transporting the wounded as the Army advanced toward Richmond, Virginia. Dalton was impressed with the fact that crude ambulances improvised during the fighting saved valuable time in caring for the wounded. In other words, he realized that time was a critical factor in survival. Returning to Bellevue after the war, he reasoned that the same considerations applied to civilian injuries. He was able to persuade the au-

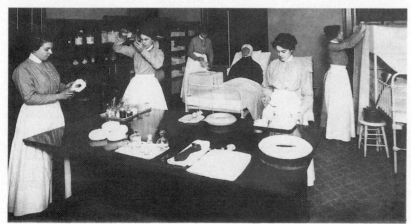

Another first for Bellevue was the recognition of the need for trained nurses; in 1873 the country's premier nurses' training school was established at the hospital. The Bellevue nursing "system" was modeled on the innovative practices instituted in Europe by Florence Nightingale—methods that raised nursing from a lowly job to a respected profession.

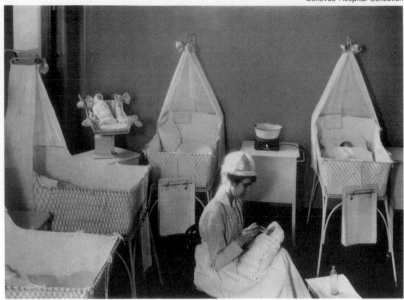

In its early years Bellevue's immigrant patients gave birth to their children at the hospital. As they grew, the children were treated at Bellevue. In 1874 Abraham Jacobi, who is known as the "father of American pediatrics," became the director of the children's ward, and Bellevue gained a reputation as an outstanding provider of pediatric care—a reputation it has maintained. In this century a cheerful environment and specialized recreation were recognized as invaluably therapeutic for hospitalized youngsters. Today the active Child Life Department is concerned with ensuring the emotional well-being of hospitalized children and their families. "Tender loving care" (TLC), in fact, was coined at Bellevue. The words of the child who created the drawing at the opening of this article sum up what the Bellevue experience is for the youngest patients: "This is a special hospital." (Right) Newborns at Bellevue, c. 1910. (Opposite page) Orthopedic ward (top), c. 1915. The circus comes to Bellevue (bottom), c. 1910, entertaining patients young and old.

thorities to try a hospital-based ambulance system, which was inaugurated at Bellevue in 1869, the first such service in the U.S.

Need for nurses, Nightingale-style. Walker Gill Wylie was a house officer on the surgical service in 1872 when he was invited by Louisa Lee Schuyler to help a women's committee to publicize and correct the lack of anything resembling adequate nursing care at Bellevue. Schuyler, a great granddaughter of Alexander Hamilton, was president of the Women's Central Association of Relief, which became the most important auxiliary of the U.S. Sanitary Commission during the Civil War. In 1872 she organized the New York State Charities Aid Association in an attempt to improve public institutions of charity and, as a branch of this committee, the Bellevue Visiting Committee.

At the time the idea of providing training for nurses was nothing short of revolutionary, and not a single trained nurse or training school existed in the U.S. It was, in fact, widely believed that training a nurse would make her dangerously disobedient and independent.

At his own expense Wylie went to England to consult with Florence Nightingale about her recently established school at St. Thomas's Hospital, London. Nightingale was indisposed at the time of his visit, but Wylie was able to study her methods at St. Thomas's, and on his return he received a long letter from her outlining practical suggestions for establishing a school. Together with Schuyler and the Bellevue Visiting Committee, he was able to overcome governmental indifference and persuade the Bellevue authorities to sponsor a nurses' training school, which opened in 1873. An imposing and formidable Anglican nun, Sister Helen Bowden, trained in Nightingale's methods, was put in charge, and the school subsequently had a powerful influence on the training of nurses in the U.S. The "Nightingale system" came to be referred to as the "Bellevue system," and the Bellevue precedent of insisting that nurses wear a clean, white uniform was soon widely adopted by hospital nurses everywhere in the country.

36

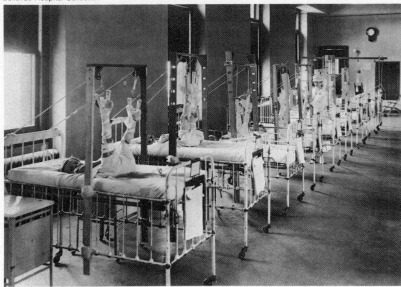

Halsted at Bellevue. William S. Halsted finished his training as house surgeon at Bellevue in 1878. After two years of study in Europe, he returned
to New York, and in 1883, at the age of 31, he was appointed visiting
surgeon at Bellevue. Long regarded as the most important figure in the
history of surgery in the United States, he is often referred to as "Halsted
of Hopkins." But he was obviously also "Halsted of Bellevue," and in the
ten formative years prior to his move to Baltimore, he became something
of a legend among New York surgeons. According to hospital records, he
participated in many operations at Bellevue between 1883 and 1887 and
made rounds regularly with the house staff.

In 1921, the year before he died, Halsted wrote to a surgical colleague
as follows: "One of the major operations performed by me under cocaine
anesthesia during the winter of 1884–1885 was the freeing of the cords
of nerves of the brachial plexus. This operation was performed in a large

Bellevue physician James Alexander Miller founded the Bellevue Tuberculosis Service in 1903—one of the first efforts to combat a rampant infection afflicting thousands of New Yorkers. Part of the therapeutic regimen established by Miller for TB patients was "fresh air treatment" on board the Southfield, *an old Staten Island ferry that was specially converted to an open-air day camp. (Above) Female TB patients are aired on a chilly winter's day in 1923, and (above right) children taking the cure for tuberculosis have classes on the boat, c. 1910.*

tent which I built on the grounds of Bellevue Hospital, having found it impossible to carry out antiseptic precautions in the general amphitheater . . . where the numerous anti-Lister surgeons dominated and predominated." Considered in the light of information now at hand, this was a curious statement. It seems likely that Halsted's illness at the time—a bile duct obstruction—plus the gap of 40 years caused his memory not to serve him faithfully. The record clearly indicates that Charles McBurney, with whom he shared a surgical service, followed antiseptic precautions that were identical to those used by Halsted, and any consideration of the attending surgeons of the time as a group of backward-looking individuals can hardly be imagined.

Combating TB. James Alexander Miller served as a "substitute" intern on the Columbia University Medical Division in 1888, the year prior to his graduation from that university's medical school. In 1903, after spending two summers helping Edward Livingston Trudeau treat patients with tuberculosis at Saranac Lake, New York, Miller left what he later referred to as the aristocratic setting of the Vanderbilt Clinic at Columbia in order to devote himself to the study and care of patients with tuberculosis at Bellevue. Finding that there was no competition for tending these patients, since no one else was or had been interested in them, he arranged to have them assigned to the Columbia division. With the financial help of some of his private patients, Miller arranged to have an old Staten Island ferryboat, the *Southfield,* refitted and tied to a dock adjacent to the hospital to serve as an open-air day camp. After treating Mayor Jimmy Walker's brother for tuberculosis, Miller was also able to persuade the mayor to include a special item in the city's budget for patients with tuberculosis. Later, as the result of a close friendship with Harry Hopkins, a former tuberculosis patient who married a Bellevue nurse and became director of the New York Tuberculosis Association, Miller obtained Pres. Franklin D. Roosevelt's support for the construction of a separate building at Bellevue for TB patients.

Nobel Prize winners. André F. Cournand was one of Miller's residents on the chest service in 1933. At the latter's suggestion he established a pul-

38

monary function laboratory at Bellevue four years later. Shortly thereafter the scope of this facility was enlarged in order that the heart, lung, and circulation could be studied as a single interrelated unit; thus, the facility became in effect the country's first cardiopulmonary laboratory. Together with Dickinson Richards, the chief of Columbia's medical division, Cournand carried out pioneering clinical studies of cardiac and pulmonary function by passing a flexible catheter via the venous system into the right side of the heart, a technique that had been newly described by Werner Forssmann in Germany. Using this approach they were able to unravel a number of previously unsolved problems ranging from the physiological effects of congenital heart disease to traumatic shock. In 1956 Cournand and Richards shared with Forssmann the Nobel Prize for Physiology or Medicine for their epochal studies.

Rehabilitating veterans. An in-hospital program designed to train disabled patients to become employable and to look after themselves was initiated at Bellevue at the end of World War II. This was the first such program in the world to be established in a nonmilitary hospital. It was set up on two wards of the hospital by Howard Rusk and George Deaver and was modeled after a rehabilitation program Rusk had initiated for servicemen during the war.

Scandal and misconception

The care of the mentally ill at Bellevue has a particularly interesting history, and for a long time there was a common misconception that Bellevue was solely a dumping ground for the insane.

From about 1839 patients considered insane were transferred to Blackwell's Island after a few days of observation at Bellevue. The facility used for this purpose at Bellevue consisted of two wards in the hospital's basement, and the service was loosely supervised by physicians who rotated from the hospital's medical divisions. In 1879, owing to an increase in the number of patients admitted for observation and to public interest in this problem, a separate pavilion was opened, followed in 1882 by the appointment of resident physicians with direct responsibility for the care of the mentally ill.

These measures did little to dispel the public's impression that serious deficiencies existed at both Bellevue and Blackwell's Island. In 1887 an editor of the *New York World* decided to get a firsthand account of conditions at both institutions by directing one of the newspaper's feature writers, Nellie Bly (Elizabeth Cochrane Seaman), to feign insanity and become a patient herself. After a few days at Bellevue followed by ten more at Blackwell's Island, Bly was "rescued" by her editor and promptly reported her ordeal in a lurid exposé titled "Ten Days in a Mad-House." Her subsequent testimony before a grand jury about the conditions she encountered led to the jurors' decision to visit these facilities. Word of the impending visit leaked, however, and many of the disgraceful conditions described by the journalist were corrected before the jurors arrived. As a direct result of the publicity attending the *World's* "investigative report," the city appropriated an additional $1 million for the care of the insane.

Nevertheless, conditions for these patients at Bellevue did not really

Although the windows are barred, a serene atmosphere dominates the softly lighted private room occupied by this Bellevue psychiatric patient. The care of the mentally ill at Bellevue has a somewhat notorious history. Quite early the hospital acquired a reputation as a dumping ground for the insane. In 1887 a journalist, Nellie Bly, posed as a patient and then wrote a lurid exposé entitled "Ten Days in a Mad-House" for the New York World. *Conditions improved markedly in 1903, when Menas S. Gregory took charge of the psychiatric division and brought the care of patients up to modern standards. In 1933 a new building for psychiatric patients was completed, abolishing the primitive old "back wards."*

39

begin to approach modern standards until 1903, when Menas S. Gregory was appointed chief of the psychiatric division. He immediately reorganized the service and gradually succeeded in abolishing an approach to mental illness that had not been changed since medieval times.

In order to care for children with postencephalitic behavior disorders, a children's division was added in 1920. This subsequently developed into a world famous center for studies of autistic children and for the training of child psychiatrists.

In 1926 Gregory was also able to persuade the city authorities to appropriate money for a new building for psychiatric patients. Completed in 1933, it was designed to accommodate 450 patients but eventually housed almost twice that number.

Bellevue beyond the shores

Preparing for the country's entry into World War I, the Army Medical Corps devised a plan for augmenting the resources of the regular corps with units from several large civilian hospitals. At the Army's request, George David Stewart, chief of New York University's surgical division at Bellevue, recruited for the "Bellevue Unit" about 20 to 30 of the hospital's physicians and 65 nurses. With additional civilians and enlisted men (mostly college students), the unit arrived in Vichy, France, in 1918. As the first such unit to organize, it received the official designation Base Hospital Unit #1. Transforming the two largest luxury hotels in Vichy into a medical and a surgical hospital, the unit received many of the casualties from the fighting at Château-Thierry and Belleau Wood.

Twenty-four years later the War Department turned again to New York University's department of surgery and asked John H. Mulholland to organize another Bellevue unit, to be designated (in honor of the 1918 unit) U.S. General Hospital #1. After training at Fort Meade, Maryland, the unit set up quarters in Hartfordshire, near London, where it cared for patients from the Army's 8th Air Force Division. Later the unit was transported across the English Channel in landing ship tanks to Omaha Beach. Reestablished in seven buildings in Paris in November 1943, the unit treated a large number of men wounded during the Battle of the Bulge.

A tradition of serving beyond the U.S. shores was established during World War I, when a fully staffed Bellevue medical unit, Base Hospital #1, served in Vichy, France (right). During World War II Bellevue units again treated the wounded in Hartfordshire (England), on Omaha Beach (Normandy, France), and in Paris.

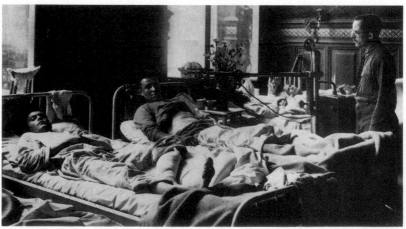

In 1975 a 25-story building replaced Bellevue's many run-down older buildings. Instead of the old large wards, the new facility was designed to accommodate patients in private rooms or rooms for two to four patients, and all departments in the medical center's large main building were supplied with state-of-the-art equipment and modern services. Today the hospital is busier than ever before, treating well over 100,000 patients a year, and—as ever—no one is turned away. At the present time nearly a quarter of Bellevue's patients are homeless; alcoholism, drug addiction, AIDS, cirrhosis, tuberculosis, diabetes, pneumonia, and psychiatric illness are some of their common afflictions.

Expanding and modernizing

Bellevue's physical plant, essentially unchanged since 1816, began to be replaced in the early 1900s. The net result of this building program, which continued for almost 15 years, was an institution spread out over ten city blocks and comprising 25 buildings, 15 of which were designed specifically to accommodate patients. The latter consisted of six- to seven-story pavilions containing large open wards, each with room for 26–30 patients. During winter months the hospital sometimes doubled this bed capacity by lining the corridors with additional beds that at times extended clear out to the elevators. The seasonal demand for additional beds was due to the influx of desperately sick patients suffering from such life-threatening infections as lobar pneumonia, meningitis, scarlet fever, diphtheria, typhoid fever, and erysipelas. With the introduction of the sulfa drugs in the 1940s and then the antibiotics penicillin and streptomycin, this demand for extra beds gradually declined.

In the 1960s, despite peeling paint and broken-down elevators and with almost every item of equipment either in short supply or malfunctioning and in need of repair or replacement, the hospital was still able to attract a superb house staff. Bellevue continued to be viewed, in the words of a *New York Times* article, as "a glittering seat of learning with the unmistakeable air of intellectual excitement that has traditionally marked it as a great teaching hospital."

In response to newspaper publicity and to repeated appeals by Bellevue's chiefs of service and a concerned group of prominent New Yorkers, the city authorities finally agreed in the 1960s to plan for a new structure. In 1975, after the expenditure of $150 million, Bellevue's shabby and decaying buildings were actually replaced by a modern 25-story air-conditioned structure. Each floor of this new building covers an area of approximately 0.6 hectares (one and a half acres), and instead of the old system of

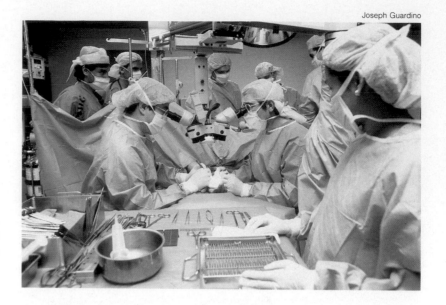

The microsurgical team of Bellevue's trauma service has become world renowned for performing delicate operations that successfully reattach severed body parts.

open wards with 20–30 beds, there are pleasant and comfortable rooms designed specifically for one, two, or four patients.

Recent history

As a look back over the more recent history of the hospital demonstrates, it is appropriate to consider separately the 10 to 20 years that have just ended. This period, really only yesterday, is a time still too close to be chronicled as history. Several developments during this period, however, seem too important to be allowed to go unmentioned.

For many years attending physicians, house officers, and medical students from Cornell, Columbia, and New York universities worked together in the crumbling old buildings and in the face of enormous difficulties to maintain the hospital's tradition of being able to handle anything at any time. In 1967, eight years before the move into the new building, two of these historic medical school ties to Bellevue were broken, and Columbia and Cornell transferred their activities to other institutions. Bellevue's patients then became the exclusive responsibility of the New York University faculty.

As far back as the 1960s the same coalition of Bellevue senior physicians and concerned citizens who had led the successful struggle for the new building had appealed to city and state legislators to develop a plan that might free the hospital from the bureaucratic mismanagement of the city's Department of Hospitals. A bill passed by the New York State legislature vested ownership and operating responsibility for Bellevue and other municipal hospitals in a quasi-public corporation, the New York City Health and Hospitals Corporation, but the final version of the bill fell far short of its proponents' original goals. It retained mayoral control over the new corporation, failed to grant to individual hospitals the authority to fully administer their own affairs, and resulted in the replacement of the old Department of Hospitals with a larger and more powerful bureaucracy.

At present Bellevue is a tertiary care hospital, certified to perform open-heart surgery and to care for patients with every kind of life-threatening

42

injury or illness (with the exception of severe burns). Its emergency department is busier today than at any time in the hospital's past, seeing in excess of 100,000 patients a year. Currently approximately 25% of these patients are homeless. Responding to their pressing health problems is thus a major challenge to Bellevue's emergency services physicians. Approximately 80% of these people are chronic alcoholics, and 20% are drug abusers. A significant but as yet undetermined number of them have active tuberculosis or one of the following disorders: cirrhosis, diabetes, pneumonia, and seizures; some have tuberculosis in addition to one of those disorders. A few have AIDS (acquired immune deficiency syndrome). In addition to providing medical care, Bellevue also houses approximately 1,000 homeless men, who are accommodated each night in a nearby building that recently was vacated when the department of psychiatry moved into quarters on the upper four floors of the new Bellevue. Viewed in historical terms, Bellevue's old psychiatry building is thus once again an almshouse—a reminder, perhaps, that the more things change, the more they stay the same.

The hospital's microsurgical team, composed of specialists from several different surgical disciplines, has become particularly well known in the last few years for its success in reattaching the severed limbs of a large number of patients. Bellevue also continues to be an institution in which research is a prominent activity. A clinical research unit funded by the U.S. National Institutes of Health opened at Bellevue in 1960 providing, for the first time, a modern well-equipped facility in which to conduct clinical studies. An almost endless succession of contributions of new knowledge continues to flow from investigations carried out in the hospital under the direction of the clinical faculty of the New York University School of Medicine. Bearing on problems as diverse as severe liver injuries, pancreatitis, and the chemical basis for mental illness, these contributions have in many cases led to an entirely new understanding of common clinical disorders. AIDS, the problem currently taxing the hospital's resources, is receiving intense study under at least seven different research protocols.

Like a rare old wine, Bellevue has acquired a special personality that seems to come only with advanced age and the right ingredients. Compensating for any imperfections in what might be called the substance of the hospital is the spirit of the place, an intangible and timeless quality to which Bellevue owes its distinctive character. This spirit is the legacy of generations of dedicated men and women who have cared for the city's sickest and poorest patients.

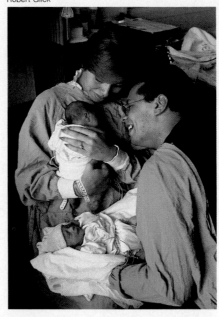

A couple share the joy of welcoming their twins, born prematurely but healthy, into the world. The obstetrical services at Bellevue ensure the best care and the brightest outlook for the 1,500 or more babies born at the hospital each year.

Ailing Continent

by Alex Poteliakhoff, M.D.

The continent of Africa, viewed as a whole, is the most disadvantaged of all continents; 29 of the world's 36 poorest countries are to be found south of the Sahara, and there the annual gross national product (GNP) is around U.S. $300 per capita, compared with over $10,000 per capita in most of the world's developed countries. In the north the situation is somewhat better and, of course, there is a relatively wealthy community in South Africa, but the overall picture is gloomy. Infant mortality rates are among the highest in the world. The continent has been racked by drought and famine. These circumstances have focused the world's attention upon Africa and its problems as never before, bringing about a growing sympathy on the part of the international community along with a desire to rectify this tragic state of affairs.

A dire situation

The Universal Declaration of Human Rights, adopted by the United Nations, places health and adequate nutrition among the basic rights of every human being, yet more than 40 years after the inception of the UN, there are huge disparities in the major indicators of health between the people in affluent developed countries and those of the world's less developed nations. Although 75% of the world's population live in the less developed countries, only 6% of world spending on health is available to them. A horrifying 98% of all child deaths between the ages of one and four occur in the less developed countries. Life expectancy on the continent of Africa itself is 48.6 years, the lowest in the world, while death rates are 17 per 1,000, the highest in the world.

The percentage of Africans living in absolute poverty rose from 82% in 1974 to 91% in 1982. Only one person in four has access to safe water. Every year 1.5 million hectares (3.7 million acres) of land are swallowed up by the advancing Sahara and, in addition, large areas of fertile land are denied to agriculture and animal husbandry by reason of such endemic dis-

Alex Poteliakhoff, M.D., is a retired physician, the Honorary Secretary of the Medical Association for Prevention of War, and coauthor of the book Real Health: The Ill Effects of Stress and Their Prevention *(1981). He resides in London.*

(Opposite page)
Photograph, David Burnett—Contact

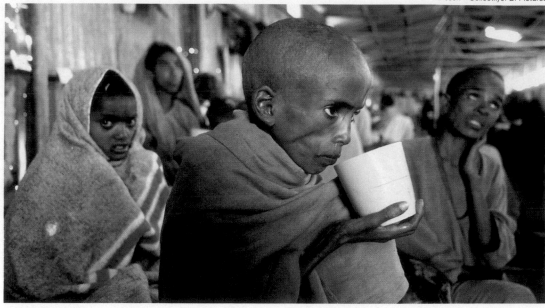

eases as those caused by the tsetse fly and the blackfly. Food production does not keep pace with the rapidly expanding population, and each year 20 million tons of cereal have to be imported.

According to the United Nations Children's Fund (UNICEF), nearly five million African children died and another five million were disabled, physically or mentally, by malnutrition and disease in 1985, and yet these deaths were preventable. Another major crisis, described at a meeting of international health experts in Nairobi, Kenya, in early 1987 as "a hidden tragedy," is the maternal death rate. In sub-Saharan Africa the number of women who die in childbirth is 6.4 per 1,000 births. This compares with 4.2 per 1,000 in Asia, 2.7 in Latin America, and less than 0.1 in northern and middle Europe. One estimate of maternal mortality in a remote part of West Africa was that there are 24 pregnancy-related deaths per 1,000 women of childbearing age. Barber B. Conable, Jr., president of the World Bank, said at the Nairobi meeting, "Common decency tells us that it is intolerable that 1,400 women die every day in the process of carrying or delivering their children."

The burden of tropical diseases is added to that of all the other diseases commonly found in more temperate climates. Malaria kills almost one million Africans a year. Some 200 million are affected by schistosomiasis, which attacks the bladder and gut. There are around five million cases of leprosy in Africa. One-third of the population is infested with worms, and anemia is so widespread that average hemoglobin levels are 15% below those of Europeans. These are just a few of the common conditions found in Africa; the list of diseases is almost endless.

AIDS: a new devastation

In the last few years AIDS (acquired immune deficiency syndrome) has significantly increased the health problems of Africa and will put a great strain on its already overstretched resources. According to Jonathan Mann,

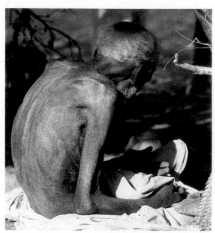

Sarah Putnam—J. B. Pictures

46

Jean Gaumy—Magnum

writing in *World Health,* a publication of the World Health Organization (WHO) in Geneva, between 2 and 20% of healthy adults are infected by the virus in different regions of Africa, and there are likely to be some one million to two million carriers in all. Assuming that 1% per year will develop clinical AIDS, with symptoms and disease (and this is a conservative estimate), he calculated that there will be 10,000 new cases per year. A far more gloomy picture is painted by the Panos Institute, London, and the Norwegian Red Cross, who forecast that one million Africans will die of AIDS in the next decade.

There are important differences in the characteristics of the disease as it affects Africans and the people of the Western world. In Africa the mode of transmission is mainly heterosexual, resulting in a ratio of 1:1 between male

The continent of Africa has been racked by drought and famine; the consequent toll on health is enormous. Infant mortality rates are among the highest in the world—in fact, higher than the average for all of the world's less developed countries, as the graph below indicates. In Mozambique up to one-third of the population have been affected by food shortages, caused first by drought and more recently by war. In 1987 it was estimated that over 400,000 people were in danger of starving to death. Emergency shipments of donated food have not reached the people; the Mozambican government estimated that as many as 1.2 million people were in inaccessible areas and 2.2 million were in areas that, owing to the presence of military forces, could be reached only by heavily guarded convoys. (Left) Uprooted Mozambicans scavenge for bits of grain that have fallen from trucks. (Opposite page) Children in a relief camp in Ethiopia in 1984 (top) subsist on a diet of gruel. The hunger that these children live with daily, reflected in their blank gazes, causes tragic damage; malnutrition may in fact be stunting the physical growth and the intellectual development of an entire generation. Ethiopia is one of the countries hardest hit by drought in this decade. It is not only the children who suffer the devastation. Dislocated by drought, an old man (bottom) has little to hope for; his existence has been reduced to near starvation in a filthy, makeshift shelter.

Pattern of child deaths—less developed countries, 1980

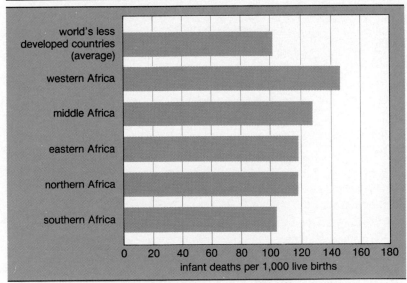

Source: United Nations, "Infant Mortality Rate by Region and Country, 1950–2025, Medium Variant," *Population Bulletin of the United Nations,* no. 14 (1982), pp. 36–41

(Left) Gilbert Brun—Gamma/Liaison; (right) World Health Organization

Tropical parasitic and infectious diseases such as malaria, schistosomiasis, filariasis, leishmaniasis, onchocerciasis, and leprosy take a huge toll on human life in Africa. The attempts to conquer these scourges, which have serious debilitating physical effects when they do not kill, have been marked by a few remarkable successes—such as the eradication of smallpox—some instances of limited progress, and many setbacks. The long and difficult struggle continues. The man shown above suffers from lepromatous leprosy. His face is covered with red nodules of leprosy, a serious complication, accompanied by fever and inflammation of the nerves, joints, testes, and eyes. The blind women above are victims of onchocerciasis, or "river blindness," which affects several million people in West Africa alone. The effort to control the blackfly vectors of the disease over the past decade has been among the most successful of the campaigns to conquer tropical infections. Happily, this success means that millions of children in West Africa no longer face the threat of losing their sight, as their parents did.

and female. By comparison, in Europe and the United States the disease is mainly transmitted homosexually; the ratio of men to women is 13:1. The African population, unable as it is to devote adequate resources to health care and subject often to malnutrition and anemia, is more vulnerable to infection with the human immunodeficiency virus (HIV). Nonsexual methods of transmission of infection are influenced by poverty and cultural factors. In the United States $60 million was spent on upgrading blood-bank screening in 1985. With an average annual expenditure of $1.75 per person, the African health services cannot monitor their transfusion services adequately, and in some areas up to 20% of blood donors have HIV antibodies. The practices of scarification and tattooing and the fact that injections, rather than oral medications, are frequently the method of treatment for patients with infectious diseases add to the problem, as needles are often reused and contaminated.

In spite of efforts by departments of health in Africa to contain the epidemic, there is evidence of a relentless progression, and the incidence of HIV infection is rising. Among prostitutes in Nairobi the incidence of HIV antibodies rose from 4% in 1980 to 59% in 1986, while in Kinshasa, Zaire, among pregnant women it increased from 0.25 to 8%. According to a 1986 report, 27 to 88% of prostitutes in the big cities have HIV antibodies and, sadly, the virus can be transmitted to newborn babies by infected mothers.

The tragedy of AIDS is that it attacks primarily young and middle-aged adults. In Kinshasa, for example, the mean age of infected subjects was 33.6 years. It is thus the most productive and valuable sector of the community that is affected. The economy of Africa is sure to be damaged as a result.

The African Regional Office of WHO has put forward proposals for coping with this immense health problem. It has urged the setting up of national AIDS committees, further epidemiological and research studies, comprehensive blood-screening programs, better laboratory facilities, and

48

(Left) Mark Peters—Sygma; (right) William Campbell—Sygma

Young girls wait to be tested for AIDS. The poster, which uses the slogan "Love carefully," is part of an AIDS education campaign sponsored by the Ugandan Ministry of Health.

training of health workers. A vast educational program is required. All this points to the need for major international commitment in financial, technical, research, and educational terms.

Recently in Zaire there has been a major campaign to end the long-held secrecy that has been typical of many African nations' reaction to the AIDS epidemic. Zaire has acknowledged the grave and serious problem and is organizing efforts to attack it openly. Not all nations in Africa have been as forthcoming.

Also in Zaire, a pioneering research project was begun in September 1986: 12 Zairians and Europeans became subjects in the first human tests

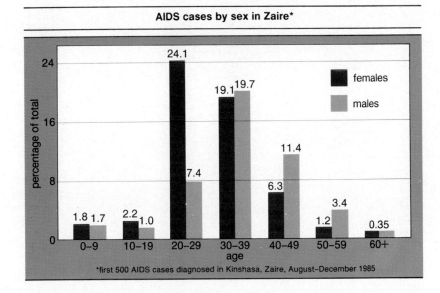

AIDS cases by sex in Zaire*

*first 500 AIDS cases diagnosed in Kinshasa, Zaire, August–December 1985

An AIDS epidemic is currently placing a new and serious burden on the already poor health status of the African people. The countries affected most by the geometric explosion of AIDS are Zaire, Uganda, Rwanda, Burundi, Tanzania, and Zambia. It has been forecast that as many as one million Africans will die of AIDS in the next decade. Unlike AIDS in Western countries, the disease afflicts nearly equal numbers of African men and women (see graph), and the main source of transmission is heterosexual. There have been some recent educational efforts, but a vast program is needed.

Adapted from Thomas C. Quinn *et al.,* "AIDS in Africa: An Epidemiologic Paradigm," *Science,* vol. 234 (Nov. 21, 1986), pp. 955–962

of a potential AIDS vaccine. The subjects, both men and women, were healthy carriers of the AIDS virus; the vaccine is designed to prevent their developing the disease. Between 1984 and 1986 researchers at the Pierre and Marie Curie Institute in Paris and at the University of Kinshasa tested the vaccine substance on African green monkeys.

Raging wars: a major health toll

Some of the problems affecting health care in Africa have been mentioned, yet there are numerous other factors to be considered. First and foremost come war and civil strife. Several conflicts are raging at this moment, as, for instance, in Ethiopia, Chad, Mozambique, and Angola. A major conflict in South Africa threatens to erupt, and huge resources that should have been used for development are poured into military preparations.

Some idea of the catastrophic effects of war can be gained from the experience of Uganda. Prior to independence in 1962, there had taken place a gradual improvement in health service provision and sanitary facilities, and indeed Uganda's health service was regarded as one of the finest in Africa. During the period of military misrule under Idi Amin (1971–79), culminating in a war of liberation, the country became impoverished; government expenditure on health decreased drastically to 6% of what it had been in 1969; immunization and maternal and child health programs came close to breakdown; expulsion of Asian doctors meant that almost half the country's physicians were lost; and in many areas the water supply became unsafe and waterborne diseases flourished. Malnutrition and disease brought about a sharp rise in infant mortality. As a result of all these setbacks, it will take great effort and investment to recover lost growth.

A more recent illustration of the calamitous effects of war in Africa was revealed by a UNICEF study; the results were reported in early 1987. The economic destabilization brought about by cross-border military strikes and

The disadvantaged status of the African continent is reflected in many ways. The level of poverty is one that makes the overall picture look particularly gloomy. Twenty-nine of the world's poorest countries are in sub-Saharan Africa, where the annual gross national product is around $300 per capita—$10,000 per capita is the average in most of the developed countries of the world—and the situation is getting worse. The percentage of Africans living in absolute poverty rose from 82% in 1974 to 91% in 1982.

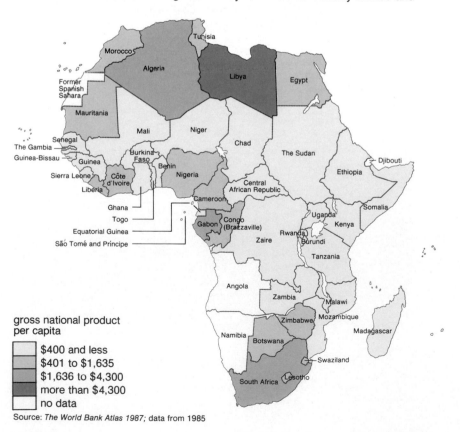

gross national product
per capita

$400 and less
$401 to $1,635
$1,636 to $4,300
more than $4,300
no data

Source: *The World Bank Atlas 1987*; data from 1985

by South Africa's support for guerrilla groups in neighboring countries has resulted in many unnecessary child deaths. It is estimated that in Angola and Mozambique 140,000 deaths a year in children under five years old, or 45% of total deaths in that age group, have been caused by war and consequent economic damage. The infant mortality rate in these two countries has reached 200 per 1,000 live births—the highest in the world.

Traditional healers: vital and valuable

In Africa as a whole, medical services are concentrated in urban areas, while rural areas are neglected. Health care is too often modeled on Western principles, with emphasis on treatment rather than prevention, and money is squandered on expensive hospitals. For instance, in Ghana 85% of health expenditure has been on hospital care benefiting 10% of the population, in comparison with 15% on primary health care (largely in rural areas) for 90% of the population.

It is patently impossible, for cultural and economic reasons, to transfer the methods of modern Western medicine to the African scene and, for that matter, it is not desirable. The various traditions, beliefs, and customs of Africa will inevitably color the choice of health care systems. Indeed, failure to recognize cultural traditions has often resulted in failure of "development" plans. A nonmedical example occurred in Zimbabwe, where a government-backed scheme for obtaining higher agricultural yields through use of appropriate pesticides and fertilizers failed because the masvikiro, or spirit mediums, had not been appealed to for support or advice and the Zimbabwean people had not been reached on a personal level. The masvikiro, who are the village leaders, defended the old farming methods of their ancestors, rejecting the modern use of artificial fertilizers. The peasants followed their trusted role models' guidance rather than accept the new way. Likewise, traditional healers have played, and continue to play, an important role in rural African health care, and their involvement in future plans is both inevitable and essential.

In many African nations war and civil strife are having a major impact as precious resources for health care are diverted for military purposes. In countries embroiled in political upheavals, all efforts to improve health services and raise the general level of development are completely undermined. Calamitous effects are currently being felt most in Ethiopia, Chad, Mozambique, and Angola. In 1985 the world community responded to urgent appeals for food for famine-racked Ethiopia. Some 500,000 tons of cereal grain were sent, but because of obstructive policies on the part of the unstable Ethiopian government, distribution of the food was hampered, and much of it was allowed to rot at port (above). In Angola war is an everyday reality, with many consequences. (Poster at left) The National Union for the Total Independence of Angola has been waging a fierce military struggle against the regime of the Popular Movement for the Liberation of Angola ever since Angolan independence in 1975. An estimated 45% of the total number of deaths of Angolan children under age five have been attributed to the presence of war.

Faith healers performing a traditional rite to cure an ailing member of the Ethiopian Orthodox Church (right) may be dubbed charlatans by Westerners accustomed to modern medicine, and the amulet "treatment" the rural Senegalese woman (opposite) is undergoing is likely to be viewed as blatantly primitive. Nevertheless, the results of what seem to be wholly unscientific practices are often quite impressive. In a continent that recognizes many diverse cultural traditions, it is both unrealistic and counterproductive to impose Western standards or to attempt to institute sophisticated medical methods. Rather, what is needed is a spirit of cooperation between traditional practitioners and Western-trained health workers.

Although techniques used by these healers strike the Western eye as unscientific and even primitive, quite often the results they produce are fairly impressive, particularly in the case of psychological disturbances and psychosomatic disease, where the psychological component is amenable to influence. The art of the traditional healer lies in his intimate understanding of his client—in particular, the role in the family and position in the community—and the healer is well aware of the cultural influences that are most likely to affect his client's mental processes. He may pronounce that the illness is due to possession by evil spirits, to a curse placed upon him by neighbors or enemies, or to certain failings on the part of the sufferer. He may go on to take action that in Western terms would be ill conceived but in the eyes of the patient is logical and appropriate, and he will often achieve a cure without recourse to complex and expensive Western technology.

Methods used by healers will vary. Some will exorcise the evil spirits by incantations and the administration of alarming concoctions, and others will induce a hypnotic trance state by the use of compelling communal music and dance. In The Sudan Muslim healers will ask the patient to drink the dissolved ink of certain religious texts. In addition to these methods of suggestion and hypnosis, however, the traditional healer will often have a profound knowledge of recognized, legitimate herbal remedies and apply these quite successfully.

In recent years practitioners of traditional medicine have begun to press for official recognition, forming national associations in countries where modern doctors and nurses do not reach the people of rural areas. As long ago as 1978, WHO had recommended that it would be better to accept reality and involve suitably trained local healers in primary health care plans. The medical profession in China has pioneered a dual approach to primary health care and has allowed traditional healers, with their experience of such long-established methods as acupuncture and knowledge of herbal medicines, to work side by side with Western-trained doctors, and this has

52

been an acknowledged success. Provided some of the harmful practices at present employed by the less responsible African traditional healers can be discouraged (for example, withholding antibiotics when these are essential or causing delay in the treatment of surgical emergencies), a similar cooperation might usefully develop in Africa.

Contacts between traditional healers and Western-trained health workers should be encouraged and would be mutually beneficial. Swaziland provides an example of a pilot project that brought nurses and traditional healers together and succeeded in improving attitudes and the involvement of traditional healers in efforts to promote good health practices.

Health and economics: hand in hand

It has long been realized that good health cannot be achieved through concentration on health issues alone. *North-South: A Programme for Survival,* the report of the Independent Commission on International Development Issues, under the chairmanship of Willy Brandt, published in 1980, points to this fact: "Improving health requires efforts far beyond medical care; it is closely linked with food and nutrition, with employment and income distribution and with the international economy." It is, however, a two-way process. A sound economy benefits health, and good health helps to achieve an expanding economy. In the words of Halfdan Mahler, director-general of WHO: "The health of a population influences economic development and is influenced by it; it is itself an element or condition of development."

On June 1, 1986, the UN General Assembly considered the critical economic situation in Africa and passed a resolution calling upon all concerned intergovernmental and nongovernmental organizations to support and contribute to the implementation of a program of action. The need was expressed as follows: "A stagnant and perpetually economically backward Africa is not in the best interests of the world community. Without durable and sustained economic development . . . there is a real danger to international peace and security and an impediment to world economic growth and development."

The international community has thus been alerted to the economic needs of Africa. Doctors and other health workers, conscious of their ethical responsibilities as expressed in many declarations of the World Medical Association and many other bodies, can play their part in promoting health, improving the quality of life, and developing human resources, which are essential for progress in economic development.

Today's Dr. Schweitzers: a special role

Accepting that the health needs of Africa are immense, the question has to be asked: Do individuals and voluntary organizations play a significant and helpful role? There is little doubt that the answer to this must be an emphatic yes. Inspired by selfless and dedicated people such as Albert Schweitzer, missionary doctors in Africa have established a long tradition of medical service. Tim Lusty, of the United Kingdom-based Oxfam, has put the work of individual doctors and voluntary organizations into perspective. In the George Armstrong lecture read at an American Ambulatory Pediatric

53

UPI/Bettmann Newsphotos

meeting in Texas in 1980, he described the work of some of the pioneers of health care in Africa and pointed to the advantages and disadvantages of the voluntary agencies. Following a symposium in Makerere, Uganda, in 1966, guidelines of primary health care for health workers had been established; *e.g.,* inappropriate high technology should be avoided while low-cost alternatives should be encouraged, the primary health care worker should be chosen by and from his or her community, and so on. In Lusty's view, the disadvantages of the voluntary agencies were that they were poorly funded, were poorly coordinated, and used a multiplicity of languages, drugs, and methods that led to confusion. In his view, though, these were easily outweighed by the advantages; for example, the ability to act quickly, to pioneer new ideas and methods, to cut through bureaucratic tangles, to distance themselves from politics, and, in general, to act in a flexible manner.

Voluntary agencies from a great many countries in the developed world are dedicated to the promotion of health care in the less developed world and have a long and distinguished history. One or two examples might convey a flavor of their efforts. The African Medical and Research Foundation Flying Doctor Service (AMREF) was founded in the late 1950s by Sir Michael Wood and Sir Archibald McIndoe of the U.K. and Thomas Rees of the U.S. with financial backing from U.S. entertainer Arthur Godfrey. Each year this now international organization makes more than 300 emergency flights on errands for the treatment of such conditions as snakebites and injuries from wild animals. The multinational team of doctors and field staff care for the people of Kenya, Tanzania, Somalia, The Sudan, Uganda, and Ethiopia. The organization also runs a health education program, publishes simple medical texts, and trains community health workers.

The UK-based Teaching Aids at Low Cost (TALC) is another very useful organization. Its task is to provide, at the lowest possible cost, a large range of simple and relevant literature on primary health care and such equipment as weighing scales for monitoring child growth.

These examples must suffice to point to the invaluable work of individual doctors and nurses and voluntary organizations, but it must be realized that their total impact cannot be great and their contributions do not absolve governments and international institutions from their responsibilities.

"Health for All by the Year 2000"

The basis for global good health was laid at Alma-Ata, U.S.S.R., in 1978, when nations met under the auspices of WHO and UNICEF and agreed on a program to achieve primary health care (PHC) for all by the year 2000. It sought to ensure adequate nutrition, safe water, and basic sanitation for all people; family-planning facilities and good maternal child care; immunization against the common infections; the prevention and control of endemic diseases; appropriate treatment for common illnesses; health education; and the provision of essential drugs. These measures strike a balance between prevention and health education on the one hand and appropriate curative treatment on the other. Finally, these services were to be accessible, appropriate, acceptable, and available.

In 1981 WHO selected 12 global indicators to help monitor progress toward Health for All by the Year 2000 (dubbed HFA2000). Here are a few that embody the principles essential for success: at least 5% of the GNP spent on health; an infant mortality rate (IMR) below 50 per 1,000 live births; a life expectancy of over 60; adult literacy in both men and women exceeding 70%; and a per capita GNP in excess of $500.

With its sights on the well-being of children, UNICEF amplifies the HFA2000 plans. Taking into account the limitation of funds, it has put forward some cost-effective proposals that are best remembered by the acronym GOBI (growth monitoring, oral-rehydration therapy, breast-feeding, and immunization). There are three additional programs. First and foremost is female education; second, family spacing; and third, food supplements. Female education has been shown to have a dramatic effect on infant mortality rates, which in many cases have been halved. The educated mother will wish to space her pregnancies and, by doing so, will improve her own health and her infant's chances of survival. A well-informed population will

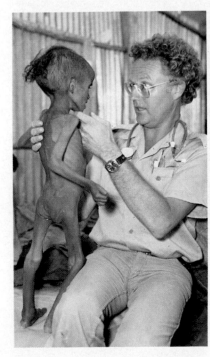

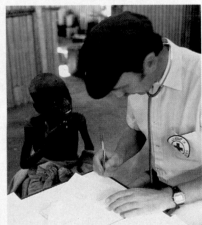

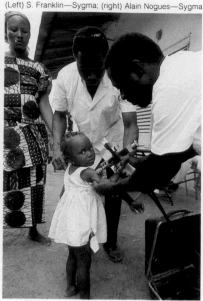

Growth monitoring (right) is an important way to prevent life-threatening complications of severe malnutrition, and it is both simple and inexpensive. Growth charts showing the results of regular monthly weighing make growth problems visible while simple remedies are still possible and long before irreversible effects take hold. Even with meager existing resources, such regular weighing is one of several "technologies" that can make enormous inroads in raising standards of child health. Immunization (far right) against the major childhood infectious diseases is another cost-effective practice that has the potential to vastly improve the outlook for millions of African children.

appreciate the factors that go toward the achievement of good health, will demand a better distribution of health care, and will work toward that goal. Food supplements in pregnancy, where indicated, will be of benefit to both mother and child, preventing low birth weight and further lowering the infant mortality rate.

What progress?

Over eight precious years have elapsed since nations made their resolutions at Alma-Ata, and it is fair to ask at this stage what progress has been made and whether HFA2000 will be achieved. A great deal of hard, devoted work has been done by UNICEF, WHO, and many governmental and nongovernmental agencies, and for this full credit must be given. Using the 12 global indicators already referred to, WHO compiled statistics from 146 member states in its seventh report on the *World Health Situation*, published in 1986. Commenting on this report in *World Health,* Sumedha Khanna, director of WHO's Office of Health for All Strategy Coordination, summarized the progress.

Steps in the right direction. In many countries there has been a great improvement as far as physical accessibility of health services to the population is concerned. There has been progress in many countries in the fields of immunization and maternity and child welfare. Infant mortality rates and life expectancy are showing improvement in the majority of countries. Khanna admits, however, certain shortcomings. The care of children under the age of five is limited and, although water supply and sanitation were improved in some areas, there was an overall deterioration because of population growth and the effect of droughts. The 1985 UNICEF report on the state of the world's children points to considerable success in the fields of their four key low-cost programs.

In 1985 a dozen African countries jointly reviewed their primary health care programs. They found some evidence of progress. For instance, in

A major African health crisis that has only recently become apparent, which has been called "a hidden tragedy," is Africa's high maternal death rate. This is in addition to infant mortality rates that are the highest in the world. In sub-Saharan Africa 1,400 women die each day in the process of carrying and delivering their children. In response to the maternal health crisis, community clinics have begun to provide comprehensive prenatal services, enabling women to help one another remain healthy during pregnancy and breast-feeding and to get advice from health workers as necessary. The pregnant women pictured here attend a clinic in Nigeria for blood pressure monitoring and prenatal instruction.

Kenya 92% of mothers received antenatal care; in Botswana 63% of one- and two-year-old children were fully immunized; Zambia succeeded in reducing the proportion of children under 80% of standard weight to about one-quarter; and in Tanzania safe water had been provided to 80% of the urban and 42% of the rural populations. In 1985 Zimbabwe had trained more than 5,000 each of community health workers and traditional birth attendants. All these are impressive achievements and show a deep commitment toward progress in health care.

The bleaker reality. So much for the positive and optimistic view of progress. Unfortunately, the full picture is not a bright one and must be painted as it is—in its uncomfortable reality. A report by the director-general of WHO to the 39th World Health Assembly in February 1986 stated: "The effects of the economic crisis have been most serious for the poorest and those whose health is most vulnerable. In countries most seriously affected, progress towards health for all has already been halted or reversed." Referring specifically to the African region, the report said: "In general the shortage of funds to pay for imported drugs and equipment has seriously disrupted services in many African countries. Fiscal retrenchment and inflation have led . . . to the disintegration of rural health service."

There are then factors mainly of a political and economic nature that hamper and even reverse progress. Large-scale famines have undone much good work in health care, and it has been shown in a UNICEF study that the nutritional status of children in Botswana and Ghana greatly deteriorated in 1983 and 1984, when between 30 and 40% of the children were found to be grossly underweight.

In fact, in 1984 a quarter more children died of malnutrition and disease in the less developed world than would have in "normal circumstances." In some countries infant mortality rates have actually increased, while public expenditure on health services has often been reduced, sometimes as a condition of obtaining loans. In addition to this there was, between 1983

Poverty is not seen only in rural and drought-stricken areas; the shantytown scene in South Africa (above) shows the kind of shabby living conditions that are prevalent throughout urban Africa. (Opposite page) Severe protein-calorie malnutrition is very dramatically visible in small children in Africa, especially in areas hit by recent famines where malnutrition and starvation had not been common previously. Mali suffered such a crisis when drought struck in 1968. A child from Mali shows evidence of the disease kwashiorkor: profound swelling of the belly, hyperpigmentation and patchiness of the skin, hair loss, and extreme lethargy and apathy. Large-scale famine has the effect of undoing progress. Both Botswana and Ghana were beginning to see some gains in overall child heath status, but then in 1983–84, owing to unwaning famine, the percentage of children found to be grossly underweight once again began to rise, as the graphs indicate.

and 1984, a 13% decline in aid from the developed countries specifically directed to health.

The situation with regard to primary health care in Ghana has been described and assessed. A health-planning unit was set up in 1976, and then a planning team was assembled, relevant sections of the population ranging from farmers and health workers to politicians were involved, and the cooperation of ministries related to the health sectors was obtained. Owing to a deterioration of the national economy linked to the global economic recession, however, many serious problems have arisen—problems of inadequate transport, scarcity of spare parts for vehicles, and shortages of essential drugs at the periphery. Similar experiences were voiced by the United States Agency for International Development. These failures and deficiencies, even when every effort is being made in planning and involvement at a grass-roots level, point—more than anything else, perhaps—to the need for greater national and international funding.

At a conference in London in September 1986, sponsored jointly by the Medical Association for Prevention of War and the United Nations Association of Great Britain and Northern Ireland, speakers wrestled with the problems of health care in Africa. They considered prospects for the future, the resources needed for adequate health care, and the means of satisfying these needs.

Predicting the future

It would require great courage and prescience to predict the future course of health in Africa. UNICEF, on one hand, takes an optimistic view, claiming that, with ideas and methods embodied in its "child survival revolution," the lives of half of the African children who die each year could be saved.

58

Ecological uncertainties: four scenarios. In contrast to UNICEF's optimism, Maurice King, senior lecturer in the department of community medicine at the University of Leeds, England, and formerly professor of social medicine in Zambia, in describing the present state of health in Africa at the London conference, was not so certain of the outcome. He pointed to doubts and fears concerning the ecology; the mismanagement of the ecosystem could mean that food production would not keep pace with population increases and might well result in death by starvation of over half a billion people by the end of the century.

King envisaged four possible scenarios. First he saw a rapid demographic transition from high fertility and population increase to lower fertility and a stabilized, sustainable population, which would allow progressive socioeconomic development in Africa. The adoption of radical family-planning methods such as those practiced in China would exert a beneficial influence; favorable economic events such as a breakthrough in alternate sources of energy would do likewise. The second scenario is a predicted population crash, of which the recent famines are a warning. The third is a state of "chronic misery" brought about by a perpetuation of the status quo—the population perhaps stabilizing at a new high figure. High fertility and population increases would be counteracted by periodic population crashes. There would be chronic poverty and possibly regression or "de-development." The fourth possibility is unthinkable; namely, a global tragedy such as a "nuclear winter," which would put an end to all human hopes.

Grandiose plans fail. King saw no easy answers to the problems of development and improved health care. Grandiose schemes such as the building of huge dams have failed to improve the economy and have often had adverse effects on health. International governmental aid has decreased. There has been no support for the proposed so-called new international economic order, which was intended to make conditions of trade between the developed and less developed countries fairer toward the latter, thereby increasing the pace of development and giving the countries of the third

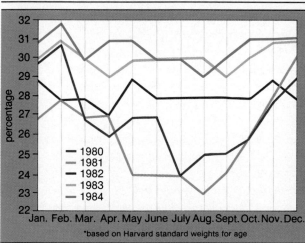

Botswana
children (1–4 years) below 80% standard weight for age*

percentage

— 1980
— 1981
— 1982
— 1983
— 1984

Jan. Feb. Mar. Apr. May June July Aug. Sept. Oct. Nov. Dec.

*based on Harvard standard weights for age

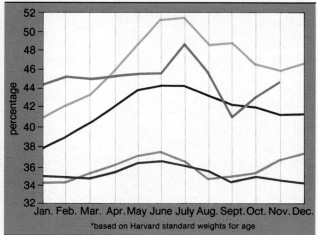

Ghana
children (7–42 months) below 80% standard weight for age*

percentage

Jan. Feb. Mar. Apr. May June July Aug. Sept. Oct. Nov. Dec.

*based on Harvard standard weights for age

Sources: (Left) "Background Papers for Workshop on Social and Nutritional Surveillance in Eastern and Southern Africa," *UNICEF Social Statistics Bulletin,* vol. 5, no. 4 (1982); (right) Catholic Relief Services, Ghana

world the opportunity to industrialize, to improve their social structures, to increase their purchasing power, and to decrease their dependence on outside assistance. The trend has, rightly, been toward smaller projects—people-oriented, participatory, low technology, and ecologically viable.

Will the children survive? All the efforts to reverse high infant mortality, unless accompanied by a demographic transition, may result in an increase in the total quantity of misery. What is the point of a child's surviving an episode of diarrhea or measles only to die of starvation later? There is, then, a clear case calling for careful scrutiny of development as a whole; in other words, health care must be considered along with social and economic development so that the quality of life is enhanced side by side with physical survival and prolonged longevity.

Help from advantaged countries

At first sight it would seem too difficult to assess the resource requirements for basic health in the continent of Africa and particularly the proportion that might be contributed by the richer and more fortunate developed world. Nevertheless, various economic assessments have been made, and these are in general agreement on the quantity of aid needed to achieve HFA2000 in the less developed countries.

There are, broadly speaking, two approaches to the problems of providing adequate global health care. The first attempts to define minimum standards of health, education, nutrition, water supply, and hygiene, which are to be applied worldwide, and then sets out to plan and implement the necessary programs. This can be called the "total approach." The second is a more modest attempt, or "partial approach," in which key elements of health care are singled out and applied to smaller communities where the needs are greatest. The latter appears to be in keeping with the methods and aims of UNICEF and many nongovernmental organizations. Therefore, both of these approaches need to be evaluated so it can be decided which offers the best chance of acceptance by the less developed countries themselves and the international community and which is more likely to be implemented.

At the September 1986 conference in London on the Medical Needs of Africa, George E. Cumper, senior lecturer in the London School of Hygiene and Tropical Medicine, agreed with the WHO position that an infant mortality rate of 50 or less per 1,000 is a valid and sensible indicator of an acceptable minimum standard of health care. It lies in between the average European IMR of about 20 and the average African IMR of about 120 and corresponds to a life expectancy of some 60 years. It can be regarded as a satisfactory advance over the present situation and yet is not overambitious and sets out an achievable target. Cumper's proposed approach may perhaps be put into the first group, *i.e.,* that of a "total approach," yet it is reasonably modest in its demands.

According to Cumper, the next step was to determine the level of health care help generally required by countries that have reached this IMR and standard of health care. He considered three main areas, namely, health care, water supply and sanitation, and basic education. In the first cate-

One way of raising current health standards is to provide trained community health workers, especially in rural settings. It is important that the medical services they provide strike a balance between, on the one hand, basic prevention and health education and, on the other, treatments that are at once appropriate, accessible, acceptable, and available. (Below) A trained midwife assists in a rural Ethiopian birth. Such help and simple child-care instruction as she is able to provide often can make the difference between life and death to both mother and infant.

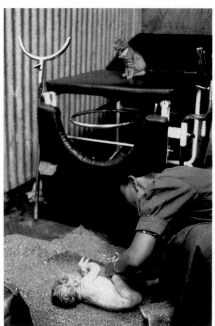

Alain Keler—Sygma

60

In some urban areas in Africa, standards of medical care are comparable to modern Western standards, as at this maternity hospital in Lagos, Nigeria. Unfortunately, however, one of the great problems plaguing African health care on the grand scale is the disproportionate distribution of available care. The vast proportion of money that is squandered on expensive hospitals that do not serve the needs of those who need care the most is such an example. Medical services are, for the most part, concentrated in urban areas, while large rural areas are neglected, and all too often health care is modeled on clearly inappropriate Western principles. The graphs below showing expenditures in Ghana and Tanzania make this clear.

gory are included such factors as the number of physicians, other health workers, and hospital beds per 10,000 of the population. In the second category is the percentage of the population supplied with safe water and excreta disposal, and in the third is the number of school places and teachers per population.

This allows a calculation of the shortfalls in each category for each less developed country and finally an estimate of the cost of making good these shortfalls. Naturally there are complicating factors that will distort the calculations, and these must be taken into account. Allowance will have to be made for population growth, the ups and downs of projected national income, inflation, and so forth. Under favorable domestic and international circumstances, the costs of remedying the resource gap will be far lower than under adverse conditions, and so it is necessary to present minimum and maximum estimates.

While it must be accepted that national per capita income is a major factor in health care provision and that, by and large, countries with a per capita GNP of over $1,000 usually reach the minimum levels of health care and countries with less do not, it must also be admitted that there are exceptions to this rule of thumb. One can point to China and Sri Lanka as examples of poorer countries that have, nevertheless, an excellent record in health care provision. These successes can, no doubt, be put down to a combination of political will, past culture, and a wise, efficient, and energetic approach to health problems in which the grass roots of the population are encouraged to play an active role.

The corollary of this is that economic aid is a necessary but not sufficient element, and success throughout the less developed world will depend on many less tangible factors. The experience and accumulated expertise of the UN, UNICEF, and other international bodies will play an important role in directing the approach to health care into wise and effective channels and, no doubt, political leaders will find it socially, morally, and economically right to strive toward adequate health goals.

Health expenditures/ population served in Ghana

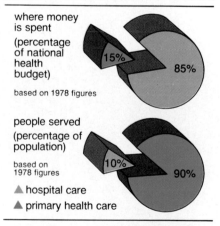

where money is spent (percentage of national health budget)

based on 1978 figures

15% 85%

people served (percentage of population)

based on 1978 figures

10% 90%

▲ hospital care
▲ primary health care

Health expenditures in Tanzania

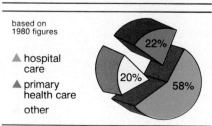

based on 1980 figures

▲ hospital care
▲ primary health care
  other

22% 20% 58%

Sources: (Top) D. Morley and H. Lovel, *My Name Is Today* (London: Macmillan, 1986), fig. 93; (bottom) Ministry of Health, Accra, Ghana, *A Primary Health Care Strategy for Ghana,* April 1978

Dollars and cents: the staggering figures. To return to the question of funding, it can be shown that the resources needed for the attainment of a target IMR of 50 in the less developed countries will on the average mean an expenditure of some 3.6% of national income on health care and 4.1% on education and the provision of some 2.3 hospital beds, 0.3 physicians, and 1.3 other health workers per 10,000 of population. At least half the people will need to be supplied with clean water, and there should be school places for 18% of the population. The shortfall for Africa is staggering. It means 1 million extra hospital beds, 155,000 more physicians, and 640,000 other health workers. Clean water and excreta disposal will need to be provided to 240 million people. In education 2.8 million teachers and 72 million school places will have to be found.

It is estimated that capital requirements for construction costs and manpower development to the year 2000 will amount to $750 million per year. Recurrent costs on health and education amount to $7.8 billion. It must be admitted that these estimates are based on minimum requirements—on the assumption of adequate growth of the economy. If, however, the present economic recession continues and terms of trade are disadvantageous to the less developed countries, then the costs could well rise to yet larger figures—as high as $3.4 billion per year and $39.5 billion for recurrent costs.

As governments control only a small proportion of the national income in the less developed countries (for southern Africa this amounts to 13.6%), they would find it difficult, if not impossible, to improve health care by redistributing defense-spending funds to health care or by increasing the proportion of the national income devoted to health. If, by some miracle, peace were to break out on the continent of Africa and security could be achieved with far smaller military expenditure, then *some* of the money needed could be so found. But the hard fact is that under present conditions international assistance will be needed.

Finding the funds. In an ideal world compassion and reason would dictate that financial resources be set aside to correct the enormous health care deficiencies of the less developed countries. But the facts are otherwise. For all manner of reasons—and particularly because of the shortsightedness of the international community—funds directed toward health care have been insufficient.

While world military expenditures are approaching $1 trillion, official development aid is a miserly 0.33% of the national product of the richer countries and amounts in all to some $35 billion. Of this total the amount devoted to health care is calculated to be only $3.9 billion.

Why are the richer countries not giving more than this? The answer may be that they perceive their own economies to be under strain and that social problems and poverty exist even in the richest countries, making it difficult to divert resources abroad. There are many competing claims they must satisfy—those of security; investment in industry and research; housing, health, and education at home; and all the numerous calls for their welfare programs. It seems that the only slack in the economy, the only sector from which transfers could be contemplated without adverse social consequences, is the military one. Yet a simple reduction of military expenditure will by no means guarantee increased spending on socially useful projects at home or abroad.

Before military budgets can be cut, it must be shown that national security will not be impaired, that the economies of the affected countries will not suffer appreciably, and that unemployment will not result. There have been many studies of these problems. Most notably, a UN panel of governmental experts considered the relationship between disarmament and development and submitted its report in 1981. The conclusions reached by these experts support the thesis that there would not be a loss of security but a gain both in military terms, by reason of a reduced threat of global annihilation, and in economic terms because security also means social and economic stability and because more resources would be available to go into the civilian sector. With properly planned mechanisms and institutions for conversion from military to civilian industrial technology, no unemployment would have to result.

A vital question thus arises: How can funds for health care be transferred from the affluent world to the impoverished nations of Africa?

Innovative proposals. There have been many attempts to establish a development fund. In 1955 Edgar Faure, then prime minister of France, put forward a plan under which the U.S., the U.K., France, and the U.S.S.R. would reduce their military spending by an increasing percentage each year and contribute a part of the savings to a development fund. A year or so later the Soviet Union suggested a reduction of 10 to 15% of the military budgets of the major powers, with a proportion of the savings going to development. In 1973 the UN General Assembly actually adopted a resolution calling for military budgets of the major powers to be reduced by 10% and one-tenth of this to be used for development, but the scheme was to apply for only one year. None of these proposals has been carried into practice.

Perhaps the most important and detailed plan was put forward in 1978 by Valéry Giscard d'Estaing, who was at that time president of France. He suggested the creation of a new UN agency—an International Disarmament

Africa desperately needs effective programs that reach the public and that educate about health matters. This billboard (opposite page) is part of a recent African health education campaign. Malaria is a major tropical infection that has proved to be stubbornly resistant to even all-out, well-organized eradication efforts. Though the battle is far from won—the development of a vaccine and the accomplishment of effective mosquito control are still needed—newer antimalarial drugs such as Nivaquine are both safe and effective—that is, provided people know about and use them. Limiting the population growth is another measure that will ensure a healthier life for those who are brought into the world.

Fund for Development. This envisaged a one-time endowment of $1 trillion, followed by a yearly disarmament dividend. The element of national security would be safeguarded by agreements on optimum security thresholds for each country.

There are problems with all these schemes. It is acknowledged that voluntary contributions cannot be relied upon. An armament levy seems to legitimize military expenditure and may not reduce the level of armaments. A disarmament dividend, by reducing armaments irrespective of the perceived needs for security, appears to compromise national security interests. (However, the above French proposal does take this factor into account.) The fact must also be faced that any contribution based solely on military expenditure would weigh unfairly on some countries and far too lightly on others. Japan, for example, although wealthy, spends relatively little on arms and would escape a heavy levy. This leads to the conclusion that assessments would also have to be made on the basis of national wealth.

Assuming that 1% of world military spending could be diverted to development, that would amount to around $10 billion, not a sum to satisfy all developmental needs but sufficient to fund a "partial approach" to health care. It is important to remember that the health needs of Africa are but one item of the overall developmental needs of that continent, and it has been estimated by the UN program of action for African economic recovery and development that these other needs would require from the international community another $9 billion annually in the years 1986–90. It must also be remembered that there are other regions in the world in need of developmental assistance. Therefore, a more realistic diversion from military spending to development would appear to be more in the region of 2% of present military expenditure.

At the September 1986 conference on the Medical Needs of Africa, Saardet Deger, an economist at Birkbeck College, London, made two important and interesting proposals. First, she suggested that the human resources of the armed forces in the less developed countries could be turned to good account by the use of those people's skills in developmental programs, as is no doubt already done in some instances; *e.g.,* disaster aid. They could help in literacy campaigns, road and medical center construction, transport, and many other areas. This would, in fact, be a way of distributing resources from military use to development. Second, she advocated that professional groups of the less developed and developed countries join hands to bring their knowledge and skills to bear on developmental problems. This would ensure that assistance was given with adequate attention to local needs and in an appropriate manner by taking account of sensible technology and ecological necessities.

New world attitudes

Medical institutions in the developed countries are showing increased interest in the health of the less developed world and increased willingness to accept some responsibility. For example, two recent public lectures at the Royal College of Physicians, London, were devoted to international health, and in 1985 the British Medical Association, at its annual general meeting,

The achievement of a raised living standard and good health is impossible without a safe water supply and major improvements in sanitation. This hand pump in Mali was installed at Galbi in the rural Zinder District to lighten the work of native women and to reduce their exposure to waterborne diseases.

UNICEF

HEALTH FOR ALL
BY THE YEAR 2000

WORLD HEALTH DAY 1983

THE COUNT-DOWN HAS BEGUN!

passed a resolution calling for "a massive and progressive reduction in world arms spending, both nuclear and conventional, with diversion of the resources thus freed to health care and welfare at home and in the developing countries." International Physicians for the Prevention of War, based in Washington, D.C., has asked U.S. and Soviet leaders to guarantee the resources for immunizing all the world's children by the year 1990 and to appropriate part of the money saved from disarmament for public health programs on behalf of children in less developed nations. One of the latter organization's affiliates, the Medical Association for Prevention of War (U.K. and Australia), believes that in addition to research into the causes and effects of war and to steps toward multilateral disarmament, there must be a positive program toward peace, including the transfer of resources from arms to development and health care.

At the World Medical Assembly in Geneva in May 1986, M. Savel'ev of the Ministry of Health of the Soviet Union said, "The attainment of the goal of Health for All is directly dependent on the preservation of world peace." Indeed, by whatever method, a way must be found *soon* to divert funds from military spending to development unless the richer countries are prepared to isolate themselves and ignore the appeal of the needy and the poor. The improvement of health care in the world's less developed countries and particularly in the most disadvantaged regions of Africa will be both a means of accelerating the pace of development and a rational humanitarian act.

Health for all Africans by the year 2000 is the goal and the challenge established at Alma-Ata, U.S.S.R., in 1978, when nations met under the auspices of the World Health Organization and UNICEF and agreed on a program of primary health care for people across the globe by the turn of the century. There have been notable steps in the right direction, but the overall picture for Africa is not bright. There is yet a very long way to go. Major help from the international community is essential if Africa's tragic state of affairs is ever to be rectified.

World Health Organization

65

The
BUSINESS
of
THINNESS
by Gina Kolata

"We have a national obsession with thinness," said Steven Blair of the Institute for Aerobics Research, Dallas, Texas, at a recent U.S. government workshop on childhood obesity. "Our society is overly concerned with body size," Norman Krasnegor commented at the same meeting. Krasnegor, a psychologist, is chief of the human learning and behavior branch at the U.S. National Institute of Child Health and Human Development, Bethesda, Maryland.

Yet this "thinness mania" appears to do little other than fatten the wallets of the promoters of diet and exercise businesses. Every year, according to the National Center for Health Statistics, Americans get fatter, and every year more Americans than ever before say they are trying to lose weight. More than a third of all Americans say they are trying to reduce. There are no reliable data on the exact size of the U.S. weight-loss business, but it is estimated that the industry takes in tens of billions of dollars each year.

Not only is the diet business more profitable than ever before, but it has never been as diverse or as robust as it is today. Although the industry is to some extent regulated by the U.S. Food and Drug Administration (FDA), the U.S. Postal Service, and the Federal Trade Commission (FTC), nothing seems to stop the outrageous claims and promises of lifelong thinness that lure the desperate and the gullible to try one weight-loss scheme after another.

Madonna did it—so can you!

"Exclusive! We've got the UCLA diet," proclaims the cover of the April 1987 *Redbook* magazine. Inside are a 1,200-calorie-a-day diet and testimonials from women whose lives were transformed when they lost weight. Susan, a 30-year-old medical assistant, wrote to the magazine's editors, "My weight loss has given me a confidence boost, which I truly needed! I feel great." "I have dieted all my life. My weight has always yo-yoed. Not anymore," wrote Judi, a 42-year-old hospital administrator.

Redbook is far from alone in its promotion of diets. In the March 1987 issue, *Prevention* magazine advertised on its cover a "new" way to diet. "Get your mate to help you lose weight," it says. The March 17 issue of the tabloid *Star* blares from the supermarket checkout line: "14 pounds thinner

Gina Kolata is a writer for Science *magazine, Washington, D.C.* *Tom D. Naughton,* sidebar author, is *a free-lance health and science writer, Chicago.*

(Opposite page) "A Light Article"— from a painting by Luise Max-Ehrler; photograph, Jean-Loup Charmet, Paris

on a popcorn diet. Madonna did it—and so can you on a doctor's great new plan." Before-and-after photos of rock singer Madonna are featured on the cover. Inside the *Star* tells how Madonna did it—not only did she eat less but she "ran six miles a day, swam 25 lengths in a pool, pedaled an exercise bike and sweated through aerobics classes."

For those who seek the easy way out, abundant ads offer miraculous products that can be ordered through the mail. A "new super-fast Japanese reducing pill," for example, will "reduce calorie absorption." The pill advertisement promises "NO diet or calorie counts" and "NO exercise. Automatic weight loss." Then there are the tablets called Cal-Ban 3000, which allow an individual to "lose up to 50 pounds without dieting!" When taking these pills, the ad claims, you can "eat all you want and still lose weight . . . lose weight whether you exercise or not . . . keep your pep without getting jittery . . . melt away flab—and keep it off."

Outrageous claims, faulty premises

The advertising pitches of diets and other weight-loss schemes are targeted to appeal to the overweight person's points of greatest vulnerability—or wildest fantasies. Vanity, fear of looking "middle aged," loss of sex appeal, abhorrence of exercise, low tolerance for feeling deprived, impatience—the weight-loss industry has managed to capitalize on each of these. A health club chain in Washington State embarrassed clients into joining, challenging, "Do you really want to look like that for the rest of your life?" The blurb on a recent book aimed at the paunchy fortyish male reads: "How a middle-aged man became a healthy hunk." Two diet books introduced in the spring of 1987, *The Popcorn-Plus Diet* and *The Feel Full Diet,* typify the appeal to the dieter's fear of being overwhelmed with hunger while trying to cut calories. Fiber supplement plans also claim to cure that empty feeling. Many ads emphasize instantaneous results. A "body wrap" cream advertised that users could "lose up to two inches from those problem areas in just one hour." Still other products offer dieters the holy grail—a way to eat all they want and not gain weight. Lotos Slimming Tea claimed to help dieters "lose weight from the very first day without cutting back on food in any way, without doing gymnastics, and without taking pills." What more could anyone ask?

Typically, the claims made by diet books and weight-loss programs are based on faulty premises. Still, there are plenty of people who are more than ready to believe them. A major problem is that most people know almost nothing about nutrition—and still less about the intricacies of metabolism—and therefore unquestioningly accept outrageous claims that are totally without scientific basis. Grapefruit burns fat, according to one popular diet program. Another says that the order in which foods are eaten makes a difference in how fattening they are. Then there is the classic "calories don't count" ploy.

In fact, calories, which are a measure of how much energy a particular quantity of food contains when metabolized by the body, are really *all* that counts in determining how fattening a food is. Calories literally measure food energy. If a person eats more calories—more food energy—than his

Obsession with weight is almost universal—especially among women. In the U.S. the first scales, early instruments of the obsession, were imported from Germany toward the end of the 19th century. These mahogany-cased platform versions, themselves weighing several hundred pounds, were indeed novelties; "penny" scales drew waiting lines in such places as banks, railroad depots, and dime stores. Before long the scale had moved into the more domestic setting of the residential bathroom; by the 1930s every affluent or middle-income family was likely to own one. Ironically, weight watchers of today get only an approximation of their true weight from most home scales. For a more accurate reading they are likely to turn to the doctor's-office-type of platform scale like the ones found in health club locker rooms.

Four By Five

68

(Left) In the late 19th century, French health authorities made sure that all children were weighed regularly and that careful records were kept of their progress to ensure that they were growing at a healthy rate. Parents took pride in their robust offspring. In the U.S. as well, chubby children were then considered to be the healthiest children.

or her body needs, the excess is stored in the form of fat. As scientific theories about fats, obesity, and exercise become more complicated, the diet hucksters follow suit by becoming increasingly sophisticated in their deployment of pseudoscientific terms and impressive-sounding justifications for schemes that have no basis in fact.

Proliferation of a vast industry

The story of the weight-loss business in the United States began in earnest around 1900 when the first "obesity tablets" came on the market. The advertisements for these products closely resembled some of the diet ads that appear today. For example, one of these early drugs was Phytolacca, a formulation that consisted of arsenic, strychnine, caffeine, and pokeberry. Its promoter, "Doctor" W. T. Baxter, claimed that the product had "a special selective action on fat cells," turning fatty tissue into muscle and sweeping away all waste.

As chronicled by Hillel Schwartz in his recent history of dieting, *Never Satisfied,* the major weight-loss fads in the U.S. between 1880 and 1920 were fasting, calorie counting, thyroid medications to speed up the metabolism, and a system called Fletcherism, which called for slowly chewing each morsel of food. In the 1930s the bathroom scale arrived on the scene, and soon every affluent and middle-income home had one; Americans became exquisitely aware of their weight. In the following years the preoccupation grew, and the kinds and numbers of products designed to promote weight

"Don't laugh, they've helped me lose 9 ounces."

69

loss proliferated. They ranged from diet pills to diet books, from low-calorie artificial sweeteners to low-fat ice cream and prepackaged frozen dinners that provide a complete meal containing no more than 300 calories. Overweight kids were sent to diet camps; their parents joined the many self-help groups designed to lend emotional support to those undergoing the ordeal of reducing. Now many have turned to exercise—fast becoming an obsession—however short-lived it may prove to be.

Diet pills. Drugs used in the treatment of obesity are officially classified by the FDA as "anorexics," or "anorexigenics." There are two categories: amphetamines (*e.g.,* Desoxyn, Dexedrine, Didrex) and nonamphetamines. All amphetamines and some nonamphetamines are available by prescription only. These are by no means innocuous drugs. Amphetamines carry a warning stating that they have "a high potential for abuse" and that long-term use "may lead to drug dependence." They are prescribed for weight reduction only for patients in whom other weight-loss therapies have been unsuccessful. While they have the effect of suppressing appetite, it is not known whether this effect is actually responsible for weight reduction. Furthermore, their ability to promote weight loss declines over time so that they are not effective for long-term use. While amphetamine and amphetamine-like prescription drugs were once commonly given by U.S. doctors to their overweight patients and represented a profitable venture for the pharmaceutical industry, these drugs are much less widely prescribed today. Until very recently some desperate American dieters would travel to Mexico to get a Mexican prescription drug called Redotex, a dangerous combination of stimulants and other active ingredients. The drug is still available in Mexico but, by FDA order, legally it cannot be taken back to the U.S. by visitors returning from that country.

Many nonprescription, or over-the-counter (OTC), drugs for weight control contain one of two active ingredients: phenylpropanolamine, a stimulant also found in many decongestants, which is supposed to suppress the appetite, or benzocaine, a topical anesthetic that numbs the gums and

One of the most successful—and enduring—strategies of the diet business is the "no effort" ploy. Ads for two products from the turn of the century (right) proclaim that unwanted fat can be made to disappear without such unpleasantries as diet or exercise. Along with reducing soaps were a variety of ointments, powders, pastes, oils, and juices that promised to remove fat from the outside of the body when used alone or in combination. While the bar of soap undoubtedly got smaller and smaller with each use, the user probably did not undergo a similar transformation!
The alternative strategy was to take something—anything—that, if swallowed, would prevent fat from accumulating. Most of the patent medicines of the late 19th and early 20th centuries fall into this category—a majority based on "botanic" ingredients, usually herbs with stimulant or laxative properties.

Despite the relative sophistication of most contemporary diet schemes, there are still numerous products that appeal to the consumer's nostalgia for remedies that are "all natural." The herbal teas at left were purchased in 1987 at a downtown Chicago outlet of a major national health-food chain.

reduces the sense of taste. These nonprescription drugs are a big business today. The Thompson Medical Co., which sells Appedrine, Prolamine, Control, and Dexatrim, had revenues of $137 million in 1985. Nonetheless, the FDA has never approved any over-the-counter drug as both safe and effective for weight loss. An FDA advisory panel recommended in 1982 that phenylpropanolamine be approved as an aid to weight loss. Some authorities, however, believe the drug may be dangerous because it raises blood pressure, and it is not clear that it really leads to weight loss. Some studies appear to indicate it is helpful, while others fail to confirm any benefit. In the meantime, the FDA has not decided whether to approve phenylpropanolamine for weight loss, although it obviously can still be sold.

The diet-book business. There are more than 300 diet books in print in English today, and at least one seems to be on the *New York Times* best-seller list every week. A recent Sunday *Times* "Book Review" examined 14 new titles (by no means representing *all* the entries of the spring diet-book "season"). The reviewer described the works under consideration as "vessels of one of the great spiritual movements of our time—gospels of the American cult of the thin." "There is the hope of heaven on earth" but, the reviewer commented, there is also the $14.95–$19.95 collection plate, "which is the only full plate you [the consumer] are apt to encounter." The amount of money made by the authors, publishers, and promoters of diet books is not inconsiderable. Two recent best-sellers, Harvey and Marilyn Diamond's *Fit for Life* and Martin Katahn's *The Rotation Diet,* sold well over two million and one million copies, respectively.

Low-cal foods. The first diet foods introduced in the U.S. market gained immediate popularity. Saccharin, the first synthetic sugar substitute, was discovered in 1879 and was widely used in the early years of the 20th century until some qualms about its safety prompted the first ban on its use. In the meantime, other artificial sweeteners were developed. Perhaps their greatest use has been in diet soft drinks, popular products whose market even now is estimated to be growing at a rate of 20% per year.

April A. Oswald

Diet books, the "gospels" of the thinness mania, proliferate at a prodigious rate. A recent count found more than 300 in print in English, and new ones appear seasonally, like crops—many making the best-seller lists. One such book, The Rotation Diet, *earned its author, Martin Katahn, a psychology professor at Vanderbilt University, Nashville, Tennessee, both fame and fortune. Today, however, most overweight Americans are beginning to wake up to the reality that dieting is not the sole answer to the problem. The importance of exercise is receiving more and more emphasis in both medical and popular literature. Here, too, there is money to be made. (Opposite page, bottom) In the U.S. the National Sporting Goods Association reported, for example, that sports footwear sales reached more than $3 billion in 1986. The display racks at a local shoe store abound with special models for running, walking, racquet sports, aerobic dancing, and hiking. Stationary bicycles, which have long been a staple at Y's and health clubs, have also come a long way. They range from simple models for home use to complex machines with computerized readings that display work load, heart rate, calories burned, and maximum oxygen uptake. Some even simulate rides up and down hills. Of course, these products will not do any good if they are not used.*

Today these drinks are sweetened with aspartame ("NutraSweet"), and G. D. Searle, the manufacturer of aspartame, took in $585 million in revenues from the sweetener in 1984 alone. Frozen "light" entrees and dinners now constitute 21% of the frozen food market and are a more than $800 million-a-year business. Sales of diet foods and beverages were increasing at three times the rate of all other foods and drinks in 1984, and industry analysts were projecting that revenues from these products would reach $41 billion by 1990.

The group approach. Diet clubs (Weight Watchers, Diet Workshop, Take Off Pounds Sensibly [TOPS], and others), many of which are patterned after the Alcoholics Anonymous self-help model, proliferate and thrive. Some of these, it must be stated, are based on sound diet and nutrition principles and offer the individual a sensible approach to lasting—but *slowly achieved*—weight reduction. The fact remains, nevertheless, that they are businesses, catering to an "ever hungry" population of consumers.

Weight Watchers, founded in 1963 by Jean Nidetch, a Long Island, New York, housewife, is the oldest and most successful of these businesses. The statistics are dizzying. The company reports that more than 25 million people have attended at least one meeting of the now-international organization, and 700,000 people in the U.S. are current members. There are more than 15,000 Weight Watchers meetings each week, and there are Weight Watchers frozen foods and a Weight Watchers magazine that has a circulation of 900,000. The *Weight Watchers Fast and Fabulous Recipe Book,* published in 1984, has sold more than 700,000 copies.

The exercise industry. According to the U.S. National Center for Health Statistics, most people who want to lose weight now say that they are trying to eat less and exercise more. This means that not only the makers of diet pills and foods and the creators of new diets but also the exercise industry is profiting from overweight. The sale of athletic shoes alone brought in more than $3 billion in the United States in 1986.

Moreover, it is not only those who are overweight who exercise and diet. More and more people of normal weight say that they are staying thin by exercising vigorously and watching what they eat. For example, thin clients at the grueling one-and-a-half-hour advanced aerobics classes at the Bodyline exercise studio in Bethesda, Maryland, talk constantly of "burning off" fat. Many are regulars at the daily class; in addition to riding exercise bicycles for as much as an hour a day, some also work out on Nautilus machines in order to keep their weight down.

Search for the miracle product continues

The diet industry includes legitimate companies, of course, which continually search for new prescription drugs to aid in weight loss. A number of biotechnology companies are currently interested in the new synthetic human growth hormone, which may allow dieters to lose fat but not muscle. This hypothesis has yet to be tested, but Genentech, a San Francisco company, has already estimated that the market for this drug as an obesity treatment would be in the billions of dollars.

Food manufacturers are working on newer and better diet foods, in-

In early 1986 the overweight citizens of Nashville, Tennessee, joined diet guru Martin Katahn in a weight-shedding scheme. Katahn appeared at weigh-ins in local Kroger stores, and the supermarket chain cooperated by labeling foods according to their place in his rotation diet plan, which calls for alternating periods of calorie cutting and "maintenance" eating.

cluding low-calorie fats, a flour substitute that can significantly reduce the calorie content of baked goods, and a synthetic sweetener that may have the ability to suppress the appetite by affecting the feedback system that regulates the feeling of satiety. Already on the market is a group of no-calorie aerosol "flavor sprays" meant to satisfy food cravings. Susan Schiffman, a psychologist at Duke University, Durham, North Carolina, invented these sprays, which provide the flavor of food but nothing else. She sold the product to Nutri/System, a company that markets an 800–1,200-calorie-

(continued on page 77)

Why Crash Diets Don't Work

In many cultures throughout history, plumpness has been considered a sign of status and beauty. In societies where food shortages and starvation were common, extra body fat was considered an indication of wealth, of a comfortable life-style that included plenty to eat. In the 17th century the painter Peter Paul Rubens portrayed the "Three Graces" as rosy, dimpled, abundantly fleshy women whose figures matched the prevailing ideal of healthy feminine sensuality. Even today, extra body fat is admired in some less developed countries. In some parts of Nigeria, for example, pubescent girls are sent to "fattening huts" to make them more desirable to suitors. Doctors working on an antiobesity campaign in Africa found that African women shown a picture of an obviously overweight woman described her as looking wealthy and happy.

In contemporary Western culture, however, thinness is the desired trait. Perhaps because modern medicine has revealed obesity to be a risk factor for potentially life-threatening diseases (*e.g.,* diabetes, heart disease, and some forms of cancer), a thin body is viewed as the healthiest body, as well as being a sign of youth and vitality. Thinness may even be equated with wealth—after all, a person who knows where his or her next meal is coming from does not have to carry around extra body fat in case of a food shortage. Models, both male and female, are generally trim—sometimes to the point of emaciation—and fashionable clothes are designed for thin bodies.

As a result, many people feel compelled to strive for this modern version of ideal beauty. Women are even more vulnerable than men to the social pressures against being overweight, and they tend to be chronically dissatisfied with their figures. In one study of college students, volunteers shown a chart of various body shapes were told to choose the figure that most resembled their own and the figure that most resembled the body they would like to have. Men generally chose as an ideal a body that closely resembled their present build. Women, however, generally selected an ideal body much thinner than their own.

Promises, promises

Because so many people want to lose weight, enterprising individuals—many of them self-proclaimed experts in nutrition who lack any real credentials—have created a booming diet industry that feeds on the desire to lose weight quickly and effortlessly. The covers of books and magazines are full of promises: Lose a pound a day! Drop 25 pounds in three weeks—and never gain it back! Take a pill and lose weight while you sleep! Fad diets tell people to eat nothing but grapefruit, to eat only on certain days, to restrict their intake of fat—or carbohydrate—or protein. Today it is the Miracle Fruit Diet, tomorrow the All-Pasta Diet, next week the Zero Carbohydrate Plan.

Books that make these promises typically become best-sellers, and mail-order diet plans have been known to make their creators wealthy. But despite the hype that accompanies each new "miracle" diet, the vast majority of the people who try them shed far more dollars than pounds.

Weight-control researchers say that crash diets—those that promise quick weight loss—not only do not work but cannot work. After all, if they did, people would lose the weight they wanted and have no reason to rush out and try the next miracle plan—which, judging by sales figures, is exactly what they do. In fact, fast, permanent loss of body fat is next to impossible. Pills or magic combinations of foods simply cannot promote a rapid, genuine loss of body fat.

Wanted: immediate results

The theory behind most of these diets is simple: people are fat because they eat more calories than they expend; therefore, if they cut back on their calorie intake until they expend more than they take in, they will lose weight. A person must achieve a deficit of 3,500 calories to lose a pound (0.45 kilogram) of fat, so a person who normally expends 2,000 calories in a day but eats only 1,000 will in seven days burn off an extra 7,000 calories and thus lose two pounds of fat.

Unfortunately, this simple theory is a little too simple—the human body is not capable of quickly burning off body fat. Still, people continue to attempt quick weight loss, perhaps because the immediate results of a crash diet seem so gratifying. For the first week or two of severely restricted calorie intake, the scale will register an encouraging loss of weight. But about half of the weight loss represents nothing more than a loss of fluid, because crash diets often upset the body's chemical balance in a way that causes water to be flushed out. This is essentially meaningless weight loss; the body will eventually recover its chemical balance, and the water weight will be regained.

Perhaps even more important, because the body cannot burn fat quickly enough to compensate for a severe restriction of calories, another large portion of the weight lost on a crash diet is the result of digestion of the body's protein stores, most of which are in the form of muscle. So while the dieter may actually weigh less and clothing may be looser, very little body fat will have been lost. Worse yet, cutting back on calories may force the body to "eat" muscle. This is counterproductive to losing body fat, because it is muscle that burns calories; having less muscle means the body

needs fewer calories. Moreover, even this misleading kind of weight loss is usually temporary. As many a frustrated dieter has discovered, after the first couple of weeks of a crash diet, weight loss usually slows down and finally stops. Weight, as measured by the scale, may even begin to creep back on.

Setpoint theory: why lost weight is regained

Weight-control researchers are not certain exactly why the dieter's lost weight is eventually regained, but they have proposed a few theories, most of which are related to the resting metabolic rate (RMR), or basal metabolic rate (BMR). Simply put, this is the rate at which the body burns calories to sustain the functions necessary for life, such as respiration, circulation, temperature maintenance, and cell growth. Apparently, cutting back on calories upsets the body's RMR. Researchers have found that when most people go on a diet, their metabolic rate declines. So when dieters suddenly begin eating less, their bodies compensate by slowing down the rate at which they expend calories to sustain life.

Researchers believe this response represents a protective mechanism. In primitive cultures an adjustable metabolism probably allowed people to survive during periods when food was scarce. The same mechanism has continued to ensure human survival throughout history. Medical studies show that during World War II some prisoners in concentration camps were able to survive on extremely limited diets because their bodies adjusted to getting by on few calories. In terms of human evolution, having too much to eat is a relatively new phenomenon, largely a result of modern methods of growing and processing food.

But this same protective mechanism works against the dieter. If, for example, a woman who normally eats 2,400 calories a day cuts back to 1,600, she will lose weight at first. But her body will soon adjust its RMR so that she can maintain her weight on 1,600 calories a day. Then, to continue losing weight, she would have to reduce her calorie intake even more. And should she go back to eating 2,000 calories a day, she would actually gain weight—at least until her body adjusted again. This ability of the body to adjust and compensate is the reason most crash diets cause people to regain weight after losing it quickly.

A theory related to RMR explains that each person's body has a "setpoint," a level of fat that it tries to maintain. This setpoint is determined by a number of factors, among them age and sex. Men seem generally to have a lower setpoint than women; older people have higher setpoints than younger people; and the setpoint for both men and women increases with age. But the most important factor seems to be heredity. Studies of adopted children indicate that they tend to be as fat or thin as their natural parents, not their adoptive parents.

According to setpoint theory, when people go on diets, their bodies adjust to maintain their normal levels of fat—that is, to return them to their setpoints. The body may do this by slowing metabolism or simply by altering the way it allocates food intake. At one time doctors believed the body used all the food it needed for tissue growth and energy, then stored any left over as fat. Now researchers believe the body may, in an effort to maintain its setpoint, allocate some intake directly to fat storage. In any case, the result is the same—the dieter regains the lost weight.

Crash dieters often respond by trying yet another quick-loss plan. However, on-again off-again dieting apparently causes the body to become resistant to losing weight. So while cutting back to 1,600 calories might have caused a dieter to lose weight during the first few attempts, losing the same amount of weight on subsequent diets may require cutting back to 1,200 and then 1,000.

The inexorable facts	
• recommended body weights (approximate*):	• calories in one gram of fat: 9

• recommended body weights (approximate*):

    women—100 pounds (45.4 kilograms) for first 5 feet (1.5 meters) of height; 5 pounds per inch (2.5 centimeters) over 5 feet

    men—110 pounds for first 5 feet of height; 5 pounds per inch over 5 feet

• average daily calorie use:

	male	female
sedentary	2,400	2,000
moderately active	2,800	2,400
very active	3,600+	3,000+

• additional calories burned in the hour after vigorous exercise: 40–60

• calories in one gram of fat: 9

• calories in one gram of carbohydrate or protein: 4

• total calories needed for adding one pound of body weight: 3,500

• net calorie restriction needed for losing one pound of body weight: 3,500

• daily calorie excess sufficient to cause 40-pound weight gain in 20 years: 20

*add or subtract 10 pounds depending on frame

"Crash" strategies

As a result of this frustrating cycle, many people end up willing to try any gimmick that is supposed to lead to permanent weight loss. The diets that have been promoted in recent years range from the merely ineffective to the outright dangerous, with a scattering of reasonably sound ones. Most weight-loss aids, schemes, and plans fall into one of the following categories.

Pills. Some of the widely marketed over-the-counter drugs sold for dieting are supposed to suppress the appetite; others claim to "burn" fat. Appetite suppressants may work at first, but weight-control researchers say that to lead to permanent weight loss, a pill would have to be taken for life, like blood-pressure pills. Doctors say most diet pills are useless, and some—in particular, the amphetamines and similar prescription drugs—are addictive. So-called starch-blocker pills, which bind to starch and make it undigestible, are now illegal in the U.S. but are still sold on the black market. They cause a number of adverse side effects, including abdominal cramps.

Low-carbohydrate diets. Severely cutting back on carbohydrates upsets the body's chemical balance in such a way that fluids are depleted. While this gives the illusion of weight loss, fat is not lost, and the water weight will eventually be regained. Besides, carbohydrates are the body's prime source of energy. Despite common opinion, starches are not fattening—rather, fat is fattening.

Fasting. Some years ago, a popular diet had people forgoing food entirely and living on liquid protein drinks and vitamins. A few people on this regime died, probably because their bodies were forced to digest so much muscle that their heart muscles failed.

Liquid diets. While some liquid diets provide sufficient protein and vitamins, they may restrict the dieter to 400 calories a day or less. Because the body cannot burn fat quickly enough to compensate for so few calories, however, muscle is also digested. Most doctors do not recommend cutting calories to fewer than 1,200 a day on any diet.

Single-category diets. These programs call for a diet restricted entirely to one kind of food, such as fruits or vegetables or rice alone. However, no single category of food provides enough nutrients to maintain healthy body tissue. Some dieters in recent years had a dramatic revelation of the inadequacy of such diets— their hair and fingernails fell out!

High-carbohydrate, low-fat diets. Most of the sound diets fall into this category. High-carbohydrate, high-fiber foods are a good source of energy and nutrients, and most are low in fat. Combined with exercise, this kind of diet promotes gradual loss of body fat. Still, the number of calories allotted per day must be sufficient to prevent the body from consuming muscle tissue. A few high-carbohydrate diet plans on the market cut calories too severely.

Cutting calories: not enough

Discouraging as all this sounds, losing body fat is not impossible. There is, however, more to the battle of the bulge than dieting alone. Studies show that though Americans have been getting fatter since the turn of the century, they are clearly eating less, not more. However, they are also far less active physically, which seems to be the crucial variable in the weight-loss equation. In fact, studies show that slim people generally eat more than fat people—not less. But they also get more exercise.

Researchers are not sure exactly how exercise keeps a person slim. One explanation is that exercise raises the RMR, so aside from burning calories during a workout, the body uses more calories all day long, even when the person is resting. A second explanation involves the setpoint. It is well known that regular aerobic exercise lowers the body's resting pulse rate; through some similar conditioning effect, exercise may lower the body's setpoint so that it "wants" to maintain a lower level of body fat.

A strategy for the long term

Whichever theory is correct, both point to the same solutions to the dieting merry-go-round. People who truly want to lose weight and keep it off need to begin an aerobic exercise program and adopt a balanced diet that they can stay with over the long term and not abandon once they have lost a few pounds. Researchers say that people who are just starting a diet and exercise program should ignore the bathroom scale at first, as weight lost in fat will likely be replaced by weight gained in muscle. The scale can be misleading, making people think they are not making progress.

Even people who exercise regularly would be wise to avoid fatty foods because they seem to raise the body's setpoint. Studies have shown that rats on a high-fat diet get fatter than rats on a lower fat diet, even if they eat the same number of calories. Some researchers also believe that alcohol may raise the setpoint.

If for no other reason, crash diets should not be considered a solution to being fat because they provide a temporary answer to a long-term problem. People do not leave crash diets with the skills necessary for maintaining the weight loss because they have made no significant changes in their life-styles, and researchers say that a change in life-style is necessary for permanent weight loss. The long-sought miracle diet simply does not exist.

—Tom D. Naughton

(continued from page 73)

a-day diet for which it provides all the foods. The sprays are meant to help dieters stick with the Spartan Nutri/System regimen and satisfy high-calorie-food yearnings. Schiffman was deluged with other offers from food companies that also wanted to market her discovery.

Meanwhile, people get fatter

Despite the plethora of weight-reducing plans, schemes, and scams, nearly a quarter of all U.S. adults are more than 20% above their desirable weight, according to the National Center for Health Statistics. The center reports that every year for the past decade, proportionately more Americans have been overweight. Moreover, statisticians have discovered that in every age group, the *percentage* of overweight people has increased; thus, the increase is not simply due to the aging of the population.

Of these obese Americans, 47.7% of the men and 64.2% of the women say that they are trying to lose weight; 35% of the population as a whole are trying to reduce. Of those trying to lose weight, 81% say they are eating fewer calories, while 57% say they are increasing their physical activity; 44% say they are doing both.

Money wasted, lives endangered

Yet if there were an effective way to lose weight and keep it off, there would be no need for the parade of ever changing diet regimes and weight-loss aids. Not only do consumers waste money on weight-loss schemes, they often endanger their lives. In the 1930s a drug called dinitrophenol was sold as a diet aid. It speeded up the metabolism, but it also killed some dieters. By 1938 it had been taken off the market. Amphetamines, obtained by prescription or illicitly, which became popular in the 1950s and '60s, also

"What are the temptations du jour?"

Despite the proliferation of diet ploys, nearly a quarter of all adults in the U.S. are overweight—that is, more than 20% above their desirable weight—according to the National Center for Health Statistics. In addition, the proportion of overweight Americans in every age group has increased every year in the past decade. Ironically, obsession with food may be the only preoccupation rivaling Americans' fixation on their weight. For every new fad diet, there is a new variety of junk food, a new fast-food chain, or a tantalizing new dessert to tempt the palate.

77

Women are much more vulnerable than men to the social and cultural forces that dictate the standards of acceptable size and shape, as witnessed by the many transformations of the "ideal" female body—from the ample frame of Lillian Russell (right, c. 1890) to the waiflike "figure" of the English model Twiggy (far right), a sensation of the late 1960s. The trend toward an increasingly slender, supple look has been gathering momentum for at least the past three decades. Recently Time *magazine made the observation that since the 1953 debut of* Playboy, *centerfolds have become progressively thinner each year. A popular adage of the day holds that a woman "can't be too thin or too rich." Apparently many women have been convinced of the truth of the former, if not of the latter. (Opposite page) Psychologists studying body image asked a group of college students to look at drawings of body shapes and choose both the figure that most resembled their own and the figure that most resembled the body they would like to have. While the men generally identified as ideal a body that closely resembled their own, women tended to select an ideal body much thinner than their own.*

speed up metabolism and suppress the appetite. In 1970 as many as two billion amphetamine pills were sold to U.S. dieters. As pointed out earlier, however, the effects of amphetamines on the appetite wear off after six to ten weeks of regular use, and the drugs are both dangerous and addictive. As a result, they have gradually fallen from popularity.

In the late 1970s there was a new threat to dieters' health. A best-selling book called—with grim appropriateness—*The Last Chance Diet* popularized a so-called liquid protein regimen. The idea was that dieters could live on 300 calories a day by consuming only prepackaged protein drinks sold at health food stores. Weight would come off fast, according to the ads, and then the newly thin dieters could learn new eating habits and stay thin for life. The FDA grew concerned because of reports that young, apparently healthy people were dying while on the liquid protein diets. It was not easy for the agency to take definitive action, however; the products were labeled as "protein supplements" with no indication that the intended use was for extremely low-calorie diets. Although the FDA was certain the diets were unsafe, it was unsure whether it could legally do anything about them. As an administrator from the U.S. Bureau of Foods stated, "Unless we can drag dead bodies into court, we won't win."

In the case of the liquid protein diets, however, the FDA did essentially have dead bodies. Investigators from the FDA and the Centers for Disease Control documented 17 cases of apparently healthy young people who died while on liquid protein diets and established in court that the diets alone were most likely responsible for these deaths. The result was a warning label on the liquid protein mixtures saying, in effect, that the diets are dangerous and should not be attempted without medical supervision. Liquid protein preparations are still being sold today, but they no longer have the popularity they once enjoyed.

Regulating the diet "industry"

Regulatory agencies frequently take action against those who sell weight-loss plans, devices, foods, and drugs, even when there is no evidence that lives are being endangered. Many of these products are hoaxes and, as such, fall under the purview of the agencies. The FDA, for example, has the authority to stop the sale of fraudulent devices and drugs. It banned the sale of "starch blockers," pills that purportedly prevented starchy foods from being digested and being turned into fat. FDA Commissioner Frank Young said at a 1985 Senate hearing, "Medical claims that these pills block the absorption of carbohydrates and nullify calories from starchy food have never been substantiated by the submission of data and, thus, they have been declared new drugs and declared illegal by several federal courts because they are unapproved new drugs." The FDA seized the product after promoters failed to comply with the agency's request to cease sales.

Recently the FTC went after a particularly specious plan called the Rotation Diet, invented by Philadelphia psychologist Barry Bricklin (not to be confused with Martin Katahn's popular book and diet, *The Rotation Diet,* mentioned above). Bricklin's plan allowed dieters to eat anything they wanted for four days of the week as long as they ate very little on alternate days, took vitamin supplements, and ate special wafers that supposedly kept the food from turning to fat. The scheme was advertised on television and radio and in newspapers and magazines, including *Reader's Digest,* one of the most widely circulated U.S. publications. To go on the Rotation Diet, a person had to pay an initial fee, which gradually was increased as the diet became more popular, until it was as high as $50. In addition, each dieter had to purchase vitamins and wafers costing about $40 a month. According to the FTC, as many as 100,000–200,000 people subscribed to the plan.

Body types: how we see ourselves

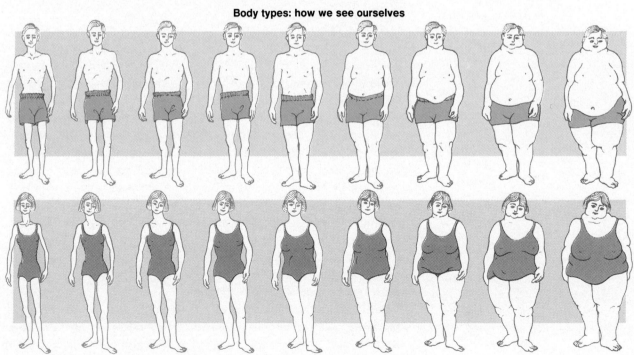

From A. Stukard *et al.,* ''Use of the Danish Adoption Register for the Study of Obesity and Thinness,''
The Genetics of Neurological and Psychiatric Disorders, ed. S. Kety (New York: Raven Press, 1983), p. 119

Not everyone is willing to accept a life sentence of self-denial. A few free spirits refuse to submit to the tyranny of thinness; they have kicked the dieting habit and found their "true image," challenging the world to accept them as they are—extra pounds and all.

The agency finally took action because the Rotation Diet ads made claims that could not be substantiated. The wafers, for example, clearly did not prevent food from being turned into fat, and the claims that women lost four to nine kilograms (8 to 20 pounds) a month on the diet and men lost 5 to 11 kilograms (12 to 25 pounds) a month were untrue. In fact, the testimonials used in the advertisements had actually been given by employees of the company that marketed the diet. As a result of the FTC's actions, the company agreed to stop making false claims, and it has now gone out of business. There are still numerous companies making equally false claims, however, and the agency has to decide carefully which ones to go after. The commission bases its selections on the egregiousness of the claims, on the size of the business, and on whether the statements are simply unsubstantiated or downright false.

The Postal Service also does its part to try to stem the tide of bogus diets. When diets or weight-loss devices are advertised through the mails, and when the advertisements are false or misleading, the Postal Service

80

can prosecute the weight-loss hucksters for mail fraud. For example, it took action against the suppliers of Citrus Industries' so-called Grapefruit Super Pill to bar its sale through the mail. The grapefruit pills supposedly "burn off" fat so that overweight people can lose weight while eating whatever they want. However, some promoters have found a way around Postal Service regulations. They are using toll-free telephone numbers for the placing of orders and are delivering their products through private package-delivery systems, thus circumventing systems regulated by federal law.

Dieting—solution or problem?

Ultimately, because there is no conclusive evidence that any weight-loss scheme is truly effective, the real question about the diet industry is why it flourishes. Why is there a continuing market for diets and weight-loss schemes? The answer, according to psychologist and weight-loss specialist Judith Rodin of Yale University, lies in the attitudes of dieters and in the false assumptions of the weight-loss specialists. According to Rodin, who has for many years been carrying out serious studies of the weight-loss obsession, dieters "blame themselves rather than the diets for their failure to lose weight. Anyone who wants to lose weight is full of self-blame for being fat in the first place." Thus, the obese assume that their overweight is based on their behavior and that this behavior should be relatively easy to correct, so they are willing to try again and again to lose weight.

A second explanation offered by Rodin is that weight-control experts continue to think that "eating behavior" is the problem behavior. More recent data, however, indicate that perhaps dieting itself is the problem behavior. Researchers are now finding that the more people diet, the less likely they are to lose weight. Furthermore, with each subsequent diet it takes the individual longer to lose weight, and whatever weight is lost is regained more quickly. Evidently, the dieter's metabolism adapts to the diet so that the individual is less and less likely to lose fat. If diet attempters do not know that they are changing their biochemistry and metabolism when they begin a new diet, they are then setting themselves up for failure as dieting becomes more and more difficult.

Inevitably, many dieters end up trying the exotic and the unusual in their quest to lose weight. The assistant director of pharmacy services at the New York University Medical Center, Samuel Uretsky, who is also a consultant to the Postal Service on fraudulent mail-order drugs, has speculated that people who buy some of the more outrageous weight-loss concoctions "very frequently are making a vote against the establishment." Traditional diets have not helped, so they turn to "magic" pills and potions.

In the end, no matter what health authorities or government agencies say, the diet business will go on. The weight-loss hucksters are selling a dream of youth and beauty. There are huge profits to be made, and an ever credulous public seems always willing to try, just one more time, to lose weight.

In the end the thinness "business" will continue to thrive. The weight-loss hucksters will fatten their wallets by selling a dizzying array of diets, potions, and pills because an ever hungry public is willing to eat up whatever is offered, as long as it promises youth, beauty, and slimness.

Randall Enos

Unlocking the Secrets of Pain

Unlocking the Secrets of Pain

The Science

by Allan I. Basbaum, Ph.D.

A patient experiences severe, unremitting pain in a region of the body that is physiologically incapable of sensing all forms of stimulation. Pinch or burn that area of the body and the person feels nothing, yet there is an unbearable pain that appears to arise from that part of the body. An equally disturbing experience is suffered by one who endures excruciating and constant pain in a limb that has been amputated. The former is a syndrome called anesthesia dolorosa ("anesthesia," meaning "no sensation"; "dolorosa," "painful"), which can arise from traumatic injury to major nerves of the body or, worse, may result from neurosurgical procedures that intentionally cut the nerves to eliminate a preexisting pain—for example, from a cancer. The latter syndrome is called phantom-limb pain. Every patient who undergoes limb amputation has a "phantom" perception of the part of the body that was removed. In some cases the patient can voluntarily "move" the phantom limb. Usually the phantom telescopes inwardly over time and disappears into the stump, but in about 10 to 20% of cases the phantom limb persists, and the patient experiences a severe burning or razor-sharp pain in the absent limb. The patient may report that the phantom fist is clenched and cannot be relaxed; the phantom fingernails often dig into the phantom hand. Anesthesia dolorosa and phantom-limb pain are not uncommon, and the pain is extremely difficult to treat. Surgical intervention usually fails to relieve the pain and may, in fact, make the problem worse. Narcotics such as morphine, the most potent pain medication available, are rarely effective.

How are such bizarre chronic pain states to be explained? More importantly, how can they be treated? Most often pain is thought of as a sensation evoked by intense, potentially tissue-damaging stimuli. That is not very different from the view of Aristotle, who proposed that pain is on the same continuum as pleasure—just the right amount of stimulation is pleasant; too much, however, yields pain. It follows that removing the stimulus when it gets too intense, or cutting the connection between the stimulus and the brain, should get rid of the pain. Unfortunately, it is not that simple. Anesthesia dolorosa and phantom limb are but two examples that illustrate that severe pain can occur without stimulation.

In fact, there is no such thing as a painful stimulus. Pain is a complex

Allan I. Basbaum, Ph.D., is Professor of Anatomy and Physiology at the University of California at San Francisco.

(Overleaf and opposite page) Victims of pain portray their torment; photographs, British Migraine Association and WB Pharmaceuticals Ltd.

Pain is often envisioned as a sensation evoked by an intense, potentially tissue-damaging stimulus, yet every person who has had a limb amputated experiences a phantom perception of the missing part. Significantly, 10–20% of these amputees develop a severe burning or razor-sharp chronic pain in the phantom limb—a pain usually unresponsive to either surgery or potent narcotics. Because pain clearly can occur in the absence of stimulation, a comprehensive understanding of pain mechanisms in the body—and effective approaches to treating pain—must deal not only with acute pain evoked by stimuli but also with chronic pain, whether so evoked or not.

perception that can, of course, be evoked by intense stimuli, but it may also be experienced in the absence of stimuli. For this reason a comprehensive analysis of pain mechanisms must not only account for how an acute, noxious (tissue-damaging) stimulus, such as a pinprick, produces pain but also how chronic pain develops whether it is evoked by stimuli or not. Pinprick pain hurts, but nobody seeks treatment for pinprick pain. The causes of chronic pain and the approaches to treating it are what need to be addressed.

Complexities of pain

In the late 19th century physiologists and anatomists recognized that the nerve fibers found throughout the body have anatomically distinct endings. About six different types of nerve ending could be recognized under the microscope. Drawing from these observations, a German physician, Max von Frey, proposed that each anatomically distinct nerve ending responds to a different type of stimulus to the body—touch, cold, heat, and pain. Pain was considered a specific sensation, transmitted along a unique class of nerve fibers in, for example, the limbs, to specific "pain pathways" in the spinal cord and from there to "pain centers" in the brain. "Pain," then, a psychological quality, was assigned to an anatomical entity. This anatomically based, telephone-line view of how pain messages are transmitted had, in fact, been articulated many years earlier. Well before nerve-conduction mechanisms were established, the early 17th-century French philosopher René Descartes wrote of the existence of specific pathways for transmitting pain information from an injured body part through the spinal cord to a pain center in the brain.

Consider the implications of the view of the so-called specificists. If there were identifiable and specific pain pathways in the periphery (*i.e.*, the regions of the body, including sense organs, muscles, and viscera, in which nerves terminate), in the spinal cord, and in the brain, then the approach to the relief of pain would be relatively simple—cut the pain pathway. In fact, there are many neurosurgical procedures that try to do just that. Sometimes the operation is successful. In many cases, however, the relief is only temporary, and far too often the pain is not relieved at all. The fact that cutting a "telephone wire" that supposedly carries pain messages does not consistently alleviate chronic pain in people reveals something very important about the generation of pain. Pain is not just a stimulus that is transmitted over specific pathways but rather a complex perception, the nature of which depends not only on the intensity of the stimulus but on the situation in which it is experienced and, most importantly, on the affective or emotional state of the individual. Pain is to somatic stimulation as beauty is to a visual stimulus. It is a very subjective experience.

Under normal circumstances it is predictable whether a stimulus will be perceived as painful; sometimes, however, it is not. Think for a moment about the football player who finds out only *after* the game that his leg is broken. Another example would be the ritual performed in some cultures requiring a young man to prove his manhood by crossing a river with a grappling hook embedded in his stomach. Pictures of these young men do not indicate that they are in pain. In yet another situation—that of childbirth—a woman who delivers a child after prenatal Lamaze training will usually experience much less pain than a woman who goes into labor unprepared; the sensory stimuli are comparable in the two births, but the severity of the pain differs.

Pathways to pain

It is because pain is a subjective experience that it is so difficult to study. Much is known about how messages from injured tissue reach the brain, but there is very little information about the location in the brain where the final decision to call something painful is made. In fact, little is known about the cortical mechanisms underlying the perception of pain. For this reason the following discussion focuses on nociception, the process through which the nervous system transmits, processes, and, in some cases, blocks signals about tissue damage.

   The peripheral nervous system: signaling tissue damage. In all sensory systems, information is transmitted by nerves of the peripheral nervous system (PNS) to the central nervous system (CNS). The PNS includes all of the nerve fibers of the body that are located outside of the spinal cord and brain. The latter two structures constitute the major components of the CNS. Three types of nerve fiber in the PNS transmit information from the body to the spinal cord and brain. The largest peripheral nerve fibers, called A beta fibers, from 5 to 12 micrometers (one micrometer equals one-millionth of a meter) in diameter, respond to nonnoxious (*i.e.,* not injurious, non-pain-producing) stimuli, such as gentle touch, pressure, joint manipulation, or movement of hairs on the skin, and transmit this information very rapidly to the spinal cord. Fibers of the second type, called A delta fibers, range from one to five micrometers in diameter and transmit information more slowly than do the largest fibers. The smallest fibers (called unmyelinated C fibers) are less than one micrometer in diameter. A delta and C fibers are predominantly nociceptors; *i.e.,* they respond only to injurious

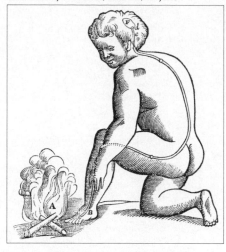

In the early 1600s French philosopher René Descartes proposed a mechanism of pain in which specific pathways transmitted pain information from damaged tissue through the spinal cord to a pain center in the brain. Were this "telephone-line" view of pain true, pain relief would always be as simple as cutting the pain pathway. That this kind of surgery often fails indicates that pain is not merely a transmitted signal but a complex perception—dependent not only on the stimulus but also on the prevailing situation and the emotional state of the individual. The Cartesian view fails to answer such questions as why some people who complain of severe pain show no tissue damage, while others in the heat of excitement—e.g., soldiers in battle or athletes on the playing field—may not be aware of even serious injuries until the frenzy has died away.

Different types of nerve fiber in the peripheral nervous system transmit sensory information from the body to the spinal cord and brain. Large-diameter (A beta) fibers carry signals from receptors, such as those in the skin, that respond to nonnoxious stimuli; e.g., gentle touch, pressure, or hair movement. Small-diameter (A delta and C) fibers bring information from free nerve endings, which respond to noxious stimuli: injurious mechanical and thermal phenomena and chemicals released by damaged tissue. Both kinds of fiber enter the spinal cord, where they terminate in the cord's inner, gray matter in the region known as the dorsal horn. (The nerve cell bodies from which the fibers extend reside in dense masses called ganglia outside the cord adjacent to the dorsal horn.) In the dorsal horn the incoming fibers form junctions with spinal cord nerve cells, whose fibers pass up the cord and into the brain. It is at these junctions that noxious "pain" signals are relayed, or in some cases are inhibited from being relayed, to the pain-transmitting spinal cord fibers. As the spinal cord fibers leave the dorsal horn, they cross to the opposite side of the cord before ascending. The pain-transmitting fibers of the dorsal horn have two major targets in the brain. Via the spinothalamic pathway one group of fibers ascends to the thalamus, where the noxious signal is relayed to other nerve cells that project to the brain's sensory cortex. Via the spinoreticular pathway a second group terminates in the reticular formations in the medulla and midbrain (parts of the brain stem) and in the thalamus. The spinothalamic and spinoreticular pathways appear to carry two different types of pain information: acute pain and diffuse, poorly localized pain, respectively.

mechanical and thermal stimuli and to the chemicals released by damaged tissue. The "first," or "fast," sharp pain that one experiences upon stubbing a toe and the "second," or "slow," diffuse, throbbing, possibly burning pain that follows seconds later and lasts longer are mediated by the A delta and C fibers, respectively.

Surprisingly, the C fibers transmit information about tissue-damaging stimuli very slowly (at one meter [3.28 feet] per second, compared with up to 72 meters per second for the A beta fibers). Perhaps this gives the brain time to evaluate the situation in which the injury stimulus is being experienced. Picture a $2,000 Limoges china coffee cup that contains steaming hot coffee. An inquisitive two-year-old might pick up the cup, reflexively drop it on the floor, and then scream. The adult, on the other hand, recognizing the value of the china, would be more likely to pick up the hot cup, quickly set it back down, and then cry out. If the C fibers were the most rapidly conducting, the reflexive response to drop the cup, which occurs in the two-year-old, would always occur before the voluntary act of putting it back down. China cups filled with steaming hot beverages would be crashing to the floor everywhere.

The physiological evidence that C fibers are specific in their response to tissue damage is supported by numerous experiments that established that the experience of pain is generated only when the small fibers are activated. For example, Swedish investigators implanted fine metal microelectrodes into a nerve in the arms of awake human subjects and studied the effects of electrically stimulating individual peripheral nerve fibers of the arm. When they stimulated a single large-diameter fiber, the subjects experienced touch and other nonpainful sensations. Whenever they electrically stimulated C fibers, pain was reported. Local anesthetics, which dentists use to numb the mouth so that they can drill painlessly, block C fibers before they block large fibers. That is why the dental patient can sometimes tell that his lip is being touched although pinching or probing it does not produce pain.

Up to this point it appears that von Frey was correct; pain is generated only when small-diameter nerve fibers of the peripheral nervous system are activated. Is there then no contribution of the large-diameter fibers to the perception of pain? Yes, the latter do play a part. Since large-diameter fibers have much greater energy requirements than small fibers, they are more susceptible to anoxia; *i.e.,* loss of oxygen. If one applies a blood pressure cuff to the arm and inflates it enough to block the blood supply to the arm, for about 20 minutes it is possible to produce a reversible block of nerve impulse conduction in the large fibers. Examination of the anoxic hand (the hand with the blood supply, and therefore oxygen supply, cut off) reveals the following: since the large motor fibers are blocked, the arm is paralyzed; the ability to perceive joint position is lost, as is the ability to localize tactile stimuli. Nor is the perception of noxious stimuli in the oxygen-deprived hand normal. The subject cannot distinguish a pin prick from ice or a pinch. In fact, all noxious stimuli are perceived by that hand as a burning sensation.

This experiment demonstrates that although small-diameter fibers are exclusively activated by and carry information about noxious stimuli, large-

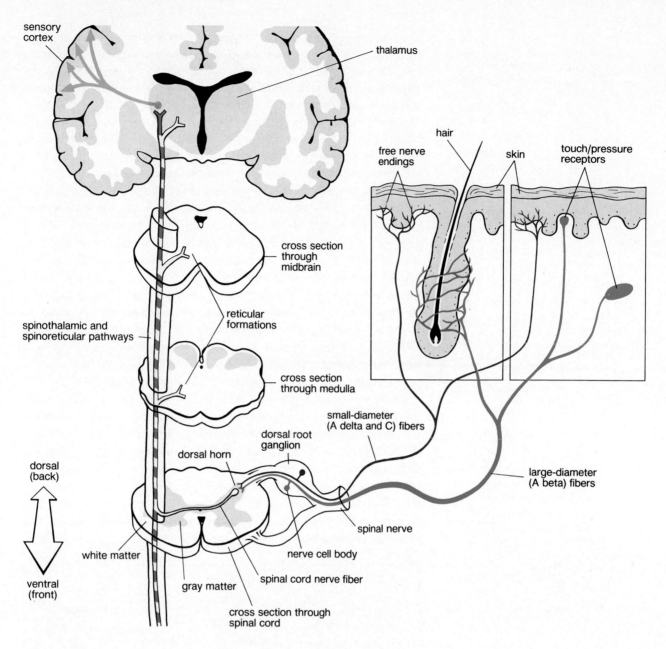

diameter fibers must be present if the quality of the stimulus is to be preserved; *i.e.,* if the stimulus is to be perceived normally. In the absence of large fibers, all tissue-damaging stimuli are perceived as painfully burning sensations. How the large fibers contribute to the perception of pain will be described later. It is not coincidental, however, that severe, continuous burning is the most common complaint of patients with peripheral nerve injury. For example, causalgia is a pain syndrome that literally means "burning" (*caus*) and "pain" (*algia*). It is often produced by gunshot wounds of major peripheral nerves of the arm or leg. Patients report that the pain is like sunburn, except it is several thousand times worse and there all the time.

Hyperalgesia: why it hurts only when you move. Although the small-diameter C fibers have the highest mechanical and thermal threshold, which

89

is what makes them specific for the pain sensation after injury and in a variety of inflammatory diseases (*e.g.*, rheumatoid arthritis), these fibers become sensitized; *i.e.*, their threshold for sending a pain signal to the spinal cord is lowered considerably. Thus, stimuli that never produce pain in normal skin (*e.g.*, a light touch with a cotton ball) now produce severe pain. Moreover, the amount of pain generated by noxious stimuli is also greatly increased. This clinical condition is called hyperalgesia; it is equivalent to tenderness. One avoids putting clothes against sunburned skin because it is hyperalgesic; even the light touch of a shirt to the skin produces pain.

Sensitization of peripheral nerve fibers results from the release of a variety of chemical mediators from injured, inflamed tissue. Among the most important substances are two breakdown products of arachidonic acid, a lipid (fatty substance) that is released from the membranes of damaged cells. Arachidonic acid is acted upon by two enzymes, cyclooxygenase and lipoxygenase, to produce prostaglandins (PGs) and leukotrienes (LTs), respectively. The latter compounds, in turn, act either directly or indirectly on the endings of the peripheral nerve fibers and lower their threshold for activation. A puff of air can cause a sensitized C fiber to transmit electrical messages to the spinal cord. The brain interprets these messages as if they were provoked by tissue-damaging stimuli and, thus, pain may be perceived, even though the stimulus was clearly not noxious.

Aspirin is one of many nonsteroidal anti-inflammatory compounds (NSAIDs) that relieve pain in inflamed tissue by blocking the cylcooxygenase enzyme that synthesizes the prostaglandins. Some pain states, however, are not relieved by NSAIDs; the lipoxygenase pathway, which synthesizes LTs, may be at fault. For patients who do not adequately respond to NSAIDs, doctors sometimes prescribe corticosteroids. The latter are powerful anti-inflammatory drugs that block synthesis of both PGs and LTs by interfering with the release of arachidonic acid. Unfortunately, the side effects of prolonged steroid use are so great that steroids cannot be used

Injured, inflamed tissue produces a variety of chemical mediators that sensitize the small-diameter C fibers. Among the most important are the prostaglandins (PGs) and the leukotrienes (LTs), two breakdown products of arachidonic acid, which is a fatty substance released from the membranes of damaged cells. These two classes of mediators in turn act either directly or indirectly (e.g., by stimulating certain white blood cells to release yet other mediators) on the sensory endings of the small-diameter fibers, lowering their threshold for activation. Aspirin and other nonsteroidal anti-inflammatory drugs (NSAIDs) relieve the pain of inflamed tissue by interfering with the breakdown of arachidonic acid to PGs, while corticosteroids work their anti-inflammatory effect higher up the breakdown pathway by blocking the release of arachidonic acid, thus interfering with both PG and LT synthesis. If drugs that specifically block LT synthesis can be developed, they should contribute in an important way to the treatment of pain from inflammation.

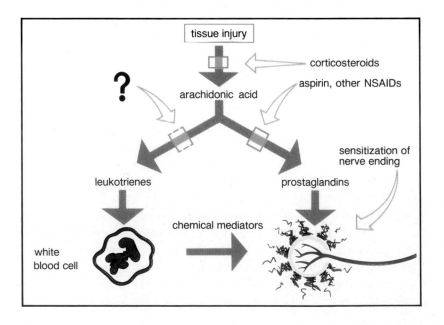

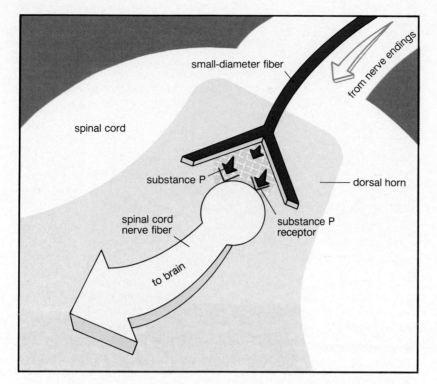

small-diameter fiber

spinal cord

from nerve endings

substance P

dorsal horn

spinal cord
nerve fiber

substance P
receptor

to brain

The peripheral nerve fibers communicate with the nerve cells of the spinal cord by releasing specific chemicals called neurotransmitters at the site where the two kinds of neurons meet in the dorsal horn. One such chemical, the peptide substance P, is released by small-diameter C fibers into the spinal cord in response to pain-producing stimulation, whereupon it binds to a specific recognition site, or receptor, on the spinal cord neurons, exciting them to transmit a message to the brain. Substance P comes closest to being a specific transmitter for noxious messages. Hence, drugs that inhibit its binding to its receptor or that deplete the C fibers' content of substance P without inducing pain themselves could have useful roles in pain control.

to treat chronic pain conditions. It is hoped that the future development of specific agents that block the lipoxygenase pathway will provide an important adjunct to the treatment of pain from severe inflammation.

Substance P: potent messenger. An alternative to blocking the sensitization and activation of peripheral nerve fibers is interrupting their communication with the second-order nerve cells (neurons) of the spinal cord; *i.e.,* where the peripheral nervous system meets the central nervous system. Neurons converse with one another when one nerve cell releases a specific chemical, a neurotransmitter, that acts on a neighboring neuron. Through the technique of immunocytochemistry, anatomists are able to use antibodies to stain neurotransmitters in the laboratory. It has been demonstrated in this way that the C fibers use one or more small peptides to communicate. Pain researchers have focused on a peptide, substance P, which contains 11 amino acids. The "p" does not stand for pain; it derives from the "p" in powder, the form in which the peptide was first isolated from horse intestine in the 1930s. The sequence of its amino acids was not established until the 1960s, however. Substance P is synthesized by about 20% of the C fibers, is released into the spinal cord by pain-producing stimulation, and excites the spinal cord cells that transmit the message to the brain. Substance P, in fact, comes closest to being a specific transmitter for noxious messages; it is, in effect, the long-sought "pain" transmitter. Like most neurotransmitters, it acts at a specific recognition site, called a receptor, on other nerve cells of the spinal cord. Accordingly, it should be possible to synthesize drugs that inhibit the binding of substance P to its receptor and specifically block its "pain-provoking" action. Success along those lines in the not-too-distant future should have a major impact on the treatment of pain.

Traditional or folk methods of pain relief—be they physical, chemical, or psychological—are valued for their insights into the nature and control of pain because at some place and time and for some people they apparently worked. In native American cultures, for example, the rhythmic chanting of the medicine man to draw out the "disease demon" and the pain it caused (right) is thought to have stimulated the sick person's own pain-control mechanisms. Many folk medicines used to relieve pain have been found to contain compounds resembling capsaicin, the active agent in hot pepper that depletes the C fibers of substance P and so decreases pain sensitivity. Recently the extract of a plant used by Brazilian Indians to treat intensely painful venomous-snake bites was discovered to block the effects of bradykinin, a peptide released from injured tissue that both activates the C fibers to cause pain and indirectly increases their pain sensitivity.

Alternatively, it might be possible to deplete the substance P. Many people have experienced the effects of a compound that exerts its actions through powerful activation of substance-P-containing peripheral nerve fibers. This compound is capsaicin, the active ingredient in hot pepper. Appropriately, capsaicin's unusual properties were discovered by two neuroscientists from Hungary, the country famous for its consumption of paprika! When capsaicin is applied to a peripheral nerve of adult rats, it massively stimulates the fibers. This is followed by prolonged depletion of the substance P content of the C fibers, with a concomitant decrease in pain sensitivity. More surprising, when capsaicin is injected into two-day-old rat pups, it is neurotoxic; the substance-P-containing nerve fibers are permanently destroyed. The animals grow up with reduced or absent pain sensitivity, although otherwise they are normal. It has, in fact, been suggested that people from cultures that love very hot, spicy dishes can tolerate such food because the C fibers in their tongues were destroyed by repeated exposure to capsaicin as infants. As a result of these observations, several laboratories are trying to synthesize a molecule similar to capsaicin that upon application might deplete substance P in areas of the body where there is severe pain. Not surprisingly, many folk medicines for the treatment of pain contain capsaicin-like compounds.

In addition to substance P and the products of arachidonic acid, many other compounds are released from injured tissue. One of the most important is bradykinin, a peptide similar in size to but very different in structure from substance P. Bradykinin is of particular interest because it not only activates the C fibers to cause pain but simultaneously stimulates the synthesis of prostaglandins, which lowers the threshold of the fibers, producing enhanced sensitivity to pain. Injection of very small amounts of synthetic bradykinin into human skin produces very severe pain. Fortunately, like substance P, bradykinin acts at a specific receptor. Pharmaceutical companies have successfully synthesized competitive blockers of the bradykinin receptor. It may soon be possible to develop a cream that contains pain-relieving peptide receptor blockers that can be rubbed over an injured, inflamed part of the body.

Inflammation, pain, and the nervous system. Rats treated with capsaicin at birth not only do not respond to "painful" stimuli but also do not show an inflammatory response to injury. This observation confirmed studies reported many years ago that concluded that the nervous system is necessary for the inflammatory response; *i.e.,* inflammation is neurogenic. When small fibers are activated by injury-provoked stimuli, substance P is released not only centrally, in the spinal cord, but also into the milieu of the injured tissue. The local release of substance P—for example, into arthritic joint tissue—activates a variety of nonneural cells that, in turn, release many inflammatory mediators. The latter cause the swelling and redness of inflammation and, by further activating the C fibers, exacerbate the pain. Pain is, in fact, the major complaint of patients with inflammatory diseases. For this reason much research is directed at interrupting the contribution of the nervous system to inflammatory responses. Capsaicin treatment, in fact, significantly reduces the inflammation seen in an experimental model of rheumatoid arthritis in the rat.

Transmission of pain messages in the central nervous system via the dorsal horn. Both the large- and small-diameter nerve fibers enter the spinal cord where they terminate in different parts of the gray matter. The latter can roughly be divided into a dorsal (or back) sensory half and a ventral (or front) motor half. Two nerve cell types predominate in the dorsal horn. One type of cell receives information only from the large-diameter fibers and thus responds exclusively to stimuli that are not noxious; a second type of cell receives convergent input from large and small fibers and as a consequence responds to both noxious and nonnoxious stimulation. The

That the nervous system is intimately tied to inflammation has become apparent from accumulated knowledge of the inflammatory response. When chemical mediators produced as the result of tissue injury activate the small-diameter fibers, substance P is released not only in the spinal cord but also into the injured tissue. This local release stimulates a variety of nonneural cells (e.g., mast cells) to secrete many mediators (e.g., histamine) that cause the swelling and redness of inflammation and exacerbate the pain by further activating the C fibers. The presence of substance P in the neural anatomy is dramatically revealed in the inset photomicrographs: the upper one, of nerve cell bodies in the dorsal root ganglion that have been stained with a fluorescent antibody to substance P; the lower one, of part of the spinal dorsal horn that has been similarly stained with antiserum against substance P.

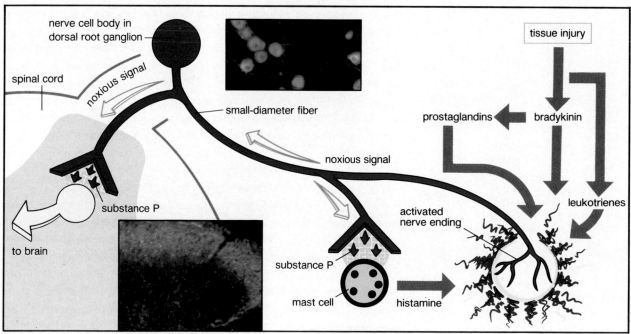

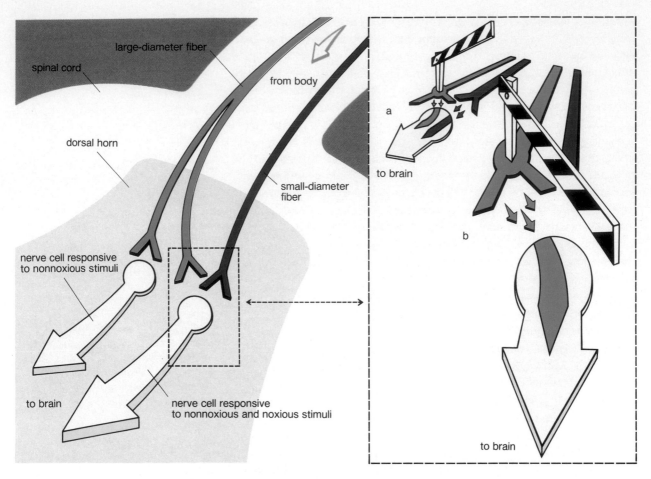

specificity of the peripheral C fiber response to noxious stimulation thus disappears in the spinal cord. Most importantly, although C fibers activate the dorsal horn cells, large-fiber stimulation can either activate or inhibit the firing of the "pain" transmission neurons in the dorsal horn. Loss of the large-diameter input, via compression block (such as with the blood pressure cuff) or after peripheral nerve injury, results in a net increase in the firing of the "pain" transmission neuron. The brain interprets the increased firing rate as due to more severe injury and, thus, greater pain is perceived. It has been suggested that the severe, burning pain of the conditions described above—anesthesia dolorosa, phantom-limb pain, and causalgia—reflects a chronic increase in the firing of nerve cells in the spinal cord secondary to a significant loss of large-fiber input.

The convergence of different types of input onto spinal cord neurons is also thought to underlie another unusual, but common, pain experience. Referred pain is the phenomenon in which patients feel pain in a somatic part of the body (*e.g.,* the shoulder) even though the injury is in an internal (visceral) structure, typically the heart. The pain is "referred" from the heart to the shoulder because some dorsal horn cells receive a convergent input from the somatic and visceral structures. Presumably, the brain misperceives the location of the injury stimulus and attributes it to the more common site; *i.e.,* the somatic body part, the shoulder.

Pain information to the brain via spinal pathways. As a result of examination of patients with injury to the spinal cord, it was recognized that the pathways for pain are crossed. That is, the pathways on the left side of the spinal cord transmit information from cells in the dorsal horn on the right side of the body. There are two major brain targets of the pain-transmission neurons of the dorsal horn. Via the spinothalamic pathway, one group of spinal cord nerve fibers ascends to the thalamus, a critical relay structure located deep in the brain, which also receives visual, auditory, and gustatory information. A second group of fibers from the dorsal horn travels in the spinoreticular pathway and projects densely to the core of the brain stem reticular formation, located between the thalamus and spinal cord. These two ascending systems appear to transmit two different types of "pain" information. Acute pain, for example, from a pinprick, is transmitted by fibers of the spinothalamic tract. In contrast, the diffuse, poorly localized pain characteristic of clinical, chronic pain states is probably mediated by the spinoreticular system.

The cortex and pain. Since pain is so clearly a complex perception, it is surprising that there is a large body of medical literature that suggests that the cortex, where the highest level of brain processing takes place, is not necessary for the experience of pain. That conclusion of scientists in the past was probably based on two observations. First, electrical stimulation of the cortex of awake patients rarely evokes a pain sensation, whereas touch and other nonpainful sensations are readily generated. Second, some patients have had large regions of cortex removed, because of cancer or epilepsy, with little impairment in the appreciation of pain. However, given the importance of learning, memories, and emotions in the experience of pain, it is impossible that the cortex is not involved. Just as the cortex must contribute to the perception of beauty, so must it contribute to the perception of pain. Careful examination of patients with cortical injury, in fact, establishes very distinct abnormalities in the perception of pain. "Pain asymbolia" is a clinical syndrome in which patients with cortical damage report, with absolutely no emotion, that intense stimuli are excruciatingly painful. It "hurts," but they do not care. In fact, seconds after reporting how unbearable the pain is, they quietly go back to reading a newspaper or doing some other activity with not the slightest signs of distress. Are these patients really experiencing pain? In the absence of normal emotions, the meaning of pain is obviously lost. The cortex integrates sensory, emotional, and cognitive features of the situation, all of which contribute to the pain experience. There can be no question about the necessity of the cortex for the normal experience of pain. At present the inability of scientists to identify the cortical areas where the nociceptive message from the thalamus is finally interpreted as painful underscores the need for more research into how memories and emotions interact with sensory stimuli to produce complex perceptions.

Children's pain

The complexity of the cognitive component of the pain experience is, in part, what makes the evaluation of pain in children so difficult. Not only

As the large- and small-diameter fibers terminate in the dorsal horn, they make contact with two types of spinal cord neurons (opposite page, left). One type receives signals only from the large-diameter fibers and thus responds only to nonnoxious stimuli. The other receives convergent signals from large and small fibers and consequently responds to both nonnoxious and noxious stimuli. Whereas the small fibers are responsible for activating the "pain" transmission nerve cells in the dorsal horn, signals from the large fibers can increase or inhibit the activation. The observation that pain appears to depend on a balance of activity in the large and small fibers led to the gate-control theory of pain (opposite page, right), wherein circuitry present in the dorsal horn works like a gate. When the balance of activity in the small and large fibers is weighted toward the small fibers, the gate is open (a), allowing transmission of the noxious signal to the brain. On the other hand, when activity in the large fibers predominates, the gate is closed (b), and the noxious signal is blocked.

Part of the difficulty in evaluating children's pain arises from their limited experience and communicative abilities, which likely make the meaning and context of their pain different from those of adults. Even more formidable is the task of evaluating pain in infants who cannot yet talk at all. One approach has been to measure infants' vocal cries with sound spectroscopy. By analyzing the pitch, loudness, length, and other variables of a cry, it is possible to develop a "vocabulary" that distinguishes between cries of pain, hunger, birth, and joy.

do children communicate less clearly (at least from the perspective of the adult) but the extent of their experience is obviously much more limited than that of the adult. Thus, the meaning and context of pain to the child must be different from those of the adult. The evaluation of pain in the preverbal infant is, of course, the most difficult. Some physicians, in fact, have argued that newborns actually do not experience pain; that, however, is a minority view.

Since the infant cannot communicate verbally, other measures must be used to evaluate pain. The infant will usually exhibit reflex withdrawal to a noxious stimulus; however, that reaction can occur without the conscious appreciation of pain. Facial expressions have been extensively studied, but these are difficult to quantitate. An alternative is to use sound spectroscopy—a way of precisely measuring the vocal cries of the infant. With this method it is possible to distinguish between cries of pain, hunger, birth, and joy. More importantly, untrained observers can readily learn to recognize the different components of the different cries.

The assessment of pain in toddlers is also difficult. Children use words differently from adults. They often characterize their pain in terms of fear. An interesting approach is to ask children to "draw" their pain or to describe their pain in terms of color. Red and black are the most common colors used to signify pain. In general, children have difficulty describing pain in language that an adult can understand. For this reason, analogies are often helpful. For example, a child can "count" the amount of "hurts" that they are experiencing. Although it is difficult to validate such scales, they do provide a number, or tally of the pain, which can be assessed before and after treatment of pain.

The problem is a very important one. If one cannot adequately evaluate pain, then one certainly cannot evaluate the success or failure of the course of treatment of the pain. How much morphine should be given to a child to block postoperative pain or pain that is likely to result from severe injury?

Physicians obviously do not want to overmedicate, but they also must not undermedicate because of an underestimate of the child's pain.

Pain-control mechanisms

Since the spinothalamic and spinoreticular tracts course together in the spinal cord, it is possible for the neurosurgeon to cut these pathways in patients who are experiencing intractable pain. This procedure, anterolateral cordotomy, was once widely used to treat chronic pain. Unfortunately, it is effective in only about 50% of patients and often for only a short time. Moreover, because almost 15% experience worse pain after the surgery, anterolateral cordotomy is now used only to treat pain in terminal cancer patients. Damage to the central nervous system (either surgical or traumatic) is irreversible; nerves in the spinal cord and brain that have been cut never regenerate normal connections. For this reason, techniques that do not destroy nerve tissue have been developed to treat chronic pain.

As described above, when large-diameter peripheral nerve fibers are blocked, a patient experiences much more severe pain, and the quality of the pain is altered. The converse is also true: increasing the activity in large-diameter peripheral fibers can decrease pain. The observation that pain is not directly related to the total activity in a peripheral nerve, but rather is a function of the balance of activity in small and large fibers, was the basis of the gate-control theory of pain, formulated in 1965 by a Canadian psychologist, Ronald Melzack, and a British neurophysiologist, Patrick Wall, who were collaborating at the Massachusetts Institute of Technology. They proposed that there is circuitry in the dorsal horn of the spinal cord that functions like a gate, opening when the balance of activity in small and large fibers is weighted toward the former and closing when large-fiber activity predominates. The reason a person vigorously shakes or rubs his or her hand when it is burned is that rubbing and shaking generate stimuli that selectively increase the activity of large fibers. Electric vibrators and a process called transcutaneous electrical nerve stimulation, or TENS (which, via a battery-powered stimulator, lead wires, and electrodes that are attached to the skin, stimulates the large fibers with a mild current), are somewhat more efficient, albeit more expensive, ways of getting the same effect.

The type of pain control generated by increased large-fiber activity is "segmental." Pain is reduced only in the segment of the body in which the large-fiber activity is increased. Rubbing one's right hand will not reduce pain of the left leg. There are, however, other pain-control systems that are not segmental; a more global control can be achieved. In 1967 David Reynolds, a scientist working at the Ames Research Center of the National Aeronautics and Space Administration (NASA) in California, implanted electrodes into the brains of rats and found that when he passed a small current through the electrodes, the rats did not respond to noxious stimuli. In fact, the pain suppression was so profound that he could perform a surgical procedure using electrical brain stimulation instead of a general anesthetic. Interestingly, although the rats were unresponsive to noxious stimuli, they were not oblivious to their environment. They would respond to light tactile stimulation of the skin and would eat and play normally while

Pain Research Clinic, National Institute of Dental Health

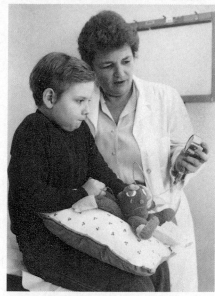

Because children usually have difficulty describing their pain in language that adults can understand, pain assessment techniques for children often make use of analogies with numbers or colors or even employ nonverbal media. In the photo above, a young cancer patient squeezes a toy octopus in proportion to how much pain he feels. A pressure sensor inside the toy sends signals to a handheld readout device. By comparing the strength of the child's squeeze before and after a treatment for pain, doctors can gain some idea of the treatment's effectiveness.

being stimulated in the brain. Apparently the electrode had tapped into an endogenous and specific pain-control system in the brain.

Subsequent studies established that electrical brain stimulation can also be used to treat chronic pain in humans. The area of the brain most often targeted for electrode implantation is located just behind the thalamus in a region called the periaqueductal gray (PAG). Electrical stimulation of the PAG activates a powerful control system that blocks the ascending transmission of the pain message from the spinal cord to higher centers of the brain. It does this by activating a complex neural circuit that extends from the brain to the spinal cord and inhibits the firing of the dorsal horn nerve cells at the origin of the spinothalamic and spinoreticular pathways. Blocking transmission of the noxious message from the spinal cord produces powerful pain control. There are few nerve cell bodies in the PAG that project directly to the spinal cord; it was determined that there is an important link with serotonin-containing cells of the medulla, a region of brain lying just in front of the spinal cord. Fibers of these serotonin cells project to the spinal cord and inhibit the firing of spinothalamic and spinoreticular neurons.

Important insights into the chemistry of this endogenous pain-control system were provided by studies using a drug called naloxone, which specifically blocks the analgesic action of narcotics, such as morphine. Working in the department of psychology at the University of California at Los Angeles, researchers Huda Akil, David Mayer, and John Liebeskind found that naloxone not only blocks the analgesia produced by morphine but can also disrupt the pain control elicited by electrical stimulation of the PAG. Other studies reported that brain-stimulation-produced analgesia is significantly reduced in animals that are tolerant to morphine; that is, in animals in which morphine, because of prolonged use, is no longer effective. Taken together, these observations suggested that the neural circuitry through which brain-stimulation-produced analgesia operates is the same as that through which morphine exerts its powerful analgesic action. How then do morphine and other narcotic drugs produce such a powerful pain control?

The type of pain control produced by increased large-fiber activity has been exploited in a process called transcutaneous electrical nerve stimulation (TENS). Generated by a compact, battery-powered device, a mild electric current is delivered via electrodes attached to the skin near the site of the pain. The current selectively boosts the activity of the large fibers, causing the noxious signal coming from the same segment of the body to be blocked or altered before reaching the brain.

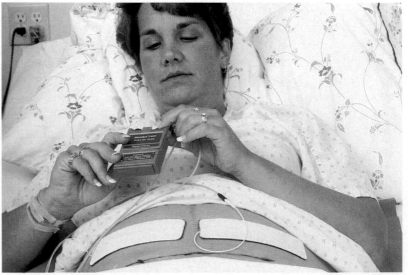

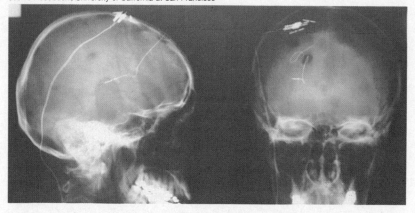

Two X-ray views of the head of a surgical patient show electrical lead wires running to the top of the skull and connecting with electrodes implanted in the periaqueductal gray (PAG), an area of the brain just behind the thalamus. Electrical stimulation of the PAG has been shown to activate a powerful endogenous pain-control system that interferes with the ascending transmission of the noxious message from the spinal cord to higher brain centers. The technique has been used to treat chronic pain.

The power of narcotics

During the time that studies of brain-stimulation-produced analgesia were being carried out, other scientists were focusing more closely on how opiates function. In 1973 Avram Goldstein, a neurochemist at the Stanford Addiction Research Foundation, Palo Alto, California, demonstrated that there are specific proteins to which morphine and its antagonist, naloxone, bind in the brain. This protein is the opiate receptor. The opiate receptor, of course, did not evolve from excessive use of morphine, a plant-derived compound. Rather, the opiate receptor is the target of a family of opiate-like (opioid) peptides called endorphins (*i.e.,* endogenous morphine), which were discovered by John Hughes and Hans Kosterlitz in Aberdeen, Scotland. Through the techniques of molecular biology, the genes that code for and the complete amino acid sequences of three endorphin families (enkephalin, dynorphin, and beta endorphin) have now been identified, and anatomical studies have mapped the location of the endorphins in the brain and spinal cord. Not surprisingly, there are high levels of the three opioid peptides in the PAG, the site from which brain-stimulation-produced analgesia is most effectively generated and from which the descending pain-control system originates. Release of the opioid peptides by electrical stimulation is hypothesized to underlie the naloxone-sensitive analgesia that is produced by electrical brain stimulation in the PAG. Since electrical-brain-stimulation-produced analgesia is produced by activation of the brain's endorphin system, it follows that injection of a chemical that mimics the action of the endorphins would also produce pain control. That, in fact, is precisely how narcotics work. When morphine is injected into the bloodstream of a patient, the drug circulates to the brain and binds the opiate receptor located in the PAG. This turns on the same descending pain-control system that is activated by electrical brain stimulation.

The major problem with injection of pain-relieving drugs, such as morphine, systemically (*i.e.,* into the bloodstream) is that pain control is not the only effect produced. Because there are opiate receptors located in many regions of the brain, severe side effects can be produced. These include depression of the cardiovascular, gastrointestinal, and respiratory systems, resulting in low blood pressure, constipation, and an arrest of breathing. Profound psychological effects of narcotics may also be produced with

The pain-control mechanism invoked by electrical stimulation of the PAG involves a complex neural circuit that descends from the brain to the spinal cord, where it blocks activation of the dorsal horn nerve cells by incoming "pain" messages from the body. Few nerve cell bodies in the PAG send fibers directly to the spinal cord; instead, they relay their control signals to serotonin-containing nerve cells in the medulla, which in turn project to the spinal cord. It is believed that electrically stimulating the PAG causes the local release of natural opiate-like peptides, which bind to receptors in the PAG and activate the descending control system. Narcotics, which also bind to these receptors, produce systemic pain relief in exactly the same way. High concentrations of opioid peptides and opiate receptors are also found in the dorsal horn, where they exert specific pain control. Again, narcotics injected spinally mimic this specific control, causing profound, long-lasting pain relief.

systemic injection, including the "high" that heroin addicts try to obtain. Is it possible to target the drug just to those opiate receptors specifically involved in pain-control circuitry? Theoretically it is possible to inject morphine directly into the PAG, but this is obviously impractical. A careful analysis of the location of the opiate receptor and the endorphins, vis-à-vis pain-transmission circuits, provided the answer.

It turns out that there are very high concentrations of both the opiate receptor and endorphins in the dorsal horn, overlapping the region of termination of the incoming, substance-P-containing peripheral fibers; *i.e.*, at the first chemical synaptic relay of the "pain" message. Tony Yaksh, a neuropharmacologist at the Mayo Clinic, Rochester, Minnesota, reasoned that injecting morphine into (intrathecally) or just around (epidurally) the fluid that bathes the spinal cord might provide direct access of the drug to the opiate receptor where it could generate a specific control of the pain, with minimal side effects. He tested his hypothesis in rats, and it worked; profound pain control could be produced. More importantly, the phenomenon carried over to people with severe pain. A single spinal injection of morphine can block pain for more than 24 hours in a patient; the same dose given systemically will provide pain relief for only a few hours. Furthermore, after spinal injection of morphine, patients are not paralyzed, as they are with spinal injection of local anesthetics, and, additionally, the bad side effects described above can be largely avoided. In fact, the patient can feel a light

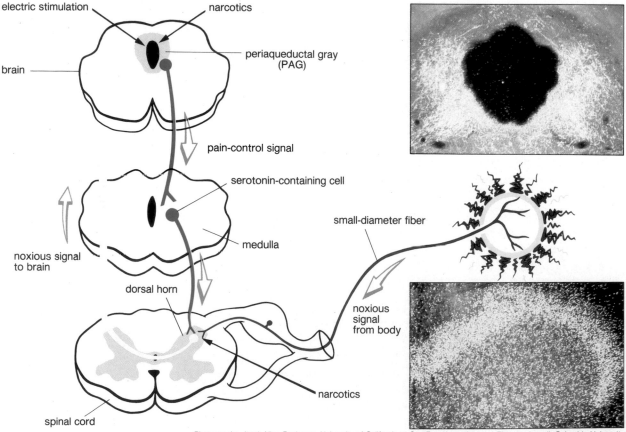

Photographs, (top) Allan Basbaum, University of California at San Francisco; (bottom) Thomas Jessell, Columbia University

touch to the skin, but pain is not experienced from the same region.

Direct spinal injection of morphine (and more recently of the endorphins themselves) is now commonly used to treat postoperative pain, especially following cesarean section. (It is of interest that spinal morphine does not provide sufficient pain relief for a woman to deliver a baby pain free. This provides some clue for male readers and others who have not had the experience of just how painful childbirth is.) With the development of implantable morphine pumps, it may also be possible to treat chronic pain conditions, such as cancer pain.

Psychological control: placebos, acupuncture, hypnosis

Do all pain-control procedures work by turning on the endorphin system? To find this out, scientists have generated pain control by various means and then determined whether the opiate antagonist, naloxone, can reverse the effect. Jon Levine and Howard Fields, neurobiologists at the University of California at San Francisco, used that approach to study placebo analgesia in human patients. The word placebo comes from the Latin verb *placere,* which means "to please"; it literally means "I will please." A placebo is a dummy medicine (such as a sugar pill) that is used to treat a medical problem even though it is not considered effective for the patient's condition. These researchers found that naloxone could indeed block the pain control exerted by such psychological factors and concluded that placebos, in part, work by activating the endorphin-mediated pain-control system. Many people mistakenly think that if a patient's pain is alleviated by a placebo, the pain must have been "imaginary." Rather, just the opposite is true. The greater the pain, the more likely the patients will respond positively to a placebo.

What about acupuncture for pain control? In one form of acupuncture, the needling is done in the area where the pain is reported. That type of acupuncture is probably comparable to rubbing one's hand when it hurts; it is another form of segmental control, like that provided by TENS. In fact, some acupuncturists attach wires to the needles and pass a small current through them. Pain control achieved by this type of acupuncture is not reversed by naloxone and thus presumably does not use the endorphins. The neurochemical basis of the segmental pain-control mechanisms is still to be discovered. On the other hand, several studies reported that pain relief from the more traditional form of acupuncture, in which points along one of 12 meridians (pathways along which the body's vital energy flows, according to acupuncture theory) are stimulated, *can* be reversed by naloxone. It should be noted, however, that the point stimulated does not appear to be critical; most acupuncturists use the so-called *hoku* point located near the junction of the thumb and forefinger. Taken together, these observations suggest that traditional acupuncture analgesia is a placebo analgesia, which, of course, would explain its reversibility by naloxone. This in no way detracts from its effectiveness, nor does it imply that the patient's pain was nonexistent. Whatever treatment the physician finds effective for treating pain is the right one. (Interestingly, traditional acupuncture for pain is rarely used in children; apparently, they do not like it.)

Insights into the body's endorphin-mediated pain-control system have led to the use of direct spinal injections of morphine and the endorphins for blocking pain without causing paralysis, numbness, or other severe side effects. Although this technique is now commonly used to treat postoperative pain, it is not sufficient for painless childbirth—a clue for those who have not experienced just how painful childbirth can be.

The Granger Collection, New York

In the illustration on the opposite page, inset photomicrographs of fluorescent-stained neural tissue demonstrate the presence of the natural opioid peptide beta endorphin in the PAG of the brain (top) and show the distribution of opiate receptors in the dorsal horn (bottom).

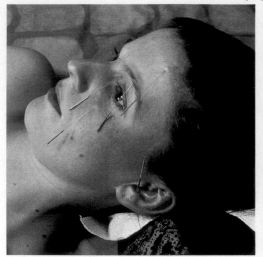 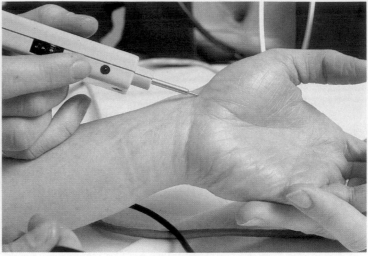

Acupuncture, an ancient Oriental technique for pain relief, appears to draw upon one or another of the body's natural pain-control systems for its success. Pain relief from the traditional form of acupuncture (above), in which thin needles are inserted and twirled at points along theoretical paths of energy flow (often quite distant from the pain site), can be disrupted by narcotic-blocking drugs like naloxone. This observation suggests activation of the endorphin-mediated system, possibly by means of a psychological placebo effect. Variations of acupuncture, in which the painful area itself is needled—sometimes with mildly electrified needles—or is stimulated at the skin surface with an electrified stylus (above right), achieve pain control that is not reversed by narcotic blockers. These variants may work by exploiting the body's segmental control system in ways comparable to TENS or to simple rubbing of the painful area.

Another powerful psychological approach to the treatment of pain is through hypnosis. Hypnotic analgesia, however, is not reversed by naloxone. What then is the mechanism? Ernest Hilgard, a psychologist at Stanford University, suggests that, in contrast to what occurs with morphine, under hypnotic analgesia the noxious input is transmitted faithfully from the peripheral nerves to the spinal cord and from there to the brain, but it is no longer perceived as painful. His experiments involved the use of a so-called hidden observer. Under hypnosis the patient reports out loud that a noxious stimulus applied to the arm is not at all painful; the "hidden observer," which presumably lies somewhere in the subject's subconscious, reports (by writing) that severe pain is, in fact, being experienced. Clearly, the noxious input got through to the brain, but somehow the perception of it as pain was altered.

The conclusions from these hypnosis studies underscore what was emphasized earlier—that pain is not a faithful transmission of a signal generated by a noxious stimulus. The input is only one of many factors that determine how much pain is perceived. Rather, pain is a complex perception that is influenced by the nature of the situation in which the stimulus is experienced, by prior experience, and by emotions. Although it is sometimes possible to block pain by surgically cutting off the input, that is often ineffective. In fact, pain may be experienced in the absence of input. Moreover, the mere fact that neurosurgery for pain usually produces irreversible damage to the nervous system demands that more conservative approaches to alleviating pain be tried first.

Future directions in understanding pain

The increasing sophistication about the neurochemistry of pain-transmission and pain-control systems points to a host of new pharmacological approaches to the treatment of pain. Bradykinin and substance-P-receptor blockers, new cyclooxygenase and lipoxygenase inhibitors, and more specific opioid peptide analgesics are all being sought or developed. The recognition that control of pain, with far fewer side effects, can be gener-

102

Major pain-control measures

measure	mechanism	limitations/comments
surgical cutting of nerve fiber	creates physical break in pain pathway	fair risk of failure or return of pain
NSAIDs (*e.g.,* aspirin)	block prostaglandin synthesis at site of injury	do not block leukotriene synthesis
corticosteroids	block prostaglandin and leukotriene synthesis at site of injury	major side effects
substance P blocker	would inhibit binding of substance P to receptors in spinal cord	still being sought
substance-P-depleting agent	would deplete substance P in pain-transmitting nerve fibers without causing pain	still being sought
bradykinin blocker	inhibits binding of bradykinin to receptors at site of pain	under development
electric vibrator; TENS	tactile or electric stimulation of large fibers blocks or alters pain signal to brain	segmental control; must be applied at site of pain
electric stimulation of PAG in brain	activates endorphin-mediated pain-control system, blocking pain signal in spinal cord	control inhibited by narcotic blockers
systemic injection of narcotics	binds to opiate receptors in PAG, activating endorphin-mediated pain-control system	severe side effects due to binding in other brain regions
spinal injection of narcotics	binds primarily to opiate receptors in spinal cord, blocking pain signal	side effects largely avoided
placebo	may activate endorphin-mediated pain-control system	control inhibited by narcotic blockers
acupuncture at site of pain	seems similar to segmental control produced by TENS	control unaffected by narcotic blockers
acupuncture distant from site of pain	form of placebo	control inhibited by narcotic blockers
hypnosis	alters brain's perception of pain	control unaffected by narcotic blockers

ated when drugs are delivered spinally instead of systemically also points to the importance of developing better drug-delivery systems.

Future research must also address the processes through which acute pain becomes chronic. Why are there such profound individual differences in the experience of pain? Given the significant cognitive and emotional contribution to the experience of pain, the need for parallel studies of the psychology of pain and pain control must not be ignored. Although much less is understood about how cognitive factors, such as learning and memory, influence complex perceptions such as pain, manipulating those processes may ultimately be the best way to treat chronic pain. The development of more effective approaches to the relief of pain will be possible when scientists have a much better understanding of how and where all of the components that contribute to the perception of pain are integrated.

Unlocking the Secrets of Pain

The Psychology

by Macdonald Critchley, M.D.

Pain is a well-nigh universal experience that is manifestly complex in character. Its vagaries are reflected in the fact that it is often described as "inscrutable," "mysterious," and "a medical enigma." Philosophers have quibbled over the problem of pain, the puzzle of pain, its challenge, and its possible purpose. William Wordsworth called it "permanent, obscure and dark," but according to Oscar Wilde it was a "revelation." For Samuel Johnson it was a "perpetual misery."

Over the years there have been arguments as to its essential nature. It has long been debated whether pain is an emotion or a sensation. Some writers have used the term perceptual experience. Others have submitted that pain should be looked upon as a "drive" in the technical sense of the word, comparable with hunger or thirst rather than a simple sensation like smell, vision, or hearing. To some theologians, however, there has apparently been no difficulty. As its etymology indicates, pain is unambiguously *poena;* that is, a penalty. Richard Chevenix Trench, archbishop of Dublin in the early 19th century, was in no doubt that pain is the correlation of sin— pain is punishment.

Pageant of pain

Despite its biologic pedigree, pain still awaits an adequate definition. Almost all painful events are accompanied by powerful feelings, their nature varying with the circumstances. Pain that steadily increases may cause feelings that differ from those following pain that is abrupt and overwhelming. Then again, there is the pain that terrifies, if only because it is inexplicable. As it continues, pain absorbs the whole of one's attention. Describing the pain she suffered during her own viral meningitis, Caroline Sullivan, a psychiatrist from Liverpool, England, recently wrote in the *British Medical Journal* (June 14, 1986): "All I wanted was pain relief. That night I became acutely aware of how pain narrows your horizons." Often the agony brings in its wake great fear. What has happened? What does it portend? How long will it last? If the pain follows injury the origin is no mystery, but will it ever cease?

Whatever the circumstances, anxiety will develop—physical agitation, mental distress, and panic. A formidable aspect of really excruciating pain

Macdonald Critchley, M.D., is Consultant Neurologist at the National Hospital, London; President Emeritus of the World Federation of Neurology; and Commander of the Order of the British Empire. He lives in Somerset, England.

(Opposite page) A migraine sufferer's depiction of pain; photograph, British Migraine Association and WB Pharmaceuticals Ltd.

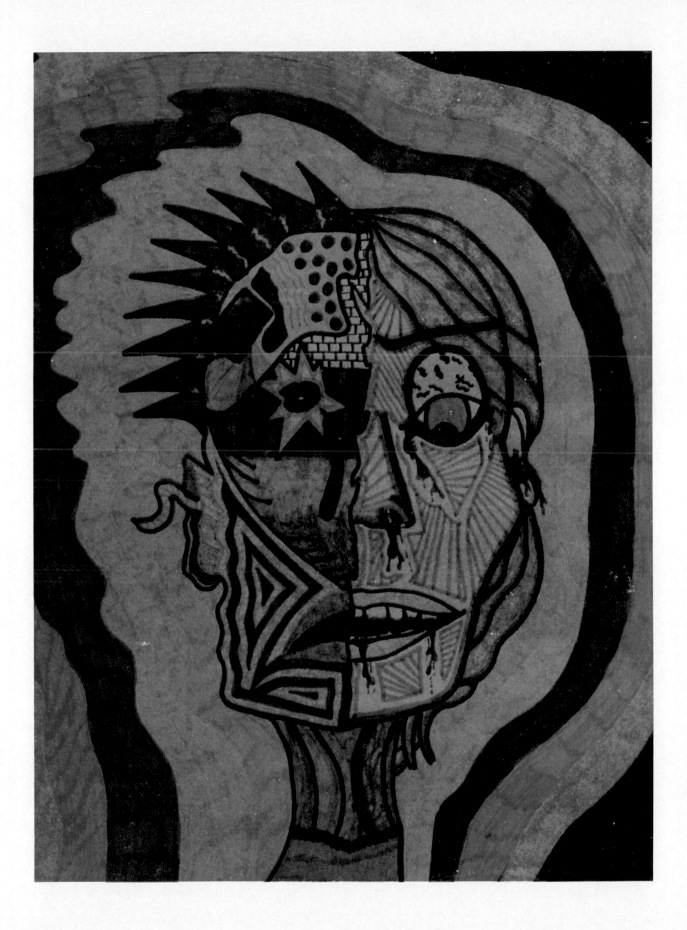

"The Cholic" by George Cruikshank; photograph, Mary Evans Picture Library, London

is the feeling it brings of utter isolation, of being forsaken. No one can help you. No one understands. The writer Peter Fleming in his "Essay on Pain" (1956) wrote: "Perhaps it is the solitariness of pain which makes it alone of man's experience incommunicable to others." As the pain builds up, so does the anguish. In clinical experience, however, fear of death may be paramount. As Samuel Johnson protested to the doctors who were tapping his hydrocele (fluid accumulation around the testicle), "I want length of life, and you fear giving me pain, which I care not for."

The endurance of pain brings about an illusory lengthening of the sense of time. "Every minute seemed an hour" is often heard in descriptions of an acutely painful episode. This is well illustrated in electrical accidents, as in the following case of a patient seen and reported on by this author in "Injuries from Electricity and Lightning to the Nervous System" (*The Lancet*, 1934). Reported the patient: "The duration of the shock could not have been more than a couple of seconds. A man riding by on a bicycle going at a good speed had only time to pass about 30 yards beyond me when the operator [of the electrical works] opened the switch (to cut off the current). Yet I could see every spoke in the bicycle and it barely seemed to me to be moving. I could feel every reversal of the current, and these reversals occurred at the rate of 60 complete cycles a minute." It is this intense activity of the brain in response to electrical impressions that makes an instant of electric shock seem hours to the sufferer.

Depression is quite distinct from anxiety, and it occupies an ambiguous place in the climate of pain. Overt or suppressed depression is not uncommon, especially when pain has been in existence for an unconscionable length of time. On the other hand, in some cases there may be deep melancholia, which is attended by a considerable rise in the threshold of pain toleration, even perhaps of actual pain perception. Procedures that are putatively agonizing are sometimes (though uncommonly) resorted to in suicidal efforts. When the attempt fails, it may come to light that the wrist

Caricaturists have had a field day with the universal subject of pain, typically portraying it as punishment inflicted by demons, devils, and other foes. Whether it is the gastrointestinal system, the head, the big toe, or some other part of the anatomy that is affected, the victim's experience of pain is invariably all absorbing. Its depiction may reflect fear, anxiety, or outright panic—especially if the pain strikes suddenly, coming as a complete surprise—or there may be doomed acceptance, as is often the case when the pain is chronic—a familiar visitant. Although artists frequently have represented pain as the source of melancholia—even as leading to the contemplation of self-destruction— its actual connection with depression is ambiguous, and rarely is pain itself known to be an inducement to suicide.

106

slashing or throat cutting was carried out with no physical distress at the time. Yet Hippocrates observed how rarely mental pain, *i.e.,* depression, and physical pain occur together. Others, too, have been impressed by a negative correlation between intractable pain and deep depression. In the considerable medical literature on melancholia, *physical* pain finds little place. The 19th-century German neuropsychiatrist Richard von Krafft-Ebing often used such terms as "painful depression," "psychic neuralgia," and "psychic pains." It is doubtful, however, that he had in mind anything other than mental anguish.

Intense pain, whether acute or long-standing, is an infrequent inducement to suicide. Precise figures, however, are lacking. The British psychiatrist Crichton Miller regarded pain as probably a less common cause of suicide

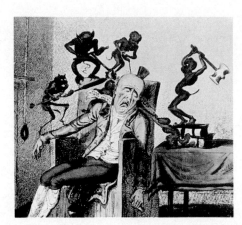

than other unpleasant sensations, and he stated that more people take their lives because of an incurable ringing in their ears than because of pain.

Obviously, the events leading up to and bringing about a state of pain largely determine what particular medley of emotions will follow. A victim's response to an accidental injury differs considerably from a trauma of similar violence inflicted deliberately. In the latter case, anger, shame, or ideas of flight or of retaliation may crowd into consciousness. The picture may be quite different when the pain is due not to injury but to disease. Now arises an additional worry, one that concerns the possible origins of the pain, its likely duration, and its potential threat to life. Pain is then the harbinger of doom. When the pain is but the reappearance of a familiar visitant like migraine or gout, however, exasperation is the response, rather than fear.

Surprise may play an important role. Expectancy may or may not lower the threshold of pain tolerance (according to psychologists, the level of pain perception does not alter). Is one reassured when the dentist says, "This may hurt a little," or is it better to be taken unawares? Perhaps the answer depends upon the length of the interval between the warning and the stimulus. There is a much-quoted case of a man who, as a stunt, used to submit deliberately to an electric current of 500 volts. When he made contact *accidentally* with the same circuit, he was killed.

One might well turn to the poets and prose writers when seeking to explore the secrets of pain. Hugh Walpole was a novelist who was obsessed with thoughts and ideas bound up with physical suffering. In his *Portrait of a Man with Red Hair* (1925), he vividly described the factor of expectancy:

Only once or twice in his life had pain actually come to him. He did not mind it so deeply were it part of an illness or natural causes but the deliberate anticipation of it— the doctor's "Now look out, I'm going to hurt!"—these things froze him with horror. . . . That [surgical] operation had been a slight one, but it had involved several weeks of the withdrawing of tubes, and the probing with bright shining instruments. Every morning for several hours before this withdrawing and probing he lay panting in bed, the beads of sweat gathering on his forehead, his hands clutching and unclutching, saying to himself that he did not care, that he was above it, beyond it . . . but closer and closer the animal came, and soon he was at his bedside, and soon bending over him, and soon his claws were upon his flesh and the pain would swoop down, like a cry of a discoverer, and the voice would be sharper and sharper, the determination not to listen, not to hear, not to feel weaker and weaker, until at length out it would come, the defeat, the submission, the scream of pity. . . .

Later, the same character reflects:

The sense of the coming pain had been more awful than anything he could have imagined. . . . One night earache attacked him. It was a new pain for him, and he thought he had never known anything as terrible. Worse than all were the intermissions between the attacks and the warnings that a new attack was soon to begin. That approach was what he feared, that terrible and fearful approach. He had said very little, had only laid there white and trembling, but the memory of all those awful hours stayed with him always.

When pain becomes excruciating or protracted, certain physical changes take place. Cautious immobility (*akinesia algera*) gives way to bodily writhings and movements of agitation. These are often accompanied by interjections and cries—loud and unrestrained. Whether these utterances

108

In this early painting (1593) by Caravaggio, the boy's expression reveals both great surprise and extreme distress at the moment of the lizard's bite.

"Boy Bitten by a Lizard" by Caravaggio; photograph, Art Resource

do anything to mitigate the suffering is open to argument. Autonomic changes occur and may attain a dangerous level, bringing about syncope (the temporary suspension of respiration and circulation) and even death.

Semantics of pain

It becomes evident that problems of pain perception are bedeviled by the handicap of language. Pain is essentially a behavioral, subjective phenomenon, the concomitants of which—verbal, autonomic, interjectional, gestural—are not reliable. Despite the efforts of psychologists and others, no system of measurement of pain has yet evolved that is wholly dependable. The clinician is still obliged to rely upon the victim's assertion that he is going through an unpleasant experience, one that is commonly called "painful," of varied quality and intensity. The power to communicate reflects not only the size of the particular sufferer's word bank but also his skill in finding and retrieving the appropriate words. In her essay "On Being Ill," Virginia Woolf wrote: "English, which can express the thoughts of Hamlet and the tragedy of Lear, has no words for the shiver and the headache. . . . The merest schoolgirl, when she falls in love, has Shakespeare and Keats to speak for her; but let a sufferer try to describe a pain in his head to a doctor and language at once runs dry."

In the English tongue (no other linguistic medium is being discussed here), relatively few terms expressing this particular unpleasant experience are in general use. "Pain," "hurt," "ache," "suffering," and "agony" are all near synonyms, though the first of these terms is the one most often employed. "Hurt" and "ache" usually imply pains that are not severe, whereas "agony" suggests pain that is both severe and protracted. Conventional habits of speech are sometimes flouted, however, and an individual may resort to his or her own personal idiom by using "agony" for even the mildest states of pain. Regional expressions may complicate matters, as when a Scot speaks of a "sore head" instead of a headache, or when one of Caribbean origin refers to a "weakness" on the "top-flat," "noggin," "dome," or "biscuit."

"Suffering" is a term that is sometimes used as a synonym for pain; when it is, it tends to imply the act of endurance of physical pain. It lacks precision, however, for it can also stand for a torment or even a state of anxiety that may or may not encompass physical pain. The familiar but lax employment of the phrase "pain and suffering" occurs repeatedly in scriptural texts but leads to ambiguity. Thus, when the theological writer C. S. Lewis, in *The Problem of Pain* (1940), wrote, "The addition of a million fellow-sufferers adds no more pain," he did not make clear whether he had in mind physical torment or mental distress.

At times there is a very fine line between the literal and metaphor. Witness the music critic who wrote of Paganini: "What a man, what a violin, what an artist! God, what suffering, torture, and pain in those four strings!"

The color of pain

Semantic difficulties increase when qualifying adjectives are considered. The thesaurus lists well over a hundred words to describe the character of pain, its severity, and its affective coloring, but this is not particularly useful because language, clearly, is not an exact science.

The investigations into "synalgia" (from the Greek *syn,* "with," and *algos,* "pain") by the two medical students Eugen Bleuler and Karl Lehmann in Zürich, Switzerland, over a century ago led them to conclude that in some persons pains are never felt or even imagined without the sufferer's entertaining an idea of color: "Violent pains are accompanied by an idea of white; still more intense and localized pains go from yellow to red and to dark brown; dull headaches give a tint which is almost black; darting pains an idea of white dots; a pinch, a yellow tint, which is clearer the keener the pain is; indigestion, a more or less clear grey; colic, a clear yellowish tint which may pass over to red or brown." Other observers have confirmed their findings.

Perhaps the earliest example of the linking of pain to a color is in Homer: "He opened his quiver and took out a fresh-winged arrow, harbinger of black pains." (*Iliad* IV). The German writer Leonhard Frank, in his novel *Brother and Sister* (1930), wrote apropos of a maternity ward: "There was nothing in the white-painted room but a white covered ottoman, a white table of instruments, and a white washstand. Lydia was white, too, and the doctors and sisters were white. Only the pains had violent colors, all colors." Describing the pains resulting from a cancer of the stomach, John Cowper Powys wrote in his novel *A Glastonbury Romance* (1932): "The pain took various shapes according to its intensity. What it resembled now was a round black iron ball of a rusty blood colour, covered with spikes."

110

Is pain ennobling? Does it serve a purpose?

Until about 50 years ago, popular belief held that long-lasting pain exercised a sort of purifying impact upon the sufferer. This mental and spiritual cleansing has been traced within the Scriptures ("perfect through sufferings," Hebrews 2:10). Early in the 19th century, many surgeons asserted that pain was a wise provision of nature; that patients *should* suffer pain; that they were all the better for it and recovered quicker. The 19th-century surgeon and anatomist Sir Charles Bell regarded pain as the companion and guardian of human life. Even in the present century, the Irish dramatist and critic St. John Greer Ervine proclaimed in his essay "Pain Is an Incentive" (1935) that suffering has stimulating powers of immense therapeutic virtue and in some persons acts as a spur to work. But does pain serve a purpose? According to tradition, a feeling of pain indicates that a particular contact is harmful and that immediate flight from danger is imperative. The stock metaphor is that of a vigilant sentinel. Matters are more complicated, however. The need to withdraw from potential tissue damage arises only with an acute pain of traumatic origin, but pain may also signal some hidden disease state, escape from which is not feasible. Pain does not assist in the healing process, although at one time the contrary view was held. Insofar as pain leads to immobilization of the injured part, it brings about a situation that is favorable for tissue repair. This was the important principle that the surgeon John Hilton, practicing at Guy's Hospital, London, in the mid-19th century, embodied within his classic work, *Rest and Pain* (1863). As a sentinel, pain must be rated inefficient, erratic, and unreliable. Once the lesion has come to light, the pain may persist; in such circumstances, it is difficult to detect any purpose or design. Some deadly ailments advancing either slowly or rapidly, in fact, run their sinister course without the victim's suffering a moment's pain.

On the other hand, there are certain intense and intractable pains devoid of any ostensible motive; they are meaningless. For examples one can

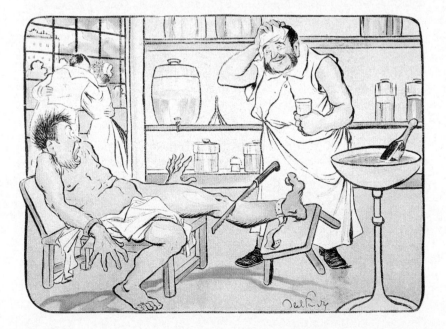

To the pains originating within the body, humans added another source of pain—that inflicted by the surgeon's knife. In the days before modern anesthesia, surgery was often performed by unskilled barbers. In the case of amputations, there was not only the pain of the excision itself but, after the part was gone, a bizarre pain known as phantom-limb pain, which was indeed felt—often excruciatingly—in the nonexistent limb. Today surgical operations are generally pain-free, but amputation patients still experience this perplexing phantom phenomenon.

National Library of Medicine, Bethesda, Maryland

turn to tic douloureux (severe, paroxysmal bursts of pain in facial nerves), cluster headaches (which are characterized by severe, intractable, unilateral pains in the eye and temple and, as the name indicates, occur in "clusters," or cyclically—*e.g.,* daily for a period of many weeks in once-a-year bouts), postherpetic neuralgia (nerve pain after a bout of herpes zoster virus), causalgia (a burning sensation affecting the skin), and certain "central" pains like those occurring in the hemialgia (pain affecting half the body) of thalamic disease and in some phantom limbs—*i.e.,* pain that is experienced in a limb that has been amputated.

Pain is surely more malefic than protective. The philosopher Friedrich Nietzsche spoke of the "senselessness of suffering." As Sir James Young Simpson, the pioneer of chloroform anesthesia, put it: "All pain is *per se,* and especially when in excess, destructive and even ultimately fatal in its actions and effects. It exhausts the principle of life. It exhausts both the system and the part. Mere pain *can* destroy life."

Very occasionally pain has been regarded as a spur. When, during a 1986 performance of *Tosca* at the Metropolitan Opera in New York City, the soprano Eva Marton sustained a dislocated jaw during a staged scuffle with her burly baritone partner, she carried on. "There is a point," she declared afterward, "when one is all keyed up. Pain is not always negative. It can also act as an elixir, a stimulant." Perhaps so, but such experiences are the exception.

Recent thinking on pain

According to John J. Bonica, a pioneer of pain management and the founder of the Seattle Multidisciplinary Pain Center, the first person to regard pain as a separate and distinct sense was the Persian physician Avicenna (980–1037). Biologic life, though, has been attended by pain ever since some form of conscious existence evolved. Over the centuries there grew up in a halting, stepwise fashion an understanding of the nature of pain and of its manner of working. The past 50 years, however, have witnessed a dramatic advancement. Three circumstances have brought this about.

First was the realization that chemical agents play an important, if not a quintessential, role in the production of pain. Substance P, a potent polypeptide that dilates blood vessels and causes muscles to contract, and is thought to function as a neurotransmitter, was isolated in 1931. Within the last decade several other pain-producing substances have been found. It has also been discovered that the human nervous system can apparently create its own painkiller chemicals, known as endorphins. Many other opioid peptides and neurohormones have since been identified, and research is proceeding at a very rapid pace.

The second step forward came about through the collaboration of a psychologist, Ronald Melzak, with a neurophysiologist, Patrick Wall. In 1965 they announced their "gate-control theory" of pain, which delineated the mode of transmission of pain as electrical impulses. This hypothesis, which they later emended and expanded, helped to explain many of the inconsistencies of pain behavior. The benefit accruing from various treatments that utilized local stimulating procedures—the application of electrical stimuli to

This British illustration, entitled "A Little Rheum Atick," bore the caption "That man should ever be obliged to exist under such panes."

National Library of Medicine, Bethesda, Maryland

112

an area of pain—had been recognized for a number of centuries. Now, at last, these homespun facts were rendered intelligible. For example, an often effective, scientifically based method of delivering a mild electrical current to the skin over the pain site, known as transcutaneous electrical nerve-stimulation (or TENS), is an important part of the present-day treatment armamentarium.

The third breakthrough was the isolation and analysis of an entity that had hitherto received scant attention. Algologists (contemporary pain specialists) became aware of the existence of a "chronic pain syndrome." This is sometimes referred to as the chronic intractable benign (nonmalignant) pain syndrome (or CIBS), since some oncologists believe patients with incurable (malignant) cancers suffer in their terminal state a type of pain that is fundamentally distinct.

The chronic pain syndrome is by no means a rarity. It often—though not always—develops out of a condition of acute pain resulting either from injury or from disease. But instead of the original pain gradually subsiding as healing proceeds, and eventually disappearing, it continues. At this stage no structural lesion may be found other than a scar, and yet the pain drags on despite analgesic drugs in doses that should have been effective. Abnormal physical signs are no longer detectable. Psychiatric symptoms begin to complicate the picture, and the patient drifts into a state of confirmed and abiding invalidism. How long must pain continue before it qualifies as chronic? Workers in pain clinics have sometimes arbitrarily decided upon six months. Usually by this time the pain is no longer a symptom; it has become a disease in its own right.

The predicament of chronic pain

According to Gerald M. Aronoff, director of the Boston Pain Center, patients with chronic pain share many of the same characteristics: preoccupation with pain, strong and ambivalent dependency needs, feelings of isolation and loneliness, masochism, inability to attend to self-needs, passivity, lack of insight, inability to deal with repressed anger and hostility appropriately, and the use of pain as a means of communication.

The typical features were also graphically described in 1985 by Philip L. Gildenberg and Richard A. DeVaul of the Chronic Pain Clinic in Houston, Texas. Symptoms continue for months or years. During this period the pain complained of is no different from that in the original acute phase, save that it responds less well to opioids. Without any reluctance the patient relates his sufferings in considerable detail and often with apparent relish. Many medications have been prescribed and are still taken even though the benefit claimed is minimal. Drug addiction is to be expected. The patient insists his pains are incapacitating and unbearable and that his case is one of urgency. In his *furor therapeuticus* he declares he will undergo any form of treatment, however drastic, contending that his problem is organic, though obscure. Often he asserts he would be perfectly well if only the doctor would rid him of his pain. Questioned as to his mental well-being and whether any personal difficulties exist, he becomes evasive or noncommittal. With his state of ill health he manipulates his family and also

113

The universality and chronicity of pain ensure that sufferers will buy any sort of remedy offered, as long as it promises relief. This has long been so—from the potions peddled by the country quack (above) and the popular, widely advertised patent medicines of the 19th century (opposite page) to the potent drugs sold today—many of which are addictive and actually compound the problem of pain.

his doctor, whom he may inveigle into injudicious measures. As Gildenberg and DeVaul have noted, "It is one of the privileges of the sick to be exempt from social responsibilities."

Indeed, the syndrome may be regarded as incurable. This nihilistic attitude is obviously unsatisfactory. Much more research into the tragic predicament of the chronic pain victim is required.

Yet those who write about the chronic pain syndrome seem to have overlooked an important and commonly recurring state of affairs. How do the symptoms alter if and when the chronic pain patient subsequently develops some mortal disease? The picture can then no longer be deemed benign. In this author's experience, a striking behavioral change comes about when a terminal illness is diagnosed. The patient is no longer difficult. He or she ceases to be truculent and loses the preoccupation with pain. The "terminal" patient is now easier to nurse and becomes relatively serene.

Remembering pain

It is possible to memorize a smell or taste, but the actual sense datum cannot be experienced. In the same way, the recall of pain is never total. However intense and however long lasting the original pain experience has been, it rarely, if ever, can be relived by an effort of will. No actual physical sensation can be evoked. One may live through all the attendant emotions of displeasure and alarm—one may even reenact the cries and contortions of the occasion—but the pain itself does not reappear.

Perhaps in exceptional cases it is possible to rekindle images so vivid that they impinge upon the boundary of awareness. The 19th-century French psychologist Théodule-Armand Ribot thought so and quoted a pupil who claimed that, by an effort of will, he could conjure up a toothache.

There is also the phenomenon of sympathetic pain; the evidence supporting this variety of experience, however, is only anecdotal. Hence, one must be skeptical of accounts of shared pain. For example, the anarchist Emma Goldman, in her autobiography, *Living My Life* (1931), quotes a letter by her comrade Alexander ("Sasha") Berkman. From prison Berkman wrote:

The death of Russell especially affected me . . . he died a terrible death (from meningitis) . . . in some manner his agony seemed to communicate itself to me, and I began to experience the pains and symptoms that Russell described in his notes. I knew it was my sick fancy. I strove against it but presently my legs showed signs of paralysis, and I suffered excruciating pain in the spinal column, just like Russell.

Memory traces of pain may lie dormant within the nervous system only to be aroused years later through another form of stimulation of the area originally involved. British neurologist Peter Nathan recently described such a case, that of an ex-soldier who had had his leg amputated after a war wound to the knee. Masses of nerve tissue resulted from abnormal regrowth of his stump, causing sensation in the stump (paresthesia). On one occasion Nathan had injected saline into the patient's stump, a procedure that had induced more paresthesia and also some pain, lasting about an hour. That same night, however, the patient was aroused by a pain in his phantom limb. This spectral pain was not the discomfort due to the saline injections, nor was it like that of his wound. It exactly reproduced a pain

114

that had occurred five years before the amputation. This earlier pain had been due to an accident during an ice-hockey match. He had fallen and another player skated over him, gashing his leg deeply. Nathan looked upon memory traces of former painful events as being reactivated by a fresh painful input. He associated the phenomenon with the group of neural activities that contribute to the process of learning.

Rarely does one hear accounts of *real* pain appearing in dream states. Those who are going through a painful illness often experience vivid and frustrating dreams that are peculiarly vexing but quite pain-free. Thus, in a severe attack of periodic migraine one becomes increasingly drowsy, and in the eventual sleep the headache lets up. It may be replaced, however, by a strange and baffling pain *equivalent* intruding within one's dreams. The French writer Marcel Proust was aware of this phenomenon; in *Remembrance of Things Past* he wrote:

When we have gone to sleep with a maddening toothache and are conscious of it only as a little girl whom we attempt time after time, to pull out of the water, or as a line of Molière which we repeat incessantly to ourselves, it is a great relief to wake up, so that we can disentangle the idea of toothache from artificial semblance of heroism or rhythmic cadence.

Pain is a form of encounter that makes its appearance throughout one's life, lingers, and then in its own time departs. The visitant may become a "familiar"—less frightening in time, no doubt, though never welcome. Pain's comings and goings are never completely forgotten. One pain influences the next, though inconsistently so. As a result, the level of pain tolerance may gradually alter, and a checkered history of severe and lengthy illness may bring about either a lowering or a heightening of the threshold.

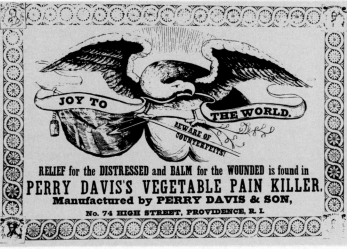

(Left) The Granger Collection, New York; (top right) Culver Pictures; (bottom right) the Bettmann Archive

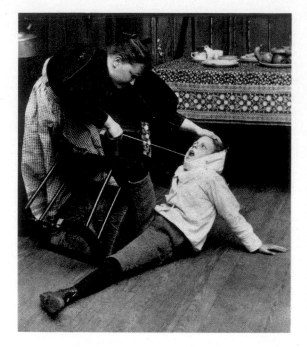

THE T VOLUME.

"Does your cyclopedy tell anything about the toothache?"
"I think so, mum; it touches on all useful information. We haven't published the T volume yet."
"Well, you can put me down for a T volume, an' if it goes ahead of our almanick on toothache cures, I'll take the whole set."

When the pain stops

No precise term exists in the English language to stand for that sensation that supervenes when pain has come to an end. Sometimes it is not easy to determine the end point of the suffering because of a lingering anxiety that all is not yet well. "Pleasure" is not the word, for it suggests a more positive state than mere cessation of pain. Despite the conventional pleasure/pain antinomy, relief from pain is a rather negative or passive feeling. Not everyone will agree, however, and it may be submitted that the letup from pain is one of release, being always attended by definite—even though transient—physical and mental gratification. The condition of *bienaise* that immediately follows the emptying of a distended bladder comes to mind. One can, in this context, evoke the reply of the "lunatic" who was asked why he was beating his head against the floor: "Because it feels mighty fine when I leave off!"

Some psychological corollaries of painful experience continue even after the pain has ceased. Literature holds many examples of this postalgic state. The philosopher William Paley said: "Pain itself is not without alleviations. It may be violent and frequent, but is seldom both violent and long continued, and its pauses and intermissions become positive pleasure. It has the power of shedding a satisfaction over intervals of ease, which I believe few enjoyments exceed."

In his novel *Hans Frost* (1929), Hugh Walpole wrote: "I am suffering tonight from a toothache, and I have always noticed that a toothache is the most unintellectual pain in one's body, just as, in all probability, a stomach-

116

ache is the most intellectual. Have you noticed, sir, how bright and clear one's brain becomes between the spasms of indigestion?"

In musical composition a discord may sometimes be inserted before a resolving harmony. In the same way, physical pain may be deliberately provoked in order to enhance the pleasurable respite that follows. For example, a person with a toothache may prod the offending tooth with the tongue, thereby temporarily increasing the discomfort. Should the pain that is incited be excessive, or prolonged, or if it is produced as an end in itself, the confines of normality are then being invaded, and one is entering the sinister sphere of algophilia.

Pursuit of pain

Algophilia (Greek *philein,* "to love"), the perverse pursuit of suffering, can be observed in four principal circumstances. First, among certain communities pain may be purposefully sought and tolerated as part of a traditional initiation ritual. The samurai of Japan, the Stoics and the Spartans of ancient Greece, and the Paramahamsas (or nomadic fakirs) of India are familiar examples. Perhaps the motive is not so much the pain as the qualities of fortitude or virility that the pain endurance symbolizes. When Scaevola thrust his arm into the fire, it was to demonstrate Roman hardihood. A widely practiced ceremony is the fire walk, which has been described and critically scrutinized on many occasions. No wholly satisfactory explanation has yet emerged as to why so little pain is felt and so little tissue damage results. Attempts have likewise been made by medical scientists to "explain" the mechanics of the practices of fakirs, such as sitting sparsely clothed on beds of nails, and of fire-eaters and glass-swallowers of the bazaars. The literature on their performances is vast, but studies have revealed little, and the complexities and perplexities inherent in the pursuit of pain abound.

The self-infliction of pain and the submission to the pains of martyrdom are two distinct aspects of religious pursuit of pain. In the former belong the practices among ascetics of the autoinfliction of torment as an act of

"St. Sebastian" by Andrea Mantegna; photograph, Scala/Art Resource

Sometimes pain is willingly submitted to—e.g., St. Sebastian's martyrdom (c. 283), a favorite subject of Renaissance artists. Pain may also be purposely sought as part of a traditional initiation ritual—e.g., the fire walk. It has not been adequately explained why so little pain is apparently felt in these cases and why so little tissue damage occurs.

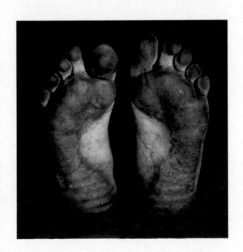

(Left) Kraipit—SIPA; (right) Lynn Goldsmith Inc.

expiation or as a means of self-purification. In the latter event the victim suffers at the hands of others. The literature of martyrology holds numerous examples of religious devotees upon whom unspeakable cruelties have been inflicted. In many cases, although not in all, the martyr has been described as submitting to the torture in a state of smiling exaltation (*e.g.,* in Edward Gibbon's *History of the Decline and Fall of the Roman Empire* and in John Foxe's *Book of Martyrs*). Such cases suggest an ecstasy arising out of a hypnotically induced trance state. The dissociation cannot be complete, however, for the victim is apparently in possession of some of his or her faculties and can move and speak.

Examples of the abnormal enjoyment of pain are familiar to psychiatrists. The most extreme instances are found among those having IQs of less than 35 and clinically designated as severely and profoundly mentally retarded, who may deliberately injure themselves by beating their heads against a wall, gnawing their wrists, or pummeling themselves. Psychotics have been known to plunge their arms into boiling water or into a fire until their charred flesh drops off. What depths of pain are thus experienced or if, indeed, there is any pain at all is difficult to gauge. Perhaps the sensations engendered are interpreted as being pleasurable, or possibly the pain that is deliberately provoked serves to assuage some other unpleasant feeling.

Finally there is sadomasochism (known clinically as algolagnia), the derivation of pleasure from inflicting pain on others or on oneself. Such a motif ran through much of the decadent literature of the 19th century. Flagrant examples are to be found in many works by the poet Algernon Swinburne and in certain revelatory passages within the *Confessions* of Jean-Jacques Rousseau. Sadomasochism crops up in the previously quoted work of Walpole, *Portrait of a Man with Red Hair:* "He had also a lot of talk about Power. . . . Some also about its being good for people to suffer . . .

Medical scientists are baffled by the mechanics of self-inflicted pain rituals, such as glass-swallowing and fire-eating (above). They likewise find it hard to explain the feats of fakirs, who are regarded as holy men possessed of inhuman thresholds of pain endurance. The East Indian fakir at right calmly rests on a bed of nails.

that life was never so intense as when we were suffering. That . . . God liked us to suffer."

Limits of endurance

There are many questions that are not asked as often as they should be. Is there any limit to the feeling of pain? Does a steady increase in the violence of the pain-invoking (nociceptive) stimulus bring about a parallel rise in the intensity of the pain? Or is there a climax that, when attained, is followed by a plateau of perception? Or by a decline? Or even a conversion into some kind of experience in which pain plays no part?

Charles Dickens believed that there was a "limit"—a certain point of mental strain beyond which no one could go—but he did not specifically refer to physical pain in this context. The novelist-philosopher H. G. Wells was one of the few to have written on the subject. In his novel *The Research Magnificent* (1915), he described the elaborate mental exercises by which his character Beham strove to overcome fear and pain and so attain the "aristocratic Life," or the "life set free":

He was clearly suggesting that in pain itself, pain endured beyond a certain pitch, there might come pleasure again, an intensity of sensation that might have the colour of delight. . . . He argued, we exaggerate the range of pain as if it were limitless. We think if we are unthinking that it passes into agony and so beyond the endurance to destruction. It probably does nothing of the kind. And following on this came memoranda on the recorded behaviour of martyrs, of the self-torture of Hindoo ascetics, of the defiance of Red Indian prisoners. These things are much more horrible when we consider them from the point of view of the easy chair . . . are they really horrible at all? Is it possible that these charred and slashed and splintered persons, these Indians hanging from hooks, have had glimpses through high windows that were worth the price . . . paid for them?

Such notions are indeed fanciful and intriguing but are not to be taken too seriously. Many elaborate theories have been advanced but, on the whole, today, as thousands of years ago, scientists and philosophers are still groping in the dark to understand pain's inmost secrets.

The essential nature of pain may never be understood—only that it is manifestly complex in character. Perhaps the creative minds of artists have come the closest. Emily Dickinson wrote:
"Pain—has an Element of Blank—
It cannot recollect
When it began—or if there were
A time when it was not—"

The Treatment
A New Era

by John D. Loeser, M.D.

When people complain of pain, they can mean many very different things. No one is born with an understanding of what phenomena should be placed in this category; using the word pain or behaving as if one has pain must be learned, and both are certainly influenced by one's family and society.

The problems concerning pain's meaning have their roots in long-held concepts that have, to a large degree, dominated thinking and practice in 20th-century health care in the Western world. René Descartes, the premier philosopher of the French Enlightenment, divided human existence into mind and body. For Descartes and his intellectual descendants, in order for there to be pain, first there must be tissue damage, which leads to a response by the person, which is then labeled "pain." However, this Cartesian concept, which so long held sway, failed to explain why athletes, for example, sustain major trauma yet do not complain and continue to play—especially when they are highly paid; why wounded soldiers may be unaware of their injuries until after the combat has ceased; why minor injuries can result in major dysfunction; why some people complain of severe pain and cannot be found to have any tissue damage; why people who have nerve injuries may report that they feel pain in uninjured parts of the body; and, even more bizarre, why there can be pains felt in absent parts of the body after an amputation.

It is clear that the Cartesian concept as a biomedical "model" is inadequate, particularly because a model that is used to explain illness also determines how the patient's problem is analyzed and what kinds of treatments are prescribed.

Components of pain

Some of the confusion surrounding the complaint of pain can be resolved with a more rational conceptual approach that discriminates four different components, namely, nociception, pain, suffering, and pain behavior.

Nociception. The activation of specific nerve endings by tissue damage affecting thermal or mechanical stimuli is termed nociception. The nerve endings are attached to nerve cell processes (axons) that conduct impulses from the skin and internal organs to the spinal cord and brain stem. Although the electrical activity in such nerves can be measured in animal or human experiments, in the clinical setting the physician can only infer

John D. Loeser, M.D., is Professor of Neurological Surgery and Director of the Multidisciplinary Pain Center at the University of Washington School of Medicine, Seattle.

(Opposite page) The persistence of pain; photograph, British Migraine Association and WB Pharmaceuticals Ltd.

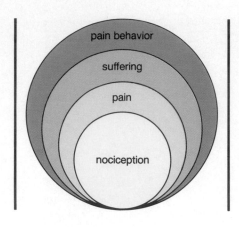

the presence of nociception by looking for signs of tissue damage. Injury
can make these nerve endings unusually sensitive to stimulation and lower
their threshold for activation. Nociception is the major cause of pain "behavior" in acute pain.

Pain. The term pain itself in this conceptual scheme refers specifically to
the perception of nociception, which begins in the first synapse (the point
at which a nervous impulse is conveyed from one neuron, or cell of the
nervous tissue, to another). Pain, then, is felt as the result of the electrical
activity as impulses are conducted through nerve cells. Anesthesiologists
earn their living by preventing nociception from becoming pain; they utilize
local or regional agents that block the passage of pain impulses along nerve
pathways to the brain. Such anesthetics have been one of the greatest
advances of medical science in the past 100 years and have made modern
surgical procedures possible.

Infants and children are just as sensitive to noxious stimulation as adults;
they may lack the verbal skills to describe their feelings. It is astonishing
that some physicians perform surgical procedures on small children without
adequate anesthesia. This is an example of inadequate dissemination of
knowledge about the management of pain.

Pain can also occur when an injury to the peripheral nerves or central
nervous system results in distorted messages reaching the higher nerve
centers. This can be seen after amputation (phantom limb pain), with herpes
zoster (shingles), with injury to a major nerve (causalgia), and in a variety
of other conditions. This type of pain is often labeled "deafferentation pain"
or "central pain." The area in which the pain is felt is not diseased; it is the
nerves themselves that are abnormal.

People tend to overlook their own innate ability to prevent nociception
from becoming pain; this does not require drugs or health care providers
but is part of the equipment each person is born with. Mammals can
modulate "afferent input" by both conscious and unconscious mechanisms,
and rituals observed in primitive societies such as walking on hot coals

and swinging from hooks inserted into muscles are ample testimony to the human's ability to block nociception from becoming pain. Evidence indicates that the performers of these rituals are not enduring pain but, in fact, are able to not sense it. More commonly in Western cultures today, people use biofeedback therapy to control certain kinds of pain; with the aid of a simple electronic instrument, they are able to record information about the physiological process causing their pain and learn to influence the felt sensation—in part by learning to relax the body and in part by regulating physiological mechanisms.

Suffering. In this conceptual scheme suffering is the component that denotes a negative affective response engendered by pain and other emotional events such as depression, fear, anxiety, and isolation. What is very misleading is that people use the language of pain and nociception for all types of suffering. Examples abound in everyday usage. In a recent issue of *Newsweek* ran the headline "No progress without pain"; in *USA Today:* "Experts . . . on how to save the troubled medicare system agreed Tuesday that only pain lies ahead for the elderly, the hospitals and physicians"; in the *Harvard Crimson:* "A monument to pain (the Vietnam Veterans' Memorial) . . ."; and in the *Wall Street Journal:* "The public doesn't get a better potato chip without a bit of pain." And how often do people refer to someone else as a "pain in the neck"? One does not mean, of course, that one's neck hurts or that the other individual resides in one's neck. Rather, the other person is causing one to suffer in some way. Suffering, like pain and nociception, is a personal and internal event whose existence can only be inferred by the doctor. Depression is closely linked to chronic pain and is clearly one of the major reasons that people suffer. The extent to which people suffer is modified by their prior experiences and their culture.

Pain behavior. Talking about pain, moaning, taking pills, going to doctors, lying down, refusing to work, and collecting compensation payments are all pain behaviors. A physician's identification of patients' pain behavior is not dependent upon any knowledge of the patient's feelings, mood, motivation, or mind-set. Rather, pain behaviors involve real gestures and blatant observable manifestations. When a physician says that a patient is "better," that clinician is really commenting upon the manifestations of pain behavior.

Pain behavior is strongly influenced by environmental consequences. When such forms of behavior lead to something "good" in the patient's view or to the avoidance of something "bad," the behavior is more likely to recur. (Conversely, the behavior is less likely to recur when it leads to something bad.) The perpetuation of the pain behavior long after the damage from a noxious event has healed may be the result of those reinforcement effects. Hence, pain behavior may start because of tissue damage (nociception), but it sometimes continues because of environmental factors. Phrased in another way, pain behaviors can be learned.

Acute and chronic pain: different as night and day

The four pain components described above enable a rational division of the types of pain seen in medical practice. "Acute pain," such as that experienced after an operation; with bone fractures, abscessed teeth, and kidney

Chronic pain: facts and figures

- chronic pain is persistent or recurrent (as distinguished from acute pain, which is limited in duration); it may be the result of a diagnosable illness but often lacks an identifiable physical cause

- chronic pain is the third leading cause of disability in the U.S., after cancer and heart disease

- approximately one-third of the population have persistent or recurring pain, and of these, one-half to two-thirds are partially or totally disabled for days, weeks, months, or years

- chronic pain is one of the most costly health problems; in the U.S. total costs and compensation exceed $70 billion per year

- 80% of the general population will experience low back pain (LBP) of a significant degree in their lifetime

- LBP is the number two cause of lost workdays, after the common cold, with 70 million days lost per year

- back pain disables an estimated 17.7 million people to an extent requiring hospitalization

- at least 40 million Americans suffer recurrent headaches and spend $4 billion on medications; migraine is estimated to occur in over 10% of the population in the Western world; headaches account for 65 million workdays lost annually

- other types of chronic pain include arthritis, cervical pain, facial pain, osteoporosis, phantom-limb pain, and myofascial syndrome

- each year arthritis costs the American economy more than $14 billion

Source: National Rehabilitation Hospital, an affiliate of the Washington Healthcare Corporation

Arthritic disorders involve inflammation of joints due to infectious, constitutional, or metabolic causes. According to a recent survey, arthritis pain accounts for well over a million workdays lost per year. The acute aspects of arthritic pain can be treated with effective analgesic medications, but the chronic aspects are better managed through an emphasis on physical rehabilitation. The participants in this "Arthritis Self-Help" group at the Stanford (California) Arthritis Center are working together to overcome their fears of pain and disability.

stones; or during prolonged labor and childbirth, is almost always due to nociception, and its treatment involves the prevention of additional injury to the damaged part, restoration of body tissues to hasten healing, and the blocking of nociception or pain to reduce suffering and pain behaviors. Narcotics, rest, and immobilization are particularly effective for this task.

"Chronic pain" is the most troublesome and pervasive type of pain. The most important fact about pain is the distinction between acute and chronic complaints. Any form of treatment that is effective for acute pain is likely to make chronic pain worse. Narcotic or sedative-hypnotic medications and rest and inactivity are the clearest examples. There are several reasons for this observation; depression is a major factor in chronic pain, and narcotics and sedatives and inactivity can, in and of themselves, have depressing effects. The medications impair cognitive functions, while inactivity rapidly leads to deconditioning and the loss of strength, flexibility, and range of motion. Moreover, taking pills and lying about tend to communicate to one's environment that one is "ill"; the environment then reinforces such pain behaviors. Thus, acute pain and chronic pain have nothing in common except the word pain. Chronic pain can be divided into at least four subtypes.

Cancer pain. Chronic pain due to cancer is really continuous acute pain and must be treated aggressively. Careful evaluation almost always reveals tissue damage, which is occurring every day and generating more nociception. Sometimes there also is nerve damage, which can produce deafferentation pain. Depression, fear, isolation, and the effects of medication, radiation therapy, or surgery can also play a role in suffering due to cancer.

Nerve-injury pain. Chronic pain due to nerve injury produces pain in the absence of nociception. This is seen after some strokes (thalamic syndrome), after spinal cord and nerve injuries, and in syndromes such as tic douloureux and postherpetic neuralgia. Since there is no nociception, narcotics and prescribed inactivity are not effective. Anticonvulsant medications are often beneficial, as they reduce the abnormal electrical activity in

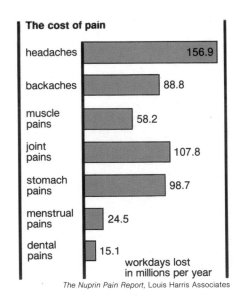

The cost of pain

	workdays lost in millions per year
headaches	156.9
backaches	88.8
muscle pains	58.2
joint pains	107.8
stomach pains	98.7
menstrual pains	24.5
dental pains	15.1

The Nuprin Pain Report, Louis Harris Associates

124

damaged nerve cells. Surgical procedures that alter central nervous system functioning either by a lesion or by electrical stimulation of the spinal cord or brain may be effective.

Disease-associated pain. Chronic pain due to a diagnosable underlying disease is most commonly seen with various forms of arthritis and some metabolic diseases (*e.g.,* diabetes and gout). Primary treatment is directed at the control of the underlying disease. In addition, the physician must also manage both the acute pain, which occurs with a flare-up of the disease, and the chronic pain, which can be due to irreparable tissue damage. It is important to treat acute pain with effective analgesic agents but *not* to treat the chronic pain similarly. The chronic pain, rather, demands a treatment program that will minimize disability and maximize functional capabilities. A very large number of people have degenerative joint diseases (arthritis and rheumatic disorders), which lead to chronic pain. Nonetheless, for reasons that are unclear, these people rarely are seen in pain clinics.

Pain in the absence of disease. The majority of patients with chronic pain who seek health care will not be found to have a diagnosable disease, although most will have had some antecedent injury or illness. Low-back pain is the complaint of two-thirds of such patients. It is possible that the medical profession is just not smart enough to uncover a source of nociception. It is more likely, however, that patients' pain behaviors are being perpetuated by environmental factors, by suffering due to things other than pain, by inappropriate prescriptions for medications and rest, and by superstitions and lack of knowledge of how the body works.

It does not make much sense to say exactly when acute pain becomes chronic pain. A better indicator is whether the complaint of pain has continued past the expected healing time for the alleged causative event. If an injury is expected to heal in three weeks, chronic pain can be diagnosed when the pain has persisted for a month or longer. Some latitude for individual variation, of course, must be allowed. Generally, the more prompt the diagnosis and management of chronic pain, the more effective treatment tends to be, with less ultimate disability.

The health care delivery system does not do well with chronic pain patients. It is this group that is causing an epidemic—one that has attracted the attention of government and business. Indeed, almost 5% of the cost of manufacturing a product or delivering a service goes to pay for low-back pain in the workers. In the United States disability ascribed to low-back pain is rapidly increasing as a major reason for Social Security payments. Physical findings, for the most part, do not correlate with the award of disability. What, then, are the government and taxpayers paying for?

Chronic pain: a sad state of affairs

There is a dramatic contrast between the number of people who report having chronic pain and the number who seek medical attention for their complaints. *The Nuprin Pain Report* (sponsored by Bristol-Myers, a major producer of analgesic medications) revealed that the majority of adults in the U.S. suffered from three or four different pains each year and that in one year (1986) those employed full time lost approximately 550 million

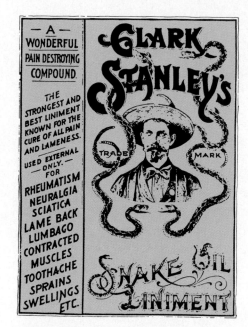

A patent medicine, c. 1895, offered immediate relief from virtually every pain that sufferers were heir to—for the price of just 50 cents.

The Granger Collection, New York

days of work, an average of five days per person. Headaches and low-back pain top the list. If all adults are included, the average respondent said that he or she was unable to perform customary activities an average of 23 days per year; a total of four billion sick-leave days can be ascribed to pain each year. These numbers are astounding, and their economic impact is immense, yet most of these people never consult a physician.

Eighty percent of people experience low-back pain at some time in their lives; recovery from at least 85% of these attacks occurs within six weeks regardless of the type of treatment. Very few treatments have any proven efficacy. In the properly selected patient, surgery may hasten recovery, but it does not improve the likelihood of being symptom-free five or ten years later. Surgery, moreover, has a significant risk of increasing disability.

Although a majority of pain victims do not seek medical care, the U.S. National Center for Health Statistics has estimated that the complaint of pain is one of the most common reasons that people go to a physician—second only to the common cold. Low-back pain is the most common reason for the initial visit and by far the most common cause of repeated visits to physicians. At least a third of these visits result in the prescription of analgesic medications, whose efficacy against chronic pain is dubious. Only normal maternity stays and deliveries were responsible for more hospital discharges in 1981 than "medical back problems," which accounted for 2.8% of all discharges from United States hospitals (to which must be added the discharges from surgical management of back pain). The medical costs of low-back pain have been estimated at $16 billion; wage-replacement costs are usually two to three times as much; low-back pain alone probably costs the U.S. at least $60 billion. The rates of surgery for low-back pain continue to increase even though the published indications for surgery are becoming more circumscribed. Additionally, the number of unorthodox "treatments," spurred by the desperation of relief seekers, continues to mushroom. Entrepreneurs market an astonishing array of alleged "back-relief" equipment from chairs, pillows, and massagers to "gravity boots"—a potentially dangerous item from which the sufferer dangles upside down.

The best answer yet: the multidisciplinary pain clinic
The existence of large numbers of chronic pain patients attests to the fact that the traditional methods of health care delivery have not been able to

126

resolve their problems. Patients typically are referred from specialist to specialist, like a billiard ball caroming off the cushions. Different physicians offer conflicting diagnoses and treatment programs. Far too much medication and surgery is prescribed. The chronic pain patient becomes progressively disabled. Health care, then, in the case of the chronic pain patient can be injurious to the patient's health!

As early as the end of World War II, anesthesiologist John J. Bonica realized that soldiers with chronic pain often did not get effective treatment. He identified part of the problem as fragmented health care and limited knowledge on the part of specialized physicians. Bonica developed a "pain clinic" in private practice in Tacoma, Washington; when he went to the University of Washington School of Medicine in Seattle in 1960, he took the pain clinic concept to academic medicine. Thus, students and other faculty could contribute experience and knowledge to the further development of the treatment of ongoing pain. The Multidisciplinary Pain Center at the University of Washington has served as the model for clinics throughout the world; its programs have evolved over 25 years. One of the most innovative developments was the behavioral approach to the management of chronic pain, which was pioneered by psychologist Wilbert Fordyce. This strategy, which, simply put, focuses upon what the patient says and does, is designed to restore chronically disabled patients to gainful activities.

The fundamental principle of a multidisciplinary treatment center is that chronic pain is a multifaceted dysfunctional state that requires treatment by a variety of health care providers. The first step is accurate diagnosis. The patient workup includes careful review of prior records, a complete history, a physical examination, and an evaluation of the patient (and possibly the spouse) by a psychologist, during which the patient completes various psychological tests.

Back pain flare-up: brief bed rest versus longer time in bed

		2 days' bed rest (90 subjects)	7 days' bed rest (99 subjects)
functional status	days absent from work	3.1	5.6
	days of limited activity	6.8	7.7
	returned to normal activities (%)	58 (67)	62 (65)
perceptions*	self-rated improvement	2.7	2.6
	clinician-rated improvement	2.4	2.2
symptoms, signs	duration of pain (in days)	11.2	10.8
	persistent neurological deficit (%)	1 (1)	1 (1)
	ability to raise straight leg (in degrees)	89	89
	spinal flexion (bending ability, measured as centimeters from finger to floor)	6.8	6.5
other care	hospital days	0	0
	sought care elsewhere (%)	2 (2)	7 (7)

*rated on a six-point scale: 1 = pain entirely gone, 4 = no change, and 6 = much worse
Adapted from Richard A. Deyo et al., "How Many Days of Bed Rest for Acute Low Back Pain?" *The New England Journal of Medicine*, vol. 315, no. 17 (Oct. 23, 1986), pp. 1064–70

Low-back pain is one of the most common and the most costly types of pain, and it accounts for the highest proportion of workdays lost. It is also the most common reason for repeated visits to physicians. Bed rest is usually recommended for back pain flare-ups, but the duration of a helpful course of rest has been uncertain. A recent study found that for many patients two days' bed rest was as effective as—or even more effective than—a week or more in bed. Thus, getting back into action as fast as possible would appear to be the most enlightened approach to managing the acute phases of chronic low-back pain syndromes and may well be the best approach to managing many other forms of chronic pain.

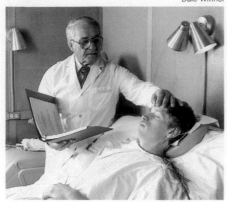

Anesthesiologist John Bonica has been called the founding father of modern pain relief. Over two decades ago he recognized that patients with chronic pain were getting very poor care, which often made them worse instead of better. He saw the need for a radical new approach and devised a kind of treatment that finally enabled long-time sufferers to begin coping and functioning again because it addressed their pain as a many-faceted problem. The Multidisciplinary Pain Center Bonica established at the University of Washington School of Medicine has become a model for such pain centers across the U.S. and in other countries.

A very small percentage (fewer than 5%) of the patients referred for multidisciplinary evaluation will be found to have a structural lesion that is amenable to surgical therapy. Of course, a pain clinic may also get referrals of patients with specific types of problems, such as cancer pain, postherpetic neuralgia, or tic douloureux, who do not need a multidisciplinary evaluation, in which case a specific treatment, either pharmacological or surgical, may be undertaken by a surgeon or other physician on the multidisciplinary staff. Some patients may need evaluation or treatment by physicians outside the clinic group, but this is uncommon, for most chronic pain patients have usually seen every type of specialist before being referred to a multidisciplinary center.

The majority of patients referred to a pain clinic do not have tissue damage to explain their pain behavior. Instead, the common findings are: (1) inappropriate use of physician-prescribed medications; (2) physical deconditioning, which includes the loss of strength, endurance, and flexibility; (3) environmental factors, which perpetuate and amplify pain behaviors; (4) superstitious beliefs about how the body functions; (5) lack of ability to deal with stress; (6) poor social skills; (7) poor educational background; and (8) lack of marketable job skills and potential employment opportunities.

The second step is to formulate a comprehensive management program that addresses all of the patient's problems at the same time. The components of such a program would include: (1) reduction of analgesic and sedative-hypnotic medications; (2) physical activation; (3) vocational assessment, counseling, and preparations for return to work; (4) education about human anatomy, physiology, and psychology; and (5) the best possible resolution of conflicts with family and at work.

Seattle's Multidisciplinary Pain Center currently uses a three-week, 12-hour-per-day inpatient program in the University of Washington Hospital to accomplish these goals. The treatment team includes physicians, psychologists, nurses, physical and occupational therapists, and vocational counselors. The center tries to avoid using any form of treatment that

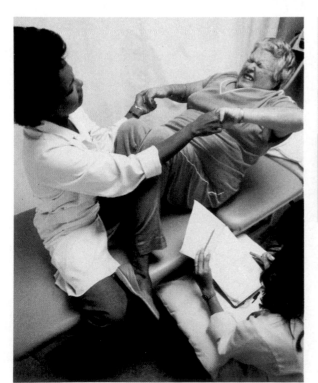

To break the chronic pain cycle, patients in a comprehensive treatment program for back pain are evaluated for fitness of stomach muscles (left) and instructed on the proper way to hold a telephone (above).

Chronic pain patients at a Minneapolis, Minnesota, clinic use biofeedback to gain control over the muscle tension that contributes to and exacerbates their pain problem.

is passive, such as diathermy, ultrasound, or massage; the restoration of normal body function requires activity in bones, joints, and muscles. Long-term use of treatment strategies that require a health care provider, such as acupuncture, trigger-point injections, nerve blocks, or manipulation, are also avoided. The goal is to teach the patients that they can gain control over the pain symptoms; treatments from health care providers tend to undermine this goal. They also can be expensive and time-consuming. In addition, since it is important that patients not call constant attention to their pain problem, electrical stimulators worn on the body are rarely used.

Biofeedback has some value, for it teaches the patients that they can gain control over muscle tension or skin temperature. The Seattle center believes hypnosis is of value only if the patients can learn self-hypnosis. Rather, the center utilizes relaxation and stress-management training and presents the patients with a broad-based array of cognitive and behavioral strategies designed to change their labeling of body sensations, their control over sensations, and their coping skills.

The typical patient seen at Seattle's Multidisciplinary Pain Center has low-back pain and has had 2.6 operations and been off work for 3.6 years. The labor-intensive program costs approximately $12,000, which is about the same as another back operation. (Most insurance plans reimburse patients for some or all of the pain center care expense.) Slightly more than half the patients are back at work six months to one year after clinic treatment.

Over and over again, specialists find that environmental factors are the major determinants of chronic pain. Depression also plays a role in many patients; antidepressant medications are helpful but by themselves do not eliminate pain behaviors. One of the major goals of treatment for chronic pain is the reduction of medication consumption. With the exception of antidepressant medications, the goal is to get the patient to be drug-free. The elimination of drug side effects, the learning of skills for coping with symptoms rather than depending on something external for relief, and the reduction of health care costs are just a few of the benefits enjoyed by

129

Three-step drug ladder for cancer pain relief

Source: World Health Organization

1 nonopioid (*e.g.*, aspirin, paracetamol)
± adjuvant (*e.g.*, anticonvulsants,
psychotropics, corticosteroids)
for specific conditions

2 mild opioids
(usually codeine)
± nonopioid
± adjuvant

if pain persisting
or increasing

freedom from
cancer pain

if pain persisting
or increasing

3
strong opioids
(usually morphine)
± nonopioid
± adjuvant

pain

The relief of cancer pain is an important but too often neglected aspect of care. Millions of cancer patients who presently suffer every day could have their pain controlled with proper doses of medication. International specialists in advanced cancer treatment have established a systematic program of drug administration that can provide respite from pain for most patients.

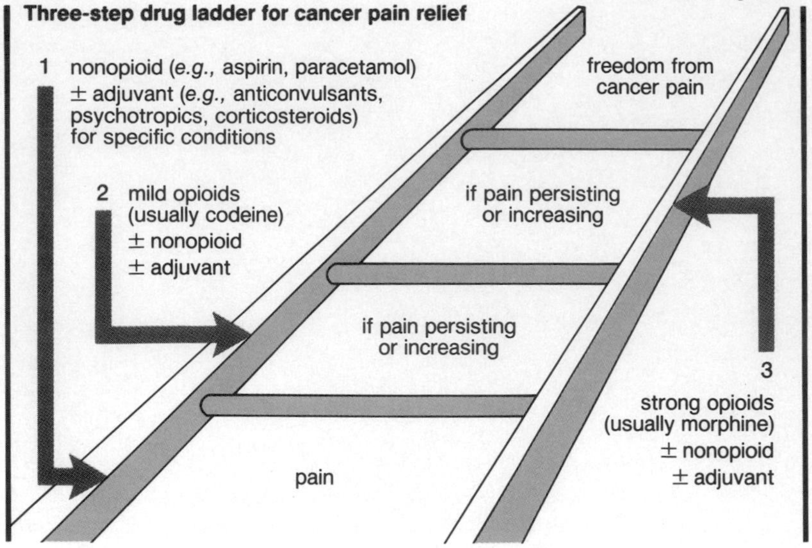

patients who are drug-free. People are bombarded daily by radio, television, and written advertisements urging them to take some sort of medication for every symptom. Patients must be taught that drugs seldom provide a solution to chronic pain.

Patients typically ascribe all of their problems to one spot in their body and deny the contributions of their beliefs, feelings, and those around them. Not every patient wishes to change; it is important to realize that this type of program works only when the patient *wants* to get better.

Cancer pain, on the other hand, is the opposite of the chronic pain described above; too little, rather than too much, health care tends to be utilized. Physicians have unwarranted fears about narcotics and often do not prescribe enough medication to provide continuous pain relief. Saint Peter is not prejudiced against those who come to the pearly gates with high serum narcotic levels, however. Newer methods of delivering narcotics directly to the spinal cord or brain via an implanted catheter can provide excellent pain relief without the side effects of oral narcotics; these techniques have been far too slowly disseminated.

Recently, in response to the inadequacy of cancer-pain relief, the World Health Organization established guidelines for the administration of medications. In a three-step "ladder" approach, nonopioids (aspirin or paracetamol) are increased to mild opioids (usually codeine) and then to strong opioids (usually morphine) until the patient is free from pain. For specific conditions or to calm anxiety, additional medications, known as adjuvant drugs, may be used. In this approach drugs are given regularly, rather than at the time of pain, and thus provide steady relief. Even with cancer pain, though, the patient's attitude and environment must be taken into consideration when a comprehensive management program is planned.

The future

The costs of chronic pain to an industrialized society have become so great that increased attention from government and industry can be expected. In

Sweden the Volvo Corp. has funded extensive research and designed the workplace so as to reduce injury and improve employee satisfaction and loyalty. Similar approaches are used in Japan. Congress and the executive branch in the U.S. recently have convened expert panels to look into the causes of the epidemic of chronic pain and disability. It is hoped that in both the Social Security disability insurance and workers' compensation laws, changes will be made that will remove the complaint of pain as a legitimate cause of disability. One of the observations made by psychologist Fordyce years ago was that people "who have something better to do do not hurt as much." There is no inherent relationship between pain and disability; it may seem harsh, but the legal system is going to have to change its approach to this problem. No longer should workers be considered permanently disabled unless they have made a vigorous attempt at rehabilitation.

When pain is alleged to be the cause of disability, treatment at a pain clinic is the most likely method for restoring the worker to gainful employment. People who fail to get better within the expected healing time will need early referral to a treatment facility so the reasons for their delayed recovery can be ascertained. Treatment in a pain clinic should precede multiple operations and habit-forming medications.

It is important to emphasize that chronic pain patients are not malingerers. They hurt. All too often this is because of their superstitions, lack of information, and bad medical advice. Much of what happens at a pain center is educational; most of the patients' improvement is due to *their* hard work.

Just as medical science's knowledge of the behavioral phenomena of pain is expanding, so is the knowledge of the anatomy and physiology that underlie nociception. Specific sites of action of various pain-relieving drugs have been identified. The discovery of the endorphins and enkephalins has dramatically expanded knowledge of how the brain controls noxious input.

New medications may improve both postoperative and cancer pain management. Research in opioid medications will lead to more effective agents. Transdermal, spinal, and other forms of administering medication will become routine and allow more precise delivery to the target area and better control of drug levels. As more is learned about the neurotransmitters, which relay information between nerve cells, it will become possible to create new drugs that are highly specific and block nociception or pain with few side effects.

A pain-free world: only a dream

Philosophers and poets have long dreamed of a pain-free world. Such a utopia seems unlikely. In many ways chronic pain without observable pathology appears to be a political, economic, and moral issue that is only masquerading as debilitating disease. Pain behavior and suffering are woven into the very fabric of society and play a major role in many important social interactions.

While acute pain is a warning that the person must heed to avoid further damage, chronic pain has no such utility. Only when research—from the cellular to sociological levels—has unraveled the mysteries of human behavior will chronic pain decrease as a major cause of disability.

"Cold Hat" invented by
Steve Mason; photograph, Cathlyn Melloan

A headache sufferer places her faith in an ice hat purchased through the mail. Because people in pain typically feel so desperate, they spend millions of dollars annually on countless remedies—many of them unorthodox, unproven, or downright bogus—in the constant search for relief. Although there has been remarkable scientific progress in the understanding and the diagnosis of pain, and although treatment has entered a new era, at present a world that is entirely free from pain and its sufferers is, regrettably, not within sight.

131

On Its Toes:
BALLET MEDICINE

by Nancy Reynolds and
William G. Hamilton, M.D.

Few professions are as stressful, both physically and mentally, as that of ballet dancing. Not only do dancers train strenuously for years, including, in the case of males, preparing to carry 45- to 54-kilogram (100- to 120-pound) ballerinas around a stage, but once they have achieved professional status, they continue intensive schooling, often while performing two or more hours a night and rehearsing up to eight hours daily, sometimes seven days a week. A study undertaken by the Institute of Sports Medicine and Athletic Trauma in New York City rated classical ballet, along with professional football and hockey, as the most demanding of 60 "sports" examined. While football and hockey players must meet extremely demanding physical requirements in order to win games and break records, however, ballet dancers not only must master a technically intricate physical vocabulary but must also manage to look beautiful while they are doing it.

An exacting, exhilarating, and ephemeral profession

Mentally as well as physically, the ballet profession is exacting. To achieve the necessary mobility in the joints—or, rather, to retain the mobility of the very young—a female student must, with rare exceptions, begin training seriously before puberty. (For men such an early start is not essential but is still highly desirable; nearly all of the great classical male dancers started classes as children.) A young girl wanting a dance career is faced with important life decisions at an age when she can make them only on an intuitive level. She must make the kind of intense commitment at the age of 12 or younger that members of the general population do not have to consider until after high school or college.

After eight to ten years of single-minded study, which have deprived her of a normal adolescence, casual friendships, and unstructured leisure time, the talented girl is taken into a professional ballet company to compete with many others whose backgrounds rival hers. All the hopes and dreams of a lifetime are centered in that imperfect and vulnerable instrument, her body, which could betray her at any time and put to waste all the years of monastic dedication.

Becoming a professional is just the beginning. A dancer must train almost daily to keep her technique finely honed; she must diet; she must learn to live with almost constant fatigue as she pursues a work schedule often

Nancy Reynolds is a former member of the New York City Ballet and the author of several books on dance.
William G. Hamilton, M.D., is Assistant Clinical Professor of Orthopedic Surgery at the Columbia University College of Physicians and Surgeons; Attending Orthopedic Surgeon at St. Lukes-Roosevelt Hospital Center, New York City; and Orthopedic Consultant to the New York City Ballet and American Ballet Theatre.

(Opposite) The foot of Patricia McBride, a member of the New York City Ballet; photograph, Daniel Sorine— Gamma/Liaison

The high levels of physical skill required for professional athletes and male ballet dancers are not dissimilar in terms of coordination, strength, fitness, stamina, etc. For the male dancer, however, there are also essential aesthetic considerations. He must, for example, be able to lift and carry his female partner high above his head with seeming ease, never losing his surefootedness or fluidness of movement. (Above) Eddie J. Shellman of the Dance Theater of Harlem elevates partner Judy Tyrus in Le Corsaire *pas de deux.*

well in excess of 40 hours a week; she must marshal extreme mental and physical resources night after night in order to appear onstage, where the justification for her existence is literally on the line with every performance; she must cope with being an adult (for which ballet school has certainly not adequately prepared her); and she will constantly have before her a paradigm of perfection that she will never attain.

On a more mundane level, hours and meals may be irregular and financial rewards almost certainly modest. Eventually, of course—and very early in comparison with other professions—her body *does* betray her; it is exceptional to be on the stage after the late thirties. The very kinetic immediacy that so thrills an audience—here for an instant and then gone—is a poignant metaphor for the ephemerality of the dancer's life and art.

The psychiatric profession has expressed amazement that under such demanding conditions, in which, in addition to complete lack of job security, most normal social contact is restricted, dancers function as well as they do. (Perhaps for this reason psychiatrists also confess bewilderment as to the best treatment of the dancer with emotional problems.) Of course, the same qualities that drive people to dance—extraordinary dedication and limitless capacity for hard work—make them survivors, and the satisfactions of their work may be particularly acute. Chief among them are the passion of involvement with an exalted cause—the cause of art; the exhilaration and release of rising to performance pitch and communicating with an audience on a "gut" level beyond words; a tremendous sense of independence or self-sufficiency brought on by physical control; and the self-discipline engendered by the profession, which becomes a part of every dancer's mental equipment and can be used in other endeavors.

Naturally, in a life embraced with such intensity, aberrations occur. The brilliant Nijinsky began a descent into madness before he was 30, never to recover. (His illness was diagnosed as schizophrenia.) More recently, the exquisite ballerina Gelsey Kirkland has written in her autobiography, *Dancing on My Grave,* that her all-consuming perfectionism led to, among other things, three years of cocaine addiction. Another example is New York City Ballet principal dancer Joseph Duell, who committed suicide in 1986 at the age of 29. Dancers are—and must be—obsessive. Those who succeed may do so in what psychiatrists call a state of "pathological equilibrium."

The new medicine of dance

In the past 15 years or so, a new medical speciality, dance medicine (a subspeciality of performing arts medicine), has evolved to treat both preventively and correctively the particular problems that can affect those whose delicate mechanisms—their bodies and their emotions—are their livelihood. The "fathers," or pioneers, of dance medicine are Eivind Thomasen of Arhus, Denmark, who recently published a book on his experiences with musculoskeletal problems in classical dancers over the past 25 years, and the late Henry Jordan, who was known as a "dance doctor" in New York City during the 1950s and 1960s.

The average dancer of today has a technical proficiency virtually unknown in the past (although it is doubtful that the world has bred another

Nijinsky). Movements are higher, bigger, and quicker, and choreographers have not hesitated to incorporate these new abilities in their ever more demanding ballets. Furthermore, because of a "dance boom" in the 1970s and federal support for dance companies, there are more professional dancers today than ever before; in turn, because the profession has become more respected and far more rewarding financially, dancers are dancing longer. (In the 1950s in the New York City Ballet, for example, it was rare for a corps de ballet member to continue for more than five years; today many enter, as they always have, as teenagers, and do not stop until middle age forces them to do so.)

Out of today's climate of heightened awareness of the dancer's problems, dance medicine was born. It is interdisciplinary in scope, consisting of a loosely knit group of physicians, surgeons, psychiatrists, and allied health professionals with a particular interest in this very specialized field. The orthopedic surgeon may have a background in sports medicine and athletic injuries. (Most major ballet companies in the U.S. and in Europe retain an orthopedic consultant.) The internist often treats endocrine (hormonal) imbalances and eating disorders. The physical therapist specializes in rehabilitation; these days large ballet companies commonly have one on staff. In addition, osteopaths, chiropractors, podiatrists, masseurs, nutritionists, exercise and technique coaches, and dance teachers may be involved. In fact, almost any measure that makes the dancer feel better and is not dangerous may be considered in prescribing treatment.

Particularly important to the professionals involved in the treatment of members of the ballet profession is a knowledge of the altered kinesiology of dancers—from their skeletal systems to their "displaced" (as well as enlarged) muscles. Also essential is a sensitivity to the psyche of these highly motivated, goal-oriented individuals, who have been trained to work through pain and who will go to almost any lengths to avoid being forced off their feet.

(Below) Students of the School of American Ballet betray their preaudition jitters as they wait to try out for the New York City Ballet's annual production of The Nutcracker. *The pressures on the young ballerina are extraordinary. A female student wanting a ballet career must begin training before puberty; she must make an intense commitment well before she is emotionally mature. In order to be accepted into the ranks of serious young ballet students, she must have both talent and natural facility— coordination, musicality, energy, an alert personality, and the intelligence to be able to comprehend and follow instructions quickly. On the purely physical side, she must have a well-proportioned body, joint mobility, and strong and flexible feet and spine. Even if she has these attributes, there remains the question of whether she will have the temperament to survive the rigors of training—an endless capacity for hard work, a healthy measure of competitiveness, and the willingness to pay ever vigilant attention to diet and to live with constant fatigue.*

Michael Tweed/The New York Times

In light of the inordinate demands on professional dancers, it is amazing that most cope and survive so well. Gelsey Kirkland (right) was an established star in major American ballet companies. She performed leading roles in her mid-twenties as a member of American Ballet Theatre, with Mikhail Baryshnikov as her partner. Many critics hailed her as the finest American Giselle and potentially one of the world's greatest ballerinas. Then began her descent: she developed severe anorexia nervosa and bulimia; she became a drug addict; and she embarked on a risky course of silicone injections and plastic surgery. In her recently published autobiography, Kirkland spares the reader none of the sordid details of how the pursuit of creativity led to her personal destruction. Happily, Kirkland recovered and is dancing again.

Joseph Duell (above), a supremely gifted dancer with the New York City Ballet, shocked fellow dancers when, at the age of 29, he took his own life.

It is the job of the practitioners of dance medicine to get dancers back to class and to performing as soon as possible and to evaluate just when the extra effort dancers so love to give is helpful to recovery—and when it is dangerous. They must be able to look into the minds of those for whom achievement and improvement come from pushing the body beyond its limits. Inevitably, "dance doctors" may be called upon to act against strictly medical logic; if a big performing opportunity presents itself to the injured dancer, whose career is so short and insecure, should the practitioner advise dancing on a sprain? Should he or she administer a risky and normally ill-advised cortisone injection?

Coauthor William Hamilton examines Marisa Cerveris (left) and Carole Divet (right) backstage during a performance of the New York City Ballet. Hamilton is one of the leading practitioners of the new medical specialty devoted to the treatment of ballet dancers; he and other "dance doctors" treat the afflictions that are inherent in such an exacting and complex discipline as that of classical ballet. Hamilton has quipped that while his partners have specialized in sports medicine and treat the Mets, his "teams" are the New York City Ballet and American Ballet Theatre.

The dance medicine field is very much in a state of development. Until recently few doctors had the opportunity to take care of enough injured dancers to gain sufficient experience or to study enough cases over a long enough period of time to derive hard data.

In New York City two specialized facilities, Miller Health Care Institute at St. Luke's-Roosevelt Hospital and the Performing Arts Center for Health (PACH) at Bellevue Hospital, have recently opened. Similarly, a performing arts clinic was begun at the University of California at San Francisco in April 1986. In the Midwest there are performance medicine clinics in Chicago at Northwestern Memorial Hospital and in Ohio at the Cleveland Clinic. They provide uniquely tailored care for members of the performing arts professions, and sometimes—in order to acquire more case histories for their data bases—they provide treatment at no cost at all.

Physical prerequisites

While there is no substitute for that indefinable element called talent— a combination of stage projection, temperament, spontaneity, motivation, and drive—it is well known that dancers work their bodies to the bone, and that some bodies are more suited to this punishment than others. Ballet technique conforms to an exacting code that has evolved over a period of 400 years. Two centuries ago Jean-Georges Noverre, then ballet's foremost theoretician, expressed the problem succinctly: "In order to dance well, nothing is so important as the turning outwards of the thigh; and nothing is so natural to men as the contrary position. . . . You see then, that to dance elegantly, . . . it is imperative to reverse the order of things and force the limbs, by means of exercise both long and painful, to take a totally different position from that which is natural to them. . . . It is impossible to bring about this change, of such vital importance to our Art, without taking it in hand in the days of childhood. That is the only time when success is possible because then all limbs are supple and may easily be made to take the desired positions." Despite the rigors of 20th-century choreography, basically very little has changed since Noverre's day.

In order to minimize injury and stress and to achieve the desired configuration of the limbs and the coordination that makes virtuoso effects possible, a dancer should have certain physical attributes.

Proportion. In ballet generally considered unaesthetic as well as impractical are physiques with combinations of long trunks, short legs, big buttocks, swayback, round shoulders, spinal curvature, large heads, and short necks. In female dancers the late George Balanchine, in particular, favored long legs and tall women, although he also had some very short dancers in the New York City Ballet. The dancers of the Royal Ballet in England are generally of medium, uniform height, with no particular attribute exaggerated. Long necks and slim ankles are prized in all females. Long feet can enhance a female dancer's "line" when she is standing on pointe, while short feet can be trained to dart about with exciting, quicksilver fleetness. Broadly generalizing, one can say that more compact bodies can move faster, with greater endurance (important for jumping), while elongated bodies often excel in lyrical roles and are more pleasing to watch in adagio movements.

It has been said that there is no great genius without a touch of madness. The brilliant Russian dancer Nijinsky's ballet career was cut tragically short in 1917, before he was 30, because of his schizophrenia. Nijinksy displayed such spectacular elevation in Le Spectre de la Rose *(above) that probably no other dancer to date has matched it.*

Dancers should be slim—although just how slim is a matter of some debate on both aesthetic and medical grounds.

Considering that pointe shoes can add nearly a foot to the height of the ballerina, the male dancer, her partner, can almost never be too tall. The most exciting male technicians—those with an explosive quality to their jumps, beats, and turns—have tended to be short, however.

Flexibility. Being loose jointed is one of the basic requirements of dancing. It is thought that this cannot be acquired through training; rather, early training maintains the natural suppleness of children. Tight dancers are predisposed to muscle pulls and tendon strains; however, overly stretched, long and loose dancers may lack the coordination for executing difficult movements and are prone to sprains, dislocations, and impingement syndromes leading to the development of bone spurs. Ideally, loose joints should be accompanied by muscles strong enough to control their excessive motion. This is especially crucial in the big jumps and multiple air turns that figure in the virtuoso roles of male ballet dancers.

Turnout. Turnout is probably the single most important fundamental in ballet technique. Ideally, the dancer should be able achieve a 180° outward rotation of the feet in the five basic positions, which will carry over with some modification to all ballet movements. However, it cannot be overemphasized that the force required for turnout of the legs and feet must come from the hip down and not from the floor up. The knee is a hinge joint and is not designed to rotate; when a dancer does not have loose enough hip joints, the knee is often called into service, and this may result in extremely severe injury. Men, who tend to be less loose jointed than women and use tremendous force in taking off and landing in big jumps, must be particularly careful about forcing the knees outward in pursuit of turnout.

While the extent of turnout is determined primarily by the bony architecture of the hip joint—by the way the "ball" fits into the "socket" and by the

As the great Romantic ballets evolved, dancing on toe became mandatory, and ballerinas aspired toward the appearance of dancing on air—becoming symbols of lightness itself. Slender and very highly arched feet became the aesthetic dream of every ballerina. Indeed, the Russian star Anna Pavlova, who was the most celebrated ballerina of the early 1900s, used to have her photographs airbrushed to make the tips of her toe shoes appear slimmer and to accentuate the curve of her arches.

La Sylphide, *which premiered in Paris in 1832, was one of the earliest in the Romantic repertoire. The genre reached its height with such ballets as* Giselle *(1841),* La Peri *(1843), and then* Swan Lake *(1877) as ballerinas attained supreme fluidity, evanescence, and even the appearance of transparency. Here American Ballet Theatre's Susan Jaffe dances the lead in* Swan Lake *at age 20.*

shape of the socket itself—achieving a turned-out look in ballet steps and positions is facilitated by a slightly bowlegged condition and some degree of hyperextension in the knee.

The ankle. The movement plié-relevé (bending the knee with the heel on the floor, followed by rising to either the high ball of the foot with the heel tucked in or to the tip of toes) is the preparation for, or a part of, the execution of almost all ballet steps. The ankle must have a good range of motion to accommodate these opposing movements. In addition, extra support from the Achilles tendon and the other tendons circumferentially around the ankle will be called on to steady the foot when it is in the pointe position. The ankle takes a tremendous amount of force in a relatively small area, and it is in the ankle that the older male dancer, in particular, is prone to the buildup of bone spurs, as bones literally bang together from the impact of landing in big jumps. (Bone spurs, often referred to popularly, and incorrectly, as "calcium deposits," can be successfully removed by surgery.)

The feet. The main functions of the foot are to provide locomotion—to impart controlled motion and energy to the ground in pushing off and to absorb energy in landing. The pointe and demi-pointe positions place a different stress on the foot, since it was designed to absorb its energy on the sole and to push off on the ball. Adaptive changes, including thickening of the metatarsal bones, occur with training to allow pointe work and high relevé. A broad, square foot will provide the best foundation for the female dancer who may have to support her entire body on the tips of her toes or for the male who is landing from multiple spins in the air.

In addition to the obvious punishment to which dancers subject their feet, the ballerina must learn to dance within the unique imprisonment of the toe shoe. This special footwear, though exquisitely lovely in appearance with its smooth, shimmering satin covering, can be the cause of blisters, corns, and bunions. While the shoes must be firm enough to provide support, they must at the same time be soft and flexible enough for the dancer to "feel" the floor and not make a clattering noise on stage. The best foot for the toe shoe will have the first three toes the same length; barring that, the big toe should be the longest.

For aesthetic reasons, flexible, slender, highly arched insteps are the dream of every would-be ballerina. Anna Pavlova, who had such feet, nevertheless had all her photographs airbrushed to narrow the tips of her toe shoes and exaggerate further the curve of her arches. These feet are not always the most practical since, being excessively flexible, they are prone to stress fractures and ankle sprains. Flat insteps, however, although they may be strong, have almost no redeeming features in classical ballet. (They are referred to by dancers as "spoons.")

Dancers' injuries: a fact of life

Dancers present something of a paradox for the orthopedist: their general loose jointedness should make them particularly injury prone, yet their superb muscle conditioning and highly developed sense of balance and timing counteract this. Moreover, injury most often results from a body trying to do what it is poorly suited to do, and the natural selectivity at work in becoming a professional dancer—the weeding out of wrong bodies and those with insufficient talent or tenacity—assures that only those with the "best" instruments make it to the stage.

Nevertheless, the conditions of the profession are usually beyond even the best trained dancer's control. Fatigue plays a great role in injury: how hard and long is a particular dancer being worked? Perhaps the dancer

Nothing is as important to dance technique as the "turnout." The force of the turnout for the legs and feet must come from the hip itself, and its extent is largely determined by the bony architecture of the hip joint—i.e., by the way the "ball" fits into the "socket" and the shape of the socket itself. When the aspiring dancer is about the age of 13, it can be determined whether he or she is suited for classical ballet on the basis of whether the anatomical structure is capable of the axial rotation necessary for proper turnout. In the test (below right), the degree of axial rotation is measured by having the dancer lie in a prone position with the hip extended and turning one leg across the other. This mimics the action of the dancer standing and extending the leg and foot in turnout.

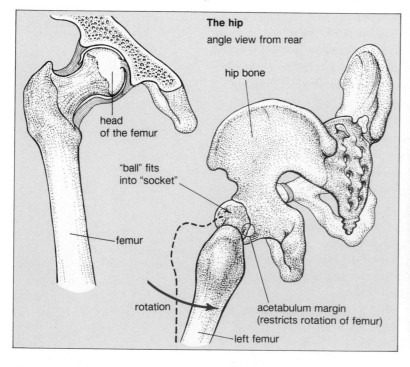

The hip
angle view from rear

hip bone

head of the femur

"ball" fits into "socket"

femur

rotation

acetabulum margin (restricts rotation of femur)

left femur

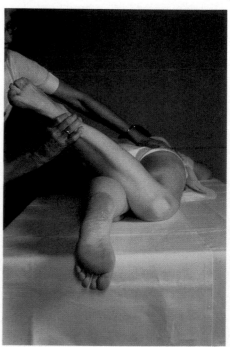

From E. Thomasen, "Forty Years of Dance Medicine," Teach 'Em Inc. educational programs, Chicago

is not performing often enough; constant layoffs require constant readjustment to new stages. Is the stage hard or soft? Too slippery? Improperly surfaced? Hard stages produce low-back pain and muscle soreness and also encourage the formation of blisters, corns, and bunions.

The type of choreography makes a difference. An informal survey reveals that the dancers of American Ballet Theatre are predisposed to stress fractures in the metatarsal, owing to the bravura showpieces in their repertory, while New York City Ballet dancers are more often plagued by tendinitis because of Balanchine's relentless use of quick footwork and speedy little jumps. (In modern dance similar observations have been made: studies show that the Martha Graham and Merce Cunningham techniques are hardest on the knees; that of Doris Humphrey-Charles Weidman, on the ankles; and that of Lester Horton, on the lower back. Also, since modern dancers perform barefoot, they have a range of difficulties with the soles of their feet, a problem that does not affect ballet dancers at all.)

The vast majority of ballet injuries occur in the lower extremities, although other areas can be affected—for example, if a dancer is accidentally dropped by a partner. There are two types of injuries to the lower extremities: those from accidents (acute "trauma") and those from chronic overuse or wear and tear, often related to incorrect technique or overloading in one area to compensate for weakness in another. Many of the injuries sustained by dancers would not be serious in the rest of the population but may interfere—sometimes in a major way—with the dancer's fine-tuning. The ability to cope sensibly, and not hysterically, with these problems is an important part of the dancer's mental arsenal because there is no dance career that does not have to take them into consideration at one time or another. The occasional injury is a fact of performing life.

Strains and sprains. A strained ("pulled") muscle is the dancer's most frequently occurring acute soft-tissue injury, particularly in the hamstrings and the groin muscles. When a muscle pulls, there is a partial tear of the muscle fibers, resulting in pain and some bleeding or hemorrhaging. The scar tissue formed as healing occurs leaves the muscle inelastic and weak, and unless it is properly rehabilitated, it will tear again when activity is resumed, resulting in more scar tissue and greater tightness.

The ankle sprain is the most common acute skeletal injury—a tear or partial tear of a ligament (one of the tough fibrous bands that hold the bones together). Acute ankle sprains, if severe, may require three or four weeks in a cast. The great hazard is that the ligaments may heal loose or stretched out, leaving the ankle unstable or poorly supported and, of course, prone to reinjury.

When muscles, ligaments, or tendons are torn, the small blood vessels that run through the body also tear, irritating the tissues and causing an inflammatory response characterized by warmth, redness, swelling, and pain. Early treatment of an acute injury should be designed to minimize the bleeding and inflammation. In fact, the same initial first-aid treatment is recommended for both strains and sprains: rest, ice, compression with a bandage, and elevation, familiarly referred to by doctors and physical therapists as RICE.

The workout dancers give their feet can be brutal, and the life of a toe shoe is notoriously short. The shimmering new satin shoe (left) is worn out (right) after just a single wearing.

141

The works of different choreographers require different skills and result in different kinds of injuries. For example, the grand jetés in many of American Ballet Theatre's bravura showpieces end abruptly and put an enormous strain on the foot, thus encouraging stress fractures. (Above) ABT's Configurations *features Mikhail Baryshnikov dancing front, center.*

Fractures. The most frequently seen acute fracture—called, in fact, "dancer's fracture"—is the spiral fracture of the fifth metatarsal bone on the outside of the foot, usually brought on by accidentally rolling outward on demi-pointe. Far more common is the stress—or "fatigue"—fracture, an incomplete break or crack in the bone caused by repeated stress or over-loading—for example, too much jumping on hard floors. These sometimes go undetected for long periods of time because they often do not show up on X-rays and can thus be difficult to diagnose.

Fractures are accompanied by pain, swelling, and bleeding in the tissues. Immediate RICE may be followed by warm soaks or Jacuzzi and taping 48 hours later. Additionally, fractures generally require splinting or setting. Treatment for stress fractures of the foot may require a walking cast for four to six weeks; acute fractures may take up to eight weeks to heal. Other stress fractures observed particularly in dancers occur in the tibia (sometimes mistaken for the tenderness called shin splints) and the lower back—called spondylolysis—where the condition may range in severity from being unnoticeable to being the cause for abandoning a career.

Tendinitis. Inflammation of a tendon occurs when it is overstrained and microscopic damage occurs in the fibers. This causes the tendon to swell, so that it no longer glides smoothly in its sheath but begins to bind. Further irritation is followed by more swelling and irritation, setting up a vicious cycle. Treatment is rest and anti-inflammatory medications. The most common areas for tendinitis in ballet dancers are the long flexor tendon to the big toe and the Achilles tendon.

The ruptured Achilles tendon is one of the most devastating accidents that can befall the dancer and often sends him into retirement (the majority of victims are men in their thirties.) Either prolonged cast immobilization or exacting surgery is required; the surgeon must take care to restore the tendon to its original length. The dancer determined to return to the stage must count on at least a year for recovery.

Injured knees. Principal injuries to this pivotal joint include subluxation and dislocation of the kneecap, in which the kneecap snaps out of place, either

142

New York City Ballet star Merrill Ashley exhibits phenomenal speed and outstanding technique in her dancing of the late George Balanchine's Donizetti Variations. *Ballets that Balanchine choreographed require exceptionally quick footwork and fast, brisk jumps. In some dancers, mastering his great ballets has led to tendinitis flare-ups.*

returning on its own or with the help of surgery; torn knee cartilage, which can cause chronic swelling, locking, buckling, or giving way; and torn knee ligaments, which, if severe, can be another catastrophic injury for a dancer.

The recently developed technique of arthroscopic surgery has revolutionized the treatment of seriously injured knees. The arthroscope contains a fiber-optic system that illuminates a field of view and a telescope that magnifies it. This instrument can be inserted in the knee and the view within projected onto a color television monitor. The surgeon can then operate without having to cut open the knee, a procedure that formerly resulted in ugly scarring and a long and painful recovery period with casts and crutches. With arthroscopy the patient is sometimes walking within 24 hours, and it is possible for dancers with torn cartilage to return to activity within three to six weeks. In the case of torn ligaments, however, while the arthroscope is useful for viewing the damage, surgical repair can usually be accomplished only by cutting the knee open. This surgery is essential for restoration of optimum function, but in the case of completely torn ligaments, the knee will never be 100% normal, and the recovery period will probably last at least a year.

Arthritis. Dancers seem to be prone to premature osteoarthritis—the wear and tear that rubs away or causes disintegration in the cartilage between the joints, sometimes exposing the bony surfaces. It is most commonly found in the older dancer's hips, knees, lower back, neck, or big toes. It is thought that the impact of landing on hard stages from jumps may contribute to arthritis. In the hip joint the lifetime pursuit of turnout can cause the head of the thigh bone to wear out. According to another theory, it is the leveraging of the head out of the socket in turnout that causes bone to impinge on bone and arthritis to develop.

Basically, there is no cure for arthritis, and taking aspirin or similar nonsteroidal anti-inflammatory medications is still the best (and least expensive) way to control the pain. Replacement of the ball and socket with metal and plastic parts is quite successful in the retired dancer, who does not need the same range of motion as the performer, but the results of the

143

From E. Thomasen, "Forty Years of Dance Medicine," Teach 'Em Inc. educational programs, Chicago

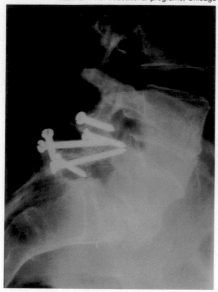

Spondylolysis, a stress fracture of the lower back that is sometimes seen in dancers, can range in severity from being unnoticeable to being the reason for abandoning a career. When this defect is not permitted to heal because of continual movement of the spine, it can result in spondylolisthesis, forward displacement of one vertebra over another. The X-ray shows what might be done in a severe case of spondylolisthesis; screws are placed into the affected area for support where there is no longer any bony support.

operation last 15 years or less, always with the risk of infection or other complications, and it is recommended only in extreme cases. Unfortunately, the ultimate "treatment" for the afflicted performer is to give up dancing.

The fine art of rehabilitation

Injuries are often accompanied by pain, stiffness, and swelling; all these symptoms go together. Any joint in the body that is stiff is usually painful, and as motion is restored, pain and swelling usually subside.

The goal in the rehabilitation of the injured dancer is the return to performing. For this, there is an orderly sequence that should be followed: motion, strength, endurance, and timing. Each step is dependent upon the achievement of a prior "plateau." For strength, there must be full motion; endurance requires strength; and the fine edge of timing—the coordination that permits the double tour en l'air landing in perfect fifth—requires all the others. Motion is restored by the frequency with which a joint is moved and not by the force that is applied. It is not how hard a stiff joint is worked but how often.

The physical therapist can help the dancer through this sometimes tedious progression, using analytical techniques to focus on the weakness that originally caused the injury as well as machines, weights, and controlled exercise that aid in prevention as well as healing. The physical therapist has been called the most important member of the dance medicine team and, unlike most others, may well figure in the dancer's life on a daily basis for years on end.

After initial first aid—RICE—heat is sometimes applied. Warmth causes local blood vessels to widen, increasing the circulation to the area, which provides nutrients and removes waste products. Heat is also a relaxant, freeing working muscles by relaxing surrounding muscle tissues. Heat may be applied by conventional "home methods"—heating pads and hot water bottles—as well as by the more sophisticated infrared lamps and microwave and shortwave diathermy machines. Moist heat is usually more effective than dry.

Soft tissue massage is another "old-fashioned" remedy that can be highly effective—the effleurage, or stroking movement, relieves fluid congestion and relaxes muscle tension; pressure on trigger points may relieve pain and tightness in seemingly unrelated parts of the body; and kneading the tissues improves fluid exchange and circulation.

Electrotherapy has been around since the time of the ancient Egyptians. In the early 20th century, electricity was used as a local anesthetic for surgery; the discovery that electric currents could stimulate muscle contractions has had widespread applications for ballet dancers' rehabilitation. Today various methods are employed: transcutaneous electrical nerve stimulation (TENS) and "inferential therapy" can relieve pain by stimulating sensory nerves, blocking painful sensations; faradism produces artificial contractions in muscles that have atrophied; and ultrasound aids in loosening and breaking up tough and inelastic scar tissue.

The benefits of using weights to provide extra resistance for weak or injured muscles are obvious; today's young male ballet students are encouraged to work out with weights to improve their partnering techniques whether they are injured or not (conventional ballet exercises do little to strengthen the arms and shoulders). It is the physical therapist who will advise how much weight and how many repetitions. Swimming back to dance health is also recommended, since the buoyancy of the water allows the injured limb to be worked with much less strain than on land. Swimming also maintains cardiovascular fitness and helps counteract the weight gain that so often accompanies injury.

Finally, there are devices that aid in dancers' rehabilitation: the triangular stretch "wedge board," on which dancers stand with toes up and heels down, is beneficial to the Achilles tendon, while the "tilt" or "wobble" board— a flat surface mounted on a half circle—tests balance by exercising the hamstrings and the inner thighs and is particularly helpful for recovery from the very common sprained ankle.

Tyranny of bodily perfection

Understandably, dancers have a unique obsession with their bodies. There is no question that this professional tool must be kept in the best possible condition. Just as no dancer has or will ever have "perfect" ballet technique, so no female or male performers have anatomically perfect bodies. The most glamorous ballerinas will tell you that their ankles are too thick, necks too short, elbows too knobby, hips too wide, and so forth; and few ever consider themselves thin enough!

Such inevitable self-focus on the body can lead to a tremendous distortion in body image. An exaggerated and neurotic case of dissatisfaction is that of Kirkland, who describes in her autobiography how she "embarked on a risky course of plastic surgery and silicone injections, major dental realignments and gruesome medical procedures," including silicone implantations in her breasts and cosmetic alteration of her insteps, ankles, and even her earlobes and lips.

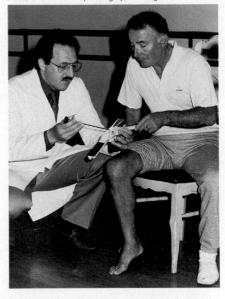

Arthroscopic surgery, or arthroscopy, has revolutionized the treatment of knee injuries common to ballet dancers and to athletes. Requiring only a minor incision, the arthroscope can be used for looking inside the knee to determine the exact extent of damage; it then can be used for accomplishing the repair. Healing is exceptionally fast in most cases and results in little or no scarring. (Above) Los Angeles orthopedist Dan Silver demonstrates the procedure on a model of a knee to dancer Stanley Holden, formerly of the Royal Ballet of England.

Peter Marshall is American Ballet Theatre's full-time physical therapist; he travels with the company and has helped many a performer stay in top condition. With quick backstage treatment during intermissions, he has enabled ABT artistic director and lead dancer Mikhail Baryshnikov (left) to continue dancing through crucial performances despite flare-ups of acute Achilles tendinitis. On a daily basis Marshall helps Baryshnikov maintain his schedule and cope with the toll it can take on his body.

Peter Martins (above) of the New York City Ballet works out in an exercise studio on equipment that helps provide resistance, helpful to male dancers in developing or rehabilitating arm and shoulder muscles. A "wobble" board (above right) is used by dancers for exercising hamstrings and inner thigh muscles and in recovering from sprained ankles. It is not surprising that dancers, who are inevitably obsessed with maintaining their sylphlike bodies, diet rigorously. (Below) A recent study of 92 female ballet students enrolled in professional ballet schools found that a significant number were consuming less than two-thirds of the recommended daily allowances (RDAs) of vitamins and minerals.

Although such drastic and dangerous steps occur among dancers, far more common is the attempt to reshape the body through food intake. There is no dancer who is not, at the very least, conscious about weight watching. To deny that this is a professional necessity would be unrealistic. Dance demands a sleek silhouette. Dancers must seek a diet that provides a maximum amount of energy but contains a low enough number of calories to allow them to maintain or even lose weight. (In fact, they usually eat heartily by the standards of others, but their energy expenditure is so high and their state of fatigue so constant that they often crave more food than they need.)

Most dancers, especially females, have at one time or another undertaken starvation or fad diets. These can set up a vicious cycle of ever greater cravings for food, leading to binges and then to more stringent dieting, along with the abuse of laxatives and diuretics and self-induced vomiting. While such behavior is symptomatic of anorexia nervosa, the starvation regimen that can create an unstoppable—and possibly fatal—spiral of weight loss (due to heart failure, low blood pressure, low body

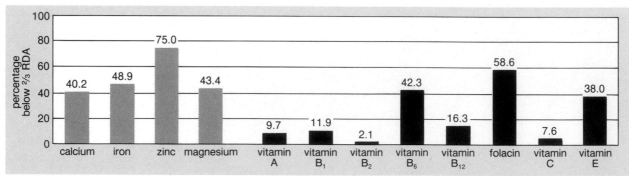

Source: J. Benson and A. Loosli, Center for Sports Medicine of Saint Francis Memorial Hospital, San Francisco

temperature, and other factors associated with true starvation), few professional dancers are victims of this disease. (Selectivity is again at work; true anorexics rarely make it to the professional level.) Rather, dancers, with their very low-calorie diets, may at times exhibit anorectic behavior. The difference is that when they allow themselves to eat normally, which most find all too easy to do, they gain weight. So, too, with bulimia—no professional could last long in her career if she were truly bulimic, although lusty overeating among ballerinas certainly occurs.

In a profession where the body takes so much punishment, the forbidden pleasures of food provide a gratification that little else can rival. Unfortunately, gorging usually affords not only instant satisfaction but instant guilt. Moreover, those who take delight in self-debasement sometimes overeat to punish themselves. Suffering through overeating can also serve to take the dancer's mind off more substantive issues and away from conditions she cannot change. (Diet, theoretically—unlike length of neck, flexibility of muscles, or the casting preferences of the ballet master—is one area over which the dancer can exert complete control.)

Menstrual irregularities, osteoporosis, and fertility

Despite their battles with food, dancers generally manage to remain extremely slim. A 1981 study of nine women in the Boston Ballet found their body weight to be far below average (although comparable to that of female runners and gymnasts), with 15% of the body weight as fat, about half the value found among healthy, nonathletic women. Despite their very low-calorie diets, there was no predisposition to anemia.

It is normal to assume that dancers, with their strenuous activity, should have particularly strong bones, while osteoporosis—thinning of the bones leading to frequent fractures—is usually associated with older adults, particularly postmenopausal women, owing to lowered estrogen production. However, low levels of estrogen, created by delayed menarche (onset of menses), irregular menstrual periods, or cessation of menstruation for a time (secondary amenorrhea), are also known to be a complication of di-

A recent survey of 75 female dancers in four professional ballet companies found a relatively high prevalance (24%) of scoliosis (curvature of the spine), which rose with increases in age at menarche (onset of menstruation), as the graph indicates. While the mean age of the dancers at menarche was 14.5 (nearly two years later than the national average), those with scoliosis had a significant increase in delayed menarche over those without scoliosis. Dancers with scoliosis also had a slightly higher prevalence of secondary amenorrhea (temporary cessation of menstruation); the duration of their amenorrhea was longer; and they scored higher on a questionnaire that assessed anorectic behavior. The dancer below has a form of scoliosis that causes the vertebrae to twist to the right side.

(Left) From M. P. Warren et al., "Scoliosis and Fractures in Young Ballet Dancers," *The New England Journal of Medicine,* vol. 314, no. 21 (May 22, 1986), pp. 1348–53; (right) from E. Thomasen, "Forty Years of Dance Medicine," Teach 'Em Inc. educational program, Chicago

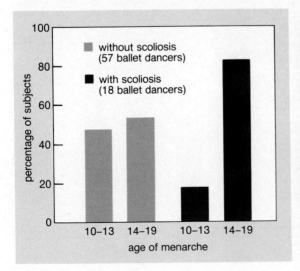

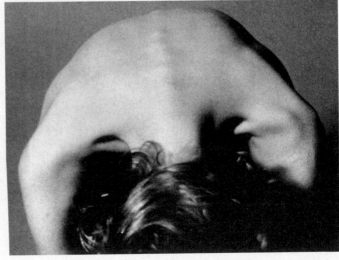

eting, weight loss, and physical training in dancers and athletes, probably because of their low body fat. Recent findings have indicated a correlation between the female dancer's low caloric intake and low estrogen and osteoporosis. In 1986 a survey of 75 female dancers in their mid-twenties in four professional companies revealed a progressively greater predisposition to stress fractures and scoliosis (spine curvature) as the ages at menarche and the length of periods of amenorrhea increased. The mean age at menarche among the 75 subjects was 14.5, nearly two years later than the national average in the U.S.

Although irregular periods, or long intervals between them, are common among ballet dancers, there is no evidence that this permanently affects fertility. Indeed, dancers in their peak physical condition probably have babies more easily than most, although occasionally their superstrong stomach muscles make the birth more difficult. Many dancers continue to exercise vigorously through the ninth month; New York City Ballet principals Melissa Hayden and Karin von Aroldingen performed on stage until halfway through their pregnancies. Getting back in shape afterward takes time and willpower but, within a year of giving birth, the body should have recovered full range of motion.

Thus, physically dancers are well equipped to be mothers. Mentally and emotionally, however, the single-minded, dedicated dancer may not find enough room in her life for children. Among ballerinas who have successfully combined a performing career with motherhood are Natalia Makarova, Patricia McBride, Allegra Kent, Antoinette Sibley, and the late Toni Lander.

Aging: the unsparing specter

Few fears, outside of overweight, torment the dancer more relentlessly than that of aging. On the one hand, dancers live for the moment—because such intense effort is involved in the execution of their work that there is time for nothing else—and on the other, they are continually aware of how

Time is the inexorable foe of dancers; only a handful defy the odds and perform beyond their late thirties. Alicia Alonso, artistic director and prima ballerina of the Ballet Nacional de Cuba, is a notable exception. She is pictured here at age 57 rehearsing for a performance of Giselle—*her most famous role.*

short their performing lives are. To this is added a panic in greater or lesser degree about what will happen afterward.

It is exceptional to have a future financial support system in place while still performing (in the United States ballet dancers' pensions, if they exist at all, begin at 65), and few ballet dancers have had time for formal education toward another career.

Only within the past 10 to 15 years has the need been recognized not only for counseling to help the ballet dancer cope with the emotional effects of retirement but for retraining for other professions. "Transition centers" with this in mind have been established in England, Canada, and the United States. In the Soviet Union, Denmark, and France, which have state-supported systems, dancers' performing-life expectancies are incorporated into their pensions, which begin at around age 40. Nevertheless, these dancers, too, may need retraining; the dance world cannot absorb them all as teachers and coaches.

By the early twenties a person has begun to age physically. Already by that time the intelligent dancer has started to compensate, to make adjustments for little things that have begun to go wrong—a "glass ankle," a "trick knee," an oddly stiff hip. They have found that it is no longer possible to work "full-out" to the point of exhaustion, as it was at 18. The wise dancer will continually reassess his or her way of working; the careless one will keep banging away, which will probably lead to injury, "burnout," and forced early retirement.

Of course, some bodies retain their resiliency longer than others, but an enlightened choice of roles can prolong performing life. Particularly for a woman, the repertory has many lyrical and dramatic ballets to which she may turn when the athletic, virtuoso showpieces are no longer possible. (In the international repertory, the full-length *Swan Lake,* with its 32 fouettés in Act III, is one of the first that ballerinas abandon, often with relief.) Margot Fonteyn, Galina Ulanova, and Alexandra Danilova danced until well into their fifties. Pavlova died at 50, still on tour. Melissa Hayden appeared in bravura Balanchine choreography at 50; Alicia Alonso performed the *Swan Lake* "white" adagio in her sixties. Ruth St. Denis could still mesmerize an audience in her late eighties with her spiritual performance of *Radha,* a solo she had choreographed over 60 years earlier.

As a rule male dancers, unless they decide to limit themselves to partnering and character roles, do not have such long lives onstage; a man begins to lose the elasticity of his jump in his late twenties, and there is simply nothing in the balletic canon to compensate. Erik Bruhn, Helgi Tomasson, and Ivan Nagy were all still considered "great" when they stopped performing, but none measured up to his own goals and earlier abilities. For Jacques d'Amboise the time to stop performing came near the age of 50, when the process of staying in condition began to take virtually all of his time and attention.

Most dancers, though, come to the end of the line physically as they approach 40. No one can tell a performer when to retire; in an art so personal, in which an entire life, body, and soul has been invested, the dancer alone must decide when to take the final bow.

Melissa Hayden, who appeared in bravura ballet repertoire until age 50, blows kisses to her audience at her farewell gala with the New York City Ballet in 1973. She is in costume for Cortège hongrois, *a ballet choreographed for her by George Balanchine.*

Jack Vartoogian

149

The Healing Touch:
GIFT
or
GIMMICK?

by James Randi

Though faith healing has been around for centuries, having its roots in many different religious philosophies, it is a striking fact that it has a remarkably undocumented success rate. In spite of this lack of sufficient evidence, many people continue to have strong belief in the efficacy of the process, perhaps because it bears semiscientific and emotional labels that lend it a considerable—though quite false—pedigree. There is a frightening tendency among believers to resist any attempts to investigate the evidence that is offered to support the claims. The glaring fact, revealed by the simplest of investigations, is that the vast majority of those who go to be healed are *not* healed except for temporary symptomatic relief—certainly none of those suffering from actual organically based diseases or disorders is "cured"—and those who believe they have been healed are simply deluded.

Faith healing's roots

The most evident style of faith healing that is practiced in the Western world today is derived from Christian philosophy. The scripture most often quoted in this regard is I Cor. 12, which cites the nine "gifts" of the "Spirit"—among them are "gifts of healing" and the "utterance of knowledge." "God has appointed in the church . . . workers of miracles" and "healers," and "to each is given the manifestation of the Spirit for the common good."

The Apostles and their successors performed the laying-on-of-hands ceremony, and later church luminaries, such as the reformer Martin Luther in the 16th century, adopted the practice. At that same time, savants such as the German alchemist and physician Paracelsus were attempting, with highly varying degrees of success, to apply "science" to medicine. Paracelsus, a vitriolic iconoclast, raged against the widely held superstitious beliefs and worthless nostrums of his day.

The Church of Jesus Christ of Latter-day Saints (Mormon) and the Protestant Episcopal Church accept faith healing as part of their theologies. Mary Baker Eddy founded her Church of Christ, Scientist, on the basis of the borrowed notion that disease and suffering are illusion and that

James Randi is a professional conjuror, author, and MacArthur Foundation Fellow. In recent years he has turned his attention to exposing charlatans who claim to be faith healers.

(Opposite page) Susan Greenwood—Gamma/Liaison

151

Faith healing derives from Christian doctrine. The Apostles and their successors performed the laying-on-of-hands ceremony to cure the sick. Historically the Christian Church has ministered to the sick both by healing and by expressing concern and compassion. Numerous miraculous healings have served as arguments for the visible presence of the Holy Spirit in the church. Miracles of healing have remained an attribute of Christian evangelists, while the religious masses have continued to yearn for personalities who can perform medical miracles— wonders that seem to satisfy a desire for the awesome and mysterious as well as a longing for personal immortality. In the above work by the 15th-century Italian painter Antonio Vivarini, Peter the Martyr is shown healing the leg of a carpenter. A Dominican friar from Verona, Peter the Martyr had an immense personal following in the early 1200s and was known for his abilities as a preacher and a miracle worker.

The Bettmann Archive

individuals have within themselves healing powers that depend on a deeper understanding of divine metaphysics. The Roman Catholic Church, though it has recently embraced faith healing and has even certified certain priests to perform it, historically relied largely on private or liturgical prayer for recovery from sickness. This would bring about the hoped-for supernatural intervention of God to effect the healing—veneration of holy relics often being a significant part of this practice. One zealous 16th-century collector of relics amassed some 17,000 of these items, among which were bones from the children slain by Herod, a hair from the beard of Christ, and a crust of bread from the Last Supper. Other enthusiasts have displayed Mary Magdalene's entire skeleton (with two right feet), pieces of the True Cross, toenails of St. Peter, and scraps ("twelve baskets full of the broken pieces left over") of bread and fish ("five loaves and two fish") left over from feeding the "multitudes" ("about five thousand men, besides women and children"). Then, among the most sacred of relics with alleged properties of healing, there are several Holy Shrouds, including the one at Turin, Italy.

Contemporary charismatic faith healing in the United States may be said to have begun with the Rev. William Branham, a fire-and-brimstone preacher from Jeffersonville, Indiana, in the 1940s. He was so convincing as a healer of the sick that when he died in 1965, his followers postponed his burial for a period of four months, until it was very evident that the reverend was not going to rise again. His methods were copied by countless other "healers," who swarmed over the countryside in their "canvas cathedrals" promising surcease of suffering to the ailing—and getting very wealthy in the process.

Radio, then television, brought the movement into full bloom. Suddenly the preachers were able to reach millions rather than thousands of people willing to accept the preached brand of faith for the relief of their troubles. In recent years, with the expansion of the television and radio media, TV channels and radio stations have been licensed solely for the purpose of broadcasting these programs, some of them seven days a week, 24 hours a day.

The placebo effect

Many people believe, with good reason, that they have been healed after what seems to the subject a dramatic encounter with a faith healer. Symptoms are often less evident, and patients often feel better emotionally after a healing ceremony. This could easily be due to the well-known "placebo effect."

A placebo effect can take place when the patient is exposed to a satisfactory "bedside manner," or medication, manipulation, or other means (any or all of which may be entirely ineffectual in themselves but are seen by the recipient as unique, special, or advanced) are applied to the problem. Such effects are also seen to take place when the patient feels in control of the situation or has surrendered that control to another in whom he or she has confidence. This is a simple case of what is known as "transference." Encouragement leads to hope, and hope to better self-care and self-interest. Many types of chronic pain, because of the emotional condition

152

of the sufferer, are associated with chronic anxiety. An efficient and caring physician, knowledgeable about the placebo effect, can largely alleviate that anxiety and thus improve at least the symptoms of certain ailments. Recent research has shown that about one-third of cases of simple illnesses (colds, chest pain, headaches, seasickness, anxiety, and postoperative pain) respond well to placebos.

Without question, a positive attitude provides a somewhat better environment for healing, if for no other reason than the fact that the patient nourishes himself or herself better and is more willing to follow prescribed procedures. Faith healers' results could also be due to certain neurological or biochemical effects of endorphin release, which can take place under stress or in highly emotional environments in any case. Endorphins, or endogenous morphines, are naturally occurring opiumlike compounds that apparently are released by the brain at certain times and circulate through the body, producing pain relief or euphoric feelings.

Faith healing and psychotherapy: similarities and differences

How long the ministrations of the faith healers will last and whether such symptomatic relief is an unmixed blessing to the afflicted, however, are other questions that must be answered. Attempts to compare the results of psychotherapy with the faith healers' impact upon their clients have demonstrated that they are roughly similar in effect. Investigators have also shown that in psychotherapy and faith healing, actual modalities of treatment and the involvement of the therapist or healer seemed to add little to the outcome. It has also been noted that the *major* result of the psychotherapists' efforts is diagnostic, and their predictions are based upon observations of the patients' characteristics. This appears to be the skill upon which certain faith healers largely depend if other, more certain methods of obtaining medical information are not available or are not preferred by the operator.

There are cases in which both psychotherapy and faith healing might be expected to have essentially similar end results since in some ways the

Paracelsus raged against the worthless nostrums of his day while believing in alchemy and the stars as healing influences. Mary Baker Eddy, founder of the Christian Science faith, believed in divine healing. The second of the advertisements below, which appeared in a New England spiritualist publication in 1868, was placed by Eddy under her married name, Mary B. Glover.

(Above) The Bettmann Archive; (below) photographs, The Granger Collection, New York

CLAIRVOYANT, Magnetic and Electric Physicians, have recently furnished a house on Quincy avenue, in QUINCY, MASS., where they are still Healing the Sick with good success. Board and treatment reasonable. Address, QUINCY, MASS. 6w*—June 6.

ANY PERSON desiring to learn how to heal the sick can receive of the undersigned instruction that will enable them to commence healing on a **principle of science** with a success far beyond any of the present modes. No medicine, electricity, physiology or hygiene required for unparalleled success in the most difficult cases. No pay is required unless this skill is obtained. Address, MRS. MARY B. GLOVER, Amesbury, Mass., Box 61 tf†—June 20.

MRS. MARY LEWIS, by sending their autograph, or lock of hair, will give psychometrical delineations of character, answer questions, &c. Terms $1 00 and red stamp.

two are very similar. The basic purposes are quite different, however. One will say that problems are generated by unresolved conflicts, and the other will declare that the problems are the doings of demons and devils who control the patients because of their lack of faith, piety, or sacrifice. The basic aim of psychotherapy is to create in patients the feeling that they are autonomous, in control of their own destinies, and assuming that control; "cures" are said to have occurred when the patients have in fact become self-sufficient and are able to function in society. The faith healers, however, promote in their victims a feeling of total dependence on the operators, based upon a mythology that the operators themselves have created by specialized interpretation of the various writings and authorities they quote.

Methods of deception

Recent investigations by this author of prominent faith healers in the United States and Canada have led to the discovery that they were using simple conjuring techniques to create the impression that they had specific "magical" powers that established their divine connections. These powers have their origins in holy writings. The most commonly used and most effective gimmick employed is a method of accomplishing the so-called word of knowledge, the supposed ability to know (by divine power) the names and ailments of and personal facts about the persons being treated. This is known in the trade as "calling out." The preacher will walk down the aisle of a crowded auditorium, suddenly stop, and extend a pointed finger at a person who is a stranger to him or her, calling out information that apparently could be known only to that person or to God. This has a great effect upon the individual—and the rest of the congregation.

As part of the deception, the preacher will usually take great care to ask the victims of this hoax whether they have ever met or spoken before. The answer is almost invariably no. What the audience does not know is that it is not at all necessary for the preacher to approach the victims for this information; it has already been gleaned from the victims by another person working for the alleged healer—either through casual conversation or by direct questioning. Those data have then been taken backstage and submitted to the preaching performer, who has the individuals pointed out to him or her and then usually uses a mnemonic system to commit the data to memory.

One of the best known of the contemporary memory artists is W. V. Grant, a Texan who, before evidence was gathered against him and published, was seen from his Eagle's Nest Cathedral in Dallas in some 216,000 households weekly via his television program, "Dawn of a New Day." He is now seen in only 95,000 homes, and that number is dropping as the news about his trickery is circulated. The information travels slowly because many persons who follow these religious figures simply do not read newspapers or watch nonreligious television programming.

The mnemonic system is often used along with "crib sheets," which are inserted, for example, into a prayer book or Bible and carried about by the preacher. Of course, there are some who cannot master such a fundamental memory system. The very influential evangelist Peter Popoff, who had

Aimee Semple McPherson had a huge following as a U.S. Pentecostal evangelist and faith healer. She established the International Church of the Foursquare Gospel in the 1920s, in which healing was one of four themes that constituted a perfect, "foursquare," full gospel; salvation, Holy Spirit baptism, and the Second Coming of Christ were the others. "Sister Aimee," as she was known, conducted her revival and healing services in great theatrical style. Like those of many of today's faith healers, her career ultimately brought her both wealth and notoriety.

The Bettmann Archive

154

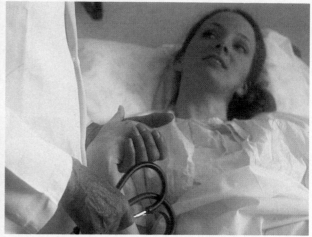

his headquarters in Upland, in southern California, and was once on 80 television stations broadcasting healing sessions continent wide (but is now on none, following exposure of his methods), used a far more technological method. His wife, who was equipped with a powerful high-frequency transmitter, would wander about the audience and interview persons there well before the show. Her husband was thus able to hear the interviews while watching the people via the television monitors backstage. He made notes, and when he later walked out to begin his healing act, wearing a tiny receiver in his ear canal, he was prompted by his wife, who was now backstage with her transmitter.

Popoff had a very powerful additional bit of technology at his disposal. He would sometimes be able to produce bits of personal information about his victims—information that had not been revealed to his wife or others who served as questioners. During all of Popoff's preaching meetings, the backstage workers, by means of a telephone modem, were able to tap into information in the Upland area mainframe computer, obtaining a wealth of personal data about some 100,000 listed individuals. Those names made up Popoff's mailing list, and in the likely event that such individuals appeared in his audience, the preacher could, on the spot, appear to know or "to divine" surprising truths. Victims of the hoax were understandably astonished at the "insights" and, lacking any other explanation, attributed the "calling out" procedure to divine sources.

There were other tricks employed, such as summoning apparently crippled persons to rise from wheelchairs as if they had been healed. Questioned later, these people admitted that they had never even been in a wheelchair before that time and had been asked by an usher to sit in one for "greater convenience."

The essence of faith

This brings up the most fascinating question of all: Why do these people go along with the deceptions? In most cases Popoff's victims and those of other faith healers are not even aware that any deception has taken place and, when they are aware, they choose to ignore that fact. They appear

It is not at all surprising that people believe they have been genuinely helped by the faith healer's laying on of hands or whatever methods he or she uses. After these dramatic encounters, ailing people often feel substantially better, and symptoms may actually be less evident. This well-known phenomenon, the placebo effect, has long been acknowledged by the medical profession. The effect can occur as the result of the proverbial "good bedside manner" or from any sort of medication (including sugar pills), manipulation, or other means that are applied for the sake of making the patient better. Encouragement from a person in whom one has placed confidence— legitimate practitioner or not—leads to hope, and such a positive attitude is conducive to healing effects.

155

The contemporary charismatic faith-healing movement in the United States was brought into full blossom via television. Suddenly faith healers were able to reach millions. One of the best known broadcasting preachers of recent years is the Texan W. V. Grant. His "Dawn of a New Day" TV show at one time reached well over 200,000 homes weekly. After some of his deceitful methods were revealed publicly, his audience was cut in half. In the televised encounter shown here, Grant receives a testimonial from a "cured" subject—a man in his audience on whom he has performed a dramatic "leg-lengthening" procedure.

to be engaging in some sort of a morality play—as actors in that drama. They have a part to play that requires unquestioned faith and submission to the director—in this case the faith healer. Doubt, they are told, leads to failure of the healing process. In fact, often when victims are questioned about their submission, they become very belligerent; when certain facts are presented to them, they suddenly reject any further participation in the questioning process. They are, in effect, shutting out the intruding reality. They seem to be a class of people disillusioned with this world and impatient for the next.

The preachers conduct massive mailings, sending out highly effective letters created by a "professional" writer—at a cost of as much as $20,000. Though it is a fairly well-known fact in this age of technology that computers can be programmed to drop first and last names into the text and thus print letters that are personalized, victims of these preachers apparently are unaware of this possibility. When questioned, they are almost universally of the opinion that the evangelist has personally written to them. On one occasion Popoff sent out a lengthy and very persuasive letter that informed each of 100,000 persons that at 5:20 AM the morning of the date of the letter, God had awakened him and had spoken the recipient's name to him as the one person selected to be a "prayer partner."

An emphasis on friendship is typical of the media preachers. The success of the modern electronic church is largely due to the millions of lonely people "out there" who are seeking a friend. They are told by the preachers that they will be prayed for and accepted as a "confidante." They receive letters regularly from these newfound "pen pals." Of course—they are told—all of this costs money and, in order to keep this friend and to assure that those welcome letters will continue, the faithful must contribute. Obviously Popoff was assured of receiving enough responses to his appeals for funds that he could afford to invest in such costly mailings.

156

Preachers quickly achieve the status of soap opera actors or rock stars pursued by "groupies." To personally witness and perhaps even touch these idols seems to be part of the goal of their admirers. Perhaps the devotees are not totally swindled when they give their money to the stars of the electronic church. The $5 or $15 or even $1,500 they surrender might be buying them just what they want and think they need: contact with a glamorous entity who has supernatural connections.

Legal deception?

All of these donations are tax free, under the position adopted by the U.S. Internal Revenue Service that religious figures may not be taxed except on their stated incomes. This must be considered in light of the fact that Popoff alone was taking in more than $1 million a month from just the mail, not to mention his "in-person" crusades.

Legally speaking, though, all the faith healers—and many evangelists who make no pretensions of healing—are at risk. The risk is incurred when the preachers promise "100-fold return" from donations, "investments," or "seed faith offerings" made to them by the faithful. By law, such financial promises cannot be made without sufficient guarantees. The preachers also either promise or strongly imply relief of ailments that medical science cannot treat effectively. In many cases the ailments they claim to "cure" are quite normal, expected effects of advancing age. By promising this kind of reward, the healers again are in violation of the law. Nonetheless, the legal risk is minimized by the widespread and strong reluctance of most law-enforcement officials to make a move against any "religious" figure.

Healing touch: too good to be true

Another variety of faith healing is known as psychic surgery. In this process, which originated in Brazil and the Philippines, the operator appears to reach

Peter Popoff's huge following has been drastically reduced after recent exposure of his methods. More than anything else, Popoff was a very convincing actor. A common "healing" ceremony he performed was summoning apparently crippled persons to rise from wheelchairs or walk without canes or crutches. (Below, left) In March 1986 at the Anaheim (California) Convention Center, Popoff "cures" an alleged arthritis sufferer. The subject was Don Henvick, a collaborator of James Randi who was planted in the audience. The man positioned behind Henvick is Popoff's assistant, who is there to "catch" the subject should he fall at any point during the act of healing. For his deceptions Popoff depended to a high degree on technological methods of trickery. (Below) Elizabeth Popoff, Peter's wife, is shown before her husband's "act" at the San Francisco Civic Center in February 1986. She would roam the audience interviewing people prior to a show—equipped with a high-frequency transmitter in her purse—while he watched and listened on a TV monitor backstage. Investigations revealed that the people Popoff randomly "called out" during his frequent, widely broadcast ceremonies had in fact been screened by his wife.

(Left) David Alexander; (right) Yves Barbero

inside the subject's body and pull forth a quantity of organic matter and blood. The miracle lies in the fact that the seeming wound heals instantly and leaves no mark whatsoever. All of this is accompanied by a great deal of hymn singing and reading from scriptures.

This author's investigations of the miraculous phenomenon have revealed that psychic surgery is actually basic sleight of hand performed in a highly emotional atmosphere. The "surgeons" use small plastic bags, fashioned from food-wrap plastic, containing animal parts (chicken livers and hearts are commonly used) and either real blood (chicken or pig) or betel-nut juice, which resembles blood and is easier to obtain and to keep fresh. These containers are introduced under cover of other actions—sometimes rather cleverly. Videotapes of the surgeons at work quickly reveal their methods, and forensic tests carried out on the materials they utilize (which have been confiscated by investigators from trash containers) have proved the true nature of the "tumors" and "bad blood" that are produced as evidence of the great miracle that has occurred during a "psychic" operation.

Psychic surgery can be classified as faith healing because the practitioners, when caught red-handed (no pun intended), have admitted their trickery but claimed that it is the drama involved that brings healing to the ill person, prompted and encouraged by the prestidigitation. Nevertheless, as with all other forms of faith healing, true cures are not seen to result from these dramatic performances.

It has been established that in this form of faith healing, victims are very much apt to throw away their medications and to refuse further orthodox treatment or advice—often with tragic consequences. They travel long distances and spend huge sums of money to undergo the highly theatrical procedures in seeking relief. With that investment, they tend to resist going back to legitimate procedures that may have promised them less.

Modern medicine's limits

A large percentage of those who turn to faith healers rather than depending on medical science have the expectation that doctors should be able to diagnose and cure, in a straightforward and speedy manner, whatever disease is presented to them. This is an erroneous expectation. Medical doctors do their best to make life longer and more comfortable and productive for their patients. They strive to cancel out and repair the effects of injuries and infections. Relief is their goal, but they seldom have the satisfaction of returning total, good-as-new function to their customers. Their promises are few, and with good reason.

There is a point beyond which medical science—at least presently—cannot go. Disease and death are part of the life process—the normal attrition of later years. The causes and the symptoms of some diseases can be combatted with specific medications and techniques that attack bacteria and viruses and either remove the invading elements or arrest their attacks upon the orderly progress of life. Death, however, often results simply and naturally from a series of failures of various smaller systems that are part of the support of people's day-to-day continued existence, and not from a catastrophic event. With years the human body breaks

158

down, with grace, it is hoped, and supported by friends and a social system that respects one's increasing failures to perform as usual. Reaction time becomes greater, perceptions are less sensitive, and memory serves people less efficiently. Perhaps the accompanying lessened awareness is an unplanned but welcome mercy of nature that eases passage; certainly it seems to be an advantage, given the inevitability of death. But there are many persons who fail to recognize these facts or refuse to accept them. They are apt to become victims of the faith healers, who promise them miracles without end.

Insights of a professional conjurer

As a professional conjurer, I possess a certain expertise—of an admittedly narrow range—that allows me to detect trickery. It would be difficult for me to describe to a nonconjurer the means whereby trickery becomes evident to me. I can give one example of my thinking that will perhaps explain it to some extent.

When a colleague and I first observed Peter Popoff in action, we had already seen W. V. Grant and knew his system was a mnemonic one. It was the sheer amount of information and the details that Popoff was able to recite that tipped us off to the fact that he had an external data source available to him and was not using a memory system. It took only a quick up-close view to determine that the preacher was wearing a hearing aid. One would not expect someone who heals the deaf to be wearing a hearing aid, we thought. We were able to substantiate our suspicions by subsequent electronic scanning in the high-frequency radio spectrum, which picked up the preacher's secret transmissions quite easily.

Also, in my role of conjurer, I am quite aware of the psychology behind the devotées of the faith healers seeing what they prefer to see. It is difficult for them to admit that they have been unobservant or that they misinterpreted what they experienced. They will often go to absurd

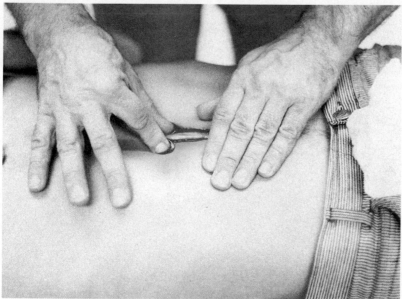

James Randi

Psychic surgeons claim to "operate" on people by piercing the skin with bare hands and plucking out, with great flourish, an offending mass such as a tumor—all without the aid of anesthetics or other surgical tools. According to its practitioners, this "miracle" involves the aid of "spiritual forces." Here James Randi demonstrates the psychic surgeon's sleight of hand: an "incision" is made and—as if by magic—"blood" appears.

The wealth of today's evangelist-healers—especially the TV evangelists—has recently been the subject of numerous scandals. The preachers do a lot more than heal the sick. When they parlay their "gift" and "healing powers" over the airwaves, they enlist their faithful congregations at a steep price. When Oral Roberts of Tulsa, Oklahoma, discovered his own "anointment" and "healing powers," he called for vast contributions. In 1981 about $250 million went toward the construction of a medical research center with a hospital "containing 777 beds," which Roberts told his 2.5 million regular viewers that God had instructed him to build. Pictured here is the glittering 60-story City of Faith medical center with its 61-meter (200-foot) glass-and-steel prayer tower in the shape of praying hands. Like many of his fellow TV evangelists, in recent times Roberts has foundered; his empire has been sorely short of funds and his hospital short of patients. A June 1987 Gallup survey found that 63% of Americans now regard TV preachers as "untrustworthy with money," and only 30% believe that so-called televangelists "have a special relationship with God." In what has been viewed as a desperate appeal to raise cash, Roberts, who received a 72% "unfavorable" rating in that same poll, put forth a new claim: that he possessed the power to raise the dead—perhaps the ultimate in faith healing.

extremes to explain away obvious paradoxes in order to keep their view of a situation—their philosophy of the moment—intact. That is often part of the instruction that believers in faith healing receive in their preparation for being deceived. They are even specifically told not to be logical in judging the claimed miracles. To quote one veteran evangelist/faith healer, Oral Roberts, of Tulsa, Oklahoma: "It requires faith to believe God can [perform a miracle]. . . . It takes faith because it goes against all human reasoning. It goes against everything our mind has been taught by Man's reasoning."

The notion that certain preachers can provide a favored few with a means of controlling God's actions—so as to bring about healing, for example—is known in theology as the "Pelagian heresy." Through publication of such best-selling books as Pat Robertson's *Beyond Reason: How Miracles Can Change Your Life*, the faithful are promised that they can learn to earn and control divine favors. It should be noted, too, that these powers are said to be reserved for Christians only. Jews and Muslims are not included.

Is there not some value to the work of these would-be healers if they bring relief of some kind to their subjects? First, it is symptomatic relief, if any, that they accomplish. This is not treating the disease but only treating the manifestations of the disease. It is much like prescribing analgesics to relieve the pain of a fracture instead of setting the broken bone. Second, the subject may decide to abandon orthodox medical treatment in favor of what appears to be a noninvasive, natural form of healing. Third, dependence upon and belief in one false notion fosters a pursuit of magical solutions in all other aspects of life. These may appeal to the imagination, but they do not give results. Fourth, total dependence on the preacher is suggested and encouraged, with obvious dangers should the preacher take advantage of that circumstance.

Despite the effective campaigns I have been able to carry out in exposing the dangerous and deceitful practices of some of the fraudulent healers who have victimized unwary and ailing people—campaigns supported by and

160

Faith healing over the airwaves has thrived largely because electronic ministries offer instant fellowship to the millions of lonely people "out there." Recent surveys indicate that anywhere from 13 million to 60 million people are regular viewers of the religious television networks. There are many reasons to believe that faith healers will continue to flourish and that they will continue to use the tricks of their trade to produce "miracles" for the unsuspecting. Most of the devotees are not aware when a deception has taken place and, if they are, they simply choose to ignore the facts. Those who turn to faith healers rather than depending on medical science tend to have highly unrealistic expectations of what physicians and medicine can and cannot actually do. The tragedy is that altogether too many are betrayed by their beliefs in the end, and some have suffered immeasurably—or died— because they disregarded proper medical advice.

in conjunction with the Committee for Scientific Investigation of Claims of the Paranormal and the Committee for Scientific Examination of Religion—I have no delusions about my ultimate ability to truly bring some sanity to this situation. The faith healers will flourish; charismatic, forceful personalities who can convincingly claim to be divinely anointed will make use of little-known technologies and psychological tricks to produce miracles for the unsuspecting—and gain power and riches in the process. Further, as long as governmental authorities continue to avoid any confrontation with the charlatans, because of their fear of violating constitutional rights, the public will go unprotected.

My investigations have led me to the conclusion that faith healing is not a positive element in society. I have witnessed the heartbreak and the disillusionment suffered by those who are betrayed by their beliefs, and I have wept with those whose loved ones died because they discarded proper medical care—imperfect though it may be—in favor of magic.

Though I have assiduously sought evidence of *any* genuine healing by faith, I have not been provided with a single example, even by the leading practitioners. Caveat emptor!

The
Treasure Troves
of
Wellcome

by Ron Champion

For medical historians and, indeed, all who aspire to trace and study mankind's mastery of the medical arts, London is Mecca. That capital city beckons to the scholar with an institute for the history of medicine containing a medical library with a historical collection that is the largest and most comprehensive in Europe and ranks internationally among the finest two or three libraries of its kind; it offers as well a "gem" of a public museum of the history of medicine containing no fewer than 125,000 artifacts.

Though they are located in fairly distant parts of the city—the latter in southwest London and the former in northwest London—and administratively independent, both are the legacy and bear the name of an inspired American-born millionaire, Sir Henry Solomon Wellcome. Wellcome was the one-man owner of the British pharmaceutical company the Wellcome Foundation Ltd. from 1895 until his death in 1936. The success of his company, which he and Silas Burroughs had founded in London in 1880 as the partnership of Burroughs Wellcome and Co., enabled him to indulge a lifelong passion to amass a vast medical and ethnographic collection illustrating the means by which people through the ages have attempted to maintain health and combat disease.

Remarkable resource for studying medical history

The Wellcome Institute for the History of Medicine is to be found discreetly housed behind the Ionic portico of the Wellcome Building at 183 Euston Road in Bloomsbury. Few of the myriad commuters and tourists who daily pass the building on their way to and from the British Rail mainline terminals—Euston, King's Cross, and St. Pancras—for which Euston Road is best known are aware of what it contains.

The library. The nucleus of the Wellcome library comprises the books collected by and for Henry Wellcome between 1898 and 1936. He regarded his library as an important ancillary to his never fully realized pet project—a "museum of man"—thus, its scope is far wider than purely medical. In addition to extensive holdings on clinical medicine, therapeutics, hospitals, and nursing, as well as case histories of patients, the library possesses large

162

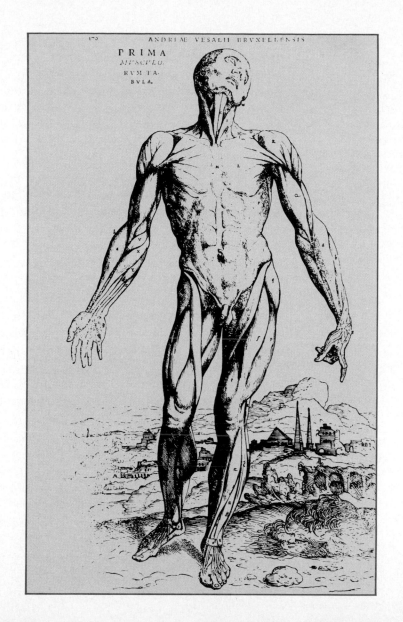

Ron Champion is a free-lance writer who resides in Essex, England.

Among the highly prized editions contained in the library of the Wellcome Institute for the History of Medicine are texts by Aristotle, Galen, Hippocrates, Vesalius, and Rhazes. The most influential Arabic contributor to medicine was Persian-born Avicenna (980–1037), a child prodigy who is reputed to have mastered the Qur'an (Koran) by the age of ten; his knowledge was indeed encyclopedic, including grammar, poetry, geometry, astronomy, anatomy, physiology, and surgery. The most renowned of his many writings was The Canon of Medicine (al-Qanun fi at-tibb), *upon which medical practitioners worldwide based their practices for hundreds of years. Even in the mid-17th century, his teachings were the basis of medical curricula of Western universities. The plate at right, from a 1632 edition of the* Canon, *shows a physician taking the pulse of a patient in a Persian garden.*

collections on the history of the biologic sciences, particularly physiology, botany, and chemistry. The development of the latter scientific fields is, of course, closely interwoven with that of the healing arts. The foundations of the modern sciences astronomy, mathematics, and physics—from the 13th century to the 18th century—are to be found in the Wellcome library in first editions of Roger Bacon, Galileo, Johannes Kepler, Descartes, Robert Hooke, Sir Isaac Newton, and Robert Boyle. There are also important sections in the library relating to travel, ethnography, alchemy, occultism, tobacco, and veterinary medicine, to name but a few.

Unfortunately, during the lifetime of Wellcome, the library always played second fiddle to his museum collection of medical artifacts. He had neither the time, the money, nor the manpower to collate, catalog, and house his prized books and other materials for public use. The library has grown steadily and developed under the direction of Wellcome's trustees, however, and today, some 50 years after his death, it is well established as an internationally recognized resource for the study of medical history and is indeed fulfilling its magnanimous founder's dreams.

The Western collection. Henry Wellcome came close to realizing his aim of acquiring a copy of every significant printed text relating to Western medical science. The library's exceptional collection of incunabula (books printed

before 1501) was largely made up from three famous private libraries, those of the British designer, craftsman, poet, and early socialist William Morris (1834–96) and the bibliophiles J. F. Payne and Kurt Wolff. Most of the great names in medicine from antiquity, the European Middle Ages, and the Renaissance are represented by original or early editions of their works.

The texts on medieval medicine cover a wide range of European languages and subjects. Books from the 16th and 17th centuries include editions of Aristotle, Galen, Hippocrates, Rhazes, and Avicenna, many of them in the highly valued editions rendered by scholar-printers. In anatomy the works of Andreas Vesalius, as well as those of his predecessors and successors, are represented; pride of place is accorded to a first edition of Vesalius's epoch-making work, *De humani corporis fabrica libri septum* ("The Seven Books on the Structure of the Human Body"), published in 1543 and carrying the author's autograph on the flyleaf. Based on meticulously performed dissections and profusely illustrated, Vesalius's *Fabrica,* as it is known, was written when he was only 28 years old. With the confidence of youth, he states in his preface: "I have done my best to this single end, to aid as many as possible in a very recondite as well as laborious matter and truly and completely to describe the structure of the human body which is formed not of ten or twelve parts, as it may seem to the spectator, but of some thousands of different parts. I bear to the candidates of medicine fruit not to be scorned."

Famous original works on subjects surgical include those of Hieronymus Brunschwig, Ambroise Paré, Paracelsus, and Della Croce—again, to name but a few. There are some 40 herbals (illustrated manuals facilitating the identification of plants for medicinal purposes), including various editions and translations of the Greek botanist Pedanius Dioscorides' *De materia medica*. The latter reigned as the world's most important work on botanical remedies for some 1,500 years.

Here, too, is the original of William Harvey's classic work on the circulation of the blood, *Exercitatio anatomica de motu cordis et sanguinis*

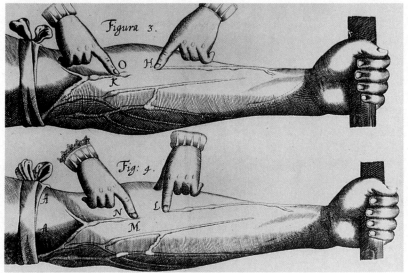

Collection, Wellcome Institute Library, London

William Harvey's Exercitatio anatomica de motu cordis et sanguinis in animalibus *("An Anatomical Experiment Concerning the Movement of the Heart and Blood in Animals"), published in 1628, is considered perhaps the foremost treatise in the history of physiology. Harvey's direct observations and experiments on animals and humans led to his revolutionary descriptions of how blood circulates and how the heart acts as a pump. An original engraving from Harvey's classic work (left) shows the way valves work in the veins.*

in animalibus (1628). Within the compass of this short treatise, Harvey presented his revolutionary description of the one-way (toward the heart) circulation of the blood (it had been thought that blood flowed back and forth, like a tide). He also gave the first example of what was then a new method of gaining knowledge: direct observation and experiment instead of the further study of what others had written. "Not from books," wrote Harvey, "but from dissections."

From later centuries there are the classic works of William Heberden, John Hunter, Edward Jenner, Joseph Lister, Louis Pasteur, Wilhelm Röntgen, and many more. The following examples highlight but three of these landmarks. Jenner, a rural physician from Gloucestershire, showed in 1798 that cowpox, a relatively harmless disease that could be contracted from cattle, not only protected against smallpox but could be transmitted from one person to another as a deliberate mechanism of protection, thereby making immunization a practical proposition. Pasteur, a Parisian research chemist untrained in medicine, discovered in the 1880s the disease-producing character of microbes and produced the first scientific vaccine for protection against the rabies virus. Lister in England in 1865 introduced the scientific principle of destroying "germs" in the operating theater by treating with carbolic acid not only the surgeons' hands, instruments, and dressings but also the air that surrounds the patient on the operating table.

Some 6,000 manuscripts dating from the 11th to the 20th century are included in this Western collection. Over 800 of these were written before 1650, the earliest being an Anglo-Saxon parchment, *c.* 1025, which describes remedies for heartache, lung disease, and liver complaints. Concerning the treatment of tumors, this rare survival from pre-Norman English literature instructs: "One shall take pure honey, such as is used to lighten porridge, boil it to almost the thickness of porridge; take radish, elder, wild thyme, cinquefoil, pound them as well as you can; then squeeze the worts so as to extract the juice from them, and when it is almost done mix in a good measure of garlic and put to it as much pepper as you think."

On the library's shelves rests a surprising collection of 15 volumes of letters and documents relating to Viscount Horatlo Nelson and his command of fleets during the years 1780–1805; two laboratory notebooks of Marie Sklodowska-Curie, the first woman to win a Nobel Prize, and one of Pasteur; and lecture notes of the brother surgeons John and William Hunter. In addition, there are prized handwritten materials including more than 100,000 letters—correspondence of notable scientific and medical figures, among them Florence Nightingale, Pasteur, Lister, Jenner, Sir James Paget, T. H. Huxley, and Alexander von Humboldt.

Americana in abundance. Henry Wellcome's North American birth and early business travels in South America stimulated his interest in primary medical literature of the American continent, and his American collection was extended after his death. His first gleanings of material relating to plant remedies, botanical exploration, and the ethnology of the American Indian were strengthened in 1927 when he purchased the library of the Mexican obstetrician and scientist Nicolás León. In 1962 the library acquired the collection of the physician Francisco Guerra, comprising many primary

The oldest text (c. 1025) in the Wellcome's Western collection is this prized Anglo-Saxon parchment. In pre-Norman English, it describes in detail remedies of the day for a wide range of common ailments—among them heartache and liver complaints.

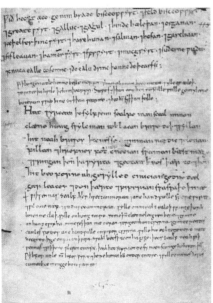

Collection, Wellcome Institute Library, London

In the library's Oriental collection is an early Hebrew manual on circumcision. The miniature at left shows the circumcision rite being performed on a male baby on the eighth day after birth, in accordance with Jewish law. The infant is held on the godfather's lap. The depiction of Queen Mahamaya giving birth to Siddhartha Gautama, the future Buddha (above), is from an Indian palm leaf manuscript. The child is emerging fully formed and clean from his mother's side.

printed materials of Mexican origin and from other Hispanic colonies in Latin America and the Caribbean. The Wellcome collection of original Mexican texts, 1577–1833, is now the most extensive in existence.

Especially well represented in the library's South and Central American and Caribbean holdings are works from Peru, Guatemala, Argentina, Brazil, Cuba, and Jamaica. Among the texts from South America are the first book on medicine published in the New World, the *Phisica Speculatio* by Alonso de la Veracruz (1557), and an original document signed by the count of Chinchón, whose name was given to cinchona, the tree bark from which quinine—an important substance in the treatment of malaria—is extracted.

North American material has been amplified by the sporadic acquisition since 1962 of some 550 printed items published in the original 13 British colonies, 1720–1820, which principally cover medical botany, travel in the United States, the ethnography of the American Indian and his medicine, and colonial and postcolonial almanacs. So extensive is the library's American collection that it has been housed in a separate room and has its own catalog.

Occidental to Oriental. The net that Henry Wellcome cast was indeed so wide that the library contains some 11,000 manuscripts and 3,000 books that are printed in Oriental scripts. For example, there are over 600 manuscripts in Persian, many of great beauty and rarity. In all, 43 languages stretching from North Africa to the Far East are represented. The Oriental collection spans some 2,500 years of civilization, from Egyptian papyri to contemporary printed books. There are over 900 palm leaf manuscripts;

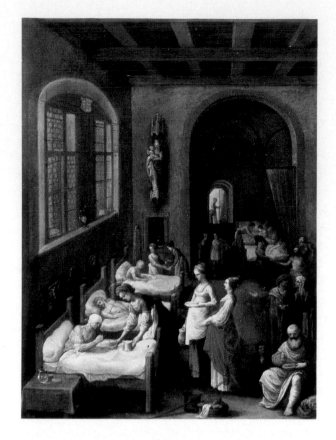

In addition to its vast collection of
books and manuscripts, the library also
possesses an impressive number of visual
materials and art. A well-preserved
painting from the late 16th century
portrays Saint Elizabeth of Hungary
tenderly ministering to a patient in
a medieval hospital. The Wellcome's
photographic collection includes some of
the very first pictures of the inside of the
human body. The radiograph below, taken
in 1895 by German physicist Wilhelm
Röntgen (the discoverer of X-rays),
is of Frau Röntgen's left hand with
wedding ring.

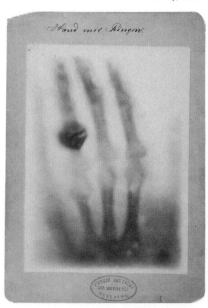

manuscripts from Burma, Indochina, and Indonesia written on metal, ivory,
and bone; and Hebrew scrolls on leather.

Indian material predominates in the library's Oriental holdings, however,
with some 6,000 manuscripts in Sanskrit and one of the largest European
collections of manuscripts in Hindi. Although Indian literary heritage is vast,
the history of Indian science and medicine remains a relatively new field of
inquiry. Indeed, the collection of Sir Henry Wellcome represents a major
step toward the preparation of such a history. For over ten years he maintained an agent in British India to gather these medical materials. Though
it is apparent in retrospect that the time was not yet ripe for such an
undertaking—and *still* much foundation work remains to be done in identifying authors and determining dates of treatises and other materials—what
Wellcome *did* amass in works of Indian literary tradition, ancient historical
writings, and contemporary medical anthropology is astounding.

Art works. Wellcome's omnivorous appetite for acquisition is further exemplified by the library's complementary holding of some 900 paintings,
100,000 drawings and prints, and 2,000 photographs. Included are first
and last portraits of Jenner; Spanish panel paintings—notably, Alonso de
Sedano's "Miracle of Saints Cosmas and Damian" (Burgos, *c.* 1500); a well-
preserved painting of St. Elizabeth visiting a hospital, recently attributed
to Adam Elsheimer (Frankfurt am Main, 1598); Dutch genre paintings of
subjects anatomical, medical, and surgical; and over 50 Tibetan *thang-ka*s,
which are paintings on woven material with religious themes and which

usually serve as aids to meditation. There are 12,000 portrait engravings and watercolors; a fine collection of English and French healing-arts-related caricatures; botanical illustrations; and so-called allegories of mortality, which portray the physical frailty and inevitable mortality of humankind.

Among many notable drawings is a pathological illustration rendered by Thomas Willis, a physician, and Christopher Wren (the latter, of course, better known as the architect of London's St. Paul's Cathedral). There is a study by the Spanish-born artist José de Ribera for his famous medical contribution, an etching of a man with goiter. There are photographs from historic scientific conferences; Röntgen's first nine radiographs made in 1895, one showing the now-famous bones of his wife's left hand; and the earliest existing clinical photographs from hospitals around the world—in all, a fascinating iconographic collection.

Kaleidoscopic and ever vital. Nothing was too small or too insignificant for Henry Wellcome to collect, provided it had relevance to the history of medicine. As a collector he was ahead of his time in recognizing the value of what are known as ephemera, items that in their day were regarded as expendable but are now prized collectibles. Among these, for example, are Victorian music hall song sheets, all pertaining in some way or other to health, a doctor, a potion, or a pill. Among the many irreverent refrains was one sung by Alf Walker:

I am a learned surgeon and my name is Doctor Quack.
My draughts and pills to cure your ills I carry on my back.
I've lotions for the measles and I've powders for the croup.
I cure the girls of whooping cough by taking off their hoop.
I've ointment for a mother-in-law, she swallows half a pound.
She'll never trouble you again for she will sleep so sound.
Who'll have a gross of leeches? Shall I put them on your back?
You won't—then he must go elsewhere to trade, must
Doctor Quack!

Virtually nothing was too insignificant for Wellcome's collections. The caricature at left, one of many from the 19th century, portrays an English country physician. He carries a bunch of flowers with him on his visit to the infirmary—presumably to sweeten the stench in the less-than-hygienic sickroom. "The Doctor" (above) is one of many Victorian music hall song sheets with medical themes. It was published in London in 1893. This practitioner's "medicine's weak," but his "fees are strong"; he has "killed thousands" and "has no idea what's the matter" with his patient.

(Left) "The Country Infirmary," attributed to Charles Williams, 1813; (above and left) collection, Wellcome Institute Library, London

THE COUNTRY INFIRMARY.

Although the overwhelming bulk of its contents was gathered by Henry Wellcome, it would be erroneous to assume that the library has remained static since its founder's death. Since the time it was first opened to readers in 1949, the library has steadily grown and developed. In addition to rarities acquired as they have become available, such as the previously mentioned 11th-century Anglo-Saxon manuscript, and an ever increasing stock of new publications, important material has been obtained in recent years from other institutions. Outstanding acquisitions include about 45% of the original library of the Medical Society of London, some 24,000 volumes of mostly 18th- and 19th-century books belonging to Britain's Royal Society of Medicine, and the entire 30,000-volume library of the Royal Society of Health. The Medical Society of London's collection provided about 200 manuscript volumes dating from the 12th century onward and also greatly strengthened the Wellcome's holdings of materials from the 15th to the 17th century.

A further example of the library's scope was the establishment in 1979 of a contemporary medical archives center as a permanent unit. Its aim is to encourage and help in the preservation of 20th-century records, documents, and archive collections relating to all aspects of medical care and medical research in Britain, from research that leads to important scientific breakthroughs to fringe and unorthodox medicine.

Those who study in the library (which is not open to the public for casual use or viewing) find accommodation and ambience in the spacious main reading room on two levels. Quiet study bays are provided by jutting bookcases on both floors. Names of the fathers of medicine and their successors through the centuries are inscribed on a frieze that runs beneath the balconies, and an impressive screen carries larger-than-life reproductions of the famed Vesalius 16th-century woodcuts of the musculature of humans. The reading room contains open-access reference books, but the rare books and manuscripts are stored within specially air-conditioned strong rooms in the building and are available to readers on application.

Those whose researches may extend beyond the library find that the Wellcome Building is conveniently situated near the British Library, the Historical Manuscripts Commission, and the Institute of Historical Research. The British Medical Association, the Royal Society of Medicine, the Royal College of Physicians, and the Royal College of Surgeons of England are also in close proximity.

Center for scholarly pursuit. The Wellcome Institute for the History of Medicine, as has been seen, has at its heart the rich resources of a library of exceptional merit. At the same time, it has developed over the past ten years an academic unit and an international center for teaching and research. In 1976 a close association was established between the institute and University College, London. As a result, a broadly based academic program has been forged, including undergraduate, postgraduate, and postdoctoral teaching and a series of symposia, seminars, classes, and lectures for the medical profession, the academic community, and the public. The principal undergraduate activity is a full-time one-year course offering an intercalated bachelor of science (B.Sc.) degree in medical history to third-year medical

Each year the institute sponsors a wide range of symposia, seminars, lectures, and various other programs that are open to the public. A recent exhibition, called "Morbid Cravings: The Emergence of Addiction," was held in conjunction with the Centenary Meeting of the Society for the Study of Addiction. One of the works on display was William Hogarth's engraving "Gin Lane," which depicts a 1750 street scene in a section of London where virtually every fourth house was a gin shop.

Collection, Wellcome Institute Library, London

170

students. Each year a number of postdoctoral research fellows, supported by grants from the Wellcome Trust and other funding bodies, are based at the institute. Many established scholars from all over the world also spend sabbatical leaves working there.

The institute's series of one-day symposia, research seminars, reading classes, and public lectures, which are open to all who are interested in the history of medicine, has gathered great momentum in the past few years. In 1985–86 alone the institute sponsored more than 100 such functions. A sampling of symposia topics in recent years conveys the breadth of interests addressed: "Medical Fringe and Medical Orthodoxy"; "Historical Hospitals: Images from Seven Centuries"; "The Black Death in Cairo (1348–49)"; "Alcoholism in History"; "The Patient's View: Lay Attitudes to Medicine, Disease, and Doctors"; "A Century of Cancer Hospitals"; "Medicine and the Five Senses"; and "Body and Soul: Bible Nurses Among the Poor in Victorian London."

Complementing these programs, exhibitions mounted by the institute are equally varied and recently have included "Morbid Cravings: The Emergence of Addiction," "Islamic Physicians and Scientists," "Five Centuries of Plague in Western Europe," and a major exhibition in 1986–87 to illustrate the contributions to medical and historical medical research of the Wellcome Trust in commemoration of its 50th anniversary.

Additionally, the academic staff of the institute publishes *Medical History*, a quarterly journal concerned with all aspects of the history of medicine from prehistory to the present day. The journal's immense value to medical practitioners and historians alike has given it an international reputation. Also published by the institute is *Current Work in the History of Medicine*, an international bibliography that lists annually over 8,000 books and articles in all major European and Oriental languages.

A clinical museum. Members of the medical and allied professions and senior students of medicine and biology who visit the Wellcome Institute for the History of Medicine will find an additional "bonus" available to

Wellcome Institute Library, London

Those who study in the library find accommodation and ambience in the spacious main reading room, with its larger-than-life reproductions of Vesalius's famous 16th-century woodcuts of the musculature of the human body. For their protection and preservation, rare books and manuscripts are not placed on the open shelves but stored in air-conditioned strong rooms.

The resources at the Wellcome Building on Euston Road are mainly for the use of specialists and professionals; however, the public can view a fascinating display of five historical pharmacies that have been reconstructed in the lobby. One of these is John Bell's Pharmacy of Oxford Street, founded in 1798. The original storefront of the London enterprise, which was dismantled in 1909, was later acquired by Henry Wellcome.

them within the Wellcome Building. This is the Wellcome Tropical Institute Museum, formerly the Wellcome Museum of Medical Science, which was founded by Henry Wellcome in 1914.

The museum is a resource of the Wellcome Tropical Institute, which was established by the Wellcome Trust in 1985 for the study of tropical medicine. Visual representations of nearly every known tropical disease have been assembled. In the early days the museum's holdings were largely restricted to exotic parasitology, epidemic bacteriology, and applied entomology, but now they include the medical disciplines of virology, inherited disorders, nutrition, immunology, cardiology, and oncology as well; the range is ever expanding as the scope of medicine itself expands apace. In the nearly 100 displays, a specific disease or condition is considered in ten aspects: a general introduction, etiology, epidemiology, immunology, pathology, clinical aspects, diagnosis, treatment, prognosis, and prevention—each category illustrated by photographs, charts, maps, diagrams, and other pictorial material. These are supplemented by displays of pathological specimens, examples of drugs used in treatment, and, for example, animals of medical importance to the transmission of a disease or insect vectors such as tsetse flies and mosquitoes. Slides and microscopes are provided at each display as well.

Pharmacies of the past. Although the resources at the Wellcome Building on Euston Road are for the use of specialists and professionals only, an attraction the public can view is on display in the entrance hall: five historical pharmacies that have been meticulously reconstructed.

They include an Italian pharmacy from the 17th century, based on the furnishings and design of the pharmacy of the Hospital of the Santo Spirito in Rome, a hospital that is still in use today. There is a genuine Andalusian pharmacy (*c.* 1790); this Hispano-Mauresque reconstruction was made possible when the whole of the contents and woodwork of the Pontes

172

Pharmacy in Granada, Spain, thought to have been in use since 1492, was purchased by Henry Wellcome in 1928. A third pharmacy, reconstructed from various sources, is a typical English pharmacy, c. 1680. An Arab pharmacy as it could have existed several centuries back, but also as it might exist today, is a gem with its exquisite glass and inlaid mother-of-pearl mosaic work. Fifth is a well-known former London enterprise, John Bell's Pharmacy of Oxford Street (founded in 1798 and dismantled in 1909), which has been rebuilt and can now be seen at the Wellcome Building.

Treasures for the public: sumptuous and unrivaled

Five kilometers (3.1 miles) southeast, on Exhibition Road, South Kensington, is the Wellcome Museum of the History of Medicine, on display to the public in two galleries on the fourth and fifth floors of the national Science Museum. Although the interested visitor will need a full day in which to absorb its fascinating presentation of humanity's progressive mastery of medical science, the material on exhibition is only the tip of the iceberg. Only 3% of the Wellcome Museum's total collection of over 125,000 objects is on display; the vast bulk of material is held in store, cataloged on computer, and available for study by research students and scholars.

Glimpses. The lower gallery of the museum, which was opened in 1980, has been designed to present what its title, "Glimpses of Medical History," implies. The time span covered by meticulously designed dioramas and reconstructions extends from Neolithic trepanning—the use of flints to bore holes in the skull—through Greek, Roman, and Islamic medicine, the Renaissance, and the New World to the beginnings of modern medicine and current medical practice.

The evolution of modern medicine is illustrated with particular effect by nonchronological displays juxtaposing the past and present. For example, Joseph Lister's surgical ward in Glasgow, Scotland, 1868, which contains some of his original equipment and furniture, contrasts with a full-scale operating theater of 1980. There is a diorama showing a 15th-century doctor-patient consultation and, a few displays away, one showing a patient consulting the doctor in 1900. Dentists treating patients are shown in the 1890s, 1930s, and 1980; dramatic differences are seen in the state of dental technology—e.g., sterilization, anesthesia, electricity, drills, and X-ray equipment—not to mention pain suffered by the patient.

Indeed, there is much to fascinate the visitor in *all* the 43 "glimpses," which illustrate medical history in its widest sense. There are models of a military hospital on the Rhine in the 2nd century AD; naval surgery in 1800; a World War I dressing station; childbirth in the 1860s; sight testing as it was done in the 1930s; aids designed to help today's disabled lead fuller lives, showing the application of sophisticated technology; and, in the 1970s, inoculation against smallpox in Ethiopia, where most of the world's last cases of this dread disease were traced. The eradication of smallpox from the face of the globe is considered one of the greatest achievements of medicine in all of time.

Most viewers are caught by surprise to learn that as long as 2,000 years ago cataracts could be treated surgically to prevent blindness. The display

A visitor to the Wellcome Museum of the History of Medicine, located in London's national Science Museum on Exhibition Road, could spend a full day or more absorbing its fascinating presentation of humanity's progressive mastery of the medical arts and sciences. In the lower gallery are "Glimpses of Medical History." Most viewers are surprised to discover that eye cataracts were treated some 2,000 years ago in Asia. A life-size diorama recreates an 11th-century Persian operating room where a surgeon and assistant carry out an "eye-couching" procedure in which the doctor pushes a patient's clouded lens aside with a needle.

The Science Museum, London

of what was known as eye-couching in Persia in the 11th century shows how a surgeon inserts a needle into his patient's eye to push the clouded lens aside. If all went well, vision was restored.

Another Persian display shows the birth of a baby in a high-ranking family in medieval times. A scene celebrating the birth includes an astrolabe, used to determine the Sun's position at the exact moment of birth so that the child's all-important horoscope could be cast.

Medicine as a science and an art. The museum's upper gallery, which is much larger, was opened in 1981. It was designed to enhance for the viewer the displays in the lower gallery, providing an in-depth look at the makings of medical history. A chronological approach has been followed, and here there is far greater emphasis on modern medicine and its development from 1800. Much care has been taken to present medicine as it evolved in its social and scientific settings.

The pre-1100 section portrays medicine in nonliterate tribal societies that left no written records. The collection of artifacts associated with tribal medicine is a particular strength of the museum. For example, a wide assortment of charms and divining objects reflect the practices of diagnosis and treatment by the summoning of supernatural powers.

Other ancient cultures represented are those of China, India, Egypt, Greece, Rome, and the Islamic world. Of ancient China one learns that opium was used as an important therapeutic drug; that acupuncture needles were used to "cure" as early as 2700 BC; that male doctors, according to Chinese etiquette, could not examine female patients—rather than disrobing for examination, women had to point to ivory dolls to reveal the location of their symptoms for the doctor to make his diagnosis and prescribe a treatment; and that the Oriental practice of foot binding was so widespread that for centuries females in China grew up virtually unable to walk.

Medicine from 1100 to 1800 traces the close relationship between medicine and religious practices, the prevalent scourges leprosy and plague,

The galleries juxtapose the past with the present in order to create a true sense of the evolution of modern medicine. Joseph Lister's surgical ward in Glasgow, Scotland, in 1868, containing some of the original equipment and furniture, was considered modern for its time. Lister revolutionized surgery by eliminating the common infections ("hospital disease") from which many surgical patients died. Lister tried new dressings for surgical wounds and used carbolic acid to aid the healing process and prevent infection. This display is near one of a full-scale operating theater of 1980 showing an open-heart procedure. Viewers thus gain a true picture of the stunning progress that has occurred in just a century.

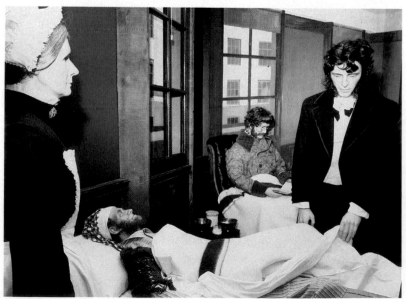

The Science Museum, London

medical knowledge derived from the introduction of dissection, the invention of early scientific instruments, and increasing concern with health matters in the 18th century.

The 19th-century exhibits present all the major scientific and medical advances of that intensive period of investigation and innovation. Among them are René-T.-H. Laënnec's invention of that all-important diagnostic tool the stethoscope, elucidation of the nature and structure of cells by Theodor Schwann and Rudolf Virchow, the germ theory demonstrated by Pasteur and Robert Koch, and hospital medicine following the introduction of anesthesia and antisepsis. There are sections, too, dealing with public health, infant care, and dentistry.

Medicine from 1900 to the present day occupies well over a quarter of the gallery, reflecting the remarkable rate of progress in the second half of this century. An introductory section on the growth of the British Health Service is followed by a large area devoted to 20th-century hospital medicine and its many specialities. A further section focuses on health and the community— *e.g.,* occupational medicine, infant welfare, and contraception, including a display of early condoms. There are displays illustrating the development of laboratory medicine, many of the subsequent notable discoveries made in labs worldwide, and current drug research. Two other sections present special topics—the influence of war on advances in medicine, and the status of medicine and the unique health needs of the third world.

Rare treasures. In a gallery that exhibits no fewer than 3,500 items, it is difficult to highlight those of special interest or rarity. Suffice it to say that nowhere else in such a concentrated space is it possible to view such treasures: the actual vaccine points prepared by Jenner along with a piece

The eradication of smallpox on a global scale is considered one of the greatest achievements in all of medicine. The diorama above shows smallpox inoculation in Ethiopia in the late 1970s, where the world's last cases were traced.

175

of horn from the cow he used to extract cowpox for human inoculation; George Washington's denture; Napoleon's monogrammed toothbrush with silver-gilt handle and horsehair bristles; microscopes used by Pasteur; a medicine chest used by David Livingstone on his last journey (1866); Florence Nightingale's dainty beaded moccasins. Objects of a more macabre ilk are here, too: skeletons from a 14th-century Danish leper cemetery; a 16th-century Peruvian mummy; 19th-century shrunken heads from South America; a collection of bladder stones; and trepanned skulls from Neolithic burials.

Behind the scenes. As mentioned earlier, the museum has rich resources available for specialized study. There are, for example, 1,600 microscopes from the 17th century to the present day, about 10,000 microscopic slides, over 40,000 surgical instruments from Roman times to the present day, 7,000 pairs of spectacles, and 10,000 botanical specimens that are known or are presumed to have medicinal properties, from all over the world. There are large holdings in medical and pharmaceutical ceramics and glassware, including no fewer than 1,200 pieces of Italian majolica of the very highest quality and around 1,500 examples of Roman and Islamic glass.

The museum operates an extensive loan service in Britain and overseas. Exemplifying this are plans to equip an Elizabethan pharmacy at Hall's Croft, Stratford-upon-Avon, the original 16th-century home of Shakespeare's physician and son-in-law. Also, the museum provides an annual exhibition based at Addenbrooke's Hospital, Cambridge, for the benefit of university medical students. Other loans have been made to Malaysia, Japan, and Australia.

Currently, the Wellcome Museum is planning a third gallery that will display the very latest medical techniques and discoveries in the ever evolving, ever exciting fields of medicine and health care.

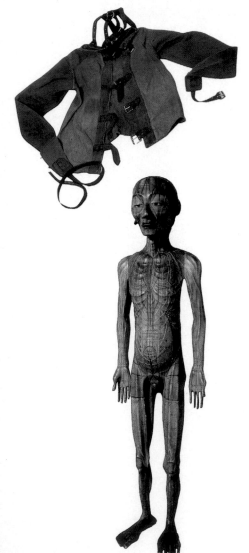

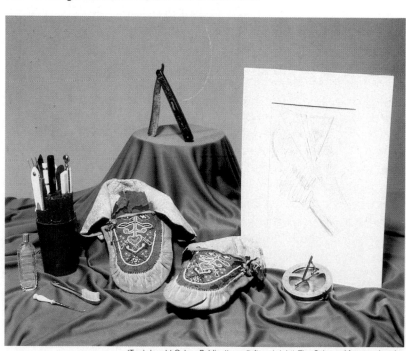

(Top) Jarrold Colour Publications; (left and right) The Science Museum, London

Medicine: Sir Henry's heir

When Henry Wellcome died in 1936, he bequeathed his sole ownership of the Wellcome Foundation Ltd., which incorporated his pharmaceutical companies, research laboratories, and historical collections, to trustees whom he nominated in his will. He stipulated that the income they would derive from the company should be used to support contemporary medical and historical research worldwide. Of the terms of Wellcome's will, the trustees wrote in a letter to *The Lancet* in January 1937: "We believe this to be the first example . . . of a testamentary disposition by which the whole of the profits from a great manufacturing and trading organisation . . . are permanently dedicated to the advancement of knowledge for the general benefit of mankind."

The Wellcome Trust, the name by which the trustees became subsequently known, has thus had responsibility for the past 50 years for what are now known as the Wellcome Institute and the Wellcome Museum. The trust transferred Wellcome's historical museum collection on permanent loan to the Science Museum in 1976, generously providing substantial seed money to cover the costs of transfer and cataloging and to assist in setting up the first, lower gallery. The reasoning behind this move was twofold. First, the Science Museum had both the facilities and the expertise to assess and catalog the vast amount of material, which had largely remained in store in its original packing cases and was poorly documented. Second, in a museum that has more than three million visitors a year viewing its four hectares (ten acres) of gallery space, the public could both enjoy and learn from a selection of objects, as Henry Wellcome intended. At the same time, the Science Museum could fulfill a further aim of Wellcome—to offer the serious student material for research by having all the material accessible.

The Wellcome Trust, which now owns 75% of the shares of the Wellcome company, is Britain's largest endowed charitable trust supporting medical research and plays a significant role both in Britain and overseas, particularly in the tropics. In 1985–86 it dispensed £40 million in support of medical research and research in the history of medicine.

The trust celebrated its 50th anniversary in 1986–87 with a series of events that included an exhibition, "Backing the Future—The Wellcome Trust 1936–1986," at the Science Museum, publication of a history of the trust, *Physic and Philanthropy*, and a film on its activities. Recognition of the trust's vital role in funding medical research was accorded by 11 British universities, including Oxford, Cambridge, and Edinburgh, which held symposia and exhibitions illustrating research work conducted at their institutions under the auspices of the Wellcome Trust.

A highlight of the celebrations was a visit to the Wellcome Building on Dec. 4, 1986, by Queen Elizabeth II and Prince Philip, the duke of Edinburgh, who toured the library, the tropical institute museum, and an exhibition featuring current research projects supported by the trust.

The trust enters its sixth decade in the knowledge that through its continuing support of research into medicine—modern and historical—it is conscientiously meeting, and with ever increasing effect, the expressed wishes of its remarkable and enormously generous originator, Sir Henry Wellcome.

When Henry Wellcome died in 1936, his immense holdings were turned over to trustees. Although during his lifetime he had neither the time nor the manpower to collate, catalog, and house his prized books, manuscripts, artifacts, and other acquisitions, both the Wellcome Institute for the History of Medicine and the public museum have grown steadily under the guidance of the Wellcome Trust. The institute has established a contemporary medical archives center and, through the Wellcome Tropical Institute, is supporting research into tropical diseases. At the same time, the library continues to acquire valuable resources, and the museum is expanding; presently a third gallery is planned that will reflect the very latest in medical accomplishments. As the Wellcome Trust entered its sixth decade in 1986, it could well be said that it was indeed fulfilling its benefactor's dreams.

177

Multiple Sclerosis:
The Puzzle and the Promise

by Donna Bergen, M.D.

Margaret M. first consulted her doctor about some puzzling symptoms shortly before her marriage. She was 24 at the time. She complained of a numb, tingling feeling in her left hand and said that several times she had inadvertently dropped objects she had been holding in that hand. The doctor examined her carefully and could find no abnormalities. They agreed that Margaret might be suffering from "premarital jitters," but she was not especially relieved by this diagnosis. She went home feeling vaguely uneasy and dissatisfied. But it seemed that the doctor had been right after all. By the honeymoon all of the young woman's symptoms had vanished. She continued to feel well until after the birth of her first child, three years later. She then consulted the physician with a different set of symptoms: her balance was poor, and she had fallen twice. In addition, strange things were happening to her vision; colors seemed dull, and she had difficulty reading fine print. She waited three weeks for an appointment with the doctor, and by the time of the examination, her visual acuity was 20/20—normal—and her balance was fine. The symptoms were again ascribed to stress, this time "new parent nerves." Margaret was glad to be better but was profoundly disturbed by these "psychosomatic" symptoms, always having considered herself a psychologically stable and healthy person.

Margaret M. is now 32. After enjoying good health for another five years, she recently returned to her doctor once again, complaining that her left leg was weak and dragging and that she was seeing double. The doctor examined her, found some abnormalities, and ordered some tests. The result: a diagnosis of multiple sclerosis and the presumption that Margaret's disease had actually started eight years earlier, when the symptoms appeared in her left hand.

This story could well be true. In fact, it is not the account of any single person; Margaret M. is actually an amalgam of many and typifies some of the problems faced by the individual, usually a previously healthy young adult, who develops multiple sclerosis (MS). The story also reflects the problems commonly faced by the physician called upon to diagnose the condition. It is a reminder of the unpredictability of the course of MS and even of MS's frequently benign nature. Further, Margaret's story suggests the frustration of both patient and doctor as they vainly search for a physical explanation for symptoms that are puzzling, evanescent, and elusive.

MS yesterday and today

Multiple sclerosis is a disease of the central nervous system that was first described by the great French neurologist Jean-Martin Charcot in the latter half of the 19th century. In his neurological clinic at the Salpêtrière Hospital

Donna Bergen, M.D., is Associate Professor of Neurological Sciences at Rush Medical College and Director of the Electroencephalography Laboratory, Rush-Presbyterian-St. Luke's Medical Center, Chicago.

(Opposite page) Color-enhanced magnetic resonance scan of an MS patient; photograph, The Cleveland Clinic Foundation

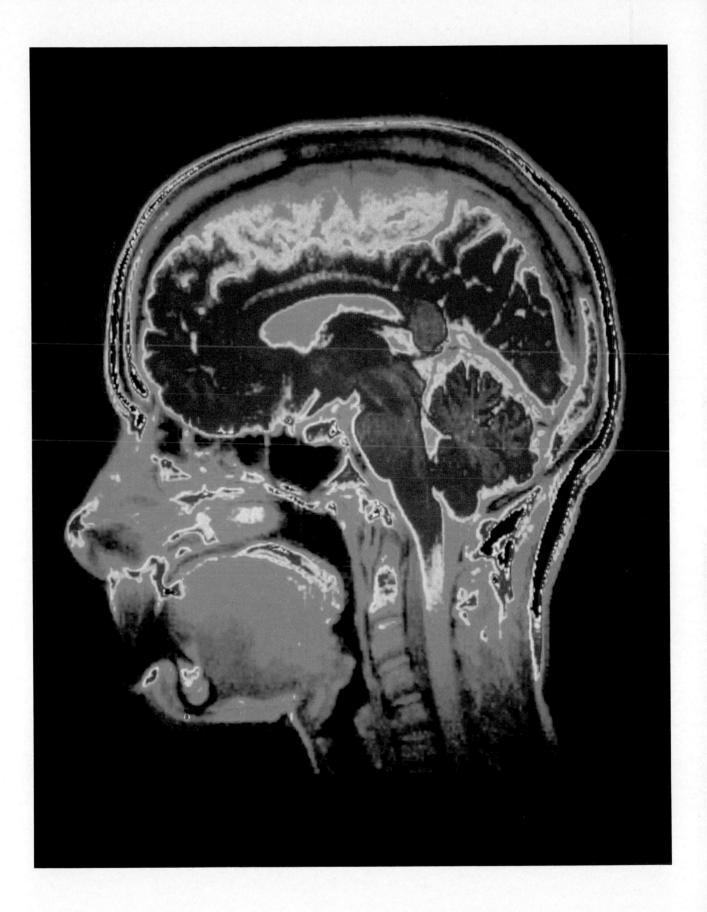

Photographs,
Cedric S. Raine, Albert Einstein College of Medicine

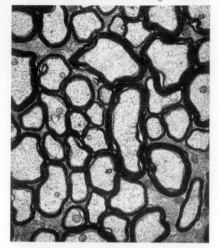

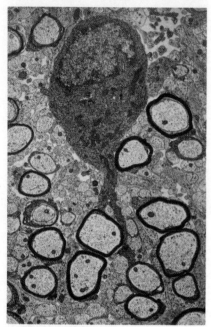

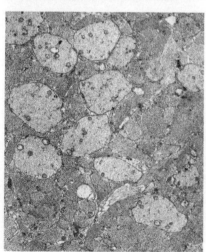

in Paris, Charcot examined the victims of madness, mental retardation, and degenerative physical disease, both while they lived and after they died. Out of a welter of diseases—paralysis agitans (Parkinson's disease), Little's disease (cerebral palsy), general paresis of the insane (dementia and paralysis caused by syphilis), and other neurological and psychiatric disorders—he discerned a group of patients who shared a diverse but characteristic group of symptoms and physical signs. At autopsy all of them were found to have the same scattered plaques, or lesions, in the brain and spinal cord. Charcot called the condition *sclérose en plaques,* after the hardened (sclerotic) patches he found in the autopsied tissue. English physicians sometimes call the disease disseminated sclerosis; in the U.S. it is known as multiple sclerosis.

In Charcot's day treatment of multiple sclerosis varied from herbal remedies to strychnine, a stimulant as well as a potent poison. The wide variety of treatments still being tried today testifies to the unsatisfactory nature of all of them, but continuing insights into the nature of multiple sclerosis are offering exciting new therapeutic possibilities based on a rational appreciation of the mechanisms and probable cause—or causes—of the disorder.

A perplexing condition

Considering the frequent dismissal of early symptoms of MS as psychogenic, it is perhaps ironic that one of Charcot's other major contributions to clinical neurology was his vivid description of hysterical or psychosomatic illnesses that mimicked organic neurological disorders. This is not to imply that Charcot himself, any more than the modern neurologist, had difficulty in distinguishing the *severely* afflicted victims of MS from people with purely psychiatric conditions. The modern practitioner, however, is often faced with an ambiguous or even insoluble problem: how to differentiate the protean, sometimes fleeting, occasionally bizarre manifestations of early multiple sclerosis from the equally "creative" symptoms of the individual suffering from psychosomatic complaints.

Once the diagnosis of MS has been made, because of the frightening implications of the disease and its variable course, the physician is presented with an even more difficult question: Should the patient be told? A lot of passion, prejudice, and personal anguish have gone into answering this question, from patients and physicians alike. As in most hotly debated questions in medicine, those who rigidly adhere to either extreme do so at the cost of causing needless suffering to patients who are either sheltered from a truth that would save them from soul-wrenching uncertainty—and even fears of insanity—or confronted with a terrifying vision of disability and deterioration that may never come to pass.

In today's medical practice, openness and frankness are the rule rather than the exception. Nevertheless, few would argue with the common sense and compassion of the doctor who does not share his or her "hunch" that the transient symptoms reported by an apparently healthy young adult are most consistent with a diagnosis of multiple sclerosis, even though the patient has already experienced a complete return to health. For the MS patient who may develop serious or long-lasting physical complaints,

180

however, few physicians nowadays would deliberately conceal the correct diagnosis without a specific, serious reason for doing so.

A demyelinating disease

Multiple sclerosis is a neurological disease that attacks the central nervous system—that is, the brain, the spinal cord, and the connection between them, called the brain stem. The characteristic plaques of multiple sclerosis are small, scarred patches that range in size from 1¼ centimeters (½ inch) or so in diameter to pinpoint lesions not visible to the naked eye. There are usually many plaques scattered throughout the central nervous system.

Viewed under a microscope, the plaques demonstrate an important feature. The nerve cells (neurons) and their threadlike extensions (axons) appear intact in most plaques. However, when a special stain is applied to the tissue, it can be seen that the insulating material of the axons, called myelin, is missing or defective in every plaque, a finding that puts multiple sclerosis into the category of the primary demyelinating diseases.

Myelin forms a sheath that "insulates" nerve fibers and facilitates the flow of nerve impulses. It is an inert, fatty and proteinaceous material that is produced by special cells, the oligodendrocytes. In addition to myelination of axons, oligodendrocytes probably also play a complex nutritive and sustaining role for the axons. It is the myelin, and perhaps the oligodendrocytes themselves, that is thought to be primarily attacked in the multiple sclerosis process. When this happens, the normal electrical conduction of nerve impulses is disrupted, and axons themselves may eventually wither. These cellular deteriorations form the basis of the numbness, incoordination, paralysis, visual disturbances, and other clinical symptoms of the disease.

The disease process in multiple sclerosis is characterized by damage to the nerve axons of the central nervous system (the brain, brain stem, and spinal cord). Myelin, a fatty material, sheathes and insulates healthy axons and facilitates nerve transmission. It is produced by special cells called oligodendrocytes. In a person with MS, the myelin is attacked by cells of the individual's immune system that gradually "eat away" this vital protective coating. This process, known as demyelination, is illustrated in the drawing below. Photomicrographs on the opposite page show normal nerve axons with myelin coating intact (top); a normal oligodendrocyte in the process of producing myelin (middle); and a section in which both myelin and oligodendrocytes have deteriorated, leaving bare axons surrounded by scar tissue (bottom).

(Below) Adapted from an illustration by Michael Rowe, *Discover* magazine, May 1985

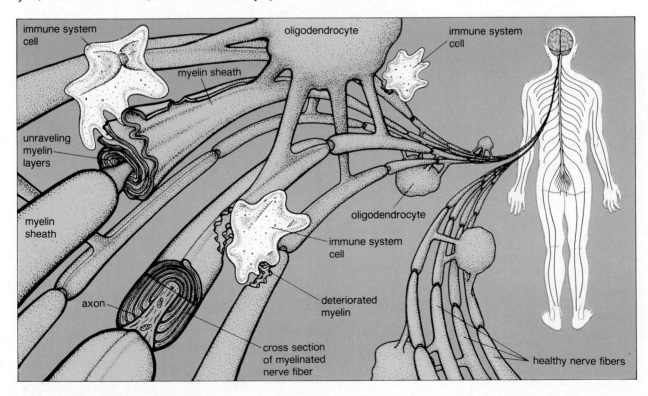

immune system cell

oligodendrocyte

immune system cell

myelin sheath

unraveling myelin layers

myelin sheath

oligodendrocyte

immune system cell

axon

deteriorated myelin

cross section of myelinated nerve fiber

healthy nerve fibers

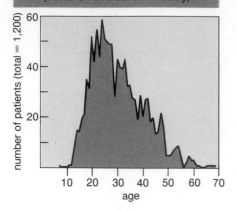

Age at onset of multiple sclerosis
(based on one Canadian study)

A capricious course

Today multiple sclerosis is one of the commonest causes of physical disability in young adults—it is a relatively common disease, with a prevalence of about one in 2,500 people in Europe and the northern U.S. It occurs less often in South America, Africa, and Asia. (More will be said later about the pattern of geographic distribution of MS and the possible significance of these findings.) It is more common in Caucasians than in blacks, even when groups living in the same area (*e.g.,* the United States) are compared.

Most multiple sclerosis typically begins in young adulthood, with incidence peaking around 30 years of age. Onset well into the sixth decade, however, has been reported. The beginning of the disease may be insidious and unalarming—tingling and numbness in the legs or slight clumsiness of a hand, as experienced by the fictitious patient described earlier. Occasionally the disorder announces itself more dramatically, with severe signs of acute spinal cord dysfunction, including paralysis of the legs and loss of bladder control.

What may happen next is unpredictable. Even the most appalling symptoms may go into remission within a matter of days or weeks. On the other hand, abnormal physical signs may progress slowly but inexorably, causing increasing disability. One of the most disconcerting features of the disease is this apparently capricious course. Even early remission does not ensure safety from subsequent episodes—one of the most common patterns of MS consists of repeated bouts of symptoms, or relapses, usually of varying lengths and at varying intervals, leaving varying degrees of permanent disability in their wake.

The diagnostic evidence

Although the scattered demyelinating lesions of MS in the nervous system produce a wide variety of symptoms and neurological dysfunction, some complaints are more typical of the disease than others. For example, in a common initial episode the victim may experience loss of vision in one or even both eyes, a condition called optic neuritis. Recovery of normal vision

within a few days or weeks is usual but not universal. It should be noted that not every case of optic neuritis predicts the subsequent development of multiple sclerosis.

Loss of balance is also common in multiple sclerosis. It may be accompanied by other signs of involvement of spinal or brain stem axons that serve the functions of coordination; these signs include incoordination or tremor of the limbs and slurred, thickened speech.

Sensation can be involved in several ways. Tingling or numbness in various body parts is common. More disabling is loss of the ability to detect the position of the limbs so that walking is difficult, particularly in the dark. Objects inside a pocket or purse may not be identifiable by touch.

Often the most obvious symptom of MS is loss of muscle power, ranging from slight fatigability of the muscles to complete paralysis. If paralysis is severe and chronic, it may be accompanied by immobility, or fixation, of joints, muscle spasms, and deformity of the limbs. Pronounced spinal cord involvement can mean impairment of urinary bladder or sexual function. Again, all of these problems can and do occur in dozens of other neurological disorders.

To make the diagnostic problem even more difficult, there is no single, reliable test for multiple sclerosis and, particularly in its early stages, the disease may cause clinical symptoms and signs that cannot be distinguished from those of other neurological disorders. Since there are other demyelinating diseases and since multiple sclerosis affects parts of the nervous system also attacked by other diseases, a definite early diagnosis, particularly during or after the initial bout, may be virtually impossible. Even well into the course of the disease, most neurologists continually and repeatedly scrutinize the diagnostic evidence to make sure that another disorder has not been erroneously mislabeled as multiple sclerosis, because the protean symptoms of the disease will continue to fit the clinical profile of many other disorders of the central nervous system, some of which demand completely different therapy.

Nevertheless, multiple sclerosis has certain broad clinical characteristics seen in no other disease, and if these are present, along with typical laboratory findings, the diagnosis can eventually be made with reasonable certainty. These clinical characteristics arise from the scattered distribution of the many sclerotic plaques and the apparent ability of the plaques to undergo full or partial healing. Symptoms therefore can originate from more than one site in the central nervous system and can go away as unpredictably as they arrive. Thus, the clinical diagnosis of multiple sclerosis is sometimes said to rest upon the occurrence of lesions that are "disseminated in time and in space." There have been attempts to increase and quantify diagnostic certainty, using scoring systems based on a combination of clinical evidence (symptoms and physical signs), spinal fluid assay and other laboratory tests, and diagnostic imaging techniques.

No "ultimate" test

Neurological laboratory tests used in the past were not always helpful in diagnosing multiple sclerosis. In fact, the electroencephalogram (EEG; a

The peak incidence of MS is in the early adult years, when important decisions are being made about the future. For many the course of life is inevitably altered. For each, however, the impact of MS is different. Jimmie Heuga (opposite page, left), a bronze medal winner on the U.S. Olympic ski team in 1964, was diagnosed with MS in 1970. Although he could not continue to compete, Heuga was determined to maintain a maximum level of physical activity. He established the Jimmie Heuga Center for the Reanimation of the Physically Challenged, Avon, Colorado, which helps people with MS and similar disorders cope with their disabilities. Cellist Jacqueline DuPré and her pianist-conductor husband, Daniel Barenboim (opposite page, right), were internationally known musicians when only in their late twenties. By the time DuPré was 30, however, her career as a performer had been tragically ended by MS. A more fortunate patient, marine biologist Richard Radtke (below), has been able to pursue his vocation despite the disease. In 1983, with the help of a National Science Foundation grant, he was able to make an expedition to Antarctica.

(Opposite page, top) Adapted from George C. Ebers et al., "A Population-Based Study of Multiple Sclerosis in Twins," *The New England Journal of Medicine*, vol. 315 (Dec. 25, 1986), pp. 1638–42; (opposite page, bottom left) Barry Staver/*People Weekly* © 1986 Time Inc.; (opposite page, bottom right) Clive Barda/*People Weekly* © 1979 Time, Inc.

Richard Radtke, Hawaii Institute of Marine Biology, University of Hawaii

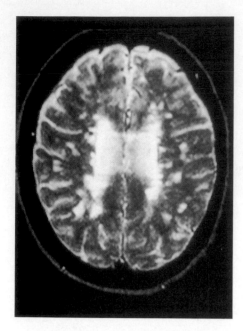

Because there is no single, reliable test for diagnosing MS, the physician must rely on a combination of clinical features— e.g., muscle weakness and problems with balance, coordination, and vision— along with diagnostic tests that are of only limited value. A relatively new imaging technique, magnetic resonance imaging (MRI), has proved invaluable in the diagnosis of this and other neurological disorders. MRI, which combines a high-powered magnet, radio frequency waves, and computerized imaging methods, produces astonishingly detailed pictures of the brain. Despite its formidable appearance, the MRI scanner (opposite page, left) is noninvasive and does not expose the patient to any X-rays. While the patient undergoes the scanning process, physicians and technicians in an adjacent area monitor the information on a video screen (opposite page, right). An MRI scan of the brain of an MS patient (above) clearly shows the scarred lesions, or plaques, characteristic of the disease.

recording of electrical activity in the brain), the skull X-ray, and the lumbar puncture, or spinal tap (to examine spinal fluid for abnormal cells and to measure glucose and protein levels), were notoriously unhelpful since in most MS victims such tests either were normal or showed very nonspecific abnormalities. Special X-rays of the back called myelograms, which employ a dye, or contrast medium, were often done in patients with symptoms of spinal cord pathology, and therefore possible multiple sclerosis, but today this test is being increasingly replaced by the computed tomographic (CT) scan and other imaging methods as a means of ruling out tumors and other types of spinal cord disorder. Nevertheless, even the CT scan of the head, so helpful in the diagnosis of other neurological diseases, shows typical plaques in only a minority of patients with multiple sclerosis.

About 13 years ago the availability of inexpensive, powerful microprocessors spurred the development of a computerized test of nerve, spinal cord, and brain electrical function called evoked potentials. Evoked potentials testing measures electrical activity in the brain, but it differs from the EEG in that the nerve impulses are deliberately elicited by means of sensory stimuli—a flash of light, a tap on the skin, a sudden noise. The electrical responses to these stimuli are processed by computer and plotted on curves that show how well the patient's nervous system receives and processes sensory information. The particular value of evoked potentials testing is that it can reveal abnormalities of sensory system function where the most thorough and careful physical examination has failed to detect any dysfunction. Patients with MS often show abnormalities of evoked potentials in parts of the central nervous system not causing obvious clinical symptoms or signs.

In recent years biochemical tests of spinal fluid have also become more varied and complex, especially those that evaluate immune activity within the central nervous system. Some of these tests are proving to be quite sensitive indicators of multiple sclerosis, although none is specific enough to be thought of as the ultimate "multiple sclerosis test."

Finally, advances in medical imaging have revealed new aspects of the disease and have proved to be of invaluable diagnostic help. Magnetic resonance imaging (MRI; also called nuclear magnetic resonance) is an entirely new method of looking inside the body of a living person, painlessly and without the use of radiation. Combining a high-powered magnet, radio frequency waves, and computerized imaging methods, the MRI scan produces an astonishingly detailed picture of the brain stem and spinal cord, showing normal and abnormal tissues. Typically, in an MS patient the MRI scan reveals many more lesions than would be predicted on the basis of clinical grounds. Although other types of lesions may look the same as a plaque on an MRI scan, the characteristic distribution of the plaques in MS, their multiplicity, and the clinical context usually enable the physician to make a firm distinction between MS and other, clinically similar disorders.

An infectious origin?

What causes multiple sclerosis? The question looms stubbornly in the path of those seeking effective treatment for the disorder, and the answer remains elusive. Observations of the disease's behavior have channeled researchers into various lines of investigation.

For some time it appeared that multiple sclerosis might be a simple infectious illness, although no infectious agent (bacteria or virus) could ever be found. Nonetheless, in many ways multiple sclerosis looked like an infection: certain white blood cells typical of inflammation were abundant in those plaques that appeared to be associated with acute symptoms, and lymphocytes, a type of white blood cell associated with immunity, were often found in the spinal fluid of MS patients during exacerbations of the disease. The lack of a single, identifiable infectious agent was bothersome to investigators, but new and unusual infectious agents were being discovered, such as "slow" viruses and prions, which had eluded traditional laboratory identification methods and which were capable of causing prolonged disease after very long incubation periods. In addition, scientists have long known of the existence of certain viruses that attack the myelin-producing oligodendrocyte. The JC virus, for instance, produces progressive multifocal leukoencephalopathy, a rare but fatal brain disease, by infecting oligodendrocytes and causing widespread demyelination even more extensive than that produced by MS but clearly similar in nature.

In the 1960s new laboratory techniques began to uncover convincing evidence of unusual infections in multiple sclerosis patients. Certain antibodies, proteins made by the immune system specifically to destroy invading organisms, were found to exist in increased numbers in these patients and were particularly abundant in their spinal fluid. Among the antibodies found in MS patients were antibodies against the measles virus. Other MS patients had high levels of antibodies against the distemper virus, which causes demyelinating disease in dogs. Subsequently some surveys found that MS victims were more likely than nonvictims to own small domestic dogs—an observation that raised the possibility that the humans had caught the disease from their pets.

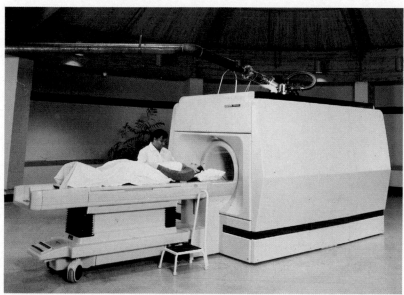
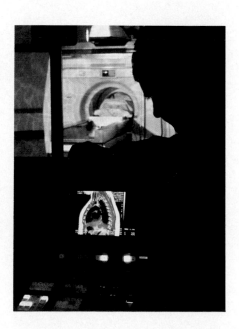

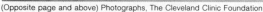
(Opposite page and above) Photographs, The Cleveland Clinic Foundation

While the disease process in MS is fairly well understood, the cause—or causes— of the disorder, effective treatment, and a possible cure remain a mystery. Epidemiological factors add to the puzzle. MS occurs more often in the northern U.S., Canada, and northern Europe than in Africa, India, or South America. This kind of regional distribution is not uncommon in diseases of infectious origin; thus, some scientists see the geographical pattern of MS as strong evidence that it must be an infectious disease. Perhaps even more intriguing is the fact that among groups of people who have emigrated from areas of high incidence to areas of low incidence— for example, European Jews who have immigrated to Israel—people who moved after the age of 15 have continued to show a high risk of the disease, while those who moved in childhood assume the lower risk associated with their new home. This pattern of disease is consistent with the theory that an infection acquired early in life causes the subsequent development of MS.

For every argument for a purely infectious origin of multiple sclerosis, however, another argument sprang up against it. Other surveys pursuing the dog-ownership theory, for example, found no disproportionate numbers of dogs in the households of multiple sclerosis victims; *i.e.,* MS patients were no more likely to have pet dogs than were members of the population at large. Repeated painstaking examination of multiple sclerosis plaques, by means of electron microscopy powerful enough to reveal individual virus particles, disclosed no infectious organisms in the plaques. Careful scrutiny of spinal fluid showed the presence of antibodies to an assortment of viruses, not just to measles or distemper, in many MS patients. Finally, the relapsing and remitting course of the disease always presented an obstacle to an infectious theory, since most infectious illnesses occur once and either go away or cause steadily progressive injury.

The lessons of epidemiology

Because multiple sclerosis is a relatively common disorder, it has been possible for researchers to examine large groups of patients in an attempt to characterize the disease. The study of the epidemiology of MS has, in fact, added to the lively controversies over the cause of the disease. Looking at large groups of people, for example, has made it clear to investigators that a person who has a close relative with multiple sclerosis has a higher chance of acquiring the disease than does a person without such a relative. Assuming that many of the affected family members shared physical space as children or adults, such an observation could be interpreted as an argument in favor of an infectious origin. On the other hand, it could just as well be used to support the theories that point to environmental influences or genetic factors.

Worldwide population studies have revealed large differences in the incidence of multiple sclerosis from place to place. Some areas have a high incidence of MS—for example, Scotland, England, northern Europe,

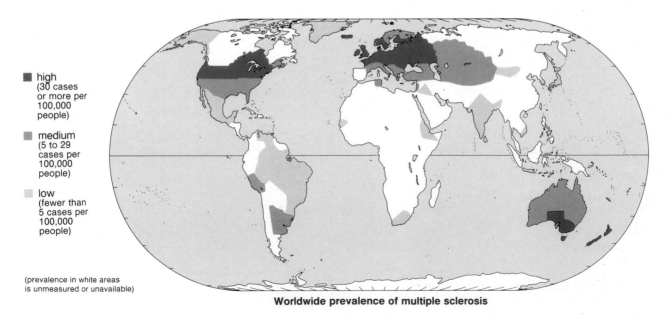

high
(30 cases
or more per
100,000
people)

medium
(5 to 29
cases per
100,000
people)

low
(fewer than
5 cases per
100,000
people)

(prevalence in white areas
is unmeasured or unavailable)

Worldwide prevalence of multiple sclerosis

Canada, and the northern United States. Other places have a very low incidence—for example, Africa, India, and South America. Infectious diseases often have such a regional distribution. Furthermore, some studies have demonstrated that where there have been large population shifts, as in the immigration of European Jews to Israel (from a high-risk area to a low-risk area), people who moved after the age of 15 continued to show a high risk of the disease, whereas those who moved during childhood continued to show a low risk. This pattern of incidence would occur if an infection acquired early in life causes MS to develop later, and it is consistent with the theory that postulates an infectious agent with a long incubation period.

Other population studies also appear to be consistent with an infectious, presumably viral, origin for the disease. The Faeroe Islands, a group of islands in the north Atlantic, for example, were found to harbor virtually no multiple sclerosis until British occupation troops landed there in 1940. The subsequent appearance of MS in some of the islanders, about six years later, seemed consistent with the theory of exposure to an infectious disease with an unusually long but precisely defined incubation period.

The intriguing phenomenon of "clustering"

The occasional reports of "clustering" of multiple sclerosis cases in relatively small areas is another intriguing aspect of the uneven geographical distribution of the disease. For example, observers in Key West, Florida, cite a local incidence of multiple sclerosis that is 40 times what would be expected in a randomly selected U.S. population of the same size in the same latitude. Other "clusters" of MS cases have been identified in small towns in Ohio and Massachusetts. Among the theories put forth to explain these high-incidence areas is that the population has been exposed to an infectious organism or a harmful substance in the environment. Infectious diseases certainly can cause local "outbreaks"; so can environmental toxins. However, the theory that MS clusters may be the result of exposure to nerve toxins is not borne out by other evidence and, like other speculations based on an infectious origin, theories that involve clustering fail to explain why only certain individuals are susceptible to the disease.

Furthermore, it should be pointed out that some clustering of cases is predictable on simple statistical grounds. In other words, one would not expect all cases of multiple sclerosis in the United States to be distributed in a perfectly even fashion throughout the country. To illustrate: one in 30 houses, or about 3%, in a particular city may be painted yellow, yet an observer might notice that of the ten houses on one particular block, three happen to be yellow—yielding a rate of 30% for that block. That is not particularly surprising, though, and very little can be concluded from it.

Genetic factors

Not all epidemiological studies of MS support the idea of a simple infectious origin. Studies of twins, for example, lend credence to the notion that genetics also plays a part in the disease. In some twins studied, only one twin had MS; in other pairs both twins were afflicted. MS was found to occur more often in monozygotic, or identical, twins than in heterozygotic, or

Selected studies of MS in twins		
	identical twin pairs	
date of study	total number	number concordant (%)
1966	39	9 (23.1)
1968	51	15 (29.4)
1978	5	1 (20.0)
1980	12	6 (50.0)
1982	22	8 (36.3)
1986	27	7 (25.9)
total	156	46 (29.5)
	fraternal twin pairs	
date of study	total number	number concordant (%)
1966	29	6 (20.7)
1968	56	5 (08.9)
1978	4	0 (00.0)
1980	12	2 (16.7)
1982	29	3 (10.3)
1986	43	1 (02.3)
total	173	17 (09.8)

Twin studies of MS show that the concordance rate (percentage of twin pairs in which both twins are affected by the disease) is higher in monozygotic, or identical, twins than in heterozygotic, or fraternal, twins. These studies lend credence to the theory that genetics must at least play a part in MS since shared childhood environments—including exposure to the same infections—would not result in a notable difference in MS incidence in the two types of twins.

Adapted from George C. Ebers et al., "A Population-Based Study of Multiple Sclerosis in Twins," *The New England Journal of Medicine*, vol. 315 (Dec. 25, 1986), pp. 1638–42

Nicole Le Douarin, Institut d'Embryologie,
Centre National de la Recherche Scientifique, France

*Finding or creating an animal model of
a disease can be crucial to understanding
the disease process in humans. One team
of researchers, exploring autoimmune
responses, grafted quail embryo nervous
system tissue onto chick embryos.
Although apparently healthy upon
hatching, the quail-chick chimeras went
on to develop a neurological syndrome
very much like MS, apparently as a result
of immune system rejection of the grafted
neural tissue. By the time the
bird is a month old, its wings are
completely paralyzed (above).*

fraternal, twins. Monozygotic twins have exactly the same chromosomal or genetic makeup in their cells; whatever physical differences exist between them are the result of different experiences or influences occurring during their lives. Heterozygotic twins, on the other hand, are genetically no more similar than any other siblings are to one another. The twin studies of MS indicate that genetics must play a role in the disease, since shared childhood environments (exposure to the same infections, for example) would not result in a notable difference in MS occurrence in the two types of twins.

In addition, the incidence of MS in women is almost twice that in men. All women differ from all men in possessing two X chromosomes rather than an X and a Y chromosome, again suggesting a genetic component in the disorder. Further evidence for a genetic element in the causation of multiple sclerosis lies in the discovery that all humans have certain gene combinations having to do with immune functions, much in the way people have different blood types. These genes, called human leukocyte antigens (HLA), have been named, and it is possible to "type" anyone in this way. When patients with multiple sclerosis were examined for these genes, more people with the gene type HLA-B7/DR2 were found than occur in a healthy population. Interestingly, this gene type is particularly common in people living in geographical regions known to be high-risk areas for multiple sclerosis, such as northern Europe, and is rare in low-risk areas, such as Africa. Not every MS patient has the HLA-B7/DR2 type, but having that gene does appear to increase one's chances of developing the disease. In addition, a second gene type, called HLA-B8/DR7, is underrepresented in multiple sclerosis patients, as though it is harder to get the disorder if that gene is present. Finally, people with a third gene type, HLA-B8/DR3, who do have multiple sclerosis tend to have particularly severe disease.

Role of the immune system

The list of diseases found to spring from abnormalities of various parts of the immune system is growing constantly. Many of these disorders are the consequence of the misidentification of some of the body's own tissues as foreign and thus subject to attack and destruction by the immune system. This category, known as autoimmune diseases, includes myasthenia gravis (a neuromuscular disease), some forms of thyroid dysfunction, and possibly systemic lupus erythematosus (a disease of the connective tissues).

One way to create an autoimmune disease in the laboratory is to inject a foreign substance, usually a protein that is similar in molecular structure to some normally occurring body protein, into an animal. In some cases the immune system, mobilized to destroy the foreign substance, will also mistakenly attack "native" structures as well, causing disease. When researchers isolated one of the proteins that constitute myelin and injected it into guinea pigs, rats, and other laboratory animals, they found that the process caused an immune response that "spilled over" into an attack against normal tissue, causing destruction of myelin, the attraction of inflammatory cells to involved areas, and signs of neurological dysfunction. The inflammatory brain and spinal cord lesions produced by this disorder, called experimental allergic encephalomyelitis (EAE), look pathologically very like those of multiple sclerosis, and many researchers think it is a helpful animal "model" of the human disease. The concept of MS as an autoimmune disease is being vigorously explored.

There are, however, major unsolved problems with the EAE model. The relapsing and remitting course characteristic of many cases of multiple sclerosis is seen in EAE only under certain experimental conditions and only in certain animal species. Moreover, if naturally occurring multiple sclerosis is fundamentally like EAE, how does a victim of the disease become "allergic" to his or her own tissue?

Despite these questions, the idea of multiple sclerosis as an autoimmune disease is supported by recent discoveries of anomalies in immune function in MS patients. It has long been known that an abnormally large number of lymphocytes are often found in the spinal fluid of MS patients during exacerbations of the disease. Lymphocytes are the white blood cells that are usually present in the body in areas being attacked by infection, and their presence in MS victims has been taken by some as an indication that multiple sclerosis is an infectious disease. Lymphocytes can also be mediators of autoimmune dysfunction, however, and as more has been learned about different subtypes of lymphocytes, their role in autoimmunity in multiple sclerosis has begun to appear particularly important.

The answer: complex and still to come

At this point, as researchers are faced with conflicting observations that favor infectious, genetic, and autoimmune origins for multiple sclerosis, attempts to synthesize some of these theories are beginning to emerge. Perhaps the answer to multiple sclerosis has been so elusive because it is complex, or even because it represents disease mechanisms heretofore unknown.

Theories combining two or even all three of the major disease mechanisms discussed here have been proposed to explain MS. The suggestively "genetic" observations can be satisfied by a theory stipulating that there are

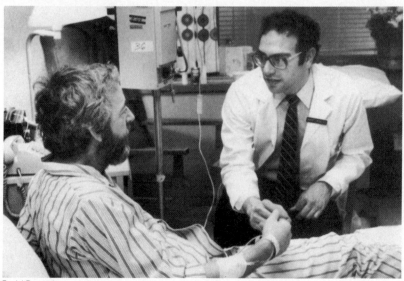

Daniel Bernstein

A number of drugs have been used, both singly and in combination, in the treatment of MS. Steroid drugs, which reduce inflammation, are a mainstay of current MS therapy. The patient pictured at left is receiving an experimental regimen consisting of injections of the steroid-enhancer ACTH (adrenocorticotropic hormone) along with high doses of the anticancer drug cyclophosphamide (Cytoxan), which suppresses the body's immune responses.

people of certain genetic types who are more susceptible to the disease than others but who, during their lifetimes, may or may not acquire it via infection by an atypical virus. Other examples of this kind of dual-factor causation are common. People who lack the gene for sickle-cell anemia, for example, are more likely to be infected with malaria than are those who possess the sickle-cell gene.

The infectious and autoimmune hypotheses of multiple sclerosis can also be combined in a plausible way. Developing MS might depend upon acquiring an autoimmune disorder, possibly through infection with an agent bearing immunologic resemblances to myelin or oligodendrocytes. The occurrence of relapses and remissions would then depend upon periodic "retriggering" of the autoimmune phenomena by infections with ordinary "run-of-the-mill" viruses such as the measles virus and those responsible for the common cold. All three mechanisms can be invoked by postulating a genetically inborn susceptibility to the original virus.

Other types of aberrant immune mechanisms have been linked to viral infections known to cause brain demyelination. For example, progressive multifocal leukoencephalopathy is seen only in people whose immune systems have been suppressed by medication or disease.

Genetics and dysfunction of the immune system have also been linked. Susceptibility to EAE, for example, varies not only among different animal species but also among genetically different strains of the same species. Possibly, susceptibility to autoimmune diseases may also vary with a person's genetic makeup. In fact, the gene type HLA-B8 /DR3, known to be associated with a risk of particularly severe multiple sclerosis, has also been found to be associated with abnormalities of immune function and is known to occur commonly in people with other diseases thought to be autoimmune in nature, such as systemic lupus erythematosus.

The search for effective treatment

Naturally, uncertainty as to the cause of MS has hampered clearly directed searches for effective therapy. In addition, the unpredictable course of the

In addition to drug therapies, a number of nondrug regimens have been used against MS with widely varying results. One of the most controversial such treatments involves subjecting the patient to prolonged sessions in a hyperbaric chamber, an iron-lung-type device into which oxygen is pumped under very high pressure. Unfortunately, specious therapies abound for MS; desperate patients are willing to try almost anything and, because of the relapsing and remitting course of the disease, some patients will experience improvement after a particular course of therapy, regardless of the efficacy of the treatment itself.

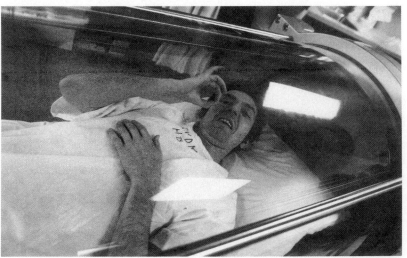

Michael Zagaris

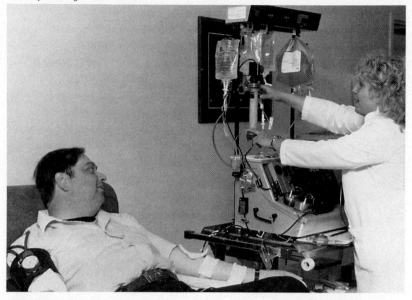

Plasmapheresis, or plasma exchange, has been under investigation for the treatment of MS and several other neurological disorders. In the process some of the patient's blood passes through a machine that separates the cellular components from the plasma, the liquid portion of the blood. After an artificial plasma is mixed with the cellular materials, it is injected into the patient's bloodstream (left). In treating MS the rationale is to remove from the blood immune system components that might be responsible for demyelination. In 1986 a U.S. National Institutes of Health consensus conference confirmed the efficacy of plasma exchange for a few neurological disorders; the data on MS were deemed inconclusive, however, and the process remains under investigation.

disorder in any single patient makes clinical trials of drugs or other therapeutic regimens difficult to construct and evaluate. Because of the tendency for symptoms to go into remission, it is possible that any patient who gets better after therapy of any kind might have done so without any intervention. Furthermore, many of the symptoms of multiple sclerosis, such as abnormalities or absence of sensation, cannot be measured objectively and are difficult to quantify. Over the years, desperate therapists and patients have tried dozens of treatments, from special diets to a variety of drugs. As in many other therapeutically resistant disorders, the all too common pattern has been for a new treatment to be tried on a few selected patients, some of whom improve—perhaps for reasons totally unrelated to the therapy. Larger trials are then designed, using two groups of patients, one of which receives the treatment under investigation while the other is given a placebo—*i.e.*, a harmless but ineffectual treatment. Finally, when the two groups of test subjects are compared at the end of the trial, the results reveal that the therapy in question is no more effective than the placebo.

Recently, however, attempts have been made to channel all potentially effective treatments into trials, conducted by several different research teams at a number of medical centers. These large, multicenter trials are conducted on the double-blind model—that is, neither the patients nor the medical evaluators know which test subjects are receiving placebo and which are receiving the test therapy. This kind of controlled clinical trial has become particularly important as proposed treatments for MS become expensive, cumbersome, and even dangerous.

Drug therapies

Recent trial therapies for MS have focused on either suppressing or enhancing various immune functions, depending on whether the investigator believes that autoimmune or infectious mechanisms predominate in producing the disease. Steroid therapy, using substances such as cortisone,

191

Many women with MS are fearful of becoming pregnant because they believe pregnancy will exacerbate the disease. Over the years a number of studies have shown that some pregnant women— between 20 and 40%—do experience a temporary worsening of symptoms within the first three months after childbirth. There is, however, no evidence that pregnancy alters the long-term course of the disease.

Adapted from Kathy Birk and Richard Rudick, ''Pregnancy and Multiple Sclerosis,'' *Archives of Neurology*, vol. 43 (July 1986), pp. 719–726

The effects of pregnancy on MS				
date of study	number of pregnancies after onset of MS	number worse during pregnancy	number worse in postpartum period	researchers' conclusions
1950	70	6	22	no effect on MS
1955	36	3	na	same as above
1959	170	6	39	increased incidence of relapse postpartum
1966	86	12	19	same as above
1981	206	34	91	improved before delivery, worse postpartum; no overall adverse effect
1983	158	13	28	same as above
1984	199	20	65	same as above

na = not available

prednisone, and methylprednisolone, as well as the steroid enhancer ACTH (adrenocorticotropic hormone), has been tested in various doses and for various periods of time. Steroids have an immunosuppressive effect and also reduce the edema (swelling) that is present in acute plaques. Some of these trials have seemed successful in shortening attacks of multiple sclerosis, and steroid drugs provide the mainstay of treatment today.

Some of the newer immunosuppressant drugs also have been or are being tried in their turn against multiple sclerosis. One such drug, Imuran (azathioprine), has shown some benefits in patients who suffer from frequent flare-ups of the disease. A large controlled study of its efficacy is currently under way in the United States, and results should be available by 1988. Another agent being tested is copolymer I, a protein that has shown some ability to reduce the frequency of exacerbations but, thus far, has demonstrated no efficacy in improving the ultimate clinical outcome of the patient with MS.

Cyclophosphamide (Cytoxan), a drug that reduces the number of lymphocytes in the blood and is used in the treatment of various autoimmune diseases, has been tried alone and in combination with steroids, with

No medication can restore lost strength, but an individualized and carefully supervised program of physical therapy can help the MS patient make maximum use of remaining muscle power. Swimming and gentle stretching exercises can help maintain flexibility and coordination.

Photographs, Randall Schapiro, Minneapolis Clinic of Psychiatry and Neurology, Ltd.

varying success. It has potentially serious toxicity, including the possible production of tumors and hemorrhage from the bladder, but is still used in treating cases of rapidly progressive, severe multiple sclerosis.

The interferons, a group of substances produced naturally by lymphocytes and other cells during infections, appear to enhance the immune system's ability to fight infection successfully. Some interferons have been tested in multiple sclerosis patients but with mixed results—in some instances they actually appear to provoke exacerbation of the disease. However, because more and more interferons are being discovered, and because their potential influence on various body tissues is still unclear, further tests will probably continue.

One of the major drawbacks to the use of immunosuppressant drugs is that they make the body more vulnerable to severe infection. However, a relatively new immunosuppressant drug called cyclosporine offers the advantage of preserving the immune system's normal ability to fight infection while fairly selectively improving the activity of the suppressor T cells, a subpopulation of lymphocytes that is reduced in multiple sclerosis. Cyclosporine has already proved invaluable in helping to prevent rejection of organ transplants. A double-blind trial of cyclosporine is now under way in more than 500 MS patients.

Drug therapy from a completely new angle is being explored with colchicine, an agent previously used to relieve the pain of gout and arthritis. This drug reduces the ability of certain scavenger cells, called macrophages, to move to body areas where lymphocytes have directed them to clear out targeted foreign material. There is some evidence that macrophages are the cells that do the "dirty work" of destroying myelin in plaques targeted by lymphocytes. One hopeful indication of its possible application to multiple sclerosis is colchicine's demonstrated ability to prevent EAE in lab animals.

Nondrug therapies

Drugs are not the only type of therapy under investigation in the battle against MS. One fairly recently developed technique that is being tried is plasmapheresis, or plasma exchange. In this process some of the patient's blood is passed through a machine that separates the red and white blood cells from the liquid part of the blood, or plasma. An artificial plasma consisting of salt water and protein is then mixed with the cellular material that was removed from the patient's blood, and the mixture is injected into the patient's bloodstream. The rationale for the treatment is to remove from the plasma abnormal immunoglobulins that might be causing demyelination. Plasmapheresis has also been used in limited trials against a number of diseases of suspected autoimmune origin, among them systemic lupus erythematosus, myasthenia gravis, and Guillain-Barré syndrome. Early trials of plasmapheresis in MS showed some promise, but the technique is uncomfortable, risky, and expensive (as much as $8,000 for a 20-week course) and certainly is not a panacea. The effectiveness of plasmapheresis in the treatment of several neurological disorders was the subject of a consensus conference sponsored by the U.S. National Institutes of Health in 1986. Although the data on MS were limited, the conference panel felt that the apparent benefits of the treatment warranted further study. Thus, plasmapheresis is still considered experimental for MS, and trials continue.

Many other treatments have been explored, sometimes with little theoretical justification. For example, MS patients have been subjected to sessions in hyperbaric chambers, contained spaces where oxygen is pumped in at high pressure. Initial reports indicated some success with this process. Several subsequent placebo trials, however, showed no difference between outcomes in patients given hyperbaric and sham treatments, and the procedure has largely been abandoned.

Fad treatments are a particular problem in MS because of the desperation of those with severe forms of the disease and the appropriately cautious approach taken by the medical establishment. Diets and vitamin therapy have ranged from the reasonable to the bizarre, and every year finds another "cure" that evaporates under close scrutiny, usually only at great cost, effort, and even risk to many MS patients.

Fears, frustrations, and making realistic choices

Given the uncertainty surrounding the cause of multiple sclerosis and the relative ineffectiveness of most treatments, it is not surprising that fear and frustration are almost ubiquitous elements of the condition. Although the diagnosis of multiple sclerosis is no longer one "of exclusion"—that is, confirmed only by ruling out every other possibility—the initial symptoms of the disorder are often so puzzling and the preliminary test results so ambiguous that a definite diagnosis may be preceded by months or even years of anxiety and uncertainty. Here the firm, compassionate guidance of a knowledgeable physician may support the patient through a difficult time.

Even after a definite diagnosis of multiple sclerosis has been made, patients are faced with a host of uncertainties—what to expect as the disease progresses, how it will affect work and family life. Should they move to a different climate? Consider a career change? Try an unproven therapy? A young woman may wonder if it would be wise to forgo childbearing. She worries that pregnancy may exacerbate the condition, and she speculates about her ability to be an active, involved mother. What will she be like in 20 years?

Again accurate, sensitive counseling is imperative. Patients must be told, quite truthfully, that a large proportion of people with multiple sclerosis continue to function normally all their lives, working and having families. It has even been postulated that many mild cases of MS are not ever diagnosed, initial symptoms resolving and no relapses occurring. In very rough terms, it has been estimated that about a third of the patients with multiple sclerosis end their lives with serious physical disability, about a third avoid significant neurological deficits, and about a third are somewhere in between these two extremes. In an individual case, the course of the disease seems to declare itself within the first three years, allowing at least some realistic planning for the future in terms of work and life-style. Climate does not have a consistent effect on the disease, other than the transient worsening of symptoms that occurs in a few patients when they become significantly overheated. The role of stress in producing or aggravating symptoms is

While research scientists labor to solve the mysteries of MS, patients and their families and friends have joined together in support of these efforts. In the United States the National Multiple Sclerosis Society, which has a membership of 450,000, celebrated its 40th year in 1986. The organization's anniversary motto, "Incurably Optimistic," eloquently expresses the determination with which the members pursue their ultimate goal— a cure for this devastating disease.

National Multiple Sclerosis Society

THE NATIONAL MS SOCIETY AT 40.
INCURABLY OPTIMISTIC.

194

not clear, and since stress is almost ubiquitous, its effect on any disease process is difficult, if not impossible, to measure.

Whether or not to undertake pregnancy is a matter that deserves very careful consideration by the patient and counseling physician. While pregnancy does not alter the long-term course of the disease, between 20 and 40% of MS patients experience a temporary worsening of symptoms within the first three months after childbirth. Whether the risk of exacerbation is worth taking depends on many factors, including the length and course of the woman's disease thus far, her general physical condition, the parenting desires of both spouses, their family resources (both personal and financial), cultural expectations, and so on.

Practical help

For those who suffer either transient or permanent neurological dysfunction, medical and physical help can make a notable difference. For example, involvement of the spinal cord can produce muscle weakness that may not remit. Although no medication can restore lost strength, drugs can stop the painful muscle spasms and reduce the muscle stiffness (spasticity) that sometimes accompany paralysis. Difficulties with balance and coordination can sometimes be ameliorated by drugs or such fairly simple mechanical devices as weights. Physical therapy can help the patient make full use of what muscle power remains; it also helps to prevent joint stiffness and abnormal postures in paralyzed limbs. Lightweight knee or ankle braces can sometimes prolong the ability to walk. Careful planning of living space and provision of strategic physical aids such as wall bars and hand grips can facilitate life's daily chores. If urinary bladder function is impaired, medications or, in some cases, surgical remedies can make a crucial difference in maintaining continence.

Coping emotionally

When the disease is severe, both patients and their families may and should be helped to cope emotionally with whatever symptoms persist. Counseling, whether in the physician's office or in the more formal setting of psychological therapy, can help strengthen family relationships and preserve marital ties. Job retraining can make it possible to remain financially independent and preserve a sense of self-esteem.

Medical personnel must always be alert to the emotional toll of the disease and be able to discriminate between psychic distress and organic symptoms caused by genuine physical involvement of the brain. Emotional and mental disorders, including depression, inappropriate euphoria, memory loss, and cognitive difficulties, may occur as a result of brain involvement, and these symptoms present practical problems as great as any other physical manifestations of disease. Antidepressant drugs are often particularly helpful. The therapist's skills in interpreting these truly physical symptoms to the patient and family may be even more helpful.

For the stricken individuals—the Margaret M.'s—the battle against multiple sclerosis may be a lifelong and difficult one, but it must not and should not be fought alone.

National Multiple Sclerosis Society, Chicago-Northern Illinois Chapter

Comedian Tom Dreesen has been in the forefront of the battle against MS ever since his sister, Darlene Bethman, was stricken with the disease. A few years ago Dreesen mobilized some of his friends in show business and professional sports to establish a "Day for Darlene," an official fund-raising event that sponsors local runs. Originating in the Chicago area, "Day for Darlene" races are now held statewide in Illinois every summer. The event has become a symbol of hope for MS patients everywhere.

195

Time Out
for the
Gift of Life

by Jake Garn

In January 1987 I spent a weekend, along with a dozen of my Senate colleagues, competing in a ski tournament to raise funds for the Primary Children's Medical Center in Salt Lake City, Utah. I was throwing all my energies into a headlong charge down the slopes, in and out of the gates, anxiously trying to break the 38-second mark on the race timer. Until someone asked, it had not occurred to me that just four months before that race I might not have imagined I would be able to do something that physically demanding.

Four months earlier, on Sept. 9, 1986, I was lying in a hospital bed in Georgetown University Medical Center in Washington, D.C. I was wide awake and apprehensive about the fact that the next morning I would go into surgery to donate a kidney to my 26-year-old daughter, Susan Garn Horne, who had lost most of her renal function as a result of a diabetic condition. As I look back on it, I was apprehensive because I was unsure about what the consequences might be for me, but I had not thought much about what impact the surgery might have on me since I had learned I was a good donor match for Sue. My only thought was that she needed my kidney, I was going to give it to her, and that was all there was to it.

Sixteen-year odyssey to hospital

It had been a long odyssey for Sue that had led us to the hospital. She had been diagnosed as a juvenile diabetic at age ten. It became a source of deep frustration for her. Like any normal child, she did not want to be held back or bound by restrictions on what and when she ate, and she certainly did not want a disease to force her to be "different" from her friends. She struggled with herself about her illness a great deal; she simply would not accept the reality of her diabetes. There were frequent occasions when she would allow herself to get dangerously close to insulin shock or even a diabetic coma, and she would almost have to be forced to take sugar water or something sweet to pull her back from the edge. My wife and I came to recognize the early symptoms of impending insulin shock, and we were constantly on the lookout for signs that Sue was slipping again.

As she grew and matured, she began to accept the fact of her condition and began to watch her diet and schedule much more carefully. Although in her own mind she finally stopped resisting her diabetes, she still wanted it to be a strictly personal and private matter—not something that was known

Jake Garn is a United States Senator from Utah.

(Opposite page) AFP Photo

197

In the hospital in September 1986 at the time of giving a kidney to his daughter Susan, Sen. Jake Garn was told by his doctors that he would not be skiing that winter. On January 15–18, 1987, however, Garn, 12 other U.S. senators, and Secretary of Energy John S. Harrington competed in a "Senator's Ski Cup" in Park City, Utah. The lawmakers were there to help raise some $35,000 for the Primary Children's Medical Center in Salt Lake City, Utah. Garn (number 1) came up with the idea and served as host for the event in order to, in his words, "express my gratitude to the Primary Children's Medical Center, which cared for my daughter Sue when she was fighting diabetes as a child."

At age ten Susan Garn was diagnosed as having juvenile diabetes. Like any normal child, she did not want to be "different" from other children, and she struggled with herself about her illness a great deal. Pictured at right are the senator and his first wife, Hazel, with four Garn children (left to right): Jake, Jr., Susan, Jeff, and Ellen.

to everyone she associated with and especially not something she wanted to have bandied about in the press. The fact that I hold public office and am occasionally in the media spotlight made that a particular concern for us. I knew how strongly Sue felt about the limelight, and I respected that desire. Throughout my public life I have tried to make a clear distinction between my public responsibilities and my family obligations, and I have always tried to help my family maintain their privacy.

By the time Sue was 24, she had begun experiencing complications from her diabetes. She had married a terrific man—our family doctor in Virginia, as a matter of fact—and they were expecting a baby. The effects of progressive diabetes can make pregnancy very difficult, and Sue was no exception. Her pregnancy was physically very hard for her, but she was excited and determined and took every precaution to minimize any complications. She gave birth prematurely on May 1, 1985, to Allison, a tiny, 1.6-kilogram (3.5-pound), but nonetheless very healthy, baby girl.

Sue was left weakened by the experience, however, and her renal function became a source of greater concern. We began to discuss with the doctors what the options were in the event of renal failure and, of course, were told that the choice would be either a transplant or lifelong dependence on dialysis. Clearly, the first choice was the former, and it was at that time that we began to discuss the question of a kidney donor.

The transplant option

We learned about the importance of tissue matching to ensure that the body's defensive mechanisms did not rise up against the "foreign" object that was transplanted into it. As one might expect, it was clear that a living related donor would be the most likely to produce a close tissue match. After a series of tests, it was concluded that my two sons and I would be the closest matches and that, although any of the three of us would be suitable, I had about a one-factor advantage.

I was delighted with the news. During the testing period I had decided in my own mind that if I proved eligible I wanted to be the donor. In the

first place, I figured that I would not be needing my kidneys as long as my sons would need theirs—Jake, Jr., was 29 years old and Jeff was 20. Besides, if I were to be the donor, Sue would have two backup potential donors in case mine was rejected by her body or her continuing diabetic condition caused the initial transplant to deteriorate to the point that it needed to be replaced.

The thought that made me most determined, though, was that this was an opportunity for me to do something for Sue that would mean almost as much as being a part of her conception had. Her mother had carried her for nine months and, if giving her a part of me now would help sustain her life, how could I pass up that opportunity?

The fact that her brothers were willing to be donors meant a great deal. There was no doubt that if for some reason, when it came time for Sue to have the transplant, I would be unable to donate, Jake, Jr., and Jeff were ready and willing to do it. That expression of love for their sister and sense of unity within the family was beautiful and touching for our entire family and was, for me, a source of great pride in my children.

Politics become secondary

Once the decision had been made, it was simply a question of timing. Since I was anticipating a senatorial reelection campaign, the question was raised about putting the transplant off until after that had been completed in November 1986. I told the doctors that my first priority was the transplant. When the time came, the Senate and the campaign would not be as important to me as Sue's health and well-being.

As it turned out, the transplant became necessary much earlier than the doctors had at first anticipated. I was in Utah during the August 1986 recess when the decision was made to do the surgery on September 10.

Office of Sen. Jake Garn

Soon after Susan Garn Horne gave birth to her daughter, Allison, in 1985, her kidney function began to deteriorate and her overall health became a matter of grave concern. Her options were a lifetime of dialysis treatments or a kidney transplant. Tests showed that the senator was the best candidate to donate a kidney and that Susan's brothers, Jake and Jeff, would be good tissue matches as well. The willingness of all the family to help and the support they gave her throughout were a moving expression of love and a great source of pride to Garn. At the time, the senator's thought was that "her mother had carried her for nine months and, if giving her a part of me now would help sustain her life, how could I pass up that opportunity?" At left, the Garn family, photographed Christmas 1985: (left to right, top row) Jake Garn, Jr., Allen Horne, Brook Bingham (Kathleen Garn's son by a previous marriage), Jeff Garn, and Todd Reich; (seated) Sharon Garn holding daughter Kirsten, Susan Garn Horne holding daughter Allison, Kathleen Garn, Sen. Jake Garn holding Jennifer (his and Kathleen's daughter), Ellen Garn Reich holding son Ryan, and Matthew Garn (Kathleen and the senator's son).

It was hoped that the kidney transplant surgery could be delayed until Garn's November 1986 reelection campaign was over. Politics became secondary, however, when the surgery was deemed necessary several months earlier than planned. The operation took place at Georgetown University Medical Center in Washington, D.C., on September 10. Father and daughter are pictured above leaving the hospital on September 17—both "feeling great." Garn went on to win his third term of office. (Below) On election night, holding grandson Ryan Reich (with other family members in the background), the fully recovered senator gives his victory speech in Salt Lake City, Utah.

I went into the University of Utah Medical Sciences Center to have some final tests done to determine my current physical condition as a prospective donor and to confirm that I could proceed.

Even though we knew that the surgery was scheduled and that the tests were a final prerequisite to my donation, I chose not to disclose the timing of the surgery. I was still very mindful of Sue's desire for privacy, especially because it had already been invaded by the press during the summer. It was obvious even at the time that other members of my family and I were undergoing the preliminary tissue-matching tests that there was great press interest and that it was going to be difficult to protect Sue from media attention, but I was determined to do whatever I could.

I went forward with my schedule, which included a three-day swing through my home state the week before the surgery to officially kick off my reelection campaign, and then returned to Washington. I instructed my staff to make no announcement about the impending surgery until Sue and I were in the hospital. The morning before the surgery we quietly drove ourselves to the Georgetown hospital and checked in. I am still amazed that we managed to slip in quietly, since for days there had been persistent and insistent inquiries from the press about the timing for the transplant. As it was, the first public comment about our entry into the hospital was that morning when the chaplain of the Senate noted in his prayer at the beginning of the day's session that I had entered the hospital that morning for the purpose of donating a kidney to my daughter; he asked for the Lord's blessings for Sue and me. My staff then issued a confirming release and organized a way of reporting the outcome of the surgery and my health status during the recovery period while protecting Sue as much as possible.

On the day of the surgery, after receiving words of encouragement from my wife, Kathleen, who had flown to Washington to be with me through the experience, I was wheeled into the operating room to be "prepped" for the transplant procedure two hours ahead of Sue. This was to enable the doctors to examine me thoroughly and to confirm that everything was intact and that no potentially complicating problems existed. After the surgeons were satisfied that I was ready to go ahead with the transplant, Sue

Jake Garn admits to experiencing great fear before the transplant. "Why was I so apprehensive?" he asked himself. He recalled going through the launch, flight, and landing of the space shuttle Discovery *in 1985 without any fright whatsoever. In retrospect he attributes his trepidation before the transplant to not knowing what to expect. He had never been very sick, had never been in a hospital as a patient undergoing major surgery, and had not even been born in a hospital. On the other hand, he had been trained extensively by NASA for his space mission; all that training and knowledge gave him a level of confidence that freed him of apprehension. Pictured at left are the* Discovery *mission crew: (left to right, front row) Jeffrey A. Hoffman, Rhea Seddon, Charles Walker; (back row) Capt. David Griggs, Col. Karol J. Bobko, Capt. Donald Williams, and Senator Garn.*

then was wheeled into the adjoining operating room. The actual transfer of my kidney to Sue's body took only 15 minutes. The entire surgery—from the time I was cut open to the time Susan's incisions were closed—was completed in six hours.

A blur of events—apprehensions and fears

Everything had moved so fast from the time the decision was made to schedule the transplant to the time we entered the hospital that it was almost a blur of events. Before the surgery Sue and I really had had little time to reflect on what was about to take place. It was actually not until the eve of the surgery that I found myself seriously thinking about what I was doing and what Sue was undergoing.

I was lying in my darkened hospital room waiting for my eyes to get tired and my mind to get settled so I could sleep. I was getting frustrated with myself for being so restless and for experiencing something that I honestly have not felt a great deal of in my life—fear.

I knew, logically and factually, that there was really nothing to worry about—that the operations that Sue and I were to undergo in the morning would be virtually routine, at least so the doctors believed. The physicians involved had been very thorough and reassuring every step of the way. They had shown us the facts and figures, and we knew from what they said, for example, that there was an eight times higher mortality rate from appendectomies than from a nephrectomy (removal of a kidney) and transplant procedure. Also, they had reassured me with statistics and anecdotes that I would not be physically impaired or have to change my life-style radically as a result of giving up the organ—except that, the doctors joked, I should not plan on doing a lot of skydiving. (I had told them I had gone skydiving once with my sons a couple of years before, but I thought I could get by without repeating the experience.)

So, why was I apprehensive? After all, I thought, a year and a half before I had sat with six others on board the space shuttle *Discovery* attached to

(continued on page 204)

Guinea Pig in Space

In the early morning of Nov. 8, 1984, I received a phone call informing me that the National Aeronautics and Space Administration (NASA) administrator, James Beggs, was formally inviting me to make an inspection flight aboard the space shuttle *Discovery*. I had been informed earlier in the year that such an invitation would be extended to me as a "congressional observer," but it was not known when or exactly under what conditions that would be done. I had told the NASA administrator in 1981, three days after *Columbia*'s historic first flight, that I would like to fly in space one day and "kick the tires," so to speak, of the orbiter for which I, as a U.S. senator who served as chairman of the appropriations subcommittee, had the responsibility of appropriating funds. To fly aboard a shuttle was the ultimate activity for the head of the oversight committee, and it was the quintessential dream of flight for an old navy aviator. Once the testing phase of the shuttle program was completed, it became more apparent that my dream could become a reality, and I continued to remind the administrator of my willingness to fly. During one hearing of my subcommittee, I even offered myself as a guinea pig for research, if that would encourage them to take me.

After the formal invitation and announcement that I was to fly in space, I went to the Johnson Space Center in Houston, Texas, for orientation on the required training program. During those sessions I learned of the interest in having shuttle crew members conduct medical experiments during shuttle missions. I was reminded of my "guinea pig" offer, and it was suggested that they were going to take me at my word. I agreed that that would be just fine with me, and they began to outline the nature of some of their proposed experiments.

Many of the tests are directed at determining the causes and possible means of avoiding so-called space motion sickness, SMS, which is experienced to one degree or another by roughly half of all space travelers. Others are directed at gaining a better general understanding of the human body's adjustment to a weightless environment, or space adaptation syndrome (SAS), irrespective of any SMS.

I agreed to participate in some of those experiments, and a series of 14 tests was incorporated into my training. Some of the tests I conducted on board the space shuttle *Discovery* STS flight 51-D, April 12–19, 1985, looked into the following:

Gastrointestinal activity. The noises my stomach and intestines made as they passed food and digestive juices were measured to document changes in gastric activity that occurred during the flight. To perform this experiment I used electronic stethoscope microphones on an ace bandage secured to my abdomen. The sounds picked up by the microphones were recorded on a voice cassette recorder and later analyzed.

This was the first time that levels of gastric activity had been documented during the earliest phases of SAS. Specifically, this was the first in-space recording of electrical activity of the stomach (the electrogastrogram, or EGG). The data revealed that my gas-

"To fly aboard a shuttle was the . . . quintessential dream of flight for an old navy aviator." Prior to orbiting in space, Jake Garn, pictured as a navy ensign in 1957, had logged some 10,000 hours of flying time as a pilot.

trointestinal (GI) activity had stopped within 15 to 20 minutes after first experiencing weightlessness. It also demonstrated that the restoration of GI function was relatively rapid, taking place within an hour once recovery from SAS began. This took place on day two of the flight. This information has contributed to the research that is examining the relationship between the sensory conflict of weightlessness and the GI tract, with particular emphasis on identifying a neurological or other pathway of the vestibular (balance) system to the GI tract.

Shifts in body fluid. In zero gravity (zero-G) body fluids shift from the legs to the upper chest and then to the head. One of the significant measurements I was asked to make was the degree of fluid movement that occurred early in flight, since this had never been documented before. The technique used to make this measurement is known as leg plethysmography. During the flight and upon return to gravity (one-G), I wore a specially designed stocking on my right leg from the ankle to the thigh. It was fitted with a series of circumferential tapes that could be marked to measure the girth of the leg at various points and at certain intervals. From this, the volume change that occurred in the leg was later calculated. In addition, I wore a blood-pressure recorder before and after flight and before and after reentry during the flight. This made a record of blood pressure and heart rate every three and one-half minutes. Leg volume, blood pressure, and heart-rate measurements taken at the same time were correlated to determine levels of orthostatic tolerance (the ability to stand after the flight without becoming faint).

Analysis of these data documented for the first time the suspected rapid shift of fluid from the legs in flight and even more rapid shift into the legs on reentry. The correlation of the other data and the observation of symptoms resulted in the appearance of orthostatic intolerance but without typical symptoms (decreased pulse and systolic pressure with increased heart rate). The physicians analyzing the recordings theorized that what was occurring was a decreased cardiac output secondary to inadequate return of circulation, or possibly inappropriate heart-rate response (my heart rate was low) with increased peripheral resistance to maintain blood pressure. NASA medical investigators have now designed further tests to examine the phenomenon more closely. The significance of this research lies in the hopes scientists have of gaining a better understanding of what is taking place when the body reacts to the weightless state and fluid shifts occur and how these reactions might be avoided, which ultimately would improve the ability of crew members to exit the orbiter rapidly in the case of an emergency after reentry and during landing.

Other studies looking into the vestibular changes included tests of my ability to manually track a moving light and the time required for me to perform certain mental tasks (called the Sternberg test). No significant differences were found between my performance on Earth and in space.

Pharmacodynamics: metabolism and activities of medications. Another test was to determine whether the doses of medication appropriate on the ground are also appropriate in flight. For this test I took one dose of acetaminophen (a substitute for aspirin, commonly marketed, for example, in Tylenol) and then took samples of saliva over several hours to measure salivary levels of acetaminophen. Saliva samples were used as a measuring technique because with acetaminophen, as with some other drugs, there is a positive correlation between plasma and saliva concentrations. What is more important is the fact that the technique is noninvasive; monitoring can be done without the withdrawal and analysis of blood samples, which is not particularly easy or practical during the sort of spaceflights contemplated in the shuttle. The investigators were looking for information concerning the rate of metabolism of this particular drug and also were testing a monitoring technique that might be used in connection with other drugs used during flight to determine whether dosages given in one-G are correct in zero-G.

The information obtained in these tests demonstrated that in my case, at least, it took twice as long to absorb the medication during flight as it did on Earth. A difference of that magnitude in the absorption rate made the drug ineffective at the given dosage level. Clearly, more study is needed—and indeed has been under way—to enable a better understanding of the dynamics of drug disposition so that the best therapeutic efficiency of drugs can be ensured and undesirable side effects of drugs that must be taken by crew members in flight can be avoided. The sampling technique, with subsequent modifications suggested by my experience, has proved to be an effective way of gaining the information needed to further that study.

In addition to experiments in which I was my own test subject, I conducted another experiment using for the first time a device that ultimately will lead to a way of carrying out unique cell separations that can be useful in the treatment of such diseases as leukemia and diabetes.

Being able to perform these fascinating experiments added a dimension to my spaceflight that I had not anticipated; it gave me a better understanding of the specific benefits to humanity that grow out of the U.S. space program. Even more meaningful to me was the satisfaction that comes from participating in something that has the potential for relieving pain or easing distress and possibly even resulting in the prevention of the development of medical problems or the cure of those that do develop. It was a taste of what I would eventually feel when I had the chance to make a direct, measurable contribution to my daughter Sue with the donation of one of my kidneys. It would be a wonderful bonus for me if, owing to my participation as a medical guinea pig who endured some trivial physical discomforts, it turned out that I was able to make a small contribution to the eventual cure of diabetes, which Sue still has to contend with.

Mealtime in space. Sen. Jake Garn offered himself as a guinea pig for research in order to encourage NASA to send him on a spaceflight. Among the many pioneering medical studies he participated in were gastric motility tests. The noises made by his stomach and intestines as they passed food and digestive juices were measured to document changes in gastrointestinal activity that occur during spaceflight.

NASA

(continued from page 201)

1.7 million kilograms (3.8 million pounds) of explosive fuel to be launched into orbit. We rode those powerful engines and boosters into space and up to a speed of 25 times the speed of sound. We hurtled through space at 6.9 kilometers (4.3 miles) a second for seven days. When the mission was finished, we thundered back through the Earth's atmosphere in a veritable furnace with outside temperatures exceeding 1,360° C (2,500° F) on a 12,872-kilometer (8,000-mile)-long glide path with only one chance to land since the 85-ton "glider" we were on had no engine power after reentry.

I had gone through that launch, flight, and landing without ever experiencing any of the kind of fear or apprehension that I felt in that hospital room. I certainly am not blessed with nerves of steel or uncommon courage, so I was struck by the difference in the way I approached the two experiences. In retrospect it is obvious that the basic difference was in how much I knew about what to expect. As a pilot with over 10,000 hours of flying time, I knew something about aerodynamics and characteristics of flight and guidance systems. I had been trained well by the National Aeronautics and Space Administration to perform the functions that were expected of me in the mission, and I had observed enough of the crew's training in shuttle operations to have the highest level of confidence in the shuttle's capabilities and the crew's mastery of them. All of that training and knowledge gave me a level of confidence that freed me of apprehension and allowed me the luxury of feeling more anticipation of and expectations about the incredibly exciting experiences I would have than any real *fear* of them.

On the other hand, I had never been in a hospital before as a patient about to undergo major surgery. I had not even been born in a hospital! The whole environment was new. I was much more frightened by something about which I had very little knowledge than by something about which I knew a great deal—going into orbit.

There are many misconceptions about organ donation. A common concern is that the donor's body will be left disfigured. People should be reassured, however, that skillful surgery leaves no noticeable change in the body's appearance. Every year thousands of people worldwide are helped by transplants of the body parts indicated below. Nevertheless, many thousands more could benefit if more people were willing to make the simple arrangements necessary so that after they died, their organs could be transplanted.

American Council on Transplantation

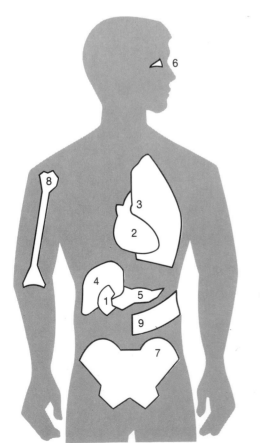

Transplants: where the need is			
organ or tissue	transplants in 1986	people waiting	success of graft after one year
1 kidney	8,973	9,000	93–96%
2 heart	1,368	300	82%
3 heart/lung	45	75	68–70%
4 liver	924	300	70%
5 pancreas	140	50	graft survival—44% patient survival—90%
6 cornea	31,000	5,000	90–95%
7 bone marrow	1,160	no waiting lists; tissues used as available	*
8 bone	bone tissue used in over 200,000 procedures	*	*
9 skin	*	*	*

*figure unavailable

For information on organ donation, contact: The American Council on Transplantation, P.O. Box 1709, Dept. Britannica, Alexandria, VA 22313, 1-800-228-4483 or 1-800-ACT-GIVE

Why would anyone hesitate to give the gift of life?

I am sure it is that same combination of ignorance and fear that results in many afflicted people's dying, or at the very least continuing to suffer, every day because they have not been able to obtain a needed organ for a transplant. Too many people are simply too fearful of the prospects of freely giving an organ to someone else who so desperately needs it.

I can understand that fear among those who are eligible to be living related donors. They cannot help but wonder about the impact their donation might have on their own lives. I certainly had those apprehensions, although I now know that the impact is minimal, if even noticeable. What I cannot understand is why anyone would be reluctant to authorize the donation of any of their vital organs or "transplantable parts" after they are dead. Of what use are those parts to them then, and what could they possibly have to fear?

I cannot help but believe that if people understood the need for organ donors, enough of them would voluntarily sign donor-authorization cards and get "donor" stamped on their drivers' licenses. I was startled to learn from one of the doctors at the University of Utah Medical Sciences Center this stark fact: if only one out of four brain-dead people in the intermountain area had authorized the donation of their organs, they would meet the transplant needs of the entire region! Just one in four!

None of us likes to think much about dying. Most of us, I think, would prefer to believe we are almost immortal and will simply outlive anyone else we know. But death is an inescapable fact of life. It seems to me that everyone, whatever they may believe about what happens after that inevitable reality, could take a great deal of comfort from the knowledge that a part of them could live on and, in so doing, extend or improve some other people's lives. Also, if they are willing to be donors themselves, they should be equally anxious to see that others are as willing. After all, those willing donors may find that they themselves need an organ transplant at some point in their lives. Their encouragement to others would result in a sort of mutual pact that everyone would enter to make sure that organs are available to whoever needs them.

Voluntary "donor-in-death" programs should never have a lack of participants. I am convinced that success in organ-donor programs lies in informing people about them and demonstrating the potential value to them by their being involved in such an active program. People need to know the value of the satisfaction of knowing that they literally may give someone else the "gift of life."

Of course, "cadaver donors," as they are called in the medical profession, are not around to see the beneficial effects of their donation. Therefore, it remains for those of us in the category of "living related donors" to try to explain to them what a terrifically self-satisfying experience it can be to improve someone else's life.

The most gratifying act of my life—bar none!

During an interview in the hospital the day before Sue and I were discharged, a reporter asked me how my donation of a kidney to my daughter

Courtesy of Ann Neimeyer

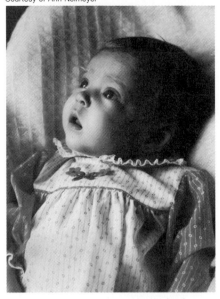

Alyssa Neimeyer's story did not have a happy ending. Only two months after her birth on June 13, 1985, doctors realized that liver disease would take her life unless she got a new liver. An urgent call went out for a donor organ, but none was found. Alyssa died Dec. 17, 1985. Alyssa's parents realized that many children who had died during that time were potential donors for their daughter, but their parents did not say yes when asked about organ donation. In spite of their own grief, the Neimeyers thought of other children who might benefit from Alyssa's body. Alyssa's corneas have given the gift of sight to two other children.

Reasons for not donating organs*			
never thought about it	31%	want body intact	7%
too old	14%	too ill	5%
religious beliefs	9%	lack of awareness	3%
general fear	9%	other	4%
distrust of medical community	7%	no answer	16%

*on the basis of 502 interviews

1987 Gallup Survey for the Dow Chemical Company Take Initiative Program

205

Giving permission for organ donation: how likely?						
	very likely	somewhat likely	not very likely	not at all likely	no answer	total
for own organs after death	30%	18%	11%	18%	23%	100%
for loved one's organs	66%	16%	5%	5%	8%	100%
for child's organs	43%	18%	8%	16%	15%	100%

1987 Gallup Survey for the Dow Chemical Company Take Initiative Program

compared with other so-called notable things I had done in my public and personal life. I did not even have to think about the answer. There is simply no other thing I have ever done that has given me greater satisfaction. Donating a kidney to Sue was something I was able to do entirely alone, and it gave me immense personal satisfaction. It gave me an opportunity to express in actions, even beyond words, my love for my daughter—and for all my seven children, since I would have done the same thing for any one of them if I were a suitable donor.

Since the transplant, many people have expressed their admiration for what I did and have said how courageous they think I am. Frankly, I have been surprised by that reaction and believe it is unwarranted. I simply cannot imagine that any parent, given the choice, would ever be reluctant to do exactly the same thing. I felt that way even before the transplant, but now, seeing the tremendous difference it has made in Sue, I realize even more completely that I could never have even considered any other course of action.

Immediately after the surgery, as soon as I was awake, I wanted to know whether Sue had accepted my kidney. My surgeon informed me that the transplant had been successful; I was indeed very eager to see Sue for myself, to be reassured that everything had gone well. Unfortunately, I had a slight fever and was not able to visit her, but I called her on the phone as soon as I was able. It had been only a few days, but it was incredible!

Did they tell family about interest in donating organs?						
	those somewhat likely to donate			those very likely to donate		
	1984	1986	1987	1984	1986	1987
yes	51%	54%	64%	65%	69%	79%
no	49%	46%	35%	35%	31%	20%
total of respondents	640	742	492	377	476	322

1987 Gallup Survey for the Dow Chemical Company Take Initiative Program

Even over the phone and even through the aftereffects of the anesthetics, I could hear a difference in her voice. I could tell she felt better already.

To date, in late summer 1987, she has not had a single rejection episode. She is very rapidly tapering off the anti-inflammatory medication that was needed after the operation. All in all, it appears to have been a very successful transplant, and surely all our family are very grateful for that.

A press release was issued from the hospital just one week after the surgery. It said simply: "Mrs. Horne has experienced no rejection activity. The kidney she received from her father is functioning normally, as is Senator Garn's remaining kidney." It all seemed so clean, so easy, yet so miraculous—that my short stay in the hospital could deliver such an enormous and precious change in Sue's life, health, and well-being!

Becoming symbols of hope

There has been another change in Sue that has taken place as a result of this experience. After the surgery we received literally hundreds of letters, telegrams, phone calls, and other kinds of best wishes from people around the country who were touched in some way by the story of our transplant. The warmth of the letters and telegrams we received was really incredible. As the heartwarming greetings continued to flow in, Sue began to realize the overwhelmingly positive nature of the widespread national media coverage of the transplant and the potential good it could do to enhance donor programs.

We learned through some very personal, candid correspondence that many people throughout the country were watching our progress and hoping for the best, not only for our well-being but because they too had some kind of difficult ordeal with which to cope. Many expressed the view that they considered us to be symbols of hope for many people. We began to feel a growing sense of responsibility to share our experience and help educate people about the need to be organ donors.

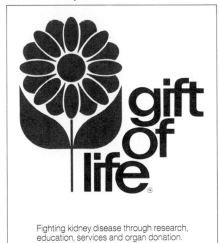

Ira Wexler

When Susan Garn Horne began to feel renewed energy and vigor, she realized that others could benefit from knowing about her experience. She and her father have made it their joint crusade to teach, motivate, and inspire other people about the personal rewards that come from giving the gift of life. Says Jake Garn, "There is simply no other thing I have ever done that has given me greater satisfaction."

Through reading about the situations of others, Sue started to catch a glimpse of just how fortunate she was not to be on an organ donor waiting list or attached to a dialysis machine, and she started to wish that others in similar situations could be so blessed. She also realized that, along with the need to educate people about organ-donation programs and how they literally save lives, there was also a very real need for someone to let the public see the success of a transplant to help allay their fears about the procedure.

Crusading for others who are ailing

As Sue thought about all of this, and as she began to feel renewed energy and vigor, she began to feel there might be a way she could turn what had seemed like a purely private struggle into a way to teach, motivate, and inspire other people. She realized that others could benefit from knowing about her experience. She thought about her mother, my first wife, Hazel Thompson Garn, who had suffered from her own very personal problem during her life. In August 1966 Hazel had been diagnosed with breast cancer, a frightening disease that was rarely talked about openly in those days. The cancer progressed to the extent that it required a mastectomy. Although it was a devastating personal setback, in her last years Hazel allowed her struggle to become a public one so that she could somehow reach out to other women experiencing the same problem. She talked candidly about how it affected her life, hoping to deliver the message that it is possible to cope and also to make people aware of the disease and the need for more research. She died tragically in the summer of 1976 as the result of an automobile accident.

While thinking about the sacrifice her mother had made by allowing the world into her most private life, Susan realized that if her mother were alive she would encourage her to do the same. She would want her to share her story, educate people, and give them some of the precious commodity of hope. It was this realization that sealed Sue's decision to share her experience.

She became very positive about participating in news shows and interviews and assisting with efforts to promote donor-awareness programs. She put aside her fears of having her life scrutinized by a demanding media and simply began to go forward and talk about her experience and her strong belief that people should not be reluctant to sign donor cards, should not hesitate to become the possible source of life for other human beings.

In the weeks that followed our initial recovery period, Sue and I made a number of appearances on the network morning talk shows and other media forums. I was so pleased at her candor and openness and the sweet, sincere, and articulate way that she came to discuss her experience. We will do more—as much as we can—to encourage people to become donors and to support research into finding cures for diabetes and kidney disease. What began as a personal struggle for my daughter has become a positive crusade. Together, what we viewed as the gift of a kidney, we now see as a gift of life and renewed vitality, and it is something we simply must share with others.

from Webster's Medical Desk Dictionary

Introductory essay
on the history and etymology
of medical English

The Language of Modern Medicine

In the past year, Merriam-Webster Inc., a Britannica company, introduced a brand new reference volume, *Webster's Medical Desk Dictionary*. This 800-page dictionary has the distinction of coming from a publisher that has had a reputation for excellence in dictionary making for nearly 150 years.

The editors of Britannica's *Medical and Health Annual*, who began using the dictionary at once, found it soon took a place among their most often consulted standard reference volumes. It readily provides authoritative guidance on the most pressing current medical language questions.

The introductory pages of *Webster's Medical Desk Dictionary* contain an instructive and thought-provoking essay on the history and etymology of the medical vocabulary—an essay that truly makes this dynamic language come alive. It chronicles how today's "rich lexical medley we call Medical English" came to comprise terms dating as far back as Hippocrates to the most current coinages (*e.g.,* the now-so-familiar acronym AIDS).

We are pleased to reprint for the *Annual's* readers this engaging examination of how words are born and how they survive, change, or are replaced.

The language of modern medicine, a vigorous, versatile idiom of vast range and formidable intricacy, expands constantly to meet the needs of a complex and rapidly evolving discipline. Medical English in its broadest sense includes not only the official nomenclatures of the basic medical sciences (such as anatomy, biochemistry, pathology, and immunology) and the clinical specialties (such as pediatrics, dermatology, thoracic surgery, and psychiatry) but also a large body of less formal expressions, a sort of trade jargon used by physicians and their professional associates in speech, correspondence, and record-keeping.

Despite the decrees of official boards and committees, medical language tends to grow and change in much the same ways as the vernacular. New terms and expressions appear as if by spontaneous generation to meet new needs, and established words readily acquire new meanings. No firm distinction can be drawn between formal terminology and argot, or between current and obsolescent nomenclature, for expressions that began as informal or shorthand terms may achieve formal status because of their aptness and usefulness, while others whose inaccuracy or inappropriateness have become obvious may survive for decades in speech and even in textbooks.

The parallel between medical English and the common speech also holds true in other ways. Just as no single person can possibly know and use all the words recorded in an unabridged dictionary, no single physician knows and uses all the terms in a medical dictionary. Purists within the profession often object to certain pronunciations and uses of technical terms, but the majority of physicians go on remorselessly pronouncing and using them in ways that seem natural and useful and, as always, it is the standard of usage that finally determines what is correct and what a word really means.

Since pronunciation, spelling, and even meaning depend on usage rather than etymology, it has often been said that the least important thing about a word is its history. And yet, to trace the history of medical terminology is to trace the history of medicine itself, for every stage of that history has left its mark on the working vocabulary of the modern physician. Each new discovery in anatomy, physiology, pathology, and pharmacology has called forth a new name, and a great many of these names, no matter how haphazardly and irregularly coined, no matter how unsuitable in the light of later discoveries, have remained in use. An etymological survey of this rich lexical medley we call medical English, where terms used by Hippocrates jostle others made up yesterday, where we find words from classical languages adapted, often ingeniously and sometimes violently, to modern concepts, and where the names

of celebrated persons, mythic figures, and remote places lend human interest and a spice of the exotic, should claim the attention of anyone having a professional or avocational concern with medicine or one of its allied fields.

For convenience, medical terms currently used by speakers of English may be grouped in eight classes: 1) terms borrowed from everyday English; 2) Greek and Latin terms preserved from ancient and medieval medicine; 3) modern coinages, chiefly from classical language elements; 4) terms based on proper names; 5) borrowings from modern foreign languages; 6) trade names; 7) argot and figurative formations; and 8) abbreviations.

Since every man is ultimately his own physician, professional practitioners of medicine have never held an exclusive right to treat diseases, much less to name and discuss them. Physicians have been borrowing "medical" words from lay English as long as the language has existed.

The history of English falls naturally into three stages. During the Old English or Anglo-Saxon period (A.D. 450–1150), a group of Germanic dialects carried into Britain from northwestern Europe by invading continental tribes including Saxons, Angles, and Jutes gradually diffused and coalesced, receiving important additions from the Old Norse of Scandinavian pirates and marauders and the Latin of Christian missionaries and lesser ones from the languages of foreign traders and the conquered Celts. As Middle English (1150–1500) evolved, most of the inflectional endings of its nouns, adjectives, and verbs weakened and were gradually lost, and it assimilated a vast number of French words brought into Britain after the Norman Conquest (1066). Modern English differs from later Middle English in many of its vowel sounds, in the stabilization of its spelling after the invention of printing, and in its increasing richness in loan words and new formations.

Many modern terms used by both physicians and laity for parts or regions of the body (*arm, back, breast, hand, head, neck*), internal organs and tissues (*heart, liver, lung, blood, bone, fat*), and common symptoms and diseases (*ache, itch, measles, sore, wart, wound*) derive from Anglo-Saxon origins. *Leg, scalp, skin, and skull,* also dating from the earliest period of English, can be traced to Old Norse. We find most of these words in the works of Geoffrey Chaucer (ca 1342–1400), the first important figure in English literary history, and in addition others that entered Middle English via Norman French from medical Latin (*canker, jaundice*) and Greek (*cholera, melancholy*). *Migraine, plague,* and *pleurisy,* also adapted by French from classical words, appear in other Middle English authors.

Though all of these structures, symptoms, and ailments have formal names in the technical language of medicine, physicians generally prefer to use the common English words. They do not, however, always use them in the same way as the laity. For example, medicine has found it expedient to narrow and fix the meanings of some words taken over from lay speech. The anatomist limits the sense of *arm* to the part of the upper extremity between the shoulder and the elbow, and of *leg* to the part of the lower extremity between the knee and the ankle. To the microbiologist and the specialist in infectious diseases, *plague* means a specific communicable disease, not just any epidemic. To the cardiologist, *heart failure* denotes a group of sharply defined clinical syndromes, not just any breakdown of heart function. Similarly, *chill, depression, joint, migraine, shock, stillborn, strain,* and *tenderness* all have more restricted meanings in medical English than in lay speech.

In discussing human anatomy, physicians use some words, such as *flank* and *loin,* that the general populace applies only to animals, and others, such as *belly* and *gut,* that many of the laity regard as impolite. On the other hand, physicians find it best to avoid certain common words of shifting or dubious meaning and to substitute others (usually borrowed from classical languages or fabricated from classical material) whose meaning can be arbitrarily limited. For example, *hip* may be undesirably vague when the context fails to indicate whether the reference is to the thigh, the pelvis, the joint between them, the entire bodily region around this joint, or, euphemistically, the buttock. A patient may complain of dizziness, but the physician cannot be content with a term whose range of meanings includes such disparate symptoms as vertigo, disequilibrium, sleepiness, and nausea.

Physicians have been accused of adopting and clinging to an abstruse terminology based on dead languages in order to keep their patients in ignorance or even to conceal their own ignorance. But apart from cases of ambiguity as with *dizziness* and *hip,* or of brand-new concepts for which the common speech can supply no suitable names, the medical profession is only too ready to borrow or modify plain English expressions. Medical English includes a great many lively and even poetic compounds and phrases built of native material, some of them involving metaphor or hyperbole: *bamboo spine, the bends, clubfoot, frozen shoulder, hammertoe, harelip, knock-knee, mallet finger, saddle block, strawberry mark,* and *wandering pacemaker.*

The enormous stock of Greek words and word elements in the medical vocabulary, a source of difficulties for physicians and laity alike, owes its origin to the fact that Western medicine, insofar as we have written records of it, began with Hippocrates in the Periclean Age of Greece. It can be said with equal truth that Western civilization itself took shape in the same era, when the world and everything in it, from the phenomena of nature to human relations and institutions, first came under the scrutiny of that soaring analytic spirit, tempered by profound wisdom, that found its most perfect expression in Socrates. The presence in modern English of such words borrowed or derived from Greek as *astronomy, character, criticism, democracy, dialogue, emphasis, idea, paragraph, problem, system, theme, theory,* and *thesis* attests to the enduring influence of ancient Greek thought on modern culture. The philosophers Plato and Aristotle, the dramatists Sophocles and Euripides, and the historians Herodotus and Thucydides were all roughly contemporary with Hippocrates.

Revered as the Father of Medicine, Hippocrates (ca 460–ca 370 B.C.) was the guiding spirit if not the founder of the world's first school of scientific medicine on the Greek island of Kos, the site of a famous temple to Aesculapius, god of healing. Tradition assigns to Hippocrates the role of separating medicine from religion by teaching that diseases have organic causes and must be combated by physical measures. He also worked out a primitive system of physiology and pathology based on the physics of Empedocles and the numerology of Pythagoras, and established the ethical directives for physicians embodied in the celebrated Hippocratic oath (which, however, is thought to be by a later hand).

The Corpus Hippocraticum, one of the wonders of ancient learning, is a collection of medical works covering a remarkable range of topics including medical history, geographic medicine, dietetics, prognosis, surgery, and orthopedics. Although no modern scholar believes that all these works are by the same author, a substantial number of them seem to show the same fertile, inquiring, incisive mind at work, and it is through these that Hippocrates has exerted so powerful an influence on all subsequent medical theory and practice. The oldest Greek medical terms in current use appear in the Hippocratic writings themselves, among them *anthrax, asthma, bronchus, condyloma, dyspnea, dysthymia, erythema, erysipelas, orthopnea,* and *tenesmus.*

These words were not, of course, invented by Hippocrates (*asthma* appears in the *Iliad*), but only borrowed by him from the common speech and adapted to serve the needs of the fledgling science. The modern physician uses all of these terms, generally with more specific meanings than did Hippocrates, and sometimes with radically different ones. The principal reason for the survival of these words from a classical language is that for centuries after Hippocrates, Greek medicine was virtually the only medicine worthy of the name in the Western world, just as Greek philosophy and science dominated Western thought until long after the beginning of the Christian era. Aristotle (384–322 B.C.), remembered chiefly as a philosopher and the formulator of the system of logic still most widely accepted today, was also a brilliant anatomist and physiologist, and a few of our medical Greek words (*alopecia, aorta, epiglottis, nystagmus, pancreas*) made early appearances in his works.

Centuries before Hippocrates, the priests of Egypt learned something about anatomy and pathology through the exercise of their duties as embalmers of the dead. Egyptian medicine, as revealed to us by tantalizingly sparse remnants of ancient writings on papyrus, seems to have been, like Greek medicine before Hippocrates, a branch of religion. There is evidence that early Egyptian science and mathematics influenced the development of these disciplines in Greece, and that, long before Alexander the Great conquered Egypt and annexed it to the Hellenic world, some Egyptian medical lore had reached Greece. A few medical terms that we customarily derive from Greek ultimately had Egyptian origins: *ammonia,* from a primitive term for ammonium chloride, of which large natural deposits were found near a shrine of the Egyptian deity Ammon (Amen) in Libya; *gum* 'vegetable exudation' from Egyptian *qmy.t* via Greek *kommi; stibium,* the chemical name for the element antimony and the basis for its international symbol, Sb, from Egyptian *stm* by way of Greek *stimmi.*

Long after Rome in its turn conquered Greece and absorbed the best of Hellenic learning and culture, most physicians in Rome and the provinces were Greek slaves or freedmen or Greek-speaking immigrants from the Near East or North Africa. Hence the lore of the craft continued to be passed on in the language of Hippocrates. Aretaeus of Cappadocia, who practiced and wrote in the first century after Christ, discussed *asphyxia* and apparently invented the term *diabetes.* His contemporary, the medical botanist Dioscorides, used the terms *eczema, kerion,* and *trachoma.* Galen (A.D. 129–199), a native of Pergamum in Asia Minor, moved to Rome early in his career, devoted many years to the study and practice of medicine, and became court physician to the emperor Marcus Aurelius. His voluminous writings in Greek on anatomy, physiology, pathology, and therapeutics have earned him second place in medicine's pantheon. Among words that first appear in his writings may be mentioned *allantois, atheroma, coccyx, epididymis,* and *peritoneum.*

In discussing parts of the body or common diseases a medical writer may find lay terms sufficient for his needs, but to write about new concepts or discoveries he must either invent new words or use old ones in new ways. From the dawn of medical history, writers on anatomy and pathology have yielded to the natural impulse to create metaphors to name new things. Thus the bone at the lower end of the spine was called *coccyx,* Greek for 'cuckoo', because of its beaklike shape, and the opening from the stomach into the small intestine became the *pylorus* 'gatekeeper'. Loss of hair was termed *alopecia* because it suggested the appearance of a fox (*alopex*) with mange, and a person with an abnormally ravenous appetite was said to have *bulimia* 'the hunger of an ox'. Perhaps none of these words was the invention of a physician, but they all appear in early Greek medical writings, setting a precedent for subsequent medical word-making in all Western languages down to the present day.

With the collapse of the Byzantine Empire, the Greek language went into eclipse as a medium of scientific and technical communication. Even the masterpieces of Greek drama, philosophy, and history dropped out of sight, to be rediscovered centuries later in the Renaissance. Meanwhile Latin, the language of republican and imperial Rome and its western provinces, flourished as both a widespread vernacular and a literary language. While the popular speech was evolving into regional dialects that would in time become Italian, Spanish, Catalan, Portuguese, French, Provençal, and Rumanian, the classical language, enshrined in the prose of Cicero and the verses of the Augustan poets, survived with changes as the international language of learning, science, jurisprudence, and the Church.

The first Roman writer on medicine, Aulus Cornelius Celsus, who lived in the first century after Christ, was probably not a physician. His eight books *De Medicina* (*On Medicine*), perhaps translated or adapted from a Greek work, review the whole subject of medical theory and practice in lucid, even elegant Latin. The immense historical value of Celsus's writings lies partly in his nomenclature, for besides recording numerous Greek medical terms for which Latin offered no suitable equivalents (*aphthae, ascites, cremaster, lagophthalmos, mydriasis, opisthotonos, staphyloma, tetanus*), he also gives the earliest medical applications of many Latin words still in use today (*angina, caries, delirium, fistula, impetigo, mucus, radius, scabies, tabes, tibia, varus, verruca, vertebra, virus*).

Celsus's contemporary, Pliny the Elder (A.D. ca 23–79), an indefatigable if somewhat incautious student of the natural sciences (he died while observing at close range an eruption of Vesuvius), was also a prolific writer. He devoted several books of his monumental *Naturalis Historia* (*Natural History*) to medical topics, and recorded for the first time the medical uses of such Latin terms as *acetabulum, pruritus, and tinea*. Whereas Celsus's rigorously scientific work remained virtually lost from about the fifth century to the fifteenth, when its rediscovery stirred the medical world to its foundations, Pliny's compendium of myth and misinformation became one of the nonfiction best-sellers of antiquity, and by the Middle Ages it was firmly established as a popular encyclopedia.

During the centuries following the decline of classical culture, the progress of medicine, as of all the arts and sciences, slowed nearly to a halt. Scientific investigation languished; education consisted largely in the uncritical memorization of ancient lore. In medicine the teachings of Galen, known through Latin translations and commentaries, maintained an unchallenged supremacy for more than a thousand years. But gradual though it was, the development of medical knowledge during the Dark Ages led to a slow accretion of technical Latin terms representing modifications of and additions to the lexical legacy of the ancients.

In the ninth century, when European letters and science were at their lowest ebb, Islamic scholars began a revival of Western learning, translating Aristotle, Galen, and other Greek authors into Syriac and Arabic and subjecting their teachings to searching analysis and impartial verification. The Persian physicians Rhazes, Haly Abbas, and Avicenna, the Arabians Averroës and Albucasis, and the Jew Maimonides performed important original research and made valuable contributions to medical literature. Traces of their influence linger in many terms of Arabic and Persian origin referring to anatomy, chemistry, and pharmacy that made their way into medical English by way of medieval Latin: *alcohol, alkali, benzoin, bezoar, camphor, nuchal, retina, safranin, saphenous, soda*, and *sugar*.

With the resurgence of intellectual activity in the Renaissance, vigorous and original thinkers arose all over Europe to overthrow the hallowed errors of ancient authorities. In medicine, the earliest revolution came in anatomy with the painstaking dissections and detailed drawings of Leonardo and Vesalius, who dared to show where Galen had gone wrong. Fallopius, Servetus, Sylvius, and many others followed their lead. Increasingly minute descriptions of the human body called for an ever more elaborate nomenclature. The printing, in 1502, of the *Onomasticon* (*Wordbook*) of Julius Pollux (2d century A.D.), a sort of dictionary that happened to include a section on anatomic terms, enabled anatomists to drop most of the Arabic names for parts of the body then commonly found in textbooks and reintroduce such classical Greek terms as *amnion, atlas, axis, canthus, gastrocnemius, tragus*, and *trochanter*.

But the system of anatomic nomenclature that had been largely codified by the end of the sixteenth century, while including a substantial body of Greek terms, was chiefly Latin. Once again metaphor played an extensive role in the choice of terms. Anatomists named body parts after plants (*glans* 'acorn', *uvula* 'little grape'), animals (*cochlea* 'snail', *vermis* 'worm'), architectural elements (*tectum* 'roof', *vestibulum* 'entrance hall'), household implements (*clavicula* 'little key', *malleus* 'hammer'), articles of clothing (*tunica* 'tunic', *zona* 'belt'), topographic features (*fossa* 'ditch', *fovea* 'pit'), and even other body parts (*capitellum* 'little head', *ventriculus* 'little belly'). By contrast, scores of other Latin anatomic terms, including many that we still use, seem almost painfully literal (*extensor pollicis longus* 'long extender of the thumb', *foramen magnum* 'big hole'). The investigation of the fine structure of the body and of disease-causing microorganisms, made possible by the invention of the simple and compound microscopes, demanded a new stock of terms, and again many of those adopted were descriptive figures (*bacillus* 'little stick', *glomerulus* 'little ball of yarn', *nucleus* 'kernel').

Medicine in the modern sense came into being only with the commencement of the scientific era. Physiology, pathology, pharmacology, and surgery, formulated on an increasingly rational basis, required increasingly rigorous and systematized language. As long as Latin was understood by all educated persons, medical textbooks and monographs continued to be written in that language and lectures to be delivered in it. New medical terms were Latin in form if not always in lexical origin. The modern vocabulary of medicine contains, besides many words known to Celsus, other terms borrowed from Latin at a much later date, such as *angina pectoris, cor bovinum, fetor hepaticus, molluscum contagiosum, placenta previa, rubeola, torticollis*, and *vaccinia*.

In the days when a doctor's prescription was a kind of recipe calling for several ingredients, prescriptions were written in an elaborate, ritualized, gramatically debased form of Latin. This pharmaceutical Latin flourished until about the middle of the present century, and many abbreviations based on it are still in use today (*b.i.d., bis in die* 'twice a day'; *p.c., post cibos* 'after meals'; *p.r.n., pro re nata* 'as the occasion arises').

Although not directly connected with medicine, the system of classificatory naming of all living things devised by the Swedish naturalist Linnaeus (1707–1778) plays an important role in medical communication. Linnaean nomenclature, fundamentally Latin with a substantial admixture of Greek stems and proper nouns, includes terms for disease-causing bacteria and fungi as well as more complex organisms of medical importance.

It is one thing for medicine to borrow a classical Greek or Latin word such as *typhus* or *scabies* and assign it a specific technical meaning, and another to combine classical stems and affixes to make entirely new words like *hypercholesterolemia* and *proprioception*. Most new medical terms formed from classical elements during the past hundred years have been of the latter kind, which we may call coinages for want of a more distinctive label.

Coinage entails two kindred processes, derivation (or affixation) and compounding. Derivation here refers to the attachment of one or more prefixes or suffixes to a word or stem, as when the prefix *endo-* 'within' and the suffix

-itis 'inflammation of' are added to the base word *metra* 'uterus' to form *endometritis* 'inflammation of the uterine lining'. Compounding is the joining of two or more adjective, noun, or verb stems, as when the English stems derived from Greek *megas* 'large', *karyon* 'nut, nucleus', and *kytos* 'vessel, cell' are combined to form *megakaryocyte* 'a bone marrow cell with a large, irregular nucleus'. Derivation is exemplified by English *outlandish* and *unfriendly*, compounding by *headache* and *windpipe*.

The combining form of a classical word consists of its stem plus, if needed, a linking vowel, usually *o* but sometimes *i* with Latin words. Thus *brady-*, as in *bradycardia*, is from Greek *bradys* 'slow'; *cortico-*, as in *corticothalamic*, from Latin *cortex, corticis* 'bark'; *hemat-* or *hemato-*, as in *hematopoiesis*, from Greek *haima, haimatos* 'blood'; *femoro-*, as in *femoropopliteal*, from Latin *femur, femoris* 'thigh'; *gastr-* or *gastro-*, as in *gastroesophageal*, from Greek *gaster, gastros* 'stomach'; *my-* or *myo-*, as in *myoneural*, from Greek *mys, myos* 'mouse, muscle'; *ov-* or *ovi-* or *ovo-*, as in *oviduct*, from Latin *ovum, ovi* 'egg'. The linking vowel is generally omitted before a following vowel: *gastritis, hematemesis, hematuria*. The final element of a classical coinage may be anglicized (*colostomy, dermatome* with silent final *e, fibroblast, herniorrhaphy*) or not (*hemochromatosis, keratoconus, polyhydramnios, asystole* with *e* pronounced).

Although in earlier times makers of new terms followed classical precedents more diligently and accurately than now, medical coinages have never adhered strictly to any rule, not even that of self-consistency. Medical language has not hesitated to shorten stems, drop awkward syllables, or use unorthodox forms of juncture. The meanings of some stems have wavered between two extremes (*carcinogenic* 'causing cancer' but *nephrogenic* 'arising in the kidney') or even gone in entirely new directions under the influence of analogy. The suffix *-itis*, in classical Greek merely a means of turning a noun into an adjective (as with English *-en* in *golden*), took on its special meaning 'inflammation of' because it often appeared in Greek phrases such as *nephritis nosos* 'kidney disease'. Even as early as the time of Hippocrates, it was customary to shorten a phrase of this kind by omitting the noun. Similarly, the Greek suffix *-ma* that was a means of forming a noun from a verb stem (as in *drama* and *diploma*) fused with the linking vowel *-o-* appeared in English as the combining form *-oma* with the medical sense of 'tumor, neoplasm' because it figured in a number of ancient terms, such as *sarcoma* and *condyloma* denoting abnormal growths.

For centuries, classical scholars thought it unscholarly to join Greek and Latin material in the same word. Since most of the living medical prefixes and suffixes, including the ubiquitous and indispensable *-itis* and *-oma*, were of Greek pedigree, matching Greek stems were dredged up from the depths of oblivion for combination with them, even when synonyms of Latin derivation were already in general use. Thus, although the common adjectives *oral, mammary*, and *renal* embody the Latin words for 'mouth', 'breast', and 'kidney' respectively, the corresponding Greek stems appear in *stomatitis, mastectomy*, and *nephrosis*. Now that objections to Greek-Latin hybrids have largely died out, many such words (*appendicitis, hypertension, radiology*) thrive without the stigma of scholarly reproach. Indeed, compounds of Greek with French (*culdoscopy, goitrogenic*), English (*antibody, hemiblock*), German (*antiscorbutic, kernicterus*), and Arabic (*alcoholism, alkatosis*) now find universal acceptance. Meanwhile the medical lexicon remains rich beyond its needs in Greek stems and in Greek-Latin synonym pairs such as *hypodermic/subcutaneous, scaphoid/navicular*, and *xiphoid/ensiform*.

The hundreds of classical stems and affixes in daily use virtually invite further coinages, and in fact physicians produce nonce words and ad hoc formations from this material at a rate that defies the lexicographer to keep pace. Each new word may become the basis of a whole dynasty of derivative or analogical formations. Nouns, equipped with appropriate suffixes, readily change into verbs and adjectives, and vice versa. Many terms arise by back-formation, the process of creating an imaginary precursor or a shortened unconventional word from an existing form, such as *to diagnose* from *diagnosis, to perfuse* from *perfusion*, and *precoridum* from *precordial*.

At all periods of history, proper nouns denoting persons and places have been incorporated into adjectives, verbs, other nouns, and phrases, as in *Jeffersonian, Americanize, Marxism*, and *Halley's comet*. Eponymy, the derivation of words from personal names, has added to the medical vocabulary such diverse expressions as *Addison's disease, chagoma, cushingoid, descemetocele, facies Hippocratica, galenical*, and *parkinsonism*. Besides terms like these honoring distinguished physicians, others stand as monuments to important patients: *bacitracin*, an antibiotic named for Margaret Tracy, from whose tissues it was first isolated; *Carrión's disease* (bartonellosis), named for Daniel A. Carrión, a Peruvian student who inoculated himself experimentally with the disease and died of it; *Hartnup disease*, a heredofamilial metabolic disorder named for an English family of which several members were so affected; *HeLa cells*, a line of cultured human malignant cells named for Henrietta Lacks, from whose cervical carcinoma they are all descended; *Legionnaires' disease*, pneumonitis due to a bacterium of the genus *Legionella*, the disease and the genus both named for the American Legion, at whose convention in 1976 the first recognized outbreak occurred.

Names of prominent figures in myth, legend, and popular fiction have also found their way into the physician's lexicon. *Atropine*, a drug extracted from belladonna and various related plants of the genus *Atropa* and used as an antispasmodic for smooth muscle, is named, in allusion to its lethal properties, for Atropos, one of the three Fates, who was reputed to cut off each person's thread of life at the moment appointed for death. *Morphine*, a narcotic extracted from the juice of the poppy, is named for Morpheus, the god of sleep. *Satyriasis*, abnormal sexual excitability in the male, refers to the Satyrs, mythic sylvan deities with a leaning toward lechery. *Pickwickian syndrome*, extreme obesity with hypoventilation, refers to Joe the fat boy in Dicken's *Pickwick Papers*.

Most of the medical terms that incorporate geographic allusions are names of infectious diseases or their causative agents and refer to sites where these diseases are specially prevalent or endemic or where they were first identified or studied. In some of these terms, the names preserve their original form, as in *Lyme disease*, a tick-borne spirochetal infection named for a town in Connecticut, and *Norwalk virus*, which causes outbreaks of diarrhea in schoolchildren and is named after a city in Ohio. For other terms the geographic origins are not so evident: *Coxsackie virus*, any of a group of human viruses causing various acute febrile syndromes, named for Coxsackie, New York; *maduromycosis*, a fungal skin disease, named after the Indonesian island of Madura; *tularemia*, an infection of rodents sometimes transmitted to man, first identified in Tulare County, California.

These terms based on proper nouns impart an element of novelty as well as a liberal dimension to what might otherwise be a depressingly prosaic assemblage of dry lexical bones gathered from the graveyard of dead languages. In a similar way, terms borrowed from modern foreign languages lend a cosmopolitan flavor to medical speech and writing. There are logical reasons why speakers of English customarily use foreign words for certain diseases, symptoms, or drugs. During the nineteenth century, the teachings and writings of Continental medical authorities played an essential part in the education of British and American physicians. Up until World War I, Americans flocked to Paris and Vienna for specialty training, and brought back French and German words and phrases for which no English equivalents seemed quite right. Numerous French words continue in use today in clinical medicine (*ballottement* 'shaking', *bruit* 'noise', *grand mal* 'big disease', *petit mal* 'little disease'), surgery (*curette* 'scraper', *débridement* 'unbridling, cutting loose', *rongeur* 'gnawer', *tamponade* 'plugging'), and obstetrics (*cerclage* 'encirclement', *cul de sac* 'bottom of the bag', *fourchette* 'little fork', *souffle* 'blowing'). The suffix *-ase*, used to form the names of enzymes, first appeared in *diastase*, a French respelling of Greek *diastasis* 'separation'. The sugar suffix *-ose* dates from French *glucose,* based on Greek *gleukos* 'sweet wine'. The phrase *milieu intérieur,* applied in French by Claude Bernard in the 1850s to his concept of internal physical and chemical equilibrium, is used in English today to designate the same concept.

German words also abound in medical English. *Mittelschmerz* 'middle pain' (that is, pain midway between menses) is a well-established term for the pain of ovulation. *Spinnbarkeit* 'stretchability' refers to the consistency of cervical mucus under the influence of estrogen. *Magenstrasse* 'stomach street' picturesquely designates a portion of the stomach whose longitudinal folds seem designed to channel food toward the intestine. A number of German terms have been retained in English for findings first reported by German or Austrian scientists: *mast* 'stuffed' *cell* in histology, *gestalt* 'shape' in psychiatry, *anlage* 'foundation' in embryology, *quellung* 'swelling' in microbiology. The term *eye ground* for the retina and associated structures as examined with the ophthalmoscope probably owes its origin to German *Augenhintergrund. Antibody* is a translation, or at least a partial translation, of *Antikörper,* and *sitz bath* bears the same relation to *Sitzbad.* The adjective *German* in *German measles,* a synonym for *rubella,* probably came into use in the sense of 'false' or 'illusory', but may allude to the German term *Rötheln,* by which the disease was widely known in the nineteenth and early twentieth centuries.

Most of the Spanish and Portuguese loans in medical use denote diseases endemic in tropical colonies established by Spain and Portugal in the Old and New Worlds, or drugs derived from plants first found in those regions. Spanish *espundia* (apparently an alteration of *esponja* 'sponge') and *pinta* 'splotch of paint' are names for tropical infections based on their appearance, and Portuguese *albino* 'little white one' was first applied to the occasional African slave without skin pigment. Spanish *curare* and Portuguese *ipecacuanha* are derived from South American Indian words, Portuguese *ainhum* from an African word. Other medical terms of African origin are *kwashiorkor* and *tsetse.*

Among Italian words in modern medical English, *pellagra* and *malaria* denote diseases once endemic in Italy. *Influenza* and *petechia* are also Italian in origin. *Kala-azar* is Hindi for 'black disease', and *beriberi* means 'extreme weakness' in Sinhalese. *Tsutsugamushi* 'dangerous bug' *disease* and *sodoku* 'rat venom' are from Japanese.

Trade names inevitably figure in workaday medical parlance, as they do in the speech of the general public. Nearly all drugs in common use and many dressing materials, instruments, and appliances bear trade names that are simpler, more euphonious, and more distinctive than their generic names. The trade name of an especially successful product may become a generic term for all similar products despite the efforts of the manufacturer to assert his legal rights in the name. *Aspirin, lanolin,* and *milk of magnesia* were once trade names; *Band-Aid, Vaseline,* and (in Canada) *Aspirin* still are.

When Jokichi Takamine isolated the hormone of the adrenal medulla in 1901 he called it *Adrenalin* and promptly patented both name and product. This created difficulties for the compilers of the *United States Pharmacopeia,* since regulations forbade the inclusion of trade names. The term *epinephrine,* the Greek equivalent of *Adrenalin,* which had been suggested in 1897 by John Jacob Abel, was therefore substituted in the *U.S. Pharmacopeia,* but meanwhile *adrenaline* (with finale *e*) had slipped into the *British Pharmacopoeia.* Nowadays *epinephrine* and *adrenaline* are generally used interchangeably for both the natural hormone and the drug, although Parke-Davis holds the rights to *Adrenalin* as a trademark for a preparation of epinephrine used as a drug.

Physicians would not be human if they never playfully made up unconventional expressions or indulged in humorous distortions of technical terminology. What motives lie behind the creation of medical argot—the natural relish for a secret group language, the poetic impulse gone astray, a spirit of rebellion against regimentation of language and thought, or a craving for comic relief—need not concern us here. As mentioned earlier, no sharp distinction can be drawn between formal terminology and medical argot. Clearly *retinitis pigmentosa* and *antihemophilic factor* belong to formal language; just as clearly *red-hot belly* in the sense of 'an abdomen showing signs of acute inflammation' and *electric lights and watermelons* as a jocular variation on *electrolyte and water balance* do not. Between these extremes lie a large number of expressions that, without being perfectly orthodox in formation or altogether serious in tone, yet hover on the verge of respectability, and occasionally achieve it.

Many terms now ratified by long use began as figures of speech, euphemisms, or experiments in onomatopoeia. An unconscious anthropomorphism has influenced the physician's way of talking about disease-causing microorganisms, which are described as *fastidious, resistant,* or *sensitive,* and about neoplasms, which may be *benign, invasive,* or *malignant.* Many expressions in daily use seem based on the notion that medical practice is a warfare waged against disease. The physician plans an *aggressive* clinical *strategy,* choosing *weapons* from his *arsenal* (or *armamentarium*) to augment the patient's *defenses* against *attacking* organisms or *foreign* substances.

Despite the nature of their calling, physicians are not much less squeamish than others about naming and discussing certain body parts and functions, nor less ready to substitute euphemisms for cruder and more explicit terms. Some expressions still in use, such as *stool* for *feces* and *void* for *urinate,* were already well established in lay speech by the end of the Middle English period. During the Victorian era, medical language copied the extreme prudishness of demotic English: childbirth was disguised as *confinement* and a leg masqueraded as a *limb.* Modern medicine continues to sugarcoat its less palatable pills, calling one kind of abortion a *menstrual extraction* and substituting *chemical dependency* for drug addiction. Even *disease, infirmity,* and *invalid* are somewhat euphemistic in tone, hinting at illness by denying wellness.

Onomatopoeia is the creation of a word whose very pronunciation seems to echo the thing named, as in the case of *screech, squawk,* and *whisper.* Any discussion of medical onomatopoeia must ignore the lines dividing languages and epochs, for the process has undoubtedly been at work since the origin of speech. In fact, at one time linguists were ready to trace all words to this source. Although that theory is no longer held, onomatopoeia still provides the most reasonable explanation for certain recurring associations between sound and sense, such as the relations between [sn] and the nose (*sneeze, sniffle, snore*) and between [gl] and swallowing (*deglutition, gullet, singultus*). Greek *borborygmus, bruxism,* and *rhonchus,* Latin *crepitus, murmur,* and *stertor,* and English *croup, hiccup,* and *wheeze* are also plainly onomatopoetic in origin. Less evidently so, because of phonetic refinements, are *eructation, rale,* and *sternutation.*

The more frequently a medical word or phrase is used, the more likely it is to undergo some kind of shortening in both speech and writing. Spoken shortenings on the order of "CA" for *cancer* and "scope" for *bronchoscope* do not often achieve formal status, but the list of written abbreviations that have become standard grows steadily longer. The most common type of written abbreviation is the initialism, consisting of the initials of the words in a phrase or of the key elements in a compound term: *BUN,* blood urea nitrogen; *ECG,* eletrocardiogram; *HMO,* health maintenance organization.

When, instead of saying the letters separately, one customarily pronounces such an abbreviation as a word (*AIDS,* acquired immune deficiency syndrome; *CABG,* pronounced "cabbage," *coronary artery bypass graft*) it is often called an acronym. An acronym may be treated as an ordinary word and combined with stems or affixes, as in *vipoma* 'a neoplasm that secretes VIP (vasoactive intestinal polypeptide)'. Other kinds of shortening to which medical terms are subject include telescoping of phrases (*arbovirus, arthropod-borne virus*) and omission of one or more words from a phrase (*steroid* for *adrenal cortical steroid*).

Not all shorthand expressions are abbreviations in the strict sense; sometimes letters or numbers are chosen arbitrarily to designate the members of a group or series. Thus the letters *A, B, C,* and so on, as used to designate the vitamins, are not abbreviations of more elaborate names (though, as an exception, *vitamin K* refers to Danish *koagulation*). Nor are the letters *P, Q R, S,* and *T,* as applied to the electrocardiogram (as in *P wave, QRS complex,* and *Q-T interval*) abbreviations for words beginning with those letters. Greek letters as well as Arabic and Roman numerals figure in many medical terms: *alpha-fetoprotein, beta-hemolysis, gamma globulin, HTLV-III, HLA-B27 antigen.*

These, then, are the ways in which nearly all of the words, phrases, and expressions in the contemporary medical vocabulary have come into being. We often forget that words are first of all combinations of sounds, and only later marks on paper. The pronunciation of a word *is* that word, no matter what it means, how it is used, or how we choose to spell it. The pronunciation of medical terms by speakers of English tends to parallel the somewhat unruly practice of the general language. Classical precedents are largely ignored in the pronunciation of Greek and Latin words, particularly as to vowel sounds and syllable stress. Words and proper names borrowed from foreign languages fare little better, and the reproduction of French phonology is usually essayed with more zeal than accuracy. Moreover, an attempt at French pronunciation is often forced on words (*chalazion, raphe, troche*) having no connection with that language.

Although medical English may give a superficial impression of order and system, it does not possess these qualities in much higher degree than the common speech. Quasi-official bodies select and ratify anatomic, pharmaceutical, and taxonomic terms to fit into schemes and classifications already established, but the bulk of medical terminology displays a remarkable lack of organization and consistency. The practice of calling diseases by common, provincial, or purely descriptive names long after their nature and causation have become clear makes for a cluttered and unsystematic nosology, or nomenclature of disease. Whereas the microbiologist has neatly classified one group of disease-causing microorganisms as the rickettsias, the infections they cause bear such heterogeneous names as *typhus, Brill's disease, rickettsialpox, Q fever, Rocky Mountain spotted fever, fièvre boutonneuse,* and *tsutsugamushi disease.*

When several competing groups of researchers are investigating a new disease, names for the causative agent may proliferate almost as rapidly as the microorganism itself only to be synonymized later. One school of research identified the retrovirus implicated in causing AIDS and called it *lymphadenopathy-associated virus* or *LAV.* Other researchers call the same virus *HTLV-III, human T-cell leukemia virus type III, human T-cell lymphotropic virus type III, human immunodeficiency virus,* or *HIV.* Meanwhile the mass media often refer to the retrovirus simply as the *AIDS virus.* It remains to be seen which of these terms will survive. The condition itself is variously denoted by *acquired immune deficiency syndrome, acquired immunodeficiency syndrome,* or simply by the acronym *AIDS.*

But although medical language cannot match the exemplary regularity of chemical and taxonomic nomenclature, it is at least no less precise and consistent than, for example, the technical vocabularies of banking, geology, aeronautics, and law, nor less useful and convenient for those who speak and write it daily in their professional work.

One might sum up the history of medical English by saying that it has grown and evolved as an integral part of the common language, choosing and even manufacturing its vocabulary to suit the special needs of medical practitioners, investigators, teachers, and writers, but generally clinging to the phonetic, semantic, and syntactic habits of plain English. The individual histories of medical words may be both fascinating and instructive, but they do not necessarily help in determining correct meanings or current spellings. Indeed, the entry of a term into the medical vocabulary is not the end of its history but only the beginning.

The meaning we accept nowadays for a word may be but the latest of many it has borne. In the Greek of Hippocrates, *aorta* refers to the lower respiratory tract and *bronchus* means the throat, gullet, or windpipe indifferently, as does *stomachos* in Homer. In classical Latin, *vulva* means 'uterus' and *uterus* generally means 'belly'. We retain the term *influenza* for a group of specific viral syndromes although we no longer attribute them to the malign influence (for that is the purport of the term) of the heavenly bodies. We preserve terms alluding to Hippocratic pathophysiology, such as *cholera, chyme, crisis, dyscrasia, humoral, hypochondria,* and *melancholia,* although the concepts for which these terms stand were rejected as invalid early in the nineteenth century. These words remain in use because over the years they have lost their original meanings and acquired others. Cholera is now a specific bacterial infection, and a blood dyscrasia is a disturbance in the formation of blood cells, both notions that would have baffled Hippocrates.

These hardy survivors illustrate the point, often overlooked and sometimes vigorously contested, that the meaning or definition of a word depends on association and analogy, not necessarily on its history or etymology. The portal vein got its name from the *porta* or gate of the liver, a cleft on the underside of the organ where this vein enters. For centuries the portal vein was believed to be the only blood vessel in the body that both begins and ends in capillaries. For this reason the term *portal* lost its earlier associations and came to mean 'beginning and ending in capillaries'. When a similar arrangement was finally discovered in the pituitary gland, the vessels there were called the *pituitary portal system.* Because the sense of *colic* (Greek *kolikos*) has shifted from the literal one of 'pertaining to the colon' to 'any intermittent, cramping pain in the lower trunk', we can speak without incongruity of *renal colic* 'the pain caused by a stone in a kidney or ureter'.

The definitions assigned to terms such as *abortion, acupuncture, chiropractic, holistic medicine, macrobiotic diet,* and *wellness* by advocates of these disciplines or practices may differ radically from the definitions of their opponents, and these again from those of disinterested observers. Our language both reflects and shapes our ways of perceiving, dividing, and classifying reality. As modern medical thought becomes less empirical and superstitious, more coherent and linear, so does modern medical language. The words may sound the same, look the same on paper, but their connotations shift with the passing years, responding to shifts in theory, doctrine, and point of view.

The quest for the exact meaning of a medical term is more than just an academic exercise. Words are our most effective means of recording and transmitting information, and almost our only way of dealing with complex and abstract subjects. The precision and perspicuity with which words are used determine the efficacy of educational and informational endeavors and the validity of written records. On the meaning of a single word in a hospital chart may hinge thousands of dollars in insurance benefits, millions in litigation settlements, even the life of the patient. In this light the importance of an accurate, up-to-date dictionary of medical English with definitions based on current usage citations can hardly be exaggerated.

JOHN H. DIRCKX. Medical Director, C. H. Gosiger Memorial Health Center, University of Dayton, Ohio. Author of *The Language of Medicine: Its Evolution, Structure, and Dynamics.*

ENCYCLOPÆDIA
BRITANNICA

MEDICAL
UPDATE

Articles from the 1987
Printing of *Encyclopædia Britannica*

The purpose of this section is to introduce to continuing *Medical and Health Annual* subscribers selected *Macropædia* articles or portions of articles that have been completely revised or rewritten in the most recent edition. It is intended to update the *Macropædia* coverage of medical and health-related topics in a way that cannot be accomplished fully by a yearly review of significant developments, because the *Macropædia* texts themselves—written from a longer perspective than any yearly revision—supply authoritative interpretation as well as pertinent data and examination of timely issues.

Two wholly new articles have been chosen from the 1987 printing: IMMUNITY and EXERCISE AND PHYSICAL CONDITIONING. Each is the work of distinguished scholars, and each represents the continuing dedication of the *Encyclopædia Britannica* to bringing such works to the general reader. New bibliographies accompany the articles as well for readers who wish to pursue certain topics.

Immunity

Immunity describes the ability of humans and other animals to resist or overcome infection by invading microbes or larger parasites. That the environment contains many potentially destructive microorganisms is obvious from the speed with which animals decay after death. It is impossible for an animal to avoid contact with microbes, many billions of which live harmlessly on the skin and in the gut, quite apart from those that are breathed in or that penetrate the skin whenever it is pricked or cut. What matters is that microbes should not grow once inside the animal's body. Humans and other vertebrates have two sorts of defenses against microbial infection. One consists of the so-called innate immune mechanisms, those that kill or inhibit a wide variety of microbes irrespective of whether these have challenged the body before. This kind of immunity is nonspecific—that is, its mechanisms can act against microbes that are not necessarily similar to one another. The other type of defense mechanisms, by contrast, provides specific, acquired immunity. Such immunity is specific in that its responses are tailored to act against a particular microbe or its products; it is acquired in that these tailor-made responses are enormously increased as a result of being stimulated by the prior presence of a given microbe or its products.

Vaccination, or active immunization, confers protection by stimulating specific, acquired immunity.

Obviously any animal that has mechanisms to destroy invaders must be able to distinguish between the materials of its own body and those that originate outside it. Considering that all living creatures are made up of basically similar building blocks, the capacity of any creature to distinguish the molecules of which it is composed—*i.e.,* "self"—from practically all others—*i.e.,* "not-self"—is remarkable. This capacity is present in all living creatures to some degree, but among vertebrates it is especially a feature of the white blood cells called lymphocytes; much of this article focuses on these cells.

Despite its obvious benefits, specific, acquired immunity can become misdirected and do more harm than good. Allergies arise when the mechanisms of immunity become exaggerated or when they are directed against otherwise harmless, nonliving materials absorbed from outside, such as pollen, dust, or food. Autoimmune disorders occur when immune responses become directed against the body's own constituents.

For the most part, this article centres on the human immune system. The discussion is divided into the following sections:

Nonspecific, innate immunity

BARRIERS AGAINST INFECTION

The skin and the linings of the respiratory and gastrointestinal tracts provide the first line of defense against invasion by microbes or parasites. Human skin has a tough outer layer of cells that produce keratin, a protein similar to that of which hair is composed. This layer of cells, which is constantly renewed from below, serves as a mechanical barrier to infection. In addition, glands in the skin secrete oily substances that include fatty acids, such as oleic acid, that can kill some bacteria; skin glands also secrete lysozyme, an enzyme (also present in tears) that can break down the outer wall of certain bacteria.

Like the outer layer of the skin, but much softer, the linings of the respiratory and gastrointestinal tracts provide a mechanical barrier of cells that are constantly being renewed. The lining of the respiratory tract has cells that secrete mucus (phlegm), which traps small particles. Other cells in the wall of the respiratory tract have small hairlike projections, called cilia, which steadily beat in a sweeping movement that propels the mucus and any trapped particles up and out of the throat and nose. As will be clear from later sections of this article, protective antibodies, which are products of specific immunity, are also present in the mucus. The lining of the gastrointestinal tract also contains cells that secrete mucus, which, in addition to aiding the passage of food, traps potentially harmful particles. This mucus also contains protective antibodies; furthermore, the stomach lining secretes hydrochloric acid that is strong enough to kill many microbes.

PROTECTIVE FACTORS

As stated above, some microbes do penetrate the body's protective barriers and enter the internal tissues. There they encounter a variety of chemical substances that may prevent their growth. Some of the chemicals are ones involved in normal body processes. For example, the blood and tissue fluids contain chemicals that inhibit the potentially damaging digestive enzymes released from the body cells that have died in the natural course of events, but these chemicals can also inhibit similar enzymes produced by bacteria. Another substance that performs normal processes but also provides protection against microbes is the blood protein transferrin. This protein binds free molecules of iron firmly and transports the metal from the gut, where it is absorbed, to those cells that use it (e.g., to make the red-blood-cell pigment hemoglobin). Bacteria need free iron to grow, and transferrin can render it unavailable to them. Probably more important than the "incidental" protective chemicals just described is the mixture of proteins termed complement, which is present in blood and tissue fluids and is discussed more fully later in this article. Many microbes can activate complement in ways that do not involve the special means used in specific immunity. If the microbes lack protective coats, complement will destroy them. Other microbes, including those that are potentially harmful (pathogenic), can evade these mechanisms. Protection against these invaders depends upon the activity of scavenger cells, together with the mechanisms to be described below under specific immunity.

Interferons

Yet another protective factor is a family of proteins collectively known as interferons; these inhibit the replication of many, but not all, viruses. Interferons are made normally by cells that are already infected by viruses or that have taken in foreign nucleic acid (nucleic acid being the essential constituent of viruses, which enables them to replicate within infected cells). When first discovered, interferon was thought to be a single substance, but scientists have learned that different cells produce different kinds. Alpha interferons are produced by white blood cells other than lymphocytes, beta interferon by fibroblasts, and gamma interferon by lymphocytes. All interferons inhibit viral replication by interfering with the transcription of viral nucleic acid, but they also exert other inhibitory effects by regulating the extent to which lymphocytes and other cells express some important constituents on their surface membranes and by stimulating the natural killer (NK) cells described below.

SCAVENGER AND NATURAL KILLER CELLS

Scavenger cells.   All higher animals, and many lower ones, contain scavenger cells capable of the phagocytosis (ingestion) and destruction of foreign particles. Most vertebrates, including all birds and mammals, possess two main kinds of scavenger cells. Their importance was first recognized by the Russian biologist Élie Metchnikoff in 1884. He named them microphages and macrophages, after Greek words meaning "little eaters" and "big eaters."

Microphages are nowadays usually referred to either as polymorphonuclear leukocytes, because their nucleus typically has several lobes, or as granulocytes, because they contain large numbers of obvious granules. Some of these granules are packets containing a mixture of powerful digestive enzymes. Others contain bactericidal (i.e., bacteria-killing) proteins that act by generating hypochlorite or hydrogen peroxide when particles have been ingested. There are three varieties of granulocytes, distinguished by the way in which their granules are stained by dyes. The differences in staining characteristics reflect differences in the chemical makeup and function of the granules. The most common granulocytes are the neutrophils, which serve as general-purpose scavengers. Less common are the eosinophils, which are particularly effective at damaging the cells that make up the cuticle (body wall) of larger parasites. Fewer still are the basophils, which release heparin (a complex sugar that prevents blood coagulation) as well as histamine and other substances that play an important role in certain allergic reactions described later in this article.

Granulocytes are continuously produced from stem (i.e., precursor) cells in the bone marrow, from which they enter the bloodstream, circulate for a few days, and then die. Granulocytes are mobile and are attracted toward foreign materials, including bacteria, which they phagocytize and in many cases digest. Bacteria deposited beneath the skin, for example, are attacked within a few minutes by neutrophils that move to the invasion site from nearby blood vessels. Various agents attract the different kinds of granulocytes. Some of these attracting agents are produced by the microbes themselves; others are released by damaged tissues. Still others result from the interaction of the microbes with proteins in the blood plasma—a particularly powerful stimulus is the activation of complement. Receptors, structures found on the surface of granulocytes, determine how these cells recognize foreign materials. The most important receptors are those that recognize and bind to antibody molecules, which have coated an invader, and those that bind to the activated form of complement. Although granulocytes make up a critical component of nonspecific immunity, some microbes produce toxins that poison granulocytes and thus prevent ingestion; other microbes are indigestible and thus are not killed. By themselves, then, granulocytes are of limited effectiveness, and they require reinforcement by the mechanisms of specific immunity.

Macrophages, the other main type of phagocytic cell, are derived from cells called monocytes. Like granulocytes, monocytes are produced by stem cells in the bone marrow and circulate through the blood, though in lesser numbers. But unlike granulocytes, monocytes then take on a maturer form—that of macrophages—and settle in many tissues, especially the lymphoid tissues (spleen and lymph nodes) and the liver, which serve as filters for trapping microbes and other foreign particles that arrive through the blood or the lymph. Macrophages live longer than granulocytes, and, although effective as scavengers, they serve a longer term and basically different function. Compared to granulocytes, macrophages move relatively sluggishly and are attracted by different stimuli; they usually arrive at sites of invasion later than granulocytes. Macrophages recognize foreign particles by mechanisms basically similar to those of granulocytes and ingest them effectively. Ingested microbes are killed and digested by much the same means as employed by granulocytes, but the process is slower and digestion is not as complete. This aspect will be shown later in this article to be of great importance for the role of macrophages in stimulating specific immune responses—something in which granulocytes play no part.

Types and functions of granulocytes

Origin and function of macrophages

Natural killer (NK) cells.   Natural killer cells were first recognized in 1975, when researchers observed cells in the blood and lymphoid tissues that, although they were neither the scavengers described above nor ordinary lymphocytes, could kill some tumour cells and cells infected with viruses cultured in vitro. (In vitro, literally "in glass," is a Latin term used for studies conducted outside the body, as opposed to in vivo studies, which are conducted in living animals.) NK cells look like lymphocytes but contain a few granules resembling those of granulocytes. They can apparently recognize some feature of dividing cells, by a mechanism that does not depend upon specific immunity; they then bind to these dividing cells and insert their granules through the outer membrane and into the cytoplasm. This causes the dividing cells to leak and die. It is not certain whether NK cells belong to a distinct lineage or are a special form of lymphocyte, but there is no doubt that they are stimulated by gamma interferon. Most immunologists feel that NK cells play an important part in checking the growth of tumour cells and cells infected with some viruses. It is likely, however, that their main biological role is to regulate the growth of stem cells in the bone marrow and elsewhere.

ACUTE-PHASE REACTIONS

Interleukin 1

Infections are commonly accompanied by a rise in body temperature, or fever. This may sometimes be protective in itself, since some microbes cannot tolerate an increase of 2°–3° C (3°–5° F) above the normal body temperature. But fever composes part of a more general effect known as the acute-phase reaction, which stems from the production of a protein termed interleukin 1 (IL-1). IL-1, which is made by infected or otherwise activated macrophages, stimulates liver cells to secrete increased amounts of several different proteins into the bloodstream. These proteins bind to products released by dying tissue cells and assist in their harmless disposal; the proteins also help in repair processes. The acute-phase reaction occurs in all warm-blooded animals that have been examined, and it can be triggered by tissue injury as well as by infections. Although not responsible for the actual elimination of infections, the acute-phase reaction is evidently an important part of the body's response once an infection has progressed so far as to make a person feel ill.

Specific, acquired immunity

It has been known for centuries that persons who have contracted certain diseases and survived generally do not catch these illnesses again. The Greek historian Thucydides recorded that when the plague was raging in Athens during the 5th century BC, the sick and dying would have received no nursing at all had it not been for the devotion of those who had already had the disease and recovered from it, since it was known that no one ever caught plague a second time. The same applies, with rare exceptions, to many other clear-cut diseases, such as smallpox, chicken pox, measles, and mumps. Yet having had measles does not prevent a child from contracting chicken pox, or vice versa. The protection acquired by experiencing one of these infections is specific for that infection; in other words, it is due to specific, acquired immunity. There are other infectious conditions, such as the common cold, influenza, pneumonia, and diarrheal diseases, that can be caught again and again; these seem to contradict the notion of specific immunity. But the reason why such illnesses can recur is that many different infectious agents produce similar symptoms (and thus the same disease). For example, more than 100 viruses can cause the cluster of symptoms known as the common cold. Consequently, even though an infection with any particular agent does protect against reinfection by that pathogen, people are still susceptible to the other agents that they have not yet encountered.

This section describes the various ways in which specific immunity operates. Although pioneer studies were begun in the late 19th century, most of the knowledge of specific immunity has been gained since the 1960s, and new insights are continually being obtained.

THE NATURE OF LYMPHOCYTES

Functions of lymphoid tissues

General characteristics.   As previously mentioned, lymphocytes are the cells responsible for the body's ability to distinguish and react to an almost infinite number of different foreign substances, including those of which microbes are composed. Lymphocytes are mainly a dormant population, awaiting the appropriate signals to be stirred to action. These inactive lymphocytes are small, round cells filled largely by a nucleus. Although they have only a small amount of cytoplasm compared with other cells, each lymphocyte has sufficient cytoplasmic organelles (mitochondria, endoplasmic reticulum, Golgi apparatus) to keep the cell alive. Lymphocytes move only sluggishly on their own, but they can travel around the body, carried along in the blood or the lymph. At any one time an adult human possesses about 2×10^{12} lymphocytes, about 1 percent of which are in the bloodstream. The great majority are concentrated in various tissues, particularly the bone marrow, spleen, thymus, lymph nodes, tonsils, and lining of the intestines. Organs or tissues containing such concentrations of lymphocytes are termed lymphoid. The lymphocytes in them are free to move but are not simply lying loose; rather, they are confined within a delicate network of connective tissue that channels the lymphocytes so that they come into contact with other cells, especially macrophages, that line the meshes of the network. This ensures that the lymphocytes—which, as discussed below, are of different sorts—come into contact with each other and with foreign materials trapped by the macrophages in an ordered manner.

Lymphocytes originate, in postnatal life, from stem cells in the bone marrow; these stem cells divide continuously, releasing immature lymphocytes into the bloodstream. Some of these travel to the thymus, where they multiply and differentiate (i.e., acquire special properties and functions) into T lymphocytes. The term T lymphocyte (or T cell) stands for thymus-derived lymphocyte (or cell), referring to the fact that these cells depend upon the maturation process that takes place in the thymus. Once they have left the thymus, T cells join the bloodstream and circulate to and within the rest of the lymphoid organs, where they can multiply further in response to appropriate stimulation. About half of all lymphocytes are T cells.

The other lymphocytes do not pass through the thymus; instead, they differentiate within the bone marrow itself and then go directly to the lymphoid organs. They are termed B lymphocytes, or B cells, and they, like T cells, can mature and multiply further in the lymphoid organs when suitably stimulated. Although it is appropriate to refer to them as B cells in humans and other mammals, because they are bone-marrow derived, the term B cell was originally used to describe the functionally analogous lymphocytes of birds, cells that differentiate not in the bone marrow but in the bursa of Fabricius, a special tissue attached to the hindgut.

Different functions of T cells and B cells

B cells and T cells differ in function. B cells secrete antibodies, proteins that attack foreign molecules. Since antibodies circulate through the humours (i.e., the body fluids—blood and lymph), the protection afforded by B cells is called humoral immunity. T cells, by contrast, do not produce antibodies. Instead, the T lymphocytes themselves directly attack specific invaders and are thus said to provide cell-mediated immunity. The distinction between these two types of specific, acquired immunity is not so clean as might be inferred from the above, however, for T cells also play a major role in regulating the function of B cells. In many cases, moreover, an immune response involves both humoral and cell-mediated assaults upon the foreign substance.

Ability to recognize foreign molecules.   The feature that distinguishes lymphocytes from other cells is their capacity to recognize foreign molecules by virtue of the three-dimensional patterns formed by the atoms of the foreign agent. To recognize a molecule, in the sense used throughout this article, a cell must have receptor molecules on its own surface. The shape of the receptors is complementary to a pattern on the surface of the molecule that is to be recognized. The great pioneer of immunology, Paul Ehrlich, used the analogy of a key fitting into a lock, and this provides a reasonably accurate and nontechnical way of imagining it—especially if the key and the lock are both regarded as made of rubber and thus somewhat flexible.

At this stage it is necessary to introduce some terms used by immunologists. An antigen is any material, usually of a complex nature, that can bind specifically to receptor molecules made by lymphocytes. If the antigen also stimulates the lymphocytes to which it binds—*i.e.,* it evokes an immune response—it is said to be an immunogen. Complex antigens have a variety of different three-dimensional patterns on different parts of their surface, each of which can be recognized separately by different lymphocytes. Each of these recognizably foreign molecular patterns constitutes an antigenic determinant, or epitope. Complex antigens thus present an "antigenic mosaic" and can evoke responses from a variety of specific lymphocytes. Some antigenic determinants are more effective than others in stimulating a response, presumably because a larger number of responsive lymphocytes is present. When two different antigens have an antigenic determinant in common, some of the responses made against one antigen are able to react against the other; such antigens are known as cross-reacting antigens. A simple chemical group that can combine with a lymphocyte receptor but does not induce an immune response is called a hapten (Greek *haptein,* "to grasp"). Haptens can become immunogenic if they are joined to a suitable complex molecule, and immunologists often utilize haptens to study various immune reactions.

As will be described below, a B lymphocyte manufactures antibodies that correspond to its specific receptor molecule. It sheds these proteins in large amounts into the body fluids, where they can be detected by their ability to combine with antigens; in fact, antibodies were discovered in the blood long before it was known what cells made them. Collectively the antibodies are known as immunoglobulins. T lymphocytes secrete little or none of their receptors into the blood, and there is no collective name for these.

Diversity of lymphocytes. The specific immune system (*i.e.,* the sum total of all the lymphocytes) can recognize virtually any complex molecule that nature or science has devised. This very remarkable ability is achieved because among the population of lymphocytes, which are being lost and renewed throughout life at a rate of some 1 percent every day, each cell develops its own specific antigen receptor, and the antigen receptor of one lymphocyte is slightly different from that of most other lymphocytes. The total number of different receptors available on all the lymphocytes cannot be measured, but most informed guesses reckon that there are at least 100,000,000. Each has a shape that can combine with a particular antigenic determinant, so that among all the lymphocytes there are at least some that can recognize any given antigen. After a lymphocyte encounters an antigen that it can recognize, the cell is stimulated to multiply, and the population of lymphocytes bearing that particular receptor increases.

The antigen receptors on a lymphocyte are proteins, and, like all proteins, they are assembled from structural building blocks called amino acids. And, as with any protein produced by any cell, the exact sequence in which the amino acids of a particular antigen receptor are assembled is specified in the deoxyribonucleic acid (DNA) that makes up the cell's genes. Since the antigen receptors on different lymphocytes each have a different—even if only slightly different—sequence, this might imply that a person's genome (the sum total of all his genes, which are common to all cells in the body except the germ cells) must contain 100,000,000 genes coding for nothing but the possible forms of antigen receptors. This far exceeds the number of genes that all the DNA in a human cell could represent, and so it must be possible to code for all of the different receptor molecules with many fewer genes than would be expected. Recent work in molecular genetics has revealed how this is done, in a way that is peculiar to lymphocytes. (To learn more about the genetic control of protein synthesis in general, see GENETICS AND HEREDITY, THE PRINCIPLES OF.)

It turns out that the protein that makes up any specific antigen receptor is coded for not by a single gene but by different genes that specify separately the sequence of amino acids in four consecutive segments of the molecule. These genes come together to provide the code that ultimately specifies the whole molecule. For each segment of the molecule encoded separately there are up to 100 alternative genes, any of which may come together with any of the genes coding for the other segments to form the final code for the whole molecule. This rearrangement of alternative genes in the final code occurs largely, though not wholly, at random, so that an enormous number of combinations can result. The genetic rearrangement takes place at the stage when the lymphocytes generated from the stem cells first become functional, and so each lymphocyte begins its active life able to make antigen receptors composed of one particular protein out of all the possible variations. Consequently, within the whole population of lymphocytes there are nearly always some that can recognize any antigen. But this is not the only way in which the diversity of receptors is achieved. Superimposed on the mechanism outlined in simplified terms above is another process, called somatic mutation. This process involves mutation—small changes in the DNA that occur spontaneously during the process of cell division (when the DNA has to be copied into the daughter cells); it is called somatic because the mutations take place in body cells (Greek *soma*) rather than in germ-line cells. Although somatic mutations can develop as a chance event in any body cell, they occur regularly in the DNA that codes for antigen receptors in lymphocytes. Thus, when a lymphocyte is stimulated by an antigen to divide, new variants of its antigen receptor can be present on its descendant cells, and some of these variants may provide an even better fit for the antigen that was responsible for the original stimulation.

ANTIBODIES AND B-CELL ANTIGEN RECEPTORS

The antigen receptors on B lymphocytes are identical to the antibodies that these lymphocytes manufacture once stimulated, except that the receptor molecules have an extra tail that penetrates the cell membrane and anchors them to the cell surface. Thus, a description of the structure and properties of antibodies (immunoglobulins), which are well studied, will suffice for both.

Basic structure. Immunoglobulins (abbreviated Ig) all have the same basic molecular structure, consisting of four polypeptide chains (*i.e.,* chains of amino acids linked together by chemical bonds known as peptide bonds). Two of the chains, which are identical in any given immunoglobulin molecule, are heavy (H) chains; the other two are identical light (L) chains. The terms "heavy" and "light" simply mean larger and smaller, but they were used in early studies of immunoglobulin structure and have stuck. Each chain is manufactured separately and is coded for by different genes, but the four chains become joined

From B. Alberts *et al., Molecular Biology of the Cell;* Garland Publishing, Inc., 1983

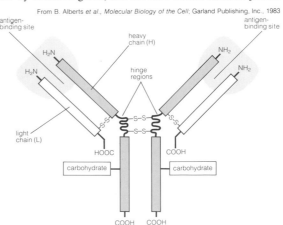

Figure 1: The basic four-chain unit of a human immunoglobulin molecule. This basic structure is composed of two identical light (L) chains and two identical heavy (H) chains, which are held together by disulfide (—S—S—) linkages to form a flexible Y-shape. The antigen-binding sites lie at the ends of each arm of the Y and are formed by a portion of both a light and a heavy chain.

Figure 2: A human immunoglobulin molecule showing the domains present in the light (L) and heavy (H) chains. The constant (C) domains are shaded, while the variable (V) domains are not. Intrachain disulfide (−S−S−) linkages maintain the folding of the molecule into domains. The variable domains account for the specific antigen-binding properties of the immunoglobulin. The constant domains of the H chain confer other biological properties, such as the ability to bind to complement and to certain nonspecific receptors on cells.

From B. Alberts *et al.*, *Molecular Biology of the Cell*; Garland Publishing, Inc., 1983

in the final immunoglobulin molecule to form a flexible Y-shape as illustrated diagrammatically in Figure 1.

At the end of each arm of the Y-shape, a portion of the H and L chains forms a region called the antigen-binding, or combining, site; each basic immunoglobulin molecule therefore has two identical antigen-binding sites. Their shape is such that part of the site can fit with a particular antigenic determinant. When two molecules fit and can approach very closely to one another, they become bound together by various weak forces. Although such forces are not as powerful as those of true chemical bonds (which bind atoms into molecules), they are nevertheless strong enough to hold the molecules together quite firmly. The two antigen-binding sites are found in those parts of the immunoglobulin molecule that differ between one antibody and another (as explained above) and are termed the variable (V) regions. The actual antigen specificity of the site depends upon the variable regions of both the H and L chains. In contrast to the variable regions, the other segments of the chains are alike from one immunoglobulin molecule to another. These segments are known as the constant (C) regions.

The variable and constant regions of both the L and H chains are structurally folded into functional units called domains. As shown in Figure 2, each light chain consists of one variable domain (V_L) and one constant domain (C_L). Each heavy chain has one variable domain (V_H) and three or four constant domains (C_H1, C_H2, C_H3, C_H4). Those domains that make up the "tail" of the basic Y-shaped molecule (in other words, all the H-chain constant domains except C_H1) are responsible for the special biological properties of immunoglobulins—except, of course, for the capacity to bind to a specific antigenic determinant.

Classes of immunoglobulins. The term "constant region" is a bit misleading in that these segments are not identical in all immunoglobulins. Rather, they are basically similar among broad groups. All immunoglobulins that have the same basic kinds of constant domains in their H chains are said to belong to the same class. There are five main classes—IgG, IgM, IgA, IgD, and IgE—each of which has special properties. Some of these main classes include a number of distinct subclasses. In addition, there are two basic kinds of L chains, either of which can be associated with any of the H-chain classes, thereby increasing still further the enormous diversity of immunoglobulins. These classes are illustrated diagrammatically in Figure 3.

IgG is the most common class of immunoglobulins. IgG antibodies are present in the largest amounts in blood and tissue fluids and are made by B cells that have been previously stimulated by antigens. Each IgG molecule consists of the basic four-chain immunoglobulin structure and thus

carries two identical antigen-binding sites. There are four subclasses of IgG, each with minor differences in their H chains but with distinct biological properties.

IgM is the earliest class of immunoglobulins made by B cells as they mature and is the form most commonly present as the antigen receptor on their surface. When IgM is secreted from the cells, five of the basic four-chain units become joined together to make a large molecule with 10 antigen-binding sites. This large antibody molecule is particularly effective at attaching to antigenic determinants present on the outer coats of bacteria.

IgA is a class of immunoglobulins especially adapted to be transferred from the body fluids to the surface of the tissues with mucous-membrane linings, such as the respiratory and gastrointestinal tracts, and into secretions, such as milk, saliva, tears, and bile. Two four-chain units become joined together and associated with a special protein that enables the IgA molecule to be passed outward through the cells that line the air passages, the gut, and the milk, salivary, tear, and bile ducts.

IgD molecules are present on the surface of most, but not all, B cells early in their development, but little IgD is ever released into the circulation. It is not clear what function IgD performs, though it may play a role in determining whether antigens activate the B cells.

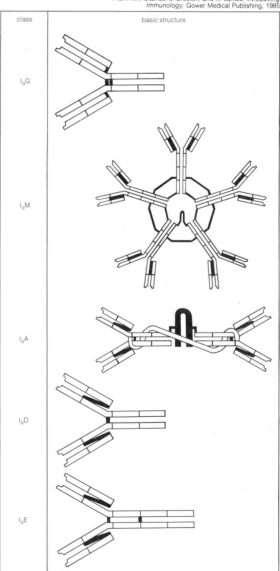

From N.A. Staines, J. Brostoff, and K. James, *Introducing Immunology*; Gower Medical Publishing, 1985

class	basic structure
IgG	
IgM	
IgA	
IgD	
IgE	

Figure 3: The arrangement of chains in the main classes of immunoglobulins. Links between the chains are represented by dark bars. The additional protein that joins the basic units in IgM and IgA is shown as a dark, inverted U-shape; and the protein required for the secretion of IgA is depicted as a twisted ribbon.

Binding of antibody to antigen

IgE is made by only a small proportion of B cells, relatively late in their development. It is present in the blood in low concentrations. Each molecule of IgE consists of one four-chain unit and so has two antigen-binding sites; each of its H chains has an extra constant domain (C_H4), which gives IgE the special property of binding to the surface of basophils, eosinophils, and mast cells (tissue cells that resemble basophils). IgE antibodies help to protect against parasitic infections, but they are also responsible for some allergies (see below *Allergies*).

Most people have fairly constant amounts of immunoglobulin in their blood, which represent the balance between continuous breakdown of these proteins and their new manufacture. There is about four times as much IgG (including its subclasses) as IgA, 10 to 15 times as much as IgM, 300 times as much as IgD, and 30,000 times as much as IgE. This implies that most active B cells make IgG and rather few make IgE.

Part of the normal immunoglobulin production undoubtedly represents the response to antigenic stimulation that happens all the time, but even animals reared in surroundings completely free from microbes and their products make substantial, though lesser, amounts of immunoglobulins. Much of the immunoglobulin therefore must represent the product of all the B cells that are, so to speak, "ticking over" even if not specifically stimulated. It is therefore not surprising that extremely sensitive methods can detect traces of antibodies that react with antigens or antigenic determinants to which an animal has never been exposed but for which cells with receptors are present.

All B cells are potentially able to use any one of the constant-region classes to make up the immunoglobulin they secrete. As noted above, when first stimulated most secrete IgM. Some continue to do so, but others later switch to IgG or IgA or IgE. Memory B cells, which (as explained more fully below) are specialized for responding to repeat infections by a given antigen, make IgG or IgA immediately. What determines the balance among the classes of antibodies is not fully understood. It is influenced by the nature and site of deposition of the antigen (for example, parasites tend to elicit IgE), perhaps through factors released locally by T cells.

T-CELL ANTIGEN RECEPTORS

Since T lymphocytes do not normally shed their antigen receptors, or do so only in very small amounts, understanding of their structure has not come from analysis of isolated receptors but from studies of the DNA that encodes them. These studies show that T-cell antigen receptors consist of two polypeptide chains, each of which, like the chains that make up immunoglobulins, is encoded by a fairly large number of alternative genes that control different parts of the receptor molecule. Also, as with immunoglobulins, these alternative genes are rearranged in any one of a very large number of possible ways to establish the final code for the receptors of any one T cell. The genes are not the same as those that control the manufacture of immunoglobulins, although the resultant molecules have a generally similar structure. So, rather unexpectedly, the body possesses two ways of generating the diversity of antigen receptors that characterize the lymphocytes. As will be mentioned later, this duplication probably resulted from the evolution of both processes from a more primitive and simpler recognition system.

Despite the structural similarities, the receptors on T cells function differently from those on B cells. This functional difference underlies the different roles that B cells and T cells play in the immune system. B cells, as has been explained, secrete antibodies that bind to antigens in the blood and other body fluids. But once an antigen—a virus, for example—succeeds in infecting a body cell, it is safely beyond the reach of the circulating antibodies. T cells, on the other hand, can bind to body cells that harbour pathogens and initiate an immune response against the infected cell. Consequently, T cells must have receptors that can detect infected cells. The way in which they do this is by recognizing foreign molecules that are expressed on the surface of an infected cell in association with normal cell-surface molecules called major histocompatibility complex (MHC) antigens. (In humans the MHC antigens were first discovered on certain leukocytes and are, therefore, often referred to as HLA [human leukocyte group A] antigens. For information on the genetic basis of the HLA antigens, see GENETICS AND HEREDITY, THE PRINCIPLES OF.) The MHC antigens are of two major types: class I antigens, which are present on the surface of virtually all nucleated body cells, and class II antigens, which are found on the surface of most B cells and on some T cells, macrophages, and macrophage-like cells.

As will be described more fully below, there are two main types of mature T cells. One type consists of helper T cells; the other is made up of cytotoxic or suppressor T cells. Helper T cells recognize foreign antigens associated with MHC class II antigens, and cytotoxic or suppressor T cells generally recognize foreign antigens associated with MHC class I antigens. This recognition is achieved by means of separate molecules on the T cells, closely associated with the specific antigen receptors but able to bind to the self antigens of MHC class I or II. To add even further to the complexity, T-cell antigen receptors are also associated with a third kind of molecule, which is necessary for activating the T cell once its antigen receptor has bound with its specific antigen. The actual arrangement of this receptor complex is not known.

LIFE CYCLE OF T AND B LYMPHOCYTES

When T-cell precursors leave the bone marrow on their way to mature in the thymus, they do not yet express receptors for antigens and are indifferent to stimulation by them. Within the thymus the T cells multiply many times as they pass through a meshwork of thymus cells. In the course of multiplication they acquire antigen receptors and differentiate into the two sorts—helper T cells and cytotoxic or suppressor T cells—mentioned in the previous section. Both kinds look alike, but they can be distinguished by their function and by the presence of special surface proteins. Most of the T cells that have multiplied in the thymus also die there. This seems paradoxical until it is remembered that the random generation of different antigen receptors is bound to produce a large proportion that recognize self antigens—*i.e.,* molecules already present on the body's own constituents—and that mature lymphocytes with such receptors would be liable to attack the body's own tissues. Nearly all such self-reactive T cells die before they leave the thymus, so that those T cells that do emerge are the ones capable of recognizing foreign antigens. These travel via the blood to the lymphoid tissues, where, if suitably stimulated, they can again multiply and take part in immune reactions. The generation of T cells in the thymus proceeds very actively in young animals, but it gradually slows down during adulthood and is much diminished in old age, by which time the thymus has become small and partly atrophied. Cell-mediated immunity persists throughout life, however, because some of the T cells that have emerged from the thymus can survive and function for a very long time.

B-cell precursors are continuously generated in the bone marrow throughout life, but as with T-cell generation, the rate diminishes with age. Unless they are stimulated to mature (as described below), the majority of B cells also die, though those that have been stimulated can survive for a long time in the lymphoid tissues. Consequently, there is a continuous supply of new B cells throughout life. Those with antigen receptors capable of recognizing self antigens tend to be eliminated, though less effectively than are self-reactive T cells. As a result, some self-reactive cells are always present in the B-cell population, along with the majority that recognize foreign antigens. The reason why these self-reactive B cells normally do no harm is explained in the following section.

ACTIVATION OF LYMPHOCYTES

The proportion of the total lymphocyte population that can recognize and respond to any given antigen is bound to be small, because most B and T cells bear receptors with other specificities. After a lymphocyte has been activated by a particular antigen, it multiplies to form a clone—that is, a population of identical progeny cells. Each member

Margin notes:

Normal production of antibody

Helper T cells and cytotoxic or suppressor T cells

Elimination of self-reactive T cells

of the clone bears the same antigen specificity as the original activated lymphocyte. This process, whereby an activated lymphocyte gives rise to a large population of cells targeted on the offending antigen, is known as clonal selection. Because the original population of lymphocytes contains so few members that recognize a particular antigen, immunologists have had to devise special techniques to unravel what goes on when the cells are activated. One such technique is the use of what are called polyclonal mitogens, most of which are plant or bacterial products whose properties were originally discovered by accident. These are molecules that react with some surface component common to all T cells or all B cells, imitating, more or less accurately, activation by an antigen. Polyclonal mitogens can thus activate large numbers of lymphocytes at one time. Another way to study lymphocyte activation is to stimulate B cells or T cells in culture and to select and propagate those that respond to a chosen antigen, thereby obtaining a sufficient population to analyze.

Activation of T cells. Antigen activation of helper T cells only takes place when (1) the foreign antigens are presented at the surface of other cells in association with MHC class II antigens and (2) the T cells have been switched on by interleukin 1 (IL-1), which is secreted by macrophages that have ingested foreign particles or have been activated in other ways (see above *Acute-phase reactions*). As mentioned earlier, MHC II molecules are made by only a few cell types, of which macrophages and B cells are the most relevant. So activation of helper T cells is largely confined to antigens that have first been taken up by macrophages. Since macrophages that have ingested foreign particles and broken down their constituents to smaller fragments return part of these to their cell surface, where MHC molecules are already present, this is an effective way of presenting the antigenic determinants so as to be recognized by receptors on the helper T cells.

Interleukin 2 and T-cell activation

The helper T cells then proceed to make another protein, called interleukin 2 (IL-2), as well as receptors that bind it. IL-2, in turn, stimulates the helper T cells to divide and to secrete several more proteins, such as gamma interferons and factors that can trigger B cells to differentiate and secrete immunoglobulins. The overall result is that the number of helper T cells that recognize the specific foreign antigen has been increased, and several T-cell factors, collectively known as lymphokines, have been produced. The lymphokines have other consequences, one of which is that IL-2 allows those cytotoxic or suppressor T cells that also recognize the same antigen to become activated and to multiply. Cytotoxic T cells, in turn, can attack and kill other cells that express the foreign antigen in association with MHC I molecules, which—as explained above—are present on almost all cells. So, for example, cytotoxic T cells can attack target cells that express antigens made by viruses or bacteria growing within them (see below *Cell-mediated immune mechanisms*). Suppressor T cells may be the same as cytotoxic T cells, but they are detected by their ability to suppress the action of B cells or even of helper T cells (perhaps by killing them). Suppressor T cells thus act to damp down the immune response and can sometimes predominate so as to suppress it completely.

Activation of B cells. A B cell is activated when an antigen binds to its specific receptors. If the B cell is newly formed and immature, the binding of an antigen prevents it from developing any further. As only B cells that recognize foreign antigens survive this stage, this is one way that the immune system prevents reactions against self proteins present in the blood and tissue fluids.

Elimination of self-reactive B cells

The surface of some antigens—notably the outer coats of many bacteria—consists of polymers (extremely large molecules composed of multiples of simpler chemical units). Such antigens present a large number of identical antigenic determinants and can stimulate the B cells to release antibodies without further ado. Most B cells, however, require the additional stimulation of lymphokines before interaction with the antigen causes them to multiply into a clone of immunoglobulin-secreting cells. These fully activated, antibody-producing cells are called plasma cells, and each can secrete several thousand molecules of immunoglobulin every second and continue to do so for several days. When a specific B cell has been switched on to multiply and make antibody, a large amount of that particular antibody will be released into the circulation. This initial burst of antibody production gradually decreases as the stimulus is removed (*e.g.,* by recovery from infection), but some antibody continues to be present for several months afterward.

The process just described takes place among the circulating B lymphocytes. But some of the B cells encounter the antigen in the germinal centres—compartments in the lymphoid tissues where few T cells are present—and are activated in a different way. They multiply extensively, especially those with the most effective receptors, but do not go on to secrete antibody at that time. Instead, they remain in the tissues and the circulation for many months or even years. If, with the help of T cells, they encounter the activating antigen again, these B cells rapidly begin to manufacture and release their specific antibody. They behave as though they "remember" the initial contact with the antigen and are therefore termed memory cells. Upon reinfection by a particular microbe, the memory cells trigger a rapid rise in the level of protective antibodies and thus prevent the illness from taking hold.

Memory cells and long-term immunity

REGULATION OF IMMUNE RESPONSES

As detailed in the previous sections of this article, specific immunity involves a complex series of interacting processes whereby activated lymphocytes multiply and become effector cells that (1) secrete lymphokines that affect other cells, (2) kill targets bearing the activating antigen, or (3) secrete antibodies that react with the antigen. The biological effects of all of these processes are discussed in later sections.

The way in which the immune system generates the diversity of antigen receptors ensures the production of lymphocytes that can recognize antigenic determinants on almost any molecule—not only those on microbes, but also those on self components and on irrelevant foreign materials that would normally never enter the body. Mechanisms whereby cells bearing receptors for self components are eliminated or suppressed have been discussed, as has the need for antigens to be presented in a special way before they actually trigger immune responses. What has not been mentioned is the fact that specific antigen receptors, being different (if only slightly) between one lymphocyte and another, might themselves be recognized as foreign and stimulate the appropriate T or B cells to respond to them. This does in fact happen. Anti-antibodies develop in the course of an immune response and then anti-anti-antibodies—and probably the process continues. In addition, certain T cells can recognize receptors on B cells and on other T cells and can act either to help or to suppress the cells recognized, thereby regulating how far and for how long the response continues. This regulatory network clearly works rather well in practice, since specific immune responses are sufficient to cope with microbial invasion of the body but fade away, apart from memory cells, once the stimulus has been removed. It is, however, as complicated as the constraints that regulate human societies and about as difficult to analyze in detail.

There is considerable interest in whether immune responses can be regulated through the central nervous system. Lymphocytes have receptors that can bind certain hormones whose production is controlled by the central nervous system. These hormones can affect immune responses—positively and negatively—both in culture and within the body. There is also evidence that an interleukin produced during immune responses can increase the nervous system's release of messengers that control the secretion of hormones by the adrenal gland. Thus some interplay between the immune system and the nervous system is certainly possible, though the importance of this interaction in regulating immune responses is unclear. Clinical and everyday experience indicates that patients with a "will to live" survive better than those who despair, but whether this higher survival rate is mediated by the impact of the nervous system on the immune system— or indeed, whether it depends upon the functioning of the immune system at all—is unknown.

ANTIBODY-MEDIATED IMMUNE MECHANISMS

Protective attachment to antigens. Many pathogenic microorganisms and toxins can be rendered harmless by the simple attachment of antibodies. For example, some harmful bacteria, such as those that cause diphtheria, tetanus, and plague, release toxins that poison essential body cells. Antibodies, especially IgG, that combine with such toxins neutralize them. Also susceptible to simple antibody attachment are the many infectious microbes—including all viruses, many bacteria, and some protozoans—that live within the body cells; these pathogens bear special molecules by which they must attach themselves to the host cells before they can penetrate and invade. Antibodies that bind to these molecules prevent invasion. Antibody attachment can also immobilize those bacteria and protozoans that swim by means of whiplike flagella or cilia. In all these instances antibodies protect simply by combining with the antigens, although they do not kill or dispose of the microbes. The actual destruction of microbes involves phagocytosis by granulocytes and macrophages, and this requires the participation of the complement system.

Activation of the complement system. Complement comprises 11 proteins that can interact sequentially to produce several biologically important results. The activation of complement makes antigen–antibody complexes attractive to phagocytes; it releases agents that cause inflammation; and, in some cases, it disrupts the outer membranes of antibody-coated cells. These 11 proteins, together with four others whose function is to damp down some of the complement interactions, form the complement system. It is beyond the scope of this article to describe the system in detail, but a brief account is needed because many of the biological effects of antibodies depend on complement activation.

The first point to make is that the complement proteins are made not by lymphocytes but by liver cells and, in many tissues, by macrophages. The second is that the action of complement is nonspecific—*i.e.,* it does not depend upon the specificity of the antigen-binding site of an antibody—and that complement proteins probably evolved before antibodies. Complement functions are similar within many species, and corresponding components from one species can replace those of another. The complement system provides a most ingenious way in which antibodies, whatever their specificity, produce the same biological effects when they combine with antigens.

Complement is activated most effectively by IgM and IgG antibodies, which are, as discussed above, the most abundant classes of immunoglobulins. The activation of the complement system by antibodies depends on the H-chain constant regions of the immunoglobulin molecules. When the antigen-binding sites of an immunoglobulin interact with the appropriate antigen, the shape of part of the H-chain constant region is distorted in such a way that it binds to one of the complement components present in the surrounding fluid. This, in turn, rearranges the complement molecule, exposing a catalytic site that can act to split the next complement component in the sequence into two pieces: a small polypeptide fragment and a larger protein part with a catalytic site exposed. This catalyst then acts similarly on the next complement component, which, in turn, acts on a protein called C3—the most abundant and biologically the most important complement component. C3 is split into a small polypeptide and a larger fragment, called C3b, which is the active form of C3.

C3b can do several different things. It can bind to antigen–antibody complexes and confer on them the property of interacting with receptors for C3b present on phagocytic cells. It can also activate the next component in the complement system. This leads to release of yet another small polypeptide and the insertion of a ringlike structure, composed of yet other complement components, into the cell membrane of the invading microbe. This structure causes the cell contents to leak out and the cell to die. Finally, C3b can combine with another protein to form a complex that converts more C3 to C3b. The small polypeptides released during the activation of complement are potent pharmacological agents that (1) cause mast cells and basophils to release histamine, (2) increase the

permeability of blood vessels, and (3) attract granulocytes and monocytes.

Thus when a microbe penetrates the body, if antibodies reactive with its surface are already present (or if it activates complement without their help), the complete complement sequence may be activated and the microbe killed by damage to its outer membrane. This mechanism is effective only with bacteria that lack protective coats and with certain large viruses, but it is nevertheless important. Persons who lack C3 and thus cannot complete the later steps in the complement sequence are liable to repeated bacterial infections.

If the microbes are not immediately killed, they nevertheless soon acquire antibody and C3b on their surface, and the small polypeptide fragments released locally divert phagocytic neutrophils and monocytes to the sites of complement activation. The C3b on the microbes binds to the C3b receptors on the phagocytic cells, and the microbes are ingested and usually killed by the digestive enzymes present in the phagocytes. Because granulocytes that have ingested foreign particles release part of their digestive enzymes and activation products into the surrounding fluid, a certain amount of local tissue damage may occur, especially if large numbers of granulocytes have accumulated at the site. This produces local inflammation, which may amount to no more than redness and swelling but can develop into an abscess. Monocytes and macrophages, which move in after the granulocytes, take part in clearing up the debris. These second-line phagocytes then carry the debris to the lymph nodes or other lymphoid tissues, where they present the antigen to lymphocytes and thus may stimulate a new or a renewed immune response. If microbes reach the bloodstream and become coated with antibody and complement there, they are also ingested in a similar fashion by granulocytes or by macrophages in the liver, the spleen, and the bone marrow.

Clearly such a biologically important chain of reactions could do more harm than good if its effects were to spread beyond the site of antigen invasion. Fortunately, the active intermediates at each stage in the complement sequence become rapidly inactivated or destroyed by inhibitors if they fail to initiate the next step. With rare exceptions, this confines the activation to the place where it is needed.

Activation of killer cells. Some cells that bear antigen–antibody complexes do not attract complement; this occurs if the antibody molecules are far apart on the cell surface or are of a class that does not readily activate the complement system. Other cells have outer membranes that are so tough or can be repaired so quickly that the cells are impermeable to activated complement. Still others are so large that phagocytes cannot ingest them. Such cells can be attacked by so-called killer (K) cells present in the blood and lymphoid tissues. K cells look like lymphocytes but are not typical T or B cells; they may, in fact, be the same as the NK cells mentioned earlier as contributing to nonspecific, innate immunity. K cells have receptors that bind to the H chains of IgG at the ends away from the antigen-binding site. These parts of the H chains are exposed on a target cell with antibody attached to it, and so K cells can bind quite tightly to them. Once bound, K cells insert something—its nature is uncertain—that causes the cell to swell and burst. K cells do not harm bacteria, but they play a role in destroying cells infected by viruses.

Other antibody-mediated mechanisms. The protection afforded by IgA antibodies, which, it will be recalled, are transported to the surface of mucous-membrane-lined passages, is somewhat different. Complement activation is not involved since there are no complement proteins on the lining of the gut or the respiratory tract. Here protection consists largely of IgA combining with microbes to prevent them from entering the cells of the lining. The bound microbes are then swept out of the body.

IgE antibodies also invoke unique mechanisms. As stated earlier, most IgE molecules are bound to special receptors on mast cells and on basophil and eosinophil granulocytes. When antigens bind to IgE antibodies on these cells, the consequence is not to cause ingestion of the antigens but to trigger the release of the cells' granules and their con-

Activation of complement by antibody

Activation of phagocytic cells by complement

tents. In the case of mast cells and basophils, this results in the sudden increase in permeability of the local blood vessels; the adhesion and activation of platelets (blood cell fragments that trigger clotting), which release their own active agents; the contraction of smooth muscle in the gut or in the respiratory tubes; and the secretion of fluids—all of which tend to dislodge large multicellular parasites such as hookworms. In the case of eosinophils, which plaster themselves onto such parasites as the flatworms that cause schistosomiasis, the granule contents are particularly effective at destroying the parasite's tough, protective skin. Therefore, IgE antibodies—although they can be a nuisance when they react with otherwise harmless antigens, as discussed below in the section on *Allergies*—appear to have a special protective role against the larger parasites.

Transfer of antibodies from mother to offspring. A newborn mammal has had no opportunity to develop protective antibodies on its own, unless, as happens very rarely, it became infected within the uterus. Yet it is born into an environment similar to its mother's, with all the potential microbial invaders to which she is exposed. Although it possesses the mechanisms of innate immunity, it has none of its mother's lymphocytes. The placenta strictly excludes the maternal lymphocytes from crossing into the fetus, where they would treat the fetal tissues as foreign antigens and thereby cause a reaction similar to the rejection of an incompatible organ transplant (see TRANSPLANTS, ORGAN AND TISSUE).

What is transferred across the placenta in many species is a fair sample of the mother's antibodies. How this happens depends upon the structure of the placenta, which varies with the species. In humans the mother's IgG antibodies (but not those of the other immunoglobulin classes) are actively transported across the placenta throughout the second two-thirds of pregnancy. In many rodents a similar transfer occurs, but mainly by crossing through the yolk sac.

Transfer of IgG antibody

In horses and cattle, which have more layers of cells in their placenta, no antibodies are transferred during fetal life, and the newborn is unprotected. There is, however, a second mechanism that makes up for this deficiency. The early milk (colostrum) is very rich in antibodies, mainly IgA but also some IgM and IgG, and during the first few days of life the newborn mammal can absorb these proteins intact from the digestive tract directly into the bloodstream. Drinking colostrum is therefore essential for newborn horses and cattle and to a somewhat lesser extent for other mammals. The capacity of the digestive tract to absorb intact proteins must not last beyond one or two weeks, since once foods other than milk are ingested the proteins and other antigens in them would also be absorbed intact and could act as immunogens to which the growing animal would become allergic (see below *Allergies*). IgA in milk is, however, rather resistant to digestion and can function within the gut even though intact absorption into the bloodstream has ended. Human colostrum is also rich in maternal antibodies, but they are less essential and are absorbed intact only during the first day or so after birth.

After a newborn has received its supply of maternal antibodies, the child is as fully protected as its mother. This means, of course, that if the mother has not developed immunity to a particular pathogen, the newborn will likewise be unprotected. For this reason, a physician may recommend that a prospective mother receive immunizations against tetanus and certain other disorders. (The active immunization of pregnant women against certain viral diseases, such as rubella [German measles], must be avoided, however, because the immunizing agent can cross the placenta and produce severe fetal complications.)

As important as the passively transferred maternal antibodies are, their effects are only temporary. The maternal antibodies in the blood become diluted as the animal grows; moreover, they gradually succumb to normal metabolic breakdown. Because the active development of acquired immunity is a slow and gradual process, young mammals actually become more susceptible to infection during their early stages of growth than they are immediately after birth. This is illustrated in Figure 4.

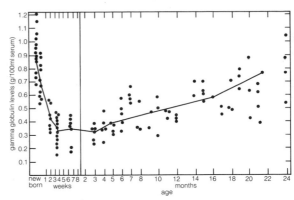

Figure 4: IgG levels in blood samples taken from children at various intervals during the first two years of life. The declining levels during the first weeks reflect the disappearance of immunoglobulins transferred from the mother before birth. The gradually increasing levels from the age of three months result from the spontaneous production of the child's own antibodies. Each point represents one measurement; the line is drawn between the means.

From O. Orlandini, A. Sass-Kortsak, and J.H. Ebbs, "Serum Gamma Globulin Levels in Normal Infants," *Pediatrics*, copyright 1955, vol. 16, p. 575

Occasionally the transfer of maternal antibodies during fetal life can have harmful consequences. A well-known example of this is erythroblastosis fetalis, or hemolytic disease of the newborn, a disorder in which maternal antibodies destroy the child's red blood cells during late pregnancy and shortly after birth. The most severe form of erythroblastosis fetalis is Rh hemolytic disease, which develops when: (1) The fetus is Rh-positive; that is, its red blood cells carry an antigen known as the Rh factor. (2) The mother is Rh-negative, which is to say her red blood cells lack the Rh factor. (3) The mother's immune system has been previously activated against the Rh antigen; this usually is the result of exposure to fetal cells during the birth of an earlier Rh-positive baby. Rh hemolytic disease can be prevented by giving the mother injections of anti-Rh antibody shortly after the birth of an Rh-positive child. This antibody destroys any Rh-positive fetal cells in the maternal circulation, thereby preventing the activation of the mother's immune system.

Erythroblastosis fetalis and Rh antibody

CELL-MEDIATED IMMUNE MECHANISMS

In addition to their importance in cooperating with B cells that secrete specific antibodies, T cells have important, separate roles in protecting against antigens that have escaped or bypassed antibody defenses. Immunologists have long recognized that antibodies do not necessarily protect against viral infections, because many viruses can spread directly from cell to cell and thus avoid encountering antibodies in the bloodstream. It is also known that persons who fail to make antibodies are very susceptible to bacterial infections but are not unduly liable to viral infections. Protection in these cases results from cell-mediated immunity. It depends upon the ability to destroy and dispose of body cells in which viruses or other intracellular parasites (such as the bacteria that cause tuberculosis and leprosy) are actively growing, as well as to dispose of the microbes themselves.

T-cell protection against viral infection

Cell-mediated immunity has two components. One depends upon the elaboration of lymphokines by helper T cells that have interacted with the appropriate antigen. In particular the gamma interferon produced by the helper T cells greatly increases the ability of macrophages to kill ingested microbes; this can tip the balance against microbes that otherwise resist killing. Gamma interferon also stimulates the NK cells mentioned in the section on nonspecific immunity. The second component of cell-mediated immunity depends upon cytotoxic T cells. These attach themselves by their receptors to cells whose surface expresses appropriate antigens (notably ones made by developing viruses) and somehow damage the infected cells enough to kill them. After a sufficient number of antigen-specific helper and cytotoxic T cells are available and the cells that act nonspecifically have been stimulated, most viral infections are rapidly overcome.

IMMUNITY AGAINST CANCER

The role of the immune system in protecting against cancer has not been fully explained. One widely held theory, called the immune surveillance hypothesis, postulates that cancer cells arise frequently but are rapidly destroyed by immune responses. This idea can be traced back to the early years of the 20th century, when Ehrlich pointed out that the enormous multiplication and differentiation of cells during prenatal life must afford many opportunities for aberrant cells to appear and grow. He speculated that immune mechanisms must eliminate such cells, since there is normally no sign of them at birth. That such mechanisms continue to function throughout life, weeding out newly arisen cancer cells, forms the basis of the immune surveillance hypothesis.

Destruction of cancer cells

Experiments have shown that cancer cells can be killed by immune processes. For example, cancer cells taken from one inbred strain of mouse or rat will grow readily when transplanted into another animal of the same inbred strain, but they are usually unable to grow for more than a few days when transplanted into mice or rats of a different inbred strain. The mechanism of rejection is the same as that responsible for the rejection of tissue transplants between different strains; it depends upon a cell-mediated immune response against the MHC antigens present on the cancer cells (see TRANSPLANTS, ORGAN AND TISSUE).

While the experiment described above shows that immune responses can kill cancer cells, it does not explain how this might happen—as the immune surveillance hypothesis says it should—when the cancer cells arise within an individual and thus bear that individual's MHC antigens. Other experiments demonstrate that many cancer cells carry unique non-MHC antigens while lacking one or more of the normal antigens, including MHC-I antigens. These cancers might therefore be expected to evoke an immune response, and frequently one can be detected. Antibodies specific for the cancer cells are often present in the blood, usually in low concentrations, and lymph nodes "downstream" from the cancer site usually contain some lymphocytes that recognize the cancer-cell antigens.

Despite the demonstrable immune responses, cancers do develop. Experiments with animal tumours have provided several possible explanations for this, any or all of which may apply to a given cancer. The simplest explanation is that the cancer grows so fast or in such a thick mass that the cytotoxic T cells or NK cells cannot get at most of the cancer cells. Another explanation is that cancer cells that have lost their MHC-I antigens can no longer be killed by cytotoxic T cells. Experiments also show that some cancer cells secrete factors that inhibit NK cells as well as interfere with the immune response; that cancer-induced immune responses often entail a predominance of suppressor T cells over helper T cells; that some cancer cells can shed their antigens, which then block the receptors on the cytotoxic T cells and thereby prevent the lymphocytes from attacking the cancer cells; and that cancer cells often resemble undifferentiated cells present during embryonic life, to which the body would not be expected to become immune.

The fact that cancers nevertheless develop does not prove that immune responses against them are useless. Transplant patients and others treated with immunosuppressive drugs over long periods of time are more liable to develop certain kinds of cancer, especially those caused by viruses. The incidence of cancer also increases greatly in old age, when immune responses are known to decline; however, the chance of having accumulated sufficient genetic mutations to cause cancer also increases sharply with age.

Although injections of interferon and other efforts to stimulate immunity in cancer patients have not been notably successful, much research has been devoted to developing effective immunotherapies against cancer. Another avenue of research has focused on finding ways to immunize healthy persons against cancer. Protection against implanted tumour cells has been induced in experimental animals by immunization with killed cancer cells or antigens from them. But this requires the use of risky procedures to increase the immune response, and it is not therefore acceptable as preventive therapy in humans.

PROPHYLACTIC IMMUNIZATION

Prophylactic immunization refers to the artificial establishment of specific immunity, a technique that has significantly reduced suffering and death from a variety of infectious diseases. There are two types of prophylactic immunization: passive immunization, in which protection is conferred by preformed antibodies; and active immunization, in which protection results from the administration of vaccines that stimulate a specific immune response.

Passive immunization.   The administration of preformed antibodies can provide lifesaving assistance in combatting poisons or infections that produce dangerous effects so rapidly that the victim does not have time to develop an immune response spontaneously. This situation may arise with victims of poisonous snakebites or botulism, as well as those in whom such infections as diphtheria, tetanus, or gas gangrene have progressed to the point where bacterial toxins have been absorbed. It is also the case with bites from a rabid animal, although active immunization is also begun at the same time since the spread of the rabies infection to the central nervous system is relatively slow. Physicians also use passive immunizations to protect temporarily persons traveling to countries where hepatitis B is prevalent and to provide antibodies to persons who suffer from B-cell deficiencies and are therefore unable to make antibodies for themselves (see below *Immune deficiencies*). As discussed earlier, physicians use passive immunizations of anti-Rh antibody to prevent erythroblastosis fetalis.

Manufacture of antiserum

Protective immunoglobulins—primarily of the IgG class—can be prepared from the blood of humans or other species (*e.g.,* horses or rabbits) that have already developed specific immunity against the relevant antigens. These preparations are known as antiserums. Human IgG is only slowly broken down in the recipient's body, the concentration falling by about one-half every three weeks, so that effective amounts of antibody can be present for two or three months. IgG from other species is far more likely to provoke an immune response that will eliminate the antibody and can lead to serum sickness (see below *Allergies*), so human antiserum is chosen whenever it is available.

Active immunization.   Active immunization aims to ensure that a sufficient supply of antibodies or T and B cells that react against a potential infectious agent are present in the body before infection occurs. So primed, the immune system either can prevent the pathogen from establishing itself or can rapidly mobilize the various protective mechanisms described above to abort the infection in its earliest stages.

Manufacture of vaccine

The vaccines used to provide active immunization need not contain living microbes. What matters is that they include the antigens important in evoking a protective response and that those antigens are administered in a harmless form and are sufficient in amount and persistence to produce an immune response similar to the natural infection. Bacterial toxins, such as tetanus or diphtheria, can be rendered harmless by treatment with formaldehyde without affecting their ability to act as immunogens. They are usually administered adsorbed onto an inorganic gel, which helps to retain them in macrophages, and they elicit effective, long-lasting immunity against the toxins themselves. In other instances, when immunization against several antigenic determinants is desirable or the important antigenic component is not known, it may be better to use the microbes themselves killed in such a way as not to alter them significantly. Such killed vaccines are used to immunize against typhoid, whooping cough, plague, and influenza, for example. In other cases researchers have developed attenuated (*i.e.,* weakened) strains of bacteria or viruses, which cause an infection but do not produce the full disease, multiply only to a limited extent in the body, and never revert to the virulent form. The use of such live microbes provides the most effective prophylaxis of all, since they truly imitate a mild form of the natural infection. Such are the vaccines for smallpox, yellow fever, poliomyelitis (oral vaccine), measles, rubella, and tuberculosis. Although attenuated so far as normal persons are concerned, live vaccines may cause the full disease in persons who have an immune deficiency.

When the same diseases can be caused by many strains of microbes, each characterized by different antigenic determinants, neither natural infection nor prophylactic immunization with any one strain protects against infection by the others. For example, it is impractical to immunize against the many viruses that cause the common cold or the numerous streptococci that produce tonsillitis. On the other hand, although there are more than 60 different strains of pneumococci that can cause bacterial pneumonia, some of the strains are much more common than others. Consequently a vaccine containing antigens from up to 14 of the most common strains has proved useful in protecting persons at special risk.

Active immunization is the most effective and cheapest way of protecting against an infectious disease. Furthermore, if 95 percent or more of the population at risk is protected and if humans are the only reservoir of infection, active immunization can even lead to the eradication of the infectious agent. This has been achieved worldwide in the case of smallpox.

PRODUCTION OF MONOCLONAL ANTIBODIES

Before turning to the disorders of the immune system, it is appropriate to discuss the artificial production of monoclonal antibodies, a technique that has emerged as one of the most important facets of biotechnology during the last quarter of the 20th century.

It was pointed out above that upon activation by an antigen, a circulating B cell multiplies to form a clone of plasma cells, each secreting the identical immunoglobulin. It is such an immunoglobulin—derived from the descendants of a single B cell—that constitutes a monoclonal antibody. The antibody response to a natural infection or an active immunization, however, is polyclonal. In other words, it involves many B-cell clones, each of which recognizes a different antigenic determinant and secretes a different immunoglobulin. Thus the blood serum of an immunized person or animal normally contains a mixture of antibodies, all capable of combining with the same antigen but with a variety of specificities. The isolation of an appreciable quantity of a particular (*i.e.,* monoclonal) antibody from this polyclonal mixture is extremely difficult.

Problem of isolating specialized antibody

There is, however, a condition in which the blood serum may contain an astonishingly high concentration of a single immunoglobulin. This results from multiple myeloma, a type of cancer in which a single B cell proliferates to form a tumorous clone of antibody-secreting cells (see below *Cancers of the lymphocytes*). The immunoglobulins made by myelomas are monoclonal, but although they must be antibodies capable of combining with some antigen, there is usually nothing to indicate what this antigen might be. Myelomas are not uncommon in species other than humans, especially in mice and rats, and they can be made to occur frequently in certain laboratory strains by injecting the experimental animal with mineral oil, which acts as a mild irritant and causes B-cell proliferation. Testing of immunoglobulins from many mouse myelomas for their capacity to bind to a very wide variety of antigens has indeed shown that some of them have recognizable antibody activity. Researchers can propagate individual myelomas by growing them in other animals of the same strain or by culturing them outside the body. Furthermore, like other lines of cancer cells, cultured myelomas can multiply indefinitely. (This stands in contrast to normal cell lines, which die out after a certain number of cell divisions.) Thus the propagation of myelomas has enabled immunologists to reap large quantities of monoclonal antibody and has been invaluable in studying the basic nature of immunoglobulins. But if an immunologist wishes to obtain large amounts of a particular antibody—say the anti-Rh antibody—the induction of myelomas is useless, for it has proved impossible to specify beforehand what antibody will be secreted by any given myeloma.

Occasionally, however, a cultured myeloma cell line continues to grow well but loses its ability to secrete immunoglobulin. In 1975 immunologists Georges Köhler and César Milstein discovered that cultured myeloma cells could be made to fuse with normal B cells from the spleen of an immunized mouse. The fusion of a myeloma cell from a line that has lost the ability to secrete immunoglobulin with a B cell known to secrete a particular antibody results in a remarkable one that makes the antibody characteristic of its B-cell component but retains the capacity of its myeloma component to multiply indefinitely. Thus it is possible to obtain hybrid cells, termed hybridomas, that grow like a myeloma but make a chosen, identifiable monoclonal antibody. Since only some of the myeloma cells fuse with the spleen B cells, and only a few of these may be making the desired antibody, researchers have devised means to select the wanted hybridomas from the rest of the cells in the mixture and to propagate them. (To learn more about these techniques, see the *Bibliography*.)

Manu- facture of specialized hybrid cells

Thanks to hybridomas, researchers can obtain—at some cost in time and trouble—monoclonal antibodies that specifically recognize individual antigenic sites on almost any molecule, ranging from drugs and hormones to microbial antigens and cell receptors. The exquisite specificity of monoclonal antibodies and their availability in quantity has made it possible to devise sensitive assays for an enormous range of biologically important substances and to distinguish cells from one another by identifying previously unknown marker molecules on their surfaces. For example, monoclonal antibodies that react with cancer antigens can be used to identify cancer cells in tissue samples. Moreover, if short-lived radioactive atoms are added to these antibodies and they are then administered in tiny quantities to a patient, they become attached exclusively to the cancer tissue. By means of instruments that detect the radioactivity, physicians can locate the cancerous sites without surgical intervention. Monoclonal antibodies have also been used experimentally as "guided missiles" to deliver cytotoxic drugs or radiation to cancer cells.

Although the preparation of monoclonal antibodies with hybridomas derived from rat or mouse cells has become routine practice, it has not proved so easy to obtain human hybridomas. This is partly because most human myeloma cells do not grow well in culture, and those that do so have not produced stable hybridomas. If, however, human B cells isolated from blood are infected by the Epstein–Barr virus (the agent that causes infectious mononucleosis), they can be propagated in culture and continue to secrete immunoglobulin. Very few of them are likely to be making an antibody with a desired specificity, even in a subject who has been immunized; but in some instances immunologists have succeeded in identifying and selecting those cells that secrete the wanted immunoglobulin. These can be grown in culture as single clones that secrete a monoclonal antibody. Researchers have used this process to obtain human monoclonal antibodies against the Rh antigen.

Disorders involving the immune system

IMMUNE DEFICIENCIES

There are several ways in which the protective mechanisms outlined above may fail. Some are inborn, due to genetic defects in the development of one or more of the cells involved in immune responses. Others result from infectious agents that damage essential immune cells. Still others are due to poisons or to drugs administered accidentally or with the intention of curing or ameliorating other diseases. In yet other cases, the immune deficiency stems from inadequate nutrition.

Some infants never develop a thymus, and consequently they cannot produce mature T lymphocytes. In others the B lymphocytes fail to secrete immunoglobulins; some infants are born with combined immune deficiency, in which the functioning of both types of lymphocytes is impaired. Other inborn deficiencies occur because the macrophages or granulocytes lack one or more of the enzymes needed to destroy ingested microbes. All these conditions are rare. . . .

Genetic deficiencies

Probably the most common cause of immune deficiency in countries with advanced medical services is the use of powerful drugs to treat cancers. These drugs work by inhibiting the multiplication of rapidly dividing cells. Although the drugs are chosen so far as possible to act selectively on the cancer cells, they are also liable to inter-

Deficien- cies caused by drug therapy

fere—even if to a lesser extent—with the generation and multiplication of the cells involved in immune responses. Prolonged or intensive treatment commonly impairs immune responses to some degree. Although this immune impairment is reversible, the physician must seek a balance between intentional damage to the cancer cells and unintentional damage to the immune system.

Medically induced suppression of the immune system also occurs when powerful drugs, which are designed specifically to interfere with the development of T and B cells, are used to prevent the rejection of organ or bone-marrow transplants or to damp down serious autoimmune responses (see TRANSPLANTS, ORGAN AND TISSUE). Although use of such drugs has greatly improved the success of transplantation, it also leaves the patient highly susceptible to microbial infections. Fortunately, most such infections can be treated with antibiotics, but the immunosuppressive drugs have to be used with great care and for as short a period as possible.

In countries where the diet, especially that of growing children, is grossly inadequate in respect to protein intake, severe malnutrition ranks as an important cause of immune deficiency. Antibody responses and cell-mediated immunity are seriously impaired, probably due to atrophy of the thymus and the consequent deficiency of helper T cells. This renders the children particularly susceptible to measles and diarrheal diseases. Fortunately, the thymus and the rest of the immune system can recover completely if adequate nutrition is restored.

ALLERGIES

As explained earlier, the immune system must be able to recognize and respond to almost any foreign molecule, since it cannot foretell which molecules will be characteristic of potentially infective agents and which will not. Consequently, an immune response can be induced by materials that have nothing to do with infection, and the mechanisms brought into play, though beneficial for eliminating microbes, are not necessarily beneficial when otherwise innocuous substances are concerned. Furthermore, even initially protective mechanisms can cause secondary disorders when they operate on too great a scale or for longer than necessary....

Type I hypersensitivity. This type of reaction, also known as atopic or anaphylactic hypersensitivity, occurs when the antigen reacts with IgE antibodies bound to tissue mast cells. Introduction of the antigen links the IgE molecules together and triggers the extrusion of granules from the mast cells and the release of the granular contents into the surrounding fluids. The granules contain histamine, which dilates small blood vessels and causes smooth muscle in the bronchial tubes of the lung to constrict; heparin, which prevents blood coagulation; enzymes that break down proteins; agents that attract eosinophil and neutrophil granulocytes; and a chemical that stimulates platelets to adhere to blood vessel walls and to release serotonin, which constricts arteries. In addition, the stimulated mast cells make chemicals (prostaglandins and leukotrienes) that have potent local effects: they cause capillary blood vessels to leak, smooth muscles to contract, granulocytes to move more actively, and platelets to become sticky.

The overall result of the antigen-IgE-mast cell reaction is an acute inflammation marked by local seepage of fluid from and dilatation of the blood vessels, followed by ingress of granulocytes. As explained earlier, this inflammatory reaction can be a useful local protective mechanism. If, however, it is triggered by an otherwise innocuous antigen entering the eyes and nose, it results in swelling and redness of the linings of the eyelids and nasal passages, secretion of tears and mucus, and sneezing—the typical symptoms of hay fever. If the antigen penetrates the lungs, not only do the linings of the bronchial tubes become swollen and secrete mucus, but the muscle in their walls contracts and the tubes are narrowed, making expiration particularly difficult. These are the symptoms of acute asthma. If the antigen is injected beneath the skin—for example, by the sting of an insect or in the course of some medical procedure—the swelling may be extensive though

IgE antibody and allergic reaction

still local. If, however, the injected antigen gets into the bloodstream and interacts with basophils in the blood as well as with mast cells in the tissues, the release of active agents can cause hives (urticaria, or nettle rash) all over the body. Or, if the reaction is more extensive and sudden, it can produce a potentially fatal condition known as anaphylaxis, or anaphylactic shock, which is characterized by a profound and prolonged fall in blood pressure accompanied by difficulty in breathing. If the antigen enters through the gut, the consequences can include painful intestinal spasms and vomiting. Since, moreover, local reaction with mast cells increases the permeability of the mucosa of the gut, in many cases the antigen enters the bloodstream and also produces hives. This sort of rash is accompanied by severe itching, which is a characteristic effect of histamine on nerve endings in the skin.

Anaphylactic shock

Most people are not unduly susceptible to hay fever or to asthma. Those who are—about 10 percent of the population—are sometimes described as atopic. They have an increased tendency to make IgE antibodies. This tendency runs in families, though there is no single gene responsible as there is in such hereditary diseases as hemophilia. Although many innocuous antigens can stimulate a little IgE antibody in the atopic individual, some antigens are much more likely to do so than others, especially if they are repeatedly absorbed in very small amounts through mucous surfaces. Such antigens are often termed allergens. They are usually polypeptides with attached carbohydrate groups and are resistant to drying....

The amount of allergen needed to trigger an acute type I hypersensitivity reaction in a sensitive person is very small: less than one milligram can produce fatal anaphylaxis if it enters the bloodstream. Medical personnel should inquire about any history of hypersensitivity before administering drugs by injection, and if necessary they should inject a test dose into (rather than through) the skin to ensure that hypersensitivity is absent. In any case, a suitable remedy should be at hand.

Another feature of type I hypersensitivity reactions is that once the immediate local reaction to the allergen has taken its course, there may occur an influx of more basophil granulocytes at the site. If the allergen is still present, a more prolonged form of the same reaction—lasting for hours rather than minutes—may supervene. This is a feature of asthmatic attacks in some subjects, in whom repeated episodes also lead to increased sensitivity of the air passages to the constrictive action of histamine. If such persons can escape exposure to the allergen for several weeks, subsequent exposure causes much less severe attacks. A prolonged IgE-induced reaction also causes atopic dermatitis, a skin condition characterized by persistent itching and scaly red patches. These often develop at sites where the skin is bent, such as the elbows and knees. The persistence is due to the influx of mast cells stimulated by the continued presence of the allergen, which is often something absorbed from the gut, such as cow's milk or egg protein.

Several drugs are available that mitigate the effects of IgE-induced allergic reactions. Some, such as sodium chromoglycate and aminophylline, prevent mast-cell granules from being discharged; others, which have effects similar to adrenaline, counteract the effects of histamine. For treatment of asthma and severe hay fever, these drugs are best administered by inhalation. The effects of histamine can also be blocked (rather than counteracted) by antihistamine agents that compete with histamine for binding sites on the target cells. Antihistamines are used to control mild hay fever and such skin manifestations as hives, but they tend to make people sleepy. Corticosteroid drugs can help control persistent asthma or dermatitis, probably by diminishing the inflammatory influx of granulocytes, but long-continued administration can produce dangerous side effects and should be avoided.

Antihistamines, corticosteroids, and other drugs

Sensitivity to allergens often diminishes with time. One explanation is that increasing amounts of IgG antibodies are produced....

Type II hypersensitivity. Allergic reactions of this type occur when cells within the body are destroyed by antibodies, with or without activation of the complement system.

Antibodies that attack body cells

By contrast with type I reactions, in which antigens interact with cell-bound immunoglobulins, type II reactions involve the interaction of circulating immunoglobulins with cell-bound antigens. Type II reactions (also known as cytotoxic reactions) only rarely result from the introduction of innocuous antigens. More commonly, they develop because antibodies have formed against body cells that have been infected by microbes (and thus present microbial antigenic determinants) or because antibodies have been produced that attack the body's cells themselves. This latter process underlies a number of autoimmune diseases, including autoimmune hemolytic anemia, myasthenia gravis, and Goodpasture's syndrome, all of which are discussed later in this article (see *Autoimmune disorders*).

Reactions against blood transfusions

Type II reactions also occur after incompatible blood transfusion, when red blood cells are transfused into a person who already has antibodies against them (either naturally or as a result of previous transfusions). Such transfusions are largely avoidable (see BLOOD: *Uses of blood grouping*), but when they do occur the effects vary according to the class of antibodies involved. If these activate the complete complement system, the red cells are rapidly hemolyzed (made to burst) and the hemoglobin in them is released into the bloodstream. In small amounts it is mopped up by a special protein called hemopexin, but in large amounts it is excreted through the kidneys and can damage the kidney tubules. If activation of complement only goes part of the way (to the C3 stage), the red cells are taken up and destroyed by granulocytes and macrophages, mainly in the liver and spleen. The heme pigment from the hemoglobin is converted to the pigment bilirubin, which accumulates in the blood and makes the subject appear jaundiced. Erythroblastosis fetalis, which was described above, also stems from a type II reaction; and the accumulation of bilirubin in the newborn baby can damage the brain.

Type III hypersensitivity. Type III, or immune-complex, reactions include the various forms of damage caused by the activation of complement in response to antigen–antibody complexes that have become deposited in the tissues or in the walls of the blood vessels. For significant damage to occur, the antigen must be present for longer periods and in greater amounts than those required to cause type I hypersensitivity. The damage results from the various consequences of complement activation already described, especially the influx and activation of neutrophils and macrophages. These scavenger cells release enzymes (which destroy tissues locally) and interleukin 1 (which, among other things, causes fever), secreting these chemicals faster than they can be neutralized or dispersed.

Type III reactions caused by repeated exposure

There are many examples of type III hypersensitivity due to the deposition of antigens in tissues where preformed IgG antibodies are present. For instance, when insects bite they inject their saliva through the skin. The first few times this occurs there may be little reaction; but later bites by the same species of insect give rise to greater and longer-lasting inflammation, owing to the supervening hypersensitivity reaction. More important are those reactions caused by the inhalation of antigens into the lung: for example, farmer's lung, due to fungal spores in moldy hay; pigeon-fancier's lung, due to proteins in powdery pigeon dung; humidifier fever, due to otherwise harmless protozoans that flourish in air-conditioning plants and become dispersed in fine droplets in the air of offices. In each case the farmer, the pigeon fancier, or the office worker will have IgG antibodies against the agent in question in their blood. Inhalation of the antigen results in tightness of the chest, fever, and malaise; these symptoms usually pass in a day or two but recur with reexposure. Permanent damage is rare unless the victims are exposed repeatedly—a situation that they normally avoid because the symptoms are so unpleasant. Some occupational diseases of workers who handle cotton, sugarcane, or coffee waste in warm countries have a similar cause, with the sensitizing antigen usually coming from fungi that grow on the waste rather than the waste itself. The effective treatment is, of course, to prevent further exposure.

The consequences of interaction of antigens with antibody within the bloodstream vary according to whether the complexes formed are large, in which case they are mostly trapped and removed by macrophages in the liver, spleen, and bone marrow, or small, in which case they remain in the circulation. Large complexes occur when more than enough antibody is present to bind to all the antigen molecules. . . .

Type IV hypersensitivity. As mentioned above, type IV hypersensitivity is cell-mediated; in other words, it does not involve the participation of antibodies but is due primarily to the interaction of T cells with antigens. Reactions of this kind depend upon the presence in the circulation of a sufficient number of T cells able to recognize the antigen. These specific T cells must then arrive and selectively accumulate at a site where the antigen is present. Since this process takes much longer than reactions involving antibodies already present throughout blood and tissue fluids, type IV reactions were first distinguished by their delayed onset and are still frequently referred to as delayed hypersensitivity reactions. They not only come on slowly, but, depending upon whether the antigen persists or is removed, they can be prolonged or relatively transient.

The T cells involved in type IV reactions are memory cells derived from prior stimulation by the same antigen. These cells persist for many months or years. . . .

AUTOIMMUNE DISORDERS

In describing the nature and origin of the antigen receptors of B and T cells, it was explained that their enormous diversity is generated by a random process that inevitably gives rise to receptors for self determinants. It was also explained that lymphocytes bearing such receptors are eliminated or rendered impotent by several different mechanisms, so that the immune system does not normally generate significant amounts of antibodies or T cells reactive with the body's own components. Nevertheless, autoimmunity can occur. . . .

BIBLIOGRAPHY. Many textbooks of immunology, all of which aim to be comprehensive, have appeared in recent years. . . . The following are listed in order of increasing complexity: J.H.L. PLAYFAIR, *Immunology at a Glance,* 3rd ed. (1984); IVAN M. ROITT, JONATHAN BROSTOFF, and DAVID K. MALE, *Immunology* (1985); JOSEPH A. BELLANTI (ed.), *Immunology: Basic Processes,* 2nd ed. (1985); and EMIL R. UNANUE and BARUJ BENACERRAF, *Textbook of Immunology,* 2nd ed. (1984). JAN KLEIN, *Immunology, the Science of Self-Nonself Discrimination* (1982), explains clearly how and why principles were discovered. For the history of immunology, see J.H. HUMPHREY and R.G. WHITE, *Immunology for Students of Medicine,* 3rd ed. (1970). . . . Evolution of the immune system is well described in ELWIN L. COOPER, *General Immunology* (1982). For genetic aspects, see H. HUGH FUDENBERG et al., *Basic Immunogenetics,* 3rd ed. (1984). At a more advanced level, clinical aspects are covered by P.J. LACHMAN and D.K. PETERS (eds.), *Clinical Aspects of Immunology,* 4th ed., 2 vol. (1982); MAX SAMTER (ed.), *Immunological Diseases,* 3rd ed., 2 vol. (1978); and G.L. ASHERSON and A.D.B. WEBSTER, *Diagnosis and Treatment of Immunodeficiency Disease* (1980). For immunochemistry, see ELVIN A. KABAT, *Structural Concepts in Immunology and Immunochemistry,* 2nd ed. (1976); and L.E. GLYNN and M.W. STEWARD, *Immunochemistry: An Advanced Textbook* (1977). A good simple account of monoclonal antibodies is given in KAROL SIKORA and HOWARD M. SMEDLEY, *Monoclonal Antibodies* (1984).

JOHN H. HUMPHREY. Emeritus Professor of Immunology, Royal Postgraduate Medical School, University of London. Coeditor of *Advances in Immunology.*

Exercise and Physical Conditioning

The terms exercise and physical activity are often used interchangeably, but this article will distinguish between them. Physical activity is an inclusive term that refers to any expenditure of energy brought about by bodily movement via the skeletal muscles; as such, it includes the complete spectrum of activity from very low resting levels to maximal exertion. Exercise is a component of physical activity. The distinguishing characteristic of exercise is that it is a structured activity specifically planned to develop and maintain physical fitness. Physical conditioning refers to the development of physical fitness through the adaptation of the body and its various systems to an exercise program.

This article is divided into the following sections:

A HISTORICAL VIEW OF EXERCISE

Prehistoric period. Hominids—human beings and their immediate ancestors—have existed on Earth for at least 2,000,000 years. For more than 99 percent of that time, hominids lived a nomadic existence and survived by hunting and gathering food. It is obvious that this way of life was enormously different from the way people live today in developed countries. Thus, evolutionary history has prepared humankind for one kind of life, but modern people lead another. This fact has profound implications for patterns of disease and for the association between living habits and health. Observation of the few remaining nomadic groups in the world indicates that they are relatively free of chronic diseases and that, in comparison to the populations in developed countries, they are leaner, have a higher level of physical fitness, eat a very different diet, and have different physical activity patterns. Data from the distant past are not available, but it is reasonable to speculate that early humans had considerably higher caloric expenditures per unit of body weight than do modern individuals.

Agricultural period. As civilization developed, nomadic hunting and gathering societies gave way to agricultural ones in which people grew their own food and domesticated animals. This development occurred relatively recently, approximately 10,000 years ago. Although many aspects of life changed during the agricultural period, it is likely that energy demands remained high, with much of the work still done by human power. Even in cities—which had evolved by about midway through the agricultural period—individuals expended more calories than do most people today.

Industrial period. The industrial period began during the mid-18th century, with the development of an efficient steam engine, and lasted to the end of World War II (1945). This relatively brief time span was characterized by a major shift in population from farms to cities, with attendant changes in many areas of life-style. Even though the internal-combustion engine and electrical power were increasingly used to perform work, the great majority of individuals in industrialized societies still faced significant energy demands. In the cities relatively more individuals walked to work, climbed stairs, and had more physically demanding jobs than do most people today.

Technological period. The post-World-War-II period has been a technological age, a period characterized by rapid growth in energy-saving devices, both in the home and at the workplace. As an example, longshoremen in the late 1940s worked hard loading and unloading ships; by contrast, most longshoremen in the late 20th century had much lower energy demands from the job, because of the containerization of cargo and the mechanization of the loading and unloading process. Also during this period, the use of labour-saving devices in the home and in yard and garden work became much more widespread. Physical activity became less and less common in industrialized countries, especially among the urban population. Although the level of general physical activity has declined, most observers feel that there have been increases in exercise participation in many countries since the late 1960s. Jogging, racket sports, cycling, and other active recreational pursuits have become much more common. In a sense this is simply humankind's returning to the more active life-style of its distant ancestors.

Effects of labour-saving devices

TYPES OF PHYSICAL FITNESS

Physical fitness is a general concept and is defined in many ways by different scientists. Physical fitness is discussed here in two major categories: health-related physical fitness and motor-performance physical fitness. Despite some overlap between these classifications, there are major differences, as described below.

Health-related physical fitness. Health-related physical fitness is defined as fitness related to some aspect of health. This type of physical fitness is primarily influenced by an individual's exercise habits; thus, it is a dynamic state and may change. Physical characteristics that constitute health-related physical fitness include strength and endurance of skeletal muscles, joint flexibility, body composition, and cardiorespiratory endurance. All these attributes change in response to appropriate physical conditioning programs, and all are related to health.

Strength and endurance of skeletal muscles of the trunk help maintain correct posture and prevent such problems as low back pain. Minimal levels of muscular strength and endurance are needed for routine tasks of living, such as carrying bags of groceries or picking up a young child. Individuals with very low levels of muscular strength and endurance are limited in the performance of routine tasks and have to lead a restricted life. Such limitations are perhaps only indirectly related to health, but individuals who cannot pick up and hug a grandchild or must struggle to get up from a soft chair surely have a lower quality of life than that enjoyed by their fitter peers.

Flexibility, or range of motion around the joints, also ranks as an important component of health-related fitness. Lack of flexibility in the lower back and posterior thigh is thought to contribute to low back pain. Extreme lack of flexibility also has a deleterious effect on the quality of life by limiting performance.

Body composition refers to the ratio between fat and lean tissue in the body. Excess body fat is clearly related to several health problems, including cardiovascular disease, type II (adult-onset) diabetes mellitus, and certain forms of cancer. Body composition is affected by diet, but exercise habits play a crucial role in preventing obesity and maintaining acceptable levels of body fat.

Cardiorespiratory endurance, or aerobic fitness, is probably what most people identify as physical fitness. Aerobic fitness refers to the integrated functional capacity of the heart, lungs, vascular system, and skeletal muscles to expend energy. The basic activity that underlies this type of fitness is aerobic metabolism in the muscle cell, a process in which oxygen is combined with a fuel source (fats or carbohydrates) to release energy and produce carbon dioxide and water. The energy is used by the muscle to contract, thereby exerting force that can be used for movement. For the aerobic reaction to take place, the cardiorespiratory system (*i.e.,* the circulatory and pulmonary systems) must constantly supply oxygen and fuel to the muscle cell and remove carbon dioxide from it. The maximal rate at which aerobic metabolism can occur is thus determined by the functional capacity of the cardiorespiratory system and is measured in the laboratory as maximal oxygen intake. As will be discussed in detail below, aerobic fitness is inversely related to the incidence of coronary heart disease and hypertension.

Motor-performance physical fitness. Motor-performance fitness is defined as the ability of the neuromuscular system to perform specific tasks. Test items used to assess motor-performance fitness include chin-ups, sit-ups, the 50-yard dash, the standing long jump, and the shuttle run (a timed run in which the participant dashes back and forth between two points). The primary physical characteristics measured by these tests are the strength and endurance of the skeletal muscles and the speed or power of the legs. These traits are important for success in many types of athletics. Muscular strength and endurance are also related to some aspects of health, as stated above.

There is disagreement among experts about the relative importance of health-related and motor-performance physical fitness. While both types of fitness are obviously desirable, their relative values should be determined by an individual's personal fitness objectives. If success in athletic events is of primary importance, motor-performance fitness should be emphasized. If concern about health is paramount, health-related fitness should be the focus. Different types of fitness may be important not only to different individuals but also to the same individual at different times. The 16-year-old competing on a school athletic team is likely to focus on motor performance. The typical middle-aged individual is not as likely to be concerned about athletic success, emphasizing instead health and appearance. One further point should be made: to a great extent, motor-performance physical fitness is determined by genetic potential. The person who can run fast at 10 years of age will be fast at age 17; although training may enhance racing performance, it will not appreciably change the individual's genetically determined running speed. On the other hand, characteristics of health-related physical fitness, while also partly determined by inheritance, are much more profoundly influenced by exercise habits.

The role of heredity

PRINCIPLES OF EXERCISE TRAINING

Research in exercise training has led to the recognition of a number of general principles of conditioning. These principles must be applied to the development of a successful exercise program.

Specificity. The principle of specificity derives from the observation that the adaptation of the body or change in physical fitness is specific to the type of training undertaken. Quite simply this means that if a fitness objective is to increase flexibility, then flexibility training must be used. If one desires to develop strength, resistance or strengthening exercises must be employed. This principle is indeed simple; however, it is frequently ignored. Many fraudulent claims for an exercise product or system promise overall physical fitness from one simple training technique. A person should be suspicious of such claims and should consider whether or not the exercise training recommended is the type that will produce the specific changes desired.

Overload. Overload, the second important principle, means that to improve any aspect of physical fitness the individual must continually increase the demands placed on the appropriate body systems. For example, to develop strength, progressively heavier objects must be lifted. Overload in running programs is achieved by running longer distances or by increasing the speed.

Progression. Individuals frequently make the mistake of attempting too rapid a fitness change. A classic example is that of the middle-aged man or woman who has done no exercise for 20 years and suddenly begins a vigorous training program. The result of such activity is frequently an injury or, at the least, stiffness and soreness. There are no hard-and-fast rules on how rapidly one should progress to a higher level of activity. The individual's subjective impression of whether or not the body seems to be able to tolerate increased training serves as a good guide. In general it might be reasonable not to progress to higher levels of activity more often than every one or two weeks.

Warm-up/cool down. Another important practice to follow in an exercise program is to gradually start the exercise session and gradually taper off at the end. The warm-up allows various body systems to adjust to increased metabolic demands. The heart rate increases, blood flow increases, and muscle temperatures rise. Warming up is certainly a more comfortable way to begin an exercise session and is probably safer. Progressively more vigorous exercises or a gradual increase in walking speed are good ways to warm up. It is equally important to cool down—that is, to gradually reduce exercise intensity—at the end of each session. The abrupt cessation of vigorous exercise may cause blood to pool in the legs, which can cause fainting or, more seriously, can sometimes precipitate cardiac complications. Slow walking and stretching for five minutes at the end of an exercise session is therefore a good practice. The heart rate should gradually decline during the cool down, and by the end of the five minutes it should be less than 120 beats per minute for individuals under 50 years of age and less than 100 beats per minute for those over 50.

Frequency, intensity, and duration. To provide guidance on how much exercise an individual should do, exercise physiologists have developed equations based on research. It is generally agreed that to develop and maintain physical fitness, the exercise must be performed on a regular basis. A frequency of about every other day or three days per week appears minimally sufficient. Many individuals exercise more frequently than this, and, of course, such additional exercise is acceptable provided that one does not become overtrained and suffer illness or injury.

The intensity of exercise required to produce benefits has been the subject of much study. Many people have the impression that exercise is not doing any good unless it hurts. This is simply not true. Regular exercise at 45 to 50 percent of one's maximal capacity is adequate to improve one's physiological functioning and overall health. This level of intensity is generally comfortable for most individuals. A reliable way to gauge exercise intensity is to measure the heart rate during exercise. An exercise heart rate that is 65 percent of a person's maximal heart rate corresponds to approximately 50 percent of his maximal capacity. Maximal heart rate can be estimated by subtracting one's age in years from 220 (or, in the case of active males, by subtracting half of one's age from 205). Thus, a sedentary 40-year-old man has an estimated maximal heart rate of 180 beats per minute. Sixty-five percent of this maximal rate is 117 beats per minute; thus by exercising at 117 beats per minute, this individual is working at about 50 percent of his maximal capacity. To determine exercising heart rate, a person should exercise for several minutes, to allow the heart rate to adjust. The exerciser should then stop exercising, quickly find the pulse, and count the number of beats for 15 seconds. Multiplying this by four gives the rate in beats per minute. The pulse

Heart rate as a gauge of exercise intensity

must be taken immediately after stopping exercise, since the heart rate rapidly begins to return to the resting level after work has been stopped. As noted above, exercising at the 50 percent level of intensity will improve physiologic functioning and provide health benefits. This level of exercise will not produce the maximum fitness needed for competitive athletics.

There is a relationship between the recommended duration of exercise and the intensity of exercise. If one exercises at a very high intensity, the duration of the exercise need not be as long to produce physiological changes. At lower intensities, duration must increase. The table presents guidelines for reasonable intensity, duration, and frequency.

Guidelines for Intensity, Duration, and Frequency of Exercise

exercise heart rate (beats/minute)	duration of session (minutes)	sessions per week
140	20	4
130	30	3
120	45	5

These values apply to a 40-year-old person.

Overall conditioning. Much emphasis has been given in the foregoing discussion to aerobic fitness, because this form of conditioning is extremely important. It should be noted, however, that other types of conditioning also have benefits. A total exercise program should include strengthening exercises, to maintain body mass and appropriate levels of strength for daily functioning, and stretching exercises to maintain joint mobility and flexibility. The specificity principle described above indicates that no one exercise is likely to produce the overall conditioning effect. In general an exercise plan should consist of aerobics, exercises that increase the strength and endurance of various skeletal muscle groups, and flexibility exercises to maintain good joint function.

Individual differences. The principles of exercise training discussed above should be viewed as general guidelines. Individuals differ in both physiological and psychological adaptations to exercise. Two people who are similar in many respects and who start the same exercise program may have entirely different impressions of it. One person may feel that the exercise is too easy, while the other may believe that it is much too hard. It is certainly appropriate that the exercise plan be adjusted to account for preferences. Likewise some individuals will progress to more intense training levels far more rapidly than others do. As mentioned earlier, exercise progress should be adjusted according to the exerciser's own assessment.

Individuals also differ in the type of exercise they like or can tolerate. Jogging, for instance, is not for everyone. Many people who dislike jogging, or who suffer running injuries, can find other satisfactory exercise activities, such as cycling, walking, swimming, or participating in a sport. Many kinds of exercise activities are appropriate and can provide physiological and health benefits to the participant. There is no one best exercise. The important thing is to be regular in exercise participation and to follow the general guidelines outlined in this section.

PHYSIOLOGICAL EFFECTS OF EXERCISE

Neuromuscular effects. *Strength and endurance.* Appropriate exercise increases the strength and endurance of skeletal muscles. Increases in muscular strength are associated with increases in muscle mass; increases in muscular endurance are associated with improved blood flow to the working muscles. These results are achieved by resistance training. Any exercise that causes the muscle to increase its tension, whether or not the muscle actually shortens during contraction, provides an appropriate strength-training stimulus. Resistance can be applied to a muscle group by attempting to move an immovable object, by working one muscle group against another, by lifting heavy weights, or by using special strength-training machines and devices. There is a wide selection of strength-training equipment

Strength training [margin note]

that, when used properly, can increase muscular strength and endurance. It is possible that some of the equipment is more efficient in developing maximal performance, which is important for competitive athletes. But for the average individual, who is training to maintain an acceptable level of muscular fitness, any one device or program is probably about as good as another.

Strength and endurance training is done by performing several "reps" (repetitions) of a given exercise, then moving on to another exercise for a different muscle group. Experts generally recommend that exercisers select a resistance that is approximately 65 percent of the maximum they can lift for that particular exercise. This load should allow the completion of 12 reps of that exercise in 24 to 30 seconds. Each group of eight to 12 reps is called a set, and two or three sets of a given exercise are recommended for each training session. The average individual should perform strength and endurance training two to three days per week. Super circuit weight training refers to a program in which running or other aerobic exercises are performed between sets; this training produces aerobic as well as strength benefits.

Flexibility. Muscles and tendons can be stretched to improve flexibility (the range of motion at a joint). Flexibility training follows a few, simple principles. To improve range of motion, the muscles and other connective tissue around a joint must be stretched. The preferred stretching technique is a slow increase in the range of motion. The exerciser should feel the muscle stretch, but not to the point of pain. The stretch should be performed gradually, and the body should be held for 10 to 20 seconds in the stretched position and then gradually returned to a relaxed posture. By stretching each muscle group in this fashion as a part of the strengthening and conditioning program, the participant will maintain good flexibility. Bouncing or explosive stretching movements should be avoided, as they can result in muscle or tendon tears.

Stretching technique [margin note]

Cardiorespiratory effects. *Cardiac effects.* Regular aerobic exercise training has a direct effect on the heart muscle. The muscle mass of the left ventricle, which is the pumping chamber that circulates blood throughout the body, increases with exercise training. This change means that the heart can pump more blood with each beat. In short, the heart becomes a bigger, stronger, and more efficient pump capable of doing more work with less effort.

Circulatory effects. Regular exercise also produces changes in the circulation. As previously discussed, muscle endurance training serves to increase blood flow to the working muscles. This increased blood flow means that more oxygen and fuel can be delivered to the muscle cells. The number of red blood cells, which carry oxygen in the blood, also increases with training, as does blood volume. Taken together, these changes indicate a greater capacity to transport oxygen to the working muscles.

Pulmonary effects. The basic function of the lungs is to facilitate the transfer (1) of oxygen from the atmosphere into the blood and (2) of carbon dioxide from the blood into the atmosphere. To accomplish this, air must pass into and out of the lungs, and the respiratory gases must diffuse through the lungs into the circulation and vice versa. Although exercise has not been shown to affect this diffusing ability, exercise training does strengthen the muscles of respiration. This means that a trained individual can move more air through the lungs per time unit, and forced vital capacity (*i.e.,* the maximum volume of air that can be exhaled after a full inspiration) may be increased.

HEALTH EFFECTS OF EXERCISE

Improved general fitness. The greatest benefit of a regular exercise program is an improvement in overall fitness. As discussed above, appropriate exercise improves muscular strength and endurance, body composition, flexibility, and cardiorespiratory endurance. The level of maximal oxygen intake or cardiorespiratory endurance is not by itself of great importance to most individuals. What is important is that one's sustained energy-spending ability is directly related to maximal levels of performance. For example, consider the simple task of walking at a rate of three miles per hour. This task involves an energy expen-

Effects on energy-spending ability [margin note]

diture of approximately three times the resting metabolic rate. Extremely unfit individuals may have a maximal aerobic power of only six times their resting metabolic rate. For such individuals, a three-mile-per-hour walk requires half of their maximal capacity. A middle-aged person who exercises regularly will have a maximal aerobic power 10 to 12 times resting, so the same walk will represent only 25 to 30 percent of maximal capacity. This example illustrates how any submaximal task is relatively much easier for the conditioned individual. Moreover, a person cannot work throughout the day at much more than about 20 percent of maximal capacity without becoming chronically fatigued. The deconditioned person who has a maximal aerobic power of six times resting can comfortably sustain a work level of only about 1.2 times resting throughout the day (6 × 0.20 = 1.2). This low capability for sustained energy expenditure can support only a very sedentary existence: for example, 20 hours of sleep and rest, two hours of personal care, one hour of housework and shopping, and one hour of activity at three times the resting rate each day.

The point of the preceding discussion is that the average energy-expenditure requirement of anyone's life can be calculated, and a person's maximal cardiorespiratory endurance determines how active a life-style can be sustained. Individuals who attempt to lead more active lives than their fitness level will support become chronically fatigued. Persons with adequate or optimal fitness levels, on the other hand, are able to meet the physical demands of an active life relatively easily. One of the most frequent observations made by individuals who have begun an exercise program is that they feel better, and research studies document an improvement in feelings of general well-being in more active people.

Decreased risk of coronary heart disease. Coronary heart disease is the leading cause of death in the developed world. Coronary heart disease is defined as myocardial infarction, or heart attack; angina pectoris, or chest pain; or sudden death due to cardiac arrest or abnormal electrical activity in the heart. The basic disease process that underlies coronary heart disease is atherosclerosis, a disorder characterized by the accumulation of cholesterol and the proliferation of smooth muscle cells in the linings of the arteries. This results in a gradual narrowing of the arterial channel, and this narrowing diminishes and may ultimately stop blood flow through an artery. When this occurs in a coronary artery—that is, an artery supplying the heart—one of the manifestations of coronary heart disease occurs.

Epidemiological evidence of exercise benefits. Studies have linked sedentary living with high rates of coronary heart disease mortality. One study found that San Francisco longshoremen who worked in jobs requiring high levels of energy expenditure had less risk of dying of heart disease than did longshoremen who performed sedentary jobs. This study showed that dockworkers and cargo handlers expended at least 1,000 kilocalories more per day than did clerks and foremen and that sedentary workers, during a 22-year observation, were about twice as likely to die from heart disease. The higher risk of death in the less active men was not due to other coronary heart disease risk factors, such as smoking, obesity, and high blood pressure; nor was it the result of less healthy men's shifting to sedentary jobs.

Another study followed the health status of approximately 17,000 male graduates of Harvard University for many years. All these men essentially had sedentary jobs, but they differed in the amount of leisure time they spent on physical activities. Men who expended at least 2,000 kilocalories per week on physical activity had only half the death rate from heart disease as did those men who expended less than 500 kilocalories per week. Not all of this energy was spent in exercise programs; some was expended during routine activities such as climbing stairs.

The effect of exercise on coronary-heart-disease risk factors. One of the important medical achievements of the 20th century has been the development of the risk-factor theory of coronary heart disease. Scientists have discovered that persons who are overweight, smoke cigarettes,

have high blood pressure, or show elevated blood levels of certain types of fat- and cholesterol-carrying molecules are much likelier to die from coronary heart disease. Furthermore, combinations of these risk factors result in exponential increases in the risk of death. The discovery and description of risk factors have led to an understanding of the atherosclerotic process and of how to prevent and treat it. Evidence suggests that regular exercise can lower a person's exposure to several of the risk factors.

Fat and cholesterol are transported by the blood in complex molecules called lipoproteins. Researchers have identified several classes of lipoproteins and have elucidated their roles in atherosclerotic progression. It is, therefore, possible to describe abnormal, or high-risk, lipoprotein profiles. Diet and heredity are key factors determining a person's lipoprotein profile, and exercise also plays an important role. Regular aerobic exercise improves the lipoprotein profile in most individuals. Although more work is needed to completely understand this association, the dose of exercise necessary to effect a beneficial change in the lipoprotein profile seems to be about eight to 10 miles of running (or its equivalent in other activity) per week.

Elevated blood pressure (hypertension) is a second powerful risk factor for coronary heart disease. Sedentary living habits and low levels of physical fitness increase the risk of developing hypertension. Exercise also appears to lower blood pressure in at least some individuals with hypertension. The greatest benefit is probably for younger people (those less than 40 to 45 years of age) whose hypertension is of relatively recent onset.

Excess body weight is considered by most experts to be an independent risk factor for coronary heart disease, although obesity also indirectly increases the risk via deleterious impact on blood pressure and the lipoprotein profile. Exercise habits are strongly related to body weight. In virtually all studies of large populations, the more active individuals weigh less. One of the most consistent results seen in exercise-training studies is the loss of body weight and fat. Weight-loss programs that incorporate exercise as well as diet are more successful than those that rely on diet alone.

Impact on other chronic diseases. Although more research is needed to arrive at definitive conclusions, some evidence has suggested that regular exercise may help in the treatment or prevention of other chronic diseases. The control of type II diabetes, for example, appears to be aided by regular exercise. This form of diabetes is a major health problem in which the patient shows elevated levels of blood sugar despite having acceptable levels of insulin, the hormone that normally clears the blood of excess sugar by facilitating its utilization by the body cells. Persons with this disease need to control their blood sugar, but not with insulin injections. Oral medications that lower blood-sugar levels are available, but their usefulness has been questioned. Consequently, dietary modifications and exercise, both of which can lower blood-sugar levels, have become the key measures in controlling type II diabetes. Exercise seems to improve the insulin sensitivity of cells, so that blood sugar can more readily be taken in and used as fuel.

A few reports have linked low physical activity with a higher risk of developing certain cancers, particularly colon cancer. These results are intriguing, but more work is needed to firmly establish that sedentary habits are an independent risk factor for cancer.

RISKS OF EXERCISE

As can be seen from the foregoing discussion, regular participation in an exercise program can provide several benefits. Yet exercise is similar to other medical or health interventions in that there are also potential costs associated with the activity. These costs range from minor inconveniences, such as time taken up by exercise, to more serious complications, including injury and even sudden death.

Injuries. It is clear that some people who participate in exercise training will develop injuries to their bones, muscles, and joints. Despite unfounded reports in the mass

Atherosclerosis

Effect of exercise on high blood pressure

Effect of exercise on diabetes

media of extremely high injury rates among adult exercisers, there have been few good studies of exercise injuries in populations. One of the difficulties in performing such studies has been the need to identify both the number of cases (individuals who become injured) and the number of persons at risk for injury (the total number of individuals exercising in the population). These two figures are necessary in order to calculate true injury rates. The best available studies on injury rates suggest that about 25 to 30 percent of adult runners will become injured over the course of a year, if injury is defined as an incident that causes an individual to stop exercising for at least one week. If only more serious injuries, such as those for which the individual seeks medical care, are considered, injury rates are much lower, perhaps in the range of 1 percent per year.

Little is known about the causes of exercise injuries. One factor that has been linked to injury is the amount of exercise; for example, individuals who run more miles are likelier to be injured than those who run fewer miles. Factors such as age, sex, body type, and experience have not been shown to be associated with risk of injury. It seems logical that structural abnormalities, sudden increases in training intensity, and types of equipment used are likely to be related to injury risk; however, data to support these opinions are not available.

How to avoid injuries

In view of the limited scientific data on injury risk, the exerciser is advised to follow commonsense practices until such time as the causes of injury are better understood. Exercisers should start their program slowly and gradually progress to more intensive training levels. They should use good equipment and pay particular attention to proper footwear. Exercisers who have had previous injuries should recognize that they may be more susceptible to similar injuries in the future. All exercisers should use caution and should monitor their bodies for the early warning signs of injury. If a problem begins to develop, it is good advice to stop exercising or to reduce the intensity of training for a few days to see if the problem disappears. Exercisers should not be afraid to experiment on themselves to find out what training practices and techniques seem to be more comfortable and less likely to produce injury. Moderation is good advice: few injuries are reported in individuals who run 10 to 15 miles per week, and this level is adequate to provide many health benefits.

Sudden death. Obviously, the most serious complication from an exercise program is sudden death. This is, fortunately, a rare occurrence. As discussed earlier, several studies have shown that individuals who regularly participate in exercise have a lower risk of dying from a heart attack. There is, however, also evidence that suggests a higher risk of dying during exercise than during sedentary activities. When one considers the total risk of sudden death over a 24-hour period, regular exercisers are much less likely to experience this catastrophe.

Virtually all individuals who drop dead suddenly have advanced coronary heart disease. It follows, therefore, that the best way to reduce the risk of sudden death during exercise is to avoid getting advanced coronary heart disease. This implies following good health practices in other aspects of life, such as not smoking, eating a prudent diet, and maintaining an ideal body weight. Individuals who are middle-aged or older can probably reduce their risk of sudden death by knowing about their coronary risk status and their general state of health before undertaking an exercise program. There are, of course, no guarantees, but if an individual has a thorough examination by a competent physician, including a maximal exercise test and other procedures that screen for coronary heart disease, that person can probably safely begin an exercise program.

SUMMARY

There has been much progress in the field of exercise and physical conditioning. Concepts about exercise have moved from faddism to scientific legitimacy, thanks to researchers in physical education, exercise physiology, and medicine. Yet much remains to be learned, and experts need to work together to further develop the study and promotion of exercise. There are many items that need further study, from the cellular level to the population as a whole. For example, more information is needed on specifically how exercise affects blood lipoprotein levels, and further research is needed on rates of injuries in populations of exercisers.

BIBLIOGRAPHY. Exercise as a key to health maintenance is found in KENNETH H. COOPER, *The Aerobics Program for Total Well-being: Exercise, Diet, Emotional Balance* (1982); MICHAEL L. POLLOCK, JACK H. WILMORE, and SAMUEL M. FOX III, *Exercise in Health and Disease: Evaluation and Prescription for Prevention and Rehabilitation* (1984); PHILIP L. WHITE and THERESE MONDEIKA (eds.), *Diet and Exercise: Synergism in Health Maintenance* (1982); BUD GETCHELL and WAYNE ANDERSON, *Being Fit: A Personal Guide* (1982); JOHN E. BEAULIEU, *Stretching for All Sports* (1980). Specific aspects of exercise for middle-aged or older people are the topic of HERBERT A. DEVRIES and DIANNE HALES, *Fitness After 50* (1982). Other special topics are treated in the *Journal of the American Medical Association*: LARRY W. GIBBONS et al., "The Acute Cardiac Risk of Strenuous Exercise," *J.A.M.A.*, 244(16):1799–1801 (Oct. 17, 1980); JOHN J. DUNCAN et al., "The Effects of Aerobic Exercise on Plasma Catecholamines and Blood Pressure in Patients with Mild Essential Hypertension," *J.A.M.A.*, 254(18):2609–13 (Nov. 8, 1985); RALPH S. PAFFENBARGER et al., "A Natural History of Athleticism and Cardiovascular Health," *J.A.M.A.*, 252(4):491–495 (July 27, 1984); and STEVEN N. BLAIR et al., "Physical Fitness and Incidence of Hypertension in Healthy Normotensive Men and Women," *J.A.M.A.*, 252(4):487–490 (July 27, 1984). See also KENNETH H. COOPER, *Running Without Fear: How to Reduce the Risk of Heart Attack and Sudden Death During Aerobic Exercise* (1985); and SIDNEY ALEXANDER, *Running Healthy: A Guide to Cardiovascular Fitness* (1980).

What happens to the body during exercise and other intense physical activity is explained in many informative sources and texts. See PER-OLOF ASTRAND and KAARE RODAHL, *Textbook of Work Physiology: Physiological Bases of Exercise*, 2nd ed. (1977); and GEORGE A. BROOKS and THOMAS D. FAHEY, *Exercise Physiology: Human Bioenergetics and Its Applications* (1984). Public health aspects of physical activities and exercise are explored in a collection of articles in *Public Health Reports*, vol. 100, no. 2 (March–April 1985). ROY J. SHEPHARD (ed.), *Frontiers of Fitness* (1971), discusses the physiology of exercise and desirable limits of fitness for people of different ages.

The usefulness of recreational exercise was studied in Greek antiquity by Galen; see ROBERT MONTRAVILLE GREENE, *A Translation of Galen's "Hygiene" (De sanitate tuenda)* (1951). For a historical treatment of exercise and sport, see RICHARD D. MANDELL, *Sport, a Cultural History* (1984), a scholarly study of physical activity as a component of culture; WILLIAM J. BAKER, *Sports in the Western World* (1982); and HISPA (INTERNATIONAL ASSOCIATION FOR THE HISTORY OF PHYSICAL EDUCATION AND SPORT), *The History, the Evolution and Diffusion of Sports and Games in Different Cultures* (1976).

KENNETH H. COOPER. President and Founder, The Aerobics Center, Dallas, Texas. Author of *The Aerobics Program for Total Well-being*.

STEVEN N. BLAIR. Director, Epidemiology, Institute for Aerobics Research, The Aerobics Center, Dallas, Texas. Chair of the editorial committee, Guidelines for Exercise Testing and Prescription.

WORLD
OF
MEDICINE

A review of
recent developments
in health and medicine

Accidents and Safety

In many countries of the world, particularly the developed countries, accidents are a major cause of death and disablement and yet are probably among the most overlooked major health problems. Accidents are the fourth leading cause of death in the U.S., after heart disease, cancer, and stroke, and they are the *leading* cause of death among those 36 years old and younger. Accidents are by far the leading cause of death among those aged 15 to 24, accounting for 54% of all deaths in that group, more deaths than all other causes combined. In addition, accidents in the U.S. cause about nine million disabling injuries each year, about 350,000 of which lead to permanent impairments.

The estimated cost of accidents to the U.S. economy—taking into account wage losses, medical expenses, insurance costs, and fire damage—was at least $107 billion in 1985, the most recent year for which statistics are available. This figure does not include the cost of public agencies such as police and fire departments, court expenses, or indirect losses to employers resulting from off-the-job accidents. None of these figures, of course, can begin to measure the toll that accidents take in human suffering. There is little wonder, then, that health experts label accidents as the most underrated health problem.

Because of differences in reporting and recording methods, it is difficult to directly compare the U.S. accidental death rate with rates in foreign countries. However, according to the statistics available, the United States appears to rank somewhere in the middle of the industrial nations, with an accidental death rate of 39.5 deaths per 100,000 population in 1985.

Japan's reported rate was 24.6, England's was 25.9, Israel's was 29.6, and Canada's was 37.5. The rate in West Germany was 38.7; in Finland it was 44.4; in Poland it was 49.9; and in France it was 66.6.

Work accidents, yesterday and today

As in several other nations, industry boomed in the United States between the Civil War period and World War I. Factories and the jobs they provided attracted men, women, and children from the farms of America and Europe.

While the factories and railroads produced and shipped goods at record levels, they also killed and maimed. Exposed gears, flying or falling steel, blast furnaces, and boilers prone to explosion made work injuries and deaths so common that the accidents were accepted as the price of progress. Miners, ironworkers and steelworkers, and railroad employees were particularly vulnerable. Steel mills were termed slaughterhouses. In just one U.S. county—Allegheny County in Pennsylvania—195 steelworkers were killed in the 12 months that began July 1, 1906. It was accepted that at least one man would be killed for each mile of railroad track laid. From 1902 through 1908 nearly 15,000 railroad workers in America were killed on the job. More than 1,200 men were killed in accidents while building the Panama Canal. One can only guess at the number of fingers, toes, eyes, and limbs lost.

Fortunately, not everyone involved in industry was willing to accept so much suffering. In 1892 the Illinois Steel Co. organized a safety department—the first in the country—at its Joliet works. In the early part of the 20th century (the exact date is not known), the Association of Iron and Steel Electrical Engineers appointed

After the Civil War, industry boomed in the U.S., employing vast numbers of men, women, and children. Injuries and deaths were so common in manufacturing establishments (such as the machine shop depicted at right) that they were regarded as an inevitable trade-off for "progress."

"The Accident in the Machine Shop," 1891 woodcut after a painting by John Bahr; photograph, the Bettmann Archive

a safety committee. In 1908 Pres. Theodore Roosevelt declared that "the number of accidents which result in the death or crippling of wage earners . . . is simply appalling. In a very few years it runs up a total far in excess of the aggregate of the dead and wounded in any major war." With presidential backing, safety laws, including the first Workmen's Compensation law for federal employees, began springing up around the U.S.

In 1912 a group of engineers gathered in Milwaukee, Wis., for the First Cooperative Safety Congress, which became the forerunner of the National Safety Council. Safety in the workplace became a priority as efforts concentrated on three major areas: machine guarding, protective equipment, and worker training. Machine guards covered previously exposed gears and moving parts so that they would no longer catch a shirt sleeve and pull a hand into the machine. Equipment such as gloves, goggles, and heavy boots protected workers from flying or falling debris. Safety experts began formally training workers on how to operate machinery safely, carry loads, and use their protective equipment.

After decades of these efforts, the American workplace has by now become much safer. While mining, construction, and certain other industries are still relatively dangerous, accident rates overall dropped by a staggering 76% between 1912 and 1985. In 1912 about 20,000 workers were killed, whereas in 1985 about 11,600 workers were killed in a work force that was twice as large and ten times as productive as that of 1912.

In 1985 the industry groups sustaining the highest proportion of deaths in work-related accidents were mining and quarrying, agriculture, and construction (50, 49, and 37%, respectively), followed by transportation and public utilities (29%); lowest were government (8%), manufacturing (6%), service—finance, insurance, and real estate—(6%), and trade—wholesale and retail—(5%). In disabling accidents in the workplace, the parts of the body injured most often were the trunk, fingers, and legs, followed by arms, head, and eyes. Today diseases of the lungs are responsible for the greatest proportion of occupational diseases.

Automobile safety: hot issues

Motor vehicle accidents today are the leading cause of accidental death. In the U.S. they kill about 45,000 each year and disable another 1.6 million. They leave more people paraplegics and quadriplegics than do all other causes combined. Traffic accidents cost the U.S. alone an estimated $40 billion a year in lost wages, medical bills, and property damage.

Safety experts agree that the traffic death toll could be cut sharply if drivers and passengers would wear their safety belts. They estimate conservatively that properly worn belts could prevent half of all traffic deaths. Unfortunately, currently only about one-fourth of the adult population in America wear safety belts.

New Mexico Gov. Garrey Carruthers (left) helps change a speed limit sign on U.S. Interstate 25 near Santa Fe after a bill raising the limit on rural highways became law in the spring of 1987.

This low use rate has sparked a heated debate over ways of reducing the highway carnage. Some safety advocates want front-seat air bags that cushion drivers and passengers in a crash installed in all cars. Others contend the three-point harnesses already in autos are the best protection and that passengers should be required *by law* to wear them. In 1984 the U.S. Department of Transportation ruled that all cars sold in the U.S. after Sept. 1, 1989, must be equipped with "passive" protection: air bags that inflate on impact or belts that automatically wrap themselves around occupants. This requirement will be dropped if states covering two-thirds of the population pass belt-use laws by April 1989.

Most industrial countries, Eastern and Western, have chosen the belt-law approach. The U.K., West Germany, Sweden, Poland, and the Soviet Union all have belt-use laws. In the U.S., though, the first mandatory belt-use law was not passed until 1984, when New York State declared that beginning in January 1985 all front-seat passengers had to wear belts. Since then 26 states and the District of Columbia have passed mandatory-use laws. (All states now require children three years old and younger to ride in child restraints.) In addition, some 18 school districts now require lap belts in school buses; pressure is mounting to make this measure more widespread.

While use laws in many countries have resulted in high rates of safety-belt use and sharp drops in traffic deaths (Sweden and the U.K. report use rates exceeding 90%), results in the United States have not been so impressive. Cities such as Dallas and Houston, Texas, report use rates as high as 71%, but only about 20–25% of all drivers buckle up in Chicago, New York City, and Atlanta, Ga. Use rates are even lower for young males driving at night—the very group most likely to be involved in traffic accidents. Proponents of air bags say these figures prove that belt laws are not effective enough. Those who favor the belt laws say stricter enforcement is needed. For now, the belt law versus air bag debate will continue.

Another issue in highway safety is the speed limit. In 1974, in the midst of an energy crisis, Pres. Richard Nixon signed legislation requiring all states to lower their highway speed limits to 55 mph (88.6 km/h) or they would lose federal highway funds. Although the lower speed limit was intended to save gasoline, it had an interesting side effect: the fatality rate on the nation's highways dropped. In subsequent years, as oil became at least temporarily abundant, politicians felt pressure to raise the limit. Safety advocates, meanwhile, insisted that the 55-mph limit should stay in place to keep the number of highway deaths down.

Early in 1987 both houses in the U.S. Congress passed a public-works highway bill that included a provision allowing states to raise the speed limit on rural highways to 65 mph (104.7 km/h). Although Pres. Ronald Reagan vetoed the bill for budgetary reasons, Congress overrode the veto. Within weeks, states began raising the speed limit on rural highways.

Alcohol accidents: the "uncounted" toll

The role that alcohol plays in traffic deaths has been well publicized, as have the efforts to fight drunken driving. Alcohol is involved in about half of all fatal traffic accidents that occur yearly. Drunk drivers are 25 times more likely than sober drivers to be in an accident.

Alcohol is also involved in nontraffic accidents. However, it is difficult to determine exactly to what extent. Unlike traffic accidents, home accidents are not usually investigated for evidence of drinking. Still, a few studies have been conducted to estimate the likely role of alcohol in specific types of accidents. Some researchers estimate that alcohol contributes to 8,000

deaths and 3.2 million injuries in homes alone—and another 7,400 deaths and 2.8 million injuries in other nontraffic settings.

Falls are the leading cause of accidental death at home, killing 6,000 Americans each year. One study of 108 accidental deaths that occurred in Sacramento, Calif., showed that of 10 people killed in falls, 7 had blood-alcohol concentrations (BACs) of 0.10% or higher—meaning they were legally drunk. In France, where alcoholism is a major problem, deaths from falls in 1984 totaled over 13,600—more than from road accidents. Although a connection was not made to alcohol use, it seems likely that a significant proportion *were* alcohol-related.

Fires account for about 4,000 accidental deaths at home each year. One study of fire deaths in Maryland showed that 35% of those killed had BACs of at least 0.10%. Another study of 155 people admitted to hospitals for fire-related injuries showed that 61% had been drinking. Still another study showed that 64% of those killed by fire were legally drunk.

Drowning is the leading cause of recreational death in the U.S.; it accounts for about 6,000 killed each year. An Australian study of drowning victims showed that 35% were legally drunk, and 75% of those who drowned after falling from a wharf or boat had BACs of at least 0.15%, which means they were very drunk. According to the U.S. Centers for Disease Control (CDC) in Atlanta, Ga., as many as 69% of all drowning victims may have been drinking.

Nine out of ten people who die in boating accidents drown. The U.S. National Transportation Safety Board estimates that 38% of all fatal boating accidents involve people who are legally drunk. However, a person can drink enough to be mentally and physically impaired without being "legally" drunk. The CDC and the U.S. National Council on Alcoholism have suggested that perhaps 70% of all fatal boating accidents involve people who were drinking.

Further studies of nonpassengers killed by cars

Flying is by far a safer mode of travel than driving. With increasing numbers of commercial flights each year, however, experts are now warning of an erosion of safety. A major cause of alarm is the sharp increase in the number of near collisions in the air.

Danger in the skies

number of U.S. commercial flights per year (in millions)

flights

near collisions

number of near collisions

1982 1983 1984 1985 1986

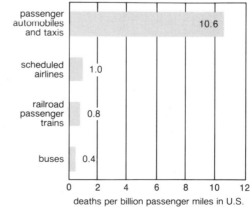

Modes of travel—how safe?

passenger automobiles and taxis	10.6
scheduled airlines	1.0
railroad passenger trains	0.8
buses	0.4

0   2   4   6   8   10   12
deaths per billion passenger miles in U.S.

(Left) Source: Federal Aviation Administration; (right) adapted from an illustration by John Pack and Marcia Scott, *Science 85*, October 1985

suggest that 30% of all bicyclists and 58% of all adult pedestrians killed by motor vehicles had been drinking.

Drinking probably also contributes to hunting, workshop, sports, and other injuries. Careful study of the effects of alcohol on human performance has clearly demonstrated that drinking reduces a person's physical coordination, balance, alertness, visual sensitivity, and ability to perform two tasks at once. Alcohol also reduces judgment and increases the willingness to take risks. Therefore, a drunk person is more likely to attempt a difficult task—at exactly the time he or she is least able to perform it.

A study reported in July 1987 of deaths in young U.S. veterans found that almost one-third had been alcohol-related—six times as many as had been so indicated on death certificates. Their duties had ranged from combat to office work.

Accident victim care

Those who are injured today often receive quicker, better treatment than they would have a few years ago, thanks mostly to recently organized trauma systems. Many countries have established trauma centers or emergency rooms that maintain a staff of injury specialists around the clock. A typical trauma center staff would include a neurosurgeon to treat head wounds, as well as a surgeon who is experienced in treating open-chest wounds.

In the United States, which has pioneered such accident care, a trauma system works basically as follows: When a person suffers a traumatic injury, those on the scene can usually telephone for help by dialing 911. Paramedics who arrive on the scene put the victim in an emergency vehicle—a so-called mobile intensive care unit, a specially equipped contemporary ambulance—and call a hospital-based trauma center. As they transport the patient to the trauma center, the paramedics assess the injuries and utilize the appropriate medical equipment to monitor the patient's vital signs. An emergency-medicine physician at the responding trauma center receives the vital signs via radio waves (telemetry) and prepares for the incoming patient's treatment.

By telemetry monitoring, the doctor can predetermine the patient's condition: Is he or she in severe shock? Has the heartbeat become irregular? Is there brain damage? The doctor can then give the paramedics instructions until they arrive at the trauma center; e.g., to begin a heart massage or other lifesaving procedures or to administer certain drugs en route. In the meantime, the doctor will know which emergency procedures will be necessary at the trauma center and can have the appropriate staff ready and waiting.

When traumatic injuries occur, every second counts. On the average, an efficient system is set up so that an injury victim will be transported to a trauma center within six minutes. Emergency personnel report that these systems have greatly improved the chances of surviving a serious accident.

Safety in the air

Because they are so often disastrous, airline crashes receive a great deal of media attention; this publicity may contribute to fear of flying. In fact, riding on an airliner is one of the safest ways to travel. An airline passenger's chances of dying on any single flight are less than one in 230,000; in terms of deaths per billion miles of travel, automobile passengers are 42 times more likely to be killed in a crash than airline passengers.

Nonetheless, critics are today contending that since the airlines were deregulated in 1978, more flights and more crowded skies have reduced the margin of safety in the air. Further, because President Reagan fired striking air traffic controllers in 1981, there are fewer experienced controllers directing air traffic today than in 1980.

Critics are also charging that people die unnecessarily even in low-impact noncatastrophic airplane crashes and that substandard spare parts mean that aircraft maintenance is seriously deficient. There is mounting evidence, for example, that better, sturdier seats would prevent deaths; according to National Transportation Safety Board statistics, 47% of all airline passenger injuries that occurred from 1976 through 1979 were caused by seat failure. Fire-resistant upholstery could prevent passengers from succumbing to smoke inhalation. In the worst airline disaster ever, two 747s crashed on the ground in 1977 in the Canary Islands; most of the 583 people who died were killed by smoke or fire.

One of the measures being proposed and researched is the creation of safer fuel tanks—having auxiliary fuselage tanks rather than wing tanks, to reduce likelihood of rupture. Another measure is providing "smoke hoods" that would have their own air supply, which would enable passengers in a burning or smoke-filled plane to exit aircraft without succumbing to deadly fumes. Several European carriers are currently pursuing the development of such hoods.

Safety groups are now addressing the matter of air safety more seriously than before and in the U.S. are pressuring the Federal Aviation Administration to adopt tougher aircraft "crashworthiness" requirements. If new safety measures were given priority treatment, the relatively impressive safety record of airline travel probably could be improved. Meanwhile, to improve chances of air travel survival, experts recommend that passengers (1) listen to flight attendants' briefings, read safety cards carefully, and read notices regarding the closest exit doors (a National Transportation Safety Board study found in one 747 evacuation that 55% of the passengers who failed to read cards were injured, whereas only 16% of those who did read them sustained injuries); (2) wear nonsynthetic (*e.g.,* wool or cotton) or nonflammable clothing and low heels aboard planes; (3) in winter, wear coats during takeoff and landing; (4) wear seat belts tight over hips, not the abdomen; and (5) if there is a fire, stay as close to the floor and breathe as little as possible.

—*Tom D. Naughton*

Adolescent Health

"Adolescence is often characterized as a negative period in life. This characterization may be because adolescents appear to place too little value on their safety and well-being and on occasion to deliberately participate in health-compromising activities. An opposing view of adolescence is that it is a period of optimal wellness and physical health." With these words Charles Irwin, a California adolescent medicine specialist, introduced a series of articles—a symposium—published in the November 1986 *Journal of Adolescent Health Care,* noting at once the best and worst health features of the second decade of life. It is precisely because adolescents generally enjoy good health that many of the events and instances for which they require medical care seem so unnecessary and avoidable: teen pregnancy, sexually transmitted disease, substance abuse, and violence (homicide and suicide). In the U.S. the rate at which adolescents visit physicians is only 165 per 100,000 of the population (compared with 281 per 100,000 visits by members of other age groups). When adolescents are hospitalized, the leading diagnoses are pregnancy and trauma or poisoning.

Physical growth and sexual maturity are the most striking changes that take place during adolescence; nearly 25% of final adult height is reached during pubertal growth, and full sexual maturity is attained by a mean age of 15–16 years. Simultaneously with the physical changes, adolescents are experiencing a new self-awareness, developing the ability for abstract thinking and a longing to achieve the autonomy that comes with adulthood. While the adolescent is in the process of changing from a dependent child to an independent, self-reliant adult, his or her peers rival parents as the most important people in their lives; however, because the adolescent is usually still financially dependent on parents (and in many instances, parents are legally responsible for teenage offspring), parent-adolescent conflict in some degree is not uncommon. Like the children they used to be, adolescents test the limits of authority, and the lessons and skills learned in childhood are brought into play, but the stakes become higher.

The major illnesses of adolescence often have their antecedents in the preadolescent period. For this reason, and because of the rapid physical development

of the adolescent, most physicians believe it to be important that the youngster have a continuous, consistent source of health care—preferably other than the local hospital emergency room. The adolescent's physician, whether a pediatrician, a family physician, or an internist, should also be his or her advocate, always assuring the patient of confidentiality; and, commensurate with the maturity of the adolescent, the physician should obtain the teenager's informed consent for any necessary diagnostic and treatment procedures. These are the major goals of those who specialize in adolescent medicine.

Rebelliousness in teen patients

Although adolescents encounter many medical problems as a consequence of their behavior, they may also have chronic illnesses, and these require continuity of medical care. The adolescents' newly acquired ability to deal with hypothetical premises, however, may make them tend to question authority, resent a diagnosis that makes them "different," and resist dependence on medicines or medical procedures. Adolescence may therefore be a particularly difficult period for an individual with a chronic illness, such as asthma, diabetes, epilepsy, chronic kidney disease, and the like. Although there are gender differences in the ways boys and girls handle this situation, there is a general conflict between cooperating with necessary treatment on the one hand and "taking over" as the master of one's fate, making one's own decisions, and telling authority figures to "butt out" on the other. Not surprisingly, teenagers are often medically noncompliant—they do not follow the physician's directions faithfully. When the directions involve taking medications that prevent asthma attacks or convulsions, the result of noncompliance can be serious. Optimal management of chronic disease in adolescents should thus include consideration of the youngster's developmental needs and special emphasis on supporting self-esteem. As soon as possible, the young person should be given responsibility for his or her own treatment.

For example, successful therapy for the youth with diabetes mellitus includes insulin administration, a special diet, a daily exercise regimen, and some sort of education and counseling. Of these, perhaps the most important are emotional support and the education that fosters the other skills. In the past the newly diagnosed young diabetic was almost invariably hospitalized. Now, however, there is increasing interest in programs of total outpatient care for diabetic teenagers. This care helps the teens become knowledgeable about their disease and acquire expertise in the self-administration of insulin and in the ability to monitor glucose levels in blood and urine. The time spent on such education in the initial days after diabetes has been diagnosed is likely to pay off in the form of increased compliance and long-range health, both physical and mental. It is also likely to help adolescent patients "accept" their conditions and not feel compromised, "different," or limited.

Are teens saying no to drugs?

Alcohol continues to be the substance most abused by teenagers; indeed, many authorities in the field argue that any use of alcohol by members of this age group is abuse. Alcohol is a contributing factor in 42% of the fatal motor-vehicle accidents that occur in the U.S. among 16–24-year-olds and is probably implicated in other forms of violence and criminal behavior. Data on the prevalence of alcohol consumption by high-school seniors, although varying by geographical location, indicate that one in 16 drinks alcoholic beverages daily, and 41% drink heavily (*i.e.,* five or more drinks on a single occasion). Cigarette smoking and alcohol ingestion are predictors of subsequent abuse of "street" drugs, such as marijuana, crack (a highly addictive form of cocaine), and others.

Current public education programs, such as the highly publicized "Just Say No" campaign—sponsored by Nancy Reagan, wife of U.S. Pres. Ronald Reagan—attempt to promote self-esteem and teach resistance to peer pressure. Just how successful such campaigns will be remains to be seen. Any future decrease in substance abuse will probably depend, in part, on a decrease in the availability of illegal drugs. In the case of alcohol abuse, the future of teenage drinking will also depend, at least in part, on a change in adult ambivalence toward drinking. The same may be said for other drugs. Addiction to tobacco should not be omitted from this consideration. It is estimated that 60% of smokers are addicted before the age of 15 and 90% before the age of 20.

Adolescent alcohol abuse is not a problem limited to the U.S., which ranks 18th among nations in alcohol consumption. Indeed, the "epidemic" is an international one. Moreover, European, Latin-American, Middle Eastern, and Asian nations are now reporting increased availability of and problems with illicit drugs as smugglers move their operations to these countries. The serious implications of this virtually worldwide problem—alcohol and substance abuse among teenagers—relate to the characteristics of the drugs themselves; some are intrinsically organotoxic (*e.g.,* toxic to the heart, as cocaine is), and some quickly produce addiction and physiological dependence. As for the use of psychotropic drugs by adolescents, to the extent that they alter perception of reality, they interfere with normal psychosocial development at a particularly vulnerable time. Therefore, whereas casual use of any substance does not in and of itself lead to abuse, high-risk adolescents—such as those doing poorly in school and those who have low self-esteem or who are from alcoholic or unstable families—may pass quickly from experimentation to addiction.

All adolescents should be assessed for risk of tobacco, alcohol, and drug abuse as part of their regular health care. The role of the physician is to provide anticipatory guidance or, if a problem already exists, to identify it and make provision for treatment. Some parents want to know if their teenage children are abusing drugs and even demand that the physician test for substance abuse; others deny that there is a problem, even in the face of good evidence. Because the support of the family will have strong bearing on the outcome of treatment, it is important that parents, siblings, and significant others become involved in the treatment of substance abuse to the extent possible. In the case of alienated adolescents or those with low self-esteem or nonsupportive families, enlisting this support may be difficult. Moreover, drugs such as cocaine are powerfully addicting; thus, by definition, the drug taker is highly motivated to continue the habit and resists all attempts at interference.

Doug Menuez—Picture Group

The issue of sex education in the schools, always a subject of controversy, has assumed even more significance with the advent of the AIDS epidemic. On one side are those parents, teachers, and administrators who feel sex education should include explicit information about birth control and "safe sex" practices. At the other end of the spectrum are those who feel that the subject has no place in the public school curriculum, that to teach about sex is to condone and even to encourage it.

Sexual activity in the teen years

Approximately 19% of U.S. teenagers are sexually active by the age of 15, 31% by the age of 16, and 44% by the age of 17, according to recent surveys. These rates are comparable to those in Western Europe (except for Sweden, where onset of sexual intercourse is earlier), yet the U.S. has a higher teenage pregnancy rate and a higher teen birthrate. Two-thirds of all sexually active teens in the U.S. do not routinely use contraceptives and, furthermore, do not understand the facts about the relative effectiveness of different methods of birth control. A variety of reasons are given by teenage girls for not using contraceptives, ranging from belief that they will not get pregnant to moral convictions against birth control. A 1986 Louis Harris poll showed that, when teens do use birth control, a majority of girls favor oral contraceptives over other methods, while a majority of boys choose condoms.

The consequences of unprotected intercourse include pregnancy, often unwanted, and exposure to sexually transmitted diseases (STDs). Of the 10 million U.S. girls between the ages of 15 and 19, each year 1.1 million become pregnant, and of these pregnancies 39% are terminated by abortion. Teenage mothers and their infants are likely to be at high risk for medical complications but, beyond that, teen parents are poorly equipped psychologically, educationally, and economically for child rearing. The slogan "children having children" eloquently expresses the double jeopardy. Studies suggest that young maternal age has an adverse effect on infant cognitive development, for example. These problems call for programs targeted at the teenage patient population, providing extensive support, education, and counseling; another vital necessity is continuity of obstetric care initiated early in the course of the pregnancy.

The implications of high rates of STDs among teenagers are also serious. In the U.S. alone, for example, the annual incidence of pelvic inflammatory disease in adolescents is estimated at 250,000 cases, 15% of which result in permanent infertility. Some STDs may be transmitted to the fetus, and if, as feared, the AIDS (acquired immune deficiency syndrome) virus spreads more widely in the general population, there will be more teenage girls infected with the virus giving birth to more AIDS babies.

Most physicians feel that periodic health checkups for adolescents should include a history of sexual activity and appropriate counseling about the risks of unprotected sex. It should be noted, however, that there is a sizable segment of the population that would prefer that sex education be carried out exclusively in the home and that there be no discussion of contraceptive use either in the school or in the physician's office or clinic. Many of these people believe that teaching about birth control condones or appears to encourage teen sexual activity, rather than promoting celibacy until adulthood. On the other side of the argument are those who say that teenagers will be sexually active, educated or not. The conflict between these two points of view has recently become manifest in the context of nationwide AIDS prevention efforts and the public endorsement by U.S. Surgeon General C. Everett Koop of sex education in the schoolroom.

Nor is the problem confined to the U.S.; the French government in 1987 also began encouraging that country's high schools to educate students on how to avoid exposure to AIDS. The available data on teenagers' ignorance of contraception and on increasing teen pregnancy rates would seem to indicate that home sex education has not been overwhelmingly successful.

The U.S. has the highest rates of teen pregnancy and teens giving birth of any country in the Western industrialized world. Two-thirds of the nation's sexually active teenagers do not regularly use any form of birth control.

(Left) Source: R. W. Blum and M. D. Resnick, "Sexual Decision-Making," *Pediatric Annals*, vol. 11, no. 10 (October 1982); (right) © Children's Defense Fund, reprinted with permission

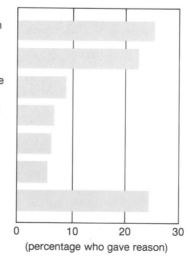

Reasons given by teenage girls for most recent nonuse of contraception (337 girls, aged 15–19)

wrong time of month to conceive

intercourse unanticipated

too young to become pregnant

contraception wrong or dangerous

infrequency of intercourse

contraceptive information lacking

miscellaneous

0   10   20   30

(percentage who gave reason)

Will your child learn to multiply before she learns to subtract?

The Children's Defense Fund.

Sports, drugs, and fitness

Adolescence, possibly the most physically active time of life, is also a time in which there is a high rate of participation in organized sports. In the U.S. alone, more than 7 million boys and girls are involved in high school sports, and at least 20 million youngsters between the ages of 8 and 16 are involved in nonschool, community-sponsored athletic programs. The health effects of exercise are undeniably positive. However, some contact sports (*e.g.,* football) are unavoidably hazardous, and at least one, boxing, has as its object the injury of the opponent. In any case, sports are important in the lives of adolescents, and so is winning. It is the desire to win that is presumably the basis for the use of performance-enhancing drugs, which include anabolic steroids and human growth hormone. There is no controversy about whether use of these drugs is medically condoned; it is not, because of their serious side effects and the unfair competitive advantage they sometimes confer. There is controversy, however, over how and when to test for use of these drugs. Like "street" drugs, they can be detected in the urine, but urine testing for any reason provokes many ethical and legal issues.

Another sports-related question of perhaps more long-term importance is that of fitness throughout life. Despite the widespread participation of school-age youngsters in sports, evaluation of the fitness of young people in the U.S. shows that there has been a steady decline. A 1986 study of 19,000 youths aged 6–17 for the President's Council on Physical Fitness and Sports found that teenage girls performed worse than those tested ten years earlier in many fitness tests and that a large percentage of both girls and boys were unable to pass a standard test: running 1.6 km (one mile) in less than ten minutes. It is possible that the emphasis in childhood and adolescence on organized team sports is a poor preparation for a lifestyle that should include some form of regular exercise. In fact, the widely publicized Harvard alumni study by Ralph Paffenbarger and colleagues, published in 1986, indicated that those individuals at greater risk of premature death were former athletes who stopped exercising after college. Perhaps the ultimate goal of athletic education should be the establishment of lifetime habits of exercise for all.

Suicide

Accidents, homicide, and suicide are now the three leading causes of death in U.S. adolescents and together account for 76% of all deaths between the ages of 15 and 24. Suicide is now the third most common cause of death among U.S. adolescents, accounting for 10.7 deaths per 100,000 per year. The suicide rate for males in this age group increased by 50% between 1970 and 1980, compared with a 2% increase for females. In all age groups firearms are used in the ma-

With suicide now the third most common cause of death among U.S. adolescents, programs to help youngsters cope with confusion and depression are springing up in communities all over the country. In Boston the Samariteens' suicide hot line is staffed by student volunteers.

jority of male suicides in the United States. The reason for the lower suicide rates in adolescent females is the method of the suicide attempt; girls tend to use drugs, which are less reliably lethal.

It has been said by some health authorities that this leading cause of death is not likely to be responsive to traditional medical intervention. For one thing, suicide in this age group may not be preceded by long-standing depression. Transient depression, however, is relatively common in adolescents. In one British study, 40 to 50% of 14–15-year-olds reported appreciable misery or depression. When their cases are examined retrospectively, some adolescents who committed suicide are found to have given signals that they were troubled. Irritability, easy anger, school failure, truancy, and drug or alcohol use or isolation, withdrawal, and indications of suicidal thoughts are forms of behavior that should surely provoke parental suspicions.

Clusters of suicide pacts among high school classmates in various cities have recently been reported by the news media, causing criticism that the media reports themselves should be curtailed in case such publicity encourages other youngsters to make similar attempts. On the other hand, some states are contemplating legislation requiring that teachers take instruction in recognizing suicidal symptoms so that youths displaying such symptoms may quickly be referred for counseling or entered into group therapy. These obviously are opposite approaches: the "say as little as possible" approach—even to the point of banning Shakespeare's *Romeo and Juliet* from school reading lists—and the point of view that says, "Let us discuss suicide openly." Neither has been tested for its efficacy. The medical rule of thumb, however, is that every suicide threat or attempt should be taken seriously and thoroughly evaluated, and treatment should be provided for the youngster in question.

—*Jean D. Lockhart, M.D.*

Fitness at Zero G

by Ralph Pelligra, M.D.

It is common in aerospace research to confine normal, healthy adults to complete bed rest in order to study the effects of weightlessness on the human body. The results of this forced inactivity, or so-called hypodynamic state, are remarkable. Within as little as 72 hours, multiple systems in the body begin to show evidence of change and deterioration. There are immediate fluid shifts within the body that lead to hormonal changes and dehydration; the heart and blood vessels begin to lose their tone and strength; and soon calcium begins to leach out of the bones. The volunteer subjects often complain of headache, backache, constipation, boredom, lethargy, and occasionally disorientation. Clearly, forced inactivity is a detrimental and unnatural condition for the healthy, uninjured body.

But what of the corollary condition, exaggerated activity? Does it necessarily follow that if forced inactivity is bad for the human body, then increased activity, or exercise, will be of benefit to it? Here again the evidence is quite clear. More than 20 years of research have proved that vigorous activity can favorably affect a person's heart, circulation, lungs, body weight, muscle tone, bowel habits, blood pressure, blood sugar, blood fats, stamina, efficiency, and general sense of well being; it can even increase longevity.

It would seem that the high degree of physical conditioning that is such a terrestrial asset would also be of benefit to the space voyager. But here the matter is not so clear. In 1973 during the fourth Skylab mission, it was observed that the scientist pilot and the mission pilot had a lower tolerance than their less physically fit commander to an inflight test that provokes fainting by applying negative pressure to the lower body (LBNP). This led to the suspicion that perhaps aerobic fitness and endurance training might cause orthostatic intolerance—*i.e.*, lowered tolerance to fainting—and that perhaps this form of exercise should be avoided by astronauts. In the late 1970s and early 1980s, investigators did begin to accumulate data showing that endurance-trained athletes might have a significantly lower tolerance to simulated spaceflight conditions than their sedentary counterparts.

Man against gravity

An understanding of the association between bed rest, space travel, orthostatic intolerance, and exercise helps explain the intriguing finding that exceptionally fit subjects may be at greater risk of suffering physically during the reentry phase of space travel, when fainting is likely to occur. Such understanding depends largely on looking first at the distant past. It was the evolutionary conquest by humans over the force of gravity that enabled them to stand upright and, in so doing, to achieve preeminence in the animal kingdom, but humans have paid a significant price for that place of distinction. In order to maintain a bipedal position in a gravitational field that attempts to keep their bellies in the mud and their noses pointed earthward, it became necessary for humans to evolve complex structural and physiological systems that are often fragile and subject to malfunction. Many human ailments, including back problems, postural abnormalities, hemorrhoids, varicose veins, certain heart conditions, and life-threatening shock syndromes, are often due to failure of the body's antigravity mechanisms.

Apart from these abnormal or pathological conditions, though, people are seldom aware that they are engaged in a moment-to-moment struggle against this silent and unseen but ever present force of gravity. For example, if one is sitting upright reading this page, blood, under the influence of gravity, is continuously draining from the head and chest down into the lower body and legs. To maintain sufficient blood (and therefore an adequate supply of oxygen) to the brain, one's heart must pump blood upward against the gravitational gradient. The pressure generated each time the heart contracts is the systolic blood pressure. To prevent the pressure in the complex network of arteries and veins in the body from plummeting to near zero every time the heart pump relaxes between beats, a tone, or tension, is maintained in the blood vessels (the diastolic blood pressure) by the action of nerves and hormones. If one stands suddenly—say, to go answer a telephone ringing in the next room—a complex series of events is triggered in response to the increased gravitational stress. Blood pressure increases, pulse rate quickens, and various reflexes come into play that cause blood vessels to constrict or dilate, depending on their location. Thus, these and other complex neuromuscular and neurohormonal mechanisms are busy working full time to prevent the individual from being knocked flat on his or her face by the force of gravity.

Surprising finding

This complex system is not in fact busy working full time; sometimes it "goes on vacation." Therein lies the connection between bed rest and space travel. In bed rest, because the body is in a horizontal rather than vertical position relative to the gravitational vector, the cardiovascular system (the heart, blood vessels, neurohormones, and reflexes) needs to work less hard to provide blood to the brain and vital organs. In space, where everything, including blood, has no weight, the cardiovascular system has an even easier time circulating oxygen and other nutrients to all the tissues of the body. In both bed rest and weightless space, the effects of gravity on the body are reduced sufficiently to allow the complex systems mentioned above to "get lazy," or decondition. Fortunately, the manner and degree to which the antigravity systems deteriorate under both these conditions are similar enough to enable prolonged bed rest to simulate exposure to weightlessness for earthbound aerospace research.

In such studies volunteers remain at total bed rest for two to four weeks or more, eating, bathing, brushing their teeth, and using a bedpan while remaining in the horizontal position 24 hours a day every day throughout the entire study. There is more to it than that, however. The foot of the bed is elevated so that the subject's body is not horizontal but tilted at a −6°, head-down angle. Soviet aerospace investigators first began to use this variation of horizontal bed-rest simulation when they realized that it caused the same sensations of fullness in the head and bloating of the face and neck that is experienced by space travelers on initial entry on orbit. These symptoms are due to the shift, or translocation, of fluids from the lower body to the upper body when the restraining force of gravity is removed (on orbit) or reversed (when the head is placed lower than the feet during bed rest).

It seems a natural enough assumption that if any muscle—whether it is in the heart, the walls of blood vessels, or the biceps—deconditions when it is not used, then the simple solution is to use it; *i.e.*, to exercise. Also, by this logic, it would appear that athletes, whose muscles are in the best possible condition, would be most resistant to the harmful effects of weightlessness and could perform more effectively in this or any natural or unnatural environment.

It is true that the antidote for muscle disuse deconditioning is exercise. Exactly what kind of exercise and how much are not clear, however, and, in fact, there have been some surprising twists. For example, in one study conducted at the National Aeronautics and Space Administration's (NASA's) Ames Research Center, in Mountain View, Calif., it was shown that static (isometric) exercises seemed to prevent aerobic deconditioning in bed-rest subjects better than did dynamic (isotonic) training regimens. This was an unexpected finding.

Isotonic versus isometric exercise

A brief explanation of the meaning of "aerobic conditioning" and the differences between isotonic and isometric exercises will help show why the researchers were surprised at the above results. One measure of a person's level of physical fitness is the efficiency with which the body's energy stores can be converted to mechanical motion, such as work or exercise. Since all sustained muscular work requires oxygen to "burn" energy supplies in the body, the amount of oxygen utilized during a maximal muscular effort is an indirect measure of the body's level of physical fitness. That is, the more oxygen the body is able to consume during a maximal-effort exercise, the better physical condition it is in. This concept is the basis for the "maximum oxygen uptake (VO_2 max) test," which, by measuring

U.S. astronaut Guion S. Bluford exercises on a treadmill during the space shuttle Challenger *mission of early September 1983. A major question that aerospace researchers are investigating is what kinds of exercise should be prescribed for the space voyager who is exposed to prolonged periods of weightlessness. Orbiting Soviet cosmonauts work out on bicycle ergometers and treadmills as part of a regular exercise program. U.S. astronauts have had access to a treadmill, but they have not been assigned any formal in-flight fitness regimen.*

NASA

Adapted from *Life Sciences Accomplishments*, NASA Technical Memorandum 88177 (September 1985)

Body fluid distribution: from Earth to space and back

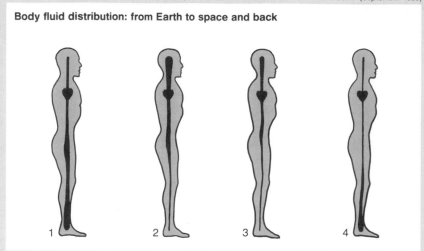

(1) Normal distribution of bodily fluids on Earth; (2) fluid distribution after entry into space: fluids shift headward and central circulatory system becomes engorged, delivering increased blood to head; (3) fluid distribution after the body has adapted to near weightlessness: blood volume is decreased, and there is a slight increase in volume of blood in leg veins; (4) immediate postflight response: decreased blood volume and increased blood vessel capacity in lower body can cause lightheadedness and dizziness as blood is drawn from head to feet.

the actual amount of oxygen consumed during maximal exercise, determines the efficiency with which the body is able to take in oxygen (lung function), deliver oxygen to the muscles (cardiovascular function), and utilize stored energy sources (metabolism). A highly fit individual is able to utilize greater than 50 milliliters of oxygen per kilogram of body weight per minute. A VO_2 max between 40 and 50 ml oxygen/kg/min is average fitness for someone between the ages of 30 and 45, and a VO_2 max below 40 is considered low fitness.

Exercises that are most likely to result in improved physical fitness (aerobic conditioning) are those that not only enlist the maximum number of the body's muscles but require that the muscles do what they do best (*i.e.,* contract). These exercises are described variously as isotonic (*iso,* "same"; *tonic,* "tension"), dynamic, or endurance exercises, and they are usually associated with movements of the body in three-dimensional space; *e.g.,* running, cycling, doing calisthenics, swimming, and playing racquetball or basketball.

By contrast, exercises that involve the application of force without movement are called isometric or static. This form of exercise was very popular in the 1950s and '60s, when it was shown that as little as six seconds of simply tensing muscle groups or applying large static loads to them at 75% of maximum effort could improve muscular strength. This form of exercise was the key ingredient in body-building regimens and was the basis of the Charles Atlas "dynamic tension" method. However, isometric exercise does not increase strength throughout the range of motion of a joint but is restricted to the joint angle at which the stress is being applied. More important, it does not make demands on the pulmonary and cardiovascular systems and can consequently lead to a large, muscular body that is essentially "out of shape."

Not all isotonic exercises result in endurance or aerobic conditioning. Weight lifting and barbell training, for example, strengthen isolated muscle groups by imposing constant loads on contracting muscles, but the demands made upon the heart and lungs are intermittent and too brief to result in an overall aerobic effect. In recent years specially designed weight machines have been developed to increase muscle strength more efficiently. Cams and pulleys permit a varying load and more uniform stress to be imposed on specific muscle groups throughout the range of motion of a joint. However, the relative value of this variable resistance method over constant resistance exercises has not yet been documented.

Investigators exposed seven healthy men (aged 19–22) to three consecutive 14-day periods of total bed rest. The men were randomly assigned to groups in such a way that by the end of the study each had participated in an isotonic exercise group, an isometric exercise group, and a no exercise group. Exercise regimens were performed in the supine position and included either two 30-minute periods daily of intermittent static (isometric) exercise at 21% of maximum leg extension force or two 30-minute periods of dynamic (isotonic) bicycle ergometer exercises daily at 68% of VO_2 max. No prescribed exercise was performed by the control group. Compared with their pre-bed-rest control values, VO_2 max decreased 12.3% in the no exercise group, 9.2% with dynamic exercise, but only 4.8% with static exercise.

Connecting the findings

Whereas it can be said that under usual circumstances dynamic exercises maintain or improve physical fitness (VO_2 max) and static exercises do not, the opposite effects occurred under the experimental conditions described above. The precise reasons for this are not known but may be related to the equally surprising observation mentioned above that endurance-trained athletes seem to have an increased tendency to faint

246

(orthostatic intolerance), as compared with sedentary or nonathletic individuals.

Fainting occurs when there is a failure to supply an adequate amount of oxygenated blood to the brain. A common cause of this condition is the pooling of blood in the lower body when a person is in the vertical position or when a force is applied from head to foot, as occurs during reentry from space. In the athlete the body has been trained to deliver large amounts of blood on demand to the muscular system. This is accomplished by a pliable and flexible network of blood vessels that expands somewhat like a balloon when stimulated by nerve and hormonal signals. During exercise a large portion of the blood volume is circulated to the legs, since they contain the largest muscle mass in the body. However, if this system is activated for some reason when the athlete is not exercising, the large amount of blood shunted to the lower extremities pools in the extremities and is made relatively unavailable to the brain.

Excessive pooling of blood in the lower body, and therefore fainting, is more likely to occur in the body with the most pliable cardiovascular system—such as that of the endurance-trained athlete. The isometric exercises in the above study increased the subjects' resistance to loss of VO_2 max because of two possible factors: a hydrostatic component that is not provided by isotonic exercise, and a reduction in vein pliability (and thus reduction of blood pooling) due to the tension support of the added limb musculature.

Exercise for space travel

Two questions need to be answered. First, is the endurance-trained body, which is normally a functional and aesthetic asset, actually a liability for space travel? Second, which, if any, exercises should be prescribed for the space voyager who will be exposed to prolonged periods of weightlessness?

Undoubtedly, there are some clear benefits for the space traveler who is in good to excellent physical condition as defined by VO_2 max. For example, working in space, especially extravehicular activity in a space suit, imposes a demanding work load on the astronaut. He or she can function much more effectively and for longer periods of time if truly fit. Also, as was mentioned above, good physical fitness is reflected in mental outlook and in the functioning of many diverse bodily systems—including the digestive, immune, and nervous systems.

The accumulated Soviet long-duration spaceflight experience has shown that an intensive inflight exercise program (2–3 hours daily) does indeed help to expedite the astronaut's recovery and adaptation on return to Earth's 1-G environment (1 G is the measurement of standard gravity on Earth). Cosmonauts currently use a bicycle ergometer (stationary bike) and treadmill for aerobic conditioning and wear a "penguin suit" made of elastic material that provides some resistive exercise during normal activities. Although U.S. astronauts are assigned no formal inflight exercise regimen, those traveling on the space shuttle have access to a treadmill for optional, informal use.

In space the one possible disadvantage of being what is usually considered especially fit is the potential hazard associated with crew who suffer orthostatic hypotension (inadequate blood supply to the brain) during reentry. Even in the absence of actual fainting, impaired blood flow to the brain resulting from pooling in the extremities could lead to critically impaired crew performance as they attempt to guide the complex, 90-ton shuttle spacecraft from orbit to a safe landing on Earth. However, this problem can be partially remedied. Thus far in spaceflights, the use of antigravity suits and fluid loading during orbit to expand the circulating blood volume (so that there is more flow to the brain) have greatly helped.

Now it appears that a further solution to the problem may be a special approach to exercise. At least in the experimental setting, dynamic and static exercises affect different components of the deconditioning process that occurs during bed rest or simulated weightlessness. Whereas dynamic exercises tend to maintain cardiovascular conditioning at the possible expense of increased orthostatic intolerance, static exercises seem to protect against the tendency toward orthostatic intolerance while providing no aerobic conditioning benefits. It seems probable, therefore, that a regimen combining both these types of exercises will offer the space voyager the greatest protection against the effects of prolonged exposure to weightlessness.

A relatively new form of exercise called isokinetics controls the rate of muscle shortening. It is sometimes called "accommodating resistance" because a specially designed "dynamometer" responds with the same amount of resistance that is applied to it by the exercising muscle during flexion and extension. This method is becoming widely used in athletic training and by physical therapists for rehabilitation of injured patients' joints because of the low risk of injury. Also, isokinetic dynamometers have important research applications because they provide speed-specific measurements of the absolute strength of a muscle group. However, optimum protocols for such use have not yet been clearly defined.

Continuing research will shed further light on some of the lingering questions about physical fitness in space. For example, is there a genetic tendency toward or predisposition to fainting that is unrelated to a person's level of physical fitness? To what extent do inherent factors related to blood pressure control such as age, gender, height, blood volume, baroreceptor sensitivity, and leg pooling contribute to orthostatic intolerance? Ultimately this research will lead to an effective and practical prescription for exercise in space.

Aging

As the number of world citizens aged 65 years or older increases and this age group constitutes a larger proportion of the population, health care systems are having to gear up to meet their medical and health needs. In addition to changes in health care delivery and financing (*e.g.,* health maintenance organizations and home care programs) and incentives for the training of more physicians with specific expertise in caring for the elderly, there have been advances in the science and art of geriatric health care. As a result, the overall approach to the elderly patient, who often has many health problems, has changed considerably. The treatment of specific diseases has also improved as a result of intense research activity.

Research in aging and geriatrics

Although geriatrics has only recently emerged as a discipline, it has become the focus of a broad spectrum of research topics from basic biologic sciences to clinical medicine. Some of these topics—for example, the effect of nutrients on the longevity of cultured rat cells—seem to bear little relevance to the care of elderly patients, but this basic science must be viewed as being the vanguard of medical scientists' understanding of the physiology and pathophysiology of aging. Other research focuses on specific diseases that are common in the elderly and on the impact of these diseases on older persons.

Geriatric research also includes the study of the delivery of health care to the elderly. Accordingly, a conference of gerontological specialists is likely to include basic scientists (*e.g.,* biologists, biochemists, and physiologists), physicians, nurses, social workers, and sociologists, all working in complementary fields in order to understand the aging process better and improve the care of the elderly. The developments in geriatric care are vast and ever increasing; some of the important basic developments in the approach to the older patient and some recent advances in the treatment of some common illnesses that affect this age group are elaborated upon below.

Differences in medical needs

Although many physiological functions, such as the body's ability to maintain levels of hemoglobin, the oxygen-carrying component of red blood cells, do not change with aging, the function of some organs, such as the kidney and some endocrine glands, declines progressively as people grow older. A classic example is the female menopause, a normal change associated with aging that may have substantial effects on the overall health of the woman. In this instance, ovarian failure and resulting falling hormone levels of estrogen are associated with loss of bone density (osteoporosis) and the progression of atherosclerosis.

Many geriatricians believe that the overall sum of changes associated with aging means older persons have a decreased ability to respond to physiological stress. When faced with the stress of a major illness, surgery, or trauma, some older persons with excellent social function and independence may abruptly develop a number of impairments, such as delirium, incontinence, or the inability to move about unaided.

Contrary to popular belief, older persons are not complainers. In fact, the converse is often true. Although they are afflicted with more disabilities and diseases than younger persons (elderly persons living in the community have, on the average, 3.5 important disabilities per person), older persons complain less frequently. This underreporting of symptoms has been noted in various settings, including hospices, where elderly terminal cancer patients complain less frequently of pain than their younger counterparts. Possible causes include decreased sensitivity to symptoms, a belief that symptoms are to be expected because they are older, or fear that reporting symptoms might lead to detection of serious illnesses or institutionalization.

On the other hand, when older persons report symptoms, these symptoms are more likely to indicate an important underlying disease. Many diseases, however, manifest themselves with different symptoms when they afflict the elderly. For example, relatively common diseases such as hyperthyroidism and heart attack may be manifested with nonspecific symptoms rather than the classic textbook signs and symptoms that physicians are taught to recognize. Accordingly, interpreting symptoms in the elderly requires an astute clinician with a high index of suspicion.

Functional assessment

Geriatricians appraise an individual's overall functional capability rather than focusing on the patient's age or specific medical diagnoses. This innovative approach assesses the older person's ability to maintain social roles and independent living. For those who have complex medical problems, a scale is used to measure their ability to perform basic activities of daily living (ADL), including bathing, dressing, going to the toilet, transferring (*e.g.,* from the bed to a chair), maintaining continence, and feeding themselves without assistance. Persons who have no difficulty completing these tasks are further assessed as to their capability to perform more complex tasks, the instrumental activities of daily living (IADL). These IADL tasks include cooking, cleaning, doing laundry, using the telephone, using public or private transportation, managing money, and taking medicines. Successful completion of these activities requires a satisfactory combination of physical capabilities, social situation, and mental capacity. A person's level of ADL and IADL can usually be assessed readily during an office visit, often with the assistance of a spouse or family member.

Recently the concept of functional assessment has been expanded beyond that which can be accomplished in a routine office visit. Thus, in the U.S. geriatric assessment units have been established countrywide, principally at acute-care hospitals affiliated with medical schools. Most of these units provide both consultant and primary care for the impaired elderly through the use of an interdisciplinary approach, as described below. Almost all provide comprehensive functional assessment, including evaluation of medical, cognitive, and psychosocial health. In addition, education, rehabilitation, and coordination of social services are important goals of these units. As a result, geriatric assessment units are believed to be more effective than routine care, especially in terms of patient and family satisfaction. Furthermore, new treatable problems are often detected in these units, and drug regimens can frequently be simplified or improved. Moreover, at least one study suggests that acute-care hospital days, nursing home days, and costs can all be reduced. To operate effectively, however, these units must be well staffed, and a substantial amount of time must be spent with each patient (an average of 2.7 hours per encounter).

Team approach

A crucial element in the success of functional assessment units, and a cardinal principle in geriatric care, is the use of a team of health care providers with diverse skills and training. No one practitioner, despite extensive training in geriatrics, can be expected to acquire or maintain all the knowledge and skills that are necessary for providing optimal care for the impaired elderly. Instead, a team approach is used; each

member contributes to a discussion that formulates the best plan for care of an individual patient. Although a physician usually heads the interdisciplinary team, this approach works best when each member is respected for his or her skills without professional rivalry. Hospital-centered inpatient teams tend to be large and most commonly include a physician, a nurse, a social worker, a dietitian, physical and occupational therapists, a pharmacist, and a psychologist; there may be an audiologist and a dentist. Teams serving outpatients are usually smaller, most commonly having three members—a physician, a nurse or social worker, and an additional health provider. Nurse practitioners and physicians' assistants are pivotal figures of many teams. In addition, many community and volunteer services (*e.g.,* Meals on Wheels and Homemakers) provide additional services and implement the team's suggestions. This interdisciplinary approach has been applied to a variety of sites and settings, ranging from community health centers to hospice care facilities.

Advances in treating diseases

Considerable recent attention has been directed to the following diseases affecting the elderly:

Dementia and Alzheimer's disease. Dementia is the term used to describe progressive deterioration of intellectual capabilities that begins with memory loss and eventually interferes with occupational or social function. In some patients dementia is the result of medical and psychiatric conditions (*e.g.,* depression, thyroid disease, and drug toxicity). Most older persons with this disorder, however, suffer from Alzheimer's disease or, less commonly, have sustained multiple strokes. Until recently the diagnostic and therapeutic abilities to

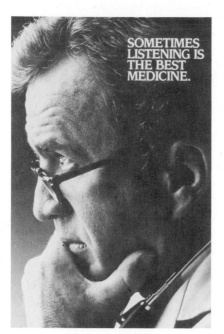

Faculty members in geriatrics for training specialists

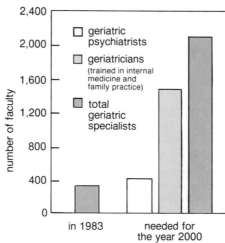

number of faculty

- ☐ geriatric psychiatrists
- ☐ geriatricians (trained in internal medicine and family practice)
- ☐ total geriatric specialists

in 1983   needed for the year 2000

As people age, their abilities decrease and medical and health needs increase. Physicians and other professionals with special training to meet the unique needs of the fast-growing segment of the population aged 65 and older are vital. The graph shows the relative dearth of geriatric specialists in the U.S. in 1983, compared with the number that will be needed by the turn of the century.

(Far left) The Center for Healthy Aging at the St. Joseph Hospital and Health Care Center, Chicago; poster design, Ketchum/Mandabach & Simms Inc., Chicago; (left) adapted from John W. Rowe *et al.,* "Academic Geriatrics for the Year 2000," *The New England Journal of Medicine,* vol. 316, no. 22 (May 28, 1987), pp. 1425–28

manage Alzheimer's disease were extremely limited. Now the origins of this disorder are being discovered. Recent evidence suggests that genetic factors may be important. For example, 10% of the siblings of patients who developed Alzheimer's disease before the age of 70 also developed the disease by age 70; an additional 35% developed symptoms by age 84. One leading theory suggests that substances called neurotransmitters, which allow brain cells to communicate with each other, may be altered. Specifically, an enzyme that manufactures acetylcholine is decreased, and this decrease has been correlated with lower scores on tests of mental capabilities. Accordingly, researchers have begun investigating treatment with drugs that increase the level of acetylcholine. Preliminary results with an oral form, tetrahydroaminoacridine (THA), have been promising, but most researchers consider it only a palliative treatment. New imaging techniques such as magnetic resonance imaging may prove valuable in establishing the diagnosis of Alzheimer's disease and, thus, define patients for whom THA or other drugs would be appropriate.

Urinary incontinence. Up to ten million Americans suffer from involuntary loss of urine, which often leads to serious adverse social and health consequences. This disorder is estimated to affect some 5–20% of elderly persons living in the community and up to 75% of those living in long-term-care facilities such as nursing homes. The cost of evaluation and treatment of these incontinent patients has been estimated at $8 billion each year. Furthermore, incontinent patients are more likely to develop pressure sores and urinary tract infections, which can be quite serious.

To begin addressing this problem, researchers have established a classification system for urinary incontinence based on the underlying causes of the disorder. First, reversible causes of incontinence, usually acute illness or the taking of certain medications, must be excluded. These "transient" causes may account for as much as 75% of incontinence in hospitalized patients. Outpatients generally suffer from chronic forms of incontinence that may stem from disorders of the nervous system, such as stroke and Parkinson's disease; anatomical abnormalities, such as an enlarged prostate gland in men or a prolapsed uterus in women; and pathophysiological changes associated with aging, such as the loss of estrogen in postmenopausal women. Some patients have "functional" incontinence in that they are limited in their ability to get to the toilet rather than their ability to control their urine. The pattern of incontinence and the amounts of urine lost and remaining in the bladder after a patient urinates voluntarily help further classify the type of incontinence and identify the probable cause.

The clinician can then direct appropriate therapy, which ranges from a urinal or bedpan near the bedside to surgical implants. Biofeedback, special exercises, and several medications have been effective in some cases. Surgical procedures are most likely to benefit patients with anatomical abnormalities. Unfortunately, some patients fail to respond to these measures and are treated with diapers and catheterization. The latter measures are probably overutilized by nursing home staff and family for their own convenience. Indwelling catheters are placed in an estimated 10–30% of incontinent patients in long-term-care facilities. Although catheters are effective for keeping patients dry, they can also predispose the patient to potentially life-threatening urinary tract infections.

Depression. At any given time, an estimated 10% of older persons are clinically depressed. This high prevalence is the result of several factors that are particularly important in the elderly. Losses, including the death of a spouse, and limitation of functional capacity may precipitate a depressive episode. Illnesses that commonly affect the elderly, including endocrine disorders, neurological diseases, and tumors, frequently have depression as a manifestation of the disease. Also common are depressions related to medications that are prescribed for other conditions, such as high blood pressure.

The diagnosis of depression is particularly important because good treatment is available and because there are serious possible sequelae, including intellectual impairment (termed "pseudodementia") and suicide. Although the diagnosis of depression is confirmed by a clinical evaluation, some researchers are investigating the use of a simple blood test of adrenal gland function (dexamethasone suppression test) to help guide therapy. Two methods of treatment are commonly employed, psychotherapy and medications. For elderly patients with prominent symptoms of depression (*e.g.,* frequent crying spells, weight loss, and disturbance of sleep patterns), many physicians favor treatment with medications; dosages must be scaled down appropriately because of changes associated with aging that affect absorption and elimination of these medicines. Side effects are of particular concern because they may aggravate other medical problems that are common in the elderly, including visual impairment, constipation, and urinating difficulties. In spite of these potential adverse effects, most patients respond, sometimes dramatically, to one of the antidepressants that are currently available. For patients with refractory or severe symptoms, electroconvulsive therapy (ECT) can be a safe and effective treatment.

Other conditions. There are numerous other age-dependent diseases and health concerns that are emerging as important and that require the special attention of geriatric specialists. As research continues, medicine is likely to be more and more able to meet the very special needs of the world's substantial and growing population of older people.

—*David B. Reuben, M.D.*

Fatal Insomnia: A Medical Mystery

by Elio Lugaresi, M.D., Pasquale Montagna, M.D., and Pierluigi Gambetti, M.D.

When, in May 1984, a doctor and his wife asked physicians who specialized in sleep disorders at the Neurological Hospital of the University of Bologna (Italy) Medical School for help for one of their relatives, the doctors who took on the patient did not know that the case—the first of an undescribed disease—would gain worldwide attention. The history that the concerned relatives related was indeed baffling. On the wife's side of the family, many members had died of a mysterious disease that started with the inability to fall asleep and, following a relentless course, ended with coma and death. Now the uncle of the wife was ill. He knew his fate. It was the patient's desire that "science" study him.

Perplexing case history

The patient, an engineer leading an active personal and working life, had always been well except for slightly high blood pressure. He used to sleep regularly for five to seven hours each night and napped habitually for a half hour in the afternoon. These hours of sleep were enough for him, and he felt refreshed, in particular, after the short afternoon nap. He reported that his first problems had begun about seven months earlier. His night sleep was not as good as before; he had difficulty in falling asleep, woke up several times, and slept for only two to three hours per night. At first, napping in the afternoon was still satisfying, but the afternoon nap also worsened and, after about three months, he was unable to sleep altogether.

From the beginning, he reported to the doctors, he also experienced sexual impotence and, later, constipation and urinary incontinence. Moreover, he was troubled by a slight and irregular unexplained fever and continuous perspiration. Sporadically and suddenly he would have increased salivation, stiffness, nasal discharge, and tears. These "vegetative storms," as the doctors called them, slowly worsened with time. When insomnia had become complete, new symptoms slowly developed; though unable to sleep normally, he would suddenly lose contact and lapse into vivid dreams that lasted minutes and that he could clearly remember when he "woke up." During these "dream attacks" he could "act"; i.e., move, gesticulate, walk, and stand according to the dream content, mimicking the complex and purposeful activities of wakefulness. For instance (at the time of the wedding of Charles and Diana, prince and princess of Wales), he had been seen by relatives to rise up from his bed with closed eyes, stand up, and give a military salute; after waking, he reported that he had dreamed of attending a coronation as one of the guard officers. Another time, he had been awakened while making gestures of scolding a secretary. These "enacted dreams" became more and more frequent, invading the patient's periods of wakefulness to a point that—as he put it—he was no longer able to distinguish between reality and dreams. By this time he had already recognized in himself the symptoms that had led to the death of two of his four sisters and his father; at that stage of his illness, he was so worried and fatigued that he decided to resign from his job.

When the sleep specialists first saw him, he was without any signs of mental impairment, but when he was left to himself, he would lose contact with the environment, shut his eyes, and gesticulate during his dreams. He underwent electroencephalograms (EEGs) to monitor the brain's electrical activity and 24-hour polysomnographic recordings that followed the activity of muscles, the heart, breathing, body temperature, and blood pressure throughout the day and night. These studies showed that the episodes of loss of contact and dreaming were associated with some changes of brain and muscle activity typically observed during rapid eye movement (REM) sleep—the sleep stage in which internal activation of the brain and dreaming occur—as opposed to the so-called slow-wave sleep, characterized by slowing and depression of brain activity. Slow-wave sleep instead was absent in the patient and could not be induced by administration of barbiturate drugs or benzodiazepines (a class of tranquilizers and hypnotics). This total lack of slow-wave sleep was associated with exaggerated levels of breathing, heart rate, and body temperature, which were persistent and did not display the fluctuation normally observed during the day and night.

This led to the investigation as well of the hormonal system, because many hormones in humans, such as the growth hormone, cortisol, prolactin, and follicle-stimulating hormone (a gonadal-stimulating hormone), are secreted in a rhythmic fashion, with peaks and dips at certain hours of the day or night (the so-called circadian rhythms). Hormonal gland function was basically normal, but normal fluctuations of the hormones during the 24-hour cycle were strikingly absent. This was true also for hormones whose secretion is not linked to sleep, so mere lack of slow-wave sleep could not explain the findings. Moreover, cortisol, a hormonal product of the adrenal glands, was constantly high, a finding typical of chronically stressful situations.

The patient was followed for two months—until his death. He became progressively less arousable; his speech became slurred; his motions coarse, uncoordinated, and tremulous; his gait unsteady; his breathing frequent and noisy, with apneas (transitory cessations of breathing); and his heart quicker. He could still be aroused for a while with strong stimulation, but by the end of his eighth month of illness, he had become comatose and shaken by continuous jerky tremors. Blood pressure, heart, and breathing rates increased progressively.

Attempts to treat him with drugs, in particular with those known to interfere with brain transmitters implicated in wake-sleep regulation (acetylcholine, dopamine, norepinephrine, and serotonin), were unsuccessful. However, the patient was aroused from his coma with a recently developed drug that antagonizes the effects of benzodiazepines, but the effect lasted only a few minutes. Then bronchopneumonia in both lungs developed and, despite intensive treatment, he died nine months after the onset of symptoms.

The family history

The family history could be reconstructed through a search of the clinical notes and the town and parish archives as far back as 1822. At least 13 family members over three generations had died from the disease, which appeared to be transmitted from parent to child in an autosomal dominant fashion (each child of either sex had a 50% probability of inheriting the disease). They had been variously diagnosed as having viral encephalitis, familial dementia, or even schizophrenia (probably because of the "hallucinations" and incongruous behavior during the "dream attacks"). All had died after a course of 7 to 12 months.

Postmortem examinations of the brains had been carried out on two sisters of the patient, but the physicians were able to retrieve only a few histological preparations from the brain of one. These and the patient's brain were studied by one of the authors at Case Western Reserve University, Cleveland, Ohio.

Unexpected findings

On the basis of the clinical signs, the investigators had anticipated some degenerative process of the hypothalamus, a region at the base of the brain in the brain stem—the brain structure that connects the cerebral hemispheres to the spinal cord. The hypothalamus intervenes in the organization of the sleep-wake cycle and, through the pituitary gland, in hormonal regulation and circadian rhythms. Certain brain stem structures,

especially the locus ceruleus and reticular substance, control wakefulness and sleep. Brain stem lesions may induce narcolepsy, a disease in which awake patients suddenly fall into a dream state similar to the "dream attacks" of the patient under investigation in Bologna.

It was therefore surprising to discover that all of these structures were microscopically normal in both the patient under investigation and the sister whose tissues were studied and that changes could be found only in the dorsomedial and anterior nuclei of the thalamus. There more than 95% of the nerve cells had died, and there were an increased number of astrocytes, nonnerve cells that proliferate after neuronal destruction.

A strange and rare disease

The thalami are the largest formations of gray substance below the cerebral cortex and have the shape and size of a small egg. They are located at the center of the brain and are separated by the ventricles (the internal brain cavities filled with liquid). Each thalamus can be subdivided into several nuclei, but the classification and function of these nuclei are still controversial. The thalami can be affected by a variety of disorders, especially tumoral, vascular, or degenerative, and the clinical pictures vary considerably depending on the nuclei involved. Two large nuclei, known as anterior and dorsomedial, which are particularly developed in humans, have intricate connections with definite regions of the cerebral cortex (the rhinencephalon, gyrus cinguli, and mammillary body of the orbital cortex). The precise functions of all these structures are still unknown, but they seem to be implicated in the function of memory and especially in the regulation of instinctive life, emotions, and vegetative responses. Isolated degeneration of only two thalamic nuclei, however, had previously never been reported.

The clinical features in this case were also peculiar. The disease started with a progressive loss of sleep and hyperactivity of the vegetative system, was later complicated by dreamlike stupor and motor abnormalities, and ended with the patient in a severely exhausted, debilitated state that was followed by coma and death. These symptoms did not correspond to any known disease, which explains why a correct diagnosis had been difficult to reach. A thorough search of the medical literature and presentation of the case worldwide confirmed that the observation represents the first instance of a disease in which the degeneration was limited to two thalamic nuclei and was genetically transmitted.

Pathological findings similar to these have recently been reported in a Vermont family in which illness had previously been wrongly classified as Creutzfeldt-Jakob disease, an encephalitis due to a transmissible "slow" virus. It is possible that still more families will be recognized as affected by the disease when appropriate investigations show that their illnesses are not true cases of dementia, sleeplessness, or mental illness.

New perspectives on sleep

The observation is of interest not only because it represents the first instance of a newly described disease but also because the correlation between the complex clinical symptoms and the thalamic degeneration suggests a new interpretation of the functions of the thalamus. It is now suspected that the thalamus plays a role in the regulation of vegetative functions and the circadian rhythms, especially in the wake-sleep cycle. The idea that the thalamus plays a role in the regulation of sleep had been suggested in the 1930s by the Swiss physiologist Walter R. Hess, who had induced behavioral sleep in cats by electrical stimulation of the medial thalamus. His work was later ignored or refuted by evidence that other centers, especially the forebrain cortex, the hypothalamus, and the reticular substance of the brain stem, regulated sleep.

The case in question confirms Hess's findings that the thalamus should be included among the other "sleep centers" with a sleep-promoting function. As to the circadian vegetative and neurohormonal rhythms, the role of the hypothalamus, particularly of the structure known as the suprachiasmatic nucleus, has been well established. Only sporadically have patients with predominantly thalamic lesions been shown to display changes in the secretion of hormones.

The normal hypothalamus and pituitary gland in the patient studied indicated that, in addition to the hypothalamic centers, a normally functioning thalamus is also needed for a regular rhythmicity of hormonal and vegetative systems. The anterior and dorsomedial thalamic nuclei thus seem to have a pivotal role in the integration of many fundamental cyclic vegetative functions, among which sleep should be included. In particular, they seem to promote those brain mechanisms (slow-wave sleep, muscle inactivity, low body temperature, and low heart and breathing rates) concerned with restoration of the body energies.

There is a functional balance (homeostasis) between the restorative metabolic processes and the energetic expenditures of the organism. Lesions of the anterior medial thalami, by inducing inordinate motor, vegetative, and hormonal hyperactivity (a condition that resembles a chronic stress syndrome), seem to alter the balance toward uncontrolled physical exhaustion and debilitation and eventually death.

Unanswered questions

What causes the selective degeneration of these thalamic nuclei? Many inherited nervous diseases are due to the lack or malfunctioning of special proteins, the enzymes needed for cell metabolism. In the Italian family's case an unknown genetic defect could have impaired a metabolic process essential only to the nerve cells of two thalamic nuclei. Investigators are currently pursuing genetic studies directed at characterizing the inborn error.

Another question relates to the fact that this defect presents itself only in adult life. Several degenerative diseases of the nervous system, such as Huntington's disease (Huntington's chorea) and Alzheimer's disease, also begin at a mature age. The mechanism by which an inborn defect becomes symptomatic only later in life is a matter of speculation. Moreover, these diseases cannot be diagnosed in early life before the bizarre symptoms strike. It is obvious that in fatal familial insomnia, as well as in other conditions, aging contributes to the expression of the disease.

Insomnia insights

Insomnia is a common complaint; about 15 to 35% of the population report some degree of trouble sleeping sometime in their lives. As far as is known, however, no patients have died solely from lack of sleep. On the other hand, sleep—slow-wave sleep in particular—is commonly regarded as a restorative process. Researchers at the University of Chicago sleep laboratory have demonstrated that rats completely deprived of sleep die for unknown reasons in a severely consumptive state. One may ask, therefore, whether the lack of sleep contributed to the fatal outcome in the case of the patient in Bologna—and in at least 13 of his family members before him.

The ultimate goal of medicine, of course, is to cure. All treatments proved ineffective in this patient because they did not reverse the ongoing degeneration of nervous cells or correct the functional impairments. Nevertheless, the effect of the experimental benzodiazepine antagonist, though transitory, was intriguing. Drugs such as the benzodiazepines, which are contained in tranquilizers and sleeping pills, act by "mimicking" the effects of endogenous benzodiazepine-like substances that are likely to be normally present in the brain. A question that should be asked, in view of the effect of the experimental antagonist, is whether those as yet little understood naturally occurring benzodiazepine-like substances have a role in regulating the wake-sleep cycle.

Although this case of apparently fatal inherited insomnia is an isolated one, it begins to shed some light on some of the mechanisms involved in the more widespread disorder insomnia. Further research, stimulated by this case, should eventually uncover many more aspects of a complex process. As Manfred Karnovsky of the Harvard Medical School concluded in an editorial, "Progress in Sleep," in the *New England Journal of Medicine*, Oct. 16, 1986: "Few will argue against the proposition that demystification of the phenomenon of sleep, though it may diminish its poetic attraction, will offer precious solutions to those who suffer from derangements of this complex activity."

AIDS

AIDS (acquired immune deficiency syndrome) continues to take its toll, with, as of September 1987, more than 41,000 victims in the United States alone—more than half of whom have died. In the six years since the disease was recognized, the causative agent has been isolated and tests for its presence have been developed. Now, however, the U.S. is faced with an estimated 1.5 million persons who have already been infected and who serve as a potential reservoir for spread of the disease. The task of caring for those infected with the virus and of preventing its spread is just starting and will increasingly demand the attention and resources of every aspect of society.

The virus: recent insights

The virus that causes AIDS was isolated at the Pasteur Institute in Paris by Luc Montagnier and colleagues in 1983; they called their discovery lymphadenopathy-associated virus (LAV). The same virus was later isolated at the U.S. National Cancer Institute by a research team headed by Robert Gallo; they named their discovery human T-cell lymphotropic virus, type III (HTLV-III). It was not initially appreciated that the two viruses were the same. After an international political and legal controversy over who had first identified the virus—and would therefore be entitled to the millions of dollars of royalties for the blood test that was subsequently developed that identifies antibodies to the virus—the suit was finally settled in April 1987, with a portion of the money going to both the French and the American investigators. In addition, it was agreed that both groups would contribute 80% of their royalties to sponsor a new foundation for AIDS research and education. Even before the legal battle was settled, the International Committee on the Taxonomy of Viruses decided to change the name of the group of viruses believed to be responsible for AIDS from the cumbersome initial compromise designation of HTLV-III/LAV to the simpler name of human immunodeficiency virus, or HIV.

HIV is a member of the retrovirus family, which is distinguished from other kinds of viruses by the presence of reverse transcriptase, an enzyme that allows the RNA of the virus to make its own DNA (a reversal of the usual replication process) after it penetrates the host cell. This viral DNA is then inserted into the infected cell's genetic structure, and the cell continues to produce more virus particles—at its own expense and, ultimately, death. With the recovery and identification of HIV, there was renewed scientific interest in HTLV-I and HTLV-II, retroviruses that have been associated with certain types of leukemia in humans and with a simian, or monkey, retrovirus that may also infect humans. The retroviruses as a group have been recognized for years as causes of disease in many different animal species the world over, but until fairly recently they were thought not to infect humans. Feline leukemia, for example, is caused by a retrovirus, but the virus is species specific to cats and poses no risk at all to humans. Quite possibly other human diseases may be attributed to retroviruses as understanding of them improves.

The origin of HIV is still a subject of debate, but the first cases of what would today be called AIDS were diagnosed in Africans more than a decade ago, and a review of laboratory-preserved serum samples from Africa indicates the presence of antibodies to the virus as early as 1959. While it is possible that HIV is a new virus that evolved suddenly a few decades ago, it seems more likely that it has been around for a much longer time but in a limited group of people or perhaps in other primates—particularly the African

As the AIDS death toll mounts, families and friends of the victims try to find new ways of dealing with grief and loss. Following a funeral service in New York City, mourners release bunches of white balloons in memory of a loved one.

The New York Times

green monkey, which is a source of meat for some peoples in Africa.

Understanding of other retroviruses has increased with the intensive study of HIV. HTLV-I, discovered in 1978 in association with an unusual form of leukemia, is now known to be present in extensive areas of Africa, Japan, and the Caribbean and more recently found its way into the drug addict population of the southeastern U.S. Another virus, designated HIV-2, has been found in West Africa and seems to be responsible for a syndrome identical to AIDS. Unfortunately, the currently available blood tests for HIV (possibly more appropriately called HIV-1) do not indicate the presence of either HTLV-I or HIV-2. The impact of these viruses is unclear, but the need for even more refined blood testing is apparent. Fortunately, these viruses seem to be spread in the same ways as the AIDS virus, so control measures for one will be effective for all.

The clinical spectrum of HIV infection

The term acquired immune deficiency syndrome was coined in 1981 when a number of young homosexual men in the U.S. were found to have a rare malignancy, Kaposi's sarcoma, or pneumocystis pneumonia, an uncommon pneumonia known to affect people with impaired immune systems. Others had a variety of infections due to unusual organisms not previously known to cause disease in apparently healthy people but sometimes found to take advantage of people whose immune systems had been weakened by disease or immunosuppressive drugs—hence, the term opportunistic infections. In AIDS patients these infections were found to result from a severe depression of immune function due to the destruction of T-helper lymphocytes, a specific type of infection-fighting white blood cell.

Today it is recognized that the AIDS epidemic as it is presently manifested is most likely only the tip of the iceberg. Scientists now estimate that for every person who has so far been diagnosed as having AIDS, some 50 to 100 people have been infected with the AIDS virus. Those who have been infected with HIV often have no symptoms, but they carry the virus and appear likely to go on to develop the various manifestations of disease associated with the virus. Some develop an acute infection—with fever, general malaise, rash, and tender lymph nodes a few days to four weeks after inoculation with the virus. This mononucleosis-like illness usually subsides as other viral infections do. Although few people have a recognizable acute illness, many go on to develop other manifestations of disease included under the designation AIDS-related complex (ARC), such as enlarged lymph nodes (lymphadenopathy), persistent fevers, weight loss, diarrhea, and abnormalities of the red and white blood cells. These conditions are seldom fatal, but the encephalitis (brain

inflammation) caused by HIV can result in personality changes, loss of memory, seizures, and dementia. The full impact of the AIDS virus on the immune system becomes apparent when any of a variety of bacteria, parasites, or viruses overwhelm the body's infection-fighting capability, eventually resulting in death.

The pattern of the progression of the HIV infection to full-blown AIDS is slowly coming to be understood. It appears that an individual's chances of developing AIDS within the first year of infection may be only 0.3%. Over the next two years the rate of conversion increases to 3–4% per year for a cumulative incidence of 10–20% over the first five years, the only time span for which reliable figures have thus far been projected. The percentage developing ARC is about the same. Other studies estimate that 20–30% will develop AIDS within five years, with another 40% developing ARC. Scientists still do not know the number of people who will eventually develop AIDS, but the conversion rate does not seem to be slowing with time. One theory is that a number of cofactors may contribute to immune suppression and possibly potentiate the development of the disease in people previously infected with the virus; cofactors may include drug abuse, poor nutrition, pregnancy, and the concomitant development of infections such as viral hepatitis, herpes, and cytomegalovirus.

The blood test

The isolation and identification of HIV and the development of tests for antibodies to the virus have allowed scientists to estimate its prevalence. In the U.S., blood tests are now readily available in every community, although some states require a signed consent form prior to testing because of the potential social, economic, and emotional consequences of an individual's positive test results. Those who wish to be tested are encouraged to discuss the meaning and value of test results with a doctor before taking the test. After blood is drawn, the sample is first examined by enzyme-linked immunosorbent assay (ELISA). A positive test usually is not reported to the doctor or patient unless a confirmatory test, using a different screening method, also yields positive results. Confirmatory testing is necessary because the ELISA test may have a false-positive rate of 0.3%—considerably higher than the actual incidence of positive results in many communities.

Once the presence of AIDS antibody has been confirmed, the patient can be assumed to have been infected with the virus and to be carrying it in his or her blood, and the virus itself can usually be cultured from the patient's blood. While the ELISA test is a good screening test, there are also some problems with false-negative results. It may take an individual two to four months to develop antibodies after being infected, even though the virus itself may be recov-

"Don't Die of Ignorance" is the slogan of the British government's massive £20 million ($29 million) public education campaign against AIDS. Posters bearing this dire warning have appeared everywhere—in subway tunnels, on the sides of city buses—and a leaflet carrying the message has been delivered to every household in the U.K.

ered from the blood before that. In a few unusual cases, people in the advanced stages of AIDS have tested negative for antibodies to the virus, evidently because their immune systems are too depressed to make any antibodies.

Recent epidemiology

While the number of AIDS cases reported to the U.S. Centers for Disease Control (CDC) continues to increase, the rate of increase is slowing. In the first few years of the epidemic, the doubling time was six months; by the late summer of 1987, it was about 14 months. As of September 1987, approximately 41,-730 AIDS cases had been reported in the U.S. With an estimated 1.5 million Americans infected with HIV, the number of AIDS cases will continue to increase and may reach 270,000 by 1991. How many AIDS cases there will eventually be depends on whether the transmission of the virus can be stopped and whether effective therapy for the disease can be developed.

As the number of AIDS victims has continued to mount, the early breakdown of groups at highest risk has shown little change in the U.S. Homosexual and bisexual men remain the largest risk group and continue to account for about 66% of the cases. Intravenous drug abusers account for 17% of AIDS cases. An additional 8% are both intravenous drug abusers and homosexual or bisexual men.

More information about the smaller risk groups is emerging as the total number of AIDS cases increases. In the U.S. as of September 1987, more than 570 children under the age of 13 had been diagnosed as having AIDS, and more than half had already died. Most of these children acquired the virus from their mothers, either during gestation or in the birth process. Most of the mothers who transmitted the AIDS virus to their babies were intravenous drug abusers or

sexual partners of drug abusers. Other children with AIDS acquired the disease via blood transfusions or blood products, such as the coagulation factors used in treating hemophilia. There were almost as many girls infected as there were boys.

Women now make up almost 7% of the AIDS cases reported in the U.S. More than half of them (52%) were intravenous drug abusers. More than one-quarter (27%) were sexual partners of men with AIDS or at risk for AIDS. Ten percent received blood or blood products that may have been contaminated with HIV. (No risk factors have yet been determined for the remaining 11%.) The increase in the number of women with AIDS will probably continue as more women already infected begin to show clinical signs of disease. One in 10,000 female blood donors and six in 10,000 female military recruits are now testing positive for the virus. The ratio of female to male AIDS cases in the United States as a whole is one to 13, while the female-to-male ratio of positive antibody tests in military recruits is one to three, reflecting the same ratio as that of the general population when homosexual and hemophiliac-associated AIDS cases are eliminated.

The heterosexual spread of HIV is of increasing concern to the average American who is neither gay, bisexual, nor an intravenous drug abuser. In Africa, where heterosexual transmission seems to be predominant, the male–female ratio is about 1:1. While the reasons for the differences in the epidemiology of HIV infection in Africa and the U.S. are not entirely clear, the percentage of Americans who acquire AIDS via heterosexual transmission does not seem to be increasing—although the number of cases among heterosexuals is increasing. The transmission rate from an HIV-infected spouse is about 20% over four years. In some U.S. cities, tests of prostitutes show that more than 50% are antibody positive.

Eric J. Aldag

Most European countries are now experiencing the epidemic spread of AIDS (SIDA is the acronym for the French name of the disease). In this Swiss poster the admonition to halt the spread of the disease is punctuated by the image of a rolled-up condom, forming the "o" in "stop."

Minority groups are particularly hard hit by AIDS. Blacks in the U.S. are three times more likely than whites to develop AIDS. Blacks and Hispanics are at greater risk for AIDS largely because of the high rate of drug abuse in these groups. While figures vary, a recent CDC study estimates that they account for 75% of heterosexual cases, 72% of female cases, and 80% of the cases of children with AIDS. It is hoped that better education and targeted prevention programs will be able to decrease the spread of the HIV infection among this population.

Although the first cases of AIDS were reported in the U.S., the disease now poses an international problem. At least 112 countries have reported cases. Some countries in Central Africa are being devastated by the disease—5–10% of the population of Zaire may be infected with the virus that causes the AIDS-like "slim" disease there. Heterosexual transmission, contaminated blood products, and the reuse of contaminated needles seem to be the major means of spread in Africa and other less developed countries such as Haiti. Malnutrition, poor hygiene, widespread venereal disease, and endemic diseases that activate the immune system are also suspected of playing a part in the epidemiology of AIDS in these countries. Intravenous drug abuse and homosexual activity are primarily responsible for the spread of the disease in Europe. In Asia, where many countries are trying to prevent AIDS by travel restrictions and limitations on U.S. military personnel, the number of reported cases is still very small. While arguments continue about which country or countries are responsible for the AIDS epidemic, the disease has finally been accepted as an international problem. Blood-testing facilities are now available even in Moscow, although the U.S.S.R. for a long time refused to admit that any cases of AIDS had been reported there.

How AIDS is and is not transmitted

There is no doubt that HIV is a formidable enemy. What is uncertain is how much of a threat it is to those not yet infected. It is important to point out that despite the rapid transmission of the virus before it was recognized and isolated, very few questions remain about how it is spread. The virus is spread in three basic ways: by sexual activity, by intravenous use of contaminated needles (or in contaminated blood or blood products), and by childbirth.

Health care workers would seem to be the most at risk of contracting the virus. However, of more than 1,000 hospital workers with puncture wounds from needles used in the care of AIDS patients, an infection rate of only 0.5% has been found—far less than the 20% rate of hepatitis B infection from needle-stick injuries. A May 1987 report of three health care workers who acquired HIV infection without evident puncture wounds aroused new fears about transmission of the virus. These cases, which involved blood contamination via minor skin wounds or the mouth (by splashed blood), underscored the need for caution in handling blood or bodily fluids from people with known or possible HIV infection. Gloves should be used routinely, along with gowns, masks, and protective eyeglasses, whenever spillage or aerosolization of blood is likely—for example, during surgery or dental work.

Studies of family and household members of AIDS patients have continued to document the lack of transmission of the virus with even close and frequent contact—unless there is sexual contact. Extensive studies have also failed to document a role for mosquitoes or other insects in transmission of HIV. There is no airborne transmission and, because of this, there is little reason to exclude an AIDS patient from school or work if he or she is well enough to attend. Infected persons pose no risk to those around them other than through the exchange of blood or bodily fluids, unlikely in any usual work or school situation.

Treatment: the critical need

Effective therapy for people with HIV infections is an urgent and pressing need. So far, efforts have been directed toward either eliminating the virus or restoring the failing immune system. In the U.S. the National Institutes of Health has developed a special program for evaluation of potential treatments for AIDS. The agency is trying to explore every drug with potential for treatment of the AIDS virus, but the process is a slow and difficult one. Although a number of aspects of the virus's replication system may be attacked, the agents that inhibit reverse transcriptase, such as zidovudine (azidothymidine, or AZT; Retrovir), hold the most immediate prospects of benefit. In 1986 the preliminary results of a controlled trial of AZT were so promising that the experiment was halted so that patients receiving a placebo could be given the new drug. As a result, AZT has already been approved by the Food and Drug Administration for limited use. Unfortunately, it has serious side effects, and it is not a cure. Half of the patients receiving AZT had such serious bone marrow suppression that the drug had to be discontinued. Some compounds similar to AZT, as well as a variety of other drugs—among them foscarnet, ribavirin, HPA-23, dideoxycytidine (DDC), suramin, and the rifamycins—are also under evaluation. So far, none appears to be any better than AZT or to have an effect other than slowing down the replication of the virus. Other substances used in attempts to treat AIDS have included the natural antiviral substances known as the interferons and natural immune modulators such as the interleukins. Even bone marrow transplants have been tried in an attempt to restore immunity, with some limited success.

While it seems unlikely that an effective treatment of HIV infection will be developed in the next few years, important strides have been made in the therapy of the secondary, so-called opportunistic infections that account for the deaths of most AIDS patients. A few years ago the life expectancy of an individual with AIDS was only six months from the time of diagnosis. Now it is more than one year. This increase is due to earlier recognition of the infections, as well as to improved treatment of them. *Pneumocystis carinii* is a parasite that may infect the lungs, causing a form of pneumonia. It is the most frequently diagnosed infection in AIDS patients and can be treated with the antibiotics trimethoprim-sulfamethoxazole or pentamidine isethionate. These antibiotics may also be useful in preventing the infection. Experimental drugs are being used for the unusual mycobacterial infections seen in AIDS patients, and antiviral drugs are under investigation for use against cytomegalovirus and herpes as well as against HIV itself. However, the slow process of development of new drugs and their limited success have led many AIDS patients to try unfounded regimens—vitamin therapy, health food products, home-cooked extracts—all of which are readily available.

Precautionary measures: the main line of defense

With some 1.5 million people carrying the AIDS virus, urgent efforts are needed to find an effective treatment. Meanwhile, efforts must also be directed toward preventing any more people from becoming infected. The development of the blood test for antibody to HIV has allowed the identification of infected people who may spread the virus even though they show no signs of disease. In the U.S. the test has been used since March 1985. This precaution has essentially eliminated transfusion-associated infection. Unfortunately, there were approximately 12,000 people who probably received transfusions of contaminated blood before testing started. Programs are now under way to identify those individuals through screening of all those who received blood transfusions between 1978 and 1985. In the meantime, even apparently healthy people who are in high-risk groups are being discouraged from donating blood because of the lag time between inoculation (*i.e.,* the actual transmission of the virus) and the ability of screening tests to detect the virus in the blood of an infected person. Anyone with a history of intravenous drug abuse or male homosexual contact since 1977 should not donate blood.

Whether a mass program of blood testing should be established remains a controversial issue; nonetheless, all U.S. military recruits are now routinely screened. Anyone at increased risk for the virus is encouraged

Like people suffering from other incurable diseases, many AIDS patients will desperately try unfounded but readily available treatments—from macrobiotic diets to a variety of home remedies.

Chuck Nacke—Picture Group

258

to have the blood test. Once a person has had a positive blood test, and thus is carrying the AIDS virus, it may be possible to alter his or her behavior to prevent further spread of the virus. The knowledge of a positive test, however, may be socially and emotionally devastating. It may, for example, be impossible for the person to get health or life insurance. Some AIDS victims have already suffered from job and housing discrimination, and some children with AIDS have been kept from attending school. The impact is potentially so great that many who may be carrying the virus choose not to know the test results or not to tell their sexual partners. What to do with irresponsible individuals who continue to spread the virus remains a major ethical and legal problem.

Until a successful vaccine can be developed, education must be the primary method of combating the spread of the virus. U.S. Surgeon General C. Everett Koop has taken a strong stand on this issue. In 1986 he issued a report, unprecedented in its explicit language, warning of the potential spread of AIDS beyond the already identified high-risk groups and advocating sex education concerning AIDS "at the lowest grade possible as part of any health and hygiene program." Sex education in elementary school has been taboo in most communities in the U.S. until recently, but many doctors and public health officials believe it may be necessary to teach children about sexual practices and intravenous drug abuse before—rather than after—they reach the age at which they might begin to engage in these activities.

Adults, too, have been the target of programs urging "safe sex" for both heterosexuals and homosexuals. Sexually active people are being discouraged from having contacts with multiple partners—or with partners who have had multiple partners. Sexual contact with prostitutes or intravenous drug abusers has been targeted as an obvious risk. Sexual practices that do not involve the exchange of blood or bodily fluids—such as "dry" kissing, massaging, hugging, and masturbation—are considered safe. Oral-genital contacts pose risk because of genital secretions. Rectal and vaginal intercourse pose the greatest risk, and public health officials have been outspoken in their recommendation that these activities not be performed without a condom. It is important to note, however, that even a condom is not 100% effective in preventing AIDS transmission. The impact of "safe sex" education programs is already being felt, as evidenced by reports that rates of sexually transmitted diseases are falling dramatically in gay communities.

Education of intravenous drug abusers is another priority. Frank information is available about the risks of drug abuse and how to avoid contaminated equipment. It has been proposed in the U.S., the U.K., and some other countries that drug addicts be provided with free needles. Indeed, free needle exchange pro-

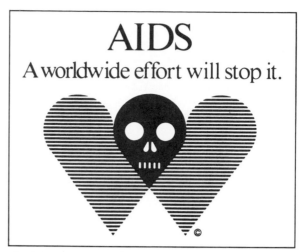

The fight against AIDS became a truly global battle in 1987 as the World Health Organization launched its first public awareness campaign against the deadly disease.

World Health Organization

grams are being tested in some U.S. cities, and some states no longer require a person to have a doctor's prescription in order to buy needles.

Creating a vaccine

In the summer of 1987, limited testing of vaccines against HIV began in France and Zaire. In the U.S. one of several requests for preliminary human trials was approved by the FDA. A truly safe and effective vaccine would have the potential to eradicate the disease worldwide—as has been done with smallpox. There are numerous obstacles, however. First, the safety of a potential vaccine would have to be proved; this is so with any vaccine, but AIDS provides a unique challenge because of the ability of HIV to incorporate itself into the genetic material of the infected cells. Furthermore, different strains of HIV have such different envelope proteins that a multivalent vaccine may well be needed. Finally, the efficacy of a vaccine can truly be tested only through the exposure of vaccinated humans to the virus itself, again a process of great risk—although homosexual men and spouses of HIV-infected persons may provide a population of willing volunteers. Thus, although a start has been made, public health officials estimate that the development of a useful vaccine will take many years. For this reason, preventive education and the search for effective therapies are all the more essential at present.

Third International Conference on AIDS

The third International Conference on AIDS met in Washington, D.C., in June 1987. It was the largest such meeting of its kind, with more than 8,000 researchers, physicians, and other health professionals from some 50 countries in attendance. The 250 papers that were presented covered a variety of clinical and patient-care issues. Robert Gallo of the National Cancer Institute reported on an apparently new virus in several Nigerian patients suffering from an AIDS-like disease. Other studies evaluated the progress of various drug treatments, followed up on the rate of AIDS transmission to spouses of hemophiliacs exposed to the virus through contaminated blood products, and evaluated the success of various educational programs among both high-risk and low-risk groups.

The biggest news, however, was made by politicians and lawmakers, rather than by researchers and clinicians. Appearing at an AIDS fund-raising event prior to the opening of the conference, U.S. Pres. Ronald Reagan urged mandatory blood testing for all persons sentenced to federal prisons, upon both entrance to and exit from such institutions, and for immigrants, refugees, and illegal aliens applying for legal status. He also recommended that the states begin a program of routine testing of marriage license applicants. These pronouncements stirred considerable controversy, and their impact seemed undiminished when they were repeated the following day by Vice-Pres. George Bush, who addressed the conferees. Perhaps the most important issues to be raised by the officials who attended the meeting, the politicians who spoke before it, and the AIDS support groups who picketed outside was the question of authority in policy-making. The AIDS epidemic, according to public health officials, is too important a global issue to be left in the hands of politicians, while to the elected officials AIDS is too crucial a social issue to be delegated to the realm of public health.

—Alan D. Tice, M.D.

Awards and Prizes

In medicine, work in several areas, including basic research, clinical discoveries, and public health advances, was lauded in the calendar year 1986. From the discovery of a factor that stimulates nerve cell growth to the establishment of a source of safe drinking water in a third world country, the honored work represents a broad spectrum of effort.

Nobel Prize: 1986

The Karolinska Institute awarded the annual Nobel Prize for Physiology or Medicine to Rita Levi-Montalcini and Stanley Cohen for their cell growth discoveries. The two scientists, who early in their careers had collaborated on research, also won the 1986 Albert Lasker Award for Basic Medical Research for this work. They were the first to discover and characterize factors that stimulate cell growth.

Levi-Montalcini was dismissed from her position at the University of Turin in her homeland, Italy, in 1939 because of the anti-Semitic policies of Benito Mussoli-

ni's government. She continued her experimental work on chick embryos in a makeshift bedroom laboratory with eggs smuggled to her by friends. After the war she went to Washington University in St. Louis, Mo., and joined the laboratory of Viktor Hamburger, where researchers were studying how nerve cells grow from the spinal cord to establish connections with internal organs and limbs. Levi-Montalcini was inspired by a colleague's demonstration that a mouse tumor could stimulate the growth of nerve fibers in a chick embryo.

She suspected that the tumor must be secreting something that induced nerve cell growth. In later work she isolated a substance from a tumor within a culture medium that stimulated the growth of embryonic nervous tissue. The substance was so potent that one-billionth of a gram per milliliter of culture medium was sufficient to promote growth; nerve cells reacted to the substance within 30 seconds. Her use of cultures was thereafter adopted in many laboratories as the standard method for studies of the substance, which came to be known as nerve growth factor (NGF).

Cohen, working in the same laboratory at Washington University, isolated and purified the compound, which he, Levi-Montalcini, and Hamburger described in a paper in 1954. To determine whether the active ingredients in the extract were proteins or nucleic acid molecules, Cohen added a type of snake venom that destroys genetic material. The venom turned out to be a more potent source of NGF than the tumor itself, with 1,000 times as much of the factor as the tumor cells. Cohen was then able to produce antibodies to the NGF. Using the antibodies, Levi-Montalcini found that with the factor blocked, nerve growth did not occur. NGF represented the first identified cell growth regulator.

Cohen, currently a professor of biochemistry at the Vanderbilt University School of Medicine, Nashville,

Rita Levi-Montalcini is pictured at her home in Rome after the Karolinska Institute announced that she had won the 1986 Nobel Prize for Physiology or Medicine for her outstanding work in cell biology.

AP/Wide World

Biochemist Stanley Cohen is pictured in his Vanderbilt University lab in Nashville, Tennessee, after learning that he would share a 1986 Nobel Prize with his longtime colleague Rita Levi-Montalcini.

Tenn., went on to discover another growth factor—epidermal growth factor (EGF). Researchers had identified the salivary gland as a rich source of NGF. When Cohen injected salivary gland extract into newborn mice, it stimulated the development of their eyelids and teeth—growth that was unrelated to the development of the nervous system. He was able to purify the responsible protein and determine the order of its genetic subunits. He and his co-workers found that EGF governs cell development in the skin and stimulates a variety of metabolic activities. EGF has been used as a component of the culture medium in which films of human skin are grown for use as grafts for victims of severe burns.

Cohen, who won the National Medal of Science in 1986 as well, also has discovered the first key step in the growth-stimulating process. At an early stage in the process of cell division, a protein on the surface of cells "catches" the EGF; the two are then absorbed into the cell, where they attach an atom of phosphorous onto a protein subunit. Several other growth factors have subsequently been discovered and found to act in a similar manner. In 1980 Cohen discovered that certain cancer "genes" produce a substance with a similar growth-stimulating function. The exact nature of the mechanism—where and when it occurs in the process of cancer development—is under investigation.

The Nobel assembly awarded the 1986 prize to Levi-Montalcini and Cohen because, as a direct consequence of their discoveries, "our understanding of many disease states such as developmental malformations, degenerative changes in senile dementia, delayed wound healing, and tumor diseases" will be significantly enhanced.

Albert Lasker Awards

In addition to Levi-Montalcini and Cohen, four other people won Lasker Awards. Luc Montagnier of the Pasteur Institute in Paris, Robert C. Gallo of the National Cancer Institute in Bethesda, Md., and Myron Essex of the Harvard University School of Public Health were honored for their research on AIDS, and New York-born Ma Haide of Beijing (Peking) was cited for public service.

In 1983 Montagnier published the first electron microscope "picture" of the retrovirus associated with AIDS. He had previously detected the enzyme reverse transcriptase in AIDS patients; this enzyme indicates that a retrovirus is present. At first uncertain as to whether the virus he had found caused AIDS or was merely another opportunistic infection associated with the disease, Montagnier named it lymphadenopathy-associated virus (LAV).

Gallo, in the U.S., also isolated the virus, which he termed human T-cell lymphotropic virus, type III (HTLV-III). (The International Committee on the Taxonomy of Viruses has since settled on the name human immunodeficiency virus, or HIV.) Using an immune system promoter that he had previously isolated, Gallo was able to grow the AIDS virus. He further found that the AIDS virus infects cells in the brain and that the virus evades the body's defenses by altering its genetic identity. The work of both Gallo and Montagnier led to the development of blood tests that identified the presence of antibodies to the virus.

Essex, a veterinarian and microbiologist, made important discoveries about AIDS retroviruses while studying feline leukemia virus, a retrovirus that can cause leukemia in cats. Essex for the first time provided evidence of how a virus can be cancer causing, and he determined the way feline leukemia suppresses the immune system. The ability of a virus to cause leukemia in free-living cats subsequently inspired Gallo to look for retrovirus-caused cancers in humans.

Essex also showed that AIDS affects T cells of the immune system and that the virus is transmissible through blood transfusions. With Gallo he developed an AIDS antibody test. Essex's lab also identified proteins and antibodies associated with the disease. He and colleagues in his laboratory identified an African green monkey virus that is similar to the AIDS virus, which led Essex to suggest that the human virus may be derived from the simian virus.

On the public service front, Ma (born George Hatem) was honored for virtually eradicating venereal disease—in particular, syphilis—in China. Ma, the senior adviser to the Ministry of Public Health in China, first went to that country in 1933 to study tropical diseases. He subsequently ministered to Mao Zedong's (Mao Tse-tung's) army after the Long March of 1934–35. After the People's Republic of China was established in 1949, Ma was authorized by Mao to begin a massive effort to wipe out venereal disease. Everyone who could be identified was treated; brothels were closed; and nonprofessionally trained health workers, or "barefoot doctors," were trained to go out in the countryside and treat people. Whereas syphilis previously infected almost one-quarter of the urban population, today there are very few cases of venereal disease in China; Ma has expressed doubt that in a group of ten million Chinese people, even one or two cases of syphilis could be found. Ma went on to focus his efforts on leprosy.

Public health

Balancing out the pioneering basic medical research awards are several important awards given in the public health field, including awards from the World Health Organization (WHO), Ronald McDonald Children's Charities, and the Rockefeller and Pew foundations.

WHO awarded the $100,000 Sasakawa Health Prize to the Ayadaw Township People's Health Plan Committee in Burma, Lucille Teasdale Corti and Pietro Corti in Uganda, and Amorn Nondasuta in Thailand. The Burmese group, which was founded in 1979, was honored for improving the township's water and sanitation supply. Whereas in 1980 only 1.6% of the population had access to safe water and proper sanitation, by 1985, 97.2% of the community had safe water and 50% had access to proper sanitation. The result in that short time span was an absence of cholera and plague—previous scourges—and a dramatic reduction in gastrointestinal infections.

The Cortis, an Italian husband-and-wife team who moved to Uganda in 1961, established a hospital there that now serves a community of 100,000 people. It provides both normal clinical services and important outreach services and sponsors primary health and prevention programs. A rehabilitation center and research facilities are now being established.

The other Sasakawa Prize winner, Amorn Nondasuta, permanent secretary for public health in Thailand, was honored for his work in rural health. He used health volunteers and community members to produce and distribute iodized salt, which decreased the incidence of goiter (a major health problem in northern Thailand) in schoolchildren from 75 to 5% within a year. Goiter, an enlargement of the thyroid gland, is associated with hyperthyroidism, a condition marked by increased metabolic and heart rates and high blood pressure.

In the United States, Julius Richmond, now a professor of pediatrics at Harvard University, received a $100,000 award from the Ronald McDonald Children's Charities for his contributions "to the health and well-being of children," in particular the creation of the Head Start program. The program, which has been in existence for more than 20 years and has involved more than ten million disadvantaged children, provides health and educational assistance to preschoolers.

The Rockefeller Foundation and the Pew Charitable Trusts have joined together to fund public health training and research efforts at up to six institutions in the United States and Canada. The institutions, to be selected in 1988, will receive a total of $10 million for work on preventive medicine and efforts toward meeting other unmet health needs of the public.

General Motors cancer research awards

Harald zur Hausen of the German Cancer Center in Heidelberg, West Germany, Donald Pinkel of the M. D. Anderson Hospital and Tumor Institute in Houston, Texas, and Phillip Allen Sharp of the Massachusetts Institute of Technology (MIT) won the 1986 General Motors Cancer Research Foundation prizes. Each received $100,000 plus $30,000 to be used for a scientific workshop or conference.

Zur Hausen is credited with relating the presence of certain types of human papillomavirus to cervical cancer. This family of viruses causes warts on the skin and particularly on the genitals. His work suggests that these viruses, which are spread primarily during sexual contact, may be involved in mouth, larynx, and lung tumors.

Pinkel's work is in the area of childhood leukemias. Pinkel found that these leukemias, previously thought to be fatal, yield to a regimen of anticancer drugs. One reason for his success in treatment is that he used drugs injected directly into the spinal fluid in combination with radiation therapy. This approach kills leukemic cells in the brain covering and spinal cord, thus wiping out a reserve that could otherwise continue to reproduce and cause a relapse of disease or exacerbation of the cancer. At one time acute lymphocytic leukemia killed more U.S. children over the age of one year than any other childhood disease. Because of Pinkel's work this form of childhood cancer is now considered curable.

Sharp was cited for more theoretical work: his discovery of genetic "nonsense," which may eventually add to the understanding of the genetics of cancer. Bacterial research had led scientists to believe that virtually all the genetic material—*i.e.,* all the DNA—of more complex forms of life was directly involved in coding for proteins. Sharp, however, showed that there are noninvolved, or nonsense, segments within the DNA of higher organisms, including that of humans. This so-called nonsense material is not used during protein production; its exact function, if it has any, is not known at present. The great difference between bacterial and other cells indicates that humans may not be on a direct evolutionary line from present-day bacteria, which was once the dominant evolutionary view. Instead, bacteria and the progenitors of higher organisms may have evolved from some common, now-extinct organism.

Lita Annenberg Hazen Award

The $100,000 Lita Annenberg Hazen Award for Excellence in Clinical Research went to Jean D. Wilson of the University of Texas Health Science Center at Dallas for his work on sex hormones. Wilson, an endocrinologist, discovered that dihydrotestosterone, not testosterone, is the primary male hormone. Because of his work, it is now known that testosterone is turned into the more potent dihydrotestosterone by an enzyme; Wilson showed that unlike its precursor, dihydrotestosterone cannot be metabolized into the female sex hormone estrogen. He also proved that it binds more tightly to the protein receptors in the cytoplasm of cells than does testosterone.

Wilson's work ascertained that beyond its activity outside the cell, the molecular complex of sex hormone and protein penetrates the cell nucleus and works directly on genetic material. He also determined how errors in the system—*e.g.,* insufficient transitional enzyme to change testosterone into dihydrotestosterone and problems in the dihydrotestosterone receptor—can cause the feminization of male genitalia, both internal and external. In mild forms such errors can cause infertility by inhibiting sperm production.

Understanding the dihydrotestosterone system has also led to the development of drugs to interrupt the process of enlargement of the prostate gland, a common health problem in aging males. Since the prostate gland depends on dihydrotestosterone for its growth, Wilson is investigating the use of a drug that interferes with the conversion of testosterone to dihydrotestosterone.

MacArthur Foundation Awards

Several biomedical researchers were accorded the 1986 MacArthur Fellowships. The "no strings attached" awards—intended to allow scientists to work without financial concerns—provide five-year stipends. Paul R. Adams of the State University of New York at Stony Brook has been working on the biophysics of Alzheimer's disease. David Page of MIT has found what may be the section of genetic material that determines maleness. Robert M. Shapely of Rockefeller University, New York City, has combined mathematics and neurobiology to understand how light goes from the eye to the brain. Allan C. Wilson of the University of California at Berkeley established that the degree of species relatedness can be determined through studies of similarities and differences in biochemistry. Such analysis can be used to estimate when individual species diverged along the evolutionary tree.

Other awards

The Louisa Gross Horwitz Prize went to two researchers at the Max Planck Institute for Biophysical Chemistry, Göttingen, West Germany. Erwin Neher and Bert Sakmann were honored for devising a procedure to monitor the flow of ions (charged particles) in cells. In the "patch-clamp" technique they invented in 1978, a tiny glass electrode is touched to a cell. The electrode senses a change in charge, and thus the passage of ions, through that section of the cell wall. Measuring the flow of ions into and out of cells is now done in many fields of biology and has proved especially valuable in the study of nerve cells.

Newest of all are the Charles A. Dana Awards; icebreakers in 1986, their first year, were Donald A. Henderson, dean of the Johns Hopkins University School of Hygiene and Public Health, Baltimore, Md., and Thomas R. Dawber and William B. Kannel of the Boston University School of Medicine. Henderson was cited for supervising WHO's vaccine program that led to the eradication of smallpox; he also received a National Medal of Science for this global achievement. Dawber and Kannel received their award for designing and sustaining the Framingham Heart Study, the most comprehensive epidemiological study of a population and its life-styles ever conducted. Inhabitants of the town of Framingham, Mass., over two generations have been the subjects. Data from the Framingham study have established that certain factors—*e.g.,* high blood pressure, high cholesterol levels, smoking, and obesity—increase the risk of heart disease. Each of the recipients of the awards received a $50,000 honorarium for the pioneering work in disease prevention and health promotion, which has been used to save millions of lives around the world.

On the horizon

Beginning in 1988 a committee of U.S. Nobel laureates will begin to select outstanding graduate students and young researchers to receive American Nobel Laureate Fellowships. These "young Nobels"—biennial prizes of $50,000—are planned for the fields of chemistry, physics, medicine, and economics. The goal is to support and encourage the stellar younger scientists who will make the important scientific discoveries of the future.

—Joanne Silberner

Cancer

According to the most recent statistics, the number of people who get cancer and the rate at which they die continue to increase. Approximately one out of every three people now living in the United States—about 74 million persons—will eventually get cancer. The American Cancer Society (ACS) estimated that in 1987 about 965,000 people would be diagnosed as having cancer and 483,000 would die of various forms of the disease, which will strike three out of four U.S. families.

What the statistics show

The chances of dying of cancer are less for people under age 55, according to National Cancer Institute (NCI) statistics showing that the death rate for patients less than 55 years old decreased between 1975 and 1984; those under 55 have a five-year survival rate of 59%, which is 10% higher than the rate for all U.S. cancer victims. This decrease does not show up in the overall death rate because the death rate for people 55 and older, who account for 76% of cancer cases, is increasing. The ACS estimated that 385,000 of those diagnosed in 1987 will be alive in 1992, but another 580,000 cancer patients will die before the end of that year if present death rates continue.

Death rates among children also have both negative and positive aspects. In the U.S. fewer than 55% of white cancer patients younger than 15 years old now die of their cancers, compared with 62% in 1975. (Not enough cases were reported in black children to allow for statistical analysis.) However, cancer kills more U.S. children between the ages of 3 and 14 than any other disease, with 2,200 deaths expected in 1987.

Encouraging progress in some areas but discouraging results in others is a pattern that also characterizes the fight against specific cancers. Because of the decline in smoking among men, both incidence of and deaths from lung cancer have been decreasing among men under 45 years of age since 1973 and among men ages 45 to 54 since 1978. More precise diagnosis and more effective drug treatments have increased the five-year survival rate for those with testicular cancer from 63% 20 years ago to 88% today. On the other hand, a surprising upswing in the death rate for breast cancer occurred in 1984, the last year for which complete statistics are available. The ACS estimated that in 1987 one in ten women in the U.S. will develop breast cancer, an all-time high. The reason for this apparent increase remains unknown, but it is possible that it may in part reflect the longer life-span of women and improved detection methods.

Women's cancers

Recent research has exonerated a high-fat diet, estrogen therapy, and oral contraceptives as causes of breast cancer. Numerous recent studies have failed to show a link between diet and breast cancer. One of the largest was a survey of more than 89,000 nurses conducted by Harvard University. The women in the study, who were from 34 to 59 years old, consumed 32 to 44% of their calories in fat, more than the 30% recommended by the NCI. Four years of examinations showed no evidence that these higher fat-intake levels increased the chances of getting breast cancer. The NCI is still studying the relationship of dietary fat and breast cancer and now intends to determine if lowering fat intake to 20% of calories can reduce the incidence of or possibly even prevent this form of cancer. In Japan, for example, where women consume diets with as little as 15% of calories as fat, breast cancer incidence is very low.

Similar investigations have also failed to conclusively link breast cancer and estrogen supplements. More than two million U.S. women take some form of estrogen, either to manage the symptoms of menopause or to adjust levels of the hormone following surgical removal of the ovaries. Scientists at the U.S. Centers for Disease Control (CDC) in Atlanta, Ga., studied more than 3,000 women with and without breast cancer and concluded that the incidence was the same in women who used estrogens and those who did not.

This was good news for the nearly nine million U.S. women who take oral contraceptives, most of which contain estrogen. Another CDC study found that long-time use of birth control pills does not increase a woman's risk of breast cancer, even if there is a family history of the disease. This and other studies also have demonstrated that taking oral contraceptives actually reduces the risk of cancer of the ovaries and endometrium (inner lining of the uterus). NCI researchers claim that the longer a woman uses the Pill, the lower her risk of ovarian cancer, a disease that will kill an estimated 11,700 U.S. women in 1987. Moreover, this reduced risk persists even after oral contraceptive use ceases. Although they cannot explain the underlying mechanism, the NCI estimates that in the U.S. alone more than 1,700 women each year avoid ovarian cancer by taking oral contraceptives.

CDC researchers have reached a similar conclusion about the protective effect of the Pill against endometrial cancer, which will kill an estimated 2,900 U.S. women in 1987. They found that women who used so-called combination pills (containing estrogen and progesterone) for at least 12 months had almost half the risk of those who had never used oral contraceptives.

On the other hand, there is evidence that use of the Pill increases the risk of cervical cancer. A recently enacted law requires that oral contraceptives be labeled with a warning about this risk and with advice that users undergo a yearly Pap smear to monitor possible precancerous changes in the cells of the cervix. The most serious side effect of the Pill, however, is an increased risk of heart disease in women users over age 35.

NCI researchers also have found that smoking 40 or more cigarettes (*i.e.*, two packs) a day or smoking for 40 years doubles the risk of cervical cancer. Any woman who smokes regularly has a 50% higher risk of the disease than her nonsmoking counterpart, according to their research. Further, they found that compared with nonsmokers, women who had quit smoking for two or more years demonstrated no excess risk, a finding that emphasized the fact that first intercourse at an early age and multiple sex partners are more important than smoking as risk factors for cervical cancer.

New data about smoking, drinking, and other life-style factors

Smokers have a 1,000% greater risk of lung cancer than nonsmokers, but what about nonsmokers who breathe the exhaled smoke? In 1986 the U.S. National Research Council (NRC) reviewed 13 studies done in different countries and concluded that they demonstrate a definite link between so-called passive smoking and lung cancer. According to the NRC report, nonsmokers married to smokers increase their risk by 30%; data gathered solely in the U.S. indicate a slightly lower risk. The NRC also found that smoking is hazardous to the fetuses and newborn children of smokers. It causes such ill effects as lowered birth weight; respiratory distress syndrome, which affects newborn premature infants and results in failure of the lungs to expand and contract properly; and, possibly, a slower rate of lung growth.

Smoking also is considered, along with high levels of cholesterol in the blood, a major risk factor for heart disease. Now two European studies have discovered a possible link between high cholesterol levels and colorectal cancer. Investigators at the Karolinska Institute in Stockholm analyzed data from more than 92,000 people over a 15-year period and found a significant statistical correlation between high blood cholesterol levels and rectal cancer in men. They also found a lesser correlation between high cholesterol and colon and rectal cancer in women and colon cancer in men. Researchers at the University of Munich, West Germany, found in 842 people "a small positive association" between high cholesterol and colorectal adenomas, tumorlike growths thought to precede cancer.

However, there are other studies that seem to show a connection between colorectal cancer and *low* cholesterol levels. A survey of more than 360,000 men, conducted by investigators at several U.S. universities, found a "significant excess" of cancer in those with the lowest cholesterol levels. The researchers who conducted this study and other investigations that reached the same conclusion were unable to explain whether the cancer caused the low cholesterol levels

or the low cholesterol caused the cancer. Those who took issue with a positive relationship between cancer and low cholesterol attributed the apparent correlation to faulty methodology or basic flaws in the design of the studies.

Added to threats posed by cholesterol levels and smoking is new evidence implicating some alcoholic beverages and agricultural herbicides as cancer risks. In 1986 the Center for Science in the Public Interest filed a petition with the U.S. Food and Drug Administration (FDA) claiming that more than 50 brands of domestic and imported liquors contain dangerous amounts of urethane, a chemical that causes cancer when large doses are fed to laboratory animals. The FDA said that no reliable data exist for determining the risks posed by the much lower levels of urethane in distilled spirits and wines. However, the agency plans

Recent cancer statistics reflect both gains and losses in the battle against the disease. A 1986 report from the U.S. National Cancer Institute showed that the death rate of patients under age 55 decreased between 1975 and 1984. The death rate for people over 55, however, was increasing.

Cancer survival: the age factor

cancer deaths per 100,000 people aged 54 or younger

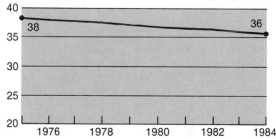

aged 55 to 64

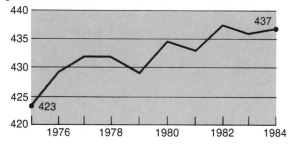

aged 65 and older

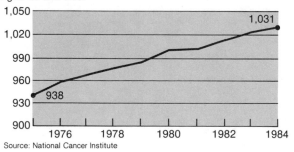

Source: National Cancer Institute

to follow the example set by Canada, which in 1985 placed limits on the amount of urethane allowed in alcoholic beverages. There was further news of an association between drinking and cancer when the *New England Journal of Medicine* in May 1987 published the data of two groups of researchers on alcohol consumption and breast cancer. The degree of risk was found to be directly related to the amount of alcohol consumed, but even moderate drinking—three–nine drinks a week—was associated with a significant increase in a woman's risk of developing breast cancer.

A clearer link exists between certain herbicides and some types of cancer. In 1986 NCI epidemiologists confirmed earlier reports from Swedish and U.S. researchers that exposure to herbicides containing phenoxyacetic acid increases the odds of developing non-Hodgkin's lymphoma (a type of blood-cell cancer) in workers who manufacture the chemicals and farmers who use it. According to the NCI findings, the risk increases significantly with the annual number of days of exposure, up to as much as sixfold for heavy users of these chemicals.

Improved testing, diagnosis, and treatment

Physicians dream of a simple, reliable test for detecting cancer in those who may be at increased risk or for screening large numbers of people. This dream may become a reality in the form of a blood analysis that detects abnormalities in lipoproteins caused by cancers. The test uses magnetic resonance imaging (MRI), a technique that is capable of showing abnormalities of function, such as decreased metabolism, in body organs or tissues. In the new blood test, MRI detects disordered structure in fat and protein molecules on the basis of their response to magnetic fields and radio waves. In tests of blood samples from 331 people, the new technique identified virtually all of those who had cancer. It gave false-positive diagnoses in only two cases, those of a pregnant woman and a man with an enlarged prostate gland. The exciting possibility is that MRI technology might eventually be used to detect cancer at its earliest stages, before it becomes visible to X-rays and before any symptoms appear.

Another recently developed procedure offers the hope of assessing a patient's chances of survival and thus indicating how aggressively he or she should be treated. Survival, researchers have determined, is related to the presence in tumors of cancer-causing genes called oncogenes. These genes are essential for such purposes as growth of fetal cells and wound healing, but they cause cancer when they are activated at other, inappropriate times. Researchers from the School of Medicine of the University of California at Los Angeles (UCLA) examined the tumor tissue of 52 breast cancer victims and discovered that 92% of the women who had a normal number of oncogenes survived at least three years. Conversely, of 11 women whose tumor cells contained five or more times the normal complement of oncogenes, only 40% survived that length of time. A normal cell may contain 1 or 2 oncogenes, a cancerous cell 10 to 20. Thus, the scientists theorize that cancer occurs when oncogenes multiply beyond their normal number. NCI investigators found the same relationship in lung cancer victims.

The pioneering work in this area was done by Robert Seeger of UCLA, who discovered multiple oncogenes in tumors from children with neuroblastoma, a cancer that affects the nervous system. Seeger and his colleagues now use this test to identify children who need higher than normal doses of drugs or radiation to fight their cancers. Further in the future is the hope of finding ways to prevent oncogenes from multiplying.

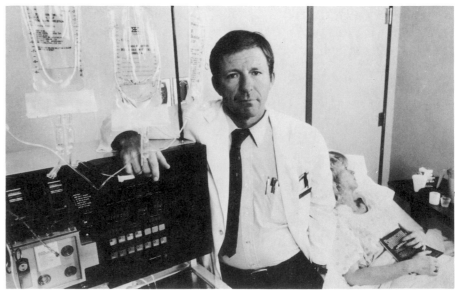

Robert K. Oldham founded Biotherapeutics, Inc., to make potentially promising but unproven therapies available to cancer patients. In a normal research setting, experimental treatment is free; Oldham's center charges a fee. The concept of test subjects' paying their own way is controversial, but some physicians believe it may become widespread.

Rob Nelson—Picture Group

Fighting drug resistance

While some cancers can be cured with drugs, others are notoriously resistant to chemotherapy. In some colon cancer cases, for example, the tumors appear to be inherently drug resistant. In other instances resistance develops in response to drugs. Thus, an attempted cure may actually assure that the cancer will return and be even harder to treat.

In an attempt to overcome this frustrating dilemma, researchers have determined one mechanism by which this resistance develops. When a patient receives the anticancer agent methotrexate, the drug inhibits the action of the enzyme dihydrofolate reductase (DHFR), essential for multiplication of tumor cells. The cancer cells respond by making more of the genes that produce the enzyme. This process of gene multiplication, called amplification, overwhelms the methotrexate, and the cancerous tumors begin to grow again. Cells with amplified DHFR genes then are resistant to the drug.

In the case of inherent resistance, cancer cells seem to possess an enhanced ability to "pump out" therapeutic drugs. One way this can happen, researchers have discovered, is via the action of a molecule called P-glycoprotein. The "P" signifies that this protein makes a cell membrane permeable. Overproduction of the protein by gene amplification may account for the expulsion of therapeutic drugs. Supporting this idea is the fact that higher than normal amounts of P-glycoprotein exist in the membranes of tumor cells that exhibit resistance to more than one drug. For example, cancers of the colon, lung, prostate, and pancreas, which resist all nitrogen mustard drugs, have high concentrations of the protein.

From such research, oncologists have learned that prolonged administration of low doses of drugs often produces resistance. This has led to a growing trend toward short-term, intensive chemotherapy. For instance, at the Dana-Farber Cancer Institute in Boston, physicians treat advanced cancers with doses so high the drugs could destroy a patient's bone marrow. As a preventive measure, they remove some of the patient's bone marrow before treatment and then replace it afterward. Thus far results have been so encouraging that the physicians plan to try the treatment on less-advanced cancers. Other researchers at Dana-Farber are testing high doses of drugs and radiation on victims of non-Hodgkin's lymphoma who have relapsed after responding initially to drug treatment. This therapy involves removing the bone marrow, treating it to destroy any lingering cancer cells, and then replacing it. Forty patients so treated have experienced complete remission. Another 24 have remained disease-free for as long as four years.

Controversy over experimental treatments

Trials of another type of intensive treatment have proved both controversial and less than encouraging.

W. C. Willet et al., "Moderate Alcohol Consumption and the Risk of Breast Cancer," *The New England Journal of Medicine*, vol. 316, no. 19 (May 7, 1987), pp. 1174–80

Drinking and breast cancer—Harvard University study

alcohol consumption (drinks per week)*	increase in risk of breast cancer
0–2	none
3–9	30%
9 or more	60%

*one drink = one 355-ml (12-oz) beer, one 118-ml (4-oz) glass of wine, or 44 ml (1.5 oz) of liquor

A new link between breast cancer and alcohol consumption was established in 1987. A Harvard University study of nearly 90,000 women found that even moderate drinking is associated with an increased risk of the disease.

In 1985 Steven A. Rosenberg and his colleagues at the NCI revealed that they had treated 25 cancer patients by removing white cells from their blood, adding to the cells a natural immune-system stimulant known as interleukin-2 (IL-2), and then injecting the treated cells back into the patient's bloodstream along with additional IL-2. In this trial 11 patients in whom no other treatment had worked experienced a 50% or more reduction in tumor size. A year later, however, Rosenberg reported that only 7 out of a total of 104 patients so treated had experienced a complete disappearance of their cancers. Another 25 experienced a measurable reduction in tumor size. Rosenberg admitted that, in addition to the poor results, the treatment is very toxic; one patient died from it.

In 1986 the same research team reported another experiment in which patients received high doses of IL-2 alone. Six people in this group were suffering from melanoma, a virulent, invasive skin cancer. Three patients who received the experimental treatment had significant tumor regressions, but two of them had to be treated again when their tumors returned. The final result was a shrinkage of tumors for three to six months in two of the patients. A third patient died.

This disappointing success rate and the unacceptable side effects of the treatment prompted Charles G. Moertel, an oncologist at the Mayo Clinic in Rochester, Minn., to call for a halt in these experimental treatments. In an editorial published in the Dec. 12, 1986, issue of the *Journal of the American Medical Association,* Moertel charged that Rosenberg's therapy was "associated with severe toxicity and astronomical costs," factors that were not balanced by "any persuasive evidence of true net therapeutic gain." Moertel criticized the researchers for encouraging extravagant attention from the press and for offering false hope to desperately ill people. Rosenberg admitted that the media coverage had been excessive, but he denied that it had been promoted by the NCI. He characterized the side effects of the new therapy as "not unacceptably severe" and denied allegations that its costs would be astronomical. Rosenberg is continuing to treat cancer patients, and he claims that a considerable number of them have responded favorably with "less treatment-related mortality than from many accepted treatments for patients with metastatic [spreading] cancer."

Traditionally, people undergoing experimental therapy at NCI facilities and university research centers receive the treatments without cost. A former NCI scientist, Robert K. Oldham, has broken this tradition by charging patients as much as $35,000 for unproven, experimental therapy. Oldham believes that conventional research programs move too slowly and turn away many terminally ill patients. Further, because these tend to be controlled studies, patients agreeing to enter a trial of a new drug can be randomly assigned to the control group, which receives a placebo (a harmless, inert substance) instead of the drug. Thus, by design, patients may not get any drug treatment at all. In 1984 Oldham founded Biotherapeutics, Inc., to provide cancer research funded by the patients themselves. He claims that his treatments are effective in about 30% of his cases. Such therapy raises ethical and scientific questions and adds to the controversy that surrounds experimental cancer treatment. Nonetheless, some authorities believe that the entry of for-profit groups into medical research is inevitable.

A genetic basis for cancer?

In 1986 researchers from the Harvard Medical School and the Whitehead Institute for Biomedical Research, Cambridge, Mass., identified a gene that they believe prevents the formation of a hereditary eye cancer known as retinoblastoma. Robert A. Weinberg, a senior member of the team that isolated and cloned the gene, said that it was the first discovery of a gene that restrains the growth of cancer. Researchers hope to identify other genes that block the development of cancer in other parts of the body, such as the lungs and breasts. Such findings would explain why, despite the fact that smoking is known to cause lung cancer, some people smoke all their lives without getting the disease.

The retinoblastoma research also points to a genetic basis for osteosarcoma, a bone cancer that attacks people 10 to 25 years old. Another member of the research team, Stephen Friend, noted that both cancers may be related to the same gene or a cluster of genes that lie close together on the same chromosome. Other scientists at the Fox Chase Cancer Center in Philadelphia have associated chronic myeloid leukemia with abnormalities on another chromosome. These discoveries make more realistic the possibility that genetic screening may someday be used to test for predisposition to certain forms of cancer.

The Outlook

Even without genetic screening, authorities believe, cancer deaths could be reduced by 35–40% if physicians and patients would take advantage of what already is known. Future advances could cut mortality by an additional 10–15%, for a total of 50% before the end of the century, according to the NCI's *Cancer Control Objectives for the Nation: 1985–2000*. Wider utilization of the newest and best therapies could reduce deaths by 10–15%, a decrease in smoking by another 8–15%, increased use of Pap smears and mammography by an additional 3%, and low-fat, high-fiber diets by 8% more.

—*William J. Cromie*

Diabetes

Owing to dramatic advances in both basic and clinical research, the outlook for people with diabetes mellitus is much better now than it was 20 or even 10 years ago. Diabetes remains a very serious and potentially catastrophic disease, but refined treatment approaches now allow far better control, and new treatments are available to minimize diabetes complications.

There is no cure, though, and in fact wide gaps still exist between what *can* be done to treat diabetes and what *is* done. It is the joint responsibility of health care professionals and individuals with diabetes to learn what can be done and to do it.

Types of diabetes: new classification

The classification of diabetes has been changed in recent years. Some 5 to 10% of the 11 million Americans with diabetes have type I, insulin-dependent diabetes mellitus (IDDM). This used to be called juvenile onset diabetes, and it is most often seen in younger people (ages 1–40 years), although it can begin at any age. By definition it is a form of diabetes that, if not treated with insulin, will lead to ketoacidosis (a medical emergency characterized by ketones in the blood and urine, with severe nausea, vomiting, dehydration, and prostration). Because people with IDDM have no pancreatic insulin secretion, they take insulin by injection every day. Their blood sugar is usually extremely variable from hour to hour.

Non-insulin-dependent diabetes mellitus (NIDDM, or type II diabetes) used to be called maturity onset diabetes because it usually comes on after the age of 40. It accounts for some 90% of all diabetes in the United States, runs strongly in families, and is very highly associated with obesity. While there may be a delay in insulin secretion, the person with NIDDM does produce some insulin from the pancreas and does not develop ketoacidosis (except under severe stress). Many people with NIDDM can be successfully treated by means of a good diet and exercise program; some need pills to stimulate insulin secretion. A somewhat confusing fact is that about 30% of people with non-insulin-dependent diabetes do require insulin by injection to control their blood sugar adequately.

There are additional forms of diabetes, classified as "other types," caused by relatively well-defined factors. Surgical pancreatectomy (following trauma, for instance), certain drugs such as steroids, other endocrine diseases such as those that result in excess cortisol or cause growth hormone secretion, and some unusual genetic syndromes may all cause diabetes by directly eliminating pancreatic insulin secretion or by opposing its action on cells.

Nearly 50% of people with diabetes do not even know they have it (so-called hidden diabetes). Sometimes the symptoms are very mild; more often, the classic symptoms (excess thirst, increased urine production, unexplained weight loss, and fatigue) are ignored.

Diabetic control: new inroads

The blood sugar concentration (plasma glucose) varies continuously in all people. For a nondiabetic person the range is normally about 60–140 milligrams per deciliter (mg/dl). Ingestion of dietary carbohydrates (simple sugars or complex carbohydrates such as starches) causes the blood sugar to increase. The normally functioning pancreas then secretes insulin, and insulin effectively brings blood sugar back to the baseline level by promoting sugar's utilization as fuel in the cells. When the pancreas does *not* secrete insulin at all (as in type I diabetes) or does not secrete *enough* insulin (as in type II diabetes), then the blood sugar often rises above normal.

Many factors other than dietary intake of carbohydrates and insulin secretion (or administration) regulate the blood sugar concentration. Chief among these other factors are exercise and stress. People who take insulin have known for years that exercise lowers blood sugar. Recent investigations attribute this to increased utilization of glucose by the muscles. Normally during exercise, adrenaline (a potent factor in raising blood sugar) increases and insulin secretion decreases in order to keep blood sugar from falling too low. The person with diabetes who has injected insulin, though, must be careful not to lower blood sugar too far during exercise. Stress, whether psychological or physical (*e.g.,* in acute illness), will tend to raise the blood sugar, again apparently owing to excess adrenaline secretion.

When the blood sugar concentration exceeds about 250 mg/dl, the blood is thickened (osmolarity is increased) to the point that thirst is stimulated in order to dilute the blood toward normal. The increased fluid intake, along with sugar in the urine, causes excess urination.

Diabetic control refers to how closely the blood sugar approximates the normal level. The person with poorly controlled diabetes may continuously have blood sugars in the 200–400-mg/dl range. Perfect diabetic control (which is rarely if ever achievable) would keep

Children's Hospital, Washington University Medical Center, St. Louis

Specialized teams are now working intensively with new teen patients, teaching them how to give themselves insulin injections and helping them cope in many ways, including getting over the initial shock of learning they have diabetes.

the blood sugar in the normal range all or most of the time. When insulin or pills are taken to treat hyperglycemia (high blood sugar), there is always a risk that they may be *too* effective, causing the blood sugar to fall too low (hypoglycemia). This problem (called an insulin reaction) may cause such symptoms as shakiness, sweating, mental confusion, or even coma, and taking sugar by mouth or by injection ordinarily will readily reverse it.

Since blood sugar does vary continuously, diabetic control is hard to evaluate. A single blood sugar value determined in a laboratory may not be representative of blood sugars at other times of the day or on other days. Testing urine glucose concentration was for years the standard approach for judging diabetic control. Urine testing is not a precise measure of blood sugar, however, and several newer approaches have revolutionized the ability to monitor, modify, and improve diabetic control.

Self-monitoring of blood glucose is now the best approach. With a lancet the person with diabetes can obtain a small blood sample from a tiny finger prick. A drop of blood is put on a special reagent stick and allowed to stay for a fixed period of time (40 to 90 seconds). The person then reads the color developed on the stick either by matching it to colors on a standard chart or by inserting the stick into a small meter that automatically measures the color developed. Some people use this simple technique four or more times daily, while others do it less often. In either case, the ability to know the exact blood sugar at any time is a tremendous advance in diabetic self-care.

Record keeping by the person with diabetes has always been important for keeping track of diabetic

269

control, for taking effective action, and for interacting with the physician. Generations of people with diabetes have kept detailed diaries, but new technology could make the diary obsolete. The new devices will automatically memorize blood sugar results or even allow the individual to record diet, exercise, and insulin doses. Use of a computer will allow averages, graphs, and other representations of the data to be printed out. This approach promises to be a real advantage, not only for the convenience of the patient but for that of physicians in analyzing patterns of diabetic control.

In addition to self-monitoring of blood glucose, another advance in measuring diabetic control is the glycosylated hemoglobin, or hemoglobin Alc. This simple blood test provides an indication of diabetic control over the previous two to three months. It actually measures the degree to which hemoglobin circulating in the red blood cells has become glycosylated (linked to glucose). The higher the glucose concentration in which the red blood cell has been circulating, the higher the glycosylated hemoglobin. A normal concentration is less than about 7.7% (different methods have different normal values), whereas poor diabetic control is indicated by glycosylated hemoglobin over about 12%.

Why control diabetes?

There is good reason to make the effort to control diabetes. To begin with, the symptoms of diabetes come on only with quite poor control. Uncontrolled thirst, excess urination, weight loss, excessive fatigue, and blurred vision are entirely avoidable with adequate treatment. Reasonable control can avoid the dangerous development of ketoacidosis or very high blood sugars and the need for hospitalization to treat these medical emergencies, but an important motivation for controlling diabetes is also the expectation that long-term complications of diabetes will be minimized.

Considerable evidence, some new and some old, suggests that poor diabetic control at least is associated with, and may well cause, such long-term complications of diabetes as retinopathy (eye disease), nephropathy (kidney disease), and neuropathy (nerve damage). Animals with poorly controlled diabetes have

many of the long-term complications seen in people; well-controlled diabetic animals have fewer complications. Clinical epidemiological studies find an increased incidence of complications in people with worse diabetic control. Short-term studies show that certain complications improve or stabilize with better control. There is no doubt that pregnancy in women with diabetes is more likely to be successful if the blood sugar is well controlled.

Nevertheless, the question of whether good control retards or eliminates diabetic complications has not been fully answered. There may be risks to achieving tight control, chief among them being the higher incidence of hypoglycemia (insulin reactions). In addition, it is not at all clear what level of diabetic control will achieve what results—whether "fair" diabetic control is adequate or "excellent" is necessary—or just how those levels are defined. Currently, a large study at the U.S. National Institutes of Health, the Diabetes Control and Complications Trial, is trying to answer some of these questions over a projected eight-year period to end in approximately 1993.

Insulin delivery: new approaches

Since the 1930s preparations of insulin have been available that last for most or all of a day (the "intermediate" or "long-acting" insulins; *e.g.,* isophane [NPH], lente, ultralente, and protamine zinc insulin [PZI]). In order to approximate normal pancreatic insulin secretion more closely, however, many people now mix NPH or lente with short-acting insulins (*e.g.,* regular or semilente). The newest approach is to use a mechanical infusion device—the external insulin pump.

External pumps have been improved greatly in the past few years. They are now small, reliable, and relatively easy to use. They all have a small syringe housed in a casing, with the plunger controlled by a battery-powered motor. Insulin is delivered through a plastic tubing to a needle inserted in the abdomen. The needle and syringe are changed every two to three days. The rate of flow is adjusted by the user, controlling a continuous basal rate, which is infused between meals and overnight, and supplemental "bolus" doses for mealtimes.

There are now several methods of achieving idealized periods of insulin effect. A "split and mixed" regimen (right) calls for mixing long-acting with regular (short-acting) insulin at breakfast time, giving regular insulin at suppertime, and delaying a further long-acting injection until bedtime. This results in peak action that coincides with the prebreakfast hours.

"Split and mixed" insulin regimen

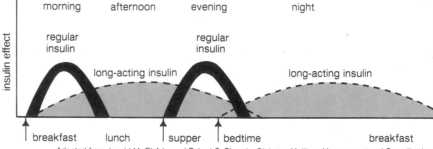

Adapted from Jerrold M. Olefsky and Robert S. Sherwin, *Diabetes Mellitus: Management and Complications* (New York: Churchill Livingstone, 1985), fig. 2-2

American Diabetes Association; photograph, Karen Richards

Blood sugar in patients with insulin-dependent diabetes is usually extremely variable from hour to hour, and monitoring the level can be tricky. Patients can now gain enhanced control over their illness by measuring their own blood glucose several times a day. With this advance they are able to achieve nearly normal glucose levels.

While the external pumps provide flexibility and convenience and can yield better diabetic control, they have limits. Pumps do not sense blood sugar, so the user must monitor blood sugar frequently every day. Use of a pump requires an understanding of insulin and diabetes, and it cannot be expected to reverse advanced complications.

Implanted insulin-infusion pumps are now being tested in human trials. They are surgically placed under the skin in the abdomen and are controlled by an external radio transmitter. Again, there is no continuous glucose sensor available, so frequent self-monitoring of blood glucose must be done. The implanted pump is only one example of exciting new research in diabetes.

Basic research advances

Basic research pursues such fundamental questions as how insulin works in the normal cell and what causes diabetes. For example, the mechanisms of normal pancreatic insulin secretion are relatively well understood, thanks to basic research in molecular biology.

The protein insulin (molecular weight 6,000 daltons) is normally synthesized in the beta cell of the pancreatic islets of Langerhans when the DNA of the insulin gene (located on chromosome 11) is "turned on." This produces a messenger RNA, which codes for the formation of a protein much larger than insulin, called preproinsulin (MW 11,500 daltons). In the rough endoplasmic reticulum of the cell, preproinsulin is broken down to proinsulin (MW 9,000 daltons), which is transported through the Golgi complex into secretory granules. The proinsulin is further divided into insulin and C-peptide, both of which are secreted into the bloodstream as the secretory granules burst through the cell membrane.

Insulin has multiple actions within the cells, affecting the metabolism of protein and fat as well as carbohydrates. Much recent research has focused on the steps that initiate these intracellular actions. Insulin itself does not enter the cell. Instead, it interacts with specific receptors at the cell surface. The receptors recognize insulin, bind it to the cell surface, and deliver its message intracellularly. The number of receptors on the surface of the cell is finely regulated. In the presence of excess circulating insulin, the number of receptors diminishes ("down regulation"), whereas when insulin is scarce, receptor numbers are increased ("up regulation").

Insulin receptors, and exactly how their effects are mediated, have been the subject of considerable basic research. Insulin binding to its receptors triggers a protein kinase reaction that initiates the intracellular insulin actions. One major effect within the cell is the recruitment of a "glucose transporter," a protein that migrates to the surface of the cell under the influence of insulin and allows the transport of glucose across the cell membrane into the cell.

Testing new treatments

Clinical studies involve the participation of patients as research subjects. Most often the object is to test a new treatment. Just as there has been strong emphasis on the necessity for treating animals humanely in research, so a great deal of attention is paid to the ethics of research on human subjects. Studies must be approved by committees charged with protecting the rights of research subjects. In the United States protocols for the study of new devices and drugs must be reviewed by the Food and Drug Administration (FDA). The studies must meet high standards for fairness, safety, and scientific significance. Finally, and most importantly, the research subject must be fully informed about the study's risks, possible benefits, alternative therapies, etc.

271

One of the more important clinical studies in recent years tested whether laser therapy is useful in reducing loss of vision from diabetic eye disease. Most people with diabetes for ten or more years show signs of "diabetic retinopathy," or changes in the tiny blood vessels that supply the eye's retina. The retinopathy consists of a weakening of the blood vessel wall that may cause it to leak slowly or burst, allowing blood to fill the vitreous portion of the eye.

The diabetic retinopathy study found that laser therapy is effective when the eye disease has advanced to the "proliferative retinopathy" stage. A follow-up study is currently testing whether laser treatment is also effective at earlier stages of disease. In order to have the advantage of laser therapy, it is therefore necessary for people with diabetes to be examined at least yearly by an ophthalmologist.

Important basic and clinical investigation has made human insulin available for routine clinical use. The basic research was the first use of recombinant DNA technology to "program" bacteria (Escherichia coli) to make insulin with the exact structure of human insulin. Then this laboratory work was extensively tested in human subjects, shown to be safe and effective, and approved by the FDA for routine clinical use. The entire process, from lab to bedside, took less than ten years. The product, human insulin, may have certain advantages for people newly treated with insulin or allergic to the usual beef/pork insulin but is not necessary for the majority of people taking the conventional preparations.

Since the discovery of insulin in 1921, people have looked for a way to administer it that does not require injections. Unfortunately, when insulin is given by mouth, stomach acid degrades it immediately. Recently insulin has been given by being sprayed into the nose. Though only at the research stage, this approach, or other new formulations that may be given by mouth, could become generally available in the future.

Another area of active research is pancreatic transplantation. Unlike kidney transplantation, which is done regularly with a high rate of success, transplantation of the pancreas has proved to be very difficult. Two broad approaches are possible: partial or total transplantation of the complete pancreas (including the body of the pancreas as well as the islet cells) or separation and transplantation of the islet cells alone. Formidable technical obstacles exist with either approach. There has been some success in transplantation of the whole pancreas, but it is apparent that more research, much of it at a basic science level, will be needed before pancreas transplantation can be considered feasible for many people with diabetes.

Taking advantage of what is available

In order to take advantage of the advances in diabetes research, patients must have a thorough understanding of diabetes, both generally and specifically. Recent studies show that most physicians have neither the time nor the expertise to provide detailed instruction on diet, foot care, glucose monitoring, and all the other necessary elements for their patients to gain a thorough understanding of diabetes. Therefore, a whole new profession has developed—that of diabetes educator.

Diabetes education programs have sprung up in many locations and with many approaches. At the Johns Hopkins Diabetes Center of the Johns Hopkins Medical Institutions in Baltimore, Md., people with diabetes and their families attend a five-day program as outpatients. They learn diabetes self-care in detail, with an emphasis on glucose monitoring, on personalized diet, and on the psychological blocks that may keep people with diabetes from doing what they know they should do. Other programs do it differently—some one-on-one, some shorter, some less personalized, but it is an integral part of good care for every person with diabetes to take advantage of the best available education program.

A psychological and emotional reaction to diabetes is normal. No one is happy to have the disease; family members and friends are often crushed to know that their loved ones have it. With thorough understanding and professional help, however, people can set reasonable goals. They can learn to live well and happily in spite of having diabetes. It has been said that the way to live a long life is to contract a chronic disease and then take proper care of it.

People with diabetes who are well-educated are able to interact well with their physicians and the health care team. Mutual trust develops. It is a help to the professional when the person can accurately report blood glucose patterns, frequency and timing of insulin reactions, early visual symptoms, or problems with foot care. The professional will probably never know as much about individuals' specific life situations as those with diabetes know themselves. On the other hand, the person with diabetes will probably never have the perspective on complications, medication options, etc., that the physician can provide. For all these reasons, an open, positive collaboration of patients and professionals is the modern way to approach diabetes care.

To a large extent, then, the improved outlook for people with diabetes is a direct result of diabetes research; a significant increase in funding over the past decade has made such research possible. Further progress will require even more research. Taking advantage of what is available now puts the person with diabetes in the best position to take advantage of future advances. With proper self-care, people with diabetes can have an outlook that is, indeed, better than ever before.

—Christopher D. Saudek, M.D.

Hyperprolactinemia: Increasingly Recognized Disorder

by James C. Sheinin, M.D.

Galactorrhea (inappropriate production of milk by the breasts) and amenorrhea (absence of menstrual periods) that persisted in women after pregnancy and childbirth were initially described in 1855. In 1932 galactorrhea and amenorrhea were reported to occur without an apparent precipitating cause. An association of galactorrhea and amenorrhea with a benign tumor of the pituitary gland (pituitary adenoma) was first observed in 1954. The fact that prolactin, the pituitary hormone that stimulates production of milk by the breasts, is present as a distinct hormone in women and men was demonstrated in 1970, but it was not until several years later that reliable laboratory methods (radioimmunoassays) for clinical assessment of prolactin levels became available. Structural details of the pituitary gland could not be evaluated directly until the computed tomography (CT; also known as computerized axial tomography, or CAT) scan became available in the late 1970s. In the relatively short time that these two techniques have been available, hyperprolactinemia (elevated levels of prolactin in the blood) has become recognized as the most common disorder of the pituitary gland.

Hyperprolactinemia in clinical disorders

Hyperprolactinemia has now been found to be significant in the pathogenesis of various clinical disorders in men as well as in women. For example, it has been found that about two-thirds of pituitary adenomas secrete prolactin (much more than any other pituitary hormone), that up to one-third of women with infertility or with secondary amenorrhea have hyperprolactinemia, and that hyperprolactinemia is found in about 5% of men with impotence.

Hyperprolactinemia may occur in patients with microadenomas (tumors of up to 10 mm [0.4 in] in diameter) or with macroadenomas (tumors greater than 10 mm in diameter) of the pituitary gland. Hyperprolactinemia also is found in patients with such other disorders as hypothyroidism, polycystic ovary syndrome, cirrhosis, and chronic renal failure. It can occur as well with compression or injury of the hypothalamus or the portal capillary system between the hypothalamus and the pituitary gland. It has been described in patients treated with various medications, in patients with physical or psychological stress, and in patients who have had breast or chest wall injury or surgery. When hyperpro-

lactinemia occurs in the absence of a demonstrable abnormality of the pituitary and the above conditions have been excluded, hyperprolactinemia is considered to be idiopathic (*i.e.,* a pathological state of unknown origin).

Hyperprolactinemia in women typically gives rise to galactorrhea and amenorrhea, as well as to anovulation (failure of the ovary to produce eggs) and infertility. What is less well known is that some women, especially those with only modestly elevated prolactin levels, may menstruate, though they rarely have regular (28-day cycle) menstrual periods, and they may even ovulate and become pregnant without treatment.

Both women and men with hyperprolactinemia may have decreased libido (sexual drive), and men may have impotence and infertility as well. Since men do not have other overt manifestations of hyperprolactinemia comparable to galactorrhea and amenorrhea, some men have been inappropriately diagnosed and treated as having psychogenic sexual dysfunction when indeed they have had hyperprolactinemia. In addition, macroadenomas may cause other symptoms by compression or invasion of adjacent tissues, including those related to compromise of normal pituitary function, headaches, and visual field defects.

Osteoporosis and emotional status

Concern has been raised that women with hyperprolactinemia who, like women following menopause, are amenorrheic and estrogen deficient may be at increased risk of developing decreased bone density and subsequent osteoporosis. Available data regarding the effects of hyperprolactinemia on bone density and on the response of bone density to restoration of normal prolactin levels are inconclusive. This may relate in part to use of different sites and different techniques for measurement of bone density. Further, as in normal women, significant variation in bone density between individual patients with hyperprolactinemia has been described.

Studies of the density of a forearm bone using the technique of single photon absorptiometry (a technique that has been available for about 25 years but is limited to bone mass measurement in the peripheral skeleton) have found a decrease in bone density in women and men with hyperprolactinemia and an increase in bone density following normalization of prolactin levels. However, vertebral bone density, which is more likely to be affected after menopause, is felt to be a more sensitive and specific index of the effects of hyperprolactinemia on bone density.

A recent study of vertebral bone density in hyperprolactinemic women using the recently available method of quantitative CT scans, which enable direct measurement of the spongy bone in the center of the spinal column, showed that although their mean (average) bone density was 10% below that of matched normal women, the bone density of all women with hyperprolactinemia was within the normal range. Moreover, their rate of loss of bone density was similar to that of normal women. Another study of vertebral bone density using the same technique found that bone density in hyperprolactinemic women was 23% below that of normal women but that normalization of prolactin was not accompanied by a significant increase in bone density.

In other work, a small group of women with hyperprolactinemia, when evaluated psychologically by means of self-rating scales, were found to be more emotionally distressed and hostile than women with normal prolactin levels. A follow-up study found that their psychological distress diminished and their sense of well-being increased as their prolactin levels fell to or near normal during treatment with the drug bromocriptine. However, the long-term effects of elevated prolactin levels on both bone density and psychological status and the implications for treatment of patients with hyperprolactinemia remain to be established.

Pathogenesis and natural history

Understanding the pathogenesis, natural history, and response to treatment of disorders associated with hyperprolactinemia is essential for formulating optimal management of the patient. Perspectives on the natural history and response to treatment of disorders associated with hyperprolactinemia have been limited owing to the relatively short time that prolactin assays and CT scans have been available. Now, however, important insights are beginning to emerge.

It has been shown that dopamine, a catecholamine (a biochemical transmitter of nerve impulses) synthesized in the hypothalamus and transported to the prolactin-secreting cells in the pituitary gland by the portal capillary system, is the primary inhibitor of prolactin secretion. There is increasing evidence that hyperprolactinemia may be due either to an abnormality of hypothalamic dopamine secretion or to resistance of the prolactin-secreting cells to the inhibitory action of dopamine. Additional evidence for an extrapituitary cause of hyperprolactinemia has been reported. In some patients with hyperprolactinemia, then, the pituitary gland may be the victim rather than the culprit. Accordingly, providing additional dopamine or a dopamine-like drug to inhibit prolactin secretion may be a more appropriate approach to treatment than surgery or irradiation of the pituitary gland.

In a recent study of 41 patients with idiopathic hyperprolactinemia who were followed clinically but not treated, it was found that 83% remained stable, spontaneously improved, or underwent spontaneous remission. When they were reevaluated after five and a half years, their prolactin levels had fallen significantly, and more than one-third had normal prolactin levels. The normal level of prolactin is up to about 20 ng/ml (nannograms per milliliter). An earlier study found that none of 25 patients with idiopathic hyperprolactinemia, microadenomas, or macroadenomas, when they were reevaluated after five years or more, had worsened clinically, and their mean prolactin level at reevaluation was significantly decreased. Further, menstruation resumed, ovulation was documented, and pregnancies occurred without treatment in some patients in both reports. Accordingly, the efficacy and risks of any therapeutic intervention must be assessed with the perspective that most patients with hyperprolactinemia appear to remain stable or improve spontaneously without treatment.

On the other hand, some patients have been described whose clinical course evolved from idiopathic hyperprolactinemia to microadenoma and subsequently to macroadenoma. A macroadenoma may compress the normal pituitary gland and thereby compromise normal pituitary function, and it may grow outside the confines of the bony pocket at the base of the skull in which the pituitary is located (sella turcica) and compress or invade surrounding tissues. In general, there has been a correlation between the size of the adenoma and the degree of hyperprolactinemia.

Prolactinomas (prolactin-secreting pituitary adenomas) in men tend to be larger and associated with higher levels of prolactin than those in women. This was thought to be because of the absence of such apparent symptoms as galactorrhea and amenorrhea, with resultant delay in diagnosis. However, a recent report suggests that there may be a difference in the biologic behavior of prolactinomas in men; i.e., these tumors may be rapidly growing ones in men more frequently than in women.

Options for treatment

Evaluation of the success of any treatment involves comparing the results of the treatment with the ultimate goal of permanent cure of the disorder without production of any untoward effects. For patients with hyperprolactinemia, whether idiopathic or associated with a microadenoma or macroadenoma, the desired outcomes of treatment include permanent restoration of the prolactin level to normal, permanent removal or destruction of the tumor if present, and permanent relief of all symptoms related to hyperprolactinemia and to compression or invasion by the tumor. Unfortunately, no treatment now available consistently fulfills these requirements.

Whenever there are several options for treatment of a disorder, each has advantages and limitations. No single treatment is optimal for all patients, and the approach to treatment should be individualized. When several options are appropriate, the patient should participate in the decision-making process. In persons with hyperprolactinemia, whether idiopathic or associated with a microadenoma or a macroadenoma, the four options for treatment are surgery, irradiation, drug treatment, and no treatment but frequent observation.

Surgery. Until several years ago, surgical removal through the sphenoid sinus (a cavity below the sella turcica) using an operating microscope was considered to be the treatment of choice for all patients with prolactinomas. Through the use of this surgical procedure (transsphenoidal microsurgical hypophysectomy), initial cure rates of over 80% in patients with microadenomas and over 30% in patients with macroadenomas commonly were reported. The best results were found in microadenoma patients whose prolactin levels were less than 100 ng/ml.

However, long-term follow-up studies of patients who had transsphenoidal hypophysectomy have shown a significant incidence of recurrence of hyperprolactinemia in patients with apparent initial surgical cures. One study found recurrent hyperprolactinemia after 4 years in 50% of the patients with microadenomas and after 2½ years in 80% of the patients with macroadenomas.

Recurrence rates in other studies have been less dramatic but may further increase with time. A prolactin level of ten nannograms per milliliter or more in the immediate postoperative period may be predictive of subsequent recurrence of hyperprolactinemia. In the hands of experienced neurosurgical and endocrine teams, surgical mortality is rare, but complications including cerebrospinal fluid leak, nasal septal perforation, sinusitis, and pituitary dysfunction have been noted.

Radiation treatment. Pituitary irradiation by various techniques has been utilized, though infrequently, in treatment of patients with hyperprolactinemia. Because response to conventional irradiation as a primary treatment has been slow and incomplete, it usually has been used as a secondary treatment for patients with large and invasive macroadenomas that were incompletely removed surgically. Heavy particle, or proton beam, irradiation, available at only a few medical centers, has been highly effective but only in patients with prolactin levels below 100 ng/ml. As yet, recurrence rates are unknown. Complications of various techniques of irradiation that have been reported include pituitary dysfunction as well as cranial nerve and brain injury and necrosis (cell death) and malignant degeneration of the brain. A recent report found that over half of the patients with pituitary tumors who were treated with conventional supervoltage radiation had one or more deficiencies in pituitary function within five years of treatment. Deficiencies were even more frequent when radiation was preceded by surgery. The incidence of such complications may increase with time.

Drug treatment. Bromocriptine, a semisynthetic ergot alkaloid that has been available for clinical use since the mid-1970s, is a specific dopamine agonist that, like the naturally occurring catecholamine dopamine, has the affinity for and the ability to stimulate dopamine receptors on prolactin-secreting pituitary cells. Bromocriptine thereby can be considered to be a pharmacological supplement or replacement for dopamine that, like the naturally occurring substance, inhibits prolactin secretion.

Numerous reports have documented the remarkable efficacy of bromocriptine in treating patients with hyperprolactinemia. Treatment with bromocriptine reduced prolactin to normal or near normal levels, suppressed galactorrhea, and restored normal menstruation, ovulation, fertility, sexual function, and libido typically in over 80%, and in some studies in 100%, of the patients with hyperprolactinemia. Success rates in patients with macroadenomas were somewhat less impressive but still clearly exceeded those of surgery. In addition, unexpectedly, bromocriptine was found to cause dramatic regression in size of macroadenomas as well as to relieve symptoms related to compression of the normal pituitary gland and adjacent tissues by the tumor, without the risk of compromise of normal pituitary function. Reduction in tumor size was thought to result from reversible reduction in size of individual tumor cells.

Hyperprolactinemia and tumor size and their associated symptoms regularly have responded to moderate, well-tolerated dosages of bromocriptine. Side effects of bromocriptine, including nausea, dizziness, fatigue, headaches, nasal congestion, abdominal cramps, and constipation, have been minimized by initiating therapy with a low dosage taken at bedtime, increasing the dosage gradually, and taking the drug with meals.

However, further reports indicated that after dramatic responses to bromocriptine, most patients experienced prompt recurrence of hyperprolactinemia and increase in tumor size following withdrawal of the drug therapy; thus, long-term therapy was required for the maintenance of the therapeutic response. As a result, many patients now have taken bromocriptine for more than five years and without untoward effects. The dosage required for maintenance of the therapeutic response often can be reduced after the prolactin level becomes normal.

Several recent studies provide important perspectives on the effects of bromocriptine therapy. A prospective multicenter study of bromocriptine as the primary therapy for macroadenomas found that two-thirds of the patients had normal prolactin levels and reduction of tumor size of about 50% or more and that visual defects improved in 40% of the patients. However, tumor reexpansion occurred in three of four patients in whom bromocriptine was discontinued after one year. Another recent study evaluated the response of patients with macroadenomas who received a dopamine agonist, usually bromocriptine, for 3½ years or more at higher than usual dosages. It was found that prolactin levels returned to normal during treatment but hyperprolactinemia recurred in 93% of the patients after treatment was discontinued. Conversely, tumor size decreased in two-thirds of the patients during treatment and did not change in 86% after treatment was discontinued. In addition, another recent study reported restitution of deficiencies of three pituitary hormones in patients with macroadenomas after treatment with bromocriptine for six months.

In contrast to the findings in patients with macroadenomas, a recent study of patients with microadenomas found that 11% who were treated for one year and 22% who were treated for two years with bromocriptine had normal prolactin levels and were in clinical remission after discontinuing treatment. This and many other studies have found that mean prolactin levels, although still elevated following withdrawal of bromocriptine, were significantly lower than before treatment.

Several recent pathological studies of prolactinomas removed after preoperative treatment with bromocriptine for only two weeks showed not only the anticipated reversible marked reduction in tumor cell size and volume but irreversible tumor cell degeneration and necrosis and an increase in fibrous tissue as well. The increase in fibrous tissue correlated with the duration of treatment with bromocriptine. These observations provide important evidence for additional effects of bromocriptine that could explain the persistent decreases in prolactin levels and tumor size that have been observed following withdrawal of treatment.

Several dopamine agonists other than bromocriptine have been used in several European countries in the treatment of patients with hyperprolactinemia, but those drugs remain unavailable for clinical use in the United States. None appears to offer a clear advantage over bromocriptine. However, any one dopamine agonist may be more effective or better tolerated than another in individual cases.

Pregnancy and lactation

Special considerations in the approach to pregnancy in women with hyperprolactinemia recently were reviewed. Treatment with bromocriptine regularly restored menstruation, ovulation, and fertility. Although there was no evidence of untoward effects of bromocriptine on the pregnancy, the fetus, or the mother, minimal exposure to the drug was advised. This can be accomplished by the use of mechanical contraception until regular menstruation and ovulation have been reestablished and by cessation of bromocriptine several days after a missed menstrual period when conception has been attempted.

Since progressive increase in prolactin-secreting cell size and number and in prolactin levels during pregnancy occurs in normal women, there is concern about tumor enlargement causing symptoms, particularly headaches and visual field defects, during pregnancy in women with hyperprolactinemia. The incidence of such symptomatic tumor enlargement in women with microadenomas was found to be less than 2%, but it exceeded 15% in women with macroadenomas. Symptomatic tumor enlargement initially was treated with emergency surgery, corticosteroids, or watchful expectancy, but now bromocriptine has become the treatment of choice. Because of the high incidence of symptomatic tumor enlargement in women with macroadenomas, surgery to reduce tumor size has been recommended by some before treatment with bromocriptine is given to restore fertility.

The effects of breast-feeding on the growth of prolactinomas have not been established, but they appear to be less than the effects of pregnancy. It is clear that women with hyperprolactinemia should be observed closely during pregnancy and lactation.

Approach to treatment

Unequivocal indications for treatment of patients with hyperprolactinemia include headaches, visual field defects, or compromise of normal pituitary function due to compression or invasion by a macroadenoma; desire for temporary or permanent restoration of menstruation, ovulation, or fertility in women; and desire for temporary or permanent restoration of sexual function or fertility in men. Whether galactorrhea, diminished libido, altered psychological status, or decreased bone density require treatment remains to be established, although elective treatment may be considered on the basis of evaluation of psychological status or vertebral bone density in the individual patient.

When treatment is indicated or is being considered electively, bromocriptine is increasingly becoming the treatment of choice. Among the options for treatment, only bromocriptine combines remarkable efficacy with no risk of long-term side effects. Maintenance of normal prolactin levels and maintenance of decreased tumor size occasionally require long-term therapy. However, bromocriptine is remarkably well tolerated, and the dosage required for maintenance is often less than that required for initiation of the therapeutic response.

It is now evident that most patients with hyperprolactinemia who are not treated remain stable or show spontaneous remission. Accordingly, in the absence of clear indications for treatment, no treatment with frequent observation may well be the most prudent approach to management of patients with this increasingly recognized endocrine disorder.

Drug Abuse

In our time, each of us confronts one of the most devastating weapons in the history of mankind: the use of illegal drugs. Simply put, marijuana, cocaine, heroin and other drugs lead to severe illness, crippling addiction, and often premature death.

Individual lives are not the only ones affected when drug use enters the home. Each time drugs cross the threshold we all lose, especially when we must fight the crime associated with use, the horror of addiction, or tragic fatalities.

These are the awful facts about drugs. The best response is to "Just Say No."

—Otis R. Bowen
Secretary, U.S. Department of
Health and Human Services, 1987

The epidemic of illicit drug use in the United States and most Western European nations continues unabated, with several frightening new trends developing that are finally causing prevention and early drug-abuse education to become worldwide priorities. For the first time, the once popular belief that illegal drugs can be used "recreationally" is being buried beneath mounting data and events to the contrary.

In the U.S. the threat to the economy and social fabric posed by illicit drugs is now accepted as a reality, and public health officials at the highest level are targeting drug abuse as one of the nation's most pressing problems. Not surprisingly, several federal government studies are linking increasing illegal drug use to increasing crime. Illegal drug profits are reported to be the number one source of income for all organized crime, generating as much as $110 billion a year.

Cocaine: the major threat

Cocaine use remains the major drug threat in the United States. Furthermore, according to a December 1986 report by the National Institute on Drug Abuse (NIDA), the most deleterious patterns of use of heroin, alcohol, sedatives, and marijuana are also cocaine-related. These drugs, the NIDA reports, are frequently used as modes of self-treatment for the cycle of euphoria and depression that results from sustained cocaine use. Furthermore, the increased purity and decreased price of cocaine in the U.S. have led to an increase in intravenous (IV) use, especially among methadone patients. This aspect of cocaine use, along with other IV drug abuse, has been an important factor in the spread of AIDS (acquired immune deficiency syndrome) into the heterosexual community, adding significantly to the magnitude of the health emergency caused by this disease.

Cocaine supplies in the United States were up from 19 metric tons in 1976 to 50–75 metric tons in 1986. During the same time period, the price of the drug dropped from $125 per gram to less than $75. The problem of cocaine is so widespread that in 1986, for the first time in 25 years, the U.S. Drug Enforcement Agency (DEA) reported that it considered cocaine to be a greater menace than heroin. According to DEA statistics, large supplies of cocaine can be found virtually everywhere in the U.S. In Minneapolis, Minn., for example, police seizures of the drug increased by 200% in one six-month period in 1986.

One positive result of increased public awareness of the dangers of drugs is the growing grass-roots antidrug movement that has drawn support from scientific studies of the highly addictive effects of several new drugs and powerful forms of drugs—most notably "crack," a highly potent smokable form of cocaine—that have entered the marketplace in the past two years. In fact, crack, more than any other drug, is responsible for changing U.S. priorities on drug abuse. The public demand for education and prevention programs is linked directly to the emergence of this drug on the national scene.

The crack epidemic

Crack is essentially a new drug in the U.S. The national cocaine hot line (800-COCAINE) had no reports of crack use through 1985. Few treatment specialists had even heard about the drug. By mid-May 1986, however, 33% of the hot-line callers reported using crack. By the end of the year, there were reports of significant crack use in Minneapolis; Boston; Phoenix, Ariz.; San Diego, Calif.; New York City; Washington, D.C.; St. Louis, Mo.; Miami, Fla.; New Orleans, La.; Seattle, Wash.; and Detroit. The vast majority of hot-line callers (81%) said they had switched from occasional intranasal cocaine use to smoking crack. Data on crack indicate that it is unlike other drugs in that age, ethnic background, and personal life-style are not factors in the onset of crack use. Rather, the major factors seem to be ease of access and prior cocaine use. Crack is also unlike other drugs in that, because of its route of administration, it seems to lead to almost immediate addiction. More than 80% of those using it reported an overwhelming compulsion to use the drug again as soon as the effect had worn off; 72% reported the onset of compulsive use and disruptive effects on their home and business lives within two months of first use. In the long run, however, the most significant effect of the crack epidemic may be a beneficial one: it has put to rest forever the question of whether cocaine—in any form—is physically addictive along with the notion that it can actually be used safely by anyone.

Cocaine and pregnancy: recent findings

Another major development in the epidemic of cocaine abuse is the epidemic of cocaine infants—the children of women who used the drug during pregnancy. While it is well known that babies born to heroin addicts may experience agonizing withdrawal symptoms, only recently has the same syndrome been observed in

Children at a South Bronx (New York) public school (above) listen attentively to a story with a moral—the perils of crack. Each page from "It's O.K. to Say No to Drugs," a coloring book (right) produced by the Major League Baseball Players Association, carries a straightforward message from a pro.

(Left) Gary Guisinger/The New York Times; (right) Susan Amerikaner, *The Pros Say It's O.K. to Say No to Drugs!*—an RGA creation (Los Angeles: RGA Publishing Group, 1986), illustration, Frank C. Smith

the offspring of women who used cocaine. Recent evidence indicates that cocaine-addicted babies often suffer a prolonged two- to three-week withdrawal syndrome. Studies also indicate that cocaine babies are three times more likely to die of sudden infant death syndrome (SIDS) than are babies born to heroin addicts. Those who survive are likely to suffer from visual impairments and develop mental retardation and strokelike symptoms. Researchers have linked the conditions caused by cocaine use during pregnancy to the rise in maternal blood pressure and the concomitant constriction of fetal blood vessels, depriving the developing fetus of vital blood flow. Current studies indicate that about 60% of the babies born to cocaine users suffer from some sort of congenital malformation or developmental defect.

Teen drug use: how widespread?

While overall drug abuse has declined slightly in the U.S. (a trend that began in the early 1980s), teen drug abuse remains a major concern. By 1986 more than half of all high school seniors admitted to using illicit drugs. Of this group, 4% said they had already tried crack, despite the publicity surrounding its dangers. Overall illicit use of drugs by U.S. adolescents continues to be extremely high in comparison with teen drug abuse in other industrialized countries.

An NIDA-sponsored study of 130 high schools, conducted by the University of Michigan's Institute for Social Research, revealed that in spite of ongoing antidrug programs in many schools, the percentage of seniors indicating that they had had any experience with drugs had fallen only from 61% in 1985 to 58% in 1986. Current abuse of all drugs—including marijuana, cocaine, phencyclidine (PCP, or "angel dust"),

and prescription drugs—has dropped somewhat more. Most of the decline in use was reported by those who had regularly used marijuana, amphetamines, or PCP, a trend that can be linked to an overall drop in the availability and increase in price of these substances. While the proportion of high school seniors using marijuana declined only 3% between 1985 and 1986, from 26 to 23%, the long-term decline from a rate of 37% reported in 1978 is significant.

Cocaine use among students, however, has remained at peak levels rather than following a downward trend. Cocaine has replaced amphetamines as the second most frequently used drug by adolescents—marijuana is the most frequently used—a trend that is directly connected to increased availability and reduced price. The acceptance and use of crack among adolescents, as well as overall cocaine use by this age group, is significant because it shows that teens are evidently ignoring the overwhelming evidence of the addictive and toxic nature of this drug. In one survey, while the majority of adolescents said they recognized that there could be great risk in regular use of cocaine, only one-third thought that "experimenting" with cocaine could endanger the user. Although only one senior in 25 had tried crack, among previous cocaine users the figure was one in three.

The increased use of cocaine among young people has also led to an increase in those who are dependent on the drug. More than 25,000 seniors in the University of Michigan survey said they used cocaine and felt unable to stop—double the number who had reported the same problem just three years earlier. In addition, many teenage cocaine abusers do not show up in the national drug-abuse statistics—some are in residential treatment programs, some have dropped

278

out of school, and a number have fallen victim to accidents or suicide. Cocaine was found in the bodies of several teenage suicide victims in New Jersey and the Midwestern states in the past year.

Ecstasy and other designer drugs

The "designer drug" industry in the U.S. is now a billion-dollar business and is still growing. Designer drugs are usually analogues—that is, similar chemical compounds slightly altered in molecular structure—of controlled substances, but they are frequently marketed on the street as entirely new drugs. They are not a new phenomenon but trace their roots back to the entreprenurial chemists of the 1960s who created LSD and other synthetic substances of abuse. Today the main designer drugs appearing in cities around the U.S. are related either to opiates such as heroin, to narcotic analgesics (painkillers) or hypnotics such as demerol or fentanyl, or to stimulants and hallucinogenic drugs such as PCP.

The designer drug that has received the most publicity over the past few years is "Ecstasy" (MDMA; 3,4-methylenedioxymethamphetamine), which, along with its structurally similar relatives MMDA and MDA, is a particularly popular recreational drug, especially among college students. Its effects are reported to be an intensely euphoric feeling of well-being, comfort, and confidence. Some proponents of the drug believe it may have a legitimate clinical use as an adjunct to psychotherapy. Although it is an illegal drug, it is still widely available.

While MDMA has been scientifically studied, its safety is doubtful, and its clinical value has never been established. A study published in 1987 in the *Journal of the American Medical Association* linked Ecstasy to five deaths in the Dallas, Texas, area. The drug's popularity has followed the same pattern as that of cocaine and marijuana when they first appeared on the scene, including widespread reports of its use by celebrities and repeated assertions of its safety, absolutely without scientific basis.

Clearly, however, drugs such as MDMA have an extremely strong potential for abuse—users repeatedly self-administer them to gain a certain effect. While their tolerance levels are unknown, drugs that stimulate their own repeated use are more likely than others to produce addiction through continual, compulsive use despite adverse consequences. At present, researchers know nothing of the long-term effects of this drug on the brain or other body systems. In addition, there are reports of all sorts of substances being marketed as Ecstasy that are in reality LSD, PCP, or other stimulants. Further complicating the situation is the fact that many people use MDA in combination with alcohol or other drugs, but scientists know little about the potentially dangerous effects of such combinations, including how to treat them.

Other designer drugs are clearly more dangerous than Ecstasy. One such drug, MPPP (1-methyl-4-phenylprionoxypiperidine), is an analogue of a relatively safe, short-acting narcotic analgesic known as fentanyl that is widely used to produce insensitivity to pain during surgery. Fentanyl also has several legally prescribed and manufactured analogues. Reproduced in a slightly different form as MPPP, it is now widely available on the West Coast; an estimated 20% of all the 200,000 heroin addicts in California are using MPPP. Fentanyl itself is 100 times more powerful than morphine; it has a rapid onset and a highly addictive nature. MPPP is reported to be almost 2,000 times more powerful than morphine; thus, even small doses can be very toxic. To date, the drug has been linked

Drug abuse among U.S. high school seniors, 1975–86

class of	'75	'76	'77	'78	'79	'80	'81	'82	'83	'84	'85	'86
marijuana, hashish	47	53	58	59	60	60	60	59	57	55	54	51
inhalants*	na	na	na	na	18	17	17	18	18	18	18	20
amyl and butyl nitrites	na	na	na	na	11	11	10	10	8	8	8	9
hallucinogens*	na	na	na	na	18	16	15	14	14	12	12	12
LSD	11	11	10	10	10	9	10	10	9	8	8	7
PCP	na	na	na	na	13	10	8	6	6	5	5	5
cocaine	9	10	11	13	15	16	17	16	16	16	17	17
heroin	2	2	2	2	1	1	1	1	1	1	1	1
other opiates	9	10	10	10	10	10	10	10	9	10	10	9
stimulants†	na	na	na	na	na	na	na	28	27	28	26	23
sedatives	18	18	17	16	15	15	16	15	14	13	12	10
barbiturates	17	16	16	14	12	11	11	10	10	10	9	8
methaqualone	8	8	9	8	8	10	11	11	10	8	7	5
tranquilizers	17	17	18	17	16	15	15	14	13	12	12	11
alcohol	90	92	93	93	93	93	93	93	93	93	92	91
cigarettes	74	75	76	75	74	71	71	70	71	70	69	68

*adjusted for underreporting   †adjusted for overreporting   na = data not available

Source: National Institute on Drug Abuse, Monitoring the Future study, 1986

The table at left shows the percentages of U.S. high school seniors from the classes of 1975 through 1986 who have ever used (i.e., at least once) various common drugs of abuse; figures are based on a nationwide survey conducted by the University of Michigan Institute for Social Research.

In a park in the Harlem neighborhood of New York City, three antidrug crusaders—the Rev. Wendell Foster, a Bronx city councilman, actor-director Ossie Davis, and social activist Dick Gregory (left to right)—spread the alarm about crack.

to more than 100 deaths on the West Coast. The amount of the drug needed to supply the entire U.S. for six months could be made in a single lab in just one week and could be stored in a small carton.

A step ahead of the law?

Because of the low-overhead, high-demand nature of the designer drug industry, its profit potential attracts many so-called entrepreneurs. A single batch of PCP, for example, can be made for around $500 and sold on the street for $300,000. The attraction of this burgeoning industry is enhanced by the fact that there are few legal pitfalls in this aspect of the drug market. In the U.S. most potentially dangerous legal drugs are classified according to their medical value and use. For example, LSD and PCP, which have no medical value, are Schedule I drugs, the most restricted federal classification, while meperidine (Demerol), fentanyl, and morphine, which are addictive but have a clear medical use, are dispensed on Schedule II. Designer drugs, however, which do not match the molecular structure of their legitimate "scheduled" analogues, were until recently subject to no legal restrictions. If one such drug became restricted, as Ecstasy did, the streetwise chemist simply made a minor alteration in the molecular structure of the drug and sold it on the street as something else. In October 1986 a federal law was passed making all analogues of illegal drugs themselves illegal—even those that have yet to be invented. However, the new law has not been tested in the courts and is not being enforced. The drug designers know that unlike the habitual cocaine or marijuana user, the designer drug customer is at once less sophisticated and more willing to be a "laboratory animal" for their products.

This situation has had deadly consequences. A recent "outbreak" of cases of evident Parkinson's disease in northern California was traced to a designer drug dealer who had altered a fentanyl analogue to produce a drug called MPTP, which was then sold as MPPP. Ironically, MPTP is a legal substance used in the production of other chemicals, so despite the fact that more than 400 people may have been exposed to MPTP in California, there was no basis for prosecution of the dealers.

Interestingly, there is no common "user profile" for designer drugs, although there have been recent reports of use among young drug abusers. In fact, detection is especially difficult because these drugs are frequently snorted rather than injected. At the same time, the side effects, such as Parkinsonian tremors, may appear after drug use has ceased; clinical analysis of the user's blood or urine yields no evidence of drugs, thus making diagnosis and treatment very difficult.

Other illicit drugs—update

Although the newspaper headlines have been captured by crack and the controversy over drug testing, the traditionally popular drugs—such as marijuana, heroin, amphetamines, and hallucinogenic drugs—are still in high demand. The trend, however, is toward higher prices and reduced supplies.

Marijuana. Treatment centers in the U.S. are reporting an increase in requests for services by marijuana smokers. Users complain of social dysfunction, family conflict, depression, and motivation and memory problems. At the same time, law-enforcement agents report a drop in supply with a corresponding increase in price. Marijuana, once the drug of choice for most

280

"recreational" users in the U.S., has been disappearing from the street scene for several reasons: dealers make more money selling cocaine, and the demand for it is greater; less marijuana is getting across U.S. borders; and the price of available marijuana varies widely, with no relation to quality.

One continuing trend in the U.S. is the increased use of a locally grown, usually powerful marijuana known as sensimilla. This drug is frequently ten times as powerful as imported marijuana with a high THC (tetrahydrocannabinol) content. In many places—among them Texas, New Jersey, Chicago, Philadelphia, and all along the West Coast—the new, exotic strains of marijuana constitute upwards of 50% of the drug sold. The price has increased from $50 an ounce to $150–$200 an ounce. Marijuana still represents a problem for both drug-abuse treatment specialists and law-enforcement agents. A sizable proportion of marijuana users are young—often under age 18 and frequently younger.

Heroin. Heroin poses an increased health threat as a result of the availability of increasingly powerful forms of the drug. One of these is "black tar," a dark, gummy type of heroin also known as "tootsie roll," which first appeared in the U.S. in the southwestern states and has since spread throughout the country. While Mexican or Asian forms of heroin have a purity level of 2–5%, black tar has been reported between 60 and 85% pure. This has led to a direct increase in emergency room admissions and drug overdoses in heroin users, not to mention an increased demand for treatment of addiction. Heroin is also frequently injected in combination with cocaine, a technique known as "speedballing." This practice, which was responsible for the death of actor John Belushi, is increasing with the spread of crack.

Treatment trends

The number of people seeking treatment also continues to skyrocket, owing largely to the number of cocaine users who have become addicts. Fewer facilities are available for most of the drug-using population, however. Federal- and state-sponsored programs are directed mainly at heroin treatment. As a result, many new private programs have been opened to meet the demand generated by cocaine and marijuana users. The question of who should bear the economic burden of the cost of treatment has become a focal point for public debate. Over the past year both the U.S. Senate and the House of Representatives have held hearings on drug-education and drug-treatment programs without any resolution of the financial issues. The ability to properly treat cocaine and other drug-abuse victims has improved, though, for both outpatients and inpatients.

Outpatient. Outpatient treatment for both drugs and alcohol is successful only when complete abstinence is a basic requirement. This goal can be achieved only by means of a regular urine-testing program that is linked to the development of a more successful drug-free life-style. Model programs usually last from six months to a year and consist of four phases: ceasing all drug use (including alcohol), entering counseling to prevent relapse, changing life-style, and forming an ongoing contact with a support group such as Narcotics Anonymous or Alcoholics Anonymous. Through these support groups, addicts can meet with and receive encouragement from peers. The most successful outpatient programs that follow this basic model also incorporate some sort of education to deal with the so-called abstinence violation effect, the feelings of remorse and failure that arise if the addict "slips" in his or her effort to achieve total abstinence.

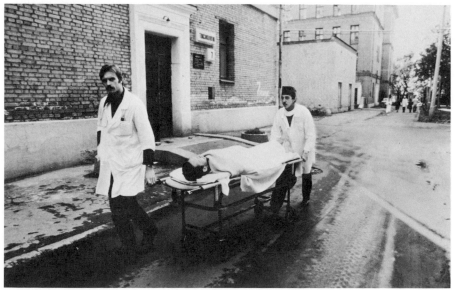

The Soviet government, which only recently took strong measures against alcoholism, has now openly admitted a growing problem with narcotics addiction. (Left) A victim of a drug overdose is rushed to a Moscow drug clinic.

Peter Turnley—Black Star

Inpatient. Inpatient treatment of drug abuse has been helped by the success of several pharmacological treatments designed to overcome the main early barriers to abstinence—the powerful cravings that drive users to compulsive use. These cravings are also a barrier to complete abstinence. Among the drugs now successfully employed in treatment of drug addiction are bromocriptine, clonidine, and naltrexone.

Bromocriptine has been shown to help users get through the most difficult period of treatment, the first few weeks, by blocking the cravings for cocaine that they experience when they abruptly stop using the drug. This allows the recovering addicts to return to work or, when necessary, to return to the environment that enabled their cocaine use. Although bromocriptine has been used only in small studies thus far, it offers great promise and hope for cocaine addicts.

Clonidine is a drug that fools the brain into thinking it is not in withdrawal from opiates (such as heroin) when in reality it is. Using this drug, a person who is addicted to heroin or methadone can be habit-free in two weeks. Unlike methadone, clonidine is not a substitute for heroin but actually blocks the withdrawal signals the brain sends out to the body when heroin or another opiate is taken away. It has been proved to be an effective tool in overcoming the classic "cold turkey" treatment for heroin addiction.

Naltrexone follows clonidine in the treatment process and is also used to defeat the cravings that accompany detoxification. Naltrexone actually blocks the effect of heroin and other opiates completely. A heroin addict taking this drug could ingest any amount of heroin without experiencing any of its effects. Naltrexone can be taken on a maintenance basis to prevent relapse, much as lithium is given to a person who suffers from manic-depressive illness. There have been some trials of tricyclic antidepressant drugs in self-help programs and residential communities as an adjunct treatment for the craving caused by cocaine cessation, but these studies have been inconclusive, and antidepressant treatment is still controversial.

Drugs in the workplace

In the U.S. the debate over how drug abuse should be stemmed has polarized society. On one side public health and safety officials—usually with the consent of private business and government—urge virtually any measure that will prevent the further spread of drugs, while civil libertarians struggle to find an answer that is consistent with the constitutional principles of protection from undue intrusion.

Workplace drug abuse has spread far beyond the glamour industries—performing arts, professional sports—into the offices of corporate America and also into factories. In the past year NIDA reported cocaine use among farm laborers and factory foremen at 10% and among craftsmen and personal service workers

at 17%. A study by the 800-COCAINE hot line found that 70% of those who were currently using cocaine had gone to work under the influence of drugs. Of that group, 21% said it was a frequent occurrence; 65% of those in the study reported using drugs on the job; 38% said they bought drugs from a co-worker; and 31% did so on the company premises.

Drug abuse has several effects on work performance. First, it leads to chronic absenteeism as a result of hangovers, respiratory infections, decline in immune function, and various minor illnesses. However, the effect of drug abuse does not end with lost productivity due to time lost from work; it also includes losses due to crime in the workplace. Eight percent of the respondents to the hot-line survey said they had stolen from their employers to support their drug use. Finally, drug use is strongly related to workplace accidents and injuries. One study revealed that 7% of drug users had had an on-the-job accident while under the influence of drugs. Of the respondents in this survey, 15% said they had been fired from at least one previous job because of their drug use.

Who should be tested?

Reduction of demand has been adopted as the front-line prevention strategy among drug-enforcement officials and treatment specialists in the U.S., but private industry, which may be losing upwards of $100 billion each year as a result of employee drug abuse, has had to take a stronger approach. Following the lead of the federal government, companies of all sizes are exploring methods of preventing drug abuse from destroying the health of their workers and the profits of their companies. Although most workplace-based drug programs have elements of education and provide for rehabilitation through either an employee assistance program or a health insurance mechanism, drug testing has become the focal point of public attention. Testing is rapidly becoming the norm in many industries, even where public safety is not an issue. The programs vary widely and may include any or all of the following: preemployment drug screening, random drug testing, testing based upon reasonable suspicion of drug use (*e.g.,* following an accident), and testing of all employees in positions affecting public safety.

Two years ago preemployment drug testing was carried out in about 25% of all Fortune 500 companies. In 1987 that number had nearly doubled. Some sources predict that within ten years 90% of all working people in the U.S. will face a drug test either on the job or before they are hired. This subject has entered the public spotlight so rapidly that very few clear-cut laws exist, and standard practices in drug testing vary widely. So new is the idea that in a 1982 NIDA booklet on drug abuse, the term drug test was not even mentioned. At that time fewer than 5% of all Fortune 500 companies had any form of testing. Now the issue is shaping up as one of the major labor-management questions of the next decade.

The public has responded to the concept of drug testing with ambivalence. Various polls show that more than 80% of those questioned favor some form of drug testing—but not necessarily for themselves. This ambivalence continues despite the fact that drug tests performed after several major recent transportation accidents revealed drugs in the blood and urine of crew members. Each time a new fatality or celebrity scandal is linked to drug use, the public responds with shock and with a short-lived enthusiasm for drug prevention. Recently, however, there seems to have been an increase in drug-related accidents. From 1975 to 1985, 48 train accidents were linked to drug and alcohol use; they resulted in 37 deaths, 80 injuries, and $34 million in property damage.

In early 1987 the United States government announced comprehensive guidelines for drug testing intended to implement Pres. Ronald Reagan's executive order issued in the fall of 1986 and to lead the way in drug prevention. Drug testing is already a fact of life for many federal government employees, including those in all branches of the military and members of investigative agencies such as the Federal Bureau of Investigation. Not surprisingly, the federal government's initiative to extend the scope of its drug-testing program was met by strong opposition, and several lawsuits on behalf of federal workers were immediately filed to block the testing.

Are drug tests legal?

The legal status of any drug-testing program ultimately will depend on the judicial system's interpretation of the protection provided to workers under the U.S. Constitution. At present there are some 40 different cases at various stages in both federal and state courts. Many of these are so-called right of privacy suits. Other base their claims on the protection from illegal search and seizure that the Constitution guarantees each citizen.

Several issues are being debated: (1) Are all workers protected equally under the Constitution? Experts differ on the answer. (2) Does the Constitution allow a person to do whatever he or she wishes outside of the workplace? The courts have issued several rulings on this point that seem to contradict each other. (3) Does the way in which the drug-testing program is structured have an impact on its validity? Yes, say many courts. In general it is now agreed that, compared with employees of private companies, people who work for either state or federal governments actually have a greater measure of constitutional protection once a drug-testing program has been imposed. The Fourth Amendment clearly and specifically protects them against unreasonable search and seizure by the government. Several courts have held that if the employer is a government agency, local or federal, and if it has no reasonable suspicion that there is ongoing drug use, it has no right to perform random tests. In other cases, however, where reasonable suspicion could be proved, government testing programs and accompanying employee disciplinary measures were upheld.

Private employees are not protected in the same way, although they do have some protection from unreasonable search and seizure. The main difference is that a private employer has more latitude in designing a random drug-testing program. For example, if employers decide to use random testing, properly inform the employees, and follow proper procedures in the testing, the courts have held that these employers are acting within their rights.

Many people mistakenly think that the Constitution guarantees them a blanket right to privacy that pre-

Drug use in U.S. military

percentage of military personnel who said they had used drugs in the last 30 days

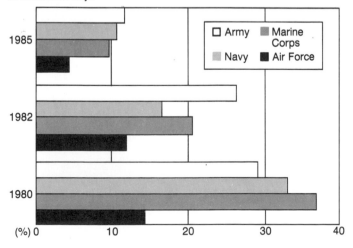

The decline in drug use among U.S. military personnel is attributed directly to the program of mandatory drug testing instituted in 1982.

(Left) Source: Research Triangle Institute;
(right) Mike Greenlar—Picture Group

vents an employer from subjecting them to drug tests. The argument is that what one does off the job is no one else's business if it does not affect work. The U.S. Supreme Court has ruled that there *is* an implied right of privacy, and it has used that decision to protect people in specific cases dealing with issues such as childbearing and marriage, but no court has yet ruled that there is a specific right of privacy that enables the individual to use illegal drugs and be free from prosecution. On this basis private employers have been given more latitude in their use of testing to detect drug use or as a preventive measure. Private employers, the courts have ruled, can set more stringent standards for their workers (*i.e.,* no smokers or no alcohol on site) than the government can set and, using proper procedures, may enforce those rules as they wish.

The Navy's example

Following President Reagan's call for a "drug-free workplace," the U.S. government in early 1987 announced detailed procedures that would cover more than two million civilian workers. Much of the government's approach is based on the success of its military programs. The U.S. military, especially the Navy, has proved that drug testing can work as a preventive measure. In early 1980 the Navy discovered that more than 48% of young enlisted sailors were using marijuana. After conducting some ten million tests, the Navy now reports a less than 10% incidence of drug abuse in the same group. The architect of the Navy's program recently stated that the sailors themselves think the pressure of drug testing is the primary, most effective measure in preventing drug abuse.

—*Mark S. Gold, M.D.*

Ear, Nose, and Throat Disorders

In the past several decades, the specialty called otolaryngology–head and neck surgery has evolved from a limited medical and surgical discipline concerned with ear, nose, and throat disorders to an expanded specialty treating the head and neck, exclusive of the eye (ophthalmology) and brain (neurology and neurosurgery). As a result of wider knowledge of head and neck disorders and the increased complexity of techniques used to treat them, the residency training requirement for board certification has been increased by the American Board of Otolaryngology from four years to five. Under the recently instituted requirements, every candidate for specialty certification must complete at least one year of residency in general surgery prior to entering a residency in otolaryngology.

General developments

Although once the most common surgical procedure in the U.S., tonsillectomy is no longer routine. It was previously a fairly common practice to operate on youngsters who suffered from recurrent tonsillitis. In some instances siblings of children with tonsil problems also underwent tonsillectomy. Today, however, stricter criteria are being used to limit the operation to those patients most certain to benefit from it. These criteria are based on the results of large-scale, long-term scientific investigations focused on identification of the diseases and conditions unquestionably helped by tonsillectomy.

Recently the results of one such study from the University of Pittsburgh (Pa.) School of Medicine documented the efficacy of tonsillectomy for the treatment of severe, recurrent tonsillitis and throat infection. A European study reported success in treating a particularly virulent type of tonsillitis, peritonsillar abscess, with unilateral tonsillectomy (removal of one tonsil). This infection can lead to a collection of pus in the tissues around a tonsil, and because of the severity of the pain and swelling, it may prevent patients from being able to swallow anything, even liquids.

Obstructive sleep apnea is another condition for which tonsillectomy has been shown to produce significant improvement. In recent years sleep has come under rigorous scientific study, with a resulting increase in the understanding of normal sleep and the disorders that interfere with it. One particularly severe sleep disorder is sleep apnea—that is, periods during sleep when breathing stops completely, as often as 100 times per night. Many individuals with obstructive sleep apnea are overweight; they tend to have excessive bulk in the tissues of the upper airway. Others have obstructions in the nose and throat that can be corrected surgically. Some combination of straightening the nasal septum, removing the tonsils, and partially removing the palate is of benefit to about half of the patients with obstructive sleep apnea. The remainder probably have an additional obstruction farther down the throat, which is not helped by currently available surgical procedures—with the exception of tracheotomy, in which a tube is placed directly into a surgical opening in the windpipe, bypassing obstructions above that point in the airway. There is ongoing research directed toward developing procedures for increasing the number of patients with obstructive sleep apnea who can be helped without resorting to tracheotomy.

Taste and smell

According to the American Academy of Otolaryngology, every year an estimated 200,000 people in the U.S. complain to their physicians about loss of the sense of smell. Nonetheless, the sense of smell and the closely associated sense of taste have traditionally received far less attention than other senses; *i.e.,* vision and hearing. Now special research centers have been organized by investigators from diverse scientific and medical disciplines to study the normal mechanisms of taste and smell and to find effective means of treating the relatively rare but distressing disorders of these senses.

The sense of smell may be affected—temporarily or permanently—by viral infections; it also tends to decline with age. Cigarette smoking also impairs a person's sense of smell. Recently methods have been developed to characterize and to quantify the magnitude of sensory loss of taste or smell that occurs in some people, often for no apparent reason. As yet, no major breakthroughs in the therapy of these disorders have been announced, but systematic research and increasing basic knowledge should lead to better methods of diagnosis and treatment of these afflictions in the future.

Cochlear implants

A cochlear implant, also known as a cochlear prosthesis, is a sophisticated electronic device that superficially resembles a large hearing aid. However, instead of using an earpiece to channel sound into the ear canal, a cochlear implant delivers electronic signals to the auditory nerve via an electrode that is implanted surgically into the inner ear. Currently the people who are candidates for cochlear implants are those who are profoundly deaf in both ears and whose hearing loss would not be helped by a traditional hearing aid.

The first such device, a single-channel cochlear implant, was approved for sale in the U.S. in 1984. In 1985 a second cochlear implant model was approved for marketing by the U.S. Food and Drug Administration. The more recently approved device is a multichannel model—i.e., one with more than a single pair of wires implanted in the inner ear. Published results of clinical testing of these units suggest a slight benefit from the multichannel device, but these preliminary findings await confirmation from larger studies, conducted over longer times. Neither of the currently available models restores the normal ability to understand speech, but both provide sound awareness to people who previously were deaf and whose residual hearing was so meager that a hearing aid did not help. A great deal of research is still in progress on the technology of cochlear implants to make them smaller and to improve the signal they produce, with the hope that someday these devices will consistently restore good hearing to the deaf.

Implantable hearing aids

Because of external ear deformities or "feedback" problems resulting from powerful amplification, many hard of hearing people cannot wear traditional hearing aids. Recently developed implantable hearing devices provide help for these individuals. Surgery is done to implant a vibrating device into the bone behind the ear. A surface coil connected to a wearable microphone and transmitter sends impulses through the skin, and the implanted vibrator stimulates the inner ear via the bone surrounding it. These devices are just now being implanted into people with serious hearing losses, and initial results seem promising. If an individual's hearing loss is profound or complete, he or she is not a candidate for an implantable hearing aid because an adequate residue of inner ear function is needed for the device to work.

Hearing loss

Fluid collection in the middle ear is a common childhood problem. The condition, known as otitis media with effusion, may affect children of all ages. Because it produces few symptoms and is usually not associated with pain, it is difficult to diagnose. Nonetheless, it may cause hearing loss. Surgery to drain the fluid and to insert a tube through the eardrum to prevent reaccumulation has become one of the most—if not the most—common surgical operations done in the United States today. It is estimated that one million such procedures are performed every year. Although the hearing loss produced by middle ear fluid is mild, recently published research indicates that children with the condition have more language-development problems and poorer school performance. It appears, therefore, that the aggressive management of otitis media with effusion by surgical means is warranted.

Although in many patients the causes of hearing loss can be determined with some certainty, in others the reason for the problem remains obscure in spite of routine clinical testing. Recent studies at the University of Illinois at Chicago suggest a cause for some of these previously puzzling cases. In some patients there appears to be an association between hearing loss and the compression of the nerve of hearing by a large blood vessel loop within the skull. Sometimes a balance disorder is also present. A sophisticated diagnostic test—computed tomography (CT) scan after injection of air into the spinal fluid space—confirms the location and placement of the blood vessel. Present studies suggest that surgical separation of the vessels from the nerve can alleviate some of the symptoms produced by these vascular loops, but more research is needed before the role that surgery should play in these cases can be determined.

There are certain ailments, known as autoimmune disorders, in which the body rejects some of its own tissues in a response that resembles an allergic reaction. Recently some rare types of inner ear hearing loss have been attributed to this mechanism, and the published results of treatment with powerful immunosuppressives, drugs that interfere with the autoimmune response, suggest that some patients benefit from drug therapy. Ongoing research at several institutions is now focusing on the development of accurate tests to identify patients with this disorder and on finding effective, safe drugs with which to treat them.

Multidisciplinary approaches. New surgical techniques continue to be developed for the removal of cancers of the head and neck, a category that includes, among others, tumors of the mouth, tongue, salivary glands, sinuses, jaw, and thyroid gland. However, the past few decades have witnessed a leveling off of cure rates produced by surgery alone. To improve head and neck cancer cure rates, combinations of supplemental radiation therapy and drug therapy are being studied. To determine the long-range success of such programs, research must follow a large patient population for many years. The early results of some of these studies suggest possible improvement in controlling the spread of head and neck cancers by the use of combinations of surgery, radiation, and drugs; however, long-term research results will be needed for clear benefit to patients to be shown in terms of extended survival and improved quality of life.

Laser surgery. Using lasers coupled to surgical microscopes, otolaryngologists are now able to vaporize cancerous tissue in locations difficult to reach by other means. Compared with other methods, this technique minimizes blood loss and allows for more sparing of normal tissue. Applications of laser surgery in the head and neck region have improved the management of some laryngeal (voice box) tumors and have enabled surgeons to reopen portions of the respiratory tract obstructed by tumor.

Photodynamic therapy. For many years it has been known that the administration of certain drugs makes some tissues more sensitive to light. Recently this phenomenon has been applied to the treatment of some head and neck cancers. A dye known as hematoporphyrin derivative can destroy cancerous tissues exposed to intense illumination, which is often delivered in the form of laser light. Normal tissues surrounding the cancer are spared. The application of photodynamic therapy is limited by the location of the tumor and by the instruments available for delivering the intense light needed for effective treatment. Because of these restrictions, such treatment is used primarily for tumors on the surface of the skin or mucous membranes and those that are accessible by endoscopy. Work is now under way to develop light probes that can be inserted into tumors, enabling the beam of light to reach beneath the surface tissues.

Inaccessible skull tumors. Previously tumors that arose in areas close to the base of the skull were considered beyond the reach of surgery and thus often incurable. Recently several surgeons have devised innovative new approaches to exposing tumors in this location, removing them safely, and reconstructing the resulting defects with results that are satisfactory from both cosmetic and functional viewpoints. These advances are due in part to dramatic developments in diagnostic imaging, such as improved CT scans and a process known as magnetic resonance imaging (MRI).

These new diagnostic techniques provide markedly better tumor localization than was previously available from standard X-ray technology.

Endoscopic nasal and sinus surgery

A refined method of examining the nose and sinuses by means of small endoscopes has become popular in the United States after several years of development in Europe. Endoscopes are fiber-optic devices that can be used to view the interior of body cavities. Inserted through the patient's nostrils, the endoscope can provide the physician with a superb view of the inside of the nose and sinuses, allowing for greater diagnostic accuracy and surgical precision than can be obtained by the unaided eye. For diagnostic purposes the endoscope can be used in the physician's office; a local anesthetic in spray form is used. Surgery under endoscopic visualization can also be performed under local anesthesia, often in an outpatient setting. The premise underlying much endoscopic sinus surgery is that the key areas of disease can be visualized while they are in the process of being removed, thereby sparing as much healthy tissue as possible; thus, a more conservative operation is possible. As with any new technique, experience will define its value and the cases in which it is likely to be most beneficial.

Partial laryngeal surgery and voice restoration

A century ago cancer of the larynx was treated by removal of the entire voice box. Since then, continuing medical research has focused on distinguishing those laryngeal cancers that definitely require radical surgery from those that can be controlled by removal of only a portion of the larynx or by use of radiation therapy or laser surgery to remove the cancer and preserve normal tissue. The advantage of partial laryngeal removal is that the patient's voice is retained. Some small cancers in early stages of development can be treated effectively with the laser. Studies now show that some large cancers of the larynx can also be removed with less than complete destruction of the structure itself. If certain critical portions of the larynx are preserved, the patient's voice can sometimes be saved.

In some cases of laryngeal cancer, however, the entire voice box must be removed. A new, relatively simple procedure, the tracheoesophageal puncture operation, restores the ability to speak in patients who have had a simple laryngectomy. An air-shunt tube with an external opening in the neck connects the remaining windpipe (trachea) and the esophagus. By covering the opening in the windpipe with a finger and exhaling air, via the shunt, into the esophagus, the patient is able to produce a sound that is much like the natural voice. Success rates for speech restoration approach 90%, according to recent studies of this procedure.

—Edward L. Applebaum, M.D.

Technology's Wonders:
New Generations of Artificial Body Parts

by Mike C. Korologos

Technologies founded on joint efforts of many disciplines—engineering, medicine, pharmacy, biology, and materials science—and supplemented by the maturing of a decade of intense research, are scripting scenarios starring a new generation of artificial organs and synthetic body tissues. Results of such unprecedented interdisciplinary collaboration include the emergence of devices once considered science fiction, such as:

- a spaghetti-sized polymer blood vessel that is flexible and pulsates with the natural vessel as blood flows through it
- an electronic chip implant that would help the blind to perceive images
- a fully implantable artificial heart, powered by either electrohydraulics or a magnetically suspended rotor
- wearable artificial kidney dialysis devices
- synthetic urinary bladders and urinary tracts
- such artificial body parts as fallopian tubes, an esophagus, skin, a urethra, a ureter, a sphincter, nerves, red cells, and blood

While the dream of developing life-extending and life-enhancing artificial body parts is deeply rooted in medical history, the modern-day genesis dates back to the 1930s, when the Dutch-born nephrologist Willem Kolff watched helplessly as his first patient died of kidney failure. That experience led the tenacious Kolff to apply engineering principles to biology and medicine, which he used to develop the first kidney dialysis (artificial kidney) machine.

Kolff did not stop after his artificial kidney made its debut in The Netherlands in 1943, however; he proceeded and indeed became the most instrumental biomedical "inventor" of other artificial body parts. Particularly notable has been his work on the mechanical heart and the Ineraid hearing device, which is commercially available and is helping the profoundly deaf to understand speech. Kolff, who carried on his pioneering work at the University of Utah, was the major catalyst in this new field specializing in body-part replacements. He became head of the division of artificial organs at the University of Utah's Institute for Biomedical Engineering. Utah is now home of one of the world's leading artificial organ development centers, which blends the talents of surgeons, physiologists, students, nurses, social workers, mechanical engineers, mathematicians, electrical engineers, anesthesiologists, chemists, dieticians, computer scientists, veterinarians, materials scientists, neurologists, and hematologists.

This extraordinary collaboration gives the institute a unique ability to carry projects from basic research and design through device development to clinical application in patients and ultimately to the marketplace. Since its founding in 1967, the institute has undertaken any problem that can be solved with an artificial organ or a mechanical or electrical device. The projects are driven by the desire to treat patients—most of whom have no other options.

Among those attracted to the University of Utah's bioengineering program by Kolff was a medical student named Robert Jarvik, who came on the scene in 1970 and spearheaded the development of the world's first permanent artificial heart, the storied Jarvik-7, now being used primarily as a bridge to transplantation. The Jarvik-7 paved the way for a new generation of man-made blood pumps.

Beyond the Jarvik-7

The very recent development of the Utah 100, a totally artificial heart device, is expected to open new avenues in replacing human hearts with mechanical ones. The device provides a new "quick connect" system that joins the artificial heart to the remaining natural heart. The elliptically shaped Utah 100 is smaller than the Jarvik-7 and can pump a required 100 ml of blood with each beat (hence its name), yet it fits into even the smallest adult chest space. If tests prove successful, the smaller heart will be made available to the large segment of the population with end-state heart failure whose chests are too small to accommodate the Jarvik-7.

Designed by a team of University of Utah researchers, the new device uses the same materials, blood-contacting surfaces, mechanical valves, and power sources (compressed air) as the Jarvik-7. The Utah 100 uses a simpler design for the housing of the ventricles, however, which makes fabrication easier and more reliable. Another advantage is that future versions of the device may be machine made rather than handmade, as is currently the case.

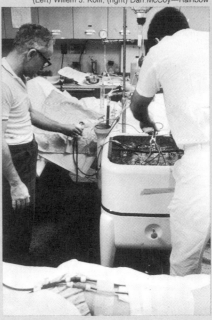

After the death of a patient from kidney failure in the early 1940s, Dutch physician Willem Kolff invented the rotating drum artificial kidney (above). By the 1960s, when the artificial kidney at right was in use, dialysis treatments were sparing the lives of patients worldwide.

Both types of artificial hearts replace the lower chambers of the natural heart and are installed by having quick-connect rings snapped onto matching fittings molded into polyester cuffs. These are sutured to the heart's upper chambers, which are left in the chest at the time of the implant.

Sausage casings to "perfect" plastics

Critically aligned to virtually every aspect of the implantation of foreign matter into the human body is the thorough understanding and modification of the interactions of certain proteins with solid surfaces. Research into the interaction between synthetic materials—in particular, certain plastics—and the body is being approached on two fronts. One is investigating the physical and chemical aspects of protein and cell absorptions and related interactions. The other is focusing on a basic understanding of the events occurring at the interface between synthetic materials and living systems in order to develop modified or new materials for specific implant applications such as a vascular prosthesis, a bile duct prosthesis, an esophagus, and other implantable body-part replacements.

In addition, the bioengineering researchers are evaluating and developing new implant biomaterials, such as fiber-reinforced composites, degradable materials, and coatings to encourage bone ingrowth. Such materials research has become the catalyst for all subsequent research in artificial body parts because in past years scientists were limited to working only with commercially available materials. In fact, Kolff used sausage casings made of thin cellophane (a new product 45 years ago) in developing his first artificial kidney machine because when they were submerged in salt solution, the casings were porous to many chemicals but not to blood.

No longer confined to such off-the-shelf products, scientists are altering the surface properties of existing materials and monitoring changes to facilitate the desired mesh between laboratory-created plastic polymers and natural body tissues. The successful linkage of human tissue to the synthetic surface can be accomplished without triggering an unfavorable response from the body and initiating clotting. Made-to-order biocompatible polymers are enabling scientists to devise such items as protein-proof coatings for bags that store human blood and for various medical devices; materials for controlling blood clotting and inflammation associated with the use of devices on artificial kidney machines; diagnostic sensors and detectors; artificial red cells and blood; and several diagnostic, filtration, and catalytic techniques based on surface absorption. Beyond the medical field, such biocompatibility research will benefit the pharmaceutical industry, as well as the cosmetics, dairy, and food-processing industries.

A world authority in the new scientific discipline of biocompatibility is Karin D. Caldwell, who is the director of the Center for Biopolymers at Interfaces at the University of Utah. Under her guidance researchers at the center are developing ways of pacifying surfaces and giving them proper qualities to prepare them for implantation. The bioengineered devices, or body parts, developed by the researchers are composed of precisely tailored ingredients that will react in predictable, and thus compatible, ways to various natural bodily fluids. Such biomedical research is thus able to eliminate the unknowns in the creation of de-

288

vices, which should lead to a generation of rejection-proof implants.

Tiny blood vessels, new fallopian tubes, and more

Exemplifying the successful use of polymer research is the development of the small-diameter artificial blood vessel. While Dacron and Teflon materials have been used successfully in limited cases, especially in replacing larger-sized coronary arteries, such surfaces are not suitable for vessels with much smaller internal diameters—those that are six millimeters (less than a quarter of an inch) or under.

Developer Donald J. Lyman, a University of Utah professor of bioengineering, materials science, and engineering and research associate professor of surgery, calls his prototype small-diameter synthetic vessel the "Model T." He expects clinical trials to continue for two years before the tubular device can be used readily to repair or replace coronary and peripheral vessels for some 500,000 likely beneficiaries in the U.S. alone whose natural blood vessels, usually in the extremities, have become diseased or damaged from atherosclerosis or trauma.

The polyurethane vessel minimizes blood clotting and is flexible enough to pulsate with the natural blood vessel as blood passes through it. Current practice finds surgeons bypassing the small obstructed blood vessels in the peripheral or coronary areas by using the patient's own vessels, usually the saphenous vein removed from the inner thigh. This process is often impossible, though, because some patients do not have veins suitable for transplant. In cases where veins are suitable, the procedure significantly increases operating time. Patients in clinical tests who are undergoing reconstructive surgery receive the artificial vessel if elsewhere in the body they have no viable natural blood vessels suitable for transplantation.

In early trials a major problem encountered was clotting originating at the junction of the graft and natural blood vessels; examination of failed grafts indicated that a mismatch in flexibility between the polymer and natural vessels was often at fault. Such a mismatch causes enough trauma at the suture site as the vessels pulsate to cause mechanical damage to the lining tissue and to initiate clotting. To combat this problem, scientists have developed a new precipitation process in order to fabricate into a graft a copolyurethane material that is opaque, white, spongy, and elastic. This allows the mechanical property of elasticity to be balanced with surface characteristics designed to minimize clotting. The precise arrangement of chemical groups on the polymer surface was engineered to bind preferentially with the protein albumin. Studies had revealed that platelets in the blood do not adhere to albuminized surfaces; hence, clotting is minimized.

In the research process, scientists are looking at other types of tubular implant materials that can be

The revolutionary portable artificial kidney above will offer new-found freedom to patients who require regular dialysis treatments. It enabled this patient to venture into the wilderness of Utah's Canyonlands National Park.

used for repair or replacement of the bile duct, ureter and bladder, and peripheral nerves. Other items evolving from this research include a new type of elastic suture that does not "pucker" when threaded; new membranes for the artificial kidney; artificial skin with appropriate permeability characteristics for burn victims; materials for the repair of ulcerated or cancerous intestines; a functioning ureter that need not vent through the skin, as is currently the case with artificial devices; the aforementioned artificial esophagus; and "scaffoldings," which facilitate the natural growth of cells and which, when they disintegrate, leave only the natural surface made of living cells. Such scaffolding makes it possible to place implants into babies because the regenerated tissue would continue to grow after the implant disintegrates.

Lyman and his coresearchers also hope to reconnect severed nerves so that the nerves will perform almost normally. They believe that this process, called "stretch neurosis," can be successful if polymer cuffs are used as bridges linking the severed nerves. The inside of the cuff would be biocompatible with its environment and allow neurons (nerve cells) to grow, while the outside surface would stimulate growth of glial cells that insulate and support the nerve cells.

Artificial fallopian tubes are yet another challenge undergoing investigation by Utah researchers, who are hoping to offer infertile couples an option to *in vitro* fertilization. As in most implant development work, the composition of biocompatible materials is the major hurdle being confronted by scientists. In this instance researchers are armed with at least nine different polymers, or combinations thereof, as they seek the harmonious combination of materials that will not trip the body's rejection mechanisms when confronted with several types of cells, including sperm, ova, an embryo, and other reproductive tissues of the body. By using cultures, scientists are attempting to determine what effect different polymers have on the sperm's structure, movement, and viability. Tests in laboratory animals are being conducted so the sperm's ability to penetrate hamster eggs can be determined and the way polymers influence the growth and division of mouse embryos can be understood.

This four-year-old project of developing fallopian tube replacements is being spearheaded by Stephen Hunter at the University of Utah College of Pharmacy. His device has the same basic design as the human counterpart and includes a built-in mechanism that supplies nutrients to the ovum as it moves from the ovary to the uterus. Prototype artificial fallopian tubes have been implanted in sheep to determine the feasibility of the device's design and surgical techniques, but more tests are necessary before it can proceed to clinical testing.

Better insulin delivery for diabetics

Other scientific advances are surfacing in the area of "targeted" and "controlled" drug-delivery systems. This research is also founded on the development of polymers, primarily their cross-linking densities that control their drug-leaching characteristics. Research has led to successful experiments in which patients with insulin-dependent diabetes inject insulin directly into the abdominal cavity.

This new insulin-delivery method utilizes a device called a subcutaneous peritoneal-access device (SPAD) leading into the abdominal cavity. It is a small container about five centimeters (two inches) across and made

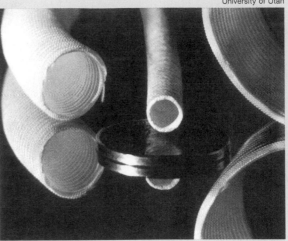

Biomedical engineers have developed tiny artificial blood vessels made of polyurethane, which enable delicate surgical repairs that were not possible with larger vascular prostheses made of dacron. The two are compared in the picture above.

of silicone rubber, polyurethane, and polyethylene glycol. Implanted just below the skin on the patient's abdomen, the SPAD has a small opening into the peritoneal, or abdominal, cavity.

Designed to imitate the normal pattern and pathway of insulin release by the pancreas, the SPAD requires patients to push a small needle, with relatively little pain, through the skin into the container and then inject insulin, which flows through the opening into the abdominal cavity, where it is drained rapidly and directly to the liver, the major chemical-processing organ of the body. There insulin metabolizes, controlling glucose and influencing at least 20 other body substances.

Contemporary medical delivery methods have people with diabetes injecting the insulin into the fatty layer under the skin, where it slowly enters the bloodstream. A relatively small amount of it makes its way to the liver, and a disproportionately large amount is directed to other organs. Two major advantages of the new subcutaneous reservoir are the virtual painlessness of the injections and the known absorption period (the time it takes the insulin to reach its target organs), which allows patients to better judge how much insulin they need and when to take it.

Still considered experimental, the SPAD implant involves a surgical procedure comparable to a hernia repair. It is estimated that the more than 1.5 million Americans whose pancreases produce almost no insulin, which leads to serious chemical imbalances, suffer from the type of life-threatening diabetes that will be aided by the new device.

On the horizon: artificial eyes

In research as sophisticated and futuristic as so much of the new body part development work is, a great

The Utah 100, a totally artificial heart, is being tested in animals. The elliptical shape of the polyurethane device allows better anatomical fit in small chests than does its predecessor, the Jarvik-7.

deal of its significance probably will not be realized for at least 15 years. On one such front a team of psychologists, pathologists, bioengineers, neurosurgeons, materials scientists, and telemetry and semiconductor experts is beginning work that aims at enabling electronic stimulation of the brains of the noncongenitally blind in order to produce "sensations" of various points of light in space.

Even after more than a decade of such research, scientists at the University of Utah are admittedly still at the "boot-strap" stage in the development of an artificial eye. The concept calls for artificially stimulating the part of the brain that controls vision—the visual cortex—with minute electronic currents. Such stimulation would be transmitted by an array containing many penetrating electrodes, each measuring three millimeters in length and less than one-tenth of a millimeter in thickness and each capable of delivering to the brain electrical currents on the order of a millionth of an amp, sufficiently large to evoke a sensation of a point of light in front of the blind individual.

The electrode array would protrude into the brain from a solid-state microprocessor chip measuring about 1.3 cm (one-half inch) square and containing miniaturized electronic circuitry, or a decoding system. The chip, or array, would be permanently implanted through an approximately 2.5-cm (one-inch)-diameter hole in the skull on a flat portion of the brain's convoluted surface. Light signals coming from the object, "seen" by a tiny television camera, would be fed to the array and translated into electrical impulses that would then stimulate the brain. It is anticipated that the visually impaired would perceive an independent light spot as each electrode in the array stimulates the brain. When these electrodes are stimulated separately, the perception would consist of many discrete points of light, one produced by each electrode, and appear similar to what one sees on an electronic scoreboard made up of hundreds of light bulbs.

One member of the Utah team involved in this investigation is bioengineer Richard A. Normann. According to Normann, an artificial eye using a compact microcomputer might eventually fit into eyeglasses in a way similar to the way hearing aids today are incorporated on the earpiece of glasses. He is optimistic but cites numerous challenges and questions ahead. The number of electrodes needed to produce a useful visual sense must be determined. Can 100 do the job, or will 1,000 or more be required? Can the electrode implant transmit current for an extended period without adverse tissue reaction? Can the electrode array measuring a mere 1.3 cm square actually be built? How strong must the electrodes be to penetrate the brain? Of what material must the tip of the electrode be so that it electronically "excites" the brain without damaging it? Because the insertion of the electrodes will damage blood vessels in the brain, this damage ob-

A deaf volunteer tests an artificial "ear" that permits him to understand speech. Electrodes implanted in his inner ear stimulate nerve fibers to produce sounds. A button behind the ear is linked to a sound processor worn on a belt.

viously must be reversible. Can this be accomplished successfully?

Experimentation is currently being conducted on cats that have been implanted with a simplified array. When current is passed through implanted electrodes, the cat "sees" points of light. As developer Normann admits, however, his is only an emerging technology, and it needs many more years of research.

Dialysis in Wonderland

In an almost storybook-like scenario, one of the most advanced artificial life-enhancing devices, after decades in the making, is the latest generation of the artificial kidney. This descendant of Kolff's original washing-machine-like contraption is a wearable artificial kidney, also known as WAK. Offering patients with renal failure new-found freedom of activity, the WAK weighs about 3.5 kg (8 lb), is battery powered, requires neither plumbing nor electrical outlets, and uses a recirculating dialyzing fluid bath.

So mobile is WAK that users are able to enjoy "therapeutic recreation," which impressively demonstrates its mobility. University of Utah scientists and staff have taken kidney-failure patients who are outfitted with the WAK on "Dialysis in Wonderland" excursions to remote wilderness areas, including white-water-rafting trips down the Colorado River through the Grand Canyon.

Lighter, more efficient WAKs are in the offing, and they will serve as additional tributes to the remarkably successful cross-pollination of diverse disciplines that has brought bioengineering from sausage casing to new skin and artificial reproductive organs and is leading it toward visual sense for the blind.

Eating Disorders

Eating disorders affect young females and occasionally males in all strata of society. Eating problems were virtually unknown to the public before the 1960s, but the 1970s saw a plethora of books and articles on the subject, especially on anorexia nervosa. Though they were thought to be modern diseases, these mysterious and frightening problems of weight control are not entirely new, as recent studies of their social and cultural history have revealed. Anorexia nervosa was named and identified in Victorian England by Queen Victoria's physician, Sir William Gull. Other scientific descriptions appeared in France and the United States at about the same time, reporting anorexia nervosa primarily in teenage girls and young women of the middle and upper-middle classes, whose social backgrounds were associated with certain emotional and material pressures and privileges. In the 19th century doctors described anorexia nervosa as a lack of appetite from nervous causes or as a form of hysteria. The outcome of the widespread dissemination of information on anorexia nervosa has resulted in earlier diagnosis and treatment, with a consequent decrease in mortality. Investigators have also isolated certain vulnerable subpopulations predisposed to developing anorexia nervosa: models, ballet dancers, jockeys, flight attendants, and others whose jobs or careers require constant attention to weight control.

Eating disorders today

Today there is general agreement that the psychological aspects of the eating disorders are manifestations of luxury and plenty, rather than of deprivation. While food advertisements lure people to try an ever new variety of tempting foods, models and actresses demonstrate that "thinness is beautiful."

Such double messages are confusing to vulnerable adolescents who are struggling with normal identity issues relating to sexuality and body image. The failure to control excessive eating and maintain thinness often leads to a sense of embarrassment, shame, and guilt, so that 70% of adolescent and young adult women, according to a recent study, believe they are overweight, even though their weight is normal for their height and body build.

A modern concept of the three primary eating disorders (obesity, bulimia, and anorexia nervosa) is that they exist in a continuum in which there is considerable overlapping. Obesity, which is generally considered separately from bulimia and anorexia nervosa, is the easiest to differentiate, but it is multidetermined, with psychological causes being only one aspect of an etiology that includes genetic predisposition, hormonal, metabolic, and physiological factors. Obesity researcher Albert J. Stunkard, at the University of Pennsylvania, believes that individuals have a biologic "set point"—a natural body weight—and have difficulty losing weight under that amount. When people force their bodies under that point by dieting, they experience depressive feelings, and their bodies press to return to their set point.

Problems with weight or with body image may lead to the other eating disorders, bulimia and anorexia nervosa. Bulimia is the most perplexing of the eating disorders; it may coexist with either obesity or anorexia nervosa or occur as a distinct entity. In the latest literature anorexia nervosa has been divided into "restrictor" and "bulimic" subtypes. The restrictor anorexics practice typical self-starvation; anorexics in another group suffer from concomitant symptoms of bulimia; and those in a third cluster develop bulimia in the later stages of their illness. Meanwhile, some investigators claim that eating disorders are secondary to mood disturbances, especially depression, instead of subscribing to an older view that the mood disturbances are secondary manifestations of the primary eating disorder.

According to the American Psychiatric Association's *Diagnostic and Statistical Manual of Mental Disorders* (*DSM—III;* 1980), the diagnosis of anorexia nervosa requires a weight loss of 25% of the original body weight

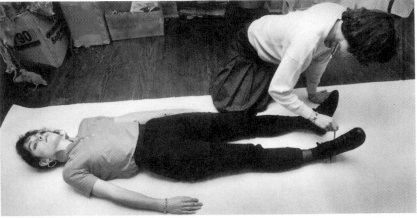

At the Renfrew Center, a residential treatment facility outside Philadelphia for the treatment of eating disorders, a bulimic patient has an outline of her figure drawn. The art therapy session is meant to help her see her body as it really is. Women with eating disorders typically suffer a disturbance of body image.

in patients with no known physical illness. Typically, patients manifest an intense fear of being obese that does not diminish as weight loss progresses; patients also suffer a disturbance of body image, claiming to "feel fat" even when emaciated, and refuse to maintain body weight over a minimal normal weight for age and height. According to *DSM—III,* "the essential features of bulimia are episodic binge eating accompanied by an awareness that the eating pattern is abnormal, fear of not being able to stop eating voluntarily, and depressed mood and self-deprecating thoughts following the eating binges." The binge is often followed by self-induced vomiting, fasting, or abuse of cathartics or diuretics.

Both anorexia nervosa and bulimia are associated with serious medical complications. Although the mortality rate in anorexia nervosa has declined significantly, clinicians must constantly monitor electrolyte balance, cardiac rhythm, endocrine function, and nutritional status. In bulimia findings of salivary gland enlargement, erosion of dental enamel, and a variety of gastrointestinal disturbances, including rupture of the stomach (following expansion due to gorging) and tearing of the esophageal wall, are not uncommon. In all eating disorders, depression with the threat of suicide is a pertinent factor, and psychotherapy and antidepressant medications may be a part of the treatment.

Bulimia: evolving concepts

Psychologists investigating bulimia have conceptualized bulimia as a multidetermined psychosomatic disorder with biologic, familial, and sociocultural components. According to researchers Craig Johnson and Karen Maddi, at the Northwestern University Medical School, Chicago, young people who are at risk of developing bulimia have a biologic vulnerability for affective (emotional) instability that is triggered by the lowered self-esteem and self-regulatory difficulties of adolescence. When they attempt to remedy this instability by the achievement of thinness, the psychological side effects of semistarvation result in a "psychobiologic impasse" that may paradoxically exacerbate the original difficulties with emotional instability and low self-esteem. University of Rochester, N.Y., neurobiologist Paul Coleman reports that brain shrinkage may contribute to some of the behavioral changes.

Richard L. Pyle and James E. Mitchell, of the University of Minnesota, have studied the incidence of bulimia and believe it to be around 2% of 18–30-year-old females. Others estimate a recent increase to as high as 15% of college women. Only a small percentage of these patients seek out treatment, but an apparent increase in prevalence may be a reflection of wider publicity of the illness, with a greater willingness of patients to discuss the intimate details of their binge-purge habit.

Neuroendocrinologic studies have revealed that hypothalamic-pituitary-thyroid-adrenal axis problems are found in both anorexic and normal-weight bulimic patients. Identification and precise understanding of the specific role of neurotransmitters that act on the hypothalamus and gastrointestinal tract hormones, such as cholecystokinin and bombesin, hold promise for furthering the understanding of feeding processes in the future. Such investigations are being carried out by Enrique Friedman at the University of California at Irvine.

The role of depression

A most controversial aspect of the eating disorders is their relationship to affective psychiatric illness, particularly depression. The findings are rather inconsistent, and it is unclear whether the depression is a mood, a symptom, or a syndrome. David B. Herzog, at the Harvard University Medical School, has delineated four basic hypotheses concerning bulimia: (1) depression causes bulimia; (2) bulimia leads to a depressive state; (3) bulimia and depression are essentially distinct and separate entities; and (4) both bulimia and depression are an outgrowth of similar genetic, biochemical, and psychodynamic predispositions.

Antidepressant drugs, utilized on the basis of an apparent link between bulimia and affective illness, have shown quite positive results. The use of these drugs is not without problems, however, in this particular patient population. The tendency toward impulsivity and acting out that is typical of such patients increases the risk of overdose and suicide. Monitoring plasma levels of patients for whom antidepressant medications have been prescribed can be very helpful in assuring compliance, attaining therapeutic levels, and detecting abuse. Although the monoamine oxidase (MAO)-inhibitor drugs (one of the two major types of antidepressants) may be quite effective, they are potentially more dangerous because of the required dietary restrictions. B. Timothy Walsh, at Columbia University, New York City, in reviewing the use of these medications, recommends commencing treatment with one of the drugs that are among the tricyclic antidepressants and switching over to the MAO group only if the former group evidences poor response or unacceptable side effects.

New treatment approaches

Of the various forms of treatment available, there has been a major shift away from psychoanalytic forms of psychotherapy, which pioneering eating disorders specialist Hilde Bruch, at Baylor College of Medicine, Houston, Texas, early in the 1980s pronounced as ineffective. The shift has been toward cognitive, group, behavioral, family, and self-help approaches.

David M. Garner, of the University of Toronto, has evolved a form of cognitive therapy for patients without a history of emaciation, a group clearly distinguish-

From H. G. Pope, Jr., *et al.*, "Bulimia Treated with Imipramine: A Placebo-Controlled Double-Blind Study," *American Journal of Psychiatry*, vol. 140, no. 5 (May 1983), pp. 554–558; reprinted with permission of the American Psychiatric Association

Changes in bulimia patients

(nine treated with imipramine antidepressant; ten given placebo)

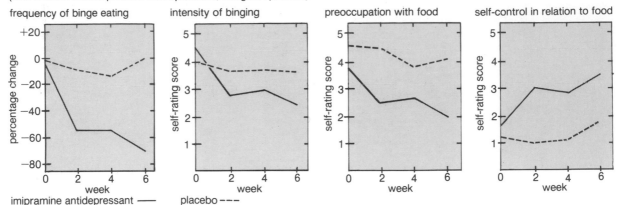

imipramine antidepressant ——   placebo - - -

Antidepressant drugs have shown positive results in some bulimic patients; treatment is based on an apparent link between bulimia and affective disorders. In one study patients showed improvement in frequency and intensity of binge eating as well as in preoccupation with food and self-control, as the individual graphs above indicate.

able from those with the bulimic subtype of anorexia nervosa. His approach involves the following steps: (1) teaching the patients to monitor their own thinking by a heightened awareness of the content of thoughts; (2) helping the patients to recognize the connection between certain dysfunctional thoughts and maladaptive behaviors and emotions; (3) examining with the patients evidence for the validity of particular beliefs, especially cultural and societal emphasis on dieting and maintaining a "perfect shape"; (4) assisting in the gradual substitution of more realistic and appropriate interpretations based upon the evidence; and (5) establishing as the ultimate goal a modification of underlying assumptions that are fundamental determinants of specific dysfunctional beliefs. Garner reports that, for some, such a treatment program may be successful within a short period of time; for others, especially those with a history of anorexia nervosa or multiple treatment failures or with particularly chaotic eating patterns, treatment may need to be more extensive.

Group therapy has become part of overall systematic and comprehensive treatment programs. The use of homogeneous group therapy—a group of individuals who share the same basic disorder or problem—is an approach widely used for other specific disorders; *e.g.*, alcoholism, drug abuse, and compulsive gambling. Such therapy is directed toward alleviating symptoms as well as gaining insight into internal and family conflicts. Katherine N. Dixon, of Ohio State University, reports significant reduction or cessation of symptoms, increased self-esteem, and improved impulse control with the group approach to eating disorders.

Harold Leitenberg and James C. Rosen, at the University of Vermont, have devised a behavioral treatment approach for patients suffering from uncontrollable binge eating and self-induced vomiting while suffering from an intense dread of weight gain or change in body appearance. They describe how binge eating is triggered by an antecedent event, dysphoric feelings, or lapses from a rigid diet. Once self-induced vomiting has been learned, it becomes the driving force that sustains the bulimic—vomiting frees the binge eater from normal inhibitions. The treatment relies heavily on anxiety reduction and uses behavioral approaches to diminish these effects rather than just dealing with loss of control or the desire to binge eat.

Laura L. Humphrey, at the Northwestern University Medical School, studies bulimia from a family systems perspective. She conceptualizes the illness as enabling family members, especially parents, to avoid dealing with the serious emotional problems contained within the family structure. Thus, the illness is seen as a homeostatic mechanism—*i.e.*, maintaining an equilibrium within the family. In the family therapy sessions, the dynamics of how individual members relate to and affect one another are delineated. In many of the families the child's eating disorder may be equated with explosive outbursts of anger evidenced in the parents or siblings. Humphrey also proposes that different family dynamics may be responsible for the development of the various subtypes of bulimia and recommends family involvement in treatment programs.

Ongoing developments in the psychoanalytic psychotherapeutic treatment of severely disturbed borderline and narcissistic patients have been applied with some success to the eating disorders. C. Philip Wilson, at Columbia University, bases treatment on a differentiation of anorexia nervosa between restrictor and bulimic subtypes; the bulimics have ineffective impulse controls where the slightest gain in weight produces panic, exercising, starving, and vomiting. Both groups struggle to avoid being overwhelmed by impulses, including voraciousness and retreat from the development of adult sexuality via a regression to the prepubertal relationship with parents.

Self-help programs have developed out of the spontaneous growth of a number of organizations dedicated to the education and provision of support services to the victims of eating disorders and their families. Group meetings of various types (*e.g.,* daily, weekly, monthly, informational, family- or sibling-oriented), with and without a facilitator, are planned to emphasize the importance of interpersonal relationships, to encourage corrective emotional experiences, and to enhance the group as a social microcosm for the isolated, desperate eating disorder sufferer. Among the established organizations in the United States from which information can be secured are the National Association of Anorexia Nervosa and Associated Disorders (ANAD), Highland Park, Ill.; American Anorexia/Bulimia Association Inc., Teaneck, N.J.; and Bulimia Anorexia Self Help (BASH), St. Louis, Mo.

Medical aspects of eating disorders

All therapeutic approaches to the eating disorders include continuous medical supervision of nutritional status. Although anorexia nervosa is a potentially life-threatening disorder, bulimia is also capable of inducing severe physical change. James C. Sheinin, at Michael Reese Hospital in Chicago, emphasizes the crucial importance of careful clinical and laboratory monitoring of patients suffering from either of these eating disorders.

In anorexic patients attention must be given to potentially serious or even life-threatening complications involving the hypothalamic-pituitary-thyroid axis, as well as gonadal dysfunction, fluid-balance alterations, electrolyte imbalance, cardiac arrhythmias, orthostatic hypotension (fainting), kidney and liver problems, and various gastrointestinal difficulties. The bulimic patient characteristically has enlarged salivary glands and erosion of dental enamel induced by repeated forced vomiting of acidic fluids. These bulimic patients are also vulnerable to developing irreparable damage to the gastrointestinal tract, cardiac arrhythmias and conduction abnormalities, skeletal and smooth muscle weakness and paralysis induced by severe protein and potassium depletion, and fluid depletion.

Ignoring these potential medical complications in a well-conceived treatment program would be a grave error. The most effective treatment plans emphasize the close collaboration of medical, psychiatric, and group approaches.

—*Sherman C. Feinstein, M.D.,*
and Arthur D. Sorosky, M.D.

Environmental and Occupational Health

The actions of nature, as well as those of humans, contributed to important recent events that called upon the expertise of specialists in the fields of environmental and occupational health. Natural disasters and unusual climatic events served as reminders that even in the late 20th century not all toxins are created within the factory gates, and even the most sophisticated technology is powerless in the face of nature.

There were several recent instances of natural events affecting the health of large numbers of people. The winter of 1986–87 saw more than 250 deaths in Europe as a result of a spell of prolonged extremely cold weather. The greatest number of deaths occurred in the U.S.S.R., where 77 people died in weather-related incidents; 36 people died in Poland and another 30 in Great Britain. Many people died of exposure, including some motorists who froze to

More than 1,700 people died in August 1986 when a cloud of noxious gases, mainly carbon dioxide, rose from Lake Nyos in northwestern Cameroon and blanketed the surrounding countryside. While the Army dug mass graves for the thousands of dead livestock, some shocked survivors refused to leave their empty villages.

T. Orban—Sygma

In November 1986 a major spill of toxic chemicals into the Rhine River near Basel, Switzerland, resulted in an ecological disaster that affected the entire Rhine basin. The incident, considered the worst nonnuclear environmental disaster in Europe in many years, was sardonically dubbed "Bhopal on the Rhine" and "Chernobasel"—references to recent catastrophes in India and the Soviet Union.

death while trapped on snowbound highways. Hypothermia, or lowered body temperature, is a special health hazard for the very young and the very old. Interestingly, temperature-related increases in death rates are, along with influenza outbreaks, among the very few causes of what public health officials refer to as "excess mortality"—that is, an increase in the number of deaths expected in a given population over and above the long-established norms. As a potentially serious secondary consequence of the severe cold in Great Britain, the safety of the London water-supply system was threatened when, throughout the city, many older water pipes burst, endangering the cleanliness of the water supply. The situation was another reminder that much that is taken for granted in the developed world—clean water, warm homes, fresh food—is in fact subject to obliteration by natural forces beyond human control.

A most unusual natural phenomenon occurred in Africa in August 1986 when more than 1,700 villagers died in the region around Lake Nyos, an inland lake in northwestern Cameroon. Large quantities of naturally generated toxic gases escaped from the freshwater lake, the toxic fumes overcoming and killing people who lived along the shore. Scientists who later investigated the incident attributed the fatalities to death by asphyxiation, caused by large amounts of carbon dioxide being released. The exact cause of the phenomenon is still under study.

Ozone and skin cancer risk

Another environmental phenomenon continuing to receive widespread attention is the possible interrelationship of certain chemicals, known as halogenated hydrocarbons, and the ozone layer surrounding the Earth. These fluorine- and chlorine-containing chemicals, also called chlorofluorocarbons or just fluorocarbons, are widely used as propellants in spray cans (although this use is almost entirely banned in the U.S.)

and as refrigerants; they are also useful for putting out fires in situations where water would be undesirable. A fire in a computer facility, for example, could be put out by halon gas, which replaces all of the oxygen in the area and, while putting out the fire, does not harm sensitive computer equipment. Fluorocarbons are believed to be ozone-attacking chemicals, and there is some evidence that they may be causing ozone depletion in the Earth's environment. In recent years environmental scientists studying seasonal changes in the Antarctic ozone layer have recorded what they believe to be an isolated but significant net loss of atmospheric ozone and an elevation of chlorine atoms in places with diminished ozone levels. Potential consequences of atmospheric ozone depletion include a general heating of the Earth's climate, with melting of polar ice and subsequent elevations in water levels, major disruptions of crop growth, and harmful effects on human health.

A recent report from the dermatology department of the New York University Medical Center noted an increase in the incidence of skin cancer, especially among young people, thought to be related to excessive exposure to ultraviolet radiation reaching the surface of the Earth through the ozone layer, which acts as a shield against ultraviolet radiation. A U.S. Environmental Protection Agency (EPA) report in November 1986 warned of a vast increase in skin cancer as a result of ozone depletion. The EPA also predicted an increase in the incidence of immune dysfunction disorders and eye cataracts due to loss of the protective effect of atmospheric ozone. International negotiations were proceeding to control the uses of chlorofluorocarbons, but an agreement was not expected to be reached soon.

Hazards of the workplace reviewed

In the United States much of the research related to occupational illnesses is conducted under the auspices

On the basis of an unpublished report linking microchip etching to high rates of spontaneous abortion, AT&T in 1987 announced that pregnant workers would no longer be permitted in "clean rooms," where nitric acid and sulfuric acid are used to engrave circuitry patterns on silicon wafers.

of the National Institute of Occupational Safety and Health (NIOSH). Recently NIOSH has been conducting a campaign to educate the work community, as well as the research community, as to what are considered by the agency to be the ten leading types of work-related diseases and injuries. They are (1) occupational lung disease; (2) musculoskeletal injuries; (3) occupational cancers (other than lung); (4) severe traumatic injuries; (5) cardiovascular disease; (6) disorders of reproduction; (7) neurotoxic disorders; (8) noise-induced hearing loss; (9) dermatologic conditions; and (10) psychological disorders.

Work-related hearing loss. Despite a concerted effort to reduce hazards in the workplace, current U.S. standards provide, in many cases, inadequate safeguards of employee health. For example, it is acknowledged by specialists in occupational health that some measurable proportion of the U.S. work force—although specific individuals cannot be identified—will suffer hearing loss because of currently allowed noise levels. Operators of heavy equipment on construction jobs, employees in underground and surface mining operations, and workers in a number of manufacturing settings, such as foundries and assembly plants, are especially at risk.

Disorders of reproduction. Studies of possible problems associated with video display terminal (VDT) use continue, although there has been no confirmation of any undue increases in birth defects, spontaneous abortions, or stillbirths among pregnant VDT users. A report published in March 1987 by the American Medical Association's Council on Scientific Affairs reviewed the recent medical literature and came to the conclusion that VDTs have not been shown to cause harm to the human fetus.

In January 1987, after an unpublished University of Massachusetts report of a high rate of miscarriage associated with microchip etching, thought to be related to solvents used in the process, AT&T announced that pregnant women would no longer be allowed to work on certain aspects of semiconductor production. The

AT&T action served to revive a controversy among health authorities over the policy of banning women—but not men—from certain work sites, as had been done several years earlier in the case of occupational lead exposure. The fact that there are known hazards to women in a given situation does not mean that there may not be other unknown harmful effects to men, say some specialists in the field. In any case, they reason, all workplaces should be safe by law.

Ten years after the first reports of the sterilizing effects on male agricultural workers of the pesticide dibromochloropropane, follow-up investigations confirmed that the sterility caused by exposure to this substance appears to be permanent in many of those affected. By emergency order of the EPA, dinoseb, a widely used phenol-derived herbicide closely related to pentachlorophenol (which at one point was totally banned because of harmful reproductive-system effects), was banned except for limited use during the 1987 growing season. Dinoseb has been linked to a high risk of sterility among farmers and farm workers and birth defects among their offspring.

Severe trauma. Traumatic injuries at the workplace have gained increasing attention, and the U.S. Centers for Disease Control (CDC) has now funded three new university-based centers whose purpose is to research the causes and prevention of such injuries. In addition, there has been an increase in funding for a wide range of injury-control projects, including the previously much neglected area of injury research related to agricultural activity. Tractor rollover injuries, amputations resulting from use of farm machinery, and other similar problems are receiving increased attention. In contrast to the study and prevention of highway accidents, research into farm-related accidents and deaths requires much more basic descriptive work on the part of investigators because such accidents have not yet been studied as rigorously and systematically as automobile accidents have.

Occupational cancers. Studies conducted in rural Sweden from 1979 to 1981 documented an association between exposure to phenoxyacid herbicides and the development of certain types of cancers, specifically soft-tissue sarcomas, Hodgkin's disease, and non-Hodgkin's lymphoma. Now U.S. researchers studying the incidence of various cancers in rural Kansas men exposed to similar herbicides have confirmed the Swedish findings regarding non-Hodgkin's lymphoma. In addition to agricultural uses, these chemical compounds have industrial applications in the manufacture of wood pulp and paper, wood preservatives, and agents used in waterproofing leather and textiles.

Occupational diseases of the lung. NIOSH has begun active consideration of extending its X-ray surveillance program to surface miners because of increasing cases of silicosis among these workers. This disease is now being appreciated as a problem separate from

297

coal workers' pneumoconiosis (also known as black lung disease), which occurs among coal miners who work underground.

Also in connection with silicosis, a long-forgotten story with an important place in American industrial history was the subject of a book published in 1986. *The Hawk's Nest Incident: America's Worst Industrial Disaster* tells of the scandalous disregard for the health of construction workers who built a tunnel near the town of Gauley Bridge, W.Va., during the Depression era. (The name Hawk's Nest refers to a roosting area on the top of Gauley Mountain, which rises above the town.) In 1929 ground was broken for construction of a tunnel through the base of Gauley Mountain for the purpose of diverting water from the New River to generate electricity for a hydroelectric plant. The rock through which the tunnel was dug contained an exceedingly high silica content. Although silicosis was well recognized by 1930 as a serious occupational health hazard, such preventive practices as the use of respirators or drilling with water (to suppress silica dust) were not employed at the Gauley Mountain tunnel site. Many workers suffered from acute silicosis, as well as the more common chronic form of the disease. Although this episode led to congressional investigations and eventually to the adoption of workers' compensation laws in many states, cases of acute silicosis associated with construction projects are, unfortunately, still being seen more than 50 years later. In the meantime, the state of West Virginia is in the process of erecting a historical marker dedicated to the workers who died constructing the tunnel.

Environmental concerns

In November 1986 a major spill of toxic chemicals entered the Rhine River in Switzerland, causing massive fish kills and affecting the life of the river for many miles downstream. This accident was considered the worst nonnuclear environmental disaster in Europe in the past decade. A continuing concern about spills such as this one is that not only is there an acute effect on wildlife and on the quality of water used for human consumption but such toxic materials may enter the ecosystem and cause problems for many years to come.

In the United States funds have been allocated for the development of training and education programs for workers who might come into contact with hazardous-waste materials. Initial appropriations at the $10 million level are expected to rise, over a period of several years, to as much as $30 million per year under the so-called Superfund legislation. The programs will be administered by the National Institute of Environmental Health Sciences (NIEHS). Workers who are to be trained regarding the health hazards and safe handling of toxic chemicals include those in facilities where such materials are generated, transportation

"Looks as if the clean-air crowd turned out in force."

workers who haul toxic-waste materials, law-enforcement personnel and other governmental employees who may be called upon for help in cases of toxic spills or fires, and members of professional and volunteer fire departments. The need for this kind of program has become increasingly urgent in the wake of the accidents at Bhopal, India, and Chernobyl, U.S.S.R., which pointed up the lack of appropriate planning for such eventualities. The worker-training effort was to be supplemented by the development of computerized systems to assist in managing accidents involving toxic materials.

Another environmental issue, acid rain, long a subject of political and economic concern, finally received some official attention from U.S. health authorities. In February 1987, testifying before a Senate committee on the environment, physicians representing several organizations—among them the American Academy of Pediatrics, the American Lung Association, and the American Public Health Association—said that acid rain and the pollutants that cause it are a significant threat to human health. Children and the elderly, both groups that are particularly vulnerable to respiratory disorders, were cited as being at greatest risk.

Tap water: dangerous to health?

Consumers in the United States were notified in the fall of 1986 that unacceptable levels of lead may be contained in some tap water. The problem is not in the water itself but in the older lead pipes of some public and private supply systems, lead water mains connecting residences to those systems, and the interior plumbing of houses and apartment buildings, which may contain lead solder (used to join copper pipes) in buildings of more recent vintage. Water sitting in the pipes causes corrosion, releasing lead into the water.

Lead that is ingested presents a significant health hazard. It can elevate blood pressure, interfere with blood formation, and cause neurological symptoms. Perhaps the greatest danger is to children and developing fetuses. A pregnant woman exposed to even moderate levels of lead runs a risk of having a low-birth-weight baby. The infant's cognitive and neurological development may also be affected. Lead exposure in children is a known cause of mental retardation.

An EPA draft report released in October 1986 detailed the potential savings of millions of dollars in medical costs that would be accomplished by a reduction of lead in drinking water. The agency's stated goal was to reduce the permissible level of lead in community water supplies from 50 parts per billion (ppb) to 20 ppb by 1988. The EPA recommendations included some that consumers could follow at home, among them checking to see if lead pipes, solder, or flux was used in the plumbing system that provides their tap water and allowing water for drinking and cooking to run from the tap for three to five minutes before use. Hot water is more likely to contain dissolved lead, so consumers were advised to use cold water for cooking purposes, especially when preparing infant formula and other baby foods.

Progress in litigation

The slow-moving litigation against the Manville Corp. (formerly Johns-Manville) continued toward resolution with a plan for establishment of a fund worth potentially more than $2.5 billion to compensate the victims of asbestosis and related diseases. The Indian government continued to proceed with litigation to compensate victims of the toxic-gas leak at Bhopal, but the replacement of the presiding judge in the case further complicated the proceedings. In the U.S.S.R. the plant director and others in charge of operations at the Chernobyl nuclear power plant at the time of the explosion and fire (April 1986) were sentenced to ten years in a Soviet labor camp. The finding that several companies operating natural gas pipelines in the United States had dumped polychlorinated biphenyls (PCBs) along their routes in various states was expected to result in several new lawsuits. Levels of PCBs up to 48,000 parts per million (ppm) were noted in soil along the pipelines (50 ppm is the threshold designated by the EPA as a health hazard). It was reported that the EPA had apparently been aware of the violation for more than a year but had not acted. In Massachusetts lawsuits regarding cases of leukemia that developed following the illegal dumping of toxic chemicals were settled out of court.

Work-site wellness

At a new Toyota plant being built near Lexington, Ky., the company expects to establish the traditional Japanese practice of work-site exercise—a program of stretching and limbering will be held prior to each work shift. The University of Kentucky Medical Center at Lexington has been asked, along with other local specialists, to help develop a medical program for the plant that addresses issues of prevention. For example, consultants have been retained to develop a program to minimize musculoskeletal problems, including hand problems such as carpal tunnel syndrome and other so-called cumulative trauma disorders, which are often associated with assembly-line work. It is expected that wellness programs addressing weight control, cigarette smoking, cardiovascular fitness, and other issues will also be established.

With the soaring costs of medical care and employee health insurance, U.S. corporations are beginning to offer their workers incentives for healthful behavior. Such incentive programs include payments for successful weight loss, extra costs to smokers on insurance policies, and the development at the workplace of fitness centers for the employees. More and more, cigarette smoking is being banned or restricted in offices, factories, and other work sites.

As heavy industry and manufacturing become established in countries not traditionally known for this output—e.g., South Korea and Yugoslavia are now becoming exporters of automobiles—occupational health authorities are watching to see if work-related health problems will be avoided in the new factories. Many typical injuries may be prevented by the application of technology and modifications of design based on lessons learned in nations with long-time experience. In particular, whether stress-related illness will increase as a "cost" of industrialization is being watched for.

AIDS testing at work?

In the United States much deliberation has been given to the issue of AIDS (acquired immune deficiency syndrome) testing in the workplace. A major pronouncement from a conference held at the CDC in the spring of 1987 took the view that AIDS testing should not be mandatory but should be encouraged on a voluntary basis. From a traditional public health point of view, this policy is consistent with one of the most basic precepts of screening examinations—that is, that screening should be applied only to medical problems for which there is an effective and generally accepted method of treatment. Although there may be some social utility in identifying employees carrying the AIDS virus, which could potentially spread to others, given the current lack of proven treatment modalities and the social stigma of identification, mandatory testing would not be useful at the current time. AIDS is a classic example of a disease in which public education—rather than reliance on poorly enforceable regulations—is vital in checking the spread of a serious health problem.

—Arthur L. Frank, M.D., Ph.D.

Chernobyl Aftermath:
Soviet Life in the Wake of Disaster

by Felicity Barringer

On April 25, 1986, the first sticky leaves were giving way to the general green of spring in the rural Ukrainian countryside surrounding the Chernobyl nuclear power plant, about 130 km (80 mi) north of Kiev. Children were going to school in the modern, 15-year-old Soviet workers' town of Pripyat, set among the old farms and marshes of the sandy, swampy region. All four 1,000-MW reactors at the power plant were operating; construction of two new reactors was under way. Before dawn the next day the landscape, the town, and the power plant were irrevocably changed. Preparations for a low-power experiment with the fourth reactor had begun in the early hours of April 25. During the experiment, which began in earnest late that night and continued into the early hours of April 26, engineers shut off or bypassed most of the existing safety systems. Forty seconds after 1:23 AM on the 26th, just after a desperate engineer tried to start an emergency shutdown, two explosions in quick succession blew the reactor's roof off.

Nuclear fuel and highly radioactive debris spewed out into the atmosphere, pumped thousands of meters into the air by the intense heat of the burning nuclear fuel and the fires it generated in the buildings around it. Squad after squad of firefighters arrived to fight the blazes. The heat of the partially molten reactor core, however, continued to push radioactive iodine, cesium, and strontium particles 1,000 m (3,200 ft) into the atmosphere, where the prevailing winds blew them toward Poland and Scandinavia. A wedge of foliage near the plant would not turn green for many springs to come.

Aftermath of the disaster

By the end of the summer of 1986, according to a Soviet government report, 31 people had died as a result of the accident, another 175 had suffered severe cases of radiation sickness, and some 135,000 people who lived either in a 1,036-sq-km (400-sq-mi) zone around the plant—or in "hot spots" up to 60 km (35 mi) away—had lost their homes, many forever. The new town of Pripyat and the old town of Chernobyl had become ghost towns. There had been scores of small villages dotted around the area, in the Gomel region of southern Belorussia and in the Kiev and Zhitomir

regions of the Ukraine; at least 163 are now deserted. Radioactive contamination mixed with the urban dust and grit in Gomel and Minsk in Belorussia and in Kiev, the capital of the Ukraine and the Soviet Union's third largest city (population 2.5 million). In addition, some 75 million people in the Ukraine, Belorussia, Russia, and Moldavia had been exposed to unusual, though in most cases small, doses of radiation.

For ten days after the accident, while the burning reactor continued to pump radioactive contamination into the atmosphere, Soviet military helicopters dropped 5,000 tons of boron, lead, dolomite, and sand to seal it off. The winds shifted toward the south and southwest, carrying the radioactive contamination over Romania and across the Adriatic Sea to Italy. By the time the emissions were finally controlled, radioactive fallout had reached the reindeer herds of the Lapps in northern Sweden and Norway, 1,770 km (1,100 mi) to the north, and lambs grazing in Wales, 2,250 km (1,400 mi) to the west. Above-average levels of atmospheric radiation were detected as far away as Israel, Japan, and North America.

From the outset some Western officials and experts, notably those in the U.S. government, reacted skeptically to the seemingly low casualty estimates cited by Soviet authorities—both the reports of the dead and injured and the projections of long-term health consequences. The skepticism was sharply aggravated by the Soviets' refusal to acknowledge the accident until 67 hours later. Nevertheless, there has been no contradiction of the Soviet reports from any source with first-hand information. Most of what is known today about the health consequences of the disaster comes from the comprehensive Soviet government report submitted to the International Atomic Energy Agency in August 1986. Western experts who reviewed the report regreted the absence of some data but expressed confidence in the general statistical and technical accuracy of the document.

The disaster left the Soviet Union facing four separate health-related crises. First was the treatment of— at the very least—some 237 people suffering from radiation exposure. The second concerned the evacuation, protection, and resettlement of the 135,000 people who lived in areas too contaminated to permit

Ukrainian women and children, evacuees from the area around the Chernobyl nuclear plant, are checked for radiation exposure by a Soviet medical technician.

further habitation, most of these within a designated danger zone of 30 km (18.6 mi) around the plant. Then came the massive task of public-health protection in the face of the radioactive fallout that dropped from the clouds with the rain and was ingested in the milk of dairy animals, eaten in agricultural produce and wild mushrooms and berries, and simply inhaled. Finally, the Soviets face the prospect of thousands of cases of radiation-induced cancers and an unknown number of genetic mutations over the next half century.

The first crisis: acute radiation illness

The first task—treating those directly exposed to radiation from the explosion and fires—was perhaps the most harrowing. Moscow Hospital Number 6, which specializes in the treatment of radiation-related disease and injury, sent two staff members to assess the disaster about five hours after the explosions. Within the next two days, 299 patients, all plant or emergency personnel, were examined for radiation sickness and 237 were hospitalized, 203 of them diagnosed as having "acute" radiation sickness. No radiation-monitoring data from the plant site itself were available to hospital personnel, so the doses of radiation suffered by the victims had to be estimated from the extent of radiation damage—the speed at which the white blood cells were destroyed, for instance, or the extent of decay of internal organs such as the liver and the intestines. Other signs and symptoms of acute radiation sickness include vomiting and diarrhea; destruction of blood platelets, predisposing to hemorrhage; drop in number of red blood cells, producing marked anemia; and loss of hair. Acute radiation illness occurs when the radiation dose exceeds 100 rads (radiation absorbed dose). Total body irradiation of 1,000 rads is

almost certain to be fatal. Of the patients hospitalized following the accident, 22 of those brought in during the first day were estimated to have received doses in excess of 600 rads. All but one died between 4 and 50 days after the accident, according to the Soviet report. A document published in January 1987 by the U.S. Nuclear Regulatory Commission (NRC) reported one subsequent death.

A fireman seriously irradiated while battling the reactor fire at Chernobyl gazes out of an isolation unit at Moscow Hospital Number 6, where those suffering from the most severe radiation injury were taken for treatment.

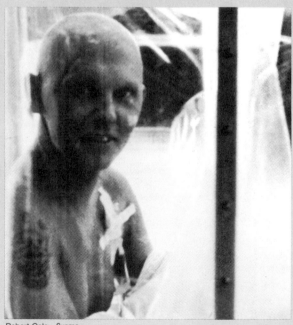

Another 23 people were estimated to have received doses between 400 to 600 rads; 7 of these died. Including the two plant workers killed at the time of the explosion or shortly afterward, the death toll had reached an official count of 31 by the first week of August. No radiation-related deaths have been reported since. Of the 158 people reported to have been exposed to doses of 80 to 400 rads, all survived.

One of the greatest dangers facing the victims of large doses of radiation is the destructive effect on the bone-marrow cells, the body's factory for producing oxygen-carrying red blood cells and infection-fighting white blood cells. One of the few treatment techniques available, itself a highly risky procedure, is bone-marrow transplantation from a donor whose blood and tissue types match those of the victim. With the help of specialist Robert Gale, a U.S. physician from the University of California at Los Angeles Medical Center, 13 bone-marrow-transplant operations were performed by teams of Soviet and American doctors. According to varying reports, one or perhaps two of these patients survived. Six other severely irradiated patients, who could not be matched with donors because their white blood cells needed for typing had been destroyed, received transplants of fetal liver cells. All of them died.

Wash and then wash again

Everywhere, from the streets of Kiev, about 130 km (80 mi) south of the reactor, to the bathhouses of collective farms of the Ukraine—where the operators of tractors and harvesters were coming home after having spent the day in newly installed airtight cabins atop their machines—everyone was required to wash and then wash again. "Our greatest enemy is dust," wrote one Soviet journalist.

In the first weeks after the accident, health authorities set absolute standards for the radioactive iodine content of various foods and food products, including milk. (The area hardest hit by the fallout was a major milk-producing area.) Leafy vegetables such as lettuce and spinach, as well as berries, mushrooms, poultry, and eggs, were among the foods involved. Checkpoints were also set up within the distribution system: at the field level, in the processing plants, and at the markets. The U.S.S.R. Ministry of Health set tolerance levels for radioactive substances for all products sold at the open farmers' markets—the goal: to limit overall individual exposure to five rads. Ice-cream stands disappeared from the streets of Kiev, and there were public warnings against eating certain home-grown or home-gathered foods, among them mushrooms, red and black currants, and gooseberries.

Leaving the native soil

As the summer of 1986 wore on, the death toll mounted slowly while other victims slowly recovered and prepared to go home. Few, however, were to return to the homes they had left in late April.

By the evening of April 27, 20 hours after the accident, the town of Pripyat was deserted. Between Saturday the 26th and Sunday the 27th, potassium iodide pills were distributed to local residents; this substance helps to prevent the uptake of radioactive iodine by the thyroid gland. First, the people of Pripyat were advised to remain indoors and keep windows closed. Then, at noon on Sunday, most of the town's 50,000 residents heard the announcement that the evacuation would begin in two hours. A fleet of some 1,100 Kiev city buses arrived on schedule, and the evacuation, according to Soviet news reports, was carried out in less than three hours. The evacuation route was itself highly contaminated, but substances to trap and damp down the roadside dust were sprayed on the roads before the buses left for Pripyat. The buses themselves were washed down before being returned to service in Kiev. According to all Soviet accounts, the Pripyat evacuation was efficient and successful and reflected careful emergency planning.

Things did not go as smoothly in rural areas. The calls for evacuation came later—up to ten days later in some areas—and the people were far less ready to comply. "This was the place of their farms, their home, their native soil, the place where their parents and grandparents were buried," said one regional Communist Party newspaper of the reluctance of these residents to leave the area. One practical concern was the outright refusal of some farmers to leave without their livestock, which to them represented their liveli-

Soviet physicians talk with a volunteer rescue worker. Despite the many casualties of the explosion and fire at Chernobyl, Western experts felt that Soviet medical authorities had coped efficiently with the disaster.

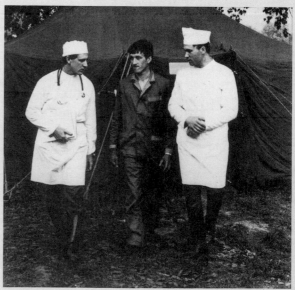

Camera Press

302

Some 50,000 people were evacuated from Pripyat and temporarily resettled in towns outside of the immediate danger zone. Families shared their quarters with the evacuees, and additional bathing facilities were hastily erected. (Left) Youngsters from the Chernobyl region adjust to their new surroundings.

hood. In the end at least 55,000 head of cattle were evacuated along with their owners. Some residents finally had to be forcibly removed; two elderly women who managed to elude authorities hid out in Pripyat until late May. Radiation doses received by some of the rural residents, according to the NRC report, were considerably higher than those of Pripyat residents—on the average about ten times higher. The Soviet report is contradictory on this point, but it does indicate that these rural residents stayed in the contaminated zone between seven and ten days. Further, they were reportedly less willing to heed warnings about the danger of drinking cow's milk. One of the most potent, though short-lived, radioactive isotopes, iodine-131, is ingested with grass by grazing dairy cows and concentrates in their milk.

The potential for uptake of radioactive iodine by the thyroid gland was one of the major concerns of the public health authorities wrestling with the disaster. Like the Pripyat residents, other inhabitants of the danger zone were given potassium iodide as a protective measure. Children underwent medical tests that monitored the iodine-uptake levels of their thyroid glands. The Soviet report indicated that most children received low overall doses of radioactive iodine, but the NRC report, extrapolating from the Soviet data, said that over time perhaps 100 thyroid cancers attributable to the Chernobyl disaster would occur in this population. It was reported later that programs were being established by the Soviet government to screen thyroid function in many people from the areas where fallout was the heaviest. There were also reports of testing for radiation-induced chromosomal damage.

One of the major problems facing Soviet emergency planners was what to do with the evacuees. Pripyat residents were taken first to villages in the Polessky

district, west of the danger zone, while evacuees from the rural northern section of the Kiev region were taken about 80 km (50 mi) to the south. Those from the southern areas of the Gomel region were taken similar distances to the north. Families moved into the small living quarters of other families; new public bathing areas were hastily erected. Radioactive clothes had to be disposed of and new clothing obtained.

During May and June 1986 rumors circulated in Moscow that pregnant women in the evacuated areas and perhaps other areas as well had been officially advised to have abortions. These rumors were never publicly confirmed, although they indicated a widespread knowledge about the mutagenic effects of radiation on susceptible fetal tissues. The rumors did prompt a reaction in the official press, however; on September 30 the Communist Party newspaper *Pravda* carried a story about 130 healthy babies having been born to evacuees in the Ukraine since the accident. A later report, published in the *New York Times* in April 1987, on the first anniversary of the accident, said that 300 normal infants had been born to women exposed to the Chernobyl radiation during pregnancy. These children will be carefully watched for signs of mental retardation—an effect of radiation exposure noted in the children of women who were heavily irradiated at Hiroshima—and for the development of radiation-induced leukemia.

A massive support system for evacuees was constructed in the receiving areas to identify them for future purposes, one of these being the eventual distribution of monetary compensation. There were, however, other reasons for keeping track of the refugees. Families separated at the time of evacuation had to be reunited. Many children in areas beyond the danger zone—60,000 children in Belorussia and 80,000 in the Ukraine, including those in Kiev—were let out of school early and sent for safety to summer camps and rest homes in uncontaminated regions in the Carpathian Mountains to the west and the Caucasus Mountains to the southeast. Most of these youngsters returned to the areas outside the general evacuation zones in time for school on Sept. 1, 1986. By that time most of the other evacuees had been resettled, if not permanently, at least for the forseeable future.

A new town for plant workers, called Zelenyi Mys ("Green Cape"), was established on the Kiev reservoir southeast of the evacuation zone. A new permanent workers' town of Slavutich was expected to be completed in the fall of 1987. Workers at the Chernobyl plant, where the number one and two reactors were restarted in the fall of 1986, live there while on duty and in some 8,500 new apartments in Kiev when they are off duty. Many of them receive as much as three times the normal pay for working at the site of the damaged reactor. Of the 179 towns and villages evacuated, only two in the Kiev region—with a total population of 213—have been resettled. Another 1,500 Belorussians have been returned to 16 villages in the Gomel region.

Decontamination—a "heroic deed"

The decontamination of the plant grounds, a prerequisite for getting workers back to start the undamaged reactors, was a massive task and was treated publicly as a *podvig*, or "heroic deed." Everything about the plant was radioactive—in many cases lethally so—even the fire engines that had been abandoned at the site the night of the explosion. The number four reactor was both an open wound and a loaded weapon. Subway workers from Kiev and miners from the Ukraine's southern coal mines were enlisted to dig a tunnel under the reactor and install reinforced shielding to prevent any nuclear fuel from contaminating the groundwater. Outside the plant, workers operated remote-controlled cranes and bulldozers to isolate and encapsulate radioactive debris; tons of topsoil were bulldozed off and buried in a nearby construction pit. Polymerizing substances were sprayed to bind the radioactive particles to the soil; other areas were simply paved over.

When there were jobs that could not be done by remote-controlled machines, men in special suits would drive up in hermetically sealed cars, run toward the pieces of debris, put them into safe containers, and sprint away. In some cases, as reported by the Soviet press, these men received the equivalent of a lifetime's worth of background radiation in a minute or less. (Background radiation is the "normal" amount of radiation present in the environment—cosmic rays, natural radioactivity, and so forth.) In that way, with radiation doses monitored by dosimeters on their suits, with clumsy mechanical arms and mad dashes, men

cleaned the site, and a massive concrete sarcophagus was erected around the reactor to enclose it for the centuries that it will take for the fuel to decompose. Decontamination work on a similar but reduced scale was going on in the deserted villages and fields—the burial of topsoil, the isolation of radioactive debris, the monitoring of wells.

The dispersal of radioactivity had gone on for so many days and the debris had been carried by so many different winds, however, that workers could make few predictions about where the "dirtiest" areas would be. They could more accurately pinpoint another possible danger: contamination of the streams and rivers. The Pripyat River, which runs by the Chernobyl nuclear power plant, flows into the Dnepr River, the main water source for the city of Kiev. In May and June dozens of artesian wells were dug around the city. As added insurance, a system of diversion was set up so that the Desna River, the subsidiary water source for the city, could replace the Dnepr as the primary source. Between June and December almost all of Kiev's water came from the Desna.

Life goes on

By winter things were returning to normal, although it was a new sort of normal. The water pipes to the Dnepr River were turned back on in Kiev. Some 8,500 homes for evacuees were completed in the fields about 50 km (30 mi) northwest of Kiev. In addition to the 8,500 apartments being readied for evacuees in Kiev, there were 500 more in the northern Ukrainian town of Chernigov. Another 8,000 families—perhaps 18,000 people—had been sent to live and work elsewhere in the Soviet Union. This population and the plant workers, cleanup personnel, bus drivers, and physicians—the inadvertent guinea pigs in one of the broadest and most brutal field tests of radiation exposure—will be monitored by Ukrainian health authorities; they will have blood tests and general medical workups at least once a year for the rest of their lives.

And what of the 75 million Soviets exposed to slight doses of radiation from Chernobyl? None of the reports specifically states what the possible number of birth defects will be, but the NRC report, extrapolating from the Soviet data, predicts at least 10,000 new cases of cancer in the Soviet population. The Soviets, when noting possible cancer incidence estimates, are quick to point out that over the next 70 years—the time during which these cancers would occur—the population would have an expected cancer incidence of 9.5 million. Also, as other public health authorities have noted, the number of cases directly attributable to Chernobyl may be so small, in a relative sense, that it will be "hidden" in the overall statistics. In any case, it will be decades before the real toll of Chernobyl—the human costs of the disaster—can be accurately measured.

Special Report

Chernobyl Aftermath: Ill Wind over Europe

by Ray Moseley

The accident that occurred on April 26, 1986, at the Chernobyl nuclear reactor in the Soviet Union was, for people in widely scattered parts of Europe, an environmental disaster of unprecedented magnitude, and one whose effects will impinge on European life and consciousness for years to come. Thousands of Europeans may be carrying the seeds of premature death from radiation exposure as a result of Chernobyl. In the vast, uncultivated Arctic lands of Sweden and Norway, where reindeer herds were seriously affected, many of the seminomadic Lapp people face the prospect of a fundamental change in their diet and a major loss of earnings. Throughout Europe the strictly economic costs of the accident were expected to run to hundreds of millions of dollars. Crops had to be destroyed; milk from dairy animals was simply thrown away; fish and wildlife became contaminated; and the tourist industry suffered heavily because of the reluctance of Americans and others from overseas to travel to Europe.

The damage from Chernobyl was by no means uniformly distributed throughout Europe. There were "hot spots" where radioactive fallout reached alarming levels and other areas that suffered little or no contamination. The contamination was heaviest in areas that experienced rainfall in the immediate aftermath of the accident. The principal hot spots were in Sweden, southern regions of West Germany, Poland, and a corner of eastern France. In some cases these spots were only a few miles wide. Parts of Scotland, the English Lake District, northern Italy, and Czechoslovakia also were seriously affected. Health authorities said there was no real danger of external irradiation for people who ventured out-of-doors in these areas; the more serious problems arose from contaminated crops and pasture lands.

Economic losses in Scandinavia

Of all of the Western European countries, Sweden was particularly unlucky—freakish wind currents, which normally would have blown in a different direction, carried radioactive material over the country. In Sweden and Norway the most serious problem involved the reindeer herds on which nearly 10% of the Lapp people depend for their livelihood. Reindeer feed on lichen, which takes its nourishment from the atmosphere

rather than the ground and consequently was heavily irradiated. Reindeer meat is a popular dish throughout Scandinavia and is a staple of the diet of the approximately 50,000 Lapps. Some reindeer meat was found to contain up to 40,000 becquerels (a measurement of radioactivity named for French physicist Henri Becquerel) of cesium per kilogram (2.2 lb), well above Norway's official safety level of 600 becquerels per kilogram and Sweden's 300. Authorities estimated that as many as 100,000 reindeer in Sweden and 40,000 in Norway had been dangerously contaminated. Initial plans called for the affected animals to be slaughtered and their meat destroyed, but officials later proposed feeding the meat to silver fox and mink. They said radiation would not affect the pelts of these animals. Fish from small lakes in the area where the Lapps live also were contaminated, some showing more than 10,000 becquerels per kilogram. It was predicted that the Lapps, who subsist by fishing and hunting, would have to become more dependent on food purchased from shops.

About 4,000 elk killed by hunters in Sweden had to be buried because their meat was found to be unfit for human consumption. The Swedish government ordered cows kept in barns in the immediate aftermath of Chernobyl so they would not ingest radioactive iodine from grazing on contaminated pastures. This action cost farmers millions of dollars in extra feed bills. While the grazing restrictions were in effect, the government also advised people to avoid eating certain green vegetables and to wash others before eating them. Some sheep and lambs were found to be contaminated, and their meat, too, was fed to mink and foxes. Christer Wiktorsson, the leader of a Chernobyl study project at the National Institute of Radiation Protection in Stockholm, said the effects of Chernobyl in Sweden were worse than originally estimated because the fallout of radioactive cesium had exceeded official expectations. He said that crops would be affected for many years, but at a low level, and milk and meat would present a problem for the next two to four years.

Norwegian authorities found high levels of radioactivity in some freshwater fish, reindeer, cattle, roe deer, elk, and bears. Thousands of tons of Norwegian vegetable crops were destroyed. The other Nordic countries, Finland and Denmark, escaped more lightly.

305

J. Donoso—Sygma

The economy of the Lapp people of Norway and Sweden was devastated by the nuclear fallout from Chernobyl. Radioactivity contaminated the reindeer grazing in local forests, as well as the lichens on which they feed. The animals were slaughtered, and the meat—unfit for human consumption—had to be either destroyed or fed to mink and other animals raised for their pelts.

Finnish reindeer were not seriously affected, and few restrictions were imposed on food consumption. Some Finnish officials said that the Swedes had been "hysterical" in their reaction to Chernobyl, but Finland had less rainfall than Sweden in the aftermath of the accident and thus may have received less fallout. In Denmark farmers were forbidden to put cattle to pasture for a few weeks, but no other restrictions were imposed. Danish officials said there was no serious contamination of milk and butter, both vital products to the country's economy.

The Soviet Union rejected all suggestions that it pay compensation for economic losses resulting from Chernobyl, but Sweden and most other affected countries compensated their farmers and others who had suffered losses. The final bill in Sweden alone was projected to be $140 million.

Anxiety, but no panic

When the true magnitude of the Chernobyl disaster started to become apparent, a few days after Swedish scientists became the first to report the event, alarm spread across Europe. While there were no reports of mass hysteria or panic, people expressed their fears in various ways. Across Europe the various countries' national radiological protection boards were sought out by the news media for comment, and because of this publicity scores of thousands of anxious citizens phoned board offices for advice. Some people also called their local doctors, but most general practitioners lacked the specific knowledge that could be of practical benefit and referred callers to the radiological protection boards or to hospitals with radiotherapy and nuclear medicine departments.

There were many calls from pregnant women worried about fetal damage and from mothers concerned about the health of young children. Some pregnant women in West Germany and other countries heavily exposed to fallout had abortions rather than risk giving birth to children deformed by radiation exposure. People who had been caught in the rain expressed concern about radioactivity on their skin and clothes. Some inquired what they could do to protect pets that had been outdoors. People planning trips to Eastern Europe called for advice on whether to go ahead with their travel. Farmers with impounded sheep wanted to know if they would get radioactive material on their hands from handling the wool.

A few of the callers were hysterical. A British expert recalled a particularly poignant conversation with a woman who was dying of cancer and was worried about the future of her two young children. Many callers also expressed an extraordinary lack of understanding about radiation. Some believed quite literally in a "China syndrome"—that is, a nuclear meltdown that would penetrate the ground at Chernobyl and melt through to the opposite side of the Earth. One woman who had been caught in the rain developed weals on her skin that she was convinced were caused by radioactivity, and others expressed similar fears about newly developed skin rashes. A dog developed fits and had to be put to sleep, and its owner suspected that radioactivity was to blame. Dead birds and fish, dead moss on rooftops, cars failing to start, and clouded waters in a garden pond were all blamed on the cloud from Chernobyl. Some people stayed indoors and sealed their homes until they were assured that it was safe to come out.

The advice from experts varied according to circumstances. In some hot spots people were cautioned to avoid drinking milk for a time and to wash fresh vegetables. In other areas they were assured that radiation levels were not high enough to worry about. Some of the more distraught callers, who imagined they were developing radiation sickness, were advised to see their doctors. A medical physicist at a hospital in Birmingham, England, said he explained to mothers and pregnant women what the levels of radiation meant by comparing them with normal levels and left it to them to decide whether to continue drinking milk or giving it to their babies. He said there was no scientific indication that fresh milk should be avoided.

Many who were visiting on the European continent at the time of the accident returned home. Some Westerners living in Poland sent their children out of the country. The British government ordered British students in Kiev and Minsk, the cities nearest to Chernobyl, to leave the Soviet Union temporarily for their own safety. They were met at London's Heathrow Airport by officials of the National Radiological Protection Board (NRPB), who used hand-held monitors to measure thyroid activity as well as to determine contamination levels of clothing and luggage. These tests found that none of the students had ingested enough radioactive material to cause concern, but some of their clothing was retained for decontamination. Seven of the students volunteered to be measured in a mobile, whole-body monitor that was taken to the airport, but these tests also found radioactivity levels insufficient to cause concern. In many other instances tourists and other travelers who happened to be in Eastern Europe

As the news of Chernobyl spread across Europe, public health officials did their best to cope with the situation. The Polish government distributed an iodine preparation to children as a precaution against thyroid irradiation.

Reuters/Bettmann Newsphotos

at the time of Chernobyl were screened at hospitals upon returning to their home countries.

No consensus on "acceptable" exposures

Chernobyl pointed up the lack of agreement on what constitutes a dangerous level of radioactivity, something that many scientists would like to see rectified. Most nations set a limit of 600 becquerels per kilogram, but France allows up to 1,000 becquerels. Gunnar Bengtsson, head of Sweden's Radiation Protection Institute, has concluded that his country's 300-becquerel limit is much too strict and resulted in the unnecessary destruction of many reindeer. The state and federal governments in West Germany differed on acceptable limits. Federal authorities set a maximum level of 250 becquerels per liter (about a quart) of milk, but two states set the limit at 20. On the day the West German government rescinded its advice to avoid drinking milk, one state halted all school milk supplies. West Berlin destroyed 24,000 liters of East German milk with a level of just 7.5 becquerels per liter, while Bavarians were drinking milk with 900 becquerels per liter.

The 12-nation European Communities (EC) imposed a temporary ban on food imports from Eastern Europe after Chernobyl, but movements of contaminated foods from one Western European nation to another were sometimes overlooked. West Germany waited until two weeks after the disaster, for example, to begin checking contaminated food arriving from Italy. The Italians banned foodstuffs from northern Europe and then seemed surprised, an EC official said, when northern European nations banned Italian vegetables in turn.

While mass destruction of crops took place in West Germany, nothing of the sort happened across the border in France. The French government assured its citizens that the increase in radioactivity from Chernobyl would have no impact on France. French conservationists, in turn, accused the government of hiding the truth. The director of France's Central Protection Service Against Radioactivity said that readings in some parts of France showed a level of radioactivity 400 times higher than normal. The government eventually acknowledged that the situation was more serious than originally had been reported but, apart from banning spinach in Alsace, took no measures concerning domestic foods.

Danger posed by fallout from the fire and explosion centers on the amounts of radioactive iodine, cesium, strontium, and other radionuclides it contained. The extent of danger posed by each of these substances is directly related to its half-life, the time required for half the amount of the substance to be eliminated by natural processes. Since radioactive iodine has a half-life of about eight days, the problems associated with it—mainly affecting milk and leafy vegetables—

307

A shopper in the Alsace region of France checks vegetables for signs of radioactivity. In the aftermath of the Chernobyl disaster, the 12-nation European Communities imposed a temporary ban on all imported foodstuffs from Eastern Europe. Because each country in Western Europe has its own standards regarding what constitutes dangerous levels of radioactivity, restrictions on specific foods varied widely.

were short-lived. Of greater concern was the fallout of cesium, which has a half-life of 30 years. Scientists, however, said a dilution effect would become apparent as time went on. Cesium that falls onto grass is filtered into the soil by rainfall. Some remains in the soil; some attaches itself to the roots of plants; and some is washed away in groundwater. One scientist said that in four years most of the cesium that fell in concentrated areas would be much more evenly distributed throughout the environment and, at lower levels, would constitute less of a health concern.

Late in 1986 West German authorities assured the public that radioactivity levels in foodstuffs were no longer dangerous. A brochure entitled "How to Eat Safely," however, warned consumers against lamb or mutton if the animals had been pastured in contaminated areas. The booklet cautioned parents against letting children eat poultry from Eastern Europe and suggested that mushroom lovers should abandon their taste for Bavarian or Polish chanterelle mushrooms. The booklet quoted a Munich toxicologist, Max Daunderer, as warning that mushrooms from Bavaria and Eastern Europe should be "absolutely taboo" for 80 years. Mushrooms, he said, can store extremely high levels of cesium and strontium.

The ultimate cost in human terms

In the aftermath of the disaster, medical experts said that radiation from Chernobyl could cause a wide range of cancers. Because radioactive iodine concentrates in the thyroid gland, they expected to see an increased incidence of thyroid cancer. Thyroid cancers have a low mortality rate though, while other radiation-associated cancers are more lethal. Cesium tends to collect in muscle tissue and could cause tumors in various parts of the body; strontium is likely to produce bone cancers. There was, however, marked disagreement among medical experts as to how many people would contract cancer, and how many would die, as a result of Chernobyl.

Britain's NRPB estimated that the disaster would cause an additional 2,000 fatalities; the board warned that cancer risks for babies and young children were at least double those for adults and could be expected to show up in an increased incidence of leukemia. Some U.S. authorities, for reasons that were not clear, offered far higher estimates. John Gofman, professor emeritus of medical physics at the University of California at Berkeley, estimated that 424,300 persons in the Soviet Union and 526,700 in the rest of Europe and elsewhere would contract Chernobyl-related cancers over the next 70 years and half would die as a result. Robert Gale, the U.S. bone-marrow specialist who treated Chernobyl victims in the Soviet Union, said that up to 75,000 related deaths could occur worldwide, including 26,000 in the Soviet Union.

The World Health Organization did not attempt to make such estimates. According to Peter J. Waight, a radiation scientist with the organization, public health authorities have no way of measuring or confirming any deaths that may occur as a result of Chernobyl. Waight and other experts agreed that the natural fluctuation in mortality rates in the various European countries would hide the number of cancer deaths directly attributable to Chernobyl, making it impossible for anyone ever to quantify the disaster in these terms. The ultimate cost of the incident—the cost in terms of human suffering—remains only one of the many questions surrounding Chernobyl that will probably never be answered.

Genetics

While scientists around the world debated the advisability of launching an accelerated international effort to create a "map" of the known human genes, small groups of researchers continued to report successful identifications of genes known to cause inherited disease. In the past year or so, gene mapping has successfully pinned down the location of two long-sought-after disease-causing genes. The first is the gene responsible for the progressive muscle-wasting disease known as Duchenne muscular dystrophy. The second is the gene responsible for retinoblastoma, the most common eye tumor in children. Recent gene mapping efforts also provided new insights into the affective disorder known as manic-depressive illness. In addition, a new discovery by U.S. and French researchers strengthened the theory that genetics plays some part in the development of Alzheimer's disease and also lent credence to the recent suggestion of a link between Alzheimer's, a form of dementia associated with aging, and Down syndrome, a major cause of congenital mental retardation.

Duchenne muscular dystrophy—new milestone

For decades investigators knew that the gene responsible for Duchenne muscular dystrophy (DMD) is on the X chromosome, but it was only with the advent of gene mapping—identifying the precise location of individual genes on the 23 pairs of human chromosomes—that they were able to undertake an all-out search for the specific gene itself. Initial gene mapping studies commonly situate a gene on an identifiable fragment of DNA that is so long it may contain 40 to 50 different genes, any one of which could be the disease-causing culprit. Subsequent mapping involves pinpointing the position of the gene in question within the suspect

fragment by identifying sequences of DNA that are progressively closer to the gene itself. Once the gene has been identified, the nature of the disease can be deduced from the sequence of the gene's chemical subunits, the resultant alterations in gene structure (as compared with normal counterparts), and the abnormalities of function found in disease sufferers.

In the case of the DMD gene, investigators recently narrowed its location to a relatively short segment on the short arm of the X chromosome, designated Xp21. While identification of the chromosomal location of the Duchenne gene was a milestone in molecular biology, delineation of the gene itself has not yet been achieved. The DMD gene appears to be either very large or extremely complex, leading some geneticists to predict that the actual isolation of the gene and description of the protein product it encodes will turn out to be even more difficult than was anticipated. In any case, progress is being made as innovative researchers continue to identify DNA sequences closer and closer to the gene itself. Several of these DNA sequences are so close to the gene that they serve as reliable markers of its presence because they are almost always inherited with it. (The smaller the distance between two sites on a chromosome, the less the chance they will be separated during the natural exchange of chromosomal material that occurs in the formation of egg and sperm cells.) Although identifying a gene by means of such markers is never as reliable as locating the exact site of the gene itself, these nearby DNA sequences have been used successfully for the detection of persons carrying the DMD gene and for the prenatal diagnosis of affected fetuses in many families with Duchenne muscular dystrophy.

In the meantime, investigators—most notably Louis Kunkel of Children's Hospital in Boston, Ronald Worton of the Hospital for Sick Children in Toronto, and

Brian Lanker

A milestone in molecular biology was attained when researchers seeking the gene responsible for Duchenne muscular dystrophy narrowed the focus of their search to a specific segment of the X chromosome. Isolation of the gene itself may someday lead to therapy for those who, like the youngster pictured at left, are born with this progressive muscle-wasting disease.

Kay Davies of the University of Oxford—continue their efforts to isolate the entire DMD gene and to sequence its genetic code. Once they succeed, it should be only a short time before they are able to identify the protein product that, when absent or defective, is responsible for the generalized weakness and eventual total muscle deterioration characteristic of the disease. Having identified the protein, scientists will be able to make predictions about the likelihood of treatment for DMD. Furthermore, this step is expected to provide important insights into the origin of other types of muscle-wasting disease.

Retinoblastoma and the first antioncogene

The recent successful isolation and cloning of the gene responsible for retinoblastoma—a malignant tumor of the eye—is of particular interest because of the insights it will bring to the study of cancer in general. It also promises to yield important advances in the treatment and perhaps even prevention of this potentially fatal eye malignancy. The most recent advance in the study of retinoblastoma was credited to researchers at the Whitehead Institute for Biomedical Research, Cambridge, Mass., and the Harvard University Medical School, including Thaddeus Dryja, Stephen Friend, and Robert Weinberg, building on the earlier work of investigators who had been studying the disease for more than a decade.

Retinoblastoma is a rare disorder; it occurs in one of every 20,000 births and affects only newborns and young children (under age four). Although the cure rate is over 95% if the malignancy is caught early, the treatment is crude, involving either removal of the eye (enucleation) or irradiation of the tumor cells, a process that may affect the growth of the skull. There are two forms of retinoblastoma, inherited and noninherited. About one-half of the children with retinoblastoma inherit the trait from one of their parents; as adults they will have a 50-50 chance of passing the trait on to each of their offspring. In the other 50% of those affected, retinoblastoma is not inherited, and the trait cannot be passed on to the next generation. However, both forms of the disease are the result of alterations, or mutations, in a gene that plays an important but as yet uncharacterized role in the growth of cells of the retina.

By 1980 scientists had narrowed the location of the retinoblastoma gene to chromosome 13 and had arrived at what they believed was a plausible explanation of the origin of the inherited and noninherited forms of the disease. The retinoblastoma gene, they hypothesized, is a rare mutation of a normal gene. Most children inherit two copies of the normal gene and never develop malignancy. Occasionally, however, a child inherits a single retinoblastoma gene from one of the parents, setting the scene for the potential development of cancer. According to the "two-hit hypoth-esis" of retinoblastoma developed in the early 1970s by geneticist Alfred Knudson, now at the Fox Chase Cancer Center in Philadelphia, retinoblastoma occurs in these children as the result of a second mutational event. Since the 1970s a great deal of research has confirmed Knudson's hypothesis. With sophisticated chromosomal banding techniques, it has been possible to substantiate his belief that the second "hit," or mutation, cannot strike just any gene; it must strike the remaining normal counterpart of the retinoblastoma gene. This second mutation is now thought to be the result of a random alteration in the gene's structure introduced during the chromosomal doubling that occurs as the cells of the retina divide and proliferate. Mutational events of this sort are fairly common in cells that are proliferating as rapidly as are the retinal cells in fetal life or early infancy. For this reason, it is not unusual to see multiple tumors in both eyes of babies who have inherited one retinoblastoma gene.

The "two-hit" theory also explains the noninherited form of retinoblastoma. Children with this form of the disease inherit two normal genes but are the victims of a rare phenomenon—the subsequent occurrence of two random errors producing mutations in both of a single retinal cell's normal counterparts of the retinoblastoma gene. Because two chance events must take place for the nonhereditary retinoblastoma to occur, this form of the disease takes longer to manifest itself and thus is generally not seen in infants. For the same reason, nonhereditary tumors usually occur singly and in only one eye.

The retinoblastoma gene is unique among the cancer-causing genes identified to date because it is the first one known to induce cancer through the inactivation or loss of a normal gene. All other cancer-causing genes studied to date—known as oncogenes—cause malignancy when they are present. The retinoblastoma gene, dubbed an "antioncogene," causes cancer by its absence. This finding suggests that the normal gene is involved in inhibiting carcinogenesis, probably by coding for substances that, at a certain point, signal the cell to stop growing. In the event that mutational alterations prevent the expression of both copies of the normal gene, manufacture of the growth-inhibiting substance is halted, and the cell is free to proceed along the destructive course of unhampered growth and proliferation.

Now that the retinoblastoma gene has been cloned (*i.e.*, identical copies have been produced in the laboratory), it is only a matter of time before researchers attempt to insert copies of the normal gene into cells that have only mutant genes to see if normal growth can be restored. Once they know what protein the gene normally codes for, this discovery will serve as a guidepost in research on similar types of cancer. There is evidence that this same process—inactivation of anticancer genes—may be responsible for other types

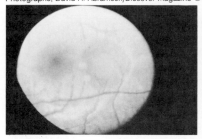 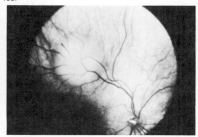 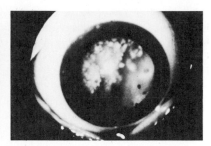

The isolation and cloning of the gene responsible for retinoblastoma, a rare malignancy of the eye, represent the latest steps in more than a decade of research. (Above, left to right) The eyes of three different children show three stages of tumor growth: early (two days old), middle (two months of age), and late (18 months).

of childhood cancer and may be involved in some common types of adult malignant disease.

Bipolar disorder: multifactorial origin?

Gene mapping promises to bring profound insights to the study of some common disorders long thought to have both a genetic and a nongenetic component. Bipolar disorder, or manic-depressive illness—an affective disorder characterized in its severest form by alternating cycles of deep depression and abnormally elevated mood with irritability and extreme hyperactivity—is one such disease. For many years researchers have believed that individuals in some families might be genetically predisposed to developing the disease, but they did not have the tools needed to confirm their suspicions. Now, as a result of gene mapping studies on large extended families in Israel and the United States, it has become clear that predisposition to manic-depressive illness is attributable to at least two different genes—one on the X chromosome and one on chromosome 11.

Many investigators believe that a sizable number of different genetic defects may eventually be linked to bipolar disorder. In fact, it is entirely possible that once more has been learned about its diverse origins, manic-depressive illness will turn out to be several different illnesses. Although it is not yet known how often either of the recently located genes is involved in the development of bipolar disorder in the general population, the current findings are expected to result in a better overall understanding of affective disorders in general and to provide the biochemical insight essential for the design of drugs more effective than those now available for controlling sudden, dramatic changes in mood.

Gene therapy—progress report

The development several years ago of efficient ways of introducing healthy genes into genetically defective cells raised hopes that gene therapy for human hereditary diseases might soon become practical. Despite considerable technical obstacles, sophisticated genetic engineering techniques have enabled scien-

tists to introduce normal genes into defective animal cells growing in laboratory cultures. In many cases they have been successful in getting the normal genes to direct synthesis of the absent protein in laboratory-grown cells. For some reason, however, it has been extremely difficult to get these newly introduced genes to continue to direct protein synthesis once the altered cells have been put back into live animals. Until scientists can maintain satisfactory expression of the inserted gene when the cells are returned to the animal, the prospect of a gene therapy trial to cure human disease remains far off.

When human gene therapy is first attempted, it will most likely be directed at defects that primarily affect red and white blood cells. New blood cells are made throughout the individual's life from a continually renewing population of cells, called stem cells, in bone marrow. Stem cells are ideal for genetic manipulation because they can be removed easily from the body by

The little girl pictured below lost her left eye to retinoblastoma, a cancer that occurs only in newborns and young children. Her right eye, which was also affected by the disease, was saved by radiation therapy.

Dana Fineman—Sygma

syringe, and they survive well in laboratory cultures. Following the introduction of the healthy gene, the altered stem cells are injected into the bloodstream and then migrate back to the bone marrow. Success of the procedure depends on the permanent incorporation of the healthy gene into enough stem cells to provide for a continuous supply of maturing red and white blood cells able to produce the missing protein that is responsible for the disease.

The first gene therapy trials in humans will be aimed at alleviating the symptoms of a hereditary disease so severe and untreatable that most of those affected die at an early age. Children lacking adenosine deaminase (ADA), an enzyme essential for immune system function, may be the first candidates. ADA deficiency devastates the immune system so completely that even the mildest infection can become a killer. Most children with this disorder die in infancy unless heroic measures are taken to isolate them from all sources of infection.

Investigators developing gene therapy techniques for the potential cure of ADA deficiency have been fairly successful in getting the human ADA gene into mouse bone-marrow cells, where it then directs the manufacture of the human enzyme. While this is an important initial step in the development of a gene therapy technique, it turns out that what works in mouse cells does not necessarily work in human cells; scientists have found it very difficult to get foreign genes to function properly after transfer into human bone-marrow cells. Recent reports indicate that redesigning the viruses used to "carry" the foreign genes into the bone-marrow cells may lead to better results. Applying this finding, researchers at several different U.S. laboratories have now successfully achieved ADA synthesis in immune system cells and connective tissue cells (fibroblasts) from patients with the enzyme deficiency. Gene therapy strategies using fibroblasts instead of bone-marrow cells are being investigated in a number of laboratories.

However, the true test of whether the technique may be capable of curing human disease is to see if the cells altered in the laboratory can continue to produce the missing enzyme after they have been reintroduced into the body. It is too early for human trials, but researchers at the U.S. National Institutes of Health have embarked on the next logical step—introducing the human ADA gene into the bone marrow of monkeys. Thus far, reports on the progress of the experiments indicate that the gene has indeed functioned as expected, directing the synthesis of human ADA in several of the monkeys treated, but at levels well below those thought necessary for curing the disease in humans. It appears that the foreign genes enter the animals' bone-marrow stem cells and remain there but for some unknown reason are subsequently inactivated. It is not understood why the newly introduced gene is "turned off" in the stem cells, though some researchers speculate that the virus used to transport the ADA gene into the stem cells may be responsible for the cessation of enzyme production. The prospect of human gene therapy trials remains far off because scientists have not yet discovered how to maintain the high level of function seen in cells in the laboratory.

In the meantime, however, some researchers are experimenting with another kind of gene therapy called germline gene transplantation. In contrast to techniques that confine the foreign gene to somatic cells, germline gene transplantation results in the new gene's presence in every cell of the body, including the sex cells (i.e., eggs and sperm). To achieve this experimentally, the researcher injects the gene under study into a single fertilized egg cell, which will eventually give rise to all of the cells in an adult animal. Because the new gene is present from the earliest stages of development onward, this experimental system is an excellent one for studying the signals that activate and inactivate specific genes at different stages of growth and in different tissues. Although the technique is considered valuable for research and may someday have applications in animal husbandry, for ethical reasons it is not being considered as a way of treating human genetic disease.

In one recent laboratory application of germline gene transplantation, scientists successfully restored fertility in mice rendered infertile as a result of an inherited absence of the gene for gonadotropin-releasing hormone, a brain chemical necessary for sexual development and fertility. Following its insertion into artificially fertilized mouse egg cells, the missing gene became incorporated into the mouse's body cells, where it functioned in a normal fashion in the expected tissues. This tissue-specific expression of the gene allowed both male and female animals to become fully capable of mating and raising healthy litters with no apparent adverse side effects. Although the research is not expected to have direct medical application, it is likely to lead to significant insights into the causes of human infertility.

In a separate set of experiments on laboratory mice, germline transplantation was used as a cure for a genetic deficiency in hemoglobin similar to the one that leads to thalassemia, a severe and sometimes fatal anemia in humans. The inserted gene was able to reduce the anemia in one mouse and completely eliminate it in another. Proper regulation of the transplanted gene demonstrated the potential of a genetic cure for inherited human anemias. Thus far, however, studies of the feasibility of hemoglobin gene transplantation into human bone-marrow stem cells have not been particularly encouraging. Therefore, it will certainly be some time before the potential is realized and clinically applicable techniques are developed.

—Jan Hudis

Special Report
A Controversy in Genetics
by Jan Hudis

Since the nature of the genetic code was first discovered—with the elucidation of the molecular structure of DNA (deoxyribonucleic acid) in 1953 and full deciphering of the code itself (the understanding of how DNA directs the synthesis of protein) about a decade later—there has been speculation about the possibility of identifying the precise order, or sequence, of the three billion chemical units that make up the 46 human chromosomes. As recently as five years ago, discussions about sequencing the entire human genome—the total complement of human genetic information—were largely speculative because the time and cost involved were prohibitive. Molecular genetics is a rapidly moving field, however, and today virtually no one doubts that sequencing the genome is a feat well within the technical capability of the present generation of scientists. Not everyone is agreed, however, on how best to proceed with such an undertaking.

The "Holy Grail" of human genetics
The prospect of sequencing the human genome—determining the linear sequence of the subunits that comprise each gene—has aroused both interest and anxiety among top scientists. While almost everyone agrees that the sequence will be of great significance, there are important questions being asked about the route being taken to discover it. On the one hand, there are those who feel that a project of such enormous scale—it could take 30,000 person-years and billions of dollars to complete the process—should be fostered through the establishment of a well-funded coordinated effort rather than left to chance. Comparing the entire sequence to the Holy Grail of human genetics and stressing its value as an incomparable tool for the study of every aspect of human function, these researchers are advocating an accelerated genome-sequencing program. With such an approach, scientists might accomplish the task in as little as five years, some authorities claim.

Presenting a slightly different point of view are those scientists who feel that more useful information is gained if sequencing goes hand in hand with genetic and biochemical studies. Sequencing, they say, is an inevitable outcome of these other investigations and therefore does not warrant the creation of new administrative bodies or solicitation of special funds. They argue against a narrowly focused sequencing project,

saying that even without a coordinated effort the entire human genome will likely have been sequenced by the year 2000.

The deciphering process
The entire human genetic blueprint resides in an estimated 50,000 to 100,000 genes, discrete units of information positioned along the length of each of the 46 human chromosomes—22 pairs of nonsex chromosomes, or autosomes, plus one chromosome pair that determines sex. Nearly every cell in the body contains within its nucleus these same 46 chromosomes. (Sperm and egg cells contain half of the full complement of chromosomes; that is, 23.)

The major constituent of chromosomes is DNA, a double-stranded molecule coiled in helical fashion. Each strand of the double helix consists of billions of pairs of chemical subunits, called nucleotides or bases, and it is these subunits that encode the instructions for the manufacture of the hundreds of different proteins essential for life.

There are four nucleotides—adenine, cytosine, thymine, and guanine (in genetic shorthand, A, C, T, and G, respectively)—in the genetic code. Strung like beads in a necklace along the length of the DNA molecule, these nucleotides are repeated in various combinations hundreds of thousands of times. The code is written in specific linear sequences of three nucleotides. Each of these triplets designates one of the approximately 20 amino acids that are the basic subunits of all proteins. For example, the nucleotide triplet GGC tells the cell that the amino acid glycine is required. The triplet AAA codes for lysine. Other nucleotide sequences signal the cell to stop or start the process that translates the genetic code into protein.

Thus, by determining the linear sequence of the nucleotides that constitute an individual gene, scientists can also discover the sequence of amino acids that make up the particular protein that the gene encodes. There are several methods for determining nucleotide sequence. One of the more popular currently used sequencing methods relies on a chemical technique that selectively destroys each of the four nucleotides, thus cutting the DNA into many fragments of differing lengths. These fragments are then sorted on the basis of length, using a process called electrophoresis, which reveals where the breaks occurred—and thus reveals the exact position of the nucleotides along the length of the piece of DNA.

Once they know the sequence of the nucleotides within a gene, researchers can begin to answer questions about how the information contained within the gene is translated to direct the manufacture of a specific protein and how very simple alterations in that information—*i.e.*, alterations in the order of subunits within a single gene—can lead to human disease. Supporters of sequencing the entire human genome believe it would be a vast contribution to the study of a wide variety of human illnesses, including those solely of genetic origin (such as cystic fibrosis or sickle-cell anemia) and those that develop as the result of complex interaction between genes and the environment (such as heart disease, diabetes, and cancer).

Genome politics

While few investigators question the advantage of sequencing a gene of known interest, there is serious question about the immediate value of knowing the precise nucleotide sequence of the entire genome. Many of the three billion subunits within the genome are repetitious or irrelevant—even the most generous estimates place the total number of chemical units that code for specific protein products at not more than 50 million, or about 2% of the total. Between these important points along the length of the chromosomes are segments of DNA that have no known function. Most researchers agree that much of this "molecular junk" may be discovered to have an important function when the information content of DNA is better understood. At this time, however, only a very small fraction of the total genome is expected to yield information that will have immediate medical value.

The fact that large portions of the human genome will contain little immediately useful information has led a number of scientists to question whether the enormous expense and coordination needed to successfully determine the entire subunit sequence are justified. A massive sequencing project could cost from $1 billion to $10 billion, putting it in the same league as other "megascience" projects with costs similar to those of the space shuttle and the Superconducting Super Collider, a huge physics research machine whose funding in the United States is currently in doubt because of budget constraints. With research dollars already in short supply, many scientists fear that even with special funding from governmental and private sources, the cost of the DNA-sequencing project would drain already limited funds. They also question the wisdom of steering biology—a science that has traditionally benefited from the creativity and innovation fostered in intimate research settings—into the kind of centrally organized, narrowly focused environment more commonly associated with disciplines such as high-energy physics, astronomy, and weapons development.

Adapted from *Washington Post Health* (Feb. 24, 1987)

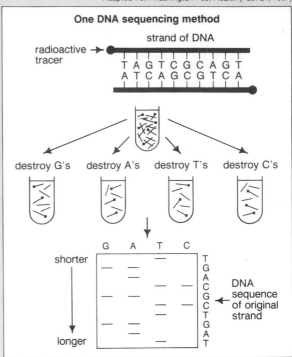

In this diagram of one sequencing method, a radioactively labeled strand of DNA is cloned to produce four identical samples. Each is treated with a chemical that selectively destroys one of the four nucleotides (A, T, G, C). The resulting smaller fragments are sorted by length, revealing where the breaks occurred and, therefore, the location of the A's, T's, G's, and C's.

Mapping: a viable alternative?

Critics of proposals to establish a genome-sequencing project have suggested alternatives that might better utilize available resources. First on the list of possible alternatives is gene mapping—a method that identifies the precise location of genes that are of known medical interest either because they are implicated in disease or because they are involved in the control of development. To date nearly 1,400 genes, portions of genes, or DNA marker sequences have been mapped, and new genes are continually being located. Once a gene has been isolated, its protein product can be identified, and its chemical subunits can be sequenced. Because the information gained through mapping is immediately relevant to the diagnosis and treatment of disease, it is a technique that will continue to be used to locate medically relevant genes regardless of the fate of a massive sequencing effort.

Gene mapping relies on the fact that genes of unknown location can be precisely located through the study of their pattern of inheritance in association with specific genes or markers, the locations of which are known. In some cases investigators study large families affected by genetic disease, looking for strong

314

associations between inheritance of the disease and inheritance of traits determined by genes of known location. In other cases they look for links between the disease in question and DNA sequences that can be used as markers because their position on a given chromosome is known. (The closer two genes lie on a chromosome, the less likely it is that they will be separated during the exchange of genetic material that occurs in the formation of egg and sperm.)

Linkage studies, as such investigations are called, have been greatly facilitated by the discovery of variations in DNA sequences known as DNA polymorphisms, which are found throughout every individual's DNA. Many of these DNA sequence changes are detected when DNA is "digested" by a class of bacterial enzymes called restriction enzymes, each of which cuts the DNA strand at a specific, known nucleotide sequence, producing a group of different but consistently patterned DNA fragments. The cutting process is usually referred to as cleavage, and the specific places cut by different enzymes are called cleavage sites. A change in the expected DNA sequence—a polymorphism—may obliterate an existing cleavage site or it may create a new one, but in either case it alters the length of the fragments produced in the cleavage process. Because polymorphic sites are common in the human genome, a set of such sites can frequently be found in the close vicinity of any given gene. Analysis of the inheritance of polymorphic sites within families affected by genetic disease provides a way to both follow the migration of the disease-causing gene from one generation to the next and, at the same time, provide ever closer landmarks to the gene itself. The ability to follow the gene's migration within a family often allows for the detection of carriers of genetic defects and prenatal diagnosis of affected fetuses, although techniques that rely on markers of this sort are never as accurate as detection based on knowledge of the precise location of the gene.

The map of the human genome as it exists today is very sketchy. With fewer than one-thirtieth of the estimated total number of genes located on specific regions of specific chromosomes, the map could be compared to a satellite photograph taken when a low cloud cover has obscured all but the highest mountain ranges. At this point the map simply is not detailed enough to allow scientists to pick out specific pieces of DNA that contain genes of interest. It will remain that way until enough genes have been mapped to provide identifiable landmarks throughout the genome. With enough genes mapped to provide a high-resolution physical map of the chromosomes, it would be a reasonably straightforward matter to pin down the location of a specific gene in question on a single fragment of DNA. And once a gene has been precisely located, it can be sequenced—*i.e.*, the order of its subunits determined—relatively rapidly.

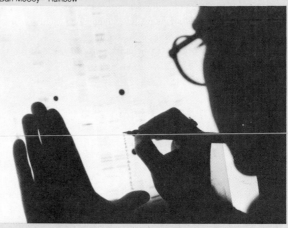

Dan McCoy—Rainbow

By studying photographic film that has been exposed to radioactively labeled, chemically "tailored" fragments of a strand of DNA, a researcher is able to determine the sequence of the nucleotide subunits.

The race to stake a claim

While creating a physical map of the human genome is not as massive a project as deriving the sequence, neither is it a trivial matter. Experts have suggested that it might take 20 scientists three to five years to complete such a map, but they estimate it could be done for a fraction of the cost of sequencing. As the pros and cons have been debated, general consensus has developed that a phased approach to the task would be best. Preparing a rough physical map of the genome would be the first step, with sequencing of specific genes organized by priority on the basis of their medical relevance or basic research interest. A phased timetable would allow the gene mappers to lay the groundwork for the project while giving the sequencers the time they need to develop the improved sequencing technology, computerized data storage capacity, and automation of laboratory procedures essential for increasing the efficiency and decreasing the cost of the project.

While many scientists support a large-scale mapping effort but oppose complete sequencing at this point, some argue that only an accelerated, centrally coordinated project will attract the funds required for developing the necessary biotechnology. Many U.S. supporters of a full-scale sequencing effort believe it is the only way to attract the money needed to keep the United States competitive in the race to dominate the biotechnology industry. Japanese researchers recently announced plans to embark on a sequencing project using an automated system capable of identifying up to a million subunits a day. The prospect of Japanese technological supremacy has added increasing urgency to the case of those U.S. scientists who want to stake their own claim to the as-yet-uncharted areas of the human genome.

315

Heart and Blood Vessels

Several major advances in the treatment of various cardiac problems have been made over the past few years, and new directions have been taken. The search for an alternative approach to surgical treatment of coronary heart disease has resulted in new information relating to the efficacy of dilating narrowed coronary arteries by inflation of balloons affixed to catheters. These are introduced into the narrowed segment of the coronary artery via an arm or leg artery. The balloon is deflated when it is inserted, but once it is at the site of narrowing, it is inflated, compressing the atherosclerotic material. When the procedure is successful, the narrowed segment dilates, thereby restoring coronary blood flow toward normal. This approach has now been demonstrated to be both safe and effective, and it is being applied to patients whose severity of coronary artery disease covers a wide range.

The balloon approach to treating operative problems has recently been broadened by its application to the treatment of valvular heart disease. Thus, balloon-tipped catheters are now being inserted through the arm or leg arteries and advanced to narrowed heart valves—either the mitral, the aortic, or the pulmonary valves. When the balloon is positioned within the stenotic valve, it is inflated, and as it dilates it opens the stenotic valve. This is an extremely exciting new approach to the therapy of valvular heart disease; however, establishing the safety and efficacy of this procedure will require additional time.

Attention also continues to be focused on the treatment of acute heart attacks. An acute heart attack develops when a blood clot forms in a coronary artery, converting a partially occluded artery to a totally occluded one and thereby stopping the blood flow. The recognition of this precipitating mechanism led to major trials to determine whether the administration of clot-dissolving drugs would effectively treat the patient in the throes of a heart attack. The data now unequivocally establish the value of this approach. Studies are focusing on how the administration of clot-dissolving substances can be combined with balloon dilation of the residual stenosis to achieve an optimal result.

Over the years many studies have demonstrated a relation between blood cholesterol and the development of coronary heart disease: the higher the cholesterol level, the greater the chances of a person's developing coronary heart disease. Recent investigations with potentially important therapeutic implications have assessed whether lowering blood cholesterol reduces the risk of coronary heart disease. Trials using cholesterol-reducing drugs and diet to decrease cholesterol in subjects with high cholesterol levels have demonstrated that cardiac deaths and heart attacks are significantly reduced in middle-aged men. Other studies in which the coronary arteries were visualized at cardiac catheterization by radiographic techniques have demonstrated that the rate of coronary artery disease progression over a two-to-five-year period is diminished when drugs and dietary restrictions succeed in lowering blood cholesterol levels. There also is some evidence suggesting that disease regression may occur. One of the chief problems with cholesterol-lowering drugs in the past has been that they are somewhat unpalatable and are associated with a relatively high incidence of unpleasant side effects. However, there are newer drugs on the horizon that not only are effective but are associated with fewer side effects. Although these developments are encouraging, it should be emphasized that there is still controversy as to whether disease regression occurs in all but the rare patient with coronary disease. In addition, although the risk of developing a coronary event is reduced by interventions that lower blood cholesterol, there still is an appreciable incidence of such events. It seems clear, therefore, that this approach alone is not the entire solution to the problem of coronary artery disease.

Perhaps one of the areas of greatest new interest in cardiology this past year has been silent myocardial ischemia. The following discussion details the interesting concepts relating to this important clinical event.

Myocardial ischemia: silent or otherwise

Atherosclerotic coronary artery disease is a modern epidemic that is most prevalent in the industrialized countries of North America and Europe. It is a disorder that causes a narrowing of the coronary arteries (the blood vessels supplying the heart muscle). In the United States its ravages afflict an estimated six million each year, and an inestimable number of middle-aged adults are developing the disease but have not yet been diagnosed. The major manifestations of coronary atherosclerosis, which are chest pain (angina pectoris) and heart attack (myocardial infarction), are due primarily to myocardial ischemia, or an inadequate supply of oxygen to the heart muscle (myocardium).

Myocardial ischemia develops when the needs of the myocardium for oxygen exceed the capacity of the diseased vessels to deliver blood and, therefore, oxygen. The major determinants of the heart's need for oxygen are the heart rate, the blood pressure, and the vigor of the heart's contraction; when any of these factors increase, myocardial-oxygen needs also increase. Under resting conditions, heart rate and blood pressure are relatively low, and the heart is not contracting particularly forcefully; therefore, the oxygen requirements of the myocardium are small, such that even coronary arteries narrowed by atherosclerotic plaques can supply adequate amounts of blood and oxygen. Ischemia, then, is not present at rest. During the stress of exercise, however, each of the determinants of myocardial-oxygen demand increases.

During maximal exercise, myocardial-oxygen demands increase markedly, leading to a fourfold to fivefold augmentation in blood flow. This large increase in flow cannot be sustained when the coronary arteries are diseased and narrowed, and the result is myocardial ischemia, which is usually sensed by the patient as chest pain, or angina pectoris.

Exercise-induced angina occurs when the coronary arteries are narrowed to between 50 and 90% of normal. However, when the coronary arteries are nearly or totally occluded, even the minimal oxygen needs of the heart muscle at rest cannot be satisfied, and rest angina then occurs. When ischemia is transient, no permanent damage to the heart muscle develops. If it is prolonged, however, death of myocardial tissue ensues, and the clinical outcome is a heart attack.

Although myocardial ischemia had always been thought to be associated with angina, it has been known for some years that it can be silent. In the absence of chest pain, the diagnosis of silent ischemia in the past was based on abnormalities detected on the resting electrocardiogram (EKG). The information conveyed by this relatively insensitive diagnostic test for coronary artery disease allowed identification of the damage inflicted by a new or old heart attack. It indicated that approximately 25% of heart attacks were clinically silent. With the advent of recent technology, which has enabled cardiologists to verifiably record episodes of myocardial ischemia (not just myocardial infarction), it has also become evident that many ischemic episodes are not perceived by patients. In recent years this finding has stimulated a tremendous amount of research into the diagnosis, pathogenesis, and management of patients with suspected or confirmed coronary artery disease and evidence of silent myocardial ischemia.

A classical history of chest pain occurring beneath the breast bone (substernally) during exercise and subsiding at rest makes the likelihood of coronary artery disease very high. When the history is not so clear-cut, other diagnostic modalities may provide important information. The EKG may show abnormalities that are diagnostic of an old myocardial infarction, and when these are present they strongly suggest the existence of coronary artery disease. Exercise stress testing, during which electrocardiographic changes are recorded, can also provide data that establish the diagnosis with a high probability.

The major electrocardiographic manifestation of ischemia is deviation of the so-called ST segment. The EKG consists of continuous electrical signals emanating from the heart during the course of the heart's cycle of contraction and relaxation. Different portions of the signal are designated by various letters of the alphabet, and one of these segments, the ST segment, is most sensitively affected by myocardial ischemia. Thus, with the onset of mild to moderately severe

From Marsha F. Goldsmith, "Cardiologists Send Up a Trial Balloon in New Efforts to Relieve Heart Failure," *JAMA*, vol. 257, no. 3 (Jan. 16, 1987), pp. 285–286; copyright 1987 American Medical Association

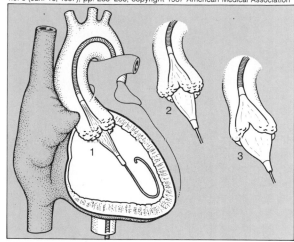

The balloon approach as a surgical alternative has been expanded to the treatment of valvular heart disorders. (Above diagram) A balloon has been inserted across the aortic valve, then inflated to open up a disease-narrowed passage.

ischemia, these ST segments deviate either upwardly or downwardly. When such changes are observed, they are usually interpreted as reflecting myocardial ischemia.

Radioisotopes: more accurate diagnosis

The use of radioisotopes in cardiac imaging has further increased the accuracy with which coronary artery disease can be diagnosed. Thallium 201 is a radioisotope that is actively taken up by myocardial cells. The amount of thallium 201 taken up when the isotope is injected into the bloodstream is directly related to the rate of blood flow perfusing the myocardial tissue and to the integrity of myocardial cell function. In patients with coronary artery disease, during peak exercise the myocardium that is perfused by the narrowed coronary arteries receives inadequate flow, and the myocardium becomes ischemic. Thus, when thallium is injected at peak exercise, its uptake into the poorly perfused ischemic myocardial cell is reduced, and imaging the heart at this time demonstrates defects in the myocardial pattern of radioactivity. Several hours after exercise, when blood flow and myocardial function have returned to normal, the isotope, which is still in the bloodstream, is taken up by previously ischemic regions of myocardium (*see* scans on following page). Thus, in late postexercise studies of the heart, transiently ischemic regions appear normal, whereas regions of the heart that are permanently damaged and have been converted to scar tissue do not take up thallium and remain as defects.

Another radioisotopic method of diagnosing myocardial ischemia employs red blood cells labeled with the isotope technetium. Since red blood cells remain within the blood vessels and the heart cavities, this

Robert O. Bonow, Cardiology Branch,
National Heart, Lung, and Blood Institute, NIH

The thallium scan (left) clearly shows reduced blood flow in the heart muscle during the stress of exercise, but after three hours of rest (right), the blood flow is uniform, thus indicating the patient's ischemia is reversible.

technique allows imaging of the blood pool so that the left ventricular cavity can be imaged continuously over time. Images of the left ventricular cavity can be obtained both at rest and during exercise. Thus, these two imaging modalities provide complementary information; imaging with thallium provides information about how the myocardium is perfused, whereas imaging with red blood cells labeled with technetium provides information about the contractile function of the myocardium. A third radioisotope-imaging technique currently available is called positron emission tomography, which uses radioisotopes with short half-lives. It enables high-resolution and repeated images of the heart to be obtained that can assay either myocardial perfusion (as with thallium 201) or the metabolic activity of the heart.

The above radionuclide techniques have provided considerable information about myocardial ischemia. For instance, great debate had centered on whether abnormalities that were not associated with chest pain were really due to myocardial ischemia. In individuals with underlying coronary artery disease, these abnormalities were recorded in the EKG periodically during the day, and the radionuclide techniques demonstrated unequivocally that many of these episodes were indeed due to myocardial ischemia, thereby substantiating the concept of silent ischemia.

Spectrum of ischemia-associated conditions

A number of clinical syndromes associated with myocardial ischemia have been recognized. Their effects and their seriousness vary quite widely.

Stable angina pectoris. First described vividly by William Heberden in 1772, stable angina pectoris remains the most common symptom occurring with myocardial ischemia. Typically, patients have a history of discomfort that strikes in the middle of the chest during or after exercise, during or after exposure to cold, or in conjunction with emotional stress or other factors that cause increases in myocardial-oxygen demand. Symptoms are relieved by removal of precipitating causes or by the administration of nitroglycerin. Most patients with classic angina pectoris have atherosclerotic narrowing of the coronary arteries. Characteristically, myocardial ischemia and angina are

precipitated at a reproducible work load during graded exercise testing. In these patients increases in myocardial-oxygen demand that exceed the capacity of the narrowed coronary arteries to deliver blood constitute the primary mechanism for precipitating ischemia.

Variant angina pectoris. Patients with anginal chest pain that usually occurs at rest rather than during exercise have what is termed variant angina pectoris. The anginal pain appears most commonly in the early morning hours. In the U.S. variant angina accounts for fewer than 1% of patients who have anginal chest pain, but it may account for up to 10% of these patients in Japan. Coronary arteriography performed in these patients during spontaneous episodes of chest pain has demonstrated transient total occlusion, or spasm, of one of the major coronary arteries. Such spasms can involve coronary arteries that appear to be normal during angiography, or they can occur at sites of atherosclerotic narrowing. In almost 80% of the patients, these spasms can be reproduced by means of intravenous administration of the drug ergonovine maleate; infusion of this drug during coronary angiography is now the way that coronary spasm is routinely diagnosed. Thus, in this variety of myocardial ischemia, the ischemia itself is precipitated not by a large increase in the myocardial-oxygen demand that exceeds the capacity of diseased, narrowed coronary arteries to deliver oxygen (as in stable angina pectoris) but by a sudden, transient decrease in myocardial blood flow caused by the coronary spasm.

Mixed angina pectoris. A number of patients with coronary artery disease and angina have a history of pain occurring at varying work loads. For instance, angina sometimes develops during rest and sometimes during exertion. The amount of exertion it takes to precipitate the pain typically varies from low to high levels. The variation in the intensity of exercise necessary for the precipitation of angina is explained by the fact that in these patients myocardial ischemia is precipitated sometimes when increases in myocardial-oxygen demand exceed the capacity of coronary arteries to deliver oxygen, sometimes when dynamic increases in coronary resistance (due to coronary vasoconstriction or spasm) decrease coronary blood flow, and sometimes by a combination of these factors.

Unstable angina pectoris. Patients with unstable angina exhibit a history of anginal chest pain that occurs more frequently, often at rest, and with increasing severity and duration and is less responsive to regular antianginal medications. The pathophysiology of the condition is multifactorial. In some patients sudden increases may occur in the severity of coronary luminal narrowing by rupture of the atherosclerotic plaque or by the formation of a blood clot on the plaque. In other patients the cause of an acute reduction in lumen diameter may be spasm at the site of atherosclerotic narrowing or platelet aggregates that form at sites of blood vessel damage and plug the vessel lumen. The importance of these various mechanisms is highlighted by the fact that studies of patients with unstable angina have shown significant beneficial effects of heparin and other drugs that are capable of dissolving blood clots, of such medications as nitrates and calcium antagonists that dilate blood vessels (vasodilators), and of aspirin (which functions as an agent that inhibits the aggregation of blood platelets).

Silent myocardial ischemia. With improvements in ambulatory electrocardiographic recording systems, it has become evident that episodes of the previously described ST-segment depression or elevation, both of which are hallmarks of myocardial ischemia, occur commonly in patients with coronary artery disease and are often *not* associated with anginal chest pain. Systems that enable accurate recording of low-frequency signals are necessary for faithful reproduction of ST-segment changes. Recent availability of these systems has made it possible to record ST-segment changes during the patient's normal daily activities, and a great deal of information is now available on silent myocardial ischemia.

Silent myocardial ischemia is common in all clinical subsets of patients with coronary artery disease. As previously noted, approximately 25% of patients with myocardial infarction have had silent events. The more recent electrocardiographic-monitoring studies have revealed that up to 70% of ischemic episodes of patients with unstable angina are entirely pain-free. Similarly, an average of 75% of ischemic episodes are silent in patients with stable exertional angina, variant angina, and mixed angina. In one study of a series of patients with coronary artery disease, the majority showed evidence of silent ischemia during a 48-hour monitoring period. Almost half of these patients had both painful and pain-free episodes, and one-fourth of the group had either painful episodes only or pain-free episodes only.

Pain usually occurs as a later manifestation of ischemia, with electrocardiographic evidence of ischemia often preceding the onset of pain by several seconds or minutes and sometimes by as long as 30 minutes. Although there is great variability from patient to patient, episodes of ischemia that are accompanied by pain are, in general, longer in duration and more severe in magnitude.

Why some patients experience predominantly asymptomatic ischemia is not known. Recent studies of these patients have demonstrated a somewhat lower perception of pain caused by a variety of painful stimuli such as cold, forearm ischemia, or electrical stimulation. Although an elevated pain threshold may partly explain why some patients have predominantly silent ischemia, it is clear that the problem is very complex and that additional, still unknown factors must play important roles.

From Elizabeth G. Nabel *et al.*, "Asymptomatic Ischemia in Patients with Coronary Artery Disease," *JAMA*, vol. 257, no. 14 (April 10, 1987), pp. 1923–28

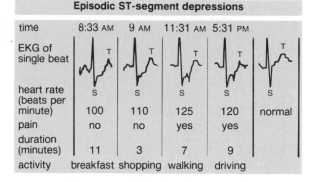

EKG recordings (top) showing significant ST-segment depression represent transient ischemia experienced over a 24-hour period, during various activities, with heart rate changes and times and duration of episodes.

Exercise testing for ischemia

A fairly close relationship exists between the ischemic threshold of a given patient, as measured by the onset of ST-segment depression during exercise testing, and the frequency and likelihood of ischemia's being detected during normal daily activities with ambulatory ST-segment monitoring. Thus, patients who exhibit ischemia at a very low exercise work load develop frequent episodes of ST-segment change (either pain-free or associated with pain) on ambulatory monitoring. These episodes are often of greater magnitude and longer in duration, compared with those of patients who develop ischemia only during intense exercise. Most of these latter patients develop little or no spontaneous ischemia during normal daily activities. Therefore, the work load to ischemia during graded treadmill-exercise testing can be used as a predictor of the frequency of ischemia during everyday activities.

Heart problems: more common in the morning

Evidence also indicates that a diurnal distribution in the frequency of ischemic episodes exists in patients with coronary artery disease. Thus, episodes of ischemia occur more frequently in the morning hours (6 AM to 12 noon) than in the afternoon, evening, or night hours. It is notable that the heart rate at the onset of ischemia in the morning hours is lower than at other times during the day. The lower heart rate would decrease myocardial-oxygen demands and therefore make it less likely that ischemia would occur. The fact that ischemia occurs most frequently at a time of lower myocardial-oxygen demands suggests that the precipitation of ischemia probably involves an important element of coronary vasoconstriction, which reduces coronary blood flow and lowers the ischemic threshold during the morning hours.

A diurnal variation in forearm blood flow also exists in normal subjects, suggesting that "vascular tone" in the peripheral arteries is higher in the morning.

This probably reflects what is occurring during sleep, although such changes are extremely difficult to measure directly. Platelet aggregability is also increased in the early morning hours, and blood fibrinolytic activity (which reflects the body's capacity to dissolve blood clots) is lower then. These findings are especially intriguing, given the recent observation that the frequency of myocardial infarction and that of sudden death are also greater in the morning hours.

Therapeutic insights and dilemmas

Several important studies have been published over the past few years that have identified subgroups of patients with coronary artery disease who are at high risk of dying and in whom surgical treatment (coronary bypass operation) would result in improved chances of survival. Prognosis can be estimated from the patient's coronary anatomy and left-ventricular function. The data suggest that patients whose narrowed coronary arteries supply a major portion of the left ventricle, and who demonstrate ischemic changes on exercise testing, constitute the high-risk group that will respond favorably to operative intervention. Those patients who do not fall into the high-risk group can be treated with medical therapy to control their anginal pain. If these patients have chest pain that seriously limits their life-style despite optimal medical therapy, an operation is necessary for symptomatic indications even though they have an excellent prognosis.

This approach to therapy is based on an understanding of coronary artery disease that is derived mainly from patients with symptomatic ischemia—that is, patients who experience angina pectoris. What is not entirely clear at the present time is whether the same indicators for surgical therapy apply to patients with silent ischemia.

The dilemma can be crystallized as follows. If an individual has a routine stress test that detects silent ischemia, and if subsequent evaluation determines that this person has the type of coronary anatomy that would categorize him or her as being at high risk (as determined by studies based predominantly on patients with angina pectoris), should the person with silent ischemia be offered surgery? In other words, is the individual with silent ischemia in the same high-risk group as the patient who has similar anatomy and exercise responses but experiences anginal pain? Although no certain answers can be given to this difficult question, there are some preliminary pieces of evidence that would suggest an affirmative answer. This evidence implies that if a patient has an ischemic response to exercise testing (an abnormal electrocardiographic or radionuclide study) and has unfavorable coronary anatomy, the prognosis is poor whether or not the ischemia is associated with anginal pain. If this evidence is substantiated by additional studies, it would appear that the patient with a silent ischemic response to exercise is at just as high a risk over subsequent years as the patient whose evidence of ischemia is accompanied by anginal pain.

A second dilemma relates to how aggressively ischemia should be medically treated in the patient who, for whatever reasons, is believed not to be an operative candidate. Currently the approach to medically treating myocardial ischemia is to administer nitroglycerin, beta-blocking drugs, or calcium antagonists so as to control the patient's symptoms. If a patient on medical therapy has only occasional anginal episodes, or if medications entirely control this symptom, medical therapy is judged to be successful. However, given the information that a large number of myocardial ischemic episodes are silent, the question arises as to whether adequacy of medical therapy should be judged in terms of eliminating all ischemic episodes, whether they are clinically silent or accompanied by anginal pain. This is not a trivial question, as expensive diagnostic testing would have to be employed to determine whether all silent episodes of ischemia have been eliminated by medical therapy. Moreover, such a goal may require administration of higher doses of medications that, while possibly eliminating the symptomatic as well as the silent episodes of ischemia, may carry a higher risk of side effects.

Another dilemma that arises is whether the patient who has *completely* silent ischemia must be detected and treated. If there are no overt clinical manifestations of underlying coronary disease, the attempt to identify and treat patients with completely silent ischemia would necessitate massive exercise or ambulatory EKG-monitoring screening programs. Estimates can be made as to the relative efficacy of such a screening program. For example, about 50 per 1,000 males aged 40 to 59 will have an abnormal exercise stress test. As many as one-third to one-half of these will turn out to have had falsely abnormal tests in that with arteriography they will be found to have normal coronary arteries. Moreover, only about three or four individuals of the 1,000 tested will have the type of high-risk coronary anatomy suitable for coronary artery bypass surgery. Thus, in order to detect the three or four patients whose prognosis may be improved by coronary bypass surgery, 1,000 exercise tests will have to be performed, and up to 50 asymptomatic patients will have to undergo the major process of cardiac catheterization.

Silent ischemia: unanswered questions

There is no doubt that silent myocardial ischemia occurs frequently in patients with coronary artery disease. However, several questions still remain to be answered as to its clinical significance, and these are currently a major focus of cardiovascular research. On the one hand, anginal pain may merely be the tip of the iceberg, and an aggressive approach aimed at diagnosing and treating all coronary artery disease and silent ischemia may be appropriate. On the other hand, it is possible that detection of silent myocardial ischemia and attempts at its total eradication may be too aggressive, with the result being exposure of some individuals to inappropriate costs, inconvenience, and risk. The questions yet to be answered about the newly recognized importance of silent ischemia to the development of coronary artery disease constitute a major challenge to cardiovascular specialists. The topic will be one of hot pursuit in the near future.

—Arshed Quyyumi, M.D.,
and Stephen E. Epstein, M.D.

Immunology

Recent advances have provided tools and information useful in furthering medical understanding of the immune system and in treating illnesses that result from its abnormal functioning. Of special interest have been new discoveries about specialized populations of white blood cells, or leukocytes, cells important in the body's defense against cancer and infections by microbes (bacteria, fungi, and viruses) and parasites.

Distinguishing different types of leukocytes

Each type of leukocyte—the granulocytes, monocytes, and lymphocytes—has specialized functions. Granulocytes are the first line of defense against infection in that they rapidly ingest and digest bacteria. The major form of granulocyte is called the neutrophil, or polymorphonuclear cell. Monocytes perform functions similar to those of granulocytes but also have other responsibilities. One of the most important is the presentation of digested bacterial proteins and other foreign proteins, known as antigens, to the white blood cells known as lymphocytes in such a way that the lymphocytes recognize these antigens as foreign and respond to them by mounting their unique immune responses. After initial contact with an antigen, lymphocytes develop the capacity to respond more quickly in the future, a phenomenon called immunologic memory. The response of these lymphocytes is specific in that they respond only to antigens that are appropriately presented to them by monocytes or similar cells and that they have an inherent ability to recognize. This ability to recognize specific antigens, called specificity, derives from the presence of molecular receptors for the antigens on the surface of the lymphocytes.

There are several populations of lymphocytes, including B lymphocytes (B cells), T lymphocytes (T cells), and natural killer (NK) cells. The ability to identify both the different types of lymphocytes, which all look the same under the microscope, and their functions is a major recent accomplishment of immunology and has been made possible by technological developments.

One new achievement of particular value in defining

Major white blood cells and some of their functions		
white blood cells	populations/ subpopulations	major functions
granulocytes	neutrophils	ingest and digest bacteria
	eosinophils	participate in allergic responses
	basophils	release histamine
monocytes		ingest and digest bacteria; present antigens to lymphocytes
lymphocytes	B lymphocytes	mature into plasma cells, which produce antibodies
	T lymphocytes helper T cells	help B cells mature and other T cells to grow and mature
	suppressor T cells	suppress antibody production
	cytotoxic T cells	kill virus-infected or malignant cells
	natural killer cells	kill malignant cells

different populations of lymphocytes is the development of monoclonal antibodies. Antibodies are proteins that specifically recognize certain other proteins and attach to them. A vital part of the immune system, antibodies circulate through the body searching for infectious agents and other foreign substances. To obtain monoclonal antibodies, scientists repeatedly inject mice with a foreign protein of interest until the immune systems of the mice respond by producing large numbers of antibody-making cells in their spleens. The mouse spleens are then removed, and those cells that produce antibody to the protein of interest are identified, separated, hybridized with certain malignant cells to extend their lives, and subsequently grown in tissue culture. Such cloned cells produce large amounts of a single antibody that reacts solely with the protein of interest. If mice are injected with human leukocytes, they make a host of antibodies that will recognize unique proteins on the surfaces of different families of these cells; for example, antibodies to granulocyte, monocyte, and lymphocyte populations and subpopulations.

Furthermore, monoclonal antibodies may be combined with certain dyes that fluoresce when exposed to bright light. A machine called a flow cytometer, which has only lately become generally available to research laboratories, passes cells through a column of laser light, one cell at a time, and measures the amount of fluorescent light emitted by that cell. If the cells are leukocytes that have been incubated with a fluorescent-labeled antibody, those populations of leukocytes to which the antibody has attached fluoresce brightly and can be counted and even sorted

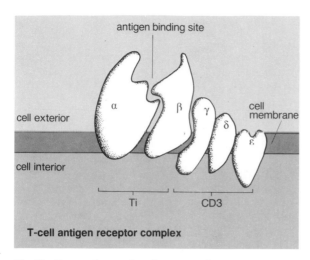

antigen binding site

cell exterior

α

β

γ

δ

ε

cell membrane

cell interior

Ti

CD3

T-cell antigen receptor complex

The T cell recognizes antigen by means of a receptor complex embedded in its cell membrane. The two major components of the receptor, Ti and CD3, are made of a total of five folded protein chains (α, β, γ, δ, and ε). The Ti component carries the site to which antigen attaches.

for study. Although it is not limited to the identification of leukocyte populations, this technology has been especially informative in the study of these cells. For instance, monoclonal antibodies distinguish between B lymphocytes, natural killer cells, and T lymphocytes. Additionally, they divide the T-lymphocyte population into helper T cells and suppressor/cytotoxic (cell-poisoning) T cells. When they are incubated with blood and passed through a flow cytometer, these antibodies allow determination of the relative proportions and numbers of specific cells present in blood. In victims of certain diseases, in particular, AIDS (acquired immune deficiency syndrome), the relative proportions of these cells are abnormal. Thus, the information obtained is useful in diagnosis. It is often not possible, however, to predict the functional capabilities of a cell from its appearance alone. In some cases cell families that have been identified as different by monoclonal antibodies have yet to reveal that difference in the form of a specialized function.

The T-cell surface receptor

One important subfamily of lymphocytes recognized by monoclonal antibodies is the thymus-derived, or T-lymphocyte, population. T cells are the primary white blood cells that protect the body against viral and fungal (as opposed to bacterial) infections and cancer. On the surface of these T cells is a protein structure called the T-cell antigen receptor complex. The receptor, whose structure was determined only within the past three years, consists of at least two major components: Ti (composed of two folded protein chains called α and β) and CD3 (made up of three chains, γ, δ, and ε).

The receptor complex is the structure that allows the T cells to recognize antigen. In this regard there is a lock-and-key relationship between a given antigen and the T cell that specifically recognizes it. The CD3 component of the receptor is common to all T lymphocytes and can be identified by monoclonal antibodies. The Ti component carries the site to which the antigen attaches. The entire receptor complex is required by the T cell to identify and respond to antigen wherever it is encountered in the body. For instance, T cells that identify viral antigens or cancer antigens on the surface of infected or malignant cells attempt to destroy the cells to rid the body of infection or tumor.

Factors that control leukocyte growth and activity

T lymphocytes are immature upon their origination in the bone marrow and complete their development in the thymus, where they acquire the ability to perform their protective functions. They are nurtured to maturity by a number of protein substances called growth factors. The activity of mature lymphocytes is regulated by similar factors termed cytokines (cell-derived factors), substances produced both by mature T cells and by other white blood cells. Cytokines made by lymphocytes are often called lymphokines. Analogous growth factors most probably control the maturation and activity of all the white blood cells, although an understanding of this complex control system is just unfolding. Cytokines of special interest in human biology include the interleukin family, the interferon family, and the tumor necrosis factors.

Interleukins is the name given to factors that act primarily between white blood cells. Interleukin-1 (IL-1), a cytokine released by monocytes, appears to be the primary signal to the brain that stimulates the production of fever during infectious illnesses. It is also a means by which monocytes interact with other cells. Interleukin-2 (IL-2) is released from T cells (in particular, from the specialized helper T cell) and is the primary growth factor for T lymphocytes. Since helper T cells are killed by the virus that causes AIDS, interleukin-2 has been used in some attempts to treat AIDS. Interleukin-3 (IL-3), also released from helper T cells, is a growth factor for mast cells, which are cells that release histamine in allergic responses. Yet another helper-T-cell product, interleukin-4 (IL-4), helps stimulate the development of B cells.

The interferons are a family of at least three different groups of proteins that regulate immune responses. One, α-interferon, has been used successfully to treat several kinds of cancer.

An interesting new group of cytokines, the tumor necrosis factors (TNFs), are released from monocytes and lymphocytes that kill tumor cells. TNF-releasing lymphocytes are called cytotoxic lymphocytes and are one of several kinds of "killer" white blood cells that have recently been identified.

Cytotoxic cells: a new weapon against cancer

Cytotoxic T lymphocytes appear to identify tumors using their T-cell receptors for tumor antigens and to use TNF to kill them. Another family of killer cells is generated when T cells are exposed to interleukin-2. These cells, called lymphokine-activated killer (LAK) cells, are effective in the destruction of otherwise difficult-to-treat tumors. In a new cancer treatment called adoptive immunotherapy, LAK cells are produced in large numbers in tissue culture when blood cells are taken from cancer patients and incubated with IL-2. The resultant LAK cells are then reinfused into the same patient, and further IL-2 is given. In some patients who have received this experimental therapy, tumor size has decreased significantly, although at the expense of unfortunate side effects. During the past year studies were under way to evaluate this treatment and to determine how interleukin-2 activates another killer-cell population, the natural killer cells. NK cells seem important in preventing the spread of tumors, although medical researchers have yet to learn how these cells recognize and kill their target cells. New ways to use these various killer cells in fighting cancer have been a major recent focus of cancer research.

Improved treatment for immune deficiency

Another important subfamily of lymphocytes is the bone-marrow-derived, or B-lymphocyte, population, which is responsible for antibody production. B cells develop directly from precursor cells in the bone marrow and proceed through a series of developmental stages until they mature into antibody-producing plasma cells. B cells recognize antigen by means of receptors—actually antibody molecules—on their surface, and they mature into cells that shed these receptors into the body fluids rather than developing into cytotoxic cells. Interaction with an antigen under the appropriate circumstances is the stimulus that triggers B-cell maturation into plasma cells. Maturation of B cells has been found to depend on growth and differentiation factors, including interleukin-4, that appear to be derived predominantly from T cells. Other factors, including interleukin-2 and γ-interferon, also play a role in this process.

For B cells to function normally and produce adequate amounts of the appropriate antibody, a complex series of cellular interactions must occur. When B lymphocytes function abnormally, for whatever reason, antibodies (which are members of the gamma globulin group of blood proteins) either are not made (a condition called agammaglobulinemia) or are defective (dysgammaglobulinemia). Individuals having either of these abnormalities are troubled with recurrent bacterial infections. For treatment the antibody missing from the blood of these patients can be replaced with antibody isolated from the blood of normal individuals. Recent improvements in the technology for extracting gamma globulin from human blood provide material of higher purity that can be given intravenously (rather than intramuscularly, as had been the case) because of the reduced risk of stimulating an undesirable immune response. Direct infusion into the bloodstream allows much more of antibody to enter the body, an advantage that appears to result in fewer infections.

Synthesizing cytokines for future research

Technological advances in molecular biology have prompted yet other exciting developments in immunology. For example, researchers have identified the protein structures of many of the cytokines discussed above and have used this information to pinpoint the genetic material in the cells responsible for the production of these substances. Then, using gene-splicing techniques, they have removed the relevant genes from their sources and transferred them into yeast cells. When the yeast cells are cultured, they synthesize large quantities of cytokines, following the genetic instructions inserted into them. The availability of interleukins, interferons, and tumor necrosis factors in quantity is providing new weapons against infection and cancer and new tools for the basic study and understanding of disease.

—Jane Morgan, Ph.D.,
and Richard D. deShazo, M.D.

Cell-derived factors (cytokines) that regulate growth and activity of other immune cells			
regulatory molecule	primary source	major function	current clinical use
interleukin-1	monocytes	causes fever; helps monocytes and lymphocytes interact	none
interleukin-2	helper T	promotes T-cell growth and development	cancer; AIDS
interleukin-3	helper T	stimulates growth of mast cells	none
interleukin-4	helper T	stimulates B cells to mature	none
interferon α	leukocytes	antitumor, antiviral, and immunoregulatory activities	herpes infections; cancer
β	fibroblasts		
γ	T cells		
tumor necrosis factors α	monocytes	kill tumor cells	cancer
β	cytotoxic lymphocytes		

Infectious Diseases

The major infectious disease concern of the past year has by far been AIDS (acquired immune deficiency syndrome). This disease, now known to be viral in origin, has the potential to become a worldwide pandemic. Because of its uniformly fatal outcome and the near impossibility of effectively preventing its spread, at the present time all the countries of the world are involved in developing some type of control measures. Because of the prolonged nature of the disease, its attendant characteristic opportunistic infections, and the need for prolonged health care, it also has the potential to consume a major portion of the already scarce health funds of the less developed countries. Either directly or indirectly, this disease will have a major health impact on the entire world. Attention will almost certainly be diverted from the more classical problems of child health and endemic parasitic diseases in the less developed countries.

On a global basis there remain many ongoing and new infectious disease problems and concerns. Beyond AIDS, some of the current major thrusts in health care center around immunization programs that are directed both at children and adults living in geographic areas where vaccine-preventable diseases are endemic and on activities that have been designated "child survival," which are those specifically directed at improving the health of infants and children in the less developed world. What follows focuses on these two major priorities; it also includes a report on legionnaire's disease, which struck a convention in Philadelphia ten years ago and caused a frightening, mysterious illness. In addition, it reviews one ongoing area of infectious diseases research that has seen recent strides: prevention of the common cold. Other areas, not detailed here, include an experimental herpes vaccine, a spreading rabies epidemic from Eastern into Western Europe, and better understanding of how viral infections can persist and produce disease long after initial exposure and symptoms.

Recent developments in immunization

October 1987 marked the tenth anniversary of the eradication of endemic smallpox from the world. By this criterion, vaccinia virus immunization (known commonly as vaccination), one of the oldest forms of immunization, has been the most successful of all immunizations. The smallpox virus itself (variola virus) is now kept alive in only two laboratories in the world (in the United States and in the U.S.S.R.). Genes from the virus have been cloned into the self-replicating DNA of bacterial plasmids, and the destruction of the last remaining intact live virus is anticipated; thus, the possibility that this disease will ever return could be eliminated.

New uses of smallpox vaccine. Paradoxically, at the same time that the main reason for the existence of vaccination has disappeared (*i.e.,* the disease smallpox is gone), its use for the immunological control of other infectious diseases is being intensively examined. The vaccinia virus is a large virus into which genetic material from other infectious agents can be cloned. When vaccination is done in the usual way, by scarification (*i.e.,* via scratches or small cuts in the skin), a genetically altered vaccinia virus can produce additional antigens controlled by the newly cloned genes, and the body thus develops an immune response to the new antigens as well as to the antigens of the original vaccinia virus. Theoretically, several antigens can be packaged in the vaccinia virus, and a single immunization could suffice for delivering a host of vaccines. This approach is presently being investigated through the use of genes from the hepatitis B virus, the herpes simplex virus, and the influenza virus, as well as genes from the AIDS virus. The vaccination, which is no longer done for smallpox prevention, may thus again become a valuable procedure for controlling other unrelated infectious diseases.

Success in cholera prevention. By way of contrast, cholera vaccine, which is one of the oldest bacterial vaccines, has been one of the poorest in terms of providing protection against the disease. Although it has been in use for the past 100 years, it is now known that its effectiveness is both low and short-lived (a matter of a few months), and it will not prevent the spread of the disease. For these reasons much effort has gone into the development of a new effective cholera vaccine that would provide adequate protection against the disease. As the first successful result

A doctor checks for malaria by feeling the spleen of an Indian patient. The global status of malaria is worsening because new parasites are resistant to chloroquine, the drug normally used to combat it.

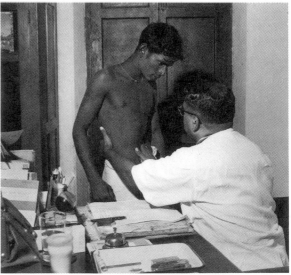

World Health Organization; photograph, N. Sharma

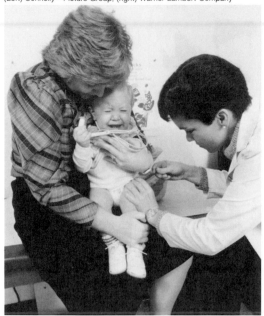
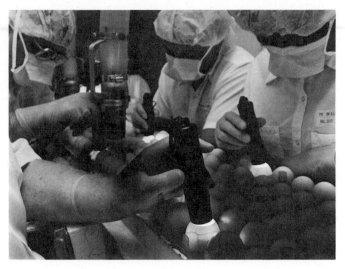

This baby in Texas (left) was vaccinated after the Taiwan flu arrived in the U.S. late in 1986 and began to take its toll. (Above) The development of vaccines that will offer better protection against yearly influenza epidemics is a high research priority.

of this recent work, an oral vaccine has been field-tested in Bangladesh during the past two years and found to be highly protective while having essentially no side effects. The oral cholera vaccine consists of a combination of killed whole bacteria and the nontoxic subunit B of the cholera toxin (which is known to be responsible for the severe diarrhea caused by the cholera infection). The degree of protection was found to be quite high (85%) during the first six months following immunization; there was a major drawback, however, in that the vaccine had to be administered at least twice in order to provide this degree of protection. In order to circumvent this problem, oral vaccines made with live attenuated (reduced in vitality) cholera organisms are being developed that should be effective following only a single dose and also should be free of side effects.

Having an effective oral vaccine would be a major achievement. Cholera has now established itself in most of the world (the only major exception being South America). It has recently been reported in the southern U.S. adjacent to the Gulf of Mexico, most cases being associated with the eating of shellfish infected with the bacteria. An outbreak of 12 cases occurred in 1986 in the New Orleans area.

Vital need for world malaria control. Malaria continues to be one of the major endemic diseases of less developed tropical countries. The global status of the disease, unfortunately, is continuing to worsen for two major reasons. First, more costly insecticides are required for the control of the mosquito populations, which have developed resistance to the earlier, less expensive agents. This high cost makes effective control measures almost beyond the financial capabilities

of many of the countries that have the most severe malaria problems. Second, the parasite that causes the most severe form of malaria, *Plasmodium falciparum,* is now frequently resistant to the standard form of therapy—chloroquine—so alternate drugs have had to be developed, most of which are less effective, more toxic, and less easy to administer. Furthermore, these resistant malaria parasites are continuing to spread around the world, so that there are few remaining countries in which the occurrence of this scourge has not become a problem.

For these reasons, and because new technology for vaccine development using molecular biology and recombinant DNA techniques has become available, major efforts are being directed toward the development of an effective malaria vaccine. Several approaches are being employed, using different life stages of the parasites, in an effort to develop a vaccine that, in a single injection, will be useful in the prevention of this disease and in the interruption of its transmission. Although there is much optimism about developing these vaccines, they are still in the experimental stages and are currently being tested in U.S. volunteers.

New flu vaccines tested. Yearly pandemics of influenza virus infections continue to occur worldwide and to result in increased mortality of infected persons, largely because of pneumonia and respiratory deaths. Infectious respiratory viral diseases, including influenza, kill four million people worldwide each year. About 40,000 die in each flu "epidemic." In the U.S. some 35 million to 70 million annually are sick with the flu, and 10,000 to 30,000 die from complications. Among Americans, however, fewer than 20% are vaccinated against the flu.

Infectious diseases

The control of the disease through immunization has not been highly effective because of the frequent variation in the antigenic aspects of the viruses, which necessitates the use of annually formulated vaccines, and because the vaccine, which is given by injection, is only about 80% effective. Major efforts are thus being directed toward developing more effective vaccines that can be given by the respiratory route (*i.e.*, via nose drops or nasal spray), which may be more directly relevant to stopping the growth of the virus in mucosal cells of the respiratory tract. In one such effort the Center for Immunization Research at the Johns Hopkins School of Public Health, Baltimore, Md., recently began tests of a new live-virus nose drop. Initial trials of this potential new preventative, which included adults and children from six months to 40 years of age, were promising.

Meningitis. The majority of bacterial meningitis cases in small children are caused by *Hemophilus influenzae* bacteria. Although there is a new vaccine (licensed in 1985) that has been shown to be effective, it is useful only in children vaccinated between the ages of 18 and 24 months. Unfortunately, the major problem of meningitis occurs in younger children, mostly those under the age of one year. These infants do not develop protective antibodies to the current vaccine, primarily because of the polysaccharide structure of the antigenic formulation of the vaccine. New vaccines are being developed that incorporate a carrier protein linked to the polysaccharide molecule, which makes it more antigenic. This formulation stimulates antibodies even in the youngest children; it thus has the potential to prevent this devastating disease, which can cause severe neurological defects in surviving children. Candidate vaccines are presently being studied in two populations in the U.S. that are known to have very high rates of severe disease due to this organism: the American Indian populations in Arizona and the Eskimo populations in Alaska.

In Britain there has been an upsurge of meningitis cases in children caused by another bacterium, *Neisseria meningitidis*, group B. A test of a new polysaccharide vaccine against this organism is under way at the Wellcome Research Laboratories. After successful tests on mice, a test of the vaccine has begun on human volunteers.

Universal immunization. The United Nations has established the goal of universal immunization of the world's children by 1990 against the six major childhood diseases: diphtheria, tetanus, pertussis, polio, measles, and tuberculosis. Safe and effective vaccines are available against these infections and are being included in the worldwide program. In 1974, prior to the widespread implementation of any immunization programs on a large scale, fewer than 4% of the children in the less developed countries had been immunized. Today the figure has risen to between 40 and 60%,

Mexican schoolchildren carry banners calling for vaccinations against polio on National Vaccination Day. The goal of the event was to promote systematic immunization of all children under the age of five.

depending upon the specific countries surveyed, and it is felt that the goal is clearly within sight. This effort has the potential to eliminate the 3.5 million deaths that occur annually because of these preventable illnesses. The important priorities now relate primarily to ensuring the availability of the vaccines, training personnel to administer them, and educating parents on the vital need for the immunizations.

Since these six major diseases have now been largely controlled in the United States and some other wealthy, developed nations, their importance on a global scale is often overlooked. Measles, for instance, which used to cause 500,000 cases annually in the U.S., was causing fewer than 3,000 cases per year, with almost no mortality, following widespread vaccination programs. By way of contrast, measles is estimated to cause two million deaths worldwide, most of them in malnourished children of the less developed world.

Measles continues to cause localized outbreaks of disease in the U.S., however, when the immune status of the population is less than optimal. In 1986 there were nearly 6,300 cases reported in the U.S. Incidence of measles in all age groups in the U.S. increased substantially between 1985 and 1986. Transmission often occurs in medical facilities; in at least one of these recent outbreaks, the initial case occurred in an unvaccinated child. Also, many measles cases are now occurring in young adults who have been less than optimally immunized.

Canada, too, experienced an increase (20-fold) in cases of measles in 1986 owing to inadequate immunization of its population. Measles-elimination strategies, if properly implemented, should decrease these proportions of preventable cases.

Polio, which has essentially been eliminated in the U.S., Canada, Japan, Australia, New Zealand, and most of Europe, is still a threat to those visitors to the less developed countries who have not been adequately immunized. In 1986 a 29-year-old California woman contracted paralytic polio while traveling and working in Asia. Worldwide about 25,000 cases of paralytic polio are being reported to the World Health Organization per year, with some 63% of those cases occurring in Southeast Asia. Federal health officials are now urging Americans traveling to certain less developed countries to make sure they have been fully vaccinated against polio.

New and improved vaccines. In addition to the vaccines mentioned above, active research is in progress toward the development of new vaccines against other infectious diseases. One group of such diseases is acute diarrheal diseases caused primarily by rotaviruses, enterotoxigenic *Escherichia coli,* and *Shigella.* All of these are major causes of diarrheal diseases in children and adults in the less developed countries. Rotavirus is also the most important cause of acute diarrhea in small children in the United States and Europe. Field trials of oral live attenuated rotavirus vaccines are currently under way. The development of conjugate vaccines for pneumococcal disease in infants (similar to that being done for *H. influenzae*) is also of high priority since pneumonia and other acute respiratory diseases take such a high toll, especially among the children of the less developed countries. In addition, new formulations of vaccines are being developed to replace presently used vaccines that can be quite toxic (for example, pertussis and typhoid vaccines) or extremely costly (for example, hepatitis B vaccine).

All newly developed vaccines must go through a lengthy series of testing before being used in field trials to determine their effectiveness in large numbers of humans. These include animal testing and then testing in small numbers of humans under carefully controlled conditions. For this latter purpose it is necessary to have human volunteer testing facilities. These presently exist in a number of medical schools, including one at Johns Hopkins University. Only after adults and children (in the case of vaccines to be used in children) have been given these vaccines can larger field trials be implemented.

Child survival worldwide

In addition to the promotion of universal immunization for children, child survival programs focus primarily on the treatment of acute diarrheal diseases with oral rehydration therapy and on the improvement of the nutritional status of children through promotion of breast-feeding and monitoring of growth by the use of simplified charts to plot height and weight.

The most dramatic results in the decrease of childhood illness and death have been seen with oral rehydration therapy for the treatment of diarrhea. This therapy is effective for acute dehydrating diarrhea caused by any organisms and in persons of any age, including newborns. It is most easily administered by the use of packets that contain the appropriate mixture of salts and glucose, which is added to water and given to the patient to drink. In spite of the fact that these packets are inexpensive (approximately ten cents for a packet that makes one liter [0.26 gal] of treatment solution), they are still not widely available throughout the world, and it is estimated that at the present time only about 25% of the world's children have access to them. In countries where they have been available (such as Egypt, Nigeria, Haiti, Honduras, and Peru) and widely promoted, there have been marked decreases in childhood deaths and a dramatic decrease in the need for hospitalization of children with diarrhea. Additional strategies for the promotion of oral therapy include the use of simple salt-sugar solutions that can be made in the home. These solutions are useful in early treatment and in the prevention of dehydration early in a diarrheal episode.

More recently, incorporation of cereals that contain large amounts of starch has been found useful in replacing the need for sugar, which may not be readily available in all homes. Such grains as rice and maize have been found to be entirely satisfactory for use in homemade oral-therapy solutions. Solutions that contain large amounts of rice (50 g [1.8 oz] per liter) may promote the absorption of water and salt to such an extent that the amount of diarrheal fluid lost may actually be diminished and the duration of the diarrheal disease may be shortened. Studies are in progress to determine whether this is indeed the case; if so, it would mean that this type of oral therapy is not only a replacement therapy but also a therapy that modifies the disease itself.

A further possibility for oral therapy is the modification of soups that are already available and widely used in the home. Such soups may already contain a source of starch (such as rice or noodles made from wheat) and are salted routinely. By measuring the electrolyte and starch contents of these soups, it may be possible to design a soup that would be palatable, adequate for rehydration, and still easy to prepare. Indeed, chicken soup with rice then may be an optimal rehydration solution if it has the correct amount of salt!

Legionnaires' disease update

It has been just over ten years since legionnaires' disease, a severe form of pneumonia, was first recognized among several hundred elderly war veterans attending an American Legion convention in Philadelphia; 29 died. There have since been a number of similar outbreaks, though on a smaller scale, in the United States, England, and Scotland. Seven hundred cases are reported yearly at present in the United States.

In 1984 in Glasgow, Scotland, 33 people became infected in the Dennistoun district in three clusters over four months. In Stafford, England, at least 28 died at a district general hospital in 1985. More recently, three patients who had received bone-marrow transplants or chemotherapy died and three others in a bone-marrow transplant program became seriously ill at the City of Hope National Pilot Medical Center in California in the spring and summer of 1986. In Sheboygan, Wis., about 30 cases and several deaths occurred in a 15-square-block area in August 1986.

Although institutional outbreaks (*e.g.,* in hospitals) are more easily identified, the vast majority of cases are probably sporadic, and most are relatively mild. The bacterium that causes the disease, *Legionella pneumophila,* is now known to be ubiquitous in nature and is found frequently in water, although most of the time it does not seem to be a health hazard. The organism has also been found to flourish and grow in instruments of advanced technology, such as air-conditioning systems, cooling towers, and room humidifiers, and thus is subject to widespread aerosolization and thereby respiratory transmission. Such air-water devices have been incriminated in most of these institutional outbreaks. It is not clear, however, exactly how virulent these organisms are or who is most likely to become ill, although older persons and those persons with compromised immune systems seem to be at highest risk.

Because the organisms are ubiquitous, it is also not clear, outside of an epidemic situation, what control efforts would be most effective. This organism almost certainly occurs worldwide, but it has been recognized as a cause of epidemic disease only in situations where there is appropriate technology (*i.e.,* air-cooling devices) for spreading the organisms. In this way the organism and the disease produced are analogous to toxic shock syndrome, also a recent epidemic disease related to advanced technology (*i.e.,* the use of commercially manufactured tampons) that is primarily limited to the developed world.

The still common cold

One of the most difficult infectious diseases either to prevent or to treat is the common cold. Although not severely incapacitating in itself, it leads to many hours and dollars lost from work and to a large amount of human suffering, albeit mild. One of the difficulties in managing colds is that they are caused by many different viruses (estimated at about 200), each with slightly different properties, which makes prevention with vaccines practically impossible. Recently there have been reports of a new approach to the prevention of colds due to one group of viruses, the rhinoviruses, which cause about 30–50% of all colds.

Infection with this group of viruses can be prevented by the nasal application of a substance called alpha interferon, a natural body substance that is produced in response to viral infections and that can prevent the establishment of viruses in cells. A large amount of this substance is needed for a therapeutic effect to be produced, and it has been only through the use of recombinant DNA technology that it has been possible to produce large amounts in the laboratory. In clinical trials using large amounts of intranasal alpha interferon for short periods of time, it has been possible to provide people with about 80% protection against developing a cold when someone in the immediate family has one and when that cold is due to a rhinovirus. About 10% of those using the nasally delivered drug develop minor nasal bleeding.

Although these protective effects are encouraging, it

Legionnaire's disease made its notorious debut in 1976 in Philadelphia at an American Legion convention. A survivor of that outbreak (right) undergoes a breathing test several years later. A variety of sources (far right) have been found to harbor the pathogen that causes the disease; several of these sources have been linked to recent legionnaire's disease outbreaks in the U.S., England, and Scotland.

Potential sources of *Legionella*

aquariums
boilers
cooling towers
dehumidifiers
evaporative condensers
fountains
hot-water tanks
humidifiers
nebulizers
potable water
respirators
saunas
shower water and shower heads
swamp coolers
hot- and cold-water taps
whirlpools

(Left) Michael Viola/The Philadelphia Inquirer; (right) source: S. M. Katz, *Legionellosis* (Boca Raton, Fla.: CRC Press, Inc., 1986)

should be noted that the overall protective effect was only about 40%, since there was no protection against the nonrhinovirus colds. Further research along this line may eventually result in a preventative or "cure" for this most elusive of infectious diseases.

—R. Bradley Sack, M.D., Sc.D.

Kidney Disease

Approximately 80,000 people in the United States and 150,000 in the rest of the world are being treated with some form of dialysis. Most use the artificial kidney in a variety of configurations, while the remainder are on peritoneal dialysis. In both methods toxic substances and excess water pass from the blood through membranes (artificial in the one instance and natural peritoneum in the other). The treatment is complex and, unlike renal transplantation, is incomplete. Advances continue to lead to an understanding of the factors involved, and as patients survive longer, more is learned of the natural history of diseases involved with dialysis.

A new disease in dialysis patients

It is well known that patients who have been on dialysis treatments with the artificial kidney for a number of years experience a multitude of aches, pains, and problems in their joints and bones. Only recently, however, has it come to light that a new disease has evolved from the dialysis treatment itself. This disease has a number of names relating to its effects on the joints (dialysis spondylarthropathy and erosive azotemic osteoarthropathy) and has as its basis a substance called B_2-microglobulin (B_2M).

B_2-microglobulin is present on every cell in the body as part of the human leukocyte antigen (HLA) system. These antigens distinguish one person from another and are used for obtaining the closest-matching tissue types (between donor and recipient) for kidney transplantation. In a healthy person, as cells age the HLA antigens from these cells break down to their components and then enter the body's circulation. The B_2M component is taken up by the kidneys from the bloodstream and is mostly destroyed there; a small amount normally appears in the urine.

Accumulation of destructive substance. In a person with failing kidneys, B_2M accumulates in the bloodstream since apparently no other organ in the body is capable of metabolizing it. When the kidneys are no longer able to deal with the task of excreting waste products and excess water, as in people who are on dialysis, concentrations of the substance reach from 20 to 50 times the normal level. This B_2M then condenses into microscopic fibers and forms deposits in the synovial linings of joints, in bones, and to a lesser extent in some body organs. This new substance is called amyloid; it is a destructive substance that ap-

Frank Gotch, Franklin Hospital
Hemodialysis Treatment and Research Center, San Francisco

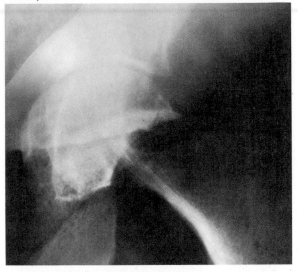

It has recently been found that a substance called amyloid accumulates in patients who have been on dialysis for many years. It appears to erode tissues and cause damage to bones, such as the hip fracture seen in the X-ray above.

pears to erode the tissues with which it comes in contact. A few years' exposure to amyloid can result in symptoms of arthritis and bone pain; this now appears to be the case for most people who have been on dialysis for ten or more years.

There are other types of amyloid substances that form in a variety of diseases, but this type has a particular propensity to deposit in the carpal tunnel in the wrist. This is a channel through which the median nerve passes from the wrist to the hand. The amyloid deposits compress the nerve, resulting initially in an unpleasant tingling sensation and eventually in severe pain and muscular weakness in the hand and arm.

It has become clear that the standard dialyzers (the apparatuses in which dialysis is carried out) that have been used for treatment of kidney failure are unable to reproduce the normal kidney function of destroying B_2M, while newly designed dialyzers may be more successful in this respect. It is therefore necessary to know why older methods fail so that patients who depend on dialysis can be treated by methods that destroy B_2M.

In a healthy functioning kidney, blood circulates through a filter that contains what could be looked upon as many tiny pores. All the unwanted, minuscule particles of waste (B_2M included) pass through the filter and are eliminated in the urine. This filter comprises two million of the basic units of the kidney, called glomeruli. It has pores large enough to accommodate particles of up to 60,000 daltons in molecular weight. B_2M has a weight of 11,800 daltons and thus passes through the glomerular filter with ease. Until recently almost all dialyzers possessed filter membranes that

329

were made of cellulosic derivatives. The pores in these membranes had a molecular weight cutoff point of about 2,000–6,000 daltons; the B_2M could not pass through and thus would accumulate throughout the body. This accounted for the eventual development of amyloidosis in long-term dialysis patients. These standard dialyzers also provoked other negative reactions that were occasionally severe. These reactions included a decrease in the white blood cell count (especially the granulocyte cells that fight infection directly) and a decrease in the activation or stimulation of the complement system, a series of substances in the blood that are involved with the body's response to infection. These and many other biochemical changes occurred in the first hour after the patient's blood was exposed to the dialysis membrane.

Seeking a safer dialysis method. New dialysis membranes that are derived from different materials are now available. These have pores large enough to admit particles with a molecular weight of 20,000 daltons and thus filter out the B_2M and remove it from the body. It is possible that the new membranes with larger pores may come closer to reproducing the filtering functions of the normal kidney and thereby improve other aspects of the health of people on dialysis treatment. Whether a sustained reduction in concentrations of B_2M will affect the amyloid that has already formed and reduce its quantity (in the same way lowering the blood uric acid reduces gouty deposits) remains to be seen. It may be that the damage to bones and joints cannot be reversed. However, this type of membrane offers the possibility of preventing the amyloid formation in the first place by reducing the concentration of B_2M. There is clinical evidence that long-term exposure to these noncellulosic membranes is associated with a lower incidence of bone and joint symptoms. The development of new dialyzers has thus made possible

marked improvement in the standard of health that may be expected for people on long-term dialysis.

Controversy over reuse of dialyzers

A matter that until lately had not been discussed outside of dialysis units and among nephrologists has now reached the public forum. Recently the U.S. Senate Committee on Aging published a report that was highly critical of the common practice of reprocessing and reusing dialyzers in dialysis treatment facilities. This was followed by dramatic television reports and newspaper articles presenting the alleged dangers of reused dialyzers to patients on dialysis.

The reuse of dialyzers is the prevailing practice in about 70% of U.S. hemodialysis units and, in fact, all published accounts examining the morbidity and mortality rates of patients in reuse units suggest that patients so treated do better than those who always use new dialyzers. This may mean only that more established units have better all-around standards, but it is also possible that the practice of reprocessing dialyzers is in itself actually beneficial in the long term. All this, of course, presupposes that the reprocessing is performed according to appropriate standards.

The Senate committee and the patients who expressed opposition to reuse methods were primarily concerned with the possible dangers of infection since it was felt that reprocessing units could not generally achieve the highest standards of sterility. Undoubtedly, incidents of infection—some of which were very serious—have been reported to have occurred in some facilities. However, in general, as stated before, the practice of reuse has proved safe.

Economic and medical incentives. The reasons why dialysis units choose to reprocess dialyzers are primarily economic—it is simply less expensive. The costs of labor and chemicals for reprocessing are lower than

A matter that recently has been the focus of considerable controversy, due to concerns about infection risk, is the common practice of reprocessing and reusing dialyzers in dialysis treatment facilities. When the highest standards of sterility are employed, however, the practice of reuse has proved safe, cost-effective, and, in fact, medically beneficial. The patient at right is undergoing dialysis at a Veterans Administration Medical Center where reuse is not employed; the chemicals and membranes for carrying out the kidney-cleansing process are replaced with each treatment.

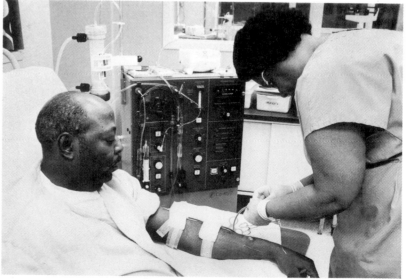

The National Kidney Foundation; photograph, Ankers Photographers, Inc.

the cost of a new dialyzer. Furthermore, if use of the newly designed dialyzers with noncellulosic membranes becomes widespread, then it will become even more expensive not to reuse these. In some cases the savings generated by reusing dialyzers are essential to the financial stability of the dialysis unit, while in other units the savings are used to supply extra services.

There is also a medical incentive to reprocessing. As was noted above, the dialyzer in common use—the cellulosic dialyzer—may engender some negative side effects in the patient; *e.g.,* decreases in the white blood cell count and in complement activation. This is accompanied by a variety of symptoms that may include chest pain, itchiness, and malaise. Once a cellulosic dialyzer has been used, however, its membrane becomes pacified by a deposit of the patient's own proteins, and the dialyzer's negative side effects are substantially decreased when the blood is exposed to the reprocessed dialyzer once again.

Establishing standards for sterility. On the other hand, if the reprocessing makes use of improper disinfectant and sterilant substances, harm can be done. The use of formaldehyde, the most popularly used disinfectant, has been criticized on the basis of its possible carcinogenicity and its unpleasant odor. Acceptable standards for formaldehyde residues remaining in reprocessed dialyzers have been suggested and are in force to various degrees. (It should be pointed out, however, that low concentrations of formaldehyde are normally found in the bloodstream.) There are also other substances known to damage cellulosic membranes under certain circumstances and thus to allow bacteria to enter circulation. One such substance has been withdrawn from sale pending a resolution of the problem. Other sterilants commonly used and deemed safe include glutaraldehyde and peracetic acid.

Recently the Association for the Advancement of Medical Instrumentation, Arlington, Va., published recommended practices for dialyzer reuse. This document is the consensus of representatives from dialysis products manufacturers, physicians' organizations, various government organizations, and kidney failure patients. The Health Care Financing Administration (of the U.S. Department of Health and Human Services) is currently using this document as the basis for establishing appropriate standards for the reuse of dialyzers in the U.S. This should help allay public concern and raise the level of practice in those facilities that do not currently observe standards. Some organizations representing patients feel that these guidelines are not enough; they maintain that a patient's consent must be obtained and that he or she has the right to receive a new dialyzer each time. Failing that, they insist that a transfer to an alternative facility must be arranged if the patient is not convinced by the physician's argument for reuse. This area is the subject of much discussion at present.

Recently the U.S. Food and Drug Administration issued a letter to manufacturers requesting that they consider removing labels on dialyzers that indicate that these products are for single use only. This step would only legalize what is already happening, but some manufacturers are wary about making such a move since this might make them responsible for events over which they have little or no control.

Although it affects a very small segment of the health care industry and total populace of medical patients, the matter of reprocessing dialyzers offers an interesting example of the increasingly common crisis in medicine today, which has been engendered by conflicts of interest in the care of sick people and in the problems inherent in applying technology for their benefit.

—Nathan W. Levin, M.D.

Medical Ethics

Over the past year, the news media have insistently—even daily—filed reports dealing with issues of biomedical ethics. The stories have usually concentrated on human dramas—the court cases and policy battles that have erupted at both the state and the federal level over fetal abuse, for example, or drug testing in the workplace. The underlying ethical dilemmas were later teased out, though, in interviews with doctors, lawyers, philosophers, and theologians.

The court case involving Baby M received the most extensive coverage. For months local and national newspapers, as well as television and radio broadcasts and talk shows, explored the social implications of surrogate parenting. By the time the lower court decision was issued, many U.S. households had received an education in artificial reproductive technologies, stimulating discussions and disagreements about the morality of this new form of parenting.

What follows is a review of some of the most controversial issues of the day and the ethical questions at stake. One recurring conflict pits the rights of individuals to make choices about their own lives and the lives of their offspring against the responsibilities of the state to protect people, including children, from harm.

Fetal abuse

In October 1986 Pamela Rae Stewart Monson became the first woman to be charged with the crime of abusing her fetus. According to the prosecution, on Nov. 23, 1985, the 27-year-old San Diego woman ignored her doctor's instructions and took amphetamines and had sex with her husband instead of getting to the hospital promptly when she began to bleed. The same day, her son Thomas was born with extensive brain damage; he died on Jan. 1, 1986.

Monson, who lived in one room with her husband and two small children, was prosecuted under a 1926

Medical ethics

California misdemeanor statute that makes it a crime for a parent to "wilfully omit, without lawful excuse," to furnish necessary medical attendance for his or her child. The statute specifies that the fetus is a person; it was intended not to punish women but to hold fathers responsible for child support. Monson, had she been convicted, faced up to a year in jail and a fine of up to $2,000. On Feb. 26, 1987, a San Diego Municipal Court judge ruled that the statute did not apply. As of late spring 1987, no decision had been made about whether to appeal.

The Monson case raises questions about the extent of a woman's obligations to her fetus and the advisability of using legal means to enforce maternal obligations. Must a pregnant woman stop drinking, smoking, working, or having sex because her doctor says so? Should she be compelled to have a cesarean section or undergo treatment for the sake of her baby-to-be and, if she fails to do so, is she guilty of "fetal abuse"?

John Robertson, a lawyer and medical ethicist at the University of Texas at Austin, argues that a woman always has the right to terminate her pregnancy, but once she decides to have her baby, she has an obligation to bring it into the world as healthy as possible. In Robertson's view, if a woman's behavior clearly puts her fetus at risk, the doctor may have a duty to seek a court order to prevent damage.

George Annas, professor of health law at Boston University Schools of Medicine and Public Health, writing in the *Hastings Center Report* (December 1986), expressed his rejection of coercive measures on the grounds that "favoring the fetus radically devalues the pregnant woman and treats her like an inert incubator or a culture medium for the fetus." His conclusion: "The best chance the state has to protect fetuses is by fostering reasonable pay and equal opportunities [for all women] and providing a reasonable social safety net, quality prenatal services, and day care programs."

Dick Locher; courtesy, Tribune Media Services

As a practical matter, support for fetal rights is growing at the expense of women's civil liberties. According to a national survey, reported in the *New England Journal of Medicine* (May 7, 1987), 46% of the heads of fellowship programs in maternal-fetal medicine favor detaining women who endanger their fetuses by refusing medical advice, and 47% support court orders for intrauterine transfusions and other procedures. Courts have ordered women to undergo cesarean sections and blood transfusions for the sake of the fetus, despite their religious objections. Women have been hospitalized against their wills and compelled to undergo drug testing and drug treatment. In most instances court orders have applied to women who are poor, unmarried, and members of minority groups.

In the future, restrictions may also apply to decisions about fetal surgery. At present, operating on the fetus is considered experimental, and the woman has no obligation to consent. However, if and when fetal surgery becomes an accepted medical treatment, a pregnant woman may lose her option to refuse the operation.

Testing for illegal drug use

On Sept. 15, 1986, U.S. Pres. Ronald A. Reagan issued an executive order requiring federal agencies to do urine testing on job applicants and an estimated one million to two million government employees in "sensitive" positions to determine whether they are taking illegal drugs. The executive order also stated that "persons who take illegal drugs are not suitable for federal employment." The announced goal is to establish a "drug-free workplace."

Despite serious doubts about the constitutionality of the order, the government has issued guidelines for implementing the program. The guidelines resemble those of a military drug-testing program that has been in effect for several years, with one exception: while the military program directly observes the person who is urinating, the federal program stations a monitor outside the bathroom door.

The issue of mandatory drug testing in the workplace pits a perceived public good against the privacy rights of employees. Supporters of random urine testing argue that it offers a reasonable way of combating drug abuse in the workplace before harm occurs. They point to the link between drug abuse and losses in productivity including accidents, injuries, theft, and absence from work. They also maintain that drug use violates the contract between employer and employee; in return for wages and a safe workplace, the worker has a duty to refrain from behavior that could harm the company.

Critics generally accept the employer's right to try to eliminate drugs from the workplace. However, they contend that urine testing is degrading and that random testing without probable cause violates the Fourth Amendment prohibition against unreasonable "search and seizure." Critics also point out that drug use does not necessarily mean drug abuse and that tests may not discriminate between the two, and they question whether the tests will be used to help employees or to fire them.

In an article on the ethics of drug testing (*Hastings Center Report,* December 1986), Morris Panner, a student at Harvard Law School, and Nicholas Christakis, a student at Harvard Medical School, cite evidence that drug testing is fallible and that even the most effective and expensive tests are subject to human and scientific error. They raise questions about the fairness of a process where, "in any given group of tested employees, athletes, prisoners, or soldiers, some individuals will unavoidably be falsely accused." They also express worry particularly about a "Kafkaesque predicament," in which "a few unlucky innocent individuals will be accused" not by a person they can confront but by "a faceless test result.

Despite such warnings, increasing numbers of public and private employers are testing their workers and job applicants for drug use. It is estimated that nearly 50% of the Fortune 500 companies do drug testing, usually in combination with drug and alcohol education and rehabilitation. More than half of the 497 national employers interviewed by the U.S. College Placement Council say that they test for drugs or plan to start testing soon. And a bill to require random testing of millions of transportation workers is being hotly debated on the floor of the U.S. Senate.

In the U.S., state and local governments have also begun testing. The city of Richmond, Va., for example, will screen all management-level employees during their annual examinations, and all employees will have

A recent poll asked full-time workers if they would submit to being tested for illegal drug use if such testing was imposed by their employers.

Support for workplace drug testing

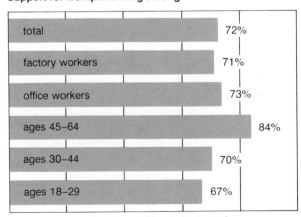

percentage willing to be tested

Source: New York Times/CBS News poll, Aug. 18–21, 1986

to undergo testing before being promoted. Washington, D.C., already asks defendants in criminal cases to undergo voluntary testing; New Yorkers who are arrested on felony charges will soon be asked to do the same. Recently the U.S. Justice Department said that it will support the efforts of local school boards to require testing for teachers who are candidates for employment.

The constitutional implications of urine testing are still unclear, and many challenges are currently working their way through the courts. Panner and Christakis believe that "given the increasing emphasis on preventing drug abuse, courts may become more willing to allow more intrusive searches." They predict that "the 'balancing' test between privacy and state interest may increasingly shift in favor of allowing mass testing for drug use and, indeed, for other medical or behavioral attributes of individuals."

Body parts: gift or property?

In the book *The Gift: Imagination and the Erotic Life of Property,* Lewis Hyde makes the point that in the "free world" most exchanges of goods and ideas are subject to the laws of the marketplace. He points out that this dominant form of exchange reinforces a sense of liberty since it "does not bind the individual in any way—to his family, to his community, or to the state."

In the U.S. one of the few exceptions occurs over transactions involving body parts. It is illegal, for example, to sell body organs in interstate commerce, and some state laws ban payment for specified organs. Such laws discourage a market in which the poor will be pressured into selling organs to the rich. The laws also constitute a tacit acknowledgment that donating body parts binds the community together.

Recently, however, body tissues and fluids have become more valuable, as potentially profitable products have resulted from research using body parts that were removed in the course of medical treatment. In 1984, for example, at the University of California at Los Angeles, the blood of a leukemia patient was used to develop a patented and commercially valuable cell line. The patient, John Moore, objected that this was done without his knowledge or explicit consent, but the doctors said that he had waived his interest in his body parts by signing a general consent form. At the University of California at San Diego, biology student Hideaki Hagiwara insisted that his family should be compensated for a cell line made from his mother's cancer cells. Although the researchers had invented the procedure and created the parent cells, the courts granted Hagiwara an exclusive license for the cell line in Japan and Asia.

Cases like Moore's and Hagiwara's raise questions about the adequacy of the gift relationship regarding the human body. Do people have the right to know that their body parts may be used for other purposes?

Should they be paid fairly for their contribution to research, diagnostics, or therapy? Should the gift relationship give way to an entrepreneurial model, which holds that a person's body is property that he or she is free to sell, or are the values attached to the gift relationship too important to surrender?

Lori Andrews, a project director in medical law at the American Bar Association, has spoken out about this matter. She argues that donors, recipients, and society will benefit from a market in body parts so long as the owners—and no one else—retain control over what happens to their bodies ("My Body, My Property," *Hastings Center Report,* October 1986). She also argues that without this control, others may decide to use a body part without the owner's permission. For example, doctors may decide to obtain eggs and embryos from women without their consent; organs may be transferred from a cadaver even though the person never granted consent during his or her lifetime; and the person or the family may suffer physical or psychological harm as a result.

Andrews also maintains that it is inconsistent and unethical to prohibit payment for a kidney or other dispensable organ since people are already allowed—and even encouraged—to donate such organs. In order to prevent coercion, she cautions that people should have the right to sell their own organs but no one else should have that right, and that donors should have the option of changing their minds until the transfer takes place.

Thomas Murray, a professor of ethics and public policy at the University of Texas Medical Branch at Galveston, rejects the notion of a property right in one's body. He believes that on the whole the system of voluntary giving has served society well since researchers and educators get the body parts they need, patients can be confident that their parts are being treated respectfully, and the public knows that medical research is proceeding without using people as commodities ("Who Owns the Body? On the Ethics of Using Human Tissue for Commercial Purposes," *IRB, A Review of Human Subjects Research,* January–February 1986). He concedes, however, that a problem arises when "someone—researcher, university, corporation—may become wealthy as a result of our gift." Murray has urged Congress to encourage biotechnology entrepreneurs to adopt ethical policies in order to preserve the dignity of the human body and the gift relationship between science and the public: "If biotechnologists fail to make provision for a just sharing of profits with the person whose gift made it possible," he warns, "the public's sense of justice is likely to be offended, and no one will be the winner."

Surrogate mothers

Over the last decade more than 500 babies have been born in the U.S. through commercial surrogacy

Mary Beth Whitehead refused to give up the baby she had contracted to bear for William and Elizabeth Stern in the celebrated Baby M case, which dramatized ethical issues surrounding surrogacy as a new form of parenting.

arrangements. In return for payment—on average, $10,000—the surrogate mother agrees to be artificially inseminated with the sperm of a man whose wife is generally infertile, to carry the baby to term, and to turn the infant over to the couple. On at least four occasions surrogate mothers apparently changed their minds and decided to keep their babies. In three instances, the fathers let the babies go. In the fourth case both the father, William Stern, and the surrogate mother, Mary Beth Whitehead, refused to give the baby up. In 1987 the dispute between the Sterns and Whitehead became the most talked-about court case in America.

Whitehead, who married at age 16 and had two children of her own before she turned 19, agreed to conceive and bear Baby M for a New Jersey couple, Elizabeth Stern, a pediatrician, and her husband, William, a biochemist, who is the child's natural father. Elizabeth Stern was not sterile, but she feared that her mild case of multiple sclerosis might worsen if she became pregnant. The baby was born on March 27, 1986. Whitehead reneged on her contract, however, and fled with the baby to Florida. About her change of mind Whitehead said, "At the end, something took over. I guess it was just being a mother. . . . It overpowered me. . . . I just cried and cried. I didn't want the $10,000. I just wanted my child."

William Stern, whose relatives had all died, wanted Baby M fiercely. She would continue the family bloodline. "Everybody is talking about mothers' rights, and nobody seems to be concerned about fathers' rights," he said. "Fathers have dreams too."

The case of Baby M has dramatized the ethical issues that strike at the heart of this new form of parenting. Key questions are: Is commercial surrogacy a form of baby selling or a legitimate service that furthers people's constitutional rights to procreate? Are surrogates entering into contracts with their eyes wide open, or are they being exploited? (Whitehead's contract took away her right to decide to abort unless it was necessary for her health, and it terminated her payments if she refused to abort an impaired fetus at the Sterns' request. The agency that made the match, however, received a nonrefundable $7,500 in advance.) Should surrogate mothers have a chance to reconsider once the baby has been born? What weight should be given to the father's genetic ties? Are surrogate arrangements threatening to family relationships and harmful to the child? Should they be regulated—or banned altogether?

The Baby M case also highlighted an important social issue, the question of class differences. Like many surrogates, Whitehead is poor and uneducated—a high school dropout; she and her husband, a sanitation worker with a drinking problem, are members of the lower socioeconomic class. Like most couples who hire surrogates, the Sterns, by contrast, are well-off and highly educated. Critics of surrogacy argue that poor women are being used as breeders for wealthy couples. Others reply that being a surrogate mother is no worse than working in the coal mines, and that it is wrong to ban surrogacy unless society provides poor women with better means for feeding their families.

On March 31, 1987, four days after Baby M's first birthday, New Jersey Superior Court Judge Harvey R. Sorkow ruled that the contract between the Sterns and Whitehead was valid and enforceable, and that it was in Baby M's best interests to remain with the Sterns. Whitehead was barred from visiting Melissa—the Sterns' name, and now the legal name, for Baby M—but her visits were reinstated, and on April 10, 1987, the New Jersey Supreme Court allowed Whitehead to see the baby for two hours a week until settlement of her appeal of the case in late 1987 or early 1988. Whatever the final decision in this case, the larger legal and ethical issues surrounding surrogacy remain.

Baby M had more than her share of devoted parents, but other babies born to surrogate mothers have too few. How then can the interests of the physically or mentally impaired baby whom nobody wants be protected? Should single people and unmarried couples be permitted to hire surrogates? Also, if commercial arrangements are to remain legal, how can the best interests of all parties involved be protected? One question will become more important as the number of surrogate children grows: Do parents have a right to withhold information about the circumstances of the child's birth?

The process of redefining motherhood is already under way. As of midsummer 1987, 26 states were considering surrogacy legislation. Some bills would outlaw commercial surrogacy altogether. Others would allow the surrogate mother a certain period after birth in which to change her mind. Still others would legalize the contracts and guarantee adoption rights for the biologic father and his wife, and some bills would make the contract enforceable at birth but would try to protect the surrogate mother's right to full and informed consent.

Similar cases are also continuing to raise questions in Great Britain, where the Surrogacy Arrangements Act has made it a criminal offense for third parties (such as agencies) to profit from surrogacy. Since Parliament passed the act in 1985, a straightforward

Paul Merideth—Click/Chicago

Surrogacy arrangements that are successful depend on scrupulous care in choosing the woman who will bear a couple's child and precisely spelling out the terms in a contract.

adoption case and a custody battle have come before the courts.

In the case of the British couple who were seeking adoption, the surrogate mother had set out to help an infertile couple. With approval from her husband, she had advertised and had chosen the couple in question; although others had offered more money, she chose the couple because she said she liked them. She then had intercourse with the father for the purpose of conceiving the child. After the child was born, she transferred it to the couple. Although she was paid £5,000 (she refused another £5,000 because she had profited from a book that was published recounting her experience), no contract had been signed; the judge agreed that this was not a commercial arrangement but one based on trust and that the adoption should proceed.

In the British custody dispute, a married woman living alone with her young child entered into a surrogacy agreement with a couple and conceived a child by means of artificial insemination by donor. The mother, who was living on social security payments, planned to use the money to help raise her child but changed her mind late in her pregnancy because of strong maternal feelings. In September 1986 twins were born, and she refused to turn them over to the couple. The babies became wards of the court and remained with the mother during court proceedings. The judge stated that, while there was nothing shameful about entering into such arrangements, the welfare of the children came first. On March 12, 1987, he awarded custody to the mother on the grounds that "these babies are bonded with their mother in a state of domestic care by her of a satisfactory nature."

Had the twins, like Baby M, remained with the contracting couple during the custody battle, the decision might have been different. In addition, there is the question of the biologic father's financial obligations; will he be expected to support his offspring without having the right to rear them?

U.S. health coverage: sad state of affairs

In the U.S. 37 million people—a numbing figure—have no public or private health care insurance. Millions more have some but not nearly enough. Government cutbacks are partially responsible. According to the American Hospital Association, over the past decade Medicaid coverage for the poor has declined from 65 to 38% of costs, while the number of poor people has risen. One-third of all workers, along with large numbers of the unemployed, have no health insurance, although the so-called COBRA Act, passed in 1986, gives some categories of unemployed workers the option of continuing coverage at group rates; when people lose their jobs, they usually lose any health insurance their companies may provide. Many elderly people (an estimated 13% of them poor, and many of them living alone) are unable to afford home help or

nursing home care, which are not reimbursed under Medicare. The AIDS (acquired immune deficiency syndrome) epidemic is straining the system further and creating new young victims of poverty. Predictions are that the situation will get worse before it improves.

Presently the issue of access to care is on the minds of many Americans. What does a society owe to its citizens in the way of health care? Is health care a basic need, such as food, clothing, and shelter? Does everyone have a right to all or some services, or are some people more "deserving" than others?

Judging from the statements of key health care providers, politicians, and policymakers, and from grass-roots polls across the country, most people say they favor universal access to a decent level of health care. There is no agreement about who should bear the financial burden, however. Presently, health care is financed largely by third-party payers through employers, with individuals, charities, state and local governments, and federal programs filling in the gaps. Should the present patchwork of public and private funding continue, or should the U.S. follow the example of every other industrialized nation, with the exception of South Africa, and institute a universal health care system at the federal level?

Citizens' groups and some unions argue that the U.S. has created a two-tiered system, where the poor go without health care and the rich can buy even the most exotic care. As evidence they point to the "dumping," or turning away, of uninsured patients by private hospitals, the lack of medical and dental care for millions of children, and the shortage of free pre-

Out-of-control costs have led to what some now see as a two-tiered health care system in the U.S.—with the poor having little access to care while the rich can buy the best. The patient below is hospitalized in a VIP suite.

Alan D. Levenson

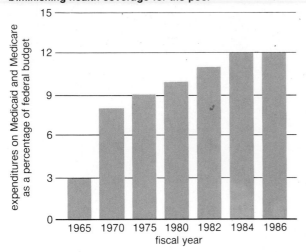

Sources: U.S. Department of Treasury, Office of Management and Budget
Diminishing health coverage for the poor

(y-axis: expenditures on Medicaid and Medicare as a percentage of federal budget; values 0, 3, 6, 9, 12, 15; x-axis: fiscal year 1965 1970 1975 1980 1982 1984 1986)

financed in part by a payroll tax, to all its citizens. State Sen. Patricia McGovern, who is sponsoring the plan, believes that it would encourage welfare recipients to enter workplaces they have been reluctant to enter because of a lack of insurance. If the plan is passed as law, Massachusetts will join Hawaii as the only states to offer health coverage to all residents.

Clinical trials and a promising AIDS drug

In the U.S. new and promising drugs must be tested, first on animals and then on human beings, in order for it to be determined whether they are safe and effective for wider distribution. Often human research subjects are patients who agree to enter a randomized controlled clinical trial to test the risks and benefits of a drug that they hope will help them. In most clinical trials about half of the patients receive the drug; the other half (the control group) receive the standard treatment or a placebo if there is no effective treatment, as is the case with AIDS. Generally, neither the research subject nor the patient's doctor is told which group the patient has been assigned to.

To enter a clinical trial, a patient must meet the researcher's strict medical criteria. If a participant is too sick or not sick enough, is too young or too old, or has the "wrong" symptoms, his or her data may skew the results of the study, and future patients may suffer from the misleading scientific information. In certain instances, however, strict criteria for eligibility and the use of placebos may clash with the best interests of patients. That is especially true if the patient is dying anyway and has no other treatment to turn to.

The ethics of clinical trials came under close scrutiny recently after the drug company Burroughs Wellcome reported that azidothymidine (AZT), which the company manufactures (and is the *sole* manufacturer of), appeared to prolong the lives of a small group of patients with AIDS and AIDS-related complex. Preliminary studies at the National Cancer Institute during

natal care for poor pregnant women. At the other extreme, they make the point that wealthy foreigners have bought their way to the top of waiting lists for organ transplants, while some Americans who cannot pay up front for costly surgery must go without.

For the most part, however, Americans continue to resist the idea of a nationalized system. A far more popular approach is that taken by the President's Commission for the Study of Ethical Problems in Medicine and Biomedical and Behavioral Research in its 1983 report to the president: "Private health care providers and insurers, charitable bodies, and local and state governments all have roles to play in the health care system in the United States. Yet the federal government has the ultimate responsibility for seeing that health care is available to all when the market, private charity, and government efforts at the state and local level are insufficient in achieving equity."

In 1987 and 1988 the U.S. Congress will discuss measures for alleviating some of the burdens on the poor. A proposal by Health and Human Services Secretary Otis R. Bowen to expand Medicare benefits may help some families facing the staggering costs of a lengthy hospital stay, but it does not address the overwhelming financial burdens imposed by a lengthy nursing home stay or other care outside the hospital, nor does it include the population under age 65, except for special categories of patients already covered by Medicare. Alternate proposals suggest lower liability rates for the elderly, as well as protection against costs of some prescription drugs. Congress may also consider strategies for expanding the Medicaid population by allowing states to include some groups that are not eligible under current law and by allowing other people to "buy into" to federal programs such as Medicaid and Medicare for a small premium.

In Massachusetts the state legislature is considering a controversial plan that would offer health insurance,

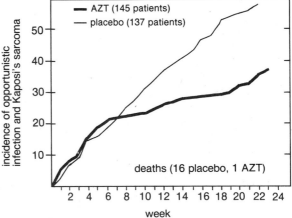

AZT trials: initial results

AZT (145 patients) / placebo (137 patients)

(y-axis: incidence of opportunistic infection and Kaposi's sarcoma; x-axis: week 2–24)

deaths (16 placebo, 1 AZT)

Source: Burroughs Wellcome Co.

Demonstrators in Manhattan in March 1987 were demanding quicker government approval of drugs that hold promise for combating the disease AIDS. The Food and Drug Administration subsequently amended its policy so that people suffering from "immediately life-threatening diseases for which no alternative therapies exist" now have access to drugs even if the drugs are considered still under investigation.

1985 had indicated that the drug did not kill the virus, but it did seem to keep it from multiplying.

In February 1986 Burroughs Wellcome decided to test the drug further on 282 patients with *Pneumocystis carinii* pneumonia (PCP), a type of pneumonia that is one manifestation of full-blown AIDS; half of the patients would get AZT, the other half a placebo. The company claimed it was limiting the trial to a small number of patients for ethical reasons; in the event that the drug should turn out to be harmful, fewer people would suffer.

In general the research community supported the need for a carefully controlled clinical trial on the grounds that it was the most efficient way of collecting accurate scientific information. Researchers pointed to previous drugs that were widely distributed before they were carefully tested and had to be withdrawn from the market when they later proved ineffective or highly toxic. Mathilde Krim, a biologist and president and founder of the American Foundation for AIDS Research, called the AZT trial "morally unacceptable," however. She argued that many people in the control group would die before the test was over. She also pushed for the release of AZT to patients outside the trial as an act of compassion.

By September 1986 the patients taking AZT were doing so much better than the others (one death, compared with 16 in the control group) that all the patients were switched to the drug. Also, despite some serious side effects (AZT has destroyed bone marrow in some patients and caused nausea, vomiting, and anemia in others), the U.S. Food and Drug Administration (FDA) allowed about 3,000 other PCP-type AIDS patients to take AZT outside the trial. Although other patients who had taken AZT have since died, in March 1987 the FDA decided that the benefits of saving lives outweighed the risks of AZT. It approved AZT (renamed

zidovudine) so that doctors could prescribe it for the thousands of other AIDS patients with PCP. Doctors who wish to try AZT for other AIDS patients are discouraged from doing so, however, because they have no guidelines for its appropriate use. AIDS patients argue that this "protection" amounts to unreasonable paternalism and that since they are dying, they should be the ones to decide whether to take the drug.

AIDS patients who are eligible for the drug now face a new problem: how to pay for it. The drug was distributed free to patients in the clinical trial; now it will cost them $8,000 to $10,000 a year. Burroughs Wellcome says that the price of the drug will help to cover the high costs of development, but AIDS patients argue that it is unethical to withhold lifesaving drugs on the basis of a patient's ability to pay.

Meanwhile, the FDA has changed its policy regarding all promising new drugs. Under the new rule, investigational drugs are no longer confined to patients in clinical trials but are available to all people suffering from "immediately life-threatening diseases for which no alternative therapies exist."

Ongoing and future issues

In the coming months, the debates that have already begun over these issues are likely to continue, if not expand. In addition, new ones will raise equally disturbing ethical questions; *e.g.,* whether further prenatal screening for genetic diseases is advisable, the difficulty of making appropriate decisions on behalf of a growing number of older patients with Alzheimer's disease about their care and their participation in research that may not benefit them directly, the morality of using human fetal tissue for research or therapy, and whether healthy organs should be "harvested" from anencephalic, or brain-absent, infants.

—Joyce Bermel

Special Report

Foreboding Trends in Health Care

by Elizabeth B. Connell, M.D.

Two major storms have been gathering, slowly at first but now with increasing speed and strength, that threaten the future health care of the U.S. public and, by extension, the rest of the world. The first of these disturbances is the professional malpractice insurance crisis, a major contributing factor to the rapidly escalating costs of medical care in the United States. Physicians are increasingly having to practice very expensive defensive medicine and, in some instances, are sharply limiting their practices in order to avoid caring for high-risk patients because they pose an increased threat of lawsuits. The overall situation is steadily worsening and is now progressively blocking access to quality medical care in a widening variety of clinical situations.

The second storm centers around product liability insurance, another factor that is adding substantially to the nation's rapidly growing medical costs. Adequate coverage is becoming unaffordable and, in some instances, totally unobtainable. As a result, pharmaceutical companies have also been forced to take a defensive stance and are now limiting their areas of activity in order to reduce their risks of being sued. The end result has been the loss of valuable drugs and devices already approved and on the market. It has also led to a sharp curtailment of the rapid advances in drug research and in the development of agents used for prevention and control of disease—advances that heretofore had established the United States as a world leader.

While the progressive deterioration of the health care system and the decreasing availability of pharmaceutical products of proven safety and effectiveness may appear on the surface to have different etiologies, a somewhat deeper look discloses that they have many basic similarities. There are at least seven major and often interacting factors that profoundly impinge upon both situations. First, there is the drug-regulatory process; second, the rise of aggressive consumerism accompanied by changing expectations and attitudes on the part of the American public; third, the frequently biased coverage given to medicolegal events by radio, television, and the various forms of print media; fourth, the increasing role of congressional hearings and Supreme Court decisions in determining the provision

of health care; fifth, the move of many individuals in the legal profession from constitutional concerns into the field of tort litigation; sixth, the appearance of unscrupulous "expert witnesses" willing to testify, often for exorbitant fees, to any required cause-and-effect relationship; and seventh, the enormous increases in the costs of malpractice and product liability insurance and its progressive unavailability. While each of these factors poses its own particular problems, taken in the aggregate they are giving rise to numerous changes that are already being felt in the current provision of health care.

All areas of medical care have been affected but none more significantly than the field of reproductive health care. Inasmuch as reproductive health care deals with some of the most vital and sensitive aspects of human life—i.e., sexual behavior, the elective control of fertility, drugs related to pregnancy and delivery, and agents used in the treatment of women, newborns, and young children—a very emotionally charged situation has developed. The above seven factors directly affect almost everyone in society and often elicit either very positive or very negative reactions from certain individuals and organizations. Because of the public's great interest in these topics, a high level of visibility has been accorded to them by the media.

The drug-regulatory process

The history of drug regulation in the United States began in this century with the Food and Drug Act of 1906. For several decades, however, jurisdiction was mainly in the category of safety, and most of the drugs evaluated were used for only short periods of time and mainly for curative purposes. Then in 1962 a major piece of legislation was enacted—the Kefauver-Harris Amendments. This law required the filing of claimed exemptions for investigative new drugs (INDs), which the Food and Drug Administration (FDA) had to approve. It further stated that informed consents, approved by Institutional Review Boards (IRBs), had to be signed by all study participants. Moreover, it mandated that not only safety but also efficacy now had to be proved by scientifically valid studies prior to the marketing of a new drug or device. In 1966 the FDA decided to evaluate the thousands of over-the-counter (OTC) drugs being sold, which had never undergone any review for safety or efficacy. Over the next few years it established more than 20 OTC panels to evaluate the safety, efficacy, and labeling claims of all of the ingredients in the products that fell within their particular area of expertise. The Medical Device Amendments of 1976 further extended the jurisdiction of the FDA by requiring the agency to review the safety and effectiveness of all existing and proposed medical devices intended for human use.

With the passage of each piece of legislation, the mandate of the FDA was progressively expanded. In order to meet these increasing responsibilities, the FDA enlarged its staff, and new individual bureaus were created to deal with all of the various agents now under its purview. During these same years the process of drug and device evaluation became ever more complicated and expensive. It moved from the era of small clinical trials, often carried out by individual medical practitioners on a few of their own patients, to large multi-institutional studies of new drugs and devices, which were conducted primarily at university medical centers. The amount of information required for approval also increased markedly as the base of scientific information continued to expand as a result of ongoing research efforts in many fields.

It has often been charged, and sometimes rightly so, that shifting study demands and numerous bureaucratic delays by the FDA have retarded the development of promising new drugs and devices in the U.S., as compared with other countries, and have sometimes even blocked their ultimate approval. Although pharmaceutical companies are required by law to prove to the FDA, prior to marketing, that their new products are both safe and effective, there are often no established guidelines that they can follow in order to do so; thus, the agency is able to continue to delay approval by asking for additional data. If this happens repeatedly, the research costs may begin to exceed the profits that can be anticipated to result from the sale of these products, and the studies may be terminated. When this occurs, the FDA is obviously spared the possibility of future problems with this particular agent because, at least in the United States, it will never be sold.

Another major deterrent to objective scientific decisions by the FDA is the almost constant intervention in FDA affairs by members of Congress. Subcommittee hearings have a major impact on the day-to-day functioning of the FDA, and some of the recent agency rulings have clearly been rendered in deference to political pressures. An ancillary but directly related difficulty has been the consistent inability of the FDA to hire and keep top-quality professionals as staff members since they have little opportunity to do good independent scientific work and have minimal chances for personal advancement. The academic community in

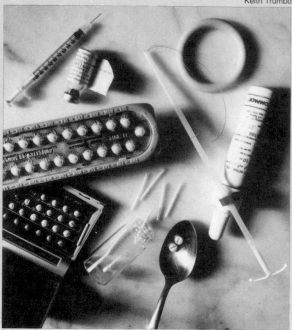

In the U.S. 1987 has been dubbed "the year of no choice" because of the sharp decline of birth control options. Contraceptives under development include (clockwise from top left): a vaccine that inhibits ovulation, a vaginal ring, a nasal spray, a progesterone-treated IUD, "morning-after" pills, implantable hormone rods, and new versions of the Pill.

general does not hold these individuals in high regard, and even work that is well done is often disregarded, which can result in serious staff morale problems.

As the mandate of the agency enlarged, the FDA set up a number of advisory committees, each with expertise in a particular scientific area. The effectiveness of these bodies has also been progressively eroded by political pressures. In the past they were composed of individuals of high professional standing who considered it an honor to serve on these committees. However, in recent years researchers who are evaluating new drugs and devices for pharmaceutical companies are often viewed as having possible conflicts of interest and thus are excluded as members. They are being replaced by political appointees with little or no scientific knowledge about the agents upon which they must render judgments.

The decisions made by the FDA have always had a major impact throughout the world. While most of the developed countries have their own regulatory agencies, many of the less developed countries do not, and they have traditionally looked to the U.S. for guidance in the use of pharmaceutical products. For many years the FDA has refused to accept any responsibility for this impact of its decisions on other countries, arguing that its role is to act on behalf of Americans and that its mandate does not extend to other nations. The failure of the FDA to approve an agent also prevents its

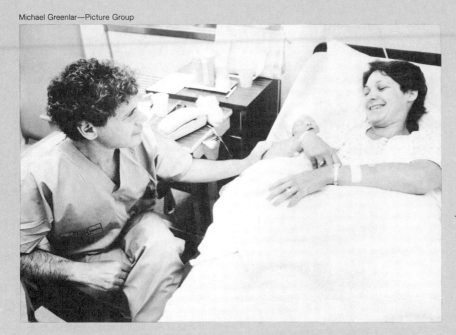

After obstetrician-gynecologist Henry Eisenberg (left) was sued for malpractice, he wrote a book to explain why he and many other doctors today must practice defensive medicine and why so many obstetricians are no longer willing to deliver babies. In the U.S. as many as seven out of ten obstetricians have faced malpractice suits.

distribution through the Agency for International Development (AID), which has long been a major supplier of medical products to health care providers working in the less developed countries. A classic example of this situation is the uncertainty about the injectable contraceptive, Depo-Provera, which is examined more fully below.

Changing public expectations

In recent years the remarkable growth in the number and power of the various consumer groups in the United States has had a major influence on the activities of the FDA. While in many ways such groups' activities have been beneficial, there has been and continues to be tremendous conflict between those groups who feel that the FDA is not demanding enough data and those in the opposite camp who say that excellent drugs, available in other countries, are being denied to the American public because of too rigid FDA guidelines and bureaucratic delay. In some instances these groups have actually blocked the approval of certain products that are believed by the scientific community to be safe and effective agents.

Today consumer advocates have been placed on most of the FDA advisory committees. These individuals have been extremely helpful in the formulation of policy, particularly with regard to labeling. In other instances, however, they have clearly not understood the medical implications involved in the committees' decisions and thus have had a very destructive effect on the outcome of certain deliberations. It also appears that certain of the more activist groups are not fully aware of the gross inaccuracy of some of the allegations they are making, nor do they seem to be aware of the implications of how their actions in partic-

ular are affecting the health care of women; *e.g.,* such actions have led to a sharp decrease in the number of contraceptive options available to women worldwide.

In fairness, it must be noted that the FDA has been forced to function under some very difficult conditions. It is a basic medical tenet that no drug or device can ever be developed that is totally safe and completely effective. However, the American public, particularly consumer advocate groups, appears to believe that there should be absolutely no risk involved in any products or practices affecting health care. Although drugs and devices today have a risk-benefit ratio that is overwhelmingly on the side of the benefits, the products are never absolutely perfect. Thus, the FDA is often forced to make value judgments as to whether the potential benefits of a new product outweigh its potential risks, sometimes putting the agency in an almost untenable position. It is asked not only to render accurate scientific judgments but also to make policy decisions as a consequence of its rulings. Moreover, since the general public has not accepted the fact that there are no perfect medical products, any adverse reaction is often quickly followed by litigation that attempts to establish which of the potential "deep pockets" would be the most logical and the most lucrative to pursue legally.

Media coverage

The subjects of reproduction, family planning, abortion, and sexual behavior have attracted major attention from the media. Although conscientious and scientific coverage of these topics has been provided by certain of the media, in many instances, unfortunately, only the most inflammatory and negative stories have been given top coverage. It has always been the case

341

that bad news is far more salable than good news. Adverse information and outcomes, whether justified by scientific data or not, are printed with alacrity, but the good news or positive results tend to receive little or no media attention. Because of this bias, certain drugs and devices have, in the public's eye, come to be perceived as dangerous medical products, whereas careful review of the scientific literature does not support these conclusions. The large numbers of product liability cases have added to the problem. As would be anticipated, large judgments against pharmaceutical companies receive wide media coverage, but cases that do not result in a settlement for the plaintiff are seldom even reported.

Congressional hearings and court decisions

In a number of instances, when the goals of the various consumer groups could not be achieved by the usual FDA process, these groups have turned to congressmen known to be receptive to their particular cause. For example, almost every method of family planning has had its day before some congressional committee. The earliest of these were the hearings on oral contraceptives held in 1970 by Sen. Gaylord Nelson's (Dem., Wis.) Subcommittee on Monopoly of the Select Committee on Small Business. The hearings demonstrated very clearly how destructive such proceedings can be.

The case of the Pill. In this instance the earlier testimonies were all given by individuals hostile to the use of the oral contraceptive pill. Many allegations were made that were totally without substance, and the media coverage was intense. Eventually, owing to the obvious bias of the hearings, the other side was allowed to present another view of oral contraceptives—one that focused on the many and clear benefits. Typically, however, media coverage of the good news was too little and too late, and the damage produced by the earlier testimony had already had a major impact. A recent survey by the Gallup organization in the U.S. and similar polls in eight other countries have shown the legacy left behind by these hearings and continuing negative publicity about the Pill. These studies documented women's unrealistic fears about the use of oral contraceptives and little understanding of their health benefits.

The Depo-Provera case. Depo-Provera, an injectable contraceptive that has been in widespread use for over 20 years in more than 90 countries, has proved to be safe and very effective. However, because of the pressure placed on the FDA by a number of consumer groups and because of two congressional hearings and extensive media coverage, this agent still has not been approved in the U.S. Over the years, the FDA's own advisory committees and numerous committees in many other countries have recommended the approval of Depo-Provera, yet in 1984 an FDA

Public Board of Inquiry refused to do so because it felt that the long-term-safety data were inadequate. The type of data it demanded far exceeded the types available on almost all drugs currently on the market and for many reasons would be almost impossible to obtain. Unfortunately, the recommendation that partial approval be given, made in a minority report filed by the only clinician on this panel (now deceased), has never been implemented. A new application, based on recently collected international data that continue to show Depo-Provera's safety and efficacy, is currently being prepared.

As a result of the successive refusals to approve Depo-Provera's use, doubts about its safety began to be engendered in the minds of people working in countries that looked to the FDA for guidance. As a result, Egypt, which had long considered Depo-Provera to be a major tool in its battle against unrestrained population growth, began to express concern about it and for a period of time even stopped authorizing its use. In fact, this situation has proved to be the prototype for a number of other drugs and devices, most notably the recent discontinuation of many intrauterine devices (IUDs).

The vaginal sponge. As a further example of the impact of congressional hearings on health care issues, shortly after the FDA approved the vaginal contraceptive sponge, two consumer groups began to petition the agency to withdraw its approval. They charged that the sponge contained three carcinogens, that the spermicide it used was dangerous, and that it carried a very high risk for the development of toxic shock syndrome. They further claimed that inadequate data had originally been presented to the FDA and that the

Malpractice insurance (average costs for obstetricians/gynecologists)

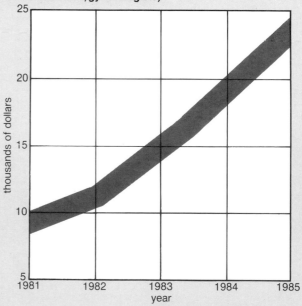

Source: American Medical Association

sponge should never have been approved. These accusations quickly culminated in congressional hearings where witnesses effectively refuted the allegations. The FDA did not take the sponge off the market, nor did it require the manufacturer to make any changes in its labeling. However, the adverse impressions that came out of these hearings still linger in the mind of the public.

A spermicide. Somewhat less well known has been the recent refusal of the Supreme Court to review, on technical grounds, a case involving a spermicidal agent. In 1985 a nonjury trial was held in Atlanta, Ga., for a woman claiming that her child's multiple congenital anomalies were caused by the use of a spermicide. Although no such scientific association has ever been demonstrated, the judge awarded her $5.1 million. This case was appealed to the Georgia courts and finally to the federal Supreme Court. Inasmuch as there is no further court of appeal, this decision may well herald the demise of one of the remaining contraceptive options because of the economic threat of unwarranted litigation and prohibitive product liability insurance costs.

A number of major decisions affecting the health care of women and their babies have also been rendered in recent years by the U.S. Supreme Court. The most publicized of these, of course, have been related to abortion. There is great concern among many health care providers that the current administration may have the opportunity to appoint to the court one or more individuals known to be opposed to abortion, and that the freedom of reproductive choice may once again be taken away from American women.

Increasingly litigious climate

In recent years there has been rapid growth in the number of attorneys practicing in the U.S. This is undoubtedly reflected in the amount of litigation currently plaguing society. Many attorneys have moved away from constitutional concerns and into the area of tort litigation—a very profitable move on their part. Some lawyers will sell information on how to sue in certain types of cases and even provide lists of "expert witnesses."

There has been a virtual epidemic of court trials related to specific medical products. Again this is particularly true in the area of reproductive health care, where the sensitivities are high and the risk of litigation is equally high. A large number of product liability suits have been initiated by a cadre of lawyers who are devoting a large percentage or all of their time to these particular types of cases. In many instances verdicts have been reached and awards have been made, not on the basis of the scientific evidence but because of the emotional impact made on a jury by a pathetic plaintiff, charismatic expert witnesses, or a plaintiff's highly articulate attorney. As a result, a num-

ber of safe and effective products, greatly affecting the health care of women and children, have recently come under attack or have actually been removed from the market.

Childhood vaccines. Vaccines given in childhood that have saved the lives of thousands and prevented serious damage to many thousands more have been on the verge of being withdrawn from the market owing to the extreme pressure of threatened lawsuits. Unquestionably, the incidence and severity of childhood diseases—particularly pertussis (whooping cough)—in early infancy are higher than at any other time of life, yet cases alleging adverse reactions to the DPT (diphtheria-pertussis-tetanus) vaccine, which are irreparable when they occur, have led to delays or nonimmunization of many children worldwide.

Today there is only one vaccine manufacturer left in the field; almost ten have withdrawn because of actual or potential litigation. Clearly it is essential that these vaccines remain available. It has been recommended that federal legislation be introduced that would set up a compensation fund to cover the rare but inevitable complications of vaccine use. This particular idea, however, has received both positive and negative reactions and has not yet culminated in specific legislation.

Antinausea drug. Another example of an agent that has been removed from the marketplace because of numerous scientifically unwarranted lawsuits is the prescription medication Benedectin. This product was used for many years by countless women in early pregnancy for the relief of severe nausea and vomiting that had been unresponsive to the usual, more conservative forms of treatment. It not only made preg-

Average product-liability verdicts

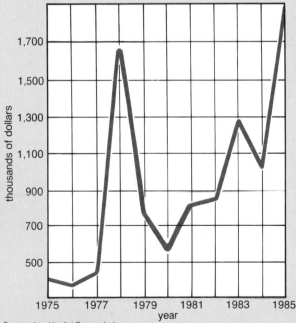

Source: Jury Verdict Research, Inc.

nancy more comfortable for these women but also improved their nutrition and thus the nutrition of their developing babies. Trial lawyers representing clients who had delivered malformed babies that they claimed resulted from Benedectin use successfully sued the manufacturer. On several occasions they received multimillion-dollar verdicts, despite a lack of any scientific evidence to support these suits. The withdrawal of this very useful medication occurred even though no other medication yet exists for the treatment of this particular disorder of pregnancy.

In March 1985 a jury in a U.S. district court in Cincinnati, Ohio, held that Benedectin was not responsible for the birth defects of children whose mothers took this drug. Moreover, in December 1986 a federal district judge set aside a verdict for $1.2 million, stating that there were no data to support any association between the use of this product and fetal damage. In fact, 21 studies to the contrary had been presented at the trial. The judge therefore concluded that the consensus of scientific opinion was contrary to the decision made by the jury, which he said was the result of "speculation and conjecture." Despite these actions, though, Benedectin still remains unavailable to American women.

IUDs. Because of the fear of litigation, many of the companies that had been working in the field of contraception have moved out, leaving only one company now putting significant amounts of money into the development of new products. The most recent, and one of the most serious, product losses for American women (in fact, for all women) has been the recent demise of all but one of the IUDs. The trouble began with the Dalkon Shield. This particular device was responsible for hundreds of cases of pelvic infection and a number of deaths. Unfortunately, it is now the perception of much of the American public (as well as people living in many other countries) that all IUDs are as dangerous as the Dalkon Shield.

After the Dalkon manufacturer filed for bankruptcy in 1985, many attorneys who had been heavily involved in litigating against this device elected to move next against the Copper-7, a popular and widely used IUD. There had been considerable adverse publicity reporting that the device was dangerous and that it caused pelvic infections because of the toxicity of copper and the faulty design of the device's tail. Although there were no data to support either contention, many lawsuits were filed. Almost all of these suits were successfully defended, but at the cost of millions of dollars. As a result, on Jan. 31, 1986, a product discontinuation of the Copper-7 and Tatum-T (also copper) intrauterine contraceptive devices in the U.S. was announced. The manufacturer stated that it regretted having to make this decision but that it had to discontinue the sale of these products because of the large number of unwarranted lawsuits and the vir-

Over the past two decades, women in less developed countries have gained access to family-planning services with aid from the U.S. Now, however, such help is being cut off, resulting in millions of unwanted pregnancies. In response, the Planned Parenthood Federation of America is waging a hard-hitting campaign against the U.S. agencies and officials responsible for the curtailment.

tual unobtainability of product liability insurance, even though both devices were still considered to be safe and effective by the company and the FDA.

This move had serious implications, particularly for older women for whom this was the method of choice. Equally unfortunate was the fact that a new IUD, the Copper TCu 380A, the best device developed to date, had been approved by the FDA and presumably was moving to the marketplace.

Following the virtual demise of the intrauterine device in the United States, though, many women began going over the border into Canada or crossing the ocean to Great Britain or Europe in order to obtain their copper IUDs, including the 380A. While this situation does not pose a major problem for women who are medically sophisticated and have the funds to go out of the country to obtain the health care that they cannot obtain at home, it clearly disenfranchises women of lower incomes who do not have this option available to them.

A decision that was made in a U.S. district court in 1986 may have some impact on the current IUD litigation scene. In this decision the judge declared that the data presented in support of a lawsuit against the manufacturer of the Copper-7 were nothing but "a series of alternative unsubstantiated theories." He therefore rendered his verdict in favor of the defendant. While this is clearly an important milestone and may well have a favorable impact on future litigation, it may not be sufficient to allow this very useful method of contraception to once again become generally available to American women. Meanwhile, there are continuing efforts to find a way to return copper IUDs, particularly the TCu 380A, to the American marketplace.

New contraceptives. The impact of the current litigation crisis is not limited to contraceptive methods that are currently available. Also affected are new methods that are well into advanced stages of research; in fact, some, such as the Silastic subdermal implant, several injectable agents, and cervical caps, are almost ready for presentation to the FDA. However, even if studies are successfully concluded and FDA approval is obtained, because of the product liability insurance crisis some of these excellent methods may never become available in the U.S.

Corporate lawyers are now increasingly unwilling to suggest or approve ventures into the field of reproductive health care since it is an area so highly sensitive and open to litigation, a fact that may seriously limit the products that will be available to American women in the future. Recently some judges have taken the position that the verdicts in certain of these cases have been "irresponsible." These judges are attempting to decrease the frequency of unjustified lawsuits and the excessive judgments that often result from such cases.

Expert witnesses

Essential to the whole process of receiving favorable judgments from juries is another group of individuals who are allied on the side of the plaintiffs. They are the so-called expert witnesses. In certain instances these are very knowledgeable scientists testifying in their areas of expertise. However, a growing number of people, primarily physicians, have begun to devote part—and in some cases all—of their time to being professional witnesses. They are testifying not in areas in which they are expert but in almost any type of medical case.

These individuals advertise their availability and, in many cases appropriately, have come to be called "hired guns." They can be relied upon to testify in a manner favorable to the plaintiff, regardless of the nature of case that is being tried. They are willing to go into court and fabricate a link between a bad outcome and something in the environment—a drug, a device, or a medical or surgical procedure—and say that this caused the problem. Very often this association is remarkably tenuous, and in many instances absolutely no such medical relationship exists. This does not deter juries, however, from feeling pity for an ill or deformed plaintiff and from awarding enormous

judgments against a particular manufacturer perceived to have an inexhaustible "deep pocket."

Insurance costs for physicians

The wildly escalating costs and increasing unavailability of product liability insurance have taken a heavy toll in the area of health care. Another important factor has been the rapid increase in the cost of medical malpractice insurance, which, in the field of obstetrics, has led many physicians to stop delivering babies, particularly in smaller communities. The amount of money that these physicians can anticipate earning from prenatal care and deliveries is now less than the cost of their insurance and, thus, it is economically unfeasible for them to continue to practice. As this situation becomes more common, it will become increasingly difficult for women to find obstetricians willing to take care of them during their pregnancies and deliveries.

Another component to this problem is the increase in lawsuits for wrongful life and wrongful birth. Even more important is the trend toward making physicians liable for any damage presumed to have been sustained during delivery. In many states a doctor is required to provide for the care of fetally damaged children up to the age of majority, which varies from 18 to 21 years. A recent study has shown that in most of these cases the abnormalities were found to be unrelated to anything done by the medical profession and, in fact, frequently occurred spontaneously long before the onset of labor. However, this has not deterred plaintiffs and their attorneys from suing physicians and in many instances, despite the lack of medical evidence, obtaining very large judgments.

It has also recently been documented that the cases of a high percentage of babies born with some sort of congenital anomaly eventually end up in court as the plaintiffs and plaintiffs' attorneys search the environment for some agent that could conceivably have produced the damage. In fact, an increasing number of attorneys now advertise for these cases, while some even list an "800" toll-free telephone number.

The future

Yet another new trend threatening health care today is the practice of suing the physician along with the pharmaceutical manufacturer in cases involving drugs and devices. The end result of the complex and very destructive trends that are brewing in the practice of medicine is the increasing difficulty that patients, particularly women, face as they struggle to obtain satisfactory medical care. Another substantial consequence is the sharp curtailment of essential medical research and the United States' loss of preeminence in the field of health care. Only when the seriousness of this alarming situation is better appreciated by the public, legislative bodies, and funding agencies will there be any hope of turning present trends around.

Mental Health and Illness

Several developments in the past year illustrate the range of current activities in the field of mental health and illness. In biologic science molecular genetic techniques were used to demonstrate a chromosomal abnormality associated with bipolar disorder (manic-depressive illness) in Amish families in Lancaster County, Pa., thus providing specific evidence of a genetic predisposition to that mental disorder. In neuroscience there has been increased use of new imaging techniques to study the brain in living subjects. This has been particularly important in revealing brain abnormalities—sometimes very subtle ones—in schizophrenic patients (see below). In treatment studies a large multisite project of the U.S. National Institute of Mental Health (NIMH) found that either of two forms of psychotherapy (cognitive therapy and interpersonal psychotherapy) could be as effective as antidepressant drug treatment for outpatients with nonbipolar depressions. Other studies have suggested that a combination of drug treatment with psychotherapy may be optimal for such patients.

On the public and political fronts, there has been concern and publicity about the pervasiveness of drug and alcohol abuse and their deleterious consequences, as well as debate about the legal and ethical issues involved in policies regarding drug-abuse testing.

There have also been important advances in the current status of understanding of the disorder known as schizophrenia, and these advances deserve focus.

A complicated and misunderstood disorder

Schizophrenia is one of the most important, disabling, costly, and misunderstood mental disorders. With a lifetime prevalence of about 1%, schizophrenia affects 1.5 million to 2 million Americans and inflicts staggering personal and financial costs. The Institute of Medicine recently estimated that lost productivity and treatment costs for the U.S. amount to $48 billion per year, but no figure can be placed on the suffering of patients and their families caused by this usually chronic disorder. Schizophrenics also constitute a substantial proportion of today's ever growing homeless population. Fortunately, there has been increased research activity on a number of aspects of schizophrenia in the past several years, but experts working in this area agree that there is a great deal that remains unknown about this complicated disorder.

Issues in diagnosing schizophrenia

The very term schizophrenia is a source of considerable public misunderstanding. The word was introduced in 1908 by a Swiss psychiatrist, Eugen Bleuler, to replace an earlier diagnostic term, dementia praecox, meaning premature mental deterioration. Schizophrenia means "splitting of the mind," and Bleuler chose this term to

By studying Amish families in Lancaster County, Pennsylvania, researchers have determined that the mental disorder known as manic-depressive illness, or bipolar disorder, is at least partly genetic in origin.

emphasize a characteristic "splitting," *i.e.,* lack of harmony or integration, of mental functions. For example, schizophrenic patients often express feelings that are at variance with simultaneously expressed thoughts (inappropriate affect) and also typically express sequences of completely unconnected ideas (loose associations—a particular type of thought disorder). It is important to emphasize that schizophrenia does not mean "split personality" and should not be confused with multiple personality, which is a completely different and far less common disorder. In multiple personality two or more distinct personalities exist within a single individual. Each personality is integrated and has its own unique behavior patterns and social relationships; the personality that is dominant at any particular time determines the individual's behavior. Several recent studies of multiple personality disorder indicate that, also unlike schizophrenia, it is almost always preceded by sexual abuse or other forms of severe emotional trauma in childhood.

The current "official" diagnostic criteria for schizophrenia contained in the latest version (1987) of the American Psychiatric Association's *Diagnostic and Statistical Manual of Mental Disorders* require a combination of (1) characteristic psychotic symptoms such as delusions (false beliefs), prominent hallucinations (*e.g.,* hearing a voice that keeps a running commentary on the patient's behavior), and loose associations; (2) deterioration from a previous level of functioning in such areas as work, social relations, and self-care; and (3) continuous signs of disturbance for at least six months. Although these symptoms typically begin in adolescence or early adulthood, the latest revision of the diagnostic criteria has dropped a previous requirement that onset had to be prior to age 45 to qualify for a diagnosis of schizophrenia.

The criteria also recognize the importance of distinguishing schizophrenia from major depression or manic syndromes, where similar psychotic symptoms can sometimes occur during an episode of illness but where a disturbance of mood (either depressed or abnormally elevated) is prominent and the course of illness is usually characterized by recurrent episodes followed by a return to normal functioning. Recently reported studies employing detailed ratings of verbal behavior have also confirmed that there are qualitative differences between the thought disorders of manic patients and those of schizophrenic patients. Manic thought disorder is characterized mainly by extravagant combinations and elaborations, whereas schizophrenic thought disorder is typically confused and disorganized, with many peculiar words and phrases.

One unresolved controversy is the question of whether schizophrenia is a single disorder with multiple manifestations or a syndrome encompassing several different disorders. An important issue in this regard is the significance of so-called negative versus positive symptoms. Negative symptoms involve *loss* of function, often hypothesized to be due to damage in some area of the brain, whereas positive symptoms reflect *release* of function, presumably due to malfunction or damage in some higher brain area that normally inhibits a particular function. In schizophrenia negative symptoms include blunting of emotional expression, social withdrawal, apathy, and impoverishment of speech and language. Positive symptoms include delusions, hallucinations, and bizarre speech and behavior. It is clear that individual patients can differ markedly in their degree of negative versus positive symptoms and also that the available drugs for the treatment of schizophrenia are far more effective for positive symptoms than they are for negative symptoms. Precise measurement and classification of patients according to positive and negative symptoms has proved to be difficult, but some studies have found correlations between biologic variables and this symptom classification.

Schizophrenic brain abnormalities

Probably the most important recent development in schizophrenia research is the growing body of evidence indicating that there is something structurally abnormal in the brains of patients. Recent studies have confirmed previous reports of an increased prevalence of (usually subtle) neurological abnormalities in schizophrenic patients compared with manic-depressive patients or normal controls. Although specific neuropathological changes in the brains of schizophrenic patients have not been established with certainty, a recent British study found tissue loss in the temporal lobes of the postmortem brains of schizophrenic patients as compared with the brains of patients with affective (mood) disorders. Most recent studies in this area have utilized the newly available imaging techniques that make possible the visualization of the structure and function of the brain.

Beginning with an initial report in 1976, a number of computed tomography (CT) studies of schizophrenia have been performed. The CT scans of most patients are read as normal by neuroradiologists; however, one fairly consistent finding of the research is the occurrence of cerebral atrophy (thinning), as indicated by dilation of the brain ventricles. The degree of atrophy varies among patients, with increased atrophy tending to correlate with negative symptoms, cognitive impairments, diminished response to drug treatment, and poor outcome. In general, no relationship has been found between the degree of ventricular dilation and the extent of previous drug treatment—an issue that has been a confounding factor in many biologic studies of schizophrenia.

Positron emission tomography (PET) is a complex technique that allows imaging of metabolic activity in the living brain. Some PET studies have found decreased activity in the frontal and prefrontal regions (hypofrontality) of the brains of schizophrenic patients, particularly those who are older and mentally deteriorated. Researchers at NIMH recently found hypofrontality in young schizophrenic patients, but only when there was a need for increased neuronal function in the prefrontal cortex. Nonschizophrenic subjects performed a card-sorting test easily and showed increased blood flow to the prefrontal cortex, whereas schizophrenic patients performed poorly on the task and did not show increased blood flow. Another important study used PET scans to demonstrate a substantial increase in the densities of receptors (specialized binding sites) for the neurotransmitter dopamine in the brains of both drug-treated and untreated schizophrenics. Along with the fact that drugs that improve schizophrenic symptoms work through the dopamine system, this finding is evidence that abnormalities in dopamine transmission play a role in the disease process, whether or not they are causative factors.

The search for schizophrenia's causes

The overview above notes the increasingly compelling evidence for brain abnormalities in schizophrenia. However, it is important to recognize that psychological and environmental factors play an important role in the course of the illness and that the causes of the biologic abnormalities remain unknown. The major current theories about biologic causes fall into three classes: genetics, birth complications, and viruses.

Genetics. The possibility that something about schizophrenia is inherited is suggested by the fact that it tends to run in families. Three main strategies are available to separate genetic ("nature") from environmental ("nurture") family influences: twin studies, adoption studies, and genetic markers.

Twin studies compare the concordance rates (the frequency with which both members of a twin pair are affected by the same disorder) for large numbers of identical and fraternal twins. A higher concordance rate in identical twins suggests a genetic component, since identical twins share the same genetic endowment. For schizophrenia the concordance rate for identical twins is over 50%—substantially higher than the rate for fraternal twins.

Adoption studies take advantage of the fact that adopted children receive their genes from one set of parents and their rearing from a different set. Several such studies in Denmark (where adoption records are particularly thorough) have shown that biologic children of schizophrenics who are adopted by nonschizophrenic parents have a higher incidence of schizophrenia than a control population.

Genetic marker studies depend on the discovery of a measurable, purely biologic trait, the inheritance of which is linked to the disorder in question. Some researchers have suggested that poor eye tracking may be a genetic marker for schizophrenia; about 65% of schizophrenics and about 45% of their first-degree relatives (parents, siblings, children) visually follow a moving object in jerky movements rather than in a smooth, fluid motion. Only about 8% of the normal population have this trait. The role of poor eye tracking as a genetic marker for schizophrenia is controversial, however, since it does not occur in all schizophrenics and is not specific for schizophrenia, occurring also in such disorders as Parkinson's disease and multiple sclerosis.

Taken together, these results suggest that genetic factors may play a role in schizophrenia but that it is not a clear-cut genetic disease such as Huntington's disease (Huntington's chorea)—a late-onset genetic affliction that ends in severe dementia and death; each child of a Huntington's disease victim has a 50% chance of inheriting the gene and eventually developing the disease. That schizophrenia is not solely an inherited disorder is illustrated by the fact that over 90% of the relatives of schizophrenics do not have schizophrenia. Some researchers have suggested that the schizophrenic syndrome may include both a "familial" form, where genetics plays an important role, and a "sporadic" form, where environmental factors are causative. Others have proposed that inheritance is just one of several "risk factors" for a disease with multiple causes, as is the case, for example, with coronary heart disease.

Complications at birth. Recent studies have reported that histories of obstetrical complications are more common among schizophrenic patients, compared with both the general population and patients with other psychiatric disorders. However, these were retrospective studies and thus must be interpreted with caution since informants (usually mothers) are biased toward identifying past problems that could be responsible for present disabilities. Not all infants who have birth complications go on to develop schizophrenia, or any other psychiatric disorder, in adult life. This question really requires a comprehensive follow-up of individuals who suffer obstetric complications, particularly those that involve periods of lack of oxygen that could lead to brain damage. For the time being, it may be appropriate to view birth complications as another possible risk factor for schizophrenia.

Viruses. Some researchers have proposed that a virus could cause the brain abnormalities observed in schizophrenia, particularly if the infection occurred before birth or in infancy, when the developing brain is vulnerable and the immune response to viral infections is deficient. One piece of indirect evidence cited in favor of this theory is that a slight preponderance (54%) of schizophrenics are born in the winter or spring months, when viral infections are frequent. However, no virus or other direct evidence of viral infection has yet been discovered, so the viral theory remains a hypothesis that still awaits proof.

Schizophrenia's treatment

Since the introduction in the mid-1950s of antipsychotic drugs that block brain dopamine receptors, which was followed by a marked reduction in the number of patients requiring chronic hospitalization, these drugs have become the mainstay of treatment for schizophrenia. They can be dramatically beneficial for acute symptomatic episodes, and a recent review of controlled studies by investigators at the Illinois State Psychiatric Institute in Chicago showed that the average relapse rate following an acute episode for patients maintained on a placebo (inactive medication) was about 60%, compared with only 16% for patients maintained on an antipsychotic drug. Although these drugs have certainly improved the previously bleak prognosis of schizophrenia, a number of problems remain unresolved. About 20% of schizophrenic patients do not respond well to the available antipsychotic drugs, which tend to be much less effective for negative symptoms (such as apathy and withdrawal) than for positive symptoms.

Also, these drugs produce some troublesome side effects, such as dizziness, muscle stiffness, and tremors. Many of the side effects can be controlled by other medications, and most are reversed when the medication is discontinued.

Increasing concerns have been expressed about a particularly serious side effect known as tardive dyskinesia, a syndrome of repetitive involuntary movements affecting the mouth, lips, tongue, trunk, or extremities. This syndrome develops in up to 25% of patients receiving long-term (over six months) treatment with antipsychotic drugs. Unfortunately, there is no effective treatment for this complication, and the abnormal

C. Vaughn and J. Leff, Institute of Psychiatry, London

Family role in schizophrenia relapse

family's "expressed emotion"*	family/patient face-to-face contact per week	patient's drug status	relapse rate
high	more than 35 hours	not on drugs	92%
		on drugs	53%
	less than 35 hours	not on drugs	42%
		on drugs	15%
low		not on drugs	15%
		on drugs	12%

* shows anger and anxious overinvolvement toward patient

movements persist in about two-thirds of the cases even after antipsychotic drug therapy has been discontinued. The U.S. Food and Drug Administration (FDA) recently ruled that all antipsychotic drugs must carry a "class warning" about the risk of tardive dyskinesia after long-term use. In most cases the movements are neither obvious to an untrained observer nor subjectively troublesome to the patient. In more severe cases the presence of readily visible abnormal muscle movements may seem more "real" than a mental disorder, but this must be balanced against the reality of the devastating effects of a disorder like schizophrenia. If the diagnosis is well established and cautious attempts to decrease or discontinue antipsychotic drug therapy are either unsuccessful or unwise in view of the patient's previous history, the benefit of continued treatment may outweigh the risks. The occurrence of tardive dyskinesia has served as one impetus for the ongoing search for drugs with a different pharmacological profile that might benefit schizophrenics. Recent studies with one such experimental drug, clozapine, have been promising.

In the past, zealous attempts to understand the environmental context of schizophrenia sometimes led to a tendency to malign or even blame the family struggling with the enormous burden of having a member with schizophrenia. One very salutary development in the treatment of schizophrenia has been a recognition of the important and very positive role the patient's family can play in the management of this chronic disorder. Specific educational and behavioral methods for enhancing the coping mechanisms and problem-solving abilities of the family have already shown considerable promise in reducing relapse rates and enhancing social adjustment. For example, research groups in England and the United States have proposed that some families are characterized by high "expressed emotion," *i.e.,* tending to evidence anger toward or anxious overinvolvement with the schizophrenic family member, and that this increases the likelihood of relapse. A program of family therapy designed to decrease expressed emotion has been shown in a recent

study to decrease relapse rates, although not all experts agree that the expressed emotion concept is the best way of explaining the benefit. Another important development regarding the families of schizophrenics is that several concerned lay and family groups (including the National Alliance for the Mentally Ill and the American Mental Health Fund, the latter founded by the parents of John Hinckley, the man who shot Pres. Ronald Reagan in 1981) are providing much-needed advocacy for increased public understanding, access to quality treatment, and research support.

The current consensus regarding the treatment of schizophrenia for most patients favors a combination of antipsychotic drug treatment with family or individual psychotherapy focused on practical support, problem solving, and stress reduction. This parallels the consensus view that causes of the disorder probably involve a combination of biologic vulnerability and psychosocial stress factors. Many patients benefit; unfortunately, some do not, and even among those who respond, improvement is often slow and incomplete. One can certainly hope that recent increases in public awareness and concern, as well as the development of new techniques of investigation in neuroscience, will lead to increased funding for research into both the causes and the treatment of schizophrenia.

—*Richard M. Glass, M.D.*

Neurology

Recent advances in knowledge of disorders of the nervous system center around three principal areas. First, new imaging techniques have been developed, allowing for more rapid and more accurate diagnosis. Second, new forms of therapy have been instituted; not all are specific, but they are effective in modifying the course of several nervous system diseases. Third, many fundamental discoveries have been made about the nature and function of the nervous system, enabling physicians to understand disease processes better. There has also been an important change in the prevalence of certain neurological disorders brought about by the increasing age of the population in most developed countries. Thus, diseases associated with degeneration of the nervous system, such as Parkinson's and Alzheimer's diseases, have received increased attention in research and therapy. Some diseases that have a profound effect on the nervous system (for example, poliomyelitis) have been largely eliminated in areas of the world where vaccination is prevalent. At the same time, diseases that were unknown a few years ago have emerged, and one of these, AIDS (acquired immune deficiency syndrome), can have devastating effects on the nervous system.

In addition to the developments in research, diagnosis, and therapy, many ethical issues have arisen because of new techniques that prolong life, advances in organ transplantation, increased ability to characterize and manipulate genes, and other such scientific achievements.

Advances in imaging techniques

Recent developments in neuroimaging techniques have provided faster, more accurate, and safer ways of visualizing various parts of the nervous system. One such major development is computed tomography (CT) scanning, which allows visualization of neural structures that ordinary X-rays cannot reveal. With CT scanning it is possible to reconstruct sectional "slices" of the body from any desired angle. This technique can reveal the size and shape of the cerebral ventricles, abnormalities in the brain tissue itself, and distortion of neural structures. It is equally useful in visualizing areas of the spinal cord. For example, the CT scan is an excellent aid to the diagnosis of herniated ("slipped") intervertebral disks, determining both the exact location and the extent of the herniation. A more recent refinement in the technology permits three-dimensional reconstruction of parts of the body. The information obtained through scanning is stored in a computer's "memory" bank, and other new techniques then allow the transmission of a holographic representation of the area of interest. The cumulated three-dimensional image obtained in this fashion can be rotated so that it can be viewed from various angles or can be distorted to bring out special features.

The application of a newer technique, magnetic resonance imaging (MRI), has allowed even better definition of neural structures, particularly within the white matter of the brain. MRI is based on the principle that atomic nuclei line up like magnets when they are placed in a magnetic field. They can then be excited in a controlled way from a radio frequency source. During the relaxation that follows excitation, the nuclei give off radio signals that can be detected and analyzed. (For medical purposes, the nuclei most commonly used are the nuclei of ordinary hydrogen atoms in body tissues.) MRI has the advantage of employing no ionizing radiation, so extensive and repeated examinations can be undertaken without any danger of radiation exposure to the patient. The MRI system is so sensitive that fluid collection in the brain may be detected. MRI can also be used to produce a three-dimensional image.

Another method of medical imaging is positron emission tomography (PET) scanning. PET scanning depends on the use of short-acting isotopes that emit positrons (the antimatter counterpart of electrons). These positrons are located by a series of detectors placed around the subject's head. Although it has been used primarily in research, the method does have some clinical applications, and these are being expanded. It is likely, for example, that PET scanning will have expanded use in the early diagnosis of neurodegenerative disorders, when metabolic changes may be evident although no structural alterations have yet occurred. For example, in Huntington's disease, an inherited neurological disorder that eventually results in dementia and uncontrolled body movements, there may be metabolic alterations in deep nuclei of the brain long before any clinical symptoms of the disease have appeared. Similarly, it has been noted in patients with Alzheimer's disease that decreased metabolism is often detectable in the parietal lobes of the brain early in the course of the disease. Such mental functions as those involving language show up on a PET scan as increased metabolic activity in the left hemisphere of the brain, the hemisphere that is dominant for language in almost all right-handed people. A variety of isotopes can be used in PET scanning to turn simple substances such as water or glucose

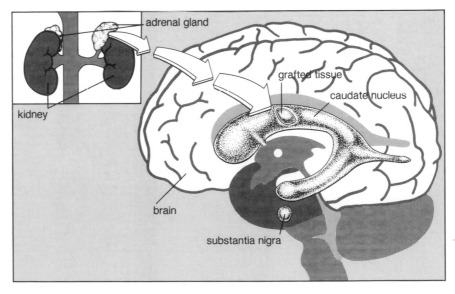

In 1987 doctors in Mexico reported the results of the first successful experiment in treatment of Parkinson's disease by means of tissue transplantation. Parkinson's patients suffer from a movement disorder believed to be caused by the loss of dopamine, a neurotransmitter produced by an area of the brain called the substantia nigra. In this pioneering surgical procedure, dopamine-producing tissue from the patient's adrenal glands is transplanted onto the caudate nucleus, an area of the brain involved in controlling body movement.

adrenal gland

grafted tissue

caudate nucleus

kidney

brain

substantia nigra

into radioactive tracer compounds. The agent that is used varies, depending on the metabolic function that is under study. Most of the recent work in neurological imaging has been done with a form of glucose, which is the important metabolite in the nervous system. As the process requires both the detection apparatus—*i.e.*, the PET scanner—and the supply of short-acting radioisotopes from either a nearby or, preferably, an adjacent cyclotron (a high-energy accelerator in which particles are propelled in a constant magnetic field), there are only a limited number of facilities able to carry out such imaging.

New and better treatments

As the scientific understanding of a disorder increases, improved methods of treatment usually follow, and such has been the case in the field of neurological disorders. For example, the discovery that there is a deficiency of neurotransmitters (the chemicals necessary for activation of nerve cells) in certain diseases has led to therapy that attempts to make up for the deficit by supplying the missing substance. Parkinson's disease is characterized by a major depletion in dopamine, a neurotransmitter, and drugs that elevate the level of dopamine or provide a substitute for it improve the patient's motor performance. There was initial hope that Alzheimer's disease would respond to drugs that increased the level of the neurotransmitter acetylcholine, but no such benefit has been clearly shown.

Neurological disorders now believed to be caused, at least in part, by immune-system dysfunction—multiple sclerosis, for example—are being treated with some success with drugs that suppress immune mechanisms.

The treatment of seizure disorders has been improved through the use of newly developed drugs that result in both fewer seizures and fewer side effects. Equally important in eliminating harmful side effects is the widespread use of monitoring procedures to maintain safe blood levels of anticonvulsant drugs. Not only does monitoring prevent overdosage but it is an effective way to judge the patient's compliance with the drug regimen. Several investigators have again emphasized that control of seizures is more effective if proper anticonvulsant medication is started early in the course of the illness. With repeated seizures, the susceptibility for seizures is increased. Therefore, disorders of long duration are more difficult to treat than those that are diagnosed and treated early.

A new approach to the treatment of seizures is an outgrowth of the discovery of naturally occurring brain substances that inhibit convulsive discharges. These substances—generally amines or peptides—have been extensively studied by researchers who record the transmission of nerve impulses at the cell level. A peptide called substance P has been found to alter transmission in the system of nerve cells activated by acetylcholine. Similarly, other naturally occurring substances may affect nerve cell transmission in other systems. Finding ways to use these natural brain chemicals may provide a completely new mode of anticonvulsant therapy.

Both the incidence of stroke and that of deaths due to stroke have continued to decline. The reason for this trend is unclear, but it may be partially explained by active detection and effective treatment of hypertension (high blood pressure), one of the greatest risk factors for stroke. Meanwhile, the treatment of various types of cerebrovascular disease remains a source of controversy. There are no clearly established modes of therapy for many forms of stroke. Recently an extremely large study of a surgical procedure called the extracranial-intracranial bypass, which links blood vessels from outside the scalp to vessels supplying the brain, found the technique to be ineffective. There has been considerable debate over this finding, based primarily on what some researchers view as faults in the design of the study itself and, specifically, in the way the test and control subjects were chosen. The procedure will continue to be studied to see if it can be demonstrated to help selected stroke victims. There is disagreement also on whether a narrowed carotid artery (the major vessel supplying blood to the brain) should be surgically reopened if the patient shows no evidence of neurological problems. Many experts feel that the use of a drug that prevents the blood platelets from aggregating (thus forming clots) is as effective as surgical treatment while eliminating the risks associated with the operation. These questions are being addressed by carefully designed controlled studies comparing the different treatment methods.

Plasma exchange therapy, also known as plasmapheresis, has been advocated for treatment of a number of neurological and nonneurological disorders and has been used experimentally in this context for several years. In 1986 a U.S. National Institutes of Health consensus conference studied the results of therapeutic plasma exchange in a variety of neurological disorders, including multiple sclerosis (MS), myasthenia gravis, amyotrophic lateral sclerosis (ALS), Guillain-Barré syndrome, and similar diseases. The conference members concluded that plasma exchange appears to reduce the duration and severity of disease in patients with Guillain-Barré syndrome, a paralytic disorder, but it is not effective in ALS and has mixed results in myasthenia gravis and MS.

Promising outlook for tissue transplants

As in other areas of scientific investigation, basic research has important implications for diagnosis and treatment of neurological illness. Nerve-tissue transplantation, a subject of research for many years, is now beginning to show some exciting results. Transplants of nerve tissue were attempted before 1900.

Early studies were poorly controlled, and there is little evidence that they were successful. However, a number of later investigators experimenting with amphibians and rodents had better results. These experiments proved that transplanted nerve tissue is capable of functioning and that transplanted fetal tissue has the greatest chance of surviving. Laboratory rats born with a defect in certain hormone-producing cells are able to synthesize the missing hormone after transplantation of these cells from a normal rat fetus. It is also possible to transplant laboratory-cultured nerve cells successfully into primates. The rejection reaction that usually occurs in organ transplantation is absent or minimal in the transplantation of tissue in the central nervous system, probably because the anatomic and physiological separation known as the blood-brain barrier prevents the circulation into the brain of the immune-system cells responsible for rejection.

In a highly publicized recent report, Mexican researchers told how they had transplanted tissue from the adrenal glands into the brains of two Parkinson's disease patients, both of whom experienced a striking improvement. It is not known exactly how the transplanted tissue functions; it may supply the necessary amount of the neurotransmitter dopamine, or it may provide stimulation that allows surviving brain cells to be more effective in dopamine production. It is too early to judge the efficacy of this therapy, but this and similar types of treatment offer new hope for people suffering from neurological disease.

Finding clues to inherited disorders

Basic research in molecular genetics has already identified the location of the genes responsible for several inherited neurological disorders, and ongoing studies are attempting to pinpoint many that are still unknown. By the use of recently developed DNA probes, characteristic fragments of chromosomes can be identified that are known to be located close to the gene responsible for a given disorder and, therefore, are usually inherited with it. Using such probes in linkage studies—investigations of large families affected by certain genetic disorders—researchers have so far identified defective genes associated with Huntington's disease, Duchenne muscular dystrophy, myotonic dystrophy, and a form of familial polyneuropathy. Once the exact site of the gene has been located, as has now been accomplished in Duchenne muscular dystrophy, the next step will be to identify the protein whose synthesis is regulated by that gene.

Progress in understanding the underlying defects in Alzheimer's disease has been accelerated by means of the study of some cases of an apparently hereditary form of the disease. Scientists estimate that 10% or more of all Alzheimer's cases may be genetic in origin, although a hereditary predisposition is believed to play a part in most—or perhaps all—cases of the disease. In the familial cases studied, the disease is inherited as an autosomal dominant trait; signs of dementia appear in patients in their fifties and sixties, much earlier than in the more typical form of the disorder.

In linkage studies of a few large families affected by Alzheimer's, using DNA markers whose location is known, scientists have now established that the defect in the familial form of the disease is on chromosome 21. This had been suspected for some time because of the already established connection between Down syndrome and Alzheimer's—nearly every Down

Using so-called linkage studies—investigations of large families in which many members have been affected by a particular disease—researchers have identified genetic factors involved in several neurological disorders. One of the latest additions to the list of syndromes believed to have a genetic component is a form of Alzheimer's disease.

Two scientists who were involved in this research, Peter H. St. George-Hyslop (left) and James F. Gusella, are pictured here viewing an autoradiograph of DNA fragments that may help locate genetic markers associated with the disease.

Massachusetts General Hospital, News and Public Affairs Office

syndrome adult develops the typical brain lesions of Alzheimer's disease—and the fact that the genetic defect in Down syndrome involves chromosome 21. There is an excessive amount of a particular protein, β-amyloid, deposited in the brain and cerebral blood vessels of patients with Alzheimer's disease, and the gene that encodes for β-amyloid, located on chromosome 21, is doubled in Alzheimer's disease, just as one of the chromosomes is doubled in Down syndrome. This finding is intriguing but perhaps raises more questions than it answers. For example, are there factors that trigger the typical changes of Alzheimer's disease in those people with a genetic predisposition for the disease? Or, conversely, are there factors that may in other people prevent these changes from taking place? While these mysteries remain, there has been additional progress toward a potential treatment for the disease and a practical method of diagnosis, both still in the experimental stage.

New thinking about the brain

Scientists' views of brain function have changed gradually over the years. For example, the traditional concept of cerebral dominance held that the anatomical basis for language resided in the left cerebral hemisphere in almost all individuals. Over the years, however, and certainly during the past 30 years, increasing evidence has indicated that the right hemisphere, generally referred to as the minor hemisphere, plays a special role in certain language and perception functions, most notably in spatial perception.

The impetus for work in this area was a series of experiments involving patients who suffered from seizure disorders. In these individuals the corpus callosum, a brain structure, was surgically cut in an effort to control the seizures. The corpus callosum is the great nerve-fiber pathway that connects the two hemispheres of the brain. If this structure is divided, much of the information passing from one hemisphere to the other is eliminated, and a certain amount of sensory input is no longer shared by both sides of the brain. It is then possible to perform tests of each hemisphere in isolation, confining the stimulus and the response to one side or the other. Such studies confirm that most—but not all—verbal processing is in the left hemisphere. Some other functions tend to be predominantly, but not exclusively, in the right hemisphere. Thus, for various functions there appears to be cerebral preponderance rather than an actual dominance. This finding accounts for the observation that various functions, including language, may show some recovery even after the left hemisphere has been damaged. Some of the regained function may be attributed to portions of the left hemisphere that have remained intact, but certainly some language function emanates from the right hemisphere.

In children who suffer brain injury at an early age, the hemisphere that is unaffected may take over functions normally provided by the damaged one. Thus, left hemisphere damage that occurs at an early age is not attended by a profound and lasting speech disturbance. With age, however, this plasticity of the nervous system lessens. Recent neurological research has also focused on systems traditionally not thought to be under neural control that may, in fact, be controlled by the brain. One of these is the immunologic system. There are, for example, studies that show that certain immune disorders and allergies are more common in left-handed individuals.

AIDS and the nervous system

The AIDS virus (human immunodeficiency virus, or HIV) directly affects certain cells of the immune system, and this accounts for the suppression of the immune reaction that is the hallmark of the disease. Immune system failure renders the individual susceptible to many secondary infections, a number of which can involve the nervous system, including toxoplasmosis, candidiasis, tuberculosis, cryptococcosis, and others. However, it has now become evident that HIV infection in itself may cause a distinct neurological syndrome, characterized by a progressive dementia, difficulty in walking, and poor balance. In some cases this neurological dysfunction is the first manifestation of AIDS. At autopsy there is evidence of shrinkage of the brain and changes in the spinal cord. The exact mechanism by which the AIDS virus destroys nerve tissue has not yet been determined.

Ethical dilemmas

Ethical issues continue to arise as a result of new drugs, procedures, and technologies. For example, the ability to detect inherited degenerative disorders early in life poses the dilemma of what to tell the healthy, asymptomatic patient who will inevitably develop an untreatable disorder. At what age should individuals at risk be tested? Does every person at risk necessarily want to undergo such tests? The confusion in values is apparent as society reduces the number of serious head and spinal cord injuries through the use of seat belts but continues to permit unsafe practices in such sports as boxing.

The nervous system is responsible to a large degree for the individual's quality of life—this viewpoint is reflected in the expanded legal definition of death that now includes brain death as well as the standard of cessation of heart activity. The issue of brain death arose as more elaborate and effective life-support systems were developed and as organ-transplant technology improved and the demand for donor organs grew. It is likely that with continuing advances in medical knowledge, similar ethical dilemmas will arise in the future.

—*Robert J. Joynt, M.D., Ph.D.*

Osteoporosis

Osteoporosis continues to be a major health problem, accounting for some 1.5 million bone fractures each year in the U.S. alone. Osteoporosis, the thinning of the bones that occurs as people age, is particularly obvious among women and is a major cause of admissions of the elderly to nursing homes. In 1984 the U.S. National Institutes of Health (NIH), recognizing the magnitude of this significant health problem, convened a consensus development conference that focused national attention on the condition. One of the conference's conclusions, that an adequate calcium intake was an important preventive step, has had far-reaching consequences, including an aggressive advertising campaign promoting the foods—especially dairy products—that are rich in calcium and a dramatic upsurge in the sales of calcium supplements in many forms. There has also been a major increase in the number of medical centers specializing in evaluating and treating osteoporosis.

In early 1987 a subsequent conference was convened by the NIH and the National Osteoporosis Foundation to evaluate data published since 1984 and to determine the most important areas for future research. The conference reviewed the changes that have occurred during the past three years in the scientific thinking about the causes, prevention, and treatment of this important bone disorder.

More than one type?

Osteoporosis (literally, "porous bone") is defined as a condition in which there is insufficient bone in the skeleton, allowing fractures or breaks to occur with minimal or no trauma. It has always been known that there are many factors that can alter an individual's risk of developing osteoporosis. Recently investigators have suggested that some of these factors might lead to one type of osteoporosis, while others may be responsible for a different form of the disease, each being manifested clinically by fractures in different regions of the skeleton. This theory has been advanced by researchers from the Mayo Clinic, in Rochester, Minn., who have suggested that loss of estrogen after menopause or oophorectomy (surgical removal of the ovaries) results in a selective decrease in the spongy (trabecular) bone that is characteristic of the spine, leading to a specific type of spinal fracture (vertebral crush fracture) that results in loss of height and kyphosis ("dowager's hump"). Fractures of the hip, the most serious complication of osteoporosis, follow the slower loss of cortical bone (the compact bone that constitutes much of the tubular framework of the long bones). Cortical bone loss is the result of abnormal calcium metabolism, caused either by an absolute deficiency in the dietary intake of calcium or by the inability of the body to metabolize an adequate supply of dietary calcium in an appropriate and efficient fashion, thus causing a relative calcium deficiency.

The classification of osteoporosis into two types, however, is not as clear-cut as this hypothesis would suggest. First, there is evidence that bone loss in women may begin before menopause, probably in relation to the gradual decline in ovarian function that occurs after age 35. Loss of bone throughout the skeleton—not only in trabecular bone—appears to accelerate after menopause or oophorectomy. Further, people with vertebral crush fracture syndrome generally have lost bone at all sites in the skeleton, which increases their risk of other fractures. Thus, postmenopausal osteoporosis can be considered to be a risk factor for hip fracture independent of other causative factors. Menopause, especially if it occurs early, is therefore a significant factor, if not the most important one, in increasing overall fracture risk in the aging female population. Other factors common to both men and women add to that risk and may be more likely to influence hip fracture than vertebral fracture. This assumption is based on evidence that the incidence of hip fracture among elderly men is half that of women, whereas the incidence of vertebral fracture

One manifestation of osteoporosis is the loss of spongy bone in the spine. This condition results in a specific type of spinal fracture (vertebral crush fracture) that is associated with loss of height and with kyphosis, or "dowager's hump."

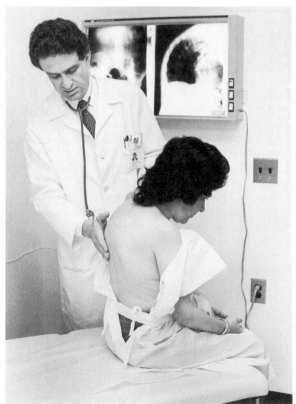

From D. W. Dempster et al., "A Simple Method for Correlative Light and Scanning Electron Microscopy of Human Iliac Crest Bone Biopsies," *Journal of Bone and Mineral Research*, vol. 1, no. 1 (1986), pp. 15–21; photographs, D. W. Dempster

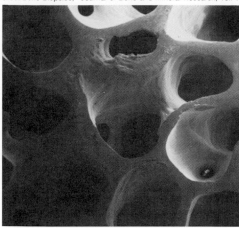
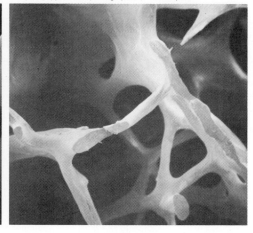

An electron micrograph of normal spongy bone (far left) shows its honeycomb-like structure, in which bony plates form the small compartments that contain the marrow. As bone is lost, the plates become thin and rodlike, and the spaces between them grow larger.

in this male population is much less than one-tenth that of the comparable female population. Finally, it is still not clear whether those who develop fractures are a specific population of aging people who have excessive loss of bone or are simply people who have less bone mass at maturity and, therefore, have an increased risk of fracture with comparatively less age-associated bone loss. Irrespective of this consideration, however, as stated above, the fact that people with vertebral crush fracture syndrome have less bone at all sites in the skeleton clearly appears to increase their risk of other fractures.

Calcium considered—and reconsidered

Calcium nutritional status is also of some importance, particularly because as people age, their bodies become less efficient in handling calcium in the diet. This is due, at least in part, to a gradual decline in the capability of the body to metabolize vitamin D into its active form, a process necessary for efficient intestinal absorption of calcium. This metabolic defect may be exaggerated in women who suffer from postmenopausal osteoporosis. For most people under the age of 70, vitamin D_3 (cholecalciferol) is normally synthesized in the skin or obtained from dietary sources in adequate amounts. Thus, the addition of vitamin D to calcium supplements is unnecessary for younger individuals. Before becoming an active hormone, cholecalciferol undergoes two enzymatically controlled metabolic steps, the first one in the liver and the next one in the kidney. The second step, in particular, is under strict biological control and is influenced by the levels of calcium and phosphorus present in the blood serum, as well as by the levels of parathyroid hormone. As aging progresses, the kidney becomes less able to produce the active hormone (1,25-dihydroxyvitamin D_3) and, in addition, the intestine may become somewhat resistant to its action. The consequence is a reduction in the efficiency of calcium absorption from dietary sources—which may already

be less than optimum—with a resulting decline in the body's supply of calcium. As a result of this kind of calcium deficiency, calcium in the bones is drawn upon to maintain the steady level of calcium in the blood that is necessary for many ongoing biologic functions. As the calcium "reservoir" in the skeleton decreases, bone loss ensues. Clearly the earlier in life that this happens, or the more severe the metabolic defect, the greater the loss of bone will be. In addition, bone loss will be exaggerated in situations where there is frank deficiency in dietary calcium intake.

The 1984 consensus conference confirmed in its conclusions the importance of an adequate calcium intake for women of all ages, particularly for postmenopausal women. The conference's recommendations that premenopausal women obtain 1,000 mg of calcium per day and postmenopausal women 1,500 mg per day were based to a large degree on the studies of calcium kinetics (the mechanisms by which calcium metabolism is effected) in women, conducted by Creighton University (Omaha, Neb.) researcher Robert Heaney. Since the average dietary calcium intake among adult women in the United States was estimated to be only about 500 mg per day, these recommendations resulted in a dramatic increase, as mentioned before, in the number of calcium supplements on the market, with aggressive advertising targeted directly at the consumer.

The 1987 conference reaffirmed the importance of adequate calcium intake, but it also reviewed specific aspects of calcium nutrition that still are unclear. First, there was general agreement that calcium deficiency is detrimental to skeletal health and may be ill-advised for other reasons as well. Conference members found, however, that the definitions of "deficiency" and "reasonable intake" are difficult to determine. "Reasonable intake" was defined by the 1984 conference as indicated above—1,000 mg for premenopausal and 1,500 mg for postmenopausal women—and in the absence of significant conflicting data, the 1987 conference elected to confirm those guidelines. However, it was noted that these levels would, at best, only slow bone loss in individuals who were previously calcium deficient and that the effects of calcium supplementation on bone loss were not nearly as marked as, for example, the effect of estrogen.

Furthermore, it has become clear that the definition of adequate calcium intake depends not only on the level of nutritional supply but also on the relative efficiency with which the individual's body can absorb and retain calcium. Thus, a woman who can absorb a high proportion of the calcium in her diet and whose kidneys do not excrete a large proportion of this absorbed calcium can achieve calcium sufficiency at a lower level of dietary intake than another woman who may be able to absorb only a small proportion of the calcium in her diet or whose kidneys cannot adequately conserve calcium. Since there is no easily applied test for calcium absorption, however, calcium intake remains the major indicator of sufficiency.

The importance of good nutrition in general was emphasized at the 1987 conference, implying that it is better to obtain an adequate calcium intake by eating foods rich in calcium than by taking calcium tablets. However, research presented in 1987, also from Creighton University, pointed out that calcium from certain dietary sources (some green vegetables, for example) that are relatively high in calcium content, may not be as available to the body as calcium from sources such as dairy products. While, on average, most people will absorb about 30% of the calcium in milk, they may absorb only 3–5% of the calcium in spinach. Thus, sufficiency, already noted to be dependent upon efficiency of utilization as well as upon adequate intake, also depends on bioavailability. This is true for calcium tablets as well, which may vary widely in bioavailability.

There appears to be no evidence that a high calcium intake, within the agreed-upon guidelines, is associated with significant adverse side effects, particularly the risk of kidney stones, as has sometimes been suggested. This risk is probably increased only in people who are able to absorb high amounts of calcium from the diet and have a family or personal history of kidney stones. For these individuals an increase in calcium intake would be contraindicated. There is also no current evidence that increasing calcium intake beyond the recommended levels will provide further benefits to the skeleton; it is possible that higher levels of calcium intake, over and above the amounts recommended, may be associated with potential adverse side effects (*e.g.,* constipation, development of kidney stones). Thus, in the last two to three years, the attitude toward calcium has become more balanced, particularly with the realization that calcium alone will not prevent osteoporosis since, among the aging population, osteoporosis has many control factors.

Assessing individual risk

Bone loss is, by itself, totally without symptoms—rather like high blood pressure before a stroke; thus, the individual is completely unaware that there may be a problem until a fracture occurs. Because the factors that increase a woman's risk of osteoporosis are relatively well known, most physicians recommend that each individual assess her own personal risks and try to alter those aspects of her life-style that increase the likelihood of suffering osteoporotic fractures. The risk of developing the disease increases with the number of risk factors present, although the relative weight given to each factor may vary from one individual to another.

When several risk factors are present, a measurement of bone mass may be a useful test. However, it must be emphasized that bone mass measurements are limited in the information that they provide. Just as the measurement of the hemoglobin level of the blood will tell whether anemia is present and how bad it is, measurement of bone mass will tell whether "osteopenia" (low bone mass) is present and how serious the problem is. Neither of these tests gives a clue as to the causes, rate of development, outlook for the future, or appropriate mode of treatment. Thus, neither measurement of hemoglobin in anemia nor measurement of bone mass in osteoporosis can take the place of a knowledgeable physician's careful evaluation and recommendations for a specific treatment program.

The prevention of osteoporosis starts with the personal assessment of risk. The most important fac-

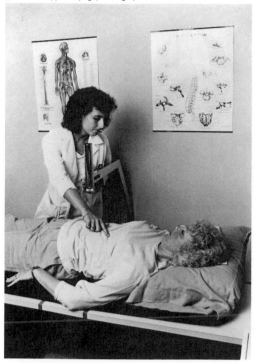

Dual-photon absorptiometry is a relatively new technique for measuring bone mass. The patient's height is measured (opposite page) before she undergoes the scanning process (left). The results are processed by a computer and are displayed on a video screen along with an image of the patient's spine (above).

tors appear to be family history of the disease, early menopause (or oophorectomy), and small, thin body build. Dietary factors that increase risk include low calcium intake, excessive use of alcohol, and excessive caffeine intake. Prolonged inactivity increases risk. Other factors include the presence of a disease process that may increase the rate of bone loss—for example, Cushing's disease (muscular weakness and obesity associated with excessive production of cortisol due to adrenal or pituitary dysfunction)—or the prolonged use of steroid drugs for conditions such as rheumatoid arthritis or systemic lupus erythematosus (SLE). Other chronic diseases that result in long-term bed rest or inactivity also increase risk because of their general effect on activity level.

At the time of menopause, if a woman feels that she may be particularly vulnerable to osteoporosis, she should consult her physician. At that point an independent assessment of the likelihood of osteoporosis, based on risk-factor analysis, perhaps together with a bone mass measurement, would constitute an appropriate evaluation process. The physician can then decide on a suitable strategy for preventing the occurrence of osteoporotic fractures.

Techniques for bone mass measurement

A variety of techniques for measuring bone mass are available. The simplest is single-photon absorptiometry, a process that has been available for about 25 years. It involves the least radiation exposure of all such measurement techniques and is less costly and time consuming than the others but is useful only for measurement of bone mass in the peripheral skeleton (usually at the wrist by measurement of the bone called the radius). However, while there is a statistical relationship between the amount of bone in the wrist and that at other sites in the body, as well as with the total amount of bone in the skeleton, the relationships are not sufficient to allow for extrapolation of the bone mass in an individual's spine or hip from a measurement of the wrist. In fact, it is possible to obtain an almost equally precise estimate of the amount of bone in the spine simply on the basis of the patient's age, sex, and ethnic background. However, because single-photon absorptiometry has relatively high precision, it is a useful procedure for following an individual patient's bone loss over time, especially if such loss is likely to be rapid.

During the past five years or so, two techniques have become available that allow a measurement of bone mass in sites of the central skeleton that are most liable to fracture—the spine and the hip. One of these techniques, dual-photon absorptiometry, is a development from single-photon absorptiometry. This procedure allows a measurement of bone in the lower part of the spine (the lumbar vertebrae) and also across the neck of the femur (the thighbone, the rounded head of which fits into the hip socket). The amount of radiation exposure in dual-photon absorptiometry is relatively low. The process takes about one to one and a half hours for both hip and spine measurements, is available at many U.S. hospitals and

357

academic medical centers, and has an average cost of between $100 and $250. The other technique that allows for bone measurement by noninvasive means is computed tomography (CT) scanning. This technique allows for direct measurement of the spongy bone in the spinal column, and it has been suggested that this is the most specific test for the development of postmenopausal osteoporosis. The CT scan, however, is associated with a higher radiation dose than either of the absorptiometry techniques and is the most expensive of the three, the average cost being from $150 to $400.

As already indicated, not every women requires a bone mass measurement, and the recommendation to undergo such testing should be made only by the physician. For example, most women starting estrogen replacement therapy after menopause need not have their bone mass measured unless they particularly wish to confirm that estrogen treatment is effectively preventing bone loss for them. Although present estimates suggest that about 5–10% of women receiving estrogen may continue to lose bone despite the treatment, for those at especially high risk of osteoporosis bone mass measurements during therapy may still be helpful to both patient and physician. Conversely, according to current evidence, a woman with no major risk factors predisposing her toward osteoporosis should not feel obliged to invest time and money in bone mass measurement. The presence of minor risk factors such as cigarette smoking may be considered insufficiently important in the increase of individual risk (although smoking is clearly a major risk factor from a public health standpoint), and bone mass measurement may not be required if this is the only factor likely to heighten risk for a given individual. Finally, it must be noted that for rate of loss to be determined, a series of bone mass measurements is generally required since a change of at least 8% must occur between any two measurements for that change to be confirmed as having real biologic significance. For this reason, on the basis of cost alone, regular bone mass measurement for individual patients is probably contraindicated unless there is a particularly strong reason to suspect that rapid bone loss is occurring.

Prevention

It is clear—and perhaps unfortunate—that prevention of osteoporosis is a more important priority and a somewhat easier approach to the problem than is the treatment of patients who have already sustained some bone fracture. This is because of the change in the skeletal architecture that occurs as bone is lost. Normal spongy, or trabecular, bone looks somewhat like a honeycomb, with bony plates separated by small spaces in which the bone marrow resides. As bone is lost, these plates of bone disappear, leaving behind remnants that look like thin rods of bone with

much larger marrow spaces between them. Individual rods eventually deteriorate completely and, thus, the template, or foundation, upon which new bone can be rebuilt is gradually lost. The point at which the process becomes irremediable is not known, but even this fact is likely to be of more help in preventing the problem than in its treatment. Furthermore, as yet there are no established, successful therapeutic methods of increasing bone mass or of preventing further fractures.

Prevention of osteoporosis is based on two major steps—first, the elimination or reduction of risk factors and, second, the evaluation of the patient for estrogen replacement therapy, which is the mainstay of prevention for the disease. It is important that a woman who is considering estrogen therapy for the prevention of osteoporosis discuss with her physician the additional benefits and the potential risks of estrogen therapy as they apply to her. For example, a large amount of circumstantial evidence suggests that estrogen may reduce the risk of heart disease among the aging population. If so, it would represent a significant benefit for the postmenopausal population. However, the effect of estrogen therapy on heart disease has yet to be scientifically evaluated in controlled clinical trials. Furthermore, the addition of progesterone (the other female sex hormone supplied by the ovary) to the estrogen treatment—to protect the endometrium (the lining of the womb) and perhaps the breast tissue as well from the potentially carcinogenic effects of estrogen—may reduce, or even negate, the beneficial effects of estrogen on cardiovascular disease. This is an area that requires further, more detailed study. The decision to embark upon estrogen replacement therapy should not be taken lightly; as for any long-term therapeutic program, the benefits and risks must be reviewed carefully with an experienced professional before the decision is made, since the commitment may be to many years—or even a lifetime—of continued therapy.

The first consideration of prevention, as noted above, is reducing individual risk. While it is clear that people who have low bone mass are at greater risk of bone fracture than are normal individuals, the risk is higher still for those who are liable to fall and injure themselves. Current evidence indicates that elderly women are more likely than elderly men to fall. The thin woman who is at risk of excessive bone loss may also be at increased risk of injuring herself after a fall, either because of reduced muscle activity due to trauma, which decreases her resistance to falling again, or because of more direct trauma to the skeleton in the absence of adequate fat and muscle tissue padding the bones. Finally, alcohol use and cigarette smoking may affect the elderly in such ways that increase the risk of falling, as does the use of tranquilizers, sedatives, and certain other medications. All of these should be avoided if possible. The elimination of hazards in the immediate environment—loose electrical wires, slipping rugs, sharp-cornered furniture—also reduces the chances of falling. In the long run such strategies may prove more beneficial than do attempts to devise medical treatment for established osteoporosis. Certainly, the public health impact of prevention is likely to be more significant than the small increases in bone mass that can be achieved by currently available therapeutic measures. Indeed, the 1987 conference on osteoporosis was disappointing in that it introduced only one new therapeutic regimen that may be capable of significantly increasing bone mass. Much additional work must be done before these preliminary experiments can be regarded as anything more than promising.

—Robert Lindsay, M.B.Ch.B., Ph.D.

Pediatrics

In September 1986 the U.S. Public Health Service (PHS) announced changes in its recommendations for the immunization schedule of normal infants and children. Previously the PHS recommendations had called for administering the combined measles-mumps-rubella (MMR) vaccine at 15 months and giving the fourth dose of diphtheria-tetanus toxoids and pertussis (whooping cough) vaccine (DTP) along with the third dose of oral poliovirus vaccine (OPV) at 18 months. However, a recent clinical trial demonstrated the safety of administering all seven vaccines simultaneously, at age 15 months or older, thus eliminating the need for a subsequent visit to the doctor. Some pediatricians may continue to advise that these vaccines be given in two separate visits, at ages 15 and 18 months, to minimize any possible augmentation of side effects that could result from the administration of all of the vaccines at one time. Nonetheless, it is reassuring to know that the vaccines may be safely given together, particularly for children who make less frequent or only irregular visits to medical facilities.

Fetal alcohol syndrome: new insights

Chronic alcohol ingestion by pregnant women, even in "moderate" amounts, may produce congenital abnormalities, known collectively as fetal alcohol syndrome (FAS), in their offspring. Moreover, it is now known that the heavier the drinking, the more severe the dysmorphic (i.e., physically malformed) features and the mental dysfunction. The principle features of FAS are:

1. growth failure, both prenatal and postnatal
2. abnormalities of the face and head, including microcephaly (small head); short palpebral fissures (small eye openings); ptosis (eyelid drop); epicanthic folds (skin folds over inside eye corner); short, upturned nose; long, smooth philtrum (area between nose and mouth); thin upper lip; micrognathia (small jaw)
3. abnormalities of the upper airways

4. cardiac defects, especially septal defects (i.e., abnormalities in the walls separating the different chambers of the heart)
5. joint and limb abnormalities
6. delayed development and mental deficiency

It was a U.S. pediatrician, David W. Smith, who, with Kenneth L. Jones and co-workers, identified these features as a syndrome in 1973 and recognized the syndrome's relationship to chronic maternal alcoholism. Current estimates of the annual frequency of fetal alcohol syndrome in the U.S. range from 0.5 to 3 per 1,000 live births. On the basis of these statistics, FAS may be the most common cause of congenital mental retardation, second only to Down syndrome (1.25 per 1,000) and spina bifida (1 per 1,000), and may account for more cases of mental deficiency than any other single cause. The effect of alcohol ingestion on fetal brain development is of special concern because—whether manifested as intellectual impairment or merely as a "learning disorder"—it is now believed to have profound and long-lasting implications. This was the conclusion of researchers who in 1986 completed a ten-year follow-up study of the first 11 U.S. children diagnosed as having FAS. Their study demonstrated that the intellectual deficits and learning problems identified among these children have continued into adolescence.

FAS occurs worldwide, but the incidence is especially high among lower socioeconomic groups, older mothers (i.e., over age 35), and American Indians, each a factor that probably reflects higher than average alcohol intake. It is not clear whether binge drinking is more detrimental to the developing fetus than is drinking on a regular basis, although animal studies indicate that the former may be. Nor are scientists certain whether the syndrome is a result of alcohol (ethanol) itself or its breakdown product, acetaldehyde. Although it is now known that maternal alcohol ingestion is embryotoxic, paternal alcohol ingestion has not been shown to be similarly teratogenic, perhaps because heavy drinking has a directly detrimental effect on male fertility.

| U.S. Centers for Disease Control revised schedule of immunization for normal infants and children ||
recommended age	vaccine(s)
2 months	diphtheria-tetanus-pertussis (DTP) and oral polio vaccine (OPV)
4 months	DTP and OPV
6 months	DTP
15 months	DTP, OPV, measles-mumps-rubella
24 months	hemophilus b polysaccharide vaccine for hemophilus influenza, type B
4–6 years	DTP and OPV

Source: Centers for Disease Control, Atlanta

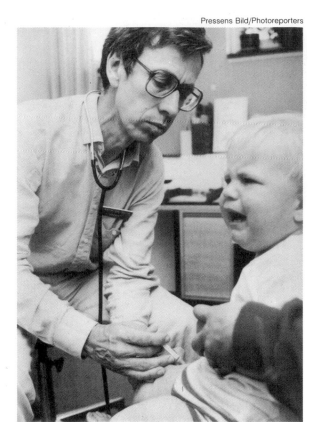

A Swedish physician inoculates an infant with a new test vaccine against pertussis (whooping cough). An epidemic of pertussis struck Sweden after the government banned the standard vaccine against the disease because of its rare but potentially serious side effects.

Not all chronic drinkers give birth to infants with FAS. In fact, only about 40% of women who drink heavily during pregnancy have a child with FAS; conversely, 11% of moderate-drinking, nonalcoholic women give birth to an affected child. It is, therefore, impossible for the physician to recommend a "safe" amount of alcohol ingestion for the pregnant woman.

Even if they escape FAS, children of alcoholic parents face another serious risk: they are four to five times more likely to become alcoholics than are other children. This tendency may be the result of a genetic predisposition, chaotic family environment, or both. Support groups such as Alateen, for teenagers with alcoholic parents, and Alatot, for younger children, have been formed to help young people deal with family members who are alcoholics and to understand their own risks of addiction.

Parent-infant bonding reevaluated

The recent trend toward less clinical, more family-oriented maternity care in U.S. hospitals can be traced, in large part, to the influence of earlier studies on parent-infant bonding, the interactional process by which attachment occurs between parents and the newborn. By the turn of the century, psychologists had noted that mothers who were separated early from their newborn infants soon lost interest in the babies. At that time, modern techniques of neonatal medicine were unknown. By the 1960s, however, advances in knowledge and technology in developed countries had made possible the survival of infants born prematurely or with serious but correctable birth defects. Unfortunately, mothers were often separated from their babies for extended periods of time during hospitalization in the neonatal intensive care facility.

The classic research of U.S. pediatricians John H. Kennell and Marshall H. Klaus sparked interest in the possible enhancement of bonding. They showed that mothers who spent additional time with their newborns immediately after delivery ("early contact" mothers) were more comforting to their infants in later months, used more mature, expressive language with their children, and had children whose IQs were measurably higher than average up to five years later. These studies seemed to support the concept of a critical period of bonding. The major components of early contact—skin-to-skin touching and eye contact between parent and newborn, with parents confronting the infant face-to-face—were described in the works of Kennell and Klaus.

Owing in large part to their influence, hospitals began to provide so-called birthing rooms, more informal and homelike than traditional delivery rooms, and to keep infants close beside their mothers for a period immediately after birth. Rooming-in—the practice of newborns staying in their mothers' hospital rooms rather than in the nursery—also gained in popularity. Parents began to request postponement of medications in newborns' eyes, a process usually performed immediately after delivery, so that the mother could hold the infant within seconds after birth. Parents also asked for more liberal visiting by family members to the new mother and infant. Bonding was compared with imprinting, an instinctual process known to occur between mother and offspring in certain birds and mammals during a critical period after birth. Less rigid, more family-oriented hospital care for mothers and newborns was not the only beneficial effect of the bonding studies; they also encouraged the return to breast-feeding, and they increased the awareness that small infants and their mothers need feedback from one another.

More recently, however, research has cast some doubt on the concept that there is a "sensitive" period after delivery during which bonding, in order to have lasting benefit, must occur. Thus, adoptive parents and parents of sick newborns who have undergone lengthy hospitalization, who may have feared that they had missed this crucial opportunity, can now be reassured. The original evidence supporting the critical importance of early bonding is now considered inconclusive, and

Photographs from Kenneth L. Jones, "Fetal Alcohol Syndrome," *Pediatrics in Review*, vol. 8, no. 4 (October 1986), p. 123

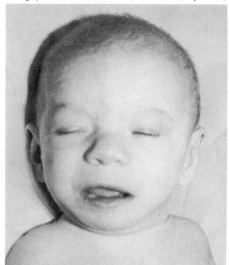 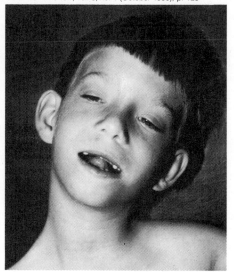

The photos at left show a victim of fetal alcohol syndrome at four months of age and at eight years. Researchers are now finding that not only do the physical abnormalities associated with the syndrome persist over time but the effects of alcohol on fetal brain development have lasting implications— for later impaired intellectual performance and learning disorders.

the prevailing belief today is that continuing loving care and day-to-day interaction can accomplish the same emotional benefits.

New anticonvulsants for children

Individuals with a convulsive disorder such as epilepsy have a chronic illness that requires daily medication for many years, sometimes for a lifetime. When they learn of the diagnosis, these patients receive two serious verdicts: the disease and the treatment. Drug therapy in many cases "controls" the convulsions— that is, convulsions do not occur as long as therapy is continued—but the drugs themselves have been found to cause some serious problems, especially for children. Now two relatively new anticonvulsants, carbamazepine (Tegretol) and valproate (Depakene), are proving useful for young people whose epilepsy is hard to control or whose previous medications impaired their mental and emotional functioning.

Until recently the mainstay drugs for the treatment of childhood seizures were the barbiturates and phenytoin. However, despite their proven ability to prevent seizures, these drugs, taken over time, produce unpleasant side effects. In fact, behavior that had heretofore been attributed to the epilepsy itself— such as drowsiness, depression, emotional instability, poor memory, mental dullness, and short attention span—was recently shown to be a side effect of barbiturate therapy. Phenytoin causes cosmetic effects: hyperplasia (overgrowth) of gum tissue and hirsutism (excess hairiness).

Carbamazepine, which has been on the U.S. market since 1968, was originally approved for the treatment of a nerve condition, trigeminal neuralgia, but is now used as initial treatment for many types of seizures, even in newborns. Its adverse reactions include rare instances of aplastic anemia (perhaps 0.5 cases per 100,000 patients per year), leukopenia (a serious drop in the number of white blood cells), and diplopia (double vision). However, it is relatively free from behavioral and cognitive effects and is therefore rapidly becoming an anticonvulsant drug of first choice. Valproate was approved for use in the U.S. in 1978 and quickly proved itself effective in preventing the short lapses in awareness known as petit mal seizures, as well as the more generalized grand mal seizures. Often it is now also the drug of choice for myoclonic seizures (those involving involuntary muscle contractions) and atonic seizures (involving loss of normal muscle tension). Its most frequent side effects are liver dysfunction, primarily in children under the age of two, gastrointestinal disturbances, tremor, and alopecia (loss of hair). It is remarkably free of effects on cognitive performance and behavior. Except for use during pregnancy (it is a known teratogen, or cause of birth defects) and in children under two, valproate is now considered a helpful and relatively safe drug. Finally, neurologists not only have new anticonvulsant drugs to offer children with epilepsy but also bring a message of hope: if seizures can be controlled for two years, 75% of the children can be weaned from medications without recurrence of seizures.

Kawasaki disease

A relatively new pediatric disease, first described in children in Japan in the 1960s, is now beginning to be reported worldwide. Kawasaki disease, also known as mucocutaneous lymph node syndrome, is unusual for several reasons: it has no definite diagnostic test; it has no definite treatment; and it may or may not be infectious in origin. Kawasaki disease is important because about 5% of the children with the syndrome develop coronary heart disease, and about 1% (usually males) die of this complication.

361

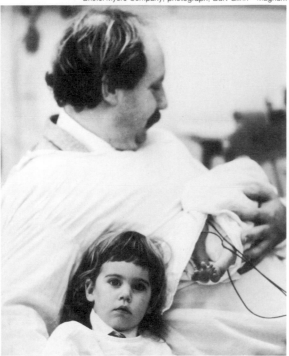

Recent insights into parent-infant bonding indicate that sick or premature newborns benefit from ongoing closeness and affection even if separated from their parents during a prolonged hospital stay.

In Japan Kawasaki disease—named for the Japanese physician who first described it—is widespread and even epidemic in some areas. In the U.S. the incidence of the disease is nearly three times higher in Asian American than in black children and more than six times higher in Asian American children than in Caucasians. More boys than girls are affected. Most victims are under the age of nine, and peak incidence occurs at about age two. Characteristically, the illness starts with high fever, accompanied by conjunctivitis ("pinkeye"); sore mouth or throat; redness, swelling, and peeling of the skin on the hands and feet; swollen lymph nodes in the neck; and general rash. After four or five days the child may appear very sick, have diarrhea or abdominal pain, and even have jaundice or swollen joints. By the 12th day the rash may disappear, to be followed by skin peeling; the electrocardiogram may show abnormalities; and there are changes in the blood count, such as increased platelets. The gallbladder may be inflamed during the course of the illness, causing pain and abdominal distension. Even after recovery from the initial illness, in three to four weeks, the child may continue to have fever and joint pain and abnormalities of the heart and coronary arteries.

For a time the chemicals in rug shampoos were thought to be associated with the disease, but sub-sequent studies showed this not to be the case, and although several biologic agents—from bacteria transmitted by house-dust mites to retroviruses—have been implicated, no environmental or infectious cause has been identified. Intravenous gamma globulin has recently been reported to help prevent coronary artery aneurysms in children with this disease. This treatment for the disease is expensive and currently only experimental, but gamma globulin may be the only agent of any real benefit in controlling the most feared complications of the illness: cardiac or coronary aneurysms or rupture. Because the cardiac complications associated with Kawasaki disease tend to develop many months after apparent recovery, children who have had the disease should have appropriate medical follow-up.

Update on sudden infant deaths

In the U.S. sudden infant death syndrome (SIDS) now occurs at the rate of two deaths per 1,000 live births (the rate is higher in blacks and American Indians). A National Institutes of Health-sponsored conference on SIDS, held in November 1986 in Bethesda, Md., was of special interest to people who have been skeptical about the efficacy of the electronic devices used to predict episodes of apnea (temporary cessation of breathing) in infants or to produce a warning in the event of prolonged apnea. The conference brought together experts from various disciplines to consider new research on the relation of neonatal and infant apnea to each other and to deaths (especially those attributed to SIDS) in infancy.

By definition, SIDS is the sudden death of an infant or young child that is unexplained by the victim's medical history or by autopsy. Many premature infants have episodes of apnea, sometimes called periodic breathing, but according to a national epidemiological study of SIDS, these episodes do not necessarily indicate that such infants are more likely to die of SIDS than are infants who do not have apneic episodes. However, this reassuring finding is offset by another: as many as 10% of infants known to have had apneic spells requiring resuscitation ultimately die of SIDS, despite the presence of electronic home monitors. In other words, apneic spells requiring resuscitation do represent a definite risk factor for SIDS and, furthermore, monitoring cannot guarantee survival. An apparent life-threatening event (ALTE) in an infant, whatever the cause—if a cause is indeed found—increases the risk of SIDS; however, infants who suffer ALTEs make up only a small proportion of total SIDS cases.

The cardiorespiratory monitors now available for home use appear to be safe, but they have been found to emit both false-positive and false-negative alarms. Care givers, therefore, need special training in the use of these devices. Cardiac monitors are more reliable and less expensive, but because they do not recognize apnea, they are not recommended for respiratory monitoring. No presently available home monitors meet all the desirable criteria as defined by the panelists at the Bethesda conference—in fact, a set of minimal standards for monitors is needed. In view of the foregoing considerations, the members of the conference panel concluded that electronic monitoring devices should not be made available to consumers without professional recommendation and supervision.

Are home monitors effective in reducing SIDS mortality and morbidity for any category of patients? Because scientifically designed studies are lacking, there is no definite answer to this question. What is known is that annual SIDS rates have not declined in the U.S. since the introduction of home monitoring. Nevertheless, for certain groups of high-risk infants, cardiorespiratory monitoring is medically indicated. High-risk individuals include infants who have had one or more severe ALTEs requiring mouth-to-mouth resuscitation or vigorous stimulation, premature infants who have had apneic spells, infants who are siblings of two or more SIDS victims, and infants who have certain diseases or conditions, such as inadequate breathing due to central nervous system disorder.

For the normal newborn, cardiorespiratory monitoring is not medically indicated. Similarly, for asymptomatic premature infants, routine monitoring is not recommended. For those in borderline groups, such as siblings of SIDS infants (whose incidence of SIDS is five to ten times greater than that of other infants), infants with less severe ALTE episodes, infants with tracheostomies (surgically created opening of the trachea), and infants of opiate- or cocaine-abusing mothers, monitoring may be advisable, although the evidence is inconclusive. Pneumograms (records of heart rate and breathing) have been widely used as a screening tool, but the opinion of the NIH panelists was that they are probably not predictive of SIDS, and the conference did not recommend their use. Finally, the panel pointed out the need for further research into specific aspects of apnea, monitoring, and sudden infant death.

This need was highlighted by the results of a study, published in the *New England Journal of Medicine* in July 1986, in which researchers made detailed investigations of a group of deaths attributed to SIDS. The study was conducted over a period of 15 months by the Kings County Hospital Center in Brooklyn, N.Y. It found that several of the deaths had other, identifiable causes, including accidental asphyxiation in the crib, smothering when sleeping in a bed with a parent or caretaker, and overheating. Critics of the study were quick to point out its limitations—small size (only 26 cases) and restriction to an economically disadvantaged population. Nonetheless, there was general agreement that the Brooklyn researchers' findings pointed up the difficulties surrounding the current diagnosis of SIDS.

Children chronically exposed to cigarette smoke are prone to develop bronchitis, asthma, and pneumonia. Some 50–75% of U.S. households contain at least one smoker; if both parents smoke, however, youngsters are at even greater risk.

Exposure to tobacco smoke: new concerns

In December 1986 the U.S. surgeon general issued a new report on the further recognized dangers of smoking. The report indicated that smoking adults inflict serious damage upon the children around them, starting in fetal and embryonal life and continuing through childhood. Within minutes of each cigarette puff taken by a pregnant woman, carbon monoxide and nicotine enter the maternal bloodstream, diminishing the oxygen-carrying ability of the blood, constricting the placental blood vessels, and speeding the fetal heart rate. These findings may help explain why pregnant women who smoke have a higher incidence of spontaneous abortions, stillbirths, and premature deliveries than nonsmokers. It is also known that the babies of smokers are smaller at birth and more susceptible to neonatal disease than are infants born to nonsmokers.

A growing child chronically exposed to cigarette smoke is prone to develop ear, nose, and throat infections; bronchitis; pneumonia; asthmatic attacks; and diminished pulmonary function. In addition, children whose parents smoke have a less-than-expected annual rate of lung growth, which may predispose them to the development of chronic obstructive lung disease, lung cancer, and heart disease in later life. Recent surveys found that between 50 and 75% of the homes in the United States contain at least one smoker; thus, as many as 12.4 million American children under five years of age are exposed to cigarette smoke in their homes. If both parents smoke, a stronger relationship exists between smoking and children's risks of lung problems than if only one of the parents in a household smokes.

Long-term effects of childhood hyperactivity

Children formerly diagnosed as "hyperactive," or "hyperkinetic," will now be officially diagnosed as having attention deficit disorder with hyperactivity (ADDH), a name that better describes their behavior problems, according to the American Psychiatric Association. Such children are characterized by a triad of symptoms—attentional deficits, hyperactivity, and impulsivity. The cause of the condition is poorly understood, although the symptoms can be effectively managed by drugs. The onset of the disorder is generally before the age of seven; it was long believed that improvement would occur spontaneously (and, therefore, that drug treatment could be stopped) during adolescence.

However, recent long-term studies of hyperactive children have led to less-encouraging conclusions. Five years after the original diagnosis of hyperactivity, about one-third of the children studied were still diagnosed as hyperactive, distractible, and impulsive; moreover, their school performance was poor. Although some had recovered, usually by about age 16, others were found to be hyperactive, and sometimes antisocial, older teenagers. Antisocial behavior took the form of stealing, truancy, and aggression. There is little information on adult performance of former hyperactive children, but at least some, as adults, continue to show antisocial behavior.

From time to time, concern is expressed by school or health professionals that the major drug used for ADDH, methylphenidate (Ritalin), is misused or overused as a "quick fix" to make schoolchildren more orderly. In fact, the U.S. Drug Enforcement Administration, which monitors prescription drug production and use, has notified states with particularly high consumption rates to review prescribing practices of doctors. Whether or not there is overprescribing of methylphenidate and similar drugs (and there may be, from place to place), it is now generally agreed by physicians who care for youngsters that the drugs, when indicated, are effective and should be continued longer than originally anticipated.

Over the years there has also been concern that hyperactive youngsters who take drugs to control their behavior might be more likely than other children to abuse drugs in adolescence. This fear has not been borne out by follow-up studies of children under treatment for hyperactivity. In fact, when drug therapy is continued into adolescence, the favorable effect it produces may mitigate against substance abuse and antisocial behavior. The drugs are, in fact, useful in enabling children and adolescents to control themselves better. Methylphenidate and the other so-called psychostimulants used in the treatment of ADDH do not produce euphoria. The one side effect they do tend to cause—retardation of growth rate—does not appear to compromise the youngsters' eventual growth to normal height.

Reye's syndrome study concluded

Reye's syndrome is a potentially fatal disorder of children and teenagers. It is usually preceded by a viral illness, especially chickenpox or influenza. The symptoms are severe vomiting, unusual drowsiness, belligerence, and delirium. Liver dysfunction is common and may progress rapidly. As the liver fails, the ammonia level of the blood rises and blood pressure increases inside the cranium, putting pressure on the brain. Reye's syndrome is fatal in 20–30% of cases, and some survivors sustain permanent brain damage. It is the increased pressure on the brain that may lead to death, and therapeutic efforts have, therefore, been directed at reducing the pressure.

In 1985 only 91 cases of Reye's syndrome were reported in the U.S., down from 204 cases in 1984 and 422 cases in 1980. One possible reason for this drop is the recognition in the early 1980s of the association between aspirin and Reye's syndrome and subsequent publicity warning against aspirin use in youngsters with flu symptoms. Two studies conducted in 1982 in Ohio and Michigan showed a link between aspirin given to children with acute febrile illnesses, particularly influenza and chickenpox, and the subsequent development of Reye's syndrome.

It was not then known—and, in fact, it still remains a mystery—why aspirin increases the likelihood of developing the syndrome. Nor is it known if aspirin plays a causal, as opposed to coincidental, role in the development of the disease. Nevertheless, the PHS, in cooperation with the Institute of Medicine of the National Academy of Sciences, began a clinical study to verify the findings of the earlier investigations, and in 1985 preliminary results confirmed the strong association between Reye's syndrome and aspirin use. The announcement of the PHS study findings was followed by governmental action to inform parents and physicians not to give aspirin products when treating children or teenagers with flu or chickenpox. The federal information campaign included public service announcements on the radio, posters in grocery stores, and notices in doctors' offices. Finally, in March 1986 the Food and Drug Administration issued a regulation requiring that a warning label appear on all aspirin-containing products.

The campaign to raise public awareness of the link between aspirin and Reye's syndrome has apparently been successful; the incidence of the disease fell to a new low in 1986, and in February 1987 it was decided to discontinue the clinical study on Reye's syndrome and medication use, in part because the association between aspirin and the syndrome had been demonstrated so conclusively and in part because of the increasing rarity of the syndrome. The final report of the PHS task force was published in the *Journal of the American Medical Association* in April 1987.

—Jean D. Lockhart, M.D.

Limiting Cholesterol: How Early to Begin?

by Myron Winick, M.D.

Atherosclerosis is the process of progressive clogging of the major arteries that deliver blood to the heart and brain. A waxy fat, cholesterol, is deposited between the thin membrane that lines the inside surface of the artery and the muscle wall of the artery itself. As more and more cholesterol is deposited, a plaque is formed, which bulges into the lumen (interior opening) of the artery, thereby narrowing the channel through which blood may flow. As this plaque slowly enlarges, the blood supply to portions of the heart or brain is gradually reduced. Eventually the plaque itself may totally occlude the artery or, more commonly, a blood clot may form around the roughened surface of the plaque, rapidly shutting off the passage through which the blood flows. This process, atherosclerosis, is the major cause of death in the United States and other Western countries. Most heart attacks and strokes are a direct result of progressive atherosclerosis. Although the occurrence of a stroke or heart attack may be sudden, the actual process leading up to it usually takes many years. What is important, then, is to interrupt the atherosclerotic process or, better still, to prevent it from ever beginning.

Autopsy studies in the 1950s and 1960s demonstrated that what is thought to be the earliest visible evidence of atherosclerosis was present among many "healthy" young Americans: soldiers killed in the Korean and Vietnam wars. In a large number of these soldiers, many as young as 18 to 20 years old, fatty streaks— thought to be the first sign of plaques—were present in the coronary arteries (the arteries that supply blood to the heart muscle). This finding suggested that at least in the American male, atherosclerosis has already begun in a significant number in the early adult years. It would follow then that any action taken to prevent atherosclerosis should take place before adulthood has been reached.

Atherosclerosis and the "prudent" diet

There are four major direct risk factors for atherosclerosis: smoking, hypertension (high blood pressure), hyperlipidemia (high levels of certain fats in the blood), and diabetes. In addition, obesity is an indirect risk factor in that it increases the risk for high blood pressure, hyperlipidemia, and diabetes. The major public health strategy for preventing atherosclerosis is to lower these risk factors within the general population.

Of the five factors mentioned above, three are in some way related to diet. High blood pressure is related to excess dietary salt (sodium) and perhaps to too little dietary calcium. Hyperlipidemia is related to excess intake of total fat in the diet, excess saturated (usually animal) fat, and, specifically, excess cholesterol. Obesity is related to excess intake of calories. Because of the relationship of these dietary factors to increased risk for atherosclerosis, some agencies and organizations—among them, the U.S. National Institutes of Health and the American Heart Association— have made specific recommendations. These guidelines for a so-called prudent diet include:

● consuming the appropriate number of calories to reach and maintain ideal weight

● reducing the total proportion of fat in the diet from the present average of 40% of total calories to 30% of total calories or less

● consuming roughly equal amounts of animal (mostly saturated) and vegetable (mostly unsaturated) fats

Autopsies of young U.S. servicemen killed in the Korean War revealed fatty streaks in their arterial walls and narrowing due to fatty plaques. This finding, suggesting that atherosclerosis had begun by the teens or early twenties, is cited as one reason for restricting dietary fat prior to adulthood.

Autopsy study of 300 U.S. servicemen killed in action in Korea	
amount/type of arterial narrowing	percentage of cases
thickening or streaking, minor narrowing	35.0
plaques causing narrowing of more than 10%	13.3
. . . 20%	6.3
. . . 30%	3.7
. . . 40%	3.0
. . . 50%	3.0
. . . 60%	1.7
. . . 70%	1.0
. . . 80%	1.3
. . . 90%	5.3
plaques causing complete obstruction of one or more vessels	3.0

William F. Enos *et al.*, "Coronary Disease Among United States Soldiers Killed in Action in Korea," *JAMA*, vol. 152 (July 18, 1953), pp. 1090–93

● reducing the amount of cholesterol from the current average of 500 mg per day or more to 300 mg per day or less

These recommendations have been made on the basis of two very strong scientific observations. The first is that a diet as outlined above—the "prudent" diet—is usually effective in lowering blood cholesterol levels. The second is that the incidence of atherosclerosis and its deadly complications is directly related to the level of blood cholesterol; further, people who manage to lower their cholesterol levels, particularly people who once had high levels, have a significantly reduced incidence of atherosclerosis and heart attacks. One study showed that for each 1% reduction of blood cholesterol level, there is a corresponding 2% reduction of risk for heart attack.

A childhood diet?

So far, the issue of the benefits of dietary modification to prevent cardiovascular disease seems relatively unclouded. Atherosclerosis begins in many people at least in the late teens to early twenties. Diet is effective in lowering serum cholesterol levels and, thereby, in reducing risk for heart attack, presumably by slowing down or even stopping the process of atherosclerosis.

On the basis of these conclusions, a committee of scientists has proposed that the dietary recommendations set forth for adults also be applied to children—specifically to all children over the age of two years. This seemingly logical extension of the scientific data has been criticized by the American Academy of Pediatrics through its committee on nutrition, and a controversy over dietary restrictions for children is now raging in the medical community. The problem is that of extrapolating data collected in an adult population to growing and developing children.

Cholesterol needs in infancy

A full understanding of this problem begins with an examination of normal nutrition in the young infant. Breast milk, the perfect food for the first months of life, is 50% fat—a higher proportion even than in the present-day average adult diet. The fat in breast milk is rich in both saturated fat and cholesterol. Nonetheless,

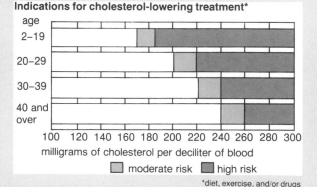

Indications for cholesterol-lowering treatment*

age

2–19	
20–29	
30–39	
40 and over	

100 120 140 160 180 200 220 240 260 280 300
milligrams of cholesterol per deciliter of blood

☐ moderate risk ■ high risk

*diet, exercise, and/or drugs

U.S. children consume more fat in their diets than most other children. Still, physicians debate the wisdom of applying the "prudent" diet—which limits fat intake, particularly cholesterol—to young children.

cholesterol does not accumulate in the infant's blood. Serum cholesterol levels are normally much lower in infants than in adults, regardless of diet. Additionally, there is considerable evidence to suggest that dietary fat may be much more important for children than for adults. Normal growth requires the accumulation of new cells throughout the body. These cells contain fat; it is a necessary component of the cell membrane. In the nervous system there is a special need for fat and particularly for cholesterol. The sheaths that surround the major nerve fibers are made of a substance called myelin, which is composed primarily of a mixture of different types of fat. The cholesterol content of myelin is very high. Thus, the young infant, whose nervous system is growing rapidly, is depositing large amounts of cholesterol and other fats in the brain and spinal cord. There is good evidence that both the quantity and the quality of the myelin in the brain and spinal cord can be affected by the amount and nature of the fat in the infant diet.

For these reasons no one has suggested that the amount of fat in the diet of the very young infant be drastically reduced. The adult dietary recommendations that were extended to include children specified that they were to apply only to children over the age of two. However, certainly during the toddler years, the central nervous system continues to develop rapidly, and myelin is still being deposited. Thus, it is possible that even during these years the child needs more fat and cholesterol than the adult. Just exactly how much more seems to be the issue. The amount of dietary fat needed by a toddler may be well supplied by the amounts as specified in the dietary recommendations for adults. In many parts of the world, at about the time of weaning, all children routinely begin to eat a diet even lower in fat than the "prudent" diet recommended above. This is standard practice for the majority of children in the less developed world. On the other hand, it is in these very populations that a variety of nutritional deficiencies are rampant. Therefore, this question has been raised: Could a deficiency in fat and cholesterol be an unrecognized part of the problem?

The dietary needs of toddlers and older children

Clearly the reason for the controversy is that there are very little data on either side that relate directly to the question being asked. How much fat is appropriate for maximum childhood growth and development to proceed and at the same time for significant protection against atherosclerosis? This question simply cannot be adequately answered. While it is known that very-low-fat diets can result in deficiency symptoms, no obvious deficiency is found at the levels being recommended. On the other hand, there is no evidence that the recommended levels afford any protection against atherosclerosis in later life—and the possibility that these low levels may be harmful, at least for some children, cannot be ruled out.

Thus, whether to recommend that toddlers aged two to five adhere to a diet based on the dietary guidelines now recommended for adults is a matter of balancing the possible benefits against the possible risks and reaching a judgment. Whatever that judgment is, it will be based on very little solid scientific information

Childhood obesity is an epidemic in the U.S., according to one study of more than 20,000 youngsters. The reasons for the growing percentage of overweight school-agers and adolescents are, quite simply, overeating and lack of exercise.

Growing percentage of obese youngsters in the U.S.

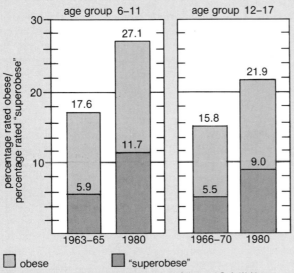

Adapted from S. L. Gortmaker, W. H. Dietz, A. M. Sobol, and C. A. Wehler, "Increasing Pediatric Obesity in the U.S.," *American Journal of Diseases of Children,* vol. 141 (May 1987), pp. 535–40

and must therefore be considered preliminary. As new evidence is gathered, it may have to be changed.

Today many physicians and nutritionists feel that there is solid evidence that too many calories may lead to childhood obesity and that childhood obesity leads to adult obesity. However, the same cannot be said for the association between fat and cholesterol intake in toddlers and the later development of atherosclerosis. Perhaps of greatest concern is the parent who reads these guidelines and then goes overboard in eliminating most fat and cholesterol from the young child's diet. In fact, recently there have been reports of several cases of failure to thrive in infants and toddlers whose well-meaning parents had severely restricted their diets, substituting skim milk for whole milk and limiting other sources of fats. Generally speaking, whenever a major change in dietary habits is suggested, the burden of proof that such change will have a beneficial effect and no adverse consequences is on those suggesting the change. In this instance, such proof has yet to be presented.

In the case of the older child, however, the facts are somewhat different. Myelination is almost entirely completed by age five or six. Hence the major theoretical reason for a possible increased requirement for fat and cholesterol is no longer present. There is also good reason to believe that adult eating patterns are developed during these years. In addition, the number of calories needed by a growing child, and particularly an adolescent, is proportionately greater for his or her size than the corresponding needs of an adult. Thus, even if the percentage of calories in the diet derived from fat is lowered to 30%, as suggested in the adult recommendations, the actual amount of fat consumed by the older child should still be more than adequate. Cholesterol is important in the formation of a number of hormones. However, the recommended daily amount of cholesterol (300 mg) is more than adequate.

Diet in the teen years

The purist may continue to argue that no direct evidence exists to show that the "prudent" diet recommended for adults actually prevents atherosclerosis if the diet is begun in the later childhood or early adolescent years. In fact, some question has been raised as to whether the fatty streak really is the first sign of atherosclerosis and, therefore, whether there is actually any evidence that the atherosclerotic process does go on in young adults. Nonetheless, there is strong evidence that in many people atherosclerosis has begun at least by early adulthood. Therefore, while there is no proof that dietary changes made during later childhood and adolescence will offer protection, it is fairly certain that any changes in eating habits instituted at that time are likely to carry over into adulthood. Thus, instituting the adult restrictions in older children or teens will, at the very most, directly

Fat children tend to become fat adults. In addition to learning to make healthy choices at mealtime, today's sedentary, television-watching youngsters ought to learn the benefits of an active life.

affect the process of atherosclerosis and, at the very least, help to form dietary habits that will be easier to adhere to in adulthood.

What of the possible negative consequences of instituting the adult recommendations in later childhood and adolescence? The majority of children in the world follow diets that conform to these guidelines, and no adverse effects have been noted. In Western countries older children and adolescents, because they eat a lot of junk food, consume diets even higher in fat and cholesterol than the levels in the average adult diet. For them, lowering fat and cholesterol intake would be a step in the right direction. Thus, many physicians feel that, given the present state of medical knowledge, it would be appropriate to extend the adult dietary recommendations to older children and adolescents.

Furthermore, moving in the direction of the adult recommendations would offer certain benefits to these youngsters even if such a change did not contribute to lowering their risk for subsequent atherosclerosis. This is because restriction of dietary fat usually results in both reduction of total calories and increase in the nutrient density of the diet. Fat has eight to nine calories per gram, compared with four calories per gram for carbohydrate and protein, and fat is comparatively low in micronutrients (vitamins and minerals). Thus, by eliminating some fat from the diet, people can bring down total caloric intake, and by replacing other fatty foods with complex carbohydrates such as cereals, pasta, and whole-wheat bread, they can benefit from valuable vitamins and minerals. In the U.S. and other more affluent countries, many older children, and especially adolescents, have a tendency to become obese; many others fail to eat foods that provide the necessary nutrients. Reducing the intake of fat is often the solution to both problems.

From a practical standpoint, lowering the amount of total fat, saturated fat, and cholesterol in the diet of an older child—and especially of an adolescent—is dependent on the education of the youngster to make proper choices when eating away from home and on the availability of foods at home that are low in fat and cholesterol. Even in fast-food restaurants, children can be encouraged to make choices that conform to the guidelines—for example, filling up at the salad bar, limiting the use of creamy dressings and sauces, and substituting fruit juices or even sugar-free soft drinks for milk shakes and ice cream sodas. As for the main course, pizza is much lower in fat than hamburger; fish and chicken, particularly broiled, are good alternatives in some restaurants. The more the public demands change, the more variety will be offered. At home, parents can emphasize fruits for snacks, use low-fat dairy products and skim milk, and serve fish and fowl more often than red meats. When red meats are served, it is wise to choose lean cuts and trim off all excess fat.

Weighing risks and benefits

Regardless of how one interprets the finding of fatty streaks in the arteries of relatively young individuals, it cannot be disputed that atherosclerosis has begun insidiously in many people at least by early adult life. Thus, the earlier the process is interrupted, the better. One major influence on the development of atherosclerosis is diet. Lowering total fat, saturated fat, and cholesterol in the diet can lower the incidence of the major complications of atherosclerosis and perhaps slow the process itself. From the point of view of prevention of coronary artery disease and stroke, the earlier a dietary change is made, the better. Fat, however, is an important nutrient, and in the young infant and toddler, fat and cholesterol are essential for normal development of the brain and nervous system.

It seems, therefore, that recommending restriction of dietary fat and cholesterol in all children over the age of two simply is not justified by the evidence now at hand. The potential risks outweigh the potential benefits. By contrast, in the older child (five through eight years old) the potential risks are less because myelin deposition has been completed. At the same time, the potential gains of a low-fat diet remain. It would, therefore, be reasonable to conclude that children aged five to eight should be gradually introduced to a diet conforming to the adult "prudent" diet, with the hope that, as they grow older, these eating habits will become ingrained. If this dietary transition is made naturally and gradually, there will be no need for radical changes later on in life.

Sexual and Reproductive Health

Many important events have occurred in the field of obstetrics and gynecology in recent years. Some of these have ultimately benefited women and their offspring; others have had quite the opposite effect. Among the major benefits are the numerous advances that have been made in the medical and surgical technology dealing with pregnancy and childbirth, allowing previously barren women to conceive and bear children. Concurrently, on the negative side, a drastic change has taken place in the patterns of social and sexual behavior, resulting in vastly different patterns of sexually transmitted diseases (STD) and, in many instances, a lowering of fertility.

In vitro fertilization developments

Less than a decade ago, the diagnosis that a woman had bilateral tubal obstruction that could not be remedied by surgery was dire news indeed for couples who had been trying unsuccessfully to achieve a pregnancy. That picture has begun to change, however, as new techniques have been developed and others are being studied that will allow some of these women to have a baby. Primary among these innovative measures is *in vitro* fertilization (IVF). In this procedure a woman's egg is allowed to mature naturally or, much more often, multiple eggs are brought to maturity in the ovary by the administration of hormones. They are removed surgically and put into a solution to which the husband's (or a donor's) sperm is added. After fertilization has occurred, the ova are incubated in the laboratory for two or three days (until they have matured to the proper size) and are then placed into the uterine cavity.

The first success in IVF, acclaimed worldwide, was the birth of Louise Brown in England in 1978. This event was the end result of extensive work carried out by reproductive scientist Robert Edwards and obstetrician-gynecologist Patrick Steptoe. Following that success, IVF programs were started by workers in a number of other countries; since then over 2,500 babies have been born by means of IVF. In the United States one of the largest and most successful programs is one that was established in 1979 at the Eastern Virginia Medical School by the husband and wife team of gynecologists Howard and Georgeanna Jones.

In the 1980s literally hundreds of IVF programs sprang up in the United States, and many more were based in universities throughout the world. With this burgeoning has come the recognition that there are certain limitations to the procedure. It is extremely time consuming on the parts of both the patients and the health care providers involved. Treatment may extend over several months if the initial implantation (or implantations) proves to be unsuccessful. In addition, repeated therapy of necessity becomes extremely expensive, costing up to $6,000.

The main reason for the high cost of IVF—and the reason it will remain costly—is that the ability to carry out the procedure successfully is dependent upon having a highly skilled, specially trained team of individuals including a gynecologic surgeon, an endocrinologist, and several reproductive scientists. IVF also requires the backup of a specially equipped and staffed laboratory. Therefore, only certain medical centers are able to offer IVF.

Although some centers have reported live births in 40 to 50% of the couples who underwent four or five cycles of treatment, the current IVF success rates generally range from 20 to 30%. This is approximately the same percentage as the natural rate of pregnancies going to term; multiple studies have shown that the spontaneous abortion rate in all pregnancies may be over 60%, the majority occurring even before the woman suspects that she is pregnant. This is nature's way of protecting the human race, since most of the abortuses (very early fetuses that are miscarried) are genetically or otherwise grossly abnormal. The same pattern appears to occur with IVF. No increase in the incidence of birth defects has been observed.

Gynecologists Howard and Georgeanna Jones, who run one of the most successful U.S. in vitro *fertilization clinics, at the Eastern Virginia Medical School, are pictured below with IVF twins Marie and Allie Snyder, born in 1984.*

Hank Morgan—Rainbow

It was inevitable that any medical procedure that dealt with the induction of human life would raise religious, moral, social, ethical, and legal questions. Despite the excitement generated by steadily increasing success rates with IVF and other new methods of achieving pregnancy, there is still considerable resistance to any "artificial" means of conception.

In an attempt to head off criticism, some facilities have restricted their programs to married couples. It has also been argued, with some justification, that IVF is just the first step leading to other forms of fetal manipulation, including the genetic engineering of human embryos. A recent accusation has been made by some feminist groups who say that IVF represents just one more way in which men are attempting to control the bodies and destinies of women.

Another type of question that has been raised centers on the fact that there are persistent and substantial unmet medical needs in the world today. Thus, it is asked: Is it appropriate to divert considerable funding and a large cadre of skilled health professionals into a field that thus far has benefited only a very small, elite population of women—particularly when the desired goal of pregnancy is achieved in fewer than half of the individuals who undergo this type of therapy?

As would be anticipated, IVF has generated considerable legal controversy. In the U.S. this has resulted in the promulgation of a variety of laws regarding the performance of IVF and other similar procedures. In fact, probably no other area in medicine has produced so many separate statutes and regulations, which vary from state to state. They encompass such areas as fetal research, protection of human subjects, and abortion procedures. In some instances there are laws regulating whether IVF can be done and, if so, under what circumstances.

The ultimate outcome, the delivery of a child, is also fraught with legal problems. Additional laws are encountered if donor eggs and sperm are utilized or if a surrogate mother carries the pregnancy to term, as has been seen in the highly publicized "Baby M" case. In some states there are laws governing artificial insemination, including procedures using sperm from both the husband and donors. In others, legislation regarding paternity and adoption has been passed, spelling out the legal relationship of the children resulting from these procedures to all of the parties involved.

New hope for infertile couples

A number of other new techniques have been developed in attempts to simplify the procedure of establishing a pregnancy and to improve the overall rate of success. Primary among these is gamete intrafallopian transfer (GIFT). This technique is used for women who have normal tubes but who suffer from conditions such as endometriosis or have unexplained infertility. Drugs are given to the woman to induce ovulation;

two hours prior to the procedure, sperm are obtained from the husband. The eggs are recovered by means of IVF techniques but are then placed in the fallopian tubes along with the sperm, as in a normal spontaneous pregnancy. While the success rate to date is about the same as with IVF, GIFT is much less complicated and does not require as large a medical team or specialized laboratory facilities.

Other techniques include ovum donation—a fertilized ovum being removed from the uterus of one woman and placed in the uterus of an infertile woman. Still another technique, known as intrauterine insemination, is the installation of sperm directly into the uterus at the time of ovulation. This method is used for women who have abnormalities of their cervical canals that block the passage of sperm. Finally, attempts are being made to remove eggs from the ovaries through the vagina under sonographic (ultrasound) guidance rather than through the abdominal wall. This method, if successful, might make IVF easier and less expensive and could possibly be done in an outpatient setting.

No matter what method is used, it is essential that care be taken not to transfer semen that is contaminated by a sexually transmitted disease. The fact that this complication has already been recorded on a number of occasions indicates the need for careful screening of all men donating sperm for these procedures. Despite the continuing controversy, it appears highly probable that programs offering IVF, GIFT, and other similar techniques will grow. When viewed from the perspective of the individual couples who have long-term and previously hopeless infertility, the need for such programs appears to be clearly indicated; they fulfill a deeply felt human need that heretofore has not been met. Indeed, it has recently been estimated that there are about 100,000 couples in the United States alone who could use IVF, GIFT, or other new means of achieving pregnancy and who could pay for the costs of the procedures. In addition, basic research in this field will also undoubtedly continue, with the probability of developing still newer techniques with even higher rates of success.

Sexually transmitted disease

Numerous STD are now assuming increasing importance. Until recently there were five conditions referred to as venereal diseases—gonorrhea, syphilis, chancroid, lymphogranuloma venereum, and granuloma inguinale—but attention was centered mainly on the first two. However, when medical research developed cures for these two major public health problems, there was a decrease in interest in their diagnosis and treatment. This period of disinterest was relatively brief. Today it is recognized that there are at least 20 different microorganisms that cause more than 50 separate disease entities that can be classified as STD. Within this category are a number of conditions that were previously not known to have a sexual route of transmission.

Thus, instead of disappearing, the problems with STD are now occurring at an increasingly rapid rate, and a number of these illnesses are present in many areas of the world in either epidemic or pandemic proportions. Part of this increase is related to the profound changes that have taken place in the sexual and social behavior of individuals. In many countries the age of first coitus has dropped progressively, and the number of sexual partners has increased. Coital patterns have moved away from the traditional genital-to-genital sex to include oral, anal, and other forms of sexual intercourse. Finally, the increased mobility of populations has permitted the rapid and widespread transmission of all types of infections.

Another factor that has had a major impact on the transmission of STD has been the change in the methods of fertility regulation being used. The use or nonuse of contraception and the particular method being employed have a direct bearing on the likelihood of contracting an STD. For example, studies of several of the major forms of STD have shown that transmission rates are higher in women who use no contraceptive method or a method that is not one of the barrier techniques. When barrier contraceptives such as condoms, diaphragms, and spermicides were the primary methods, individuals had at least a partial block to the transmission of these infectious agents, but the major switch to oral contraceptives (OCs) and intrauterine devices (IUDs) has altered this pattern of protection.

The oral contraceptives have varied effects on different organisms, decreasing the risk of gonorrhea but possibly increasing the risk of chlamydial infection. IUDs, on the other hand, have been shown to produce an increase in the risk of pelvic inflammatory disease (PID) in young women who are sexually active with multiple partners. This disease is the result of infection that is most commonly transmitted by intercourse. The severe inflammation and infection of the fallopian tubes, unless vigorously treated at an early stage, often result in permanent infertility. However, the IUD danger has a direct relationship to the number of sexual partners, and recent studies have shown no increased risk with the use of copper-bearing IUDs if the couple is monogamous.

A major problem with a number of the currently epidemic STD is the fact that the majority of individuals harboring these infections are totally asymptomatic and, therefore, the diseases are unwittingly being spread by people who are unaware that they are infected. As a result, the diagnosis is not being made, and treatment is not being instituted. Moreover, there still is no effective therapy for several of the most important STD, including genital herpes and AIDS (acquired immune deficiency syndrome). While a number of new drugs have been developed that initially appeared to be of value, several of them have been found to have serious side effects. In addition, there is little information as yet on their long-term safety and their potential effects on a developing fetus. Even in the case of a disease such as gonorrhea, for which medical science presumably had found a cure, there are three new organisms that have appeared in recent years. These new strains of gonorrhea are totally resistant to the antibiotic therapies used successfully in the past.

Two STD in particular are producing growing evidence of their immediate and long-term ill effects on both women and their children. These infections—chlamydia and genital warts—rather unfortunately have been overshadowed by human immunodeficiency virus infections, especially AIDS. They too deserve exhaustive attention.

Chlamydia: major threat to women's health

The first of these, chlamydia, which is caused by *Chlamydia trachomatis* (from the Greek word *chlamys,* "to cloak"), has been shown to infect almost all species of birds and mammals. Although classified as a bacterium, it also has many properties normally attributed to viruses. As a result, it is one of the most highly successful parasitic organisms identified to date: it is extremely infectious; it can live only inside cells; it is easy to transfer; resistance to this organism is generally poor; and it rarely kills the host. These characteristics have allowed the infection to spread rapidly and widely in humans.

Chlamydia trachomatis (CT) is now the most common genital infection in the Western world, and it has been estimated that there are 300 million cases worldwide. Between three million and ten million new cases

Sexually transmitted diseases

(estimated new cases, 1986)

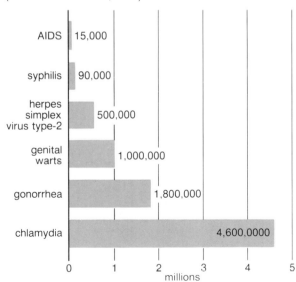

AIDS	15,000
syphilis	90,000
herpes simplex virus type-2	500,000
genital warts	1,000,000
gonorrhea	1,800,000
chlamydia	4,600,0000

millions

Source: Centers for Disease Control, Atlanta

occur in the United States each year, compared with two million cases of gonorrhea, 200,000 to 500,000 cases of genital herpes, one million cases of venereal warts, and 90,000 cases of syphilis. The U.S. Centers for Disease Control (CDC) now considers chlamydia control a top priority. CT is a major health threat to women; it has been estimated that these infections result in 250,000 cases of PID, 30,000 cases of infertility, and 10,000 cases of ectopic pregnancy every year. The problem is much more severe in women, but it is also a leading cause of medical problems in men; chlamydia can cause infections of the urethra and testes and possible sterility.

The incubation period of chlamydia is 7 to 21 days. Once the organism is within the body, the infectious particle (elementary body) is engulfed by a cell. The particle then develops a membrane that is highly protective against the body's normally effective defense mechanisms. Thus, it may remain within the cell for months or even years. Whereas most bacteria divide every two to four hours, CT replicates very slowly, taking 24 to 30 hours. The cell then ruptures, releasing 300 to 1,000 new elementary bodies, beginning the cycle again by infecting other cells.

Evasive and complex. Chlamydial infections are much more difficult to cure than such other bacterial infections as gonorrhea because antimicrobial agents (antibiotics) cannot get into the cell to kill the protected organisms. Because of CT's prolonged reproductive cycle, it is extremely important that patients who have this infection comply with the long-term therapy that is required for ridding the body of all of the infectious particles. Both male and female sexual partners must be treated if one is found to be infected.

Because so often CT infections are asymptomatic—it is often dubbed the silent disease—it is very difficult to estimate the actual incidence of the disease. A number of studies that have been carried out in college student health clinics have shown an incidence of up to 10%. Some of the students come complaining of symptoms of genital or urinary tract infections, but most are entirely asymptomatic, their infections being diagnosed only when they are found by history to be at high risk.

It is important to identify those women who are at high risk. There are two important factors to look for—young women with a history of the recent onset of sexual activity and multiple sexual partners. Studies have shown that infections occur relatively soon after starting sexual intercourse; women under 20 years of age have two to three times the infection rates of those over 20. In addition, infection rates have been found to be five times higher if a woman has three or more sexual partners. Even if a woman is monogamous, she is at increased risk if her partner has multiple partners.

It is particularly important to identify women who have a sexual partner or partners with a previous history of gonorrhea. It has been found that almost half of the women with CT infections also have gonorrhea. For this reason, the current guidelines established by the CDC call for treatment of both diseases if one is found to be present. It is also essential to evaluate women whose sexual partners have nongonococcal urethritis (NGU), a disease that is also caused by CT. Studies show that almost all women with partners infected with NGU harbor the CT organism; the organism is present in their reproductive tracts, and half of them have clinically obvious cervicitis (inflammation of the cervix).

There is new but as yet inconclusive evidence that these organisms may be carried "piggy-back" on sperm. They have been found to adhere to sperm in laboratory tests, but whether this phenomenon plays a role in the transmission of CT infections in humans remains unknown. Also unknown is the number of organisms that would have to reach the uterus and the fallopian tubes in this fashion in order to produce a pelvic infection.

All the barrier methods of birth control have been demonstrated to decrease the risk of developing this infection. On the other hand, there is considerable controversy at the present time as to the possible role of oral contraceptives in the development of chlamydia. While it has been known for several years that their use protects against PID in general, it has more recently been shown that the frequency with which chlamydial organisms can be recovered from the cervix is increased as much as ten times in women using OCs. However, these hormonal agents produce an overgrowth of cervical tissue known as ectopy, which may simply allow the organisms to be present in greater numbers. Any condition that increases cervical ectopy has been found to increase the incidence of cultures positive for chlamydia. What is unknown at present is whether these individuals have an increased risk of developing infection of the upper genital tract. As a result of these observations, it is currently assumed that the protection OCs offer against PID and resultant infertility is limited primarily to gonorrhea. Whether there is no protection or even an enhanced susceptibility to chlamydia in oral contraceptive users remains unclear.

Reproductive health risks. It is now well established that CT infections have a profound effect on reproductive health. In fact, this disease is currently believed to be more serious than all the other STD combined. There is also some new evidence that chlamydia, along with genital herpes and condylomata, may be implicated as cofactors in the development of cervical cancers.

In the adult female the most common manifestation of chlamydia is an inflammatory condition of the cervix known as mucopurulent cervicitis. This disease may occur in an acute form but much more often is chronic and asymptomatic. Of the women who have this condition, 10% will develop acute inflammation of the fallopian tubes; it has been estimated that between 20 and 60% of all PID diagnosed today is due to chlamydia. While the symptoms of chlamydia are similar to those seen with gonorrheal infections, they tend to be much milder.

The most dangerous types of chlamydial disease are the insidious infections of the fallopian tubes that are either entirely asymptomatic or cause symptoms so mild that women fail to seek medical care. These untreated infections can result in either infertility or ectopic pregnancy. When it was realized that chlamydia might be playing a previously unrecognized key role

in infertility, a number of studies were undertaken. It was found that 75% of patients with damaged tubes had increased levels of antibodies to chlamydia. Tubal disease is a major cause of infertility. Recent data indicate that 11% of women have involuntary tubal occlusion following one attack of PID; this number increases to 33% with the second attack and 66% with the third.

Chlamydia is now also believed to be a key contributor to the increasing incidence of ectopic pregnancy, a potentially very dangerous condition in which a pregnancy develops outside the womb. In the U.S. this condition has tripled in frequency in the past 20 years. These patients, too, have been found to have a high incidence of positive antibodies to chlamydia. The risk of developing an ectopic pregnancy is increased tenfold by one attack of chlamydial salpingitis (inflammation of the fallopian tubes). Each subsequent attack of PID further increases the accumulated risk.

A major concern about chlamydial infections is their possible impact on pregnant women. Surveys have shown a 10 to 20% prevalence rate of chlamydia in pregnancy, compared with a 1 to 2% rate of gonorrhea. The vast majority of these women are completely asymptomatic. Several recent studies have indicated that this organism may induce premature rupture of the fetal membranes, thereby increasing the number of premature births. It has also been noted that these infections may be associated with a greater risk of having a stillborn child. Moreover, there are data that indicate a neonatal death rate that is as much as ten times higher than normal.

While some studies have shown an increased likelihood of having a low-birth-weight infant when a woman is infected with chlamydia, others have not shown this association; thus, the connection remains unclear. If it is a factor, it is probably of concern only for those women who have recently acquired the disease, not for women who are chronically infected. Unfortunately, treating this quite small minority who have acute disease would not have any major impact

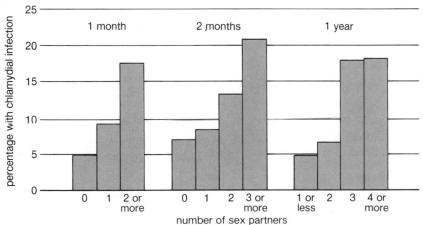

Chlamydia, an especially serious threat to reproductive health, is most likely to occur in women who have recently become sexually active and have multiple sexual partners. The graph at left indicates how infection rates rose with the increase in the number of sexual partners among young women treated at two urban clinics.

H. Hunter Handsfield *et al.*, "Criteria for Selective Screening for *Chlamydia trachomatis* Infection in Women Attending Family Planning Clinics," *JAMA*, vol. 255, no. 13 (April 4, 1986), pp. 1720–34

on the overall incidence of low-birth-weight babies—a major and serious current obstetrical problem in much of the world today.

It has further been established that CT can be transmitted to a baby during the process of delivery Within the first two weeks of life, between 40 and 50% of babies born to mothers with this disease will develop conjunctivitis (an eye infection), and 4 to 10% of the babies will develop pneumonia. In newborns both of these infections generally are not serious and will resolve without active therapy.

While all women need not be screened for CT, it is currently recommended that all pregnant women have routine cultures taken. Any woman, pregnant or not, who is at high risk or who has cervicitis or urethritis should be evaluated and treated if she is found to harbor the organism. In one study it was shown that erythromycin treatment of infected women at 36 weeks of pregnancy prevented the development of eye infections in their newborns but had minimal effect on the incidence of infant pneumonia.

Two other possible associations of CT and pregnancy have been found. The first is the occurrence of the infection late in the postpartum period, up to two weeks after delivery; the second is after elective abortions, when the CT organisms may cause PID in 20% of women.

Diagnosis and treatment. It was very difficult to diagnose chlamydia in the past. The diagnosis is best made by culture, but this is expensive and not always available. There are a number of new techniques now becoming available and others under study that may make the diagnosis simpler and more accurate in the future. While CT infection has been suggested by Pap smears, it is now clear that the Pap smear alone cannot be used as a definitive means of diagnosis.

Antibiotic treatment of chlamydia with either tetracycline or erythromycin is effective, but therapy must take into consideration the fact that almost half of the individuals who have chlamydia also have gonorrhea (which may be resistant to these drugs). In the past, women with both infections were often diagnosed and treated for gonorrhea, but their chlamydia went undiagnosed and untreated and therefore produced considerable damage to their reproductive tracts. For this reason patients with either one of these diseases should receive therapy for both.

Genital warts: neglected STD in both sexes

Genital, or venereal, warts, also known as *Condyloma acuminata,* are caused by the human papillomavirus (HPV). As many as 46 distinct human papillomaviruses have been identified; 12 of them have been associated with lesions of the genital tract. Genital warts are generally painless fleshy growths that may occur in clusters and have a cauliflower-like appearance. However, although the virus was identified by means of electron microscopy in 1969, it has been only in the past decade that the actual significance of these lesions has become increasingly evident and consequently more ominous. The prevalence of this disease has been increasing in both men and women, in some areas reaching epidemic proportions. The actual incidence is unknown, mainly because, like chlamydia, approximately 75% of the cases are asymptomatic, but it is currently estimated that between 2.5 and 10% of women under the age of 30, and approximately 3% of pregnant women, have this infection. Twice as many men are affected. The U.S. National Disease and Therapeutic Survey, based in Washington, D.C., reported that office calls to private practitioners concerning genital warts increased 460% from 1966 to 1981, from 169,000 to 946,000.

Workers in the STD field believe that these infections have not received an appropriate amount of attention, given their serious implications. This neglect is unfortunate because over one million new cases of genital warts will probably occur in the U.S. alone each year. Previously these lesions were regarded somewhat casually and were considered primarily as a nuisance. Continued research into their behavior, however, has shown them to be considerably more dangerous than had been thought. Papilloma infections are extremely difficult to treat and can cause extensive damage and even death. In addition, under the stimulus of pregnancy the warts may become greatly enlarged and actually obstruct a vaginal delivery.

It has been estimated that the period of incubation for genital warts infections ranges from 3 weeks up to as long as 18 months, the average time being approximately 3.5 months. The infectious particles are transmitted during sexual intercourse and are highly contagious, although there are fewer viruses present in older genital warts. Therefore, the diagnosis of condylomata in an individual clearly indicates the need for evaluation of all sexual partners. It is particularly important to evaluate the male partners of women who have these lesions because 60% of them will be found to have penile condylomata.

The same factors that place a woman at high risk for many other STD—young age, low socioeconomic status, multiple sexual partners or partners with multiple sexual contacts, and partners who have or are at high risk for STD—place her at increased risk of acquiring the papillomavirus.

These organisms prefer and grow best in an environment that is moist and warm. Therefore, the skin of the perineum, the area around the anus, the vagina, and the cervix—all of which can be traumatized during intercourse, allowing the entrance of the virus—are the most common sites for this infection. The viruses, however, are not exclusively confined to the genitals; they also may invade the urinary tract, including the urethra, bladder, and kidneys, causing bleeding, infection, and actual obstruction to urinary outflow. In addition, they may occur as far away from the pelvis as the nipples, lips, oral cavity, cheeks, esophagus, and skin. When the virus involves the reproductive tract, HPV can also be transmitted to an infant by an infected mother during delivery, with the child later developing papillomas of the larynx. This condition has recently been renamed pulmonary papilloma, since the lesions have been found to extend well down into the child's lungs.

In men genital lesions occur in specific anatomical areas depending on the sexual practices of the individual. In heterosexual men warts are found most often on the genitals. However, in homosexual men they are most frequently noted in or around the anal canal.

A cancer risk. The 12 different subtypes of HPV that have been associated with genital warts have different potential effects. Two subtypes of papillomaviruses have been found to be associated with genital tumors that are essentially benign. A source of major concern in recent years, however, has been the growing evidence that as many as four of the other subtypes are associated with neoplastic (cancerous) change, some of the lesions ultimately developing into frank malignancies.

In homosexual men the presence of anal condylomata is associated with 25 to 50 times the increased risk of the subsequent occurrence of anal cancer. In the female the cervix is the organ at highest risk. Changes have been observed to occur over a period of months to years, progressing from benign lesions to precancerous conditions, finally ending with invasive carcinoma. It has been estimated that a woman who has condylomata has up to 2,000 times the relative risk of developing invasive squamous cell cancer of the cervix. It has recently been shown that HPV is the most frequent cause for abnormal Pap smears. In recent studies between 1.2 and 10% of smears showed early neoplastic changes that were later confirmed to be due to this virus. The presence of HPV increases fourfold the risk of the precancerous condition known as cervical dysplasia. This potentially dangerous lesion is becoming progressively more common in younger women, probably owing to their earlier sexual activity and increased numbers of sexual partners.

It is currently believed that HPV alone will not produce cancer. However, in conjunction with another infection—particularly herpes simplex virus type 2 or chlamydia—or exposure to X-rays, HPV may stimulate the growth of a malignancy.

New treatments. As the seriousness of this STD became more apparent, an increased amount of attention was given to attempts to find a therapy that would consistently eradicate genital warts. In the past multiple therapies were used; primary among these was the local administration of podophyllin, which has a caustic effect. More recently the topical application of agents such as the antimetabolic cytotoxic agent 5% fluorouracil cream, which disrupts the infectious process within cells, has been employed.

Numerous surgical approaches have been tried, including local excision, cryotherapy, electrocautery, and electrosurgery. Most recently the carbon dioxide laser has been used successfully in treatment; it has the advantage of being relatively bloodless surgery, with rapid healing and a high success rate. The equipment is quite expensive, however, and requires surgeons with special training. While chemical agents should not be used in the treatment of pregnant women, cryotherapy has been found to be safe and effective, often eliminating the need for cesarean delivery. The U.S. National Cancer Institute is studying interferon as a form of therapy, but early results look only moderately promising.

It is now generally appreciated that ridding the body of the papillomavirus is not a simple matter; recurrence rates are in the neighborhood of 20%. Recent studies have indicated the probable reason for this: the virus has often been found in normal-appearing skin immediately adjacent to the warts. In one study all of the individuals who had a recurrence within three to six weeks after therapy were found to have residual virus. Therefore, it is clear that a wider area must be treated at the time of the original therapy.

Above all, patients should not assume, even if it appears that their genital warts have been adequately treated, that they are free of the disease, that they may not ultimately develop a malignancy, or that they cannot transmit the disease to another individual. In fact, it would appear that all individuals who have ever had genital warts must be followed very carefully for the rest of their lives.

As the STD epidemic grows

The alarming increase in STD today—and certainly the emergence of the deadly disease AIDS—is beginning to cause what may be a reversal of the sexual revolution. It appears that the sense of urgency resulting from the epidemic is spurring a new movement toward safer sexual practices—with increased motivation to use condoms and other barrier methods of contraception and to have fewer sexual partners. There is evidence of this change in homosexuals and heterosexuals. Furthermore, it is now recognized that even young school-age children should be educated about sexual matters in a frank manner. Additionally, it is now clear that men and women from all socioeconomic classes are at risk. Because women tend to have more severe complications from many common STD, it is in women's interest to take the lead in primary prevention. As the incidence of and alarm about STD increase, clear changes in societal mores and practices seem inevitable.

—*Elizabeth B. Connell, M.D.*

Choosing a Child's Sex: Possibilities and Problems

by Raphael Jewelewicz, M.D.

The desire to determine the sex of one's offspring is as old as recorded history. Folkloric notions exist in many cultures about ways to bring about sex preselection; none has been proved, and most are harmless. Methods for sex preselection were described in Greek mythology, the Bible, and the Talmud, but it is difficult to assess them because, as one would expect, given nature's sex ratio, approximately half of all methods practiced yielded the desired results. Generally, among humans and many other animal species, the average sex ratio at birth is 105 males to 100 females. However, it is also true that females live longer than males. The death rate from the time of birth is higher for males than for females in many species. In humans the average length of life for males is about five years less than for females. Consequently, toward the end of the human life-span, the sex ratio shifts to a preponderance of females versus males.

Renewed interest in preselection of gender is influenced by economic, cultural, and personal factors, but the current approach is more scientific and promises better results. If sex preselection were possible, however, it could have far-reaching social, demographic, and genetic consequences.

Medical indications for sex preselection

Approximately 200 genetic diseases are known to be sex linked. Many of these are fatal or result in lifelong deformities, retardation, major health complications, or severely compromised life and well-being. Among the more common are hemophilia, glucose-6-phosphate-dehydrogenase deficiency, several types of muscular dystrophy, and retinitis pigmentosa. Sex-linked genetic diseases can be prevented if the child is of the unaffected sex. Thus, by preconceptional sex selection, the problems involved in rearing an affected child can be avoided.

The ability to influence the sex ratio in domestic and laboratory animals as well as in humans is not only of academic interest but of considerable clinical, practical, and economic value. Since sex is determined by the spermatozoa, various techniques of separation or enhancement of X- or Y-bearing spermatozoa have been studied. Separation techniques involve sophisticated laboratory procedures, manipulation of sperm outside the body (in vitro), and artificial insemination of the female eggs. Enhancement—"natural manipulative" (in vivo)—methods include coital timing in the menstrual cycle, manipulation of cervical mucus pH, and special diets. To be clinically applicable, any methods must assure the integrity, quality, and fertilizability of the sperm. Methods that may damage the sperm in any way are, of course, not acceptable.

In vitro methods for sperm separation

As early as 1932 it had been found that when rabbit spermatozoa were placed in a vessel with an anode and a cathode (cells with positive and negative electrical charges), the X sperm migrated to the anode and the Y to the cathode. Insemination of rabbits with sperm separated in this manner resulted in 80% of the offspring being of the expected sex. However, further and more sophisticated studies failed to distinguish any differences in surface electrical charges between X and Y spermatozoa.

In 1969 researcher Love Zech at the Karolinska Institute in Stockholm discovered that the long arm of the Y chromosome, but not the X chromosome, could be stained with a kind of hydrochloride (quinacrine hydrochloride), thus enabling visual differentiation of X and Y sperm. This new technique made it possible to evaluate objectively the various methods of sperm separation before insemination.

Then in 1973 Ronald J. Ericsson, then at the Schering Co. laboratories in West Berlin, reported a method of separation of X and Y spermatozoa based on differential centrifugation techniques and migration of the sperm through progressively denser solutions of a liquid bovine serum albumin (6, 10, and 20%). Samples containing up to 85% Y spermatozoa were recovered from the higher (20%) bovine albumin fraction. This method, which was patented by Ericsson, or its modifications are used extensively today for sex preselection. The latest modification is the use of human serum albumin instead of bovine serum albumin. Clinical trials with the Y fraction resulted in 75–79% male babies. The method involves treatment of sperm and artificial insemination with the X or Y fraction. When this sperm-separation technique was used in combination with quinacrine staining, it was discovered that men who had three or more daughters produced a lower number of Y spermatozoa.

Another method of sperm separation was reported by Omer P. Steeno, an endocrinologist at University Hospital, Louvain, Belgium. By a special laboratory method, sperm suspended in solution were filtrated, and the X spermatozoa were increased to 74% in the final fraction. Thus, this method is suitable for X-sperm enrichment in order to conceive a female offspring.

In 1982 James F. Daniell and colleagues at Vanderbilt University, Nashville, Tenn., reported a method of so-called convection counterstreaming galvanization for separating X and Y spermatozoa. Prepared semen was placed in a specially designed apparatus through which an electric current was run. After separation the anode-collected (positive-charged) fraction contained an average of 77% Y spermatozoa and the cathode (negative-charged) fraction an average of 76% X spermatozoa. Thus far this method has not been tested clinically.

In vivo methods for sex preselection

Direct, nonlaboratory methods of preselecting sex—in living bodies of animals and humans—have also been investigated. In 1954 Sophie J. Kleegman, of the department of obstetrics and gynecology at the New York University School of Medicine, reported the effect of timing of coitus on the sex ratio in 150 births following a single exposure in the cycle of conception. When insemination occurred at the time of ovulation, as judged by the basal temperature, 80% of babies born were male. When insemination occurred 48 hours prior to ovulation, there was an 80% preponderance of female offspring. This study had no controls, and the evidence of time of ovulation was based on the basal temperature only.

In 1960 Landrum B. Shettles, then an assistant clinical professor of obstetrics and gynecology at Columbia University's College of Physicians and Surgeons, New York City, reported that two different structural types of human sperm could be distinguished: large, oval-headed sperm that correlated with the X chromosome and smaller, round-headed sperm that correlated with the Y chromosome. Shettles also reported that males from families that had only male offspring for several generations tended to produce higher proportions of the smaller, round-headed sperm, while males with several female offspring produced a preponderance of larger, oval-headed sperm. These findings, however, have been strongly disputed by other investigators. Shettles speculated that the smaller, Y-bearing sperm, which have less mass, may move faster in the cervical mucus than the heavier, X-bearing sperm, while the X-bearing sperm may survive longer. On the basis of these assumptions and certain observations about the cervical mucus—*i.e.,* at ovulation the cervical mucus is copious, alkaline, and of low viscosity, while preovulatory mucus is more acidic, sparse, and less favorable to sperm—Shettles suggested certain practices that may favor one type of sperm or the other and enhance natural preconception selection of gender.

According to his method, a couple wanting to have a male should follow the following practices: (1) sexual abstinence prior to ovulation, with intercourse occurring at ovulation time only; (2) a water and baking soda vaginal douche used by the female partner prior to intercourse (two tablespoons of baking soda to one quart, or one liter, of water); (3) female orgasm timed either simultaneously with or before the male; (4) deep penetration by the male at the time of orgasm, thus assisting the faster, smaller sperm (Y bearing) in entering the cervix more quickly; and (5) vaginal penetration from the rear to help ensure deposition of sperm at the cervix.

Practices, according to the Shettles method, favoring female offspring include: (1) no abstinence, except

George Gerster—Photo Researchers

In China, where one-child families are a top priority, chorionic villus sampling (which determines sex at eight to nine weeks' gestation), followed by pregnancy termination when the fetus is of the undesired sex, has been used with high success. While male babies were previously the most highly desired, today female children are also esteemed—indeed welcomed—by parents.

Accurate methods of gender preselection are likely to become available in the near future so that parents will be able to determine the sex of their children with a high degree of certainty. How will this affect family composition? In the U.S. surveys have shown that a vast majority of couples prefer a two-child family, with a son as the firstborn and a daughter as the second child.

intercourse should stop two to three days before ovulation; (2) intercourse is preceded by an acid vaginal douche (two tablespoons of white vinegar per quart of water); (3) no female orgasm; (4) shallow penetration by the male at the time of ejaculation, presumably to help the heavier, X-bearing sperm survive; and (5) face-to-face intercourse.

Shettles reported that when these methods were used, 22 attempts at conceiving a male offspring resulted in 19 successes, and 19 attempts at conceiving a female offspring resulted in 16 successes. Others who followed his suggestions could not repeat his results, however. To date there have been no large-scale, well-controlled studies that could confirm his recommendations as being valid ones. Another investigator, Robert H. Glass of the department of obstetrics and gynecology at the University of California at San Francisco, studied the effect of pH on sperm motility by allowing sperm to migrate into capillaries containing media of different pH. The results contradicted Shettles's, and Glass concluded that the motility of Y-bearing sperm is not influenced by the pH of the media.

Can diet influence gender?

A possible connection between diet and the sex of offspring has been postulated throughout history and may be found, among other places, in the Chinese yin-yang philosophy. Animal studies have suggested that variations in the relative concentrations of sodium, potassium, magnesium, and calcium may affect the sex ratio at birth in various animals and humans. Studies in frogs demonstrated that when tadpoles were raised in a balanced solution (Ringer's type), the male-female ratio of the resulting frogs was 1:1. When potassium was increased in the solution, 70% were males, while when calcium or magnesium or both were increased, 70% were females. An experiment carried out in cattle in France in the late 1960s demonstrated

that a balanced diet resulted in equal numbers of male and female calves. When the diet was rich in alkaline earth elements, the proportion of females was higher. In 1980 Joseph Stolkowski at the Centre Hospitalier in Puteaux, France, applied the same principles to humans. A diet rich in potassium and sodium, including sausage, meat, potatoes, beans, artichokes, peaches, apricots, and bananas, and excluding calcium-rich foods such as dairy products, eggs, and greens, produced mostly boys, while the opposite, a diet rich in calcium and vitamin D, produced mostly girls. The treatment was started at the beginning of the first menstrual cycle in which conception was desired and continued until pregnancy was confirmed (a minimum of one and a half cycles). There were no restrictions regarding the timing of intercourse. The success rate—*i.e.*, conception of a child of the preferred gender—was 81–86%. Although several similar studies have been reported, the number of cases involved is quite small. No large-scale, adequately controlled studies have been done to substantiate the effect of diet on sex preselection.

Gender selection after conception

Another possible method of gender selection is determination of sex after pregnancy has been established, with termination of pregnancy when the conceptus is of the undesired sex. At present, sex can be determined by placental sampling, known as chorionic villus sampling (CVS), at as early as eight to nine weeks' gestation. This method has been widely used in China, where birth control is a top priority and there is a nationwide campaign to limit most families to one child. A recent Chinese study reported 93% accuracy in 100 cases where fetal sex was determined through CVS within the first six to eight weeks of pregnancy. Fetuses of the undesired sex were then aborted. It should be noted that in China male children

378

were traditionally regarded more highly than females, a preference that came into conflict with the one-child limit and encouraged fetal sex selection. Today, however, females are also held in high esteem, and the practice of sex selection favoring males is probably declining. This method may not be acceptable in the United States and in many other countries, especially Roman Catholic nations, where abortion is prohibited or controversial. The method is, nevertheless, a practicable one.

Attitudes and ethics

Undoubtedly within a few years, safe, accurate techniques for gender preselection will become available, and parents will be able to determine the sex of their children with a great degree of certainty. When combined with other techniques of family planning, sex preselection will make it possible to realize the "ideal" family with respect to spacing, number, and sex composition. Demographically, three important population variables could be influenced: family size, gender of the firstborn child, and sex ratio.

If sex-selection techniques were available, to what degree would they be employed? Demographic studies in Asia and the Far East indicate that parents prefer a male child who will carry on the family name and provide for the parents in their old age. And in agricultural societies, a male is prized more than a female.

Studies in the U.S. in the 1960s also indicated a preference for boys as the firstborn. A survey of unmarried college students in 1964 revealed that if a couple were to have only one child, 91% of men and 66% of women would prefer a boy. In 1968 Amitai Etzioni of Columbia University hypothesized that the availability of sex preselection would increase the sex ratio of male children in the U.S. by 7%. Extensive studies in 1970 and 1975 revealed that most U.S. couples preferred a son as the firstborn and a daughter as the second child, while at the same time, there was a clear preference for a balanced sex composition within the family. Thus, presumably, if sex preselection were to be practiced widely, initially there might be an increase in the ratio of males, but later the sex ratio would balance out. Except for the firstborn, there is no strong son preference in the U.S. Many couples indicated that they would not use sex preselection for their first child but, rather, would use sex preselection for the second child in order to achieve a balanced family. The majority of women in the U.S. did not approve of control of sex of their offspring. Thus, it would appear that the use of sex preselection methods would have little overall effect on the sex ratio of the population in the U.S., but it might have different results in other parts of the world.

A method for sex preselection with high probability of success was recently reported from Japan, where medical ethicists expressed concern about a high tendency to choose male offspring if use of the method were allowed. The technique utilizes separation in a centrifuge of sperm that carry X chromosomes and those bearing Y chromosomes. On egg fertilization in vitro, the X sperm produce females and the Y sperm males. The technique's developers, led by Rihachi Iizuka at Keio University, Tokyo, claim a 95% success rate in producing females and 85% success in producing males (because Y-carrying sperm are more difficult to separate). The ethical controversy focuses on apparently unauthorized and indiscriminate use of the technique. Guidelines were set by a Japanese medical ethics advisory committee limiting the procedure to use to avoid hereditary and sex-linked disorders. The guidelines are not legally binding, however, and physicians who are familiar with the method can continue to use it if there is public demand.

The ability to predetermine gender may have far-reaching social and economic consequences. It could lower the birthrate and limit family size to two children—one of each sex. It has been speculated that societies that prefer male offspring may regress to "frontier-like" social practices. Some predict lower moral standards and even increased lawlessness—possibly increased prostitution and male homosexuality as well as disorganization of marital norms. However, these are speculations; no one can really predict the outcome. Alaska, with a male/female ratio of 132:100, has no increase in criminality or homosexuality.

The last point that should be discussed is the acceptability of the method of sex preselection. The most successful methods are likely to require laboratory manipulation of the sperm and artificial insemination, however objectionable these procedures may seem to the public. Coital techniques or other "natural manipulative" methods are not ultimately reliable. The latter is true of gender-choice kits that have recently been marketed in the U.S. These kits consist of a three-month supply of disposable thermometers to measure basal temperature changes that indicate ovulation, vaginal mucus sampling materials, and instructions for timing and style of intercourse, use of douches, etc. The kits, which sell for about $50, have been investigated by the U.S. Food and Drug Administration, which has found them to be "a gross deception of the consumer." The agency maintains that the method promoted for choosing gender is not supported by adequate scientific data.

Access to sex preselection may not be uniform either across or within cultures. In any given nation, couples in different social classes may not have the same opportunities to exercise the option of gender preselection. From published social surveys, it is evident that economic progress and the level of education are important factors. In addition, many ethical and legal questions will be raised for which, at present, society has no answers.

Smoking

The terms nicotine addiction and tobacco dependency may sound a bit dramatic when used to describe an act as common as cigarette smoking, yet since the late 1970s a great deal of research has focused upon the addictive nature of nicotine to explain smoking behavior. The U.S. National Institute of Drug Abuse lists four criteria that define a drug as having dependency-producing potential; the substance must (1) be psychoactive, (2) produce objectively defined euphoric effects, (3) be biologically reinforcing (have the ability to establish and maintain compulsive ingestion), and (4) be characterized by a tendency for users to relapse after successfully stopping for a time. According to research that was conducted in animals and humans, nicotine meets these criteria. Any smoker who has tried to quit can attest to the strength of this dependency.

Until recently, people who tried to stop smoking and failed were said to lack willpower. The tobacco industry reinforces this idea by referring to smoking as a personal choice. The 1981 U.S. surgeon general's report on the health consequences of smoking, however, states that one of every three adult smokers tries to quit each year, yet 80% return to smoking. This relapse rate is similar to the rates for other highly addictive drugs.

Viewing cigarette smoking as only an addiction to nicotine, however, is also inaccurate. If smoking behavior were a matter of nicotine addiction only, substitution of nicotine in other forms would have a better chance of resulting in all people's quitting. Unfortunately, the most recent research on nicotine replacement has failed to document this effect. Thus, smoking must be seen as a complex behavior based upon an addictive substance but accompanied by powerful psychological rewards.

The undisclosed facts

Despite the fact that over 20 years have passed since the initial U.S. surgeon general's report in 1964 warned of the dangers of smoking, tobacco use continues to be a part of life. Statistics on the risk of smoking are numerous, and the widely publicized list of diseases attributed to tobacco use is expanding.

The public, however, is too often protected from the reality of death by tobacco use. Obituaries rarely refer to smoking as the cause of death but cite such problems as heart attack, emphysema, or lung cancer. The public hears about the high numbers—about 50,000 people each year—who die in motor vehicle accidents. Seven times that number, 350,000, die prematurely each year as a direct result of cigarette smoking, yet this news is hidden. The Worldwatch Institute concluded in 1986 that "tobacco causes more death and suffering among adults than any other toxic material in the environment." Worldwide, the cost in lives is now estimated at 2.5 million per year.

Aside from the thousands who die each year, millions of people live disabled by heart or lung diseases as a result of smoking. While loss of life and disability are critical social costs, the economic impact of tobacco use in the U.S. is also substantial. An estimated $25 billion is spent each year in direct medical care costs related to smoking. Much of this cost is paid for by businesses through health insurance premiums. Smoking's impact on absenteeism, productivity, and indoor air quality have also made it a major corporate concern. Marvin Kristein, a noted health economist, estimates that each smoker costs business at least an extra $350 per year.

Millions of Americans have quit smoking since the 1964 surgeon general's report. Some of the most dramatic reductions have been in middle-aged white males in general and in certain professional groups such as physicians. Not all health professionals have seen the same reduction pattern. Nurses, for example, still have high rates of smoking. In fact, a recent extensive study at the John Hopkins Medical Institutions found that nurses' smoking habits may interfere with patients' attempts to kick their own habits.

Since 1965 the percentage of the population who smoke has dropped from about 42% to slightly over 33%. There has been a gradual increase, however, in the average number of cigarettes per day consumed by those who continue to smoke. At the rate of 30 cigarettes per day and ten puffs per cigarette, the average U.S. smoker receives over 100,000 reinforcing blasts of nicotine a year. No other form of substance abuse is administered as frequently.

Social status has bearing on smoking habits. The rich and well educated have the lowest rates. The highest rates are among minority populations and the working class. In young people, 8% of college-bound high school seniors are half-a-pack or more daily smokers, but among the non-college-bound 21% are regular smokers.

Current treatment methods

Five general categories describe efforts to help people quit smoking. These are (1) broad-based public intervention and information campaigns, (2) self-help approaches, (3) group programs, (4) individualized behavioral interventions, and (5) drug therapy. Each is described briefly below.

Public intervention and information campaigns. These are population-wide efforts to discourage smoking and help people quit. They include news coverage of studies citing the benefits of quitting and the dangers of continuing to smoke, publicity surrounding release of such documents as the surgeon general's reports, and events like the Great American Smokeout, sponsored annually by the American Cancer Society. Included in this category would be tax increases (which discourage consumption) and warning labels on the products.

To some extent mass media focus on smoking has resulted in a population that knows more consequences of smoking than it knows skills for quitting. To help rectify this, the National Cancer Institute, the American Lung Association, and the National Heart, Lung, and Blood Institute have sponsored televised smoking-cessation programs. As cable television expands, such approaches will likely increase. Recent studies suggest that mass media approaches to helping people quit may be the most cost-effective of all the traditional methods.

Self-help. Self-help approaches are consistent with the high value many people place on independence, free will, and self-control. This approach generally relies upon a manual or guide to help the smoker in the quitting process. Recently, videotaped programs have become available through home video outlets. These efforts call for a motivated smoker who is willing to follow a prescribed step-by-step program. Some of the programs require a high level of reading skill and therefore may not be appropriate for all groups. The self-help approach is one of the least costly methods and is often used as a first step by people who are not interested in attending group programs.

Group programs. Perhaps the best known approach to quitting smoking is joining a group of other smokers in a structured program. Most approaches consist of exercises and lectures aimed at giving the smoker skills for quitting and social support during the process. Participants analyze their own smoking behavior, examine the conditions under which they smoke, and identify alternatives to smoking. Many groups use record keeping as a method of detecting cues to smoking and of forming strategies for reducing the urge to smoke. Groups generally meet for four to eight two-hour sessions. Maintenance is achieved by follow-up sessions or telephone contact after the sessions have ended.

Individualized behavior modification. It has been relatively uncommon for smokers to seek help from professionals for individualized behavioral programs, although more stop-smoking clinics are opening, offering multidimensional therapies to individual clients and "guaranteeing" success. Individualized programs are a costly alternative but may be the only acceptable choice for some people. Quite often the techniques used in group programs are employed in the individualized approaches.

Drug therapy. The search for a drug to help smokers quit has been in progress for years. The ineffective practice of prescribing sedatives for people who complain of nervousness after quitting has declined rapidly. Since nicotine is the psychoactive drug that alone or in combination with other substances pro-

Mark Twain claimed that quitting smoking was easy— he had done it a thousand times. Staying *quit is the issue, however. Successful quitting is generally defined as total abstinence for one year.*

duces the desired effect in smokers, various nicotine substitutes have been tried. The most effective drug to use in cessation efforts, however, is nicotine itself, administered as nicotine gum or in other forms such as smokeless cigarettes that emit nicotine. In the U.S.S.R. pharmacologists have recently developed an antismoking drug called gambasine (from an isomer of nicotine obtained from a plant grown in central Asia). It tastes like nicotine but is 30 times less toxic. In the mouth it suppresses the desire to smoke. In preliminary trials more than 75% of those who used it in gum or tablet form reportedly stopped smoking.

Other approaches to smoking cessation include hypnosis, acupuncture, adjustable filters to reduce smoke consumption, yoga, exercise, and meditation. Aversive conditioning techniques, such as forced rapid smoking, being confined in a smoke-filled room while smoking, or imagining a painful or distasteful occurrence each time a cigarette is desired, are also used as part of many individualized or group programs. While it is convenient to classify smoking-cessation efforts into five categories, in practice, combinations of many of the above approaches predominate.

Success rates

One does not have to be an authority to know that success rates for quitting smoking are not high. Sadly, neither is the success rate of lung cancer treatment. What constitutes success? Mark Twain is well known for having boasted that quitting smoking was the easiest thing in the world—he had done it a thousand times. The issue, of course, is not quitting but *staying* quit. Claims of success attributed to various methods

Bonnie Vierthaler, artist and director of the Badvertising Institute, has exhibited a series of takeoffs on cigarette ads in schools and workplaces, at medical society meetings, and at the U.S. Senate Office Building.

range from zero to 100%. To assure standardization, major health organizations concerned with smoking jointly defined successful quitting as total abstinence from smoking for one year.

The problems in evaluating the success of various methods are considerable. Many studies are poorly designed or reported. Variations in group leaders' skills, poor descriptions of the target group (*e.g.*, whether they were all three-pack-a-day smokers, 20-year smokers, or teens with less than a year's smoking experience), and incomplete descriptions of what was done in treatment sessions are all factors that complicate evaluation research.

Despite these problems, however, a number of excellent evaluations have recently been conducted on self-help, group, and drug-assisted cessation programs. Self-help programs have reported success rates of nearly 20% after one year. Some group approaches have documented nearly 60% quit rates. Group or individualized programs supplemented by nicotine gum have demonstrated higher success rates than group programs alone. In general, smoking-cessation efforts are considered to be successful if they achieve quit rates between 20 and 40% after one year.

According to the available data, a few points are clear. Single-method approaches are rarely effective. Multiple methods of achieving and maintaining cessation are the most promising. Follow-up initiatives for at least four months after quitting may reduce relapse. Management of stress and emphasis on weight control are also important long-term success factors for many ex-smokers.

Nicotine gum

Few advances in smoking cessation have achieved the level of professional and public interest of nicotine gum. First used in the early 1970s in Sweden, the gum has been available on the U.S. market by prescription since 1984. It is one of the only prescription drugs advertised in the lay press. The sole U.S. producer, Merrill Dow, has undertaken a massive effort at professional and public education to assure that the gum, like any other drug, is prescribed and used appropriately.

Nicotine gum is clearly not the "magic wand" for solving the problem of smoking. The manufacturer is probably the most ardent proponent of the use of the gum as part of an organized behavioral program. In its literature on the product, the producer states: "It is emphasized that Nicorette (nicotine gum) is an adjunct to smoking cessation. Given the complex, strongly reinforced, conditioned response nature of tobacco dependence, a single stratagem will rarely suffice to overcome it."

While nicotine gum is not a panacea, impressive quit rates have been obtained when it is used in a behavior modification program. Quit rates after one year are one and a half to five times higher in the group receiving the nicotine gum, compared with the group receiving a placebo (gum without nicotine). Also, as an adjunct to individual physician counseling, nicotine gum is successful and cost effective, compared with other medical approaches. Long-term dependence on the gum does not appear to be a problem. Ironically, one needs a physician's prescription for the gum, but cigarettes may be purchased by almost anyone who has the $1.25 or more to spend on a package. The gum is not expensive; it costs about $20 for 96 pieces, but as the American Institute for Preventive Medicine has calculated, the pack-a-day smoker will spend $4,565 and the two-pack-a-day smoker $9,130 over ten years.

Taking cigarette addiction seriously

The past decade has seen dramatic expansion in the treatment system for substance abuse. Inpatient facilities (some hospital based), outpatient clinics, residential facilities, and halfway houses for the rehabilitation of alcohol- and drug-dependent patients are found throughout the United States and in other countries. Some facilities cater to the unique needs of special populations such as adolescents or women. These facilities are usually professionally staffed and managed. They employ a variety of techniques for addressing alcoholism and addictions to sedatives, barbiturates,

This woman is undergoing aversion conditioning to stop smoking. Every time she takes a puff on a cigarette, she receives a mild but irritating electrical impulse, delivered by a therapist who observes through a one-way screen. The impulses build unpleasant associations with smoking. The confined booth, the mirror in which the addicted smoker watches herself, the overflowing ashtrays, and the barrage of cigarette ads are meant to reinforce the ugly aspects of smoking.

opiates, and a variety of other substances. Licensing systems are established to assure that they meet generally recognized standards of care. In many U.S. states substance abuse counselors must undergo special training and are certified by a board of registration.

A number of states have recently required that substance abuse treatment services be reimbursed by group health insurance plans. This has helped to propel treatment for substance abuse into the mainstream health care system. The change has also brought with it new requirements for assuring quality care. Indeed, by removing psychological and financial barriers to care, these laws have opened the treatment system to many more addicted people. Reimbursement for substance abuse treatment in effect identifies the problem as the equivalent of heart disease, a broken leg, or appendicitis.

Absent from these recent advances in the substance abuse field is treatment for tobacco dependency. This situation exists despite the fact that nicotine is six to eight times more addictive than alcohol (when measured by the percentage of users who lose control of their intake).

Smoking-cessation programs, then, are not part of a system. No quality-control mechanism certifies that they are effective or reputable. Few, if any, insurance companies will reimburse smoking cessation as a covered service, and many programs may be prohibitively costly. What this means is that tobacco dependency tends to be viewed as different from, or less serious than, other forms of substance abuse.

The need for change is demonstrated by the following hypothetical case. An employee in a state where group health insurance offers substance abuse coverage can receive treatment for marijuana abuse from a certified provider and be reimbursed. If that employee seeks help for a three-pack-a-day tobacco dependency, he or she may have to pay for assis-

tance that is questionable at best in terms of quality. If the smoker fails to quit and eventually progresses to severe heart or lung disease, many health insurance policies still will not cover the cost of a smoking-cessation program as part of therapy but will cover the high costs of hospital, medical, and surgical treatment of the serious diseases that are a direct result of smoking.

In the United States the treatment of substance abuse has been shaped as much by political and moral forces as by scientific evidence of effectiveness. Among experts there are divergent perspectives on substance abuse. Some feel that the problem is internal to the individual; others proclaim that it is a by-product of social and economic conditions and failure to control access to drugs. Still others view the problem as one in which the special effects of the drug itself are damaging to a small number of vulnerable people. Each perspective leads to a different assumption about treatment. Public policy toward supporting substance abuse treatment has been rationalized by the need to prevent crime, to save middle-class youth, or to protect the moral fabric of the nation. Therefore, smoking is not treated as manifestly harmful. Despite recent substantial evidence of the harm caused by "passive smoke," it is argued that smokers are not a hazard to others when they are behind the wheel of a car. Nor do they enter a life of crime to support their daily habit.

Treatment for tobacco dependency is a relatively recent concept. The first documented smoking-cessation clinics were established in 1955 in Sweden; not until the early 1960s did similar clinics appear in the United States. Voluntary health agencies, the U.S. Public Health Service, religious groups such as the Seventh-day Adventists, and independent agencies such as the American Health Foundation were major forces in establishing the U.S. smoking-cessation efforts.

383

Smoking

While cessation efforts got a major boost with the surgeon general's report in 1964, public demand for the treatment of smokers was not overwhelming. Perhaps the lack of data on the social costs of smoking helped reinforce its image as an individual concern. Also, perhaps many less dependent smokers quit shortly after the surgeon general's report, thus giving the false impression that quitting smoking would be easy for anyone.

A new proposal

In light of the awesome health toll and the high social costs of smoking, which are borne by nonsmokers and smokers, why not open up the treatment system to address tobacco dependence? The treatment system has shown its ability to respond quickly and effectively to such "new" problems as phencyclidine (PCP, or "angel dust") and cocaine abuse. These problems, compared with tobacco dependency, involve a small percentage of the population. Why is there not such enthusiasm for helping users of a drug that kills 350,000 prematurely each year and costs the economy billions of dollars?

Some of those addicted to alcohol or "real" drugs may fail to see the logic in this proposal. However, it is precisely such a cavalier attitude that perpetuates the myth that tobacco dependence is somehow less serious than other drug dependencies. As one-third of the adult population smoke, tobacco dependence is clearly the most prevalent drug problem.

Because denial is a major barrier to seeking help for other drug problems, opening treatment facilities to a relatively stigma-free drug habit like tobacco could provide a sizable population with a safe first step for seeking help with other problems. Heavy drinkers are much more likely also to be heavy smokers. Some studies have shown this to be particularly true among women. Certainly there are priorities in treatment. In treating an alcoholic smoker, the alcoholism should be addressed first. But ignoring smoking as part of long-term treatment may simply be trading one health problem for another. The use of treatment facilities by a broader population could result in making treatment for those who need it consistently available.

Importantly, changes in treatment for tobacco dependency would also remove financial barriers by allowing health insurance reimbursement for the service. Before insurance companies would cover the costs, however, quality-control measures would be required, including reporting of treatment effectiveness and assurance of counselor competence. These measures also would help prevent smokers from spending huge amounts for dubious methods that only lead to failure.

Smoking could also be incorporated into many existing treatment programs. As mentioned before, some alcohol-treatment programs are specifically designed to help women. Although the reason is unknown, women have a more difficult time than men in quitting smoking. It is likely that the same targeted approach could especially help women smokers.

In addition, some benefits of mainstreaming tobacco-dependency treatment would accrue to society rather than the individual. The inclusion of tobacco in substance abuse treatment would send a clear message to young people about the seriousness of smoking and the difficulty of quitting. Further, an expansion of the advocacy groups for social action on all addictive substances is possible. There are strong social action groups for nonsmokers' rights and others addressing alcohol, but they rarely join forces or consist of the same people. In the extreme these groups argue about which dependency is worse. The power gained by joining these two movements against the two most damaging and costly influences on health would be considerable.

Countercurrents

Not everyone will rally behind this concept. Some smokers will rebel against being labeled tobacco dependent or addicted. While most people who have quit have done so without help, those continuing to smoke may, as a result of past failures, be more physically or psychologically dependent and more in need of assistance.

The substance abuse field itself may not endorse the concept. It could be seen as diverting attention and resources away from "real" drug problems or placing an extra load on an already overburdened system. No successful application of this idea will come about without additional resources. Implementation costs could be offset by funding through health insurance reimbursement or raising tobacco excise taxes, which would also reduce consumption.

Another possible criticism of the idea is that it threatens existing methods of smoking cessation; however,

Recent surveys indicate that some 80% of those who quit smoking resume the habit within a year— a relapse rate similar to those for other highly addictive drugs.

Relapse rates over time

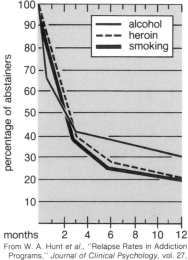

From W. A. Hunt *et al.*, "Relapse Rates in Addiction Programs," *Journal of Clinical Psychology*, vol. 27, no. 4 (October 1971), pp. 455–456

Mick Stevens © 1987 Hippocrates Magazine

SMOKING AREA OF THE FUTURE

the latter would continue to be offered but would compete with other systems on the basis of price, success rates, convenience, methods used, and, most importantly, patient preference. With more than 50 million current smokers in the U.S., there would be more than enough business for everyone. Proposing to expand the number of people providing a service is never popular with those already in the business. The public's best interest, however, must be the guiding principle.

The time has come

Until tobacco dependency is brought into the mainstream of substance abuse treatment, what will continue to be offered will often be simplistic appeals to the smoker's willpower. Physicians, who daily treat the consequences of smoking, must be primary advocates of increased services for patients who wish to stop. Laudably, the American Medical Women's Association, a group of women physicians with 10,000 members, recently launched a nationwide antismoking campaign aimed specifically at women and teenage girls. The effort focuses on women's health issues and the particularly high toll of deaths and illnesses among female smokers. Additionally, U.S. Surgeon General Everett C. Koop's call for a "smoke-free society by the year 2000" has become a positive unifying theme for the American Lung Association, the American Cancer Society, and the American Heart Association.

Employers, too, have a humanitarian and economic interest in helping their employees quit. Plainly and simply, employees who smoke cost more. Public health policymakers, the government, and the nonsmokers' rights groups who have successfully worked for legislation restricting smoking in such locations as workplaces, public buildings, and restaurants have a responsibility to help smokers quit. The latest data on the effects of environmental tobacco smoke on healthy nonsmokers confirm it as a health hazard, not just an annoyance. This information will increase legislation and pressure for more smokefree areas.

Smokers are the victims of a sophisticated industry that spends billions of dollars each year promoting the illusion that tobacco use is not a serious prob-

lem. Restricting tobacco use without assuring help to smokers who want to quit is unfair to the victims of a dependency-producing process that most initiated as teenagers.

Historically there has been a time lag between the recognition of a drug's addictive properties and action to curtail habitual use. It has been well over 30 years since the first reports in the scientific literature appeared linking smoking to health problems, 23 years since the first surgeon general's report on smoking and health, and over 30 years since the first organized smoking-cessation efforts began in Sweden. Now is the time for action.

—*Edward F. Miller*

Sports Medicine

The continued growth of the specialty of sports medicine in the United States reflects an increased demand for services by a nation apparently obsessed with fitness. Meanwhile, the field's scope has broadened to include not just prevention, diagnosis, and treatment of sports-related injuries but the entire gamut of activities related to exercise and fitness. Researchers have learned that regular exercise is associated statistically with avoidance of some diseases and with increased longevity, but they have changed their thinking about the intensity of exercise needed to produce those effects.

Recent technical advances in the field included successes in using synthetic materials to replace injured or destroyed anterior cruciate ligaments of the knee. During the past year subjects that raised controversy included the usefulness of preparticipation physical exams for preventing injury to youthful athletes and questions related to athletes' attempts to gain a competitive edge by tinkering with their bodies—for example, through steroid use and blood doping. Use of such techniques led to concerns about the need for drug testing—not only for steroids but for other potentially abused substances—among athletes. Yet another new controversy surrounds the recent publication of guidelines for exercise during pregnancy.

Pathogenic weight-control measures used by female athletes have been a concern for some time. This is not a problem that is restricted to girls and women, however; some male-dominated sports—such as wrestling—are notorious for the hazardous techniques participants use to "make weight" in lighter classifications.

Benefits of light to moderate exercise

Virtually every exerciser knows that the benefits of exercise, especially aerobic exercise, depend on the frequency, duration, and intensity of the activity. While it is easy to control frequency and duration, intensity is to a great extent dependent upon the type of exercise

385

From R. S. Paffenbarger *et al.*, Correspondence, *The New England Journal of Medicine*, vol. 315, no. 6 (Aug. 7, 1986), pp. 400–401

Added life from an active life-style* (Harvard alumni, 1962–78)

age at entry	days spent exercising	estimated days gained	estimated hours gained per hour of exercise
40	260	533	2.05
50	195	493	2.53
60	130	380	2.92
70	65	208	3.20

*active life-style = exercising 3 hours per week and expending at least 2,000 cal

one engages in. Running, cycling, and vigorous swimming clearly provide demonstrable aerobic benefits. Recently, however, researchers have found that other forms of exercise can also induce a training effect (defined as producing a sustained heart rate greater than or equal to 70% of maximal heart rate). Fast walking, for example, can produce a training effect even in people who already are fit.

Perhaps a more important issue is that of whether one must attain a training heart rate to derive general health benefits (as opposed to training-induced aerobic fitness) from exercise. The answer seems ever more clearly to be no. Activity, as distinguished from exercise, is what has been associated with increased life expectancy.

In 1980 the United States Public Health Service (PHS) published "1990 Objectives for the Nation," which included the expectation that 60% of adults 18–65 years old would "participate regularly in vigorous exercise"; *i.e.*, they would exercise for three times each week for at least 20 minutes at an intensity level that reached 60% or more of their maximum capacity. In response to more recent research, however, the PHS has altered its expectations; it proposed in 1985 that only 30% of the population would achieve the original goal, while others might well aspire to the same frequency and duration but would engage in less intense exercise, such as walking rather than running. To its original goals the PHS added the objective of encouraging more people to improve the nonendurance aspects of fitness such as flexibility, strength, and body composition.

This new emphasis on low-intensity activity may come as welcome news to those who try to improve the general fitness and health of the population. The belief that high-intensity work is necessary for any noticeable benefits to accrue has undoubtedly dis-

couraged some, if not many, people from even trying to improve their fitness. There is increasing evidence, though, that high intensity is not necessary for fitness, health, and longevity.

An ongoing study of mortality and longevity among more than 16,000 Harvard University alumni has found that subjects who expended only 2,000 cal of energy per week in normal activities such as walking and climbing stairs reduced their death rate from all causes by 28%. The risk of death continued to decline up to an expenditure of 3,500 cal per week, beyond which the trend reversed. This major study has been conducted and overseen by Ralph Paffenbarger of the Stanford University School of Medicine, who has noted that there are too many variables involved in the findings to consider either 2,000 cal a minimum or 3,500 cal an optimal weekly energy expenditure (although, on the basis of the research findings thus far, these numbers would appear to be reasonable guesses). Nevertheless, while there is no known "magic number" of calories that one must expend in order to promote longevity, the gradient clearly suggests that up to the as yet unknown limit, more activity is better than less as far as longevity is concerned.

It seems quite clear, therefore, that one need not push one's body to its limits to benefit from activity. A person who normally expends 1,000 cal per week in daily living can add 8–11¼ km (5–7 mi) of walking a week to get up to the 2,000-cal level. Most people could easily do that, for example, by walking instead

"Miriam keeps me young."

Drawing by Weber; © 1987 The New Yorker Magazine, Inc.

of driving on a few errands each week or by using stairs instead of an elevator.

It also is important to remember that the kind of vigorous activity that benefits the cardiovascular system may be detrimental to the musculoskeletal system. Where exercise is concerned, each individual requires his or her own prescription.

Finally, there is evidence that exercise, even at moderate levels, can slow or reverse some of the effects of aging. Some of the detrimental effects of aging may be related more to changes in behavior than to increased years. The Harvard Alumni Study seems to indicate that one's current level of exercise is more important than one's past level of participation; those alumni who became active later in life also decreased their mortality rates.

Blood doping

Blood doping, like steroid abuse, is one of a host of techniques that athletes obsessed with winning have devised in order to gain a competitive edge. Although the practice has long been deemed unethical, it was not until 1985 that the International and United States Olympic committees declared it illegal in response to the revelation that seven members of the U.S. Olympic cycling team (four of whom won medals, one a gold) had used the procedure in the 1984 summer Olympic Games in Los Angeles.

Blood doping—also known as blood boosting, blood packing, and induced erythrocythemia—involves transfusing additional red blood cells into an athlete's body in order to improve oxygen delivery and thus endurance. The usual procedure is to extract a quantity of the athlete's blood, separate and freeze the red cells for several weeks, and then reinfuse the red cells shortly before a competition, after the athlete's hemoglobin count has returned to normal.

The theory behind blood doping is as follows: In an elite endurance athlete, the number of red cells in the bloodstream increases, as does plasma volume. The increase in plasma volume is somewhat greater, so there is more blood, but that blood is thinner (a condition sometimes called "runner's anemia"). The increased red cell mass combined with reduced blood viscosity results in easier pumping of more red cells—and oxygen—to muscles. The athlete's maximal oxygen consumption and, therefore, performance improve. Presumably, if an athlete can artificially add even more red blood cells (blood doping) without increasing blood viscosity, he or she could improve performance even further.

There is reason to believe that competitive pressures have made blood doping a common practice among world-class endurance athletes for some time. (Indeed, "staying competitive" was one of the rationales used by the Olympic cyclists to justify their actions.) Unfortunately, it may remain widespread for

From A. J. Brien and T. L. Simon, "The Effects of Blood Cell Infusion on 10-Km Race Time," JAMA, vol. 257, no. 20 (May 22–29, 1987), pp. 2761–65

Effect of blood doping on performance

runner	race	race time at recorded intervals (minutes and seconds)			
		1,600 m	4,800 m	8,000 m	10,000 m (10 km)
1	1	5:00	15:49	27:02	34:02
	2*	5:03	16:01	27:24	34:32
	3†	5:03	15:32	26:18	33:02
2	1	5:00	15:32	26:21	32:51
	2*	5:01	15:31	26:13	32:42
	3†	5:00	14:59	25:16	31:33
3	1	5:00	15:45	26:40	33:30
	2*	5:00	15:49	26:49	33:37
	3†	5:00	15:20	25:50	32:20
4	1	5:01	15:21	26:00	32:31
	2†	5:00	15:00	25:00	31:12
	3*	4:59	14:58	25:02	31:14
5	1	5:14	16:09	27:16	34:09
	2†	5:03	15:31	26:13	32:48
	3*	5:03	15:32	26:13	32:51
6	1	5:07	15:56	27:05	33:46
	2†	5:00	15:31	26:28	33:04
	3*	5:03	15:33	26:26	33:03

1 = control time   *placebo
†red blood cell infusion

A recent study of six distance runners determined that the highly controversial practice of blood doping did in fact improve race times by approximately one minute in the ten-kilometer race. The table indicates times recorded at 400-meter intervals and at the end of the race.

some time to come; even though it is illegal, and has always been considered a form of cheating, it is difficult, if not impossible, to detect, and the fact remains that for the athlete, it does promise to provide that all-important "edge."

Laboratory studies bear out the theory behind blood doping. The performance of athletes tested in controlled settings does actually improve after infusion of preserved red cells. One controlled study implied that it might work, but it is unclear whether the subjects' improved performances resulted from blood doping, training, or placebo effects.

Whether the controversial practice works in competition is another matter. Not all athletes who resort to blood doping win medals, and some athletes who reject the practice do win. However, a recent study at the University of New Mexico, conducted under competitive rather than laboratory conditions, found that reinfusing blood did improve the subjects' times in ten-kilometer races. Furthermore, as long as winning is deemed to be everything in the eyes of athletes, and if they believe that blood doping can help them win, the practice is likely to remain a problem in the sports world until there are simple tests to detect it.

Drug testing

Drug testing of athletes takes two forms: testing for performance-enhancing substances such as steroids and testing for recreational drugs. Few would argue against the validity and importance of the former. Using chemicals to enhance performance is unethical, is in many cases illegal, and is often physically dangerous to the athlete. A sense of "fair play" as well as sound medical practice demand that abuse of performance-enhancing drugs be curtailed.

Testing athletes for use of so-called recreational drugs, such as marijuana and cocaine, is a more controversial matter, however. The highly publicized cocaine-related deaths of basketball player Len Bias and defensive back Don Rogers shocked the sports world and reinforced demands for mandatory drug testing for college and professional athletes.

It has even been suggested that athletes be subjected to genetic testing, on the grounds that some may be biologically susceptible to the potentially lethal effects of certain drugs. Presumably, an athlete who is at risk should know about it. The implication appears to be that athletes are a special class who are more likely than other people to fall into patterns of drug use and abuse and are more deserving of protection from self-destructive impulses or genetic imperfections.

While testing for performance-enhancing drugs is an exercise in ensuring fairness in competition, testing for recreational drugs raises numerous questions. Why, for example, is it more important to test college football players for cocaine use than to test members of the debating team, philosophy students, or the entire faculty? Some have argued that drugs will inevitably impair the performance of an athlete, and in a team sport this could subject teammates to unnecessary hazards. Even if this is true, however, should not the impaired performance, rather than membership on the team, be the criterion for testing? In a free society should an entire class of individuals be subjected to an invasion of privacy so that a few who may be acting illegally can be detected?

Some have also questioned the motives of those attempting to institute mandatory drug-screening programs for football and baseball players at the professional level. Do they want to protect the athletes from the deleterious effects of drug use, or do they want to protect the team owner's investment in the athletes? Is there a real concern for players (and for the devoted fans, many of whom are children, who may look to players as role models), or is the concern for what might happen to attendance figures if fans became disenchanted with their heroes (or if the heroes simply could not play up to expectations)? Clearly, it is tragic when an athlete suddenly dies from drug abuse. It seems no less tragic when a young scholar, an anonymous high school student, or anyone else dies from the same cause. There are serious questions about whether mandatory drug screening will solve the problem.

Exercise and pregnancy

Most pregnant women are as likely to benefit from regular exercise as any other subgroup of the population. Carrying a fetus imposes numerous changes on a woman's body, however, including increased heart rate and blood volume, greater joint laxity, and decreased respiratory reserve. Thus, like other groups with special physical needs (*e.g.,* children during their growth spurt, patients in cardiac care, the elderly), pregnant women need exercise guidelines that take into account the special needs and demands of their physical condition.

Pregnant women are likely to benefit from exercise; debate centers around how much and what kind. Guidelines have been issued by the American College of Obstetricians and Gynecologists; however, many of the recommendations have been criticized by sports medicine specialists and women. One controversial recommendation is that after the fourth month of gestation, women should not do any exercises while lying on their backs.

John Danicic, Jr.

The American College of Obstetricians and Gynecologists (ACOG) has produced just such guidelines. The guidelines suggest a program that includes a mild form of aerobic exercise. Prior to publication such a program was tested on a group of ten pregnant women and was refined on the basis of the women's reactions (e.g., complaints of discomfort or boredom).

Although generally well received, the ACOG guidelines have nevertheless generated controversy within the sports medicine community and among some women's groups. Some physicians feel that the guidelines are too general and fail to account for individual differences in fitness and ability. Other critics argue that they are not sufficiently challenging for women who are already physically active, while more conservative detractors think the guidelines may be *too* challenging for women whose life-styles have been largely sedentary.

In fact, the ACOG guidelines were designed for the average woman, who is neither sedentary nor an elite athlete. The "average woman," is, of course, an abstraction and may not exist in reality. Thus, it is important to remember that the guidelines are just that—guidelines—and not hard and fast rules. Most physicians, including those responsible for creating the guidelines, would agree that women should consult their physicians before exercising during and just after pregnancy and that exercise programs should be tailored to an individual's own needs and abilities. Those who established the ACOG guidelines seem to have intended them as merely a step in that direction.

Ironically, one of the more serious criticisms of the very existence of these guidelines is that attorneys may choose to interpret the guidelines otherwise, as a rigid standard of care. There exists a fear that a physician who prescribes an exercise program for a very fit and active woman, and who in the process advises activities exceeding the guidelines, could end up in litigation should the woman develop any problems with her pregnancy. If a court were to interpret the guidelines as representing a standard of care, the physician could be found liable for injury.

It is possible that the committee that developed the guidelines for exercise during pregnancy was cognizant of the danger of appearing to set standards for medical care in a litigious society, and that might explain partly why the guidelines are so general.

Because the guidelines are generalized goals, a pregnant woman should use common sense when she applies them. If she engaged in regular, intense exercise before becoming pregnant, she can probably continue, though in greater moderation. If she was basically sedentary, pregnancy is probably not the time for her to begin a vigorous running program. In any case, she should consult her physician, with whom she shares a common goal: to promote the health and well-being of both herself and the fetus.

"Making weight" is important to wrestlers. Unfortunately, many wrestlers, especially at high school and college levels, turn to hazardous weight-control methods that seriously jeopardize their health and strength.

Pathogenic weight control in males

The use of potentially health-threatening techniques for reducing weight typically has been associated with females, especially gymnasts, dancers, distance runners, field hockey players, and others engaged in strenuous physical performances. Pathogenic weight-control behavior is also common among some groups of males as well, most notably high school and college wrestlers.

Presumably, a wrestler will gain a competitive edge over an opponent by wrestling in a lower weight class than that for which his "normal" weight would qualify him. Unfortunately, wrestlers at the high school and college level most often turn to teammates, rather than to health professionals, for advice on "making weight" at a lower level. Too often the advice is simply to restrict food intake to perhaps 500 cal or less per day—a dangerous level that represents only one-third to one-fourth of what is required for a balanced diet for a competing wrestler. The athlete will thus starve himself prior to the weigh-in, despite solid scientific evidence that such diet restriction will reduce both strength and endurance.

In addition to restricting calorie intake, wrestlers may resort to dehydration to lose significant weight in the week before a competition. As a result, they may still be in a dehydrated state when they compete, even if they rehydrate immediately after the weigh-in and do not wrestle for five hours or longer. Like severe food restriction, dehydration can impair muscle performance; it can also reduce sweating and thus impair regulation of body temperature. This becomes especially dangerous when athletes attempt to accelerate weight loss by exercising in a sauna. Sauna heat can combine with the body heat generated by exercise to produce potentially dangerous—or even lethal—core temperatures of 40° C (105° F). Consequently, the American College of Sports Medicine recommends "prohibiting the single or combined use of rubber suits, steam rooms, hot boxes, saunas, laxatives, and diuretics to 'make weight.'"

Cutting weight is sufficiently ingrained in scholastic wrestling that, as is the case with other risky procedures athletes subject themselves to, it is unrealistic to expect it to disappear. Nevertheless, the team physician can play an important role by educating the coach—who probably has the greatest influence on the athletes—about safe weight and nutrition practices. Coaches can in turn educate student-athletes to the fact that starvation and dehydration threaten health and diminish performance, and they can encourage those athletes to accomplish weight loss by more sensible means, including sound diet and nutrition practices.

Other suggestions for promoting less perilous weight-control behavior include creating more weight classes, with smaller gradations between them, and allowing two or more wrestlers to compete in each of the middle levels, thus making weight cutting less attractive.

The long-term health effects of the practices described here are not known. It is certain, however, that cutting weight is unhealthy in the short term if it involves neglecting the nutritional needs of the athlete.

Better knee repair

Injuries to the anterior cruciate ligament (ACL), usually resulting from combined rotation and flexion of the knee, are among the most common leg injuries in sports. Downhill skiers who catch an inside edge, football players who are victims of clipping, and basketball players or gymnasts who land in awkward positions are among the athletes most susceptible to this type of injury. A torn or otherwise weakened ACL causes knee instability. This is not necessarily a problem for everyone, and surgery is done in only about one-third of the cases seen by orthopedists. The most likely candidates for corrective surgery are those whose livelihood might be threatened by an unstable knee—competitive amateur or professional athletes or such people as construction workers. Treatment of ACL injuries traditionally has involved the use of autogenous tissue; *i.e.,* tissue from elsewhere in the patient's body. Repair of an acute injury using autogenous tissue to augment the ACL is likely to heal well. In a bad injury autogenous tissue may be used to reconstruct the knee. The failure rate has been relatively high, however, because (1) the blood supply to the area is tenuous; if the ligament's blood supply is actually torn, healing simply cannot happen; (2) in some cases the tissues used for repair stretch after a time, thus reintroducing instability; and (3) the grafts used—from the patellar tendon, the semitendinosus, or the iliotibial tract—are only one-third to one-half as strong as the original ACL.

To counter the drawbacks of repair using live tissue, researchers have developed synthetic devices such as the Gore-Tex ACL Prosthesis. Made of the same material used in skiwear and rainwear, the prosthesis has two major advantages over autogenous tissue: it is two to three times as strong as a normal ligament, and its continued function is not dependent on blood supply to the ACL. Early clinical investigations reported device failure rates as low as 1.8%.

Another advantage is that use of a synthetic prosthesis may reduce rehabilitation time. A patient can begin physical therapy within a week to ten days (rather than the usual three months after a standard knee operation using human tissue) and may be able to return to a normal activity level within three months instead of in nine months to a year. Finally, the Gore-

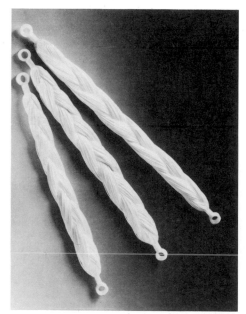

Damage to the anterior cruciate ligament, a common sports injury, can be repaired with the use of a braided synthetic prosthesis made of Gore-Tex. This method appears to have a number of important advantages over previous methods that utilized tissue from elsewhere in the body. The prosthesis comes in three standard sizes.

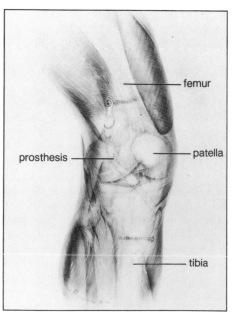

femur

prosthesis

patella

tibia

Photographs, W. L. Gore & Associates; illustration (right) Frederick Harwin

Tex material has been used for some time in vascular grafts and has an admirable safety record and, because it contains no living tissue, it can simply be removed if the ligament repair fails.

The Gore-Tex prosthesis was the first to receive U.S. Food and Drug Administration approval, but the number of other companies seeking approval for similar prosthetics testifies to the need for alternatives to autogenous repair. Nevertheless, many physicians argue that the decision to employ this type of repair is not one to be made lightly. Because the device is new, no one yet knows how it will withstand the ravages of time and use. Also, although no carcinogenic effects have been reported, some researchers consider this a potential problem. Finally, there is a possibility, though not serious, that pieces of such a device may wear off and migrate to other parts of the body. Like any other new technique for improving medical care, this one must be monitored closely until it has proved itself over time.

Preparticipation physical examinations

Parents, coaches, and school officials—not to mention school-age athletes themselves—have a strong interest in determining beforehand that a youngster's participation in sports will be safe and appropriate. Virtually everyone agrees that it is important to screen out students whose health or physical well-being would be imperiled by athletic activity and that some form of preparticipation physical exam can help accomplish this. There is considerable disagreement, however, about what such exams should include, how and at what intervals they should be administered, how comprehensive they should be, and how much they should cost.

As suggested, the most obvious purpose of these exams is to disqualify students for whom some or any athletic activities would be dangerous. Another purpose of testing is to discover problems that may not disqualify a student but do require special management in a sports environment. The choice of antihistamines for an allergic runner, for example, will differ from the management of allergies in a nonathlete. A third purpose of examining a child prior to sports participation is the prevention of injuries. If the examination reveals that a youngster is tight-muscled, stretching exercises can be prescribed to prevent pulls and tears.

Traditionally, the type of exam aimed at accomplishing these goals has involved an annual check of a student's musculoskeletal system combined with a quick look at the chest, abdomen, and (in boys) inguinal canals. Sometimes quantitative measurements are included—blood count, urinalysis, blood pressure—as are such sport-specific tests as examination of the eardrums of potential swimmers. If the results, combined with a brief medical history, show no abnormalities, the child is OK'd for participation.

This approach to the preparticipation exam usually works fine—in part because most children are basically healthy. Some physicians, however, believe that preparticipation exams should be performed less often but in much greater detail.

For example, another test that may be included as part of a preparticipation exam for adolescents—though in most cases it is not—is maturity assessment. This can be used to protect children by ensuring that those engaging in contact sports are matched according to their level of physical maturity and by determining when a given child is experiencing the growth spurt, which renders him or her more susceptible to injury. The most common approach to assessing maturity is circumpubertal evaluation. The technique involves use of the so-called Tanner stages (developed by and named after the physician J. M. Tanner), based on pictorial standards for genitalia and pubic hair rating in boys and breast development and pubic hair rating in girls. Use of the assessment technique can help ensure that children who are at widely disparate stages of physical maturity will not compete against one another. A coach who has been made aware that a student is in his or her period of fastest growth (Tanner stages 3 and 4 for boys, stages 2 and 3 for girls) can reduce the training load.

Cost is an important factor determining the content and frequency of preparticipation physicals. Relying solely on physical examinations to screen for disqualifying conditions can be very expensive since 1% or fewer of the children examined have such conditions. (One study of 763 children found significant problems in only 16 and disqualifying conditions in only 3.) The cost per child of identifying athletes with major problems could conceivably be in the thousands of dollars. Of course, some think that spending several thousand dollars to prevent a single major injury—or a death—is well worth the cost.

There are several approaches to the preparticipation physical. Often it is conducted annually; in some areas it is conducted biennially, and medical histories are taken in alternate years. A physical may be conducted when a child enters an activity; then, subsequently, medical histories are used to select only a few children for more detailed screening.

There are proposals for reducing the costs of protecting young athletes via preparticipation exams. One scheme would have children examined before their first year of participation, then at intervals of two, three, or more years. A written medical history would be submitted in nonexam years, and only the children with identified risks would be given physicals. (A 1980 study showed that the vast majority of disqualifying conditions show up on a history.)

Another approach is to perform mass screenings with on-site consultants in such specialties as orthopedics and internal medicine. This would save the

391

expenses incurred in referring to private physicians those children with suspected problems outside the examiner's area of expertise.

Sports medicine—here to stay

As mentioned at the outset, the field of sports medicine is continuing to grow; in the U.S. this is spurred by the national obsession with fitness and by a growing recognition of the beneficial effects of exercise on several medical problems.

As more people become involved in fitness-related activities—be they competitive or purely recreational— the number of injuries attendant upon participation increases as well. Sports medicine professionals thus see more patients and are stimulated to find more effective ways of rehabilitating injured athletes.

On the other hand, the medical community has discovered that an increase in the number of sports- and fitness-related injuries is only part of the picture. The other part is that patients are more fit and are reaping the rewards of that fitness: enhanced self-esteem, increased sense of well-being, and enjoyment. In addition, the medical community is discovering that exercise can prevent or ameliorate some problems and thus avoid drug therapy or surgery. In this sense sports medicine is part of preventive medicine, aimed at promoting health as well as, or instead of, treating sickness and injury.

—*Douglas C. Benson*

Surgery

The surgical treatment of disease progresses slowly and haltingly, with new and better approaches usually coming after years of careful development and evaluation. Much of surgical research is intended to simplify operations, to make them safer, to develop new techniques for presently untreatable problems, or on occasion to eliminate the need for an operation. In the treatment of breast cancer, for example, the recent emphasis has been on reducing the amount of body tissue surgically removed; with gallstones it has been on dissolving or disintegrating them without an operation; and with heart disease it has been on decreasing the need for coronary artery bypass grafts while encouraging a burgeoning new area of cardiac surgery.

Stones in the kidney and gallbladder

The treatment of kidney stones has undergone a revolutionary change in the past few years because of a device that pulverizes the stones with shock waves generated outside the body. Developed in Munich, West Germany, the apparatus, a lithotripter, makes use of a high-current, underwater spark discharge to produce powerful shock waves that can be directed and focused through a water bath in which a patient has been immersed. The shock waves pass safely

through the body, reach the stone, and fragment it into tiny pieces, which are then flushed out with the urine. The patient is anesthetized during the procedure and given hundreds to thousands of shocks over a period of as long as an hour. After careful experimentation in animals, this technique was first used clinically in Munich in the early 1980s. Today many centers in the U.S. possess lithotripters, and it is estimated that more than 90% of patients with stones in the upper urinary tract can be successfully treated with shock waves.

Following up on their earlier success, medical investigators in Munich then began applying the technique to the treatment of gallstones. They reported on animal studies in 1983, and by mid-1986 they had treated 14 patients with stones in either the gallbladder or the common bile duct. There were no adverse effects, and in 10 of the 14 patients the stones disappeared. Some patients reported pain when the small fragments passed into the duodenum. It also appeared possible or likely that the stones would recur in future years. At present it is estimated that only one of ten patients with gallstones would benefit from this approach, but the indications for its use may expand as experience is gained.

Work also continued on the possibility of dissolving stones in the gallbladder or common bile duct with solvents; *i.e.,* without a major operation. Early work using solvents such as chenodiol, taken by mouth, showed that such substances required a long time to dissolve stones and were often ineffective or associated with complications. An agent currently being evaluated, mono-octanoin, requires 3 to 21 days to dissolve cholesterol stones. Another solvent, methyl-tert-butyl ether, has been used in several patients to dissolve cholesterol stones in the gallbladder and in the common bile duct within a few hours; administration of this volatile liquid must be done through a catheter inserted through the skin into the gallbladder or the bile duct.

Cancer

Although malignant disease remains a vexing and catastrophic problem, medical researchers have made considerable recent progress in a number of different areas. Of particular importance have been the development and reporting of randomized clinical trials to compare the effectiveness of two or more treatments for the same affliction. Such trials also have allowed evaluation of multimodal (combination) therapy or adjuvant therapy (therapy that enhances the effectiveness of the primary treatment) for many kinds of tumors. The various options in multimodal therapy now include surgery to remove the tumor, radiation therapy, chemotherapy, hormonal therapy, hyperthermia, and immunotherapy.

Multimodal cancer therapy is presently being used against a number of difficult tumors, particularly of the esophagus. Cancer of the esophagus has been notoriously resistant to therapy because it is difficult to detect early, a problem that also raises the likelihood that by the time it is first treated, the malignancy has already spread. A combination of preoperative chemotherapy and irradiation for the common variety of esophageal cancer (squamous-cell carcinoma), by reducing obstruction of the esophagus, has allowed many patients to eat better until a successful operation to remove the esophagus and tumor could be carried out. Long-term results of this approach are promising. It is also being used for certain tumors of the lung and of the lower colon and rectum.

Several lines of surgery-related cancer research hold promise for the future. One is a tumor-locating technique that uses monoclonal antibodies labeled with a radioactive isotope. Appropriate monoclonal antibodies will bind preferentially to tumor cells, concentrating the isotope at the tumor site and allowing its detection by diagnostic radiology techniques. By means of genetic engineering, bacteria have been given the ability to produce in quantity a tumor necrosis factor that will be evaluated in the laboratory and in patients for its effects on tumors. The body carries certain populations of T cells, a type of white blood cell, that will attack tumor cells when activated by natural control factors in the blood called lymphokines. Referred to as cytotoxic, or killer, T cells, they have been shown effective in animal studies and have been used—with encouraging early results—in an initial clinical trial against metastatic solid tumors. With further development such presently experimental studies may one day reduce or even eliminate the need for certain types of cancer surgery.

Accidental injury

Accidental injury is presently the fourth most common cause of death in the U.S., exceeded only by deaths from cardiovascular disease, cancer, and stroke. It is the leading killer of those under age 40. Accidental injury is also a major killer on a worldwide scale.

Important advances in the care of accident victims have been made in recent years. These strides owe less to technological or clinical improvements and more to the development of an organized plan of care for the injured.

For treatment of the injured, several developments deserve emphasis. One is a sophisticated system of in-hospital care, a surgical intensive care unit for monitoring and treating critically injured patients. Another is the increasingly widespread recognition of life-threatening injuries and the need for their early diagnosis and treatment. These include injuries to the neck and spinal cord, which may quickly produce quadriplegia (paralysis below the neck) if not promptly and correctly handled; major blood vessel injuries; and bone fractures. Early, complete fixation of fractures by the surgical insertion of rods and other stabilizing devices has been shown to decrease the likelihood of complications and improve the chances of survival in patients with multiple injuries.

Half of all accident fatalities can be traced to central nervous system (head) injuries. Although progress has been made in treating such injuries, severe cases remain a problem and are best "treated" by prevention. Further development of passenger restraints in automobiles, including more effective seat belts, air cushions, and other devices; continued regulation of driving speed; and gun control should all lead to fewer deaths from injury.

Lasers

The highly directional and concentrated energy of laser light has been employed successfully in eye surgery for some years for treating retinal detachment, cataracts, and diabetic retinopathy. More recently, lasers have

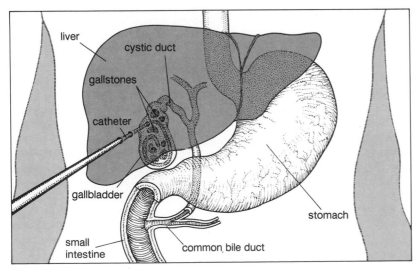

Gallstones are dangerous when they leave the gallbladder and lodge in the cystic and common bile ducts, blocking drainage. By injecting an ether solvent through a thin catheter, doctors have been able to dissolve cholesterol gallstones quickly without major surgery.

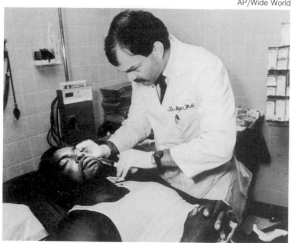

Sophisticated surgical intensive care is providing lifesaving emergency treatment and has greatly improved the outlook for accident victims.

been used to treat patients with diminished hearing from otosclerosis (a bony overgrowth of the stapes, one of the ear's tiny bones) or with small tumors of the larynx, vocal cords, or other parts of the throat. The laser's major advantage is its ability to reach and coagulate or remove lesions in otherwise inaccessible places. In thoracic surgery lasers have succeeded in opening cancerous obstructions in the lung and esophagus, which can then be attacked with chemotherapy and radiation. A new approach, photodynamic laser therapy, requires a special dye that accumulates selectively in the tumor. When a laser beam that is tuned to the proper frequency strikes the tumor, the dye absorbs most of the light energy, heating the tumor and destroying it. Laser beams are also being evaluated experimentally for opening blocked arteries both in the legs and in the coronary circulation.

Other uses of laser technology include repair of blood vessels and treatment of hemorrhoids, bleeding peptic ulcers, cancer of the rectum, gastrointestinal and vascular abnormalities, and various skin lesions. In fact, most surgical specialists (urologists, neurosurgeons, otolaryngologists, gynecologists, and general surgeons) now employ lasers for certain problems where tissue removal or destruction is needed.

Pediatric surgery

The practice of pediatric surgery has changed remarkably in recent years owing to the increased use of ultrasound in diagnosing congenital defects in infants before birth. Prenatal detection of such life-threatening defects as an omphalocele (herniation of the intestine within a thin membrane through the abdominal wall) allows the surgeon, the obstetrician, and the pediatrician to prepare a carefully planned sequence of delivery, resuscitation, and corrective surgery shortly

after birth. Medical research is revealing that a number of congenital abnormalities can damage organs or prevent their proper development as the fetus grows in the uterus. For example, an obstruction in the urethra, the outlet of the bladder, may put pressure on the kidneys and destroy them prior to birth. Doctors can now diagnose a urethral obstruction before birth and treat it by inserting a catheter through the abdominal wall of the mother into the bladder of the fetus to drain the urine.

Other types of fetal manipulation or operations are being studied experimentally. For example, a congenital defect in the left side of the diaphragm (Bochdalek's hernia) allows the intestines to move up into the chest and compress the left lung, preventing its normal development. Even though the hernia can be corrected after birth, the stunted lung reduces the likelihood of survival. If such a defect could be corrected in the uterus, the lung would develop normally, and the infant would have a much better chance of survival.

Newborn infants often develop respiratory failure because of immaturity or certain problems associated with delivery. A technique recently introduced in a number of medical centers assists such infants during the period following delivery and allows the lungs to rest and gain strength. In this technique, called extracorporeal membrane oxygenation (ECMO), blood is transported through tubes from the infant's body into an instrument that oxygenates the blood, removes carbon dioxide, and then returns the blood to the body, relieving the lungs of this function. The gas exchange takes place through a membrane in the instrument, obviating the need to expose the infant's blood to the outside world. Infants who have been treated with ECMO have shown improvement in two to seven days, although some have needed such support for as long as two weeks.

Colon and rectal surgery

Surgeons have devoted considerable effort in recent years to preserving the rectum and anus when it has been necessary to remove all or part of the colon because of inflammatory disease or cancer. For retention of the function of the lower portion of the rectum and the anus when the entire colon must be removed for such illnesses as ulcerative colitis or Crohn's disease (inflammatory bowel disease), reconstruction of a pouch of small intestine into a reservoir or connection of the lower portion of the small intestine—the ileum—with the rectum is required. Most patients would prefer surgical preservation of an intact gastrointestinal tract rather than a colostomy or ileostomy, which are surgically created openings of the colon or ileum on the abdominal wall. Such an operation, however, can produce complications, and results may not be totally satisfactory. Furthermore, if the disease process is chronic, such as in Crohn's disease, it may return or recur if the rectum is left in. In contrast, most patients receiving an ileostomy or colostomy can return to a normal and productive life, although some have continuing difficulty and are bothered by the presence of the opening on the abdominal wall and the need to wear a collecting bag. Continued evaluation and development of such techniques for improving gastrointestinal function, decreasing complications, and relieving the disease process are necessary.

As with carcinoma of the lip, squamous-cell carcinoma of the anus can be treated adequately by local surgery, particularly for small lesions. Combined therapy using 5-fluorouracil as a major drug along with mitomycin-C and radiation therapy for anal carcinoma has been quite successful. Thus, it is unnecessary to remove the rectum and anus for small squamous-cell cancers in this region.

Stroke

Strokes result most commonly from the partial or total blockage of blood vessels in the neck or within the skull that supply the brain. The common carotid and internal carotid arteries, the blood vessels in the neck that supply the brain, are quite susceptible to the development of fatty arteriosclerotic plaques that narrow or obstruct the vessel. In addition, these plaques can develop ulcerations such that small fragments break off and lodge in narrower vessels downstream, likewise producing a stroke.

It has been clearly established that if an arteriosclerotic plaque is causing trouble and if it can be surgically removed before a stroke occurs, the patient will fare much better. Such lesions frequently announce themselves in the form of a "ministroke," or transient ischemic attack (TIA), in which the patient experiences temporary blurring of vision, faintness, light-headedness, or weakness of one portion of the body. Patients experiencing a TIA should be evaluated for a carotid endarterectomy, an operation designed to open the

carotid artery and remove the plaque. In some cases plaques can be detected when the sound of obstructed blood flow in the artery is heard through a stethoscope; in other cases such routine screening tests as ultrasound imaging are needed. It is not clear that the finding of a plaque in a patient who has no symptoms should be regarded as sufficient reason for surgical removal. Although the consensus among vascular surgeons and neurologists is that the presence of a small plaque does not require an operation, if the plaque narrows the blood vessel to a considerable extent or in diagnostic studies seems to be ulcerated, then its removal by a qualified vascular surgeon may reduce the likelihood that a stroke will occur in the future.

A recent study evaluated the stroke-reducing benefits of an operation in which the superficial temporal artery outside the skull is joined, or anastomosed, with a branch of the middle cerebral artery inside the skull, thereby bypassing the internal carotid artery. Patients with significant symptoms of reduced blood flow to the brain were assigned randomly either to a group treated only with aspirin and for control of hypertension or to a group receiving the extracranial-intracranial bypass operation. Seventy-one neurosurgical centers were involved, and 1,377 patients were studied. The final conclusion was that no basic difference exists between the two treatments in protection from the development of stroke. Although there has been some as-yet-unresolved debate over the findings, the study did point up the importance of demonstrating the effectiveness of new operations by means of randomized trials before the operations become widely performed.

Bone and joint surgery

The continued development of implants and artificial joints has been a boon to individuals with diseases and injuries of bones and joints. The artificial hip, artificial knee, and other prosthetic joints have allowed patients with severe fractures or arthritic diseases greater mo-

Cerebral bypass surgery

external carotid artery

bypass

site of blockage

common carotid artery

internal carotid artery

The EC/IC Bypass Study Group, "Failure of Extracranial-Intracranial Arterial Bypass to Reduce the Risk of Ischemic Stroke," *The New England Journal of Medicine,* vol. 313, no. 19 (Nov. 7, 1985), pp. 1191–1200

Follow-up functional status*		
	treatment groups	
	medical	surgical (carotid artery bypass)
number of patients	714	663
impairment		
none	61%	61%
minor	23%	23%
major	5%	6%
death	11%	10%

*patients followed for an average of 55.8 months after treatment

In patients with symptoms of reduced blood flow to the brain, there was no basic difference between those treated medically or surgically (with carotid artery bypass). The table indicates follow-up functional status (minor impairments = difficulty in functioning; major = inability to function without assistance).

bility with less discomfort. In spite of good results in most patients, unsolved problems have limited the use of these devices to older patients. The artificial materials used in their manufacture can fracture, fail, loosen, or become sites of infection. Concern also exists about the long-term behavior of the methylmethacrylate cement used to bond the devices in place, about osteoporosis (loss of bone substance) developing in the surrounding bones, and about wear and tear on metal parts and local corrosion on metallic surfaces.

Some of these problems should be overcome as better methods of fixing prostheses in place are developed. Changing the surface characteristics of the implant can promote biologic fixation, by which the ingrowth of bony and fibrous tissue serves to anchor the implant. Other implant modifications and improved cementing techniques are also being evaluated. If successful, they would make it reasonable to consider the use of total joint implants and long-bone substitutes for children, in whom at the present time the stresses of increased activity and growth decrease the likelihood of good long-term results from such devices.

Attention has also turned to the use of bone substitutes in younger individuals to replace bone that has been destroyed or must be removed. These materials fall into three categories: autogenous bone, osteochondrous allografts, and such osteo-inducing substances as decalcified bone and hydroxyapatite.

Autogenous bone (bone from the patient's own body) can be transplanted comparatively easily from one site to another when only small sections of bone are involved. When a large bone segment is needed, however, its blood supply must be preserved; for this, the blood vessels that service the bone graft must be connected to vessels at the transplant site. Today, because of advances in microvascular surgery, surgeons using a microscope for magnification can suture blood vessels as small as one millimeter (four hundredths of an inch). Among bones that can serve as grafts are ribs, the fibula in the lower leg, and a portion of the pelvis called the iliac crest. Since the tissue is the patient's own, there is no problem of rejection.

Osteochondrous allografts are bones and joint surfaces taken from cadavers and preserved by freezing or by freeze-drying or used fresh to substitute for bone that must be removed, usually because of cancer. Since malignant bone tumors occur in young individuals, this technique can be extremely helpful in treating childhood cancer. Use of fresh bone, including the cartilage of the joint surface, may produce problems of rejection, but previously frozen tissue has been found to induce less of an immune response. Nevertheless, in one out of three cases in which frozen bone has been used, the bone has broken or deteriorated. Another useful technique is a shell graft, in which only the bone and cartilage of the joint surface are used to resurface a joint that has been destroyed.

Several osteo-inducing (bone-inducing) substances are being developed. One is bone segment taken from another individual, decalcified, and used to replace a defect. As healing progresses, the implant serves as a framework for the ingrowth and development of surrounding bone. Another substance, hydroxyapatite, is a complex calcium mineral that functions as the chief structural material in natural bone. Easily synthesized from calcium carbonate, it has a large pore size and can be formed in a number of sizes and shapes. Like decalcified bone, it serves as a latticework for the formation of new bone, within which it becomes totally incorporated.

Vascular surgery

In spite of extensive research and the development of a number of artificial substitutes for arteries, the best replacement remains the patient's own veins taken from the lower extremities. The saphenous vein in the leg continues to be the best long-term conduit for bypassing an arteriosclerotic obstruction in an artery, whether it be in the legs or in the coronary arteries of the heart. Improved design of prosthetic devices, the possibility of lining plastic vessels with living cells, and other approaches to making the inner surface of the artificial vessel more like living tissue are all being evaluated, but so far they either have not been practical for clinical use or have not been an improvement over the patient's own veins. When plastic tubes are substituted for such small-caliber vessels as coronary arteries, which measure only one to three millimeters in diameter, they gradually become blocked and function less satisfactorily. On the other hand, when such a large blood vessel as the aorta must be replaced because of an aneurysm (weakness in the vessel wall), then plastic grafts function quite satisfactorily and have a low incidence of infection and complications.

Cardiac surgery

Recent progress has been made in the development of surgical techniques, instruments, and technology for treating various forms of heart disease that, although uncommon, are serious. In complex forms of congenital heart disease, for example, it is clear that many of these defects are best corrected surgically soon after birth or at least during infancy. Nevertheless, new advances have now made possible nonoperative treatments for certain defects, such as stenosis, or narrowing, of the pulmonary valve. Stretching, or dilatation, of the pulmonary valve by means of a catheter introduced into a large blood vessel has been performed successfully in a number of children. Using fetal lambs as subjects, surgeons have developed procedures for repairing congenital cardiac defects. If such techniques could be adapted to the human fetus, surgeons could correct certain abnormalities before birth, obviating the need for an open-heart operation later.

Adapting technology developed for adults to children can be fraught with problems. For instance, the use of pig heart valves to replace the aortic and mitral valves in adults has proved quite satisfactory; these valves function for a surprisingly long time, although deterioration does begin to take place in some of them after six to ten years. When porcine valves are implanted in young children, however, they deteriorate much more rapidly and become calcified, and another operation is required within a few months to a few years.

Arrhythmias, disturbances of the heart rate or rhythm, are produced by a number of factors, including stress, drugs, coronary artery disease, and abnormal conduction systems of nervous tissue within the heart. Electrophysiological studies of these problems have led to the development of operations to treat such abnormalities. One example is rapid heartbeat, or tachycardia, produced by the presence in some individuals of an accessory nerve pathway between the atria and ventricles of the heart. Patients with this abnormality, called Wolff-Parkinson-White syndrome, have recurrent attacks of rapid heart action. Many such patients will respond to drugs, but others will not or cannot tolerate the medication. An operation to disconnect the abnormal pathway was first developed in 1969; recently modified, it now enjoys a success rate of 99%. This advance has opened an entirely new field of surgery for cardiac arrhythmias and spurred new approaches, including techniques for destroying the accessory nerve pathway by freezing and thereby avoiding an open-heart operation.

People suffering from ventricular fibrillation have benefited from a device called an implantable automatic cardioverter-defibrillator. Ventricular fibrillation is an abnormality of the heart rhythm in which a rotating wave of electrical activity disrupts the natural pacemaker; as a result, the heart quivers but does not beat. This arrhythmia is fatal unless defibrillation is carried out within five minutes. For unmanageable ventricular arrhythmias, implantation of an automatic defibrillator, which detects the abnormal rhythm and delivers necessary correcting shocks, has been associated with one-year survival of 90–95%.

Cardiac transplantation has now been carried out in over 3,000 patients with improved early and long-term survival. Mechanical ventricular assistance devices are being used increasingly to provide temporary support until a donor heart is available for transplantation. However, the use of an implanted artificial heart is not recommended as a permanent replacement.

Anesthesiology

It has become recognized that when a patient prior to an operation is given a general anesthetic through a tube inserted into the windpipe, the oxygen concentration of the arterial blood may fall and ventricular function may decrease. In some patients these conditions have been associated with the development of cardiac arrest. Foreknowledge of this possible hazard now allows the anesthesiologist to support such patients properly. Catheters inserted through the neck into the pulmonary circulation of the lungs provide careful monitoring of the heart and of oxygenation so that normal physiological functioning can be maintained during complex and difficult operations involving loss of blood or other disturbances to the circulation or to the lungs.

The technique of inserting a small catheter into the back, alongside but not through the membrane surrounding the spinal cord, allows repeated injections of a local anesthetic agent both during an operation and in the postoperative period. Called continuous epidural anesthesia, it has proved excellent for both abdominal and thoracic operations. In countries such as China, in which medical technology is still comparatively unavailable, use of an epidural catheter for abdominal operations allows the patient to be awake and eliminates the need for respiratory support. In operations on the chest and on the heart and lungs, continual epidural anesthesia can also be employed for the first few days after an operation to relieve pain and decrease the amount of narcotic needed.

Anesthesiologists, by virtue of their duties in supporting respiration during an operation, have become experts in the treatment of respiratory failure after injury and after operations. Their skills have been appreciably enhanced by improved techniques for maintaining respiration mechanically. New artificial respirators feature microprocessor-controlled inspiratory and expiratory valves that help automate the regulation of flow rate and flow patterns for optimum ventilation. Another recently developed technique, called high-frequency ventilation, delivers a very low volume of gas to the lungs at a very low pressure but at rapidly alternating rates to provide ventilation and oxygenation. Although the physical mechanism by which this technique succeeds is not completely understood, it has been helpful during such diagnostic procedures as laryngoscopy and bronchoscopy and in the treatment of fistulas (abnormal openings) between the windpipe or lungs and the outside world.

Recently it has come to light that patients occasionally report hearing and remembering conversations in the operating room when they supposedly have received a general anesthetic and are "asleep." This may occur with light anesthesia or when a paralyzing drug (such as curare) has been used. Usually the patient has no pain in spite of this awareness, but some reports have noted subsequent awareness by patients of what was said about them by the operating team during the operation. Such occurrence is usually not a problem when the operating team, as is the rule, is above all concerned for the patient's well-being.

—Arthur E. Baue, M.D.

Special Report

Reshaping the Eye for Better Vision

by George O. Waring III, M.D.

Since spectacles and contact lenses were invented, nearsighted and farsighted individuals have been grateful for them but have wished that they could see normally without them. Advances in refractive corneal surgery—operations that attempt to permanently change the focus of the eye by changing the shape of the clear cornea on the front of the eyeball—are increasing the likelihood that some individuals can discard their corrective lenses. All types of refractive eye surgery—including radial keratotomy, the most popular of these operations—are in an active phase of change, evolution, and development.

Basic facts about eyes and vision

The human eye consists of a series of lenses that bend light rays and focus images of the environment on the retina, the nervous tissue in the eye that conducts impulses down the optic nerve to the brain. As long as the strength of the lenses and the length of the eyeball match, the image is clear. If the lenses are too strong or the eyeball too long, the image falls in front of the retina, creating nearsightedness, or myopia. Conversely, if the lenses are too weak or the eyeball too short, the image falls behind the retina, creating farsightedness, or hyperopia. If the lenses distort the image, astigmatism is present. Spectacles and contact lenses correct the focus of the eye.

The strongest lens in the eye is the cornea, the clear tissue that arches over the front of the eye like a watch crystal; it has the thickness of a credit card and the diameter of a dime. Surgery can make the cornea steeper and therefore a more powerful lens to treat farsightedness, flatter and thus a less powerful lens to treat nearsightedness, or steeper in one meridian and flatter in another to treat astigmatism. The power of a lens is measured in diopters. A lens with 1 diopter of power bends light rays to a focal point one meter (3.3 ft) away. Because the refractive surgery changes the focusing—that is, the refractive power—of the cornea, it is called refractive corneal surgery, or refractive keratoplasty.

Evolution of refractive corneal surgery

There are two ways to change the refractive power of the cornea. The first is to change the curvature of the anterior surface. This process is analogous to changing a spectacle lens or a contact lens to a different shape for a different focus. The second is to change the density (the refractive index) of the cornea. The higher the refractive index, the greater the focusing power of the cornea.

Eye surgeons have devised five basic types of refractive corneal surgery, all of which attempt to change the corneal curvature: (1) keratotomy, in which incisions are made in the cornea; (2) lamellar refractive surgery, in which a disk of cornea is ground to a new shape and sutured to the surface of the eye (much like a contact lens), or in which a disk of tissue or plastic is inserted within the cornea to change its shape (one type of plastic has a high refractive index); (3) keratectomy, in which tissue is removed from the cornea; (4) thermokeratoplasty, in which the eye is treated with focal applications of heat; and (5) corneal transplant (penetrating keratoplasty), in which a human donor cornea is used to eliminate a corneal scar and to create a proper focus.

The development of these procedures spans the past century. Eye surgeons in the mid-19th century attempted to restore a more normal shape to distorted corneas by applying chemical or heat cautery, which shrank and flattened the cornea. In the 1880s William H. Bates in New York and Leendert J. Lans in Leiden, Neth., in experiments on humans and animals, used keratotomy to treat astigmatism. Their discoveries lay dormant until the 1940s, when Tutomu Sato in Tokyo used a series of radially placed incisions in both the anterior and posterior surfaces of the cornea to treat astigmatism and myopia. Unfortunately, many of these patients developed swelling and scarring of the cornea an average of 20 years later because the posterior incisions had damaged the delicate, nonregenerating layer of endothelial cells that maintain corneal clarity. Before this complication became apparent, a new optical invention—the contact lens—had led Sato and his colleagues to abandon this type of keratotomy.

During the 1950s and 1960s, José I. Barraquer in Bogotá, Colombia, developed lamellar refractive keratoplasty. Barraquer devised two variants of this surgery. In the first, keratomileusis (from the Greek *keras,* "cornea," and *mileusis,* "to carve"), the surgeon

398

uses a miniature vibrating plane called a microkeratome to remove a thin slice of the anterior cornea, places the tissue on a lathe where it is frozen, carves it into a new shape, thaws it, and sutures it back onto the surface of the cornea. This technique is now being refined, but its expense and complexity have limited its application to only a score of surgeons who currently use it in practice. In the second procedure, keratophakia (from the Greek *keras,* "cornea," and *phakos,* "lens"), the surgeon places a lens carved from a donor cornea within the patient's cornea. Barraquer also implanted lenses made of glass and plastic, but they eroded through the cornea.

In the late 1960s and throughout the 1970s, Svyatoslav Fyodorov in Moscow modified the Japanese approach to radial keratotomy, making incisions only in the anterior surface of the cornea, and devised a multifactorial formula that attempted to tailor the operation to each individual. In the late 1970s surgeons in India, Eastern Europe, and the United States studied with Fyodorov and adopted his basic techniques, which have become the most popular of the refractive keratoplasty procedures.

The placement of a plastic lenticule within the cornea to change its shape or its refractive power was revived by V. Mester in the 1970s in Bonn, West Germany, because hydrophilic plastics, the type soft contact lenses are made of, became available. These materials could transmit water and nutrients through the cornea and create a refractive change. Like keratophakia using a human donor lenticule, the use of a hydrophilic plastic lenticule requires that the surgeon shave off the front layers of the patient's cornea with a microkeratome, a complex procedure. This complexity and the increasing use of plastic intraocular lenses in cataract surgery have slowed the application of this technique in humans.

In 1980 Herbert E. Kaufman of New Orleans, La., simplified the keratomileusis technique by using lenticules of eyes from human eye banks, preparing them in a commercial laboratory, freeze-drying them, and shipping them to the surgeon, who made a circular incision in the cornea and sutured the rehydrated lenticule onto the surface of the cornea. This procedure is called epikeratoplasty because the tissue lens is attached to the surface of the cornea. It is undergoing continued improvement and clinical investigation.

In the early 1980s D. Peter Choyce in London used a polysulfone plastic to make lenticules of high refractive index that could be slipped into a small pocket in the cornea, an operation now being tested in laboratory animals.

In 1983 Stephen L. Trokel and Rangaswamy Srinivasan in New York City used a shortwave-length excimer laser (the type of laser used to cut fine grooves in microcircuit chips) to make incisions in the cornea, leading many investigators in the field of ophthalmology

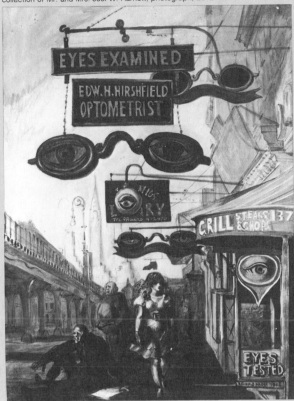

"Eyes Examined," by Reginald Marsh, 1946; collection of Mr. and Mrs. Joel W. Harnett; photograph, Eeva-Inker

Nearsighted and farsighted people may be thankful for the corrected vision that spectacles and contact lenses can give them, but many long for a way to do without any sort of optical devices at all.

to explore the possibility of using computer-directed, robot-driven lasers to carve a patient's cornea into a new shape and to do so within a few seconds. Years of research will determine whether this futuristic surgical device will make glasses and contact lenses historical curiosities.

The ideal operation to change the focus of the cornea would be (1) safe, not only when it worked properly but also when mistakes or problems occurred, so that the chance of permanent damage to the patient's eye would be minimized, (2) predictable, so that the patient's best possible visual acuity could be obtained with reasonable certainty, as it is with corrective lenses, (3) reversible, so that if the outcome of the operation was not desirable or the patient's refractive error changed after the surgery, further modifications could be made to keep the eye in focus, (4) simple, so that a reasonably trained ophthalmic surgeon could perform the operation without highly specialized training or complex machines and patients would not have to travel to specialized centers for surgery, and (5) stable soon after surgery, to prevent fluctuating vision. Active research is modifying the currently available techniques to meet these goals.

399

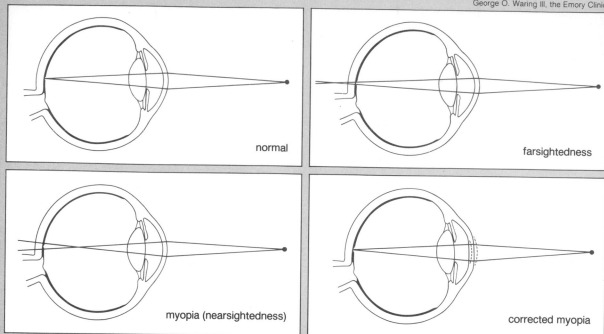

In the normal eye (top left), the cornea and lens focus light rays onto the retina. In the farsighted eye (top right), the lens and cornea are not strong enough for the length of the eyeball; light rays focus behind the eye. In the nearsighted, or myopic, eye (bottom left), the cornea and lens are too strong; light focuses in front of the retina. After refractive corneal surgery to correct myopia (bottom right), optical power is reduced in the cornea, and light rays focus onto the retina.

Radial keratotomy

The most popular of refractive keratoplasty procedures is radial keratotomy. In the late 1970s interest in the U.S. mounted when coverage of the operation by the lay media attracted the attention of myopic individuals. (About 25% of North American adults are myopic.) Many ophthalmologists became interested in the procedure because of its potential for helping their myopic patients, because of fascination with the new field of refractive corneal surgery, because radial keratotomy was less complex than other refractive operations, and because of its possible economic benefit to their practices. The popularity spiraled in spite of a paucity of published data documenting the safety and efficacy of the procedure. Therefore, nine clinical centers collaborated under the direction of George O. Waring of Atlanta, Ga., to carry out the Prospective Evaluation of Radial Keratotomy (PERK) study, which was funded by the U.S. National Eye Institute in 1980.

In early 1982 two ophthalmologists and seven patients filed a class-action antitrust lawsuit against selected members of the PERK study, the National Advisory Eye Council, the American Academy of Ophthalmology, and the National Eye Institute claiming that these individuals had conspired to interfere with interstate commerce in radial keratotomy and had attempted to corner the market in the procedure. The defendants viewed the accusations as preposterous,

pointing out that neither informing the public that this was an experimental procedure nor establishing a clinical scientific trial of the operation constituted violations of antitrust laws. The suit was resolved in a no-fault out-of-court settlement in 1985 and did not interfere with the functioning of the PERK study.

Patient selection. Two psychological studies of patients requesting radial keratotomy showed that the most common reason for seeking the surgery was the desire to see well without depending on corrective lenses; only a minority expressed an occupational need, a cosmetic reason, or a recreational reason. For those who are interested, a warning is necessary because radial keratotomy has received extensive coverage in the popular press and is the subject of advertising campaigns by some ophthalmologists; myopic individuals must take a "buyer beware" attitude when evaluating this procedure.

To be eligible for radial keratotomy, a patient must have a stable refractive error so that the amount of nearsightedness does not continue to increase after the operation. Usually the refraction changes little after the age of 20. The cornea should be normal—without scars or distortions, as occur in diseases like keratoconus. Contact lenses should not be worn for at least two weeks before the definitive examination because they can warp the shape of the cornea and lead to misleading calculations by the surgeon.

Individuals with smaller amounts of myopia, ranging from approximately 1.5 to 5 diopters, are the best candidates because they have the best chance of eliminating almost all of their myopia, whereas individuals with larger amounts of myopia, from approximately 6 to 10 diopters, have a much smaller chance of reducing their nearsightedness to the point where they can go without glasses or contact lenses. Individuals with more than 1 diopter of astigmatism may have residual astigmatism after the operation unless special techniques are used to correct the astigmatism in addition to the myopia.

Each patient must have a full understanding of the risks and benefits of the procedure and be able to give a truly informed consent not clouded by unrealistic claims on the part of friends or physicians or by their own unrealistic desires.

Practical aspects of the surgical procedure. Although practices vary from one surgeon to another, most perform radial keratotomy in an outpatient, ambulatory surgical center using full precautions to ensure a sterile operating field. On the operating room table, the patient receives topical anesthetic eyedrops and—in some cases—injection of anesthetic adjacent to the eyeball. The patient remains alert throughout the procedure but feels little of what is going on. After surgery the patient may use eyedrops, pain medication, and an eyepad for a day or two to decrease pain and light sensitivity. Most individuals can return to their normal activities in a couple of days.

Surgical technique. The surgeon makes a series of radial incisions in the cornea in a pattern that resembles spokes in a bicycle wheel. There are three variables that can be altered during surgery: the number of incisions, the length of the incisions, and the depth of the incisions. The depth of the incision is expressed as a percentage of the thickness of the cornea, so that an incision 100% deep would actually perforate the cornea and penetrate the eyeball.

The surgeon adjusts these three factors on the basis of the amount of nearsightedness to be corrected and the age of the patient, older patients needing less extensive surgery than younger ones. Other factors, such as the shape of the cornea and the pressure within the eyeball, may exert a minor influence.

Historically the number of incisions effective in radial keratotomy has declined, from 40 used by Sato in the 1940s, to 16 and 12 used by Fyodorov in the 1970s, to 8 and now 4 incisions used by most surgeons. Approximately 75% of the effect is achieved by the first four incisions. The length of the incision is defined by the diameter of the central clear zone of the cornea. Surgeons avoid cutting into the central clear zone so that the scars from the incisions do not impinge upon the direct line of vision. The diameter of the central clear zone varies from 3 to 5 mm (0.12 to 0.2 in) in most cases; the smaller the diameter, the longer the

incision and the greater the effect from the surgery. The deeper the incision, the greater the resultant flattening of the cornea. However, because the incisions are made manually, it is difficult to ensure that the depth is uniform from one end to the other and from one incision to the other. This explains some of the variability in the procedure.

Two instruments are important in determining the depth of the incision in the cornea: the pachymeter, with which the surgeon measures the thickness of the cornea, and the surgical knife. Most surgeons currently use an ultrasonic pachymeter that works like radar, sending ultrasonic waves from the tip of a three-millimeter probe into the cornea and receiving them back. On the basis of these measurements, the surgeon sets the knife blade at a length that will incise approximately 90% of the corneal thickness.

The scalpel consists of a specially designed micrometer handle that advances a diamond knife blade between two flat guards so that when the knife is inserted into the cornea, the blade will penetrate only to the depth determined by its extension beyond the flat guards. The surgeon tries to avoid a full thickness incision, through which the fluid within the eye can leak and through which infection can enter the eye.

To make the incisions, the surgeon steadies the eyeball with a pair of forceps or a fixation ring, marks the central clear zone with a dull circular marker, sets the knife blade, inserts the blade into the cornea at the edge of the clear zone mark, and makes an incision radially out to the edge of the cornea.

Surgery for astigmatism. Astigmatism, too, can be corrected by radial keratotomy. Astigmatism refers to corneas that have a different refractive power in one meridian than another. The surgeon can flatten the steeper meridian of the cornea by making transverse incisions between the radial incisions. The length and number of these transverse incisions is proportionate to the amount of astigmatism to be corrected.

How radial keratotomy works. Most of the cornea consists of collagen fibrils that extend from one side to the other, like cables over a bridge. The incisions cut these fibrils and weaken the structure of the cornea, allowing the pressure within the eyeball to push the periphery of the cornea between the incisions forward. This movement pulls the central uncut cornea flatter, decreasing its optical power and moving the point of focus back toward the retina, where a sharper image creates better vision.

Healing and stability of vision after radial keratotomy. Unlike most tissues in the body, the cornea has no blood vessels and receives its nourishment by diffusion from the surrounding fluids. Therefore, the cornea heals more slowly than most tissues, as the collagen fibrils heal with scar tissue. Fibrils themselves do not reattach end to end. During the first six months after surgery, when the wounds undergo most of their

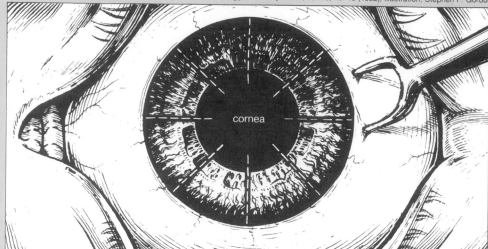

From *Highlights of Ophthalmology*, Triweekly Letter, vol. 10, no. 18 (1982); illustration, Stephen F. Gordon

In this radial keratotomy procedure, the surgeon fixates the eyeball with double-pronged forceps and makes eight radial incisions (dotted lines) from the edge of the central clear zone across the cornea to its edge.

cornea

healing, the shape of the cornea changes and the vision fluctuates. After six months approximately two-thirds of the patients have reasonably stable vision, but one-third continue to experience some fluctuation. This fluctuation can continue for many years.

Although it is unknown exactly when the cornea achieves a stable, fully healed state, it can take at least four years for some individuals. During this time, however, the fluctuation in vision is not usually great enough to impair daily function.

Outcome of radial keratotomy. The most accurate method of reporting radial keratotomy results should include statistics for varying degrees of myopia, since patients with smaller amounts of myopia are more likely to experience the best surgical outcome. The PERK study, therefore, divided individuals into three groups: lower myopia (−2 to −3.12 diopters with a 4-mm [0.16-in]-diameter clear zone), middle myopia (−3.25 to −4.37 diopters with a 3.5-mm [0.14-in] clear zone), and higher myopia (−4.5 to −8 diopters with a 3-mm [0.12-in] clear zone). There are two ways to represent the results. The first is to use the amount of residual refractive error, and the second is to use the visual acuity of the patient without correction. Since these two measures do not correlate exactly, both are cited, on the basis of results of the PERK study, reported three years after the surgery.

A reasonable, expected outcome after surgery is a residual refractive error within one diopter of zero refractive error (emmetropia), a goal achieved in 75% of the lower group, 62% of the middle group, and 39% of the higher group. In terms of visual acuity, 20/20 or better acuity was achieved in 74% of the lower group, 50% of the middle group, and 33% of the higher group. A level of 20/40 visual acuity—that generally required for obtaining a driver's license—was achieved in 90% of the lower group, 81% of the middle group, and 60% of the higher group.

Expressing these results in less technical terms, one can say that all patients achieved some decrease in their nearsightedness. However, it was not possible to predict the exact amount of decrease that would be achieved by any individual patient. In fact, the published studies indicate that the best prediction that can be made for an individual patient is that the final refraction will be within a range of approximately 3.50 diopters; that is, approximately 1.75 diopters on either side of the value predicted before surgery. This contrasts with the accuracy of fitting glasses or contact lenses, which is a range of approximately 0.50 diopter.

It is difficult to measure exactly the percentage of individuals who could go without glasses or contact lenses after surgery because many wear corrective lenses part of the time if the surgery has not been 100% successful. In general, after radial keratotomy approximately two-thirds of the patients can perform most daily functions without corrective lenses.

Satisfaction with the surgery has been measured by psychological tests and, of course, a satisfactory outcome for one person may be unsatisfactory for another. In the PERK study, after one year 48% of the patients were very satisfied, 42% were moderately satisfied, and 10% were dissatisfied with the results of surgery in one eye. As expected, individuals with a lower residual refractive error, better uncorrected visual acuity, and less fluctuation of vision were the most satisfied.

Complications. The most common complication of radial keratotomy is an undercorrection with persistent nearsightedness or an overcorrection with conversion to farsightedness. In the PERK study an undercorrection of more than 1 diopter occurred in 8% of the lower group, 19% of the middle group, and 48% of the higher group, while an overcorrection of 1 diopter or more occurred in approximately 16% of the eyes. Undercorrected patients are likely to have to wear

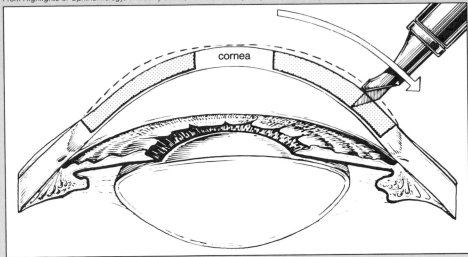

From *Highlights of Ophthalmology*, Triweekly Letter, vol. 10, no. 18 (1982); illustration, Stephen F. Gordon

A cross-sectional view of the anterior of the eye. In a radial keratotomy procedure, incisions (shaded area) made by a diamond-bladed micrometer surgical knife cause the cornea to bulge forward peripherally and flatten centrally (dotted line), thus reducing the amount of myopia.

glasses or contact lenses for nearsightedness. Over-corrected patients are more likely to need reading glasses when they reach their early forties.

After radial keratotomy, patients with residual near-sightedness or farsightedness can usually achieve good visual acuity with spectacles, and most of the time the glasses are thinner than they were before surgery. Fitting contact lenses after radial keratotomy is more difficult than fitting them on a normal cornea. Soft contact lenses should not be worn after radial keratotomy because they induce the growth of blood vessels into the scar in many patients. Hard contact lenses can be successfully worn but tend to slide off to the side of the cornea more readily than in a normal eye.

Because radial keratotomy is performed on an anatomically normal eye that is capable of good corrected vision, a major question is: What is the chance that vision will be damaged so that the patient cannot see as well after surgery as before? Fortunately, blinding complications are rare after radial keratotomy, and cases of severe infection, cataract formation, rupture of the eyeball after blunt trauma, severe persistent irregularity of the cornea from the surgical scars, and disabling glare have occurred in fewer than 1% of the cases.

Roughly 2% of the patients do not have as good a corrected visual acuity after surgery as they did before. Fortunately, most lose only two or three lines of the fine print on the vision-testing chart, but the quality of their vision may drop slightly. This may occur because the final shape of the cornea is not always perfectly smooth, with the resulting astigmatism reducing the uncorrected visual acuity.

People who wear glasses or contact lenses are familiar with glare that occurs when these lenses become scratched or dirty and with glare that is accentuated at night when the pupil is dilated and the eye is directed toward a particular light source, such as a streetlight or the headlight of an automobile. A similar phenomenon occurs when light scatters from the radial keratotomy scars. Many patients see a radiating pattern of lines around lights at night, but it seldom interferes with their visual function. Fortunately, because the fine scars do not extend to the center of the cornea, very few patients experience disabling glare after radial keratotomy.

Because the incisions heal very slowly after radial keratotomy, delayed infection and traumatic rupture of the cornea have occurred in a few patients. There presently is no indication that severe complications will arise 20 to 40 years after surgery, but only long-term follow-up can document the extended condition of corneal cells, the effect of future surgery (*e.g.*, cataract surgery), and the stability of vision over a prolonged period of time.

Current and future status of radial keratotomy

Even though radial keratotomy has been refined to the point where it can be an effective procedure for carefully selected patients, the outcome cannot be accurately predicted for an individual. Two major factors contribute to this lack of predictability. The first is the inability of the surgeon to perform the exact same operation case after case, and the second is the variability in healing of the incisions from one patient to another.

Two advances, now in the stage of animal experimentation, may help solve these problems. The first is the use of a finely tuned laser to make the incisions, which will increase the surgical precision. The second is the use of growth factors that rapidly stimulate healing of the radial keratotomy wounds. The field of surgical treatments that correct refractive errors is clearly in a state of flux, intriguing ophthalmologists and patients alike about the possibilities.

HEALTH INFORMATION UPDATE

Instructive and practical
articles about common
health concerns

Hazards of the High-Tech Kitchen
by Tom D. Naughton

Thanks to today's high-technology kitchen, cooking has never been easier or faster. Microwave ovens make it possible to cook an entire meal, including baked potatoes, in minutes instead of hours. Food processors allow cooks to slice, dice, and chop food in seconds instead of minutes. These time-savers are becoming increasingly popular, especially among two-career couples who might otherwise eat dinner out after a long, tiring day (when they would really prefer not to) or settle for TV dinners. As some microwaves are now dipping below $100 in price and food processors below $60, sales of these laborsaving and timesaving items are expected to keep increasing.

However, like all products of new technologies, microwave ovens, food processors, and other appliances that have recently become so popular have raised questions about safety: Are there any health hazards involved in using them? Can they cause injuries? If so, how can the injuries be avoided? Microwave ovens probably raise the most questions in the minds of consumers, if only because microwave cooking is somewhat mysterious. Many consumers do not know how a microwave heats food; they know only that radiation is involved—and "radiation" is a word that tends to arouse grave fears or, at the very least, make some people nervous.

How a microwave oven works

A microwave is an electromagnetic wave that falls into a certain frequency range. Television and radio signals are also electromagnetic waves; in fact, many television transmitters use microwaves. Microwaves are reflected by metal, but they pass through glass, paper, plastic, and similar materials and are absorbed by food.

In a microwave oven the microwaves are produced by an electron tube known as a magnetron. The interior of the oven is made of metal. Thus, when food is placed in a microwave oven, the microwaves bounce around the interior of the oven until they are finally absorbed by the food. As the microwaves bombard the food, they agitate the water molecules in the food. As these agitated water molecules begin to rub into and bump against each other, they create friction, which in turn creates heat. The heat then cooks the food. Because of the nature of the process, foods with a high water content generally become heated more quickly than other foods.

The radiation issue

Although microwave ovens have been in general use for about 20 years, at first some consumers were worried that the radiation they emit could be harmful over time, that cumulative exposure to them might be dangerous, as with X-rays. But there has not been a single documented case of an injury caused by the radiation from a microwave oven. In 1971 the U.S. Food and Drug Administration (FDA) set standards for permissible radiation leakage from microwave ovens. The standards state that over its lifetime, an oven may not leak more than five milliwatts of radiation per square centimeter (mw/cm^2). Leakage is measured at five centimeters (two inches) from the exterior surface of the oven.

Because microwaves can pass through glass, it would seem natural to assume they can pass through the glass doors on microwave ovens. However, the oven doors contain a perforated metal shield that, while allowing the cook to view the food inside, prevents microwaves from passing through. As long as the door, the hinges, and the seals are intact, there is no reason to worry about radiation exposure. Several varieties of devices for monitoring microwave leakage are available, but most of these are not reliable, according to the FDA, and therefore are not recommended.

Microwaves also diminish drastically in strength over short distances. Therefore, even if a microwave oven were leaking at the maximum allowable level, a person standing just a foot away would be exposed to only a minuscule amount of radiation. Of course, people are exposed to small amounts of radiation every day—from the Sun.

405

Hazards of the high-tech kitchen

One of the few legitimate concerns originally raised about microwave ovens was that they might interfere with the operation of cardiac pacemakers. (Other electronic devices, such as metal detectors at airports and some other public installations, diathermy equipment that is used in hospitals, and some electric razors and tools, have raised the same fear.) To prevent possible problems, most pacemakers are now shielded against electronic interference. However, it is still wise for people who have pacemakers to inform their physicians before they purchase or use a microwave oven.

Possible dangers of microwave ovens

While radiation concerns are minimal, microwave ovens can and do cause burns, albeit indirectly. In fact, *Burn Care International* reports that more than 90% of all people who use microwave ovens have been burned at least once by the foods cooked in them. The most common cause of these burns is overheated liquids. A person reheating a cup of cold coffee, for example, may not realize the coffee has reached a scalding temperature and may swallow a big gulp instead of sipping first. Another frequent injury is a scald caused by overheated baby formula. Many people do not realize that microwave ovens heat liquids unevenly; even if the parent dribbles a few drops of heated formula on his or her wrist to test the temperature, formula in another part of the bottle may have reached scalding temperatures and pose a serious danger to the baby. Anyone heating formula in microwaves should, upon removing the bottle from the oven, shake or stir it to ensure an even dispersion of heat, then test for temperature. Some pediatricians advise against using microwaves to heat baby formula or any other baby foods.

Food cooked in a microwave oven in a pot, pan, or dish may also contain "hot spots." After it has been removed from the oven, it should always be thoroughly stirred before it is tasted. Another common cause of

Source: Burns Institute, Cincinnati Unit, Shriners Hospitals for Crippled Children, Cincinnati, Ohio

Burn injuries associated with microwave ovens		
injury cause	number of cases (and ages of victims)	
	U.S.	U.K.
heating baby bottles	6 (under 7 months)	1 (46 years)
spilled liquid	3 (17 and 22 months, 24 years)	5 (4, 18, 26, 40, and 46 years)
hot vapor (steam)	0	4 (16, 22, 36, and 43 years)
splashes	1 (10 years)	2 (31 and 35 years)
exploding egg	3 (18, 30, and 49 years)	1 (37 years)
drinking hot liquid	1 (4 years)	0
contact with hot item	1 (40 years)	4 (20, 26, 43, and 50 years)
exposure to microwaves*	7 (10, 23, 25, 32, 33, and 40 years)	2 (38 and 53 years)

*oven did not shut off when door was opened

The table above, compiled by the Burns Institute of the Shriners Hospitals for Crippled Children (Cincinnati, Ohio), is based on a 1986 survey of selected burn treatment hospitals in the United States and the United Kingdom.

burns is unevenly heated food. When a jelly donut is heated in a microwave for 30 seconds, for example, the outer pastry portion may just feel warm; the jelly center, however, having a much higher water content, may have reached a temperature of more than 90° C (200° F). The unsuspecting eater then bites into the donut and burns his or her mouth.

Facial burns, including at least one report of serious eye injury, have been caused by the steam released from bags of a popular microwave product, popcorn, which is popped in a paper bag or cardboard container that expands during the process. Any food cooked in a microwave oven in any sort of closed container should be opened very carefully, away from the face.

Depending on the material they are made of, certain pots, pans, and plates can become heated in a

Should not be prepared in microwave	
eggs in shell	will burst in microwave
whole, peeled cooked eggs; foods with nonporous skins	will burst if not pierced before microwaving
deep-fat-fried foods	temperature difficult to control; fat will spatter; may cause fire
home-canned foods	surface cooking necessary to maintain safe internal temperature
popcorn	microwaving popcorn in paper bag not designed for this purpose may cause fire

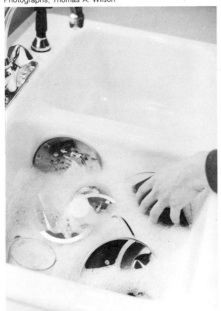

Food processors and blenders can cause injury even when unplugged. Cleaning the sharp blades requires special care. Cuts are often inflicted when the blades are retrieved from a sinkful of soapy water. For safety's sake used blades should be kept on the kitchen counter and washed one by one. Another common mistake is trying to clean a sharp blade with a finger; nylon brushes and rubber spatulas are the recommended tools for this task.

microwave and cause burns. A person may, for example, put leftover food on a plate that is not safe for microwave use; as the food is heated, so is the plate. The person then grabs the plate and burns his or her hand. Cooking utensils that will not become hot in a microwave oven are usually sold in packages labeled "microwave safe." Cooks who are not sure whether a dish is microwave safe can find out by placing it in the microwave on the highest setting for 15 to 20 seconds. If the container feels warm when it is removed from the oven, it is absorbing microwaves and is not safe to use.

No dishes or utensils that contain any metal should be used in a microwave oven. Metal can cause an electric arc to occur in a microwave, which can in turn cause a fire. Some metal racks are designed by manufacturers to be safe in microwave ovens, but any such rack not specifically labeled as microwave safe should not be used. Likewise, metal twist ties should not be used in a microwave. A cook who wants to use metal or aluminum foil in a microwave oven should first check the owner's manual that comes with the appliance to see which materials are safe. Even microwave-safe dishes can become heated by the food cooked in them. Before removing any dish from a microwave oven, the cook should touch the dish lightly to see if it has become hot and, if it has, use pot holders to remove it.

Another potential problem associated with microwave ovens is food that explodes. Heat produces steam, so foods that confine the steam—such as eggs cooked in the shell—can explode. While exploding foods may not necessarily be dangerous, cleaning them off the inside of the oven is not an enjoyable task.

The owner's manual that comes with the microwave oven will warn cooks which foods can explode if not prepared properly. It is also possible for certain foods such as potatoes and popcorn to become overheated and catch fire. The best way to avoid this type of fire is to carefully follow the cooking directions in the manufacturer's instruction booklet.

Like any electrical appliance, a microwave oven must be used cautiously to avoid shocks or electrical fires. It should be placed on a sturdy surface—not a flimsy cart—and should be surrounded on all sides by at least five centimeters (two inches) of space for ventilation. Most microwave ovens require a three-prong plug so they can be grounded and must be plugged into a compatible outlet; consumers should not use an adapter to override the third prong, as this takes the grounding wire out of the circuit. Microwave ovens draw up to 1,600 w of power, so it is best to operate them on a separate 15- or 20-amp circuit. If this is not possible, the consumer should nonetheless avoid using a microwave oven on the same circuit as another high-wattage appliance, such as a toaster or an electric skillet. Overloading the circuit can, at best, trip a circuit breaker or blow a fuse, cutting off all current in that circuit; at worst, it can cause an electrical fire.

Manufacturers of microwave ovens suggest these additional tips for safe use and care:
● Do not operate an oven if the door is cracked or does not close tightly.
● Do not let anything get between the oven door and the sealing surfaces.
● Do not operate an empty oven; this can damage it.
● Do not use the oven for anything other than cooking, defrosting, or reheating foods. Microwaves do not kill

407

all the disease-causing bacteria that may be present in food, so the ovens are not suitable for sterilizing jars for canning food or any other food-preservation equipment. The microwave oven is not a dryer; it should never be used to dry wet clothes and is not the place to put a small dog or cat whose coat is wet.

● Use only the cleaning materials recommended in the owner's manual. Abrasive materials such as steel wool can scratch the surface of the oven and leave areas that may eventually burn.

Food processors, mixers, and blenders

Food processors and blenders chop and mix food with sharp blades that rotate at speeds as high as 30 revolutions per second; obviously, these appliances have the potential to cause injuries. In fact, according to the Consumer Product Safety Commission (CPSC), in the U.S. alone about 7,000 people each year are treated in hospital emergency rooms for injuries associated with food processors, mixers, and blenders.

Most of these injuries are not due to faulty design of the appliances, which generally feature a number of built-in safeguards. A food processor, for example, will not operate unless the cover is in place. The motors that turn the blades and disks are designed to stop within seconds after the machine has been turned off, or about the time it takes to remove the cover. Food processors are supplied with a food pusher so cooks can "feed" food into the appliance without getting their hands near the blades.

Unfortunately, consumers sometimes ignore warnings not to reach into the chute—often they do so in an attempt to unclog food that has become stuck. When they push against the food, it may suddenly give way, and the hand's own momentum carries it down into the blades. If food does become stuck, the person using a food processor should first make sure the food processor is turned off and then clear the chute. Likewise, the user should never use a fork, knife, or any other utensil in an attempt to clear the chute when the machine's motor is still on.

It is far easier to reach the blades of a blender than those of a processor, and cooks are frequently injured while feeding food directly into a running blender or while using a finger or utensil to redistribute food that has become stuck in the blades. As with a food processor, a running blender should never be fed by hand, and food that is stuck should be removed only when the appliance is turned off. The blender should be operated only when the top is in place. To feed in

food, the cook should shut off the motor, put the food in the jar, replace the top securely, and then restart the blender.

A blender can also cause injuries if the jar is not securely in place. A typical accident happens this way: a blender jar that is not screwed down tightly starts to fall off while food is being blended; the cook, reacting impulsively, grabs for the jar and ends up catching a finger in the whirling blades.

All kitchen appliances should be unplugged when they are not in use or when they are taken apart for cleaning. If they are plugged in, they can be turned on accidentally and cause injuries. The CPSC reports one case in which a woman was removing the beaters from her electric mixer when she accidentally turned it on; the result was a severely lacerated broken finger.

Even a properly unplugged appliance can cause an injury indirectly—the sharp blades can inflict a cut during cleanup. One way this commonly occurs is that a person washing dishes drops the blades from a food processor or blender into a sinkful of soapy water, then reaches into the water later and is cut. To avoid this type of injury, one should keep the blades on the counter until they are ready to be washed. It is best in any case to avoid cleaning sharp blades with bare hands. Using a finger to remove food from a blade is likely to result in a cut. Most owner's manuals recommend using a brush with nylon bristles or a plastic or rubber spatula to clean the blades.

As is the case with microwave ovens, consumers need to treat small electrical appliances properly to avoid receiving shocks. The cord from an appliance should not be allowed to hang over the edge of a counter or to touch hot surfaces. If the cord becomes frayed or damaged, the appliance should not be used until the cord has been replaced by a qualified service technician.

The portion of an appliance that contains the electric motor should never be immersed in water. If this section accidentally becomes wet, the appliance should not be used until it has been checked and repaired if necessary. Nor should an appliance that has been dropped be used until it has been checked for damage.

One way consumers who are looking for a new electrical appliance of any kind can ensure that it has been thoroughly tested for safety is by looking for the Underwriters Laboratories (UL) label. UL are independent laboratories that test and certify both U.S. and foreign-made appliances.

Behavior Therapy
by Alan E. Kazdin, Ph.D.

Behavior therapy, sometimes also referred to as behavior modification, is an approach to the treatment of a variety of psychological and behavioral problems. The approach includes many different treatment techniques that can be applied to a wide range of psychological disorders and problems of everyday living. For a given clinical problem such as depression or anxiety, a number of behavioral treatments are available.

Behavioral techniques make use of many different procedures. For example, among the different techniques, exercises to promote relaxation, imagery (mental picturing of real-life situations), self-administered verbal statements (positive verbal reinforcement), or special incentives may be used in the therapy. Nonetheless, these different techniques share a common set of underlying assumptions. First, the way in which the clinical problem and treatment are conceptualized is a central feature of behavior therapy. Behavior therapists focus on how behaviors develop, are maintained, and can be altered—or more simply, how behaviors are learned. Treatment consists of providing specific learning experiences for the development of more adaptive ways of behaving.

Second, in behavioral treatments emphasis is placed on behavior, or on what a person does. How people feel (affect) and think (cognition) also are important and often are central to the specific problems brought to treatment. For example, depressed people often feel sad (affect), believe they cannot do anything right (cognition), and engage in only a few activities (behavior) in their everyday lives. Although all three—affect, cognition, and behavior—are important, behavioral treatments focus on behavior as a means of altering the clinical problem. Thus, a depressed patient may be encouraged to engage in specific activities involving interactions with others and to set goals for accomplishing tasks at home or at work. Increases in activity and completion of tasks are some of the behaviors that have been found to alter the many feelings and thoughts that constitute depression. Consequently, the behavioral approach often focuses on behavior both as an end in itself and as a means of changing different facets of the clinical problem.

Third, in behavior therapy the goals and the means to obtain them are usually well specified. Before initiating treatment the therapist must conduct a careful assessment to identify what the problem is, how the patient is affected by it, and circumstances under which the problem emerges. Once the problem has been carefully identified, the therapist can state the specific procedures and the goals toward which they will be directed. The explicit nature of the procedure is an important characteristic of therapy.

Finally, evaluation of the progress and outcome of treatment is an essential feature. There is a strong emphasis on research examining the effectiveness of given treatments and comparing one treatment with another. Evaluation measuring the progress the patient is making during the course of treatment is also important. The evaluation might be accomplished by having the patient complete questionnaires about specific symptoms or keep a diary or record of activities.

Ideally, of course, the information gathered through questionnaires and written records reveals that the patient is improving and that treatment is working. However, one of the most useful features of the evaluation is that both patient and therapist can identify when treatment is not working. This information can be used by the therapist to alter the treatment program and, if necessary, to try different techniques.

An example of a treatment

As an illustration of the behavioral approach and how it is carried out in practice, there is the case of a 35-year-old married woman who suffered from agoraphobia (fear of open spaces). People with agoraphobia tend to remain at home as much as possible. When they leave their homes, they experience high levels of anxiety, reflected in agitation, high levels of physiological arousal (sweating, trembling, dizziness, rapid heartbeat), and, in general, extreme discomfort. Many patients fear that they will lose control, faint, or even go insane in the presence of others. It is not clear how agoraphobia develops, although many different theories exist. However, even in the absence of specific knowledge about the cause of the problem, effective behavioral treatments have been developed for agoraphobia.

For the woman described above, the techniques of graduated exposure and relaxation training were used. She was introduced to a variety of different situations outside of her home on a graduated basis—that is, those encountered at first provoked relatively little anxiety and were not seen by the patient as too demanding or threatening. The presence of the therapist also mitigated some of the anxiety. As the patient progressed, more difficult situations were introduced, without the immediate support of the therapist.

In this particular case, before beginning specific tasks the patient was trained to engage in deep muscle relaxation so that she would have a technique to help herself remain relaxed when she felt anxiety coming on. Developing the ability to relax deeply is usually accomplished in only a few training sessions. The first step is for the patient to close his or her eyes and become very quiet. The patient is then instructed by the therapist to focus attention on various groups of muscles (*e.g.,* lower arm, upper arm, neck and shoulders). Muscle groups of the major skeletal muscles are alternately tensed and relaxed in response to instructions given by the therapist. The exercise helps the patient learn to recognize and identify these different sensations and to achieve a state of relaxation in specific muscle groups. As the tensing and relaxing cycle is completed for each of the major groups, the patient becomes very deeply relaxed. After a few sessions the patient can induce a state of relaxation relatively quickly with little or no assistance from the therapist.

After the patient in question had learned how to relax, her treatment continued with the assignment of a series of specific tasks or behavioral exercises. At first she was required to take a short walk with the therapist, staying close to her home, thus in a relatively nonthreatening locale. If she did feel herself becoming anxious, she was assisted by the therapist in engaging in relaxation exercises. The brief walks, the presence of the therapist, and the use of relaxation techniques decreased the likelihood that high levels of anxiety would arise.

In subsequent sessions the woman was exposed to situations that involved going farther and farther away from home, including walking to various local stores, driving a car to a shopping mall, riding a bus, and accomplishing other tasks related to situations she found anxiety provoking. She was given "homework" assignments, activities to carry out on her own without the therapist. For example, the first assignment was to visit a friend, another woman who lived a few houses away. The patient and her friend usually spoke on the telephone for extended periods each day. The assignment was to visit the friend in person for at least 30 minutes on two separate occasions during the week. After three such visits the patient was assigned to go

on an errand at a store with her friend and to walk to a mailbox two blocks away from home by herself. After the practice trials with the therapist and the homework assignments, the woman reported feeling less anxiety. Eventually her anxiety was eliminated, and she was able to resume several activities outside of the home.

Throughout the course of treatment, she systematically evaluated her progress in a diary that detailed both her activities and the amount of anxiety elicited. In the diary were places to record where she went, how long she was out of the house on each trip, and how much anxiety she felt—the latter rated on a scale from one (perfectly relaxed) to ten (extremely uncomfortable and anxious). Throughout the course of the therapy, the information provided by the diary was useful in deciding when to proceed to more difficult tasks, evaluating the progress of the patient, and judging whether the treatment was achieving its goals.

Comparison with other therapies

Behavior therapy emerged in part as a reaction to traditional forms of psychotherapy that focus on unconscious processes and sources of personality conflict that are believed by some to explain psychological problems. Traditionally, psychotherapy has focused on psychological processes, particularly those that develop in childhood, and on conflicts that have arisen and need to be resolved. The task of therapy typically has been to develop a close interpersonal relationship between therapist and patient and to use this relationship as the basis for delving into unconscious processes. The forms of psychotherapy that take this general approach often are referred to as "insight therapies" because of the focus on revealing the connections between long-existing underlying personality processes and current psychological problems.

Behavior therapy, with its emphasis on overt behavior and current functioning, differs from insight therapies in its focus and goals. First, behavior therapy is less likely than traditional psychotherapy to focus on past determinants of behavior. In the case of the agoraphobic patient, for example, the therapist is likely to focus on what the problem is now and how the patient wishes to change.

Second, as noted earlier, behavior therapy is likely to focus on specific behaviors per se rather than on how these behaviors became established. Within treatment, the therapist and patient will talk about the problem so that the therapist learns precisely what is wrong. Once this is understood, practice experiences both inside and outside of therapy are likely to be used in the treatment. In traditional forms of psychotherapy, the focus often is on underlying processes or conflicts, the assumption being that once these have been "worked through," the effect will be reflected by changes in behavior.

Third, behavior therapists often make specific recommendations of what action to take and what the patient should do in treatment. These are not generalized prescriptions regarding how one should live or suggestions regarding major decisions in one's life. Instead, the therapist is likely to be directive in the sense of making concrete recommendations for engaging in new learning experiences that will affect the clinical problem. This is quite different from traditional psychotherapy in which the patient is encouraged to talk about a problem and how he or she feels about it and the therapist's role is to encourage the expression and examination of feelings but to refrain from suggesting any specific course of action.

In behavior therapy others in the patient's life may be actively involved in treatment. These people may work with the therapist to learn how to help the patient engage in the new, adaptive behaviors. For example, the husband of the agoraphobic patient was asked to help by going on brief outings with her two or three times a week. A close friend also played an important role. In some applications of behavior therapy, for example, in treatment of childhood problems such as bed-wetting, parents are trained to carry out the procedures at home.

Problems treated and selected techniques

Behavior therapy encompasses a number of treatment techniques that have been successfully applied to many different clinical problems, among them fears and phobias, panic disorders, obsessions and compulsions, depression, shyness and social withdrawal, childhood hyperactivity, marital discord, sexual dysfunction and deviance, obesity, cigarette smoking, substance abuse, and eating disorders. Treatment is based on variations of a number of techniques, among them desensitization, flooding, modeling, reinforcement, and cognitive therapy. Some of these techniques are described briefly below.

Desensitization and flooding. These are processes in which the patient is exposed to anxiety-provoking cues for the purpose of overcoming various fears and phobias. Exposure may take the form of imagining anxiety-provoking situations or confronting them directly. For example, the agoraphobe may be asked to imagine herself shopping in a large department store, or she may actually make the trip to the store. *In vivo,* or real-life, variations of these treatments tend to be more effective than mental picturing. In desensitization the patient is exposed in a graduated fashion so as to minimize the degree of anxiety that is aroused. In the example above of the agoraphobic patient, she may think first only of leaving her house. Subsequently she imagines getting into the car. Later she pictures herself in the crowded store. Relaxation is used to help minimize anxiety. In flooding the patient is exposed to the situation without gradual preparation, in a way that arouses anxiety. The patient remains in the

situation—real or imagined—until anxiety decreases. Flooding may initially produce intense anxiety, but repeated exposure to the situation eventually ceases to provoke any fear, and the phobia is eliminated.

Modeling. Modeling consists of demonstrating specific behaviors to the patient. The therapist may show how to engage in the desired behavior. For example, working with a socially withdrawn youngster, the therapist may "role play" or act out how to approach a classmate or how to respond to a request from a teacher. The child then tries to imitate what was demonstrated. The therapist evaluates the patient's "performance," perhaps with suggestions for improvement.

Reinforcement. Reinforcement techniques consist of a variety of methods of rewarding specific behaviors with praise, attention, or points that can be exchanged for prizes or privileges. Although the use of rewards as incentives is quite common in everyday life, the manner in which they are used significantly influences their effects. In behavior therapy the use of divers rewards, their immediate and consistent application, their application in different situations, and evaluation of their effectiveness constitute a set of techniques that have enjoyed particularly widespread use for motivating adaptive behavior in children, adolescents, and adults in day-care facilities, schools, hospitals, nursing homes, prisons, and other institutional settings.

Cognitive therapy. In cognitively based treatments, the focus is on the beliefs, perceptions, and thoughts of the patient that may underlie maladaptive behavior. The therapist helps to identify those assumptions about the world that influence the patient's actions and relationships. The patient may be instructed to practice thinking new thoughts and to do so by making specific statements to himself or herself. For example, a patient who is socially withdrawn may be operating under the assumption that no one could ever like him or that he is boring to be with. In cognitively based treatment both these beliefs and their basis in fact are challenged. New, more positive beliefs and self-statements are encouraged and are directly practiced; for example, the patient may be asked to say to himself on a number of occasions during the day that he is a likeable person and has some unique experiences to share with others. The behaviors that follow from these new beliefs are encouraged—the patient may try approaching others at school or work and talking to people in public places.

Behavioral approaches have made important inroads in treating people for whom effective therapy has been largely unavailable, including autistic children, schizophrenics, and the mentally retarded. While none of these approaches claims to have been successful in restoring these people to entirely normal functioning, behavioral techniques have helped them to develop specific skills and to adjust to life in institutions, at home, and in the community. For example, for mentally retarded people of all ages, behavioral techniques have been very effective in developing eating, grooming, and language skills, learning how to use public transportation, and learning how to perform various occupational tasks. Behavioral techniques have also been used in the elimination of such maladaptive behaviors as rocking, head-banging, temper tantrums, and hitting oneself, often seen in autistic or severely retarded people.

Many applications of behavior therapy focus on physical illness and health-related problems; for example, reducing anxiety related to surgery and medical procedures, reducing the side effects of chemotherapy in cancer treatment, controlling pain, and increasing compliance with medical regimens such as taking medication, engaging in exercise, following a specific diet, and quitting smoking.

Limitations

Although behavior therapy has made remarkable inroads in providing new, effective, and practical treatment options, the approach is not a panacea. As stated earlier, for many problem areas—the treatment of fears, phobias, compulsions, social withdrawal, aggression, and self-abusive behaviors, to mention a few—behavioral techniques have been shown to be superior to traditional approaches. For many other areas, however, sufficient comparisons are not available on which to base claims about the relative effectiveness of behavior therapy as opposed to other forms of treatment. Many behavior therapy treatments have been the object of research studies to test the effects of different methods. In its favor as a treatment approach is the fact that some behavioral techniques have been well tested and subjected to this type of scrutiny. In contrast, traditional forms of therapy have been less frequently tested in controlled clinical studies, and evaluation of their results tends to be subjective rather than objective.

Behavior therapy is not always the treatment of choice. For some clinical problems many different techniques are available and appear at present to be similar in their effects. For example, in the treatment of depression some forms of behavioral treatment, interpersonal psychotherapy, and medication have produced similar effects. Furthermore, a number of different behavioral treatments used for depression have not been shown to differ in their effects. This is not to say that all treatments for depression are equally effective; many treatments in use in clinical practice simply have not been subjected to such study.

Although behavior therapy is usually used as a treatment in its own right, it may also be used in conjunction with other techniques. For example, for a schizophrenic patient, medication may be used for controlling hallucinations. At the same time, behavior therapy may be used for adapting to community living, developing social and job skills, and even complying in taking medications. In this case medication can control specific symptoms, while behavior therapy fosters the development of adaptive behaviors that help the patient function in everyday life. In the instances of medical diseases where behavior therapy is used as an adjunct, behavioral techniques are not substitutes for primary medical care. In the treatment of cancer and diabetes, for example, medical treatments such as chemotherapy and insulin are essential. The role of behavior therapy is in alleviating side effects and encouraging adherence to diet and exercise regimens.

Seeking qualified therapists

There is no special degree that qualifies an individual to practice behavior therapy. Professionals who administer behavior therapy usually have an advanced degree that permits them to conduct psychological treatment. Usually the degree is a doctor of philosophy (Ph.D.) in psychology, with a specialty in clinical psychology. A doctor of medicine (M.D.) with specialization in psychiatry, a Ph.D. in counseling, and a master's degree in social work (M.S.W.) are other advanced degrees that behavior therapists may have. In the United States the individual states regulate the certification of professionals who engage in psychological therapy. Typically, an aspiring therapist must have an advanced degree that attests to training in one of the mental health professions and must pass the state's licensing exam. However, these exams do not test the person's competence to conduct a specific type of treatment, such as behavior therapy, family therapy, or psychoanalysis. Since there are more than 400 different recognized therapy techniques, it is clearly not feasible to test individuals on their competence to administer a specific treatment.

In any given city, local mental health centers, clinics, and hospitals can be consulted for the name of trained professionals who conduct behavior therapy with adults, adolescents, or children. In the U.S. the national organization known as the Association for Advancement of Behavior Therapy (15 W. 36th Street, New York, NY 10018) can be of assistance as well.

Once a prospective therapist has been identified, it is valuable to the patient to schedule an initial consultation to see exactly what the treatment will entail. The prospective patient or client will want to ask what sorts of problems the therapist treats, what techniques are used, how long the treatment might take, and so on. Without full knowledge of the problem, the therapist cannot answer all of these questions definitively. Nonetheless, the specific treatment technique, methods of evaluation, and prospects for the success of the treatment are reasonable issues to address at the initial meeting. The patient may want to consult a few different therapists before making a final choice.

Marfan Syndrome
by Reed E. Pyeritz, M.D., Ph.D.

In January 1986 Flo Hyman, age 31, a star of the 1984 U.S. Olympic volleyball team, died during a game in Japan. An autopsy showed that her aorta—the largest artery in the body and the conduit for all blood pumped from the heart—had ruptured. In addition to determining the cause of Hyman's death, the postmortem examination revealed that the first several inches of the aorta were greatly enlarged and the wall of the vessel weakened. An aneurysm—a ballooning out of the vessel wall—had formed, and the rupture was inevitable. Because enlargement of the aorta to the degree of formation of an aneurysm is characteristic of the hereditary connective tissue disorder known as the Marfan syndrome, consideration focused on whether Hyman had had other features of the disorder. The conclusion was unequivocal: Flo Hyman was a Marfan victim.

In the interval since this tragedy, three crucial questions have been asked about Flo Hyman's life and death: Given the presence of the Marfan syndrome, how could she have been such a superb athlete? In view of the physical and emotional stress of her 15-year competitive athletic career, why did her aorta suddenly and without apparent warning rupture? And finally, given that Hyman had undergone the numerous medical examinations attendant to participation on national, Olympic, and professional teams, how was the diagnosis missed? These questions cut to the center of current understanding of the syndrome.

Nature of the disorder

The connective tissue may be thought of as "the scaffolding and the glue of the human body." No cell in the body exists without contact with connective tissue, and some structures, such as bone and cartilage, are made up almost exclusively of connective tissue. The composition of connective tissue is highly complex. Some of the better studied components include the large family of collagen molecules (type I collagen, the principal protein of bone, is the most common protein in the body); elastin and microfibrils that interact to form elastic fibers; and glycosaminoglycans, gelatinous materials that cement cells together and lubricate joints.

There are two major groups of connective tissue disorders. The first includes conditions such as rheumatoid arthritis, systemic lupus erythematosus, and scleroderma, which are caused by some process extrinsic to connective tissue (*e.g.,* autoimmunity) that disrupts normal function. In these conditions the constituents of connective tissue are not abnormal in themselves, and while familial factors may confer a predisposition, the disorders are not classified as genetic.

The second group encompasses close to 200 separate conditions that are caused by a mutation in one or another gene that specifies a structural component of or a metabolic process crucial to connective tissue. The conditions in this category are extraordinarily diverse. Some cause dwarfism; others, tall stature. Patients with some die in infancy; those with other disorders have a normal life expectancy. Some of these diseases affect the skin primarily; others affect only bone. One condition (familial mitral valve prolapse syndrome) is extremely common; many occur only rarely. The Marfan syndrome is one of these so-called heritable disorders of connective tissue.

The cause—or, more likely, causes—of the Marfan syndrome is not known. An important medical principle, called genetic heterogeneity, holds that what appears clinically to be the same condition in different patients could be due to fundamentally different mutations. Thus, it is highly probable that not everyone diagnosed as having the Marfan syndrome has the same underlying genetic mutation, and perhaps not even a mutation in the same gene. Over the past decade several constituents of the connective tissue have been found to be abnormal in Marfan patients, but whether the abnormalities are the fundamental defect or simply a secondary result of it has not been clarified.

Discovery and diagnosis

In 1896 a French professor of pediatrics, Antoin-B.-J. Marfan, published a brief case report of a five-year-old girl who had unusually long fingers and toes, limitation of joint motion, and curvature of the spine. In the few decades afterward, other abnormal features were described in people who had the skeletal features thought to be similar to those of Marfan's young patient. Gradually a syndrome (*i.e.,* a collection of signs and symptoms that "run together") of associated features was defined, and Marfan's name was attached to it. Today a wide range of features are recognized as potential consequences of the mutation that presumably causes the syndrome. In the absence of clear understanding of the basic defect, however, the diagnosis of the Marfan syndrome depends entirely on the physician's recognizing enough of these features, particularly in the eye, skeleton, heart, and aorta, and on determining if a close relative of the patient in question has been affected.

However, diagnosis can be difficult for three reasons. First, few people with the Marfan syndrome have all of the features, and many have relatively few, a phenomenon termed variability. Second, many of the features—such as tall stature, double-jointedness, protrusion or depression of the breast bone, scoliosis (curvature of the spine), nearsightedness, and mitral valve prolapse—are common in the general population and may not even be considered medical problems. It is only when many of these characteristics "run together" in the same person that a diagnosis of the Marfan syndrome should be considered. Also, several

of the features, in particular, dislocation of the lens of the eye and enlargement, or dilatation, of the aorta, are rare outside of the Marfan syndrome, so their presence is much stronger evidence of the diagnosis. Finally, in perhaps a third of the cases, no one else in the family has or has had the Marfan syndrome. The finding of negative family history means that more clinical evidence of the condition must be present for the physician to be confident of diagnosis than if, for example, a parent of the patient is known to be affected. In the case of a patient who has a close relative with the syndrome, the physician may make the diagnosis on the basis of fewer or subtler features.

Thus, when a person displays many of the features of the Marfan syndrome described in the medical texts, diagnosis is straightforward. It is when a patient lacks some of the typical features that the physician expects, and therefore incorrectly requires, to be present that the diagnosis is overlooked. Flo Hyman, for example, was not particularly double-jointed, did not apparently have dislocated lenses (although subtle displacement can be missed if the pupil of the eye is not fully dilated before examination), did not have a major chest or back deformity, and had no significant heart murmur. But she did exhibit some characteristics of the syndrome: tall stature (she was more than 1.8 m [6 ft] tall at the age of 13), an enlarged aorta (not recognized until autopsy), and other affected family members (also unknown until after her death). Ironically, as for many other Marfan victims who grow up excelling at sports, Flo Hyman's tall stature contributed to her athletic prowess and was indirectly responsible for her sudden death. Her case also illustrates the point that the Marfan syndrome is not necessarily associated with poor muscular development or incoordination.

A number of unusual skeletal features may be associated with the Marfan syndrome, among them extremely long fingers, a condition known as arachnodactyly, and elongated arms and legs. Another manifestation of the disorder is an indentation of the breast bone known as "funnel chest."

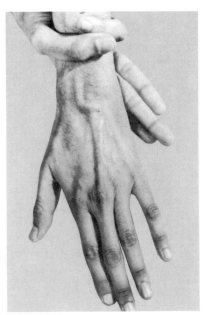

Photographs from Reed E. Pyeritz, "The Marfan Syndrome," *Principles and Practices of Modern Genetics,* ed. A. E. H. Emery and D. L. Rimoin (New York: Churchill Livingstone, 1983)

In the early 1970s a medical imaging technique was introduced that revolutionized the diagnosis of the Marfan syndrome. Echocardiography, as the technique is called, involves recording the reflections of high-frequency sound waves (ultrasound) off the structures of the heart and blood vessels. By this method the diameter of the aorta can be measured accurately, noninvasively, with no discomfort, and at modest expense. Because progressive dilatation of the aorta is painless and difficult to detect by a conventional chest X-ray, echocardiography offers the most reasonable and accurate method for detecting this abnormality, especially at an early stage, before serious complications develop. These complications are uncommon in the moderately dilated vessel—that is, up to about 50 mm (2 in), which is 50% greater than normal. Therefore, in someone suspected of having the Marfan syndrome, the diagnosis cannot be excluded until an echocardiogram has been performed.

Incidence

The Marfan syndrome occurs in about one out of every 10,000 people, regardless of race or ethnic origin. Men and women are affected with equal frequency and severity. Any man with the condition has a 50-50 chance of passing on the mutant gene with any sperm that participates in the conception of an offspring. Similarly, any woman with the Marfan syndrome has a 50-50 chance of producing an ovum that carries the mutant gene. Each new conception carries the same risk, and the odds are not modified by the diagnosis of the Marfan syndrome in children born previously to the parents or by the severity of the condition in an affected parent. This pattern of transmission is termed autosomal dominant.

As mentioned above, roughly one-third of the people with the Marfan syndrome do not have an affected parent. The mutation responsible for the disorder was not present when either parent was conceived and must have arisen in either the ovaries of the mother or the testes of the father of the affected child. As far as is understood, mutations occur constantly in human germ cells (eggs and sperm); most are never recognized, but occasionally one will occur that so disrupts development or function that a clinical disorder results. A prospective parent who has the Marfan syndrome should receive genetic counseling so that he or she fully understands the risks of having a child with the condition.

The most serious features

"Serious" is a relative term and depends not only on the severity of symptoms but also on their impact on health and life-style and on the ability of a person to cope. For example, being considerably taller than her seventh-grade peers may seem an overwhelming burden to a young girl with the Marfan syndrome, while a boy of the same age and height who is intent on playing basketball may feel blessed. In any event, poor vision, marked curvature of the spine, leakage of heart valves, and stretching and weakening of the aorta produce the most serious, and sometimes even fatal, consequences.

Poor vision in Marfan patients is caused by near-sightedness, dislocation of the lens of the eye, retinal detachment, and failure to correct vision in childhood. Most retinal detachments can be prevented if the lens is not removed. Early correction of vision with spectacles will prevent amblyopia, or "lazy eye" (decreased acuity in one eye). Anyone with the Marfan syndrome should have a detailed ophthalmologic evaluation. This is true for infants as well as for adults.

Abnormal curvature of the spine progresses during periods of growth, but unless it is severe, it rarely worsens in adulthood. The pediatrician should screen routinely for any lateral, or side-to-side, curve (scoliosis) and refer to an orthopedic surgeon any child who develops a curve of more than a few degrees. Deformity of the spine can be largely prevented through a combination of regular examination, bracing, and surgical stabilization; most people with the Marfan syndrome never need back surgery.

The mitral valve, which allows passage of blood from the left atrium to the left ventricle (but not the reverse), is abnormal in more than 80% of people with the Marfan syndrome. For Marfan patients, backward leakage of blood through the valve (mitral regurgitation) is the most serious cardiovascular problem in childhood. The leakage occurs because of worsening of a peculiarity of valve motion called mitral valve prolapse. This leakage is much more common in people with the Marfan syndrome than in the millions of people in the general population who have this same valvular characteristic. When leakage progresses to a certain point, the mitral valve must be repaired or replaced.

The aorta is a large blood vessel that grows as an individual matures, eventually reaching 0.6–0.9 m (2–3 ft) in length in adults. In the youngster with the Marfan syndrome, the diameter of the first several centimeters of the aorta may either be enlarged at birth or become enlarged during childhood; in rare cases it remains within the normal range of dimensions into early adulthood. Most of the life-threatening complications of the Marfan syndrome are related to progressive dilatation of the aorta. As the caliber of the vessel increases, the aortic valve, which prevents blood that has been pumped out of the left ventricle from leaking back, becomes stretched. Eventually the valve cannot cover the opening of the ventricle, and leakage (aortic regurgitation) results. The ventricle copes with the leakage for a while, but eventually heart failure results.

As the aorta dilates, its wall becomes thinner and weaker. A tear can develop in the inner layer, leading to separation of the layers either for a short distance or for the entire length of the vessel. This separation, called dissection, often occurs suddenly and is associated with severe pain in the chest or back. Branch vessels from the aorta can become blocked by the dissection, resulting in heart attack, stroke, or kidney failure. Not all dissections are fatal, and some are even silent—that is, the victim is unaware of its occurrence. Sudden death occurs most often when the dissection allows blood into the pericardium (the sac surrounding the heart), producing a condition called tamponade, in which effective pumping of blood to the peripheral circulation is prevented.

Management

The prime consideration in management of the Marfan syndrome is prevention of life-threatening and disabling complications. Thus, the requirements are routine evaluations, preventive measures, and multidisciplinary care. The key member of the treatment team is the physician who oversees and coordinates care. Family physicians, pediatricians, internists, and medical geneticists generally can fulfill this role. Echocardiography, which revolutionized diagnosis of this disorder, is also important to its management. Anyone who has the Marfan syndrome should have routine, periodic echocardiograms to monitor the size of the aorta.

The surgical procedure for repair of the dilated or dissected aorta has been tremendously improved since the early 1970s. Patients who formerly would have died because of an acute dissection, or who would have been considered too ill for surgery, can now often be saved. The key innovation was development of the composite graft, a Dacron conduit with an artificial valve in one end, which is used as a replacement for the most severely weakened portion of the aorta. By performing this operation before a dissection occurs, the surgeon can replace all of the dilated aorta and the leaking aortic valve. The physicians at the Johns Hopkins Hospital, Baltimore, Md., who applied this procedure to the Marfan syndrome, recommend prophylactic repair when the aorta attains a diameter of 60 mm (2.4 in). This measurement represents a compromise between the risks of dissection and the technical considerations of reimplanting the coronary arteries into the graft, which becomes easier as the aneurysm grows larger. Operative deaths at Johns Hopkins have been under 2% in all elective and emergency operations using the new technique, and long-term survival has been encouraging—over 85% after five years. The Hopkins surgeons have predicted that of 100 patients operated on, nearly all would have died within a year or two had the surgery not been performed.

Preventive strategies

As much as surgical treatment has improved, the ideal goal is to prevent the need for surgery by preventing aortic dilatation and injury. Several approaches hold promise. The first involves restriction of activity, beginning in childhood. The child with the Marfan syndrome should not participate in contact sports such as basketball and should not be encouraged to exercise at maximal capacity. Isometric exercises (in which opposing muscles are contracted, thereby increasing the blood pressure) and weight lifting should also be discouraged. Most patients can, however, participate in activities such as noncompetitive swimming and bicycling. Some children will be limited to begin with because of muscular underdevelopment and double-jointedness. The physician should work with the child, parents, and school to arrange for an appropriate exercise program. These restrictions pertain throughout life, even after replacement of the ascending aorta with a composite graft. The entire length of the aorta is affected by the same connective tissue defect that led to enlargement of the first few centimeters.

The second approach to prevention involves the use of a medication that reduces stress on the aorta. There are sound theoretical reasons for suspecting that blocking one portion of the sympathetic nervous system, the beta-adrenergic receptors, will delay the onset of serious cardiovascular problems. Recently a clinical trial of the beta-blocker drug propranolol (Inderal) produced encouraging results. Both the rate of aortic dilatation and the risk of serious complications were reduced significantly. Current medical thinking holds that unless there are evident reasons why such therapy should not be used, any person with the Marfan syndrome should be considered for treatment with a beta-adrenergic-blocking drug.

Future outlook

It is too early to know what impact the recent publicity, interest, and investigation will have on the health and life expectancy of all those who have the Marfan syndrome. However, in individual cases the answer is clear. Because of Flo Hyman's death, her siblings were screened for the Marfan syndrome. Her brother was found to have an asymptomatic aneurysm of the ascending aorta; he underwent composite graft surgery and now looks forward to an active, healthy life.

Despite the outlook for Marfan patients, the syndrome remains a serious condition that is a burden medically, financially, professionally, socially, and psychologically. In the U.S. the National Marfan Foundation is a voluntary organization of people with the Marfan syndrome and health professionals who treat and study the condition. The foundation has established local chapters and has published educational material for both lay and medical audiences. Further information can be obtained from the National Marfan Foundation, 382 Main Street, Port Washington, NY 11050.

Breakfast: How Important Is It?

by Myron Winick, M.D.

Everyone has probably heard the sayings "A good breakfast is the most important meal of the day" and "Start the day right with a hearty breakfast." Theodore Roosevelt even made breakfast a moral issue: "A good man eats a hearty breakfast." Not long ago syndicated columnist Russell Baker reminisced about his youth, when "the only thing available was the Breakfast of Champions, which [he] ate, though with skepticism." Said Baker, "I couldn't help wondering why, since the Breakfast of Champions was available to millions of people in stores all over the land, the country wasn't swarming with champions."

Is there any real evidence that breakfast is important and, if so, what kind of breakfast is best? There are three fundamental factors to consider in assessing the importance of breakfast. The first has to do with the timing of this particular meal. Breakfast, as the word implies, is the first meal after a long fast, and it is also the first meal after a long rest. The second has to do with the age, physiological condition, and health status of the person consuming the breakfast. The third concerns life-style. How active is the person? What kind of work does he or she do? Is he or she trying to control calories, cut down on fat and cholesterol, maximize dietary intake of calcium?

The first food of the day

For most people breakfast comes after a 6- to 12-hour fast. Even if one has had a snack before retiring, it is often 10 to 12 hours between the last substantial food intake and the time one gets up in the morning. During this period, particularly during the sleeping phase, the body is resting and expending only a minimum of energy. Thus, the evening meal is digested, and the energy it contains is stored and released relatively slowly during the ensuing hours. Even with this minimal use of energy, however, the body continues to carry out certain physiological processes, and as time

goes on energy stores can become depleted. Thus, characteristically, a person's blood sugar is lowest after a prolonged fast and, for most people, it is lowest when they get up in the morning. In times of famine, it is not unknown for people consuming very limited quantities of food over a long period of time to go to bed one night and fail to get up the next morning; their already low blood sugar level has dropped even farther during the night, so that by morning they are in a hypoglycemic coma and simply do not wake up.

Of course, this is an extreme example. People do not die from not eating breakfast—but skipping breakfast has its physiological effects even if the rest of the day's diet provides the necessary nutritional requirements. The importance of eating in the morning—or after any prolonged period of fasting—has been demonstrated scientifically. One such investigation was carried out in the late 1960s at Iowa State University. In an evaluation of volunteers who skipped breakfast for several weeks, researchers found that the test subjects' blood sugar continued to drop throughout the morning, reaching significantly lower levels than those of the control subjects who had eaten breakfast. More significant, perhaps, was that the ability of the test subjects to solve problems in school, to compete in athletics, and to carry out certain prescribed tasks also declined, particularly during the morning hours. Studies of school-age children have shown similar results. It would seem, therefore, that in almost all populations some sort of breakfast is important for maintaining optimum blood sugar levels and for achieving maximum performance during the morning hours. For some people, however, this is even more important than it is for others.

Who needs breakfast?

Anyone who must perform particularly well in the morning—whether in school, at work, or in sports—

417

should not skip breakfast. School-age children are particularly at risk. They are expected to be able to solve problems and maintain a high level of concentration in the morning, and they require relatively more calories (in relationship to body size) than adults require. This combination of factors makes them especially vulnerable to lower blood sugar levels and poor school performance if they skip breakfast. There are some data that suggest that the elderly need their meals more evenly spread than do younger individuals. Skipping any meal, but especially breakfast, may be particularly detrimental to them. A study conducted in the late 1970s at Vanderbilt University, Nashville, Tenn., suggested that older people intuitively know the importance of breakfast. When asked by researchers what was the most important meal for them, the majority chose breakfast, stating that if they had a good breakfast, they felt better for the rest of the day.

Pregnant and lactating women constitute another group for whom a good breakfast is particularly important. Both of these conditions increase a woman's caloric requirements. It is difficult to meet this increased need if the morning meal is skipped. In addition, during pregnancy and while a woman is breast-feeding, her body is constantly being drained of calories by the baby, and these calories should be replaced regularly throughout the day.

Finally, there are people with certain chronic illnesses for whom skipping breakfast may be particularly dangerous. The most striking example, of course, is the person with diabetes. A primary objective in managing this condition is to minimize pronounced swings in blood sugar. Eating regularly spaced meals and between-meal snacks is a mainstay of treatment. For the diabetic, missing breakfast is clearly detrimental. There are other conditions, such as peptic ulcers and other gastrointestinal disorders, in which frequent and regularly spaced meals are important. Again, people suffering from these conditions must eat breakfast.

Life-style and eating patterns

Eating patterns in the United States and in many other Western countries have changed radically over the years. Today, particularly in urban areas, a small breakfast followed by a light lunch and a relatively heavy dinner is the most common pattern of food consumption. Many people often eat a snack in the late morning and again in the evening.

Around the world the pattern of food intake varies considerably from one country to another. In Bali and other Pacific islands, for example, there is an absence of organized meals. People eat whenever they are hungry, often consuming a series of snacks during the day. This pattern is similar to the habitual nibbling of certain animal species, and there is evidence that this type of eating pattern consumes calories more efficiently than the feast-and-famine pattern of two or three "regular" meals a day. In rural areas of Europe and Great Britain, a large meal is consumed in the morning. Often this is not the very first food of the day, which may be only a cup of tea or coffee or a bowl of soup consumed at dawn. The morning meal is followed by a light midday meal and a moderately light evening meal. In certain Latin countries breakfast is small, often consisting only of coffee and bread or rolls; lunch is the main meal of the day, followed by a sort of "tea" at about five in the evening and a light dinner at nine or ten o'clock. In many parts of Africa

Nutritional value of selected cereals (per one-ounce serving)					
cereal	calories	sugar (g)	fat (g)	dietary fiber (g)	sodium (mg)
All-Bran	70	5	1	9	260
Cap'n Crunch	120	12	2	trace	220
Cheerios	110	1	2	2	290
Cocoa Puffs	110	11	1	trace	200
Corn Flakes	100	2	0	1	290
Fiber One	60	2	1	12	230
Frosted Flakes	110	11	0	trace	200
Fruit & Fibre (Harvest Medley)	90	7	1	4	200
Grape-Nuts	100	3	1	3	170
Life	120	6	2	1	180
Natural Raisin Bran	80	9	0	4	180
Rice Krispies	110	3	0	trace	290
Shredded Wheat (spoon size)	110	0	1	0.7	trace
Shredded Wheat 'N Bran (spoon size)	110	0	1	4	0
Special K	110	3	0	trace	230
Total	110	3	1	2	280
Wheat Chex	100	2	0	2	200
Wheaties	110	3	1	2	270

Compiled from nutrition information on box labels (September 1987)

only one major meal is consumed each day, and this occurs in the evening; during the day, while people are working at home and in the fields, only casual snacks may be consumed. Thus, among different cultures, depending on the life-style of the people, the quantity and quality of the morning meal varies enormously, influenced particularly by what kind of work the people do, how far they travel during the day to and from work, what kinds of food are available, and the times of the day when it is possible to eat a large, leisurely meal.

Even within the Western industrial culture, different life-styles dictate different breakfast needs. Activity patterns are an important determinant. The early morning jogger needs a relatively high-calorie breakfast, preferably high in complex carbohydrates. Some joggers split this into two meals: juice and coffee before the exercise and more substantial fare after they return. A good breakfast is even more important for the serious competitive athlete or the person who leaves home to perform hard physical labor.

Regardless of age or profession, however, there are always some people—busy mothers, shift workers, people who commute long distances—who feel that they simply do not have time for breakfast. Typically, they have a cup of coffee or two first thing in the morning and "make up" for missing breakfast by having a donut or sweet roll later, at a midmorning break. In such people blood sugar levels will gradually fall, and irritability and difficulty in concentrating could result later in the morning. In addition, eating a high-calorie, low-nutrient snack in place of breakfast will make it harder for them to balance their nutritional intake during the rest of the day.

People who are trying to control their caloric intake also should eat breakfast. Many people who are dieting have a tendency to skip meals in order to eat less during the day. However, studies have shown that spreading out the caloric intake over the entire day may utilize calories more efficiently and may prevent the dieter from overeating at the next meal.

Meeting nutritional requirements

Given, then, that for most people breakfast is an important meal, what kind of foods should it consist of? In the United States and many other Western countries, people are being urged to try to conform to certain dietary guidelines in order to decrease their intake of saturated fats, sodium, and sugar and increase their intake of dietary fiber. Both the American Heart Association and the National Cancer Institute have made specific recommendations designed to reduce people's risk of cardiovascular disease and certain kinds of cancer. These recommendations include the following: keeping calories at an appropriate level; consuming no more than 30% of the day's calories as fat; keeping saturated (animal) fat to no more than 15% of caloric intake; consuming 300 mg or less of cholesterol per day; reducing salt (sodium) intake; consuming 55% or more of calories as carbohydrates, with less than 15% as simple sugar; increasing the intake of fruits and vegetables; and increasing the intake of fiber. If properly chosen, the foods eaten at breakfast can contribute significantly toward fulfilling these requirements.

After using the above guidelines for choosing from the different categories of food available, one would next ask how many calories one should consume at breakfast. As noted earlier, the caloric intake will vary

Nutritional values of selected fast-food breakfast items

item	calories	protein (g)	fat (g)	carbohydrates (g)	sodium (mg)	cholesterol (mg)
McDonald's						
Egg McMuffin	327	18	15	31	885	229
scrambled egg breakfast (scrambled eggs, sausage, English muffin with butter, and hash brown potatoes)	697	28	44	47	1,463	412
hotcakes and sausage (with butter and syrup)	706	17	29	94	1,685	90
English muffin (with butter)	186	5	5	30	318	13
hash brown potatoes	125	2	7	14	325	7
orange juice (6 oz)	80	1	0	20	0	0
Roy Rogers						
crescent sandwich	401	13	27	25	867	148
with bacon	431	15	30	26	1,035	156
with sausage	449	20	30	26	1,289	168
with ham	557	20	42	25	1,192	189
apple Danish	249	4	12	32	255	15
cheese Danish	254	5	12	31	260	11
Wendy's						
breakfast sandwich	370	17	19	33	770	200
French toast	400	11	19	45	850	115
home fries	360	4	22	37	745	20

Source: *Fast Food and the American Diet: A Report by the American Council on Science and Health*

somewhat with the individual's physiological state and life-style. A good rule of thumb for most healthy adults is between 20 and 25% of the total daily requirement. For a dieter on a 1,200-cal-a-day regime, this would mean a breakfast of only about 300 cal. Certainly on some days a person may consume fewer calories and on others, more—on weekends or during a vacation, for example. For the person who is trying to keep total fat intake to 30% or less of daily calories, the two "breakfast" foods that require the most caution are eggs and dairy products. Fifty percent of the calories in whole milk are supplied in the form of fat. For eggs the percentage is even higher. Both are high in cholesterol—one egg yolk contains 250 mg, almost a whole day's supply. Substituting skim milk and other low-fat dairy products helps. With eggs, however, the problem of restriction is more difficult, as it involves strictly limiting the number one may eat. Usually two to three eggs per week is considered acceptable. A person who eats more than three should have his or her serum cholesterol level checked annually. If the level is under 200, the person can probably safely continue the higher egg-consumption pattern. Breakfast meats such as bacon or sausage are also high in saturated fat and cholesterol and are relatively poor sources of protein compared with other meats. Thus, the typical American bacon-and-egg breakfast no longer fits into the diets of health-conscious people who are trying to reduce their intake of fats—especially cholesterol—salt, and, for many, total daily calories. The fast-food counterparts of the typical breakfast, which are extremely popular among people who feel pressed for time in the morning and those who like food that is "portable," often have more fat, more sodium, and more calories than the meal they replace.

On the other hand, cereal, particularly "old-fashioned" cooked cereal, is an excellent breakfast food, as are many of the newer brands of high-fiber whole-grain cold cereals, especially those that contain raisins and other dried fruits. Such cereals are low in calories, high in complex carbohydrate and fiber, fortified with added vitamins and minerals, and, when eaten with skim milk, rich in calcium and vitamin D. In addition, in recent years many brands of breakfast cereal have reduced or eliminated salt and sugar. Citrus juices are also good for breakfast, containing large amounts of vitamin C and certain minerals. Whole-grain breads, rolls, muffins, and the like are also high in complex carbohydrates. Thus, a breakfast of juice, cereal and fruit with skim milk, and whole-wheat toast or a muffin is an excellent choice. Substituting margarine for butter is another step toward controlling saturated fat and cholesterol.

The excuse some people give for not eating breakfast is that they do not like any of these typical breakfast foods. But breakfast can be a more original, imaginative meal if one does not feel bound to the more or less traditional menu. Europeans often eat a variety of cheeses at breakfast; the British have kippers; and the Scandinavians eat herring. In Israel a typical breakfast may include a variety of yogurts and fruits. In fact, breakfast can vary as much as dinner while still conforming to the guidelines for good nutrition. Interestingly, most people tend to eat the same things for breakfast every day. Imagine if they did this with lunch or dinner. Mealtime would quickly become a boring event.

In planning the breakfast menu, people should not be afraid to experiment. Soups, rice dishes, peanut butter sandwiches, even some of the previous night's leftover pizza—all are appropriate for breakfast once in a while. Then, of course, there are such traditional dishes as pancakes, French toast, and waffles, all acceptable on occasion, with some caution about the amounts of butter and syrup that are used. On the other hand, some people like "breakfast" foods better than any others and would be happy having French toast for dinner or a bowl of cereal as a before-bed snack. In many restaurants fancy omelettes on luncheon and dinner menus are among the entrées that are specialties of the house.

Breakfast is often an ideal meal for providing necessary calcium and fiber, which are in short supply in the diets of many Americans and Europeans. Most of the calcium in the U.S. diet comes from dairy products. Skim milk, low-fat cheeses, and yogurt are all good sources of calcium. Some nuts, such as almonds, and small bony fish, such as sardines, are also good sources. These foods can easily be incorporated into an appetizing breakfast. As for fiber, bran and other high-fiber cereals, dried fruits, and the skin and pulp of many fresh fruits are rich sources of this essential substance.

For individuals with special needs, only a few slight modifications are necessary. The athlete can consume more calories at breakfast in the form of complex carbohydrates—cereals, rice, potatoes, pancakes and waffles, and even pasta—which provide the major, most efficient fuel for active muscles. The person restricting calories needs to reduce the amount of fat to even less than 30%. Fat is the most concentrated source of calories. Increasing bulk by adding more fiber not only confers the health benefits of a high-fiber diet but also makes the meal more filling, thus helping to curtail appetite.

The old clichés stated at the outset are essentially correct. Breakfast is a very important meal—but it need not be a boring or unpleasant one. The number and combinations of foods that can be included are large enough to accommodate all tastes. All that is required for planning a healthful and appealing breakfast is some basic nutritional knowledge and a bit of imagination.

Chest Pain
by Paul Cutler, M.D.

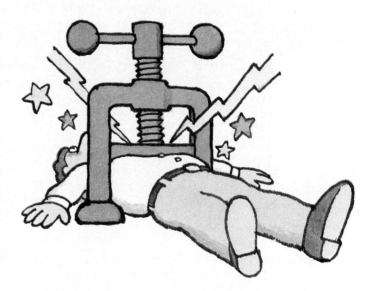

For people experiencing chest pain, one of the first thoughts is that they are having a heart attack. Usually this fear of the worst is unfounded; disorders involving the musculoskeletal system (muscles, bones, ligaments) are by far the most common causes of chest pain. Indeed, most people with chest pain who consult their physicians thinking that they have a "heart condition" do not have heart problems at all.

The chest is basically a large cage composed of muscles, bones, fibrous tissue, and ligaments. Inside this cage are the heart and its covering layers (pericardium), the lungs and their covering layers (pleura), the major artery known as the aorta, the esophagus, and the trachea. Diseases or disorders that affect the function of any of these organs and tissues can cause chest pain of varying severity and seriousness. In many cases it is easy to distinguish the cause of the various types of chest pain by observation of the pain's characteristics—the nature and location of the pain; what causes it; what makes it worse; what alleviates it; when it occurs; its relation to physical activity, meals, body position, and deep breathing; and accompanying signs and symptoms, such as nausea, fever, or localized tenderness. In some instances this differentiation is not so simple, and further observation and tests may be necessary.

Heart pain

Pain caused by coronary artery disease is the most feared because it is the most lethal. The heart itself is a muscle and cannot function without an adequate blood supply. This blood is carried to the heart via the coronary arteries. If one or more coronary arteries are sufficiently narrowed by fatty deposits (atherosclerosis), the individual may experience angina pectoris (literally, "pain in the chest") whenever the heart muscle needs more blood and oxygen. This type of pain is usually brought on by physical exertion or acute emotional stress; in both of these circumstances the heart muscle has an increased need for oxygen because it must work harder.

In the past two decades, it has been recognized that an uncommon form of angina pectoris may occur in an individual who is at rest. It results from spasm of a normal (i.e., not narrowed or blocked) coronary artery or spasm superimposed upon an artery already substantially narrowed by atherosclerosis. The chest pain resulting from this "atypical" angina is identical to the pain associated with the more common form, although it differs in that it occurs at rest rather than upon exertion.

In both kinds of angina, the pain is typically under the sternum (breast bone); covers a wide area of the central portion of the chest; cannot be pointed to with a single finger (i.e., is diffuse rather than localized); is described as a tightness, burning, pressure, crushing, squeezing, or heavy weight on the chest; and often radiates to the neck, the lower jaw, or the inner aspect of one or both arms. Usually the pain subsides in several minutes, either spontaneously as the spasm or stress abates or after the patient dissolves a nitroglycerine tablet under the tongue. This medication causes blood vessels to dilate, relieves the shortage of blood flowing through the coronary arteries, and also decreases the heart's work load.

Patients with this type of anginal pain should promptly consult their physicians. Even though the description of pain is enough to suggest angina pectoris with reasonable diagnostic certainty, the seriousness of this disorder warrants absolute confirmation. An electrocardiogram may suffice, but often an exercise stress test is performed as well. The stress test can be done alone or in addition to cardiac imaging that produces pictures of the heart's performance. At times the physician may even request coronary arteriography, a more invasive, costly—and, in some cases, potentially risky—procedure, if an imminent catastrophic event is thought to be probable. Early treatment with drugs that dilate the coronary arteries (nitrates, calcium-channel blockers), drugs that decrease the heart's requirements for oxygen (beta-blockers), modification of diet, cessation of cigarette smoking, and regulation of physical activities and emotional stresses may halt the progress of coronary artery disease.

When obstruction of the coronary arteries becomes

421

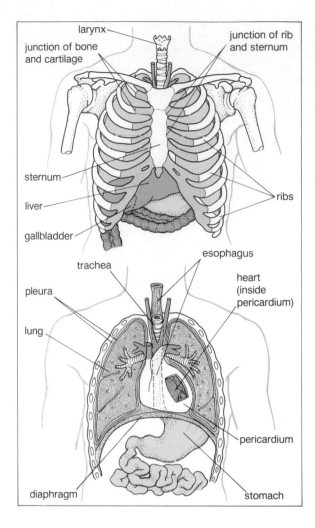

junction of bone
and cartilage

larynx

junction of rib
and sternum

sternum

liver

gallbladder

ribs

trachea

esophagus

pleura

heart
(inside
pericardium)

lung

pericardium

diaphragm

stomach

severe enough, a coronary occlusion, or blockage of an artery, may occur. Under these circumstances the pain is similar to the pain of angina pectoris, but it is continuous and more severe, it does not subside for several hours, and the portion of heart muscle supplied by the obstructed artery "dies" for lack of oxygen and nutrition. This kind of tissue death is called necrosis. This event is known as a myocardial infarction (the word infarct means "an area of necrosis"), or "heart attack." The patient experiencing this kind of pain tends to lie still rather than move about, and the pain requires potent analgesics or narcotics for relief. (It should be noted that a heart attack can also occur without any accompanying pain.)

Angina pectoris that gets progressively more severe, occurs more often, and is increasingly easy to provoke often culminates in a heart attack. In addition to experiencing continuous chest pain, the heart attack victim may perspire freely, appear pale, be nauseated, vomit, and generally seem to be quite sick. Immediate hospitalization is indicated. Emergency measures may include administration of oxygen as well as anticoag-

ulants and clot-dissolving medications and attempts to open obstructed vessels with expandable balloons or laser beams. If applied early enough, usually less than three hours after the onset of chest pain, some of these measures may limit or even eliminate consequent heart muscle damage.

Muscle, bone, and ligament pain

Knowing the seriousness of heart attacks, many people apprehensively attribute all instances of chest pain, regardless of their nature or location, to the heart. For example, one may injure a muscle, tendon, or ligament of the chest wall during exercise or a sudden stretch or pull. Because the pain may become more noticeable many hours after the causative event, the patient may not be aware of the relationship. This kind of chest pain does not resemble heart pain in either nature or location—the site can usually be precisely located, and certain motions or activities that use the injured area can cause the pain to be reproduced. Often the painful area is tender when pressed.

A special type of chest wall pain that often confuses both doctor and patient is called Tietze's syndrome. This condition does not result from injury, and its cause is not clearly understood; it is associated with pain, inflammation, and severe tenderness at the junctions of one or more ribs with their connecting cartilage close to the breastbone. The pain may be constant but is aggravated by voluntary motion or reflex actions such as sneezing and coughing that cause movement of the chest wall. The pain of Tietze's syndrome is almost invariably associated with considerable tenderness when pressure is applied to the inflamed site.

Pain in the lungs and pleura

Interestingly, the lungs do not have sensory nerves and, therefore, diseases within the lungs themselves are not associated with chest pain unless the pleura are involved. The pleura are two pairs of concentric baglike structures, one of which encases the lung while the other lines the inside of the chest wall. Acute pleuritis, or pleurisy, can result from an inflammation of the lung (i.e., pneumonia), a blood clot—or embolus—originating in the legs and traveling to the lungs (pulmonary embolus), or other causes. In most cases the patient has a preexisting illness. The pain is characteristically sharp and knifelike. Most commonly, it occurs in the back and sides of the lower chest, usually on only one side. The distinctive feature of pleural pain is that it becomes worse upon breathing, especially deep breathing, or coughing—whenever two pleural surfaces rub together. Other symptoms, such as cough, fever, or leg pain, often accompany pleuritic pain.

The physician examining a patient with pleuritis may hear the characteristic sound of a "friction rub" when a stethoscope is applied over the area of lung involved. Since this type of pain almost invariably results from

422

disease of the underlying lung tissue, a chest X-ray is sufficient to confirm the diagnosis. If the X-ray is normal yet pleuritic pain resulting from a pulmonary embolus is suspected, a special radioisotope study will furnish positive evidence.

Pericardial pain

The heart is encased in two thin layers of tissue called the pericardium. Inflammation of the pericardium can be a source of chest pain. Such inflammation results most commonly from a bacterial or viral infection and is called acute pericarditis. The pain is quite similar to that of a heart attack and is often mistaken for such, but pericarditis differs in that it is much less common than heart attack, frequently occurs in young, healthy people, and is usually accompanied by fever. The pain does not tend to radiate into the neck or arms, as heart attack pain may do; it is often worse upon deep breathing because of inflammation of the adjacent pleura and may be relieved if the patient sits up and hunches forward.

This type of pain is frequently accompanied by a special type of friction rub heard over the lower portion of the heart. The electrocardiogram may offer proof-positive evidence, and the chest X-ray may show signs of fluid in the pericardial sac. Often both the pain and the electrocardiogram reading are initially indistinguishable from the picture of a heart attack, and patients with pericarditis usually require hospitalization.

Gastrointestinal pain

Disorders of the gastrointestinal tract may be associated with chest pain. Notable are diseases of the esophagus associated with esophageal spasm (achalasia), inflammation (esophagitis), narrowing (stricture) of the esophagus, and esophageal ulcers. The pain may be similar to heart pain but tends to radiate less to the arms and neck and more to the upper abdomen and usually is not associated with physical exertion. Related symptoms include so-called heartburn, caused by the backflow (reflux) of acidic stomach secretions, and difficulty in swallowing. In the case of esophagitis caused by acid reflux, antacids often relieve the pain.

Esophageal problems are now known to be more common than was once thought, and at times a number of diagnostic studies may be needed for the differentiation of cardiac from esophageal pain. Their treatments and seriousness differ greatly. Procedures sometimes needed for the confirmation and distinguishing of esophageal disorders include perfusion of the esophagus with a solution of hydrochloric acid, which reproduces the pain of acid reflux; barium-contrast X-rays to determine structural or functional problems in swallowing; measurements of esophageal motility and sphincter pressure; direct visualization of the esophagus with a flexible fiber-optic instrument called an esophagoscope; and the swallowing of a

dilute radioactive solution, the amount of which, if regurgitated back into the esophagus, can be measured with a Geiger counter.

Old-fashioned "indigestion," consisting of gas, belching, nausea, and sometimes vomiting, is associated with vague discomfort very high in the abdomen but is not ordinarily associated with chest pain. Confusion exists primarily because prior to the early part of the 20th century, genuine heart attacks were labeled as "acute indigestion." There should be no difficulty in distinguishing the two. Indigestion is caused and exacerbated by overeating or overindulgence in alcoholic beverages and often occurs after an especially heavy meal. It can be aggravated by certain foods and beverages and some drugs, including aspirin.

Under unusual circumstances, pain arising from duodenal or gastric ulcers or from gallstones can radiate to the uppermost portion of the abdomen, even overlapping into the lower chest. This is uncommon, however, and the distinction can usually be easily made by means of associated symptoms and the physical examination. Patients with ulcers usually also have heartburn and epigastric (high abdominal) pain and discomfort, and this pain is frequently timed to meals, occurring one or more hours after eating, when the stomach is empty of food but full of acid. Patients with gallstones may have repeated attacks of sharp pain in the right upper portion of the abdomen under the rib cage and may also have intolerance to fatty or fried foods. In both these instances the pain is predominantly abdominal. Confirmatory evidence is offered by barium-contrast X-rays of the upper and lower gastrointestinal tract (a "GI series") in the case of ulcer and an ultrasound study in the case of gallbladder stones.

Nerve pain

Another source of chest pain lies in the spine and the nerves emanating from it. For example, a herniated ("slipped") disk in the spinal column of the neck can press on a nerve root going to the chest wall. In this instance the pain is usually worsened by neck movement, and the distribution of the pain conforms to the area to which the affected nerve distributes its sensory fibers. This pain is intermittent, relieved by certain neck positions, and does not have the nature, distribution, radiation, or relation to exertion that cardiac pain has. Arthritis affecting the parts of the spine that pass through the neck (cervical spine) or chest (thoracic spine) has the same characteristics. X-ray studies of the spine, sometimes aided by computed tomography (CT) scans, may determine the diagnosis, but caution must be exercised in interpreting abnormal spine X-rays.

Herpes zoster—more commonly known as shingles—is another type of nerve disorder that may cause chest pain. In this case there is a viral infection of a sensory nerve root causing pain in the area of that nerve root's distribution. If the nerve carries fibers of sensation from the chest, pain in the chest results. This pain may be quite severe, is continuous for several or more days, is usually associated with peculiar tingling or pricking sensations (paresthesias), and is confined to the area of the nerve's distribution. It may be accompanied by chills, fever, upset stomach, and general malaise. The pain caused by shingles should not be confused with heart pain, and it can be diagnosed with certainty when, on the third or fourth day after the onset of the infection, small reddish blisters erupt on the skin along the nerve's course.

"Café coronary"

So-called café coronary, which is actually a choking spell, should not be confused with a true heart attack. The former situation results when a wad of swallowed food—commonly an inadequately chewed piece of meat—becomes lodged in the larynx; it usually occurs at the table, frequently in a restaurant, where the diner has had too much to drink, is not chewing carefully, and "swallows" food into the respiratory tract rather than into the esophagus. The choking victim cannot talk or breathe, becomes agitated, and eventually turns blue from a lack of oxygen. These signs may be mistakenly interpreted by fellow diners as signs of heart attack—hence the term café coronary. The true heart attack victim can speak, tends to hold still, and becomes pale rather than bluish. The choking person, on the other hand, does *not* have chest pain and almost invariably is pointing to or grasping his or her throat. The alert bystander should quickly comprehend the situation, and anyone who is properly trained should perform the Heimlich maneuver, or hug, a procedure that dislodges impacted food.

Other causes

Some singularly occurring episodes of chest pain may be quite serious, even fatal. Although uncommon, they invariably cause the patient to seek medical attention because of the pain's severity and because of associated symptoms. A tear in the lining of the aorta, the main artery leading out of the heart, allows blood to flow in between the layers of tissue that compose this vessel. This kind of hemorrhage is called a "dissection" of the thoracic aorta and is a catastrophic event; it is usually accompanied by cold, clammy skin and physiological shock. The pain of aortic dissection is severe and continuous, may resemble the pain of a heart attack very closely, and requires hospitalization and diagnostic studies for verification and differentiation. Such studies include a simple chest X-ray, an X-ray of the aorta with an intra-arterial injection of radiopaque dye (aortography), and an ultrasound image of the vessel's layers. A simple physical examination sometimes furnishes the key diagnostic clue.

A tear of the surface of the lung permits large quantities of air to escape into the pleural space (the space between the two layers of pleura). This phenomenon is called a pneumothorax. Spontaneous pneumothorax usually occurs in young, healthy males but is also seen in older persons whose lung surfaces are thin and overstretched because of diseases such as asthma or chronic obstructive lung disease. Traumatic pneumothorax, as the name implies, is the result of an accident or injury, such as a needle puncture or stab wound. While sharp chest pain on either the right or the left side is the initial feature of pneumothorax, shortness of breath soon follows. The physical exam may provide the physician with good reason to suspect pneumothorax, but a chest X-ray will offer ultimate proof. Urgent medical attention is needed.

Finally, if the pain fits no pattern of distribution or causation and is vague, recurring, and variable in nature, anxiety and emotional factors must be considered. As more is learned about the various causes of chest pain, fewer incidences are attributed to emotional disorders, but certainly the latter causes still exist.

Some generalizations

Chest pain, as the above distinctions indicate, can be classified into three types. The first is characterized by severe, onetime, enduring pain usually associated with other evidence of serious illness, such as cold, clammy skin, shortness of breath, or fever. Such pain requires a physician's immediate attention.

The second type is brief, episodic, and recurrent and is not as severe as the first. It usually conforms to a pattern that can be detected from the timing of the episodes and the precipitating factors, the location of the pain, and the measures that relieve it. In this case, too, a visit to the physician is indicated.

The third type of chest pain is also mild and recurrent but does not conform to any known pattern insofar as timing, location, and precipitating or relieving factors are concerned. It may vary in location from time to time. These pains are usually inconsequential and benign, and they may be psychosomatic in origin.

In most instances the cause of chest pain can be clearly distinguished by the physician, who considers the preceding determinants in making a diagnosis. Patients frequently can do the same. But, as in all aspects of the practice of medicine, there are often patients whose disease manifestations do not conform to textbook descriptions, whose symptoms are not clear-cut or conclusive, for whom a definite diagnosis cannot be made with an acceptable degree of certainty, or whose symptom complex can be caused by more than one disease. In these instances, if the patient's medical history and the physical examination cannot clearly define the causative disorder, further diagnostic studies will be performed.

Delivering the Right Dosage
by Joseph Wartak, M.D.

The Western societies' appetite for drugs has been a driving force for the development of some 10,000 pharmaceutical preparations that are on the market today. Despite that overwhelming number of drugs, they all have one thing in common: a substance or agent that is capable of producing therapeutic effects is accompanied by one, two, or more inactive substances called excipients, or vehicles. The amount of an active agent is usually very small, and the bulk must be provided by a vehicle. For example, the dose of a potent cardiac drug, digoxin, is frequently only 0.125 mg, and such an amount is too small to be accurately weighed and conveniently administered. Because it is impractical to administer drugs in their natural, or pure, state, various pharmaceutical preparations, or "dosage forms," such as tablets, capsules, suppositories, injections, and others must be prepared using "vehicles."

Vehicles not only provide a suitable bulk or volume but also are used to carry the active agent to the site of absorption; to bind, suspend, or solubilize the active agent; to add flavor or color; and to protect the active agent's potency. Commonly used vehicles for tablets and capsules include starch, sugar, gelatin, chocolate, and various flavoring and coloring agents. Proper coloring and flavoring result in a better acceptance, especially by children. Unfortunately, the candylike appearance of many tablets and capsules frequently leads to poisoning among children if drugs are not securely stored. To prevent accidental poisoning, tablets and capsules are frequently dispensed in containers that are designed so that they cannot be easily opened by children.

Drug action
The majority of drugs are used to provide relief for such symptoms as all kinds of pain (e.g., headache, abdominal pain, chest pain, back pain), cough, nasal congestion, shortness of breath, constipation, diarrhea, insomnia, and anxiety (i.e., unspecified or unfounded fear). Such drugs cannot change the natural course of the disease. Rather, they bring some form of temporary relief. If a disease—for example, a common cold—is self-limiting (i.e., it can cure itself), then the use of drugs is rarely indicated or justified. This rationale has been best expressed by the following saying: "A common cold lasts one week if treated and lasts seven days if not treated." When a disease is progressive, for example, angina pectoris or chronic bronchitis, then despite symptomatic treatment it will run its natural course, often leading to complications and even to death.

Only a small number of drugs change the natural course of a disease. Antibiotics are capable of killing bacteria or other biologic agents (except viruses) that cause infectious diseases and thus bring a cure. (They are often, however, used indiscriminately against viral infections for which they are not effective.) Other drugs, such as insulin (for diabetes) or dopamine (for Parkinson's disease), can control the disease process and delay complications.

In addition to a specific biochemical action, all drugs produce a psychological or psychophysiological effect that is manifested by a temporary relief of the patient's symptoms. This so-called placebo effect can be best demonstrated with capsules containing nothing more than sugar. When patients complaining of pain are given such capsules, they will experience relief, provided they expect the capsules to contain the pain-relieving substance. In order for the placebo effect to occur, patients must believe that the use of the drug will make a symptom or disease disappear and have faith in the physician's capability to cure disease.

425

Administration of drugs

Some drugs can be formulated in only one way, or into one dosage form. For example, insulin, noradrenaline, streptomycin, immune sera, and vaccines can be used only as solutions for injection. Most drugs, however, can be manufactured into several dosage forms suitable for different routes of administration. For example, many antibiotics and corticosteroids are available as tablets, capsules, injections, creams, ointments, drops, aerosols, and other forms.

To derive the maximum benefit from the medication, the patient must use the dosage form properly; if such information is not provided by the physician, the patient should ask the pharmacist for instructions. Instructions on how to use medication are especially important for some tablets, capsules, and aerosols. In general, drugs should be taken on an empty stomach in order to ensure optimal absorption. However, those drugs that irritate the gastric mucosa (e.g., aspirin, iron salts) may be taken immediately before, during, or after meals and snacks in order to avoid or minimize gastric irritation and its symptoms (nausea, vomiting, heartburn). All drugs can be taken with a drink of water to lessen any disagreeable taste and to assist in swallowing.

To produce therapeutic effects, the drug must reach the target cells in the appropriate organ or tissue. When the organ or tissue is readily accessible (e.g., skin, eyes, body orifices), the target cells can be reached by drugs applied locally. However, the target cells in most organs and tissues can be reached only by drugs that enter the bloodstream either directly by an injection into the vein or indirectly by means of absorption from the alimentary tract or the site of an extravascular (i.e., intramuscular or subcutaneous) injection.

From pure drug to dosage form

active substance (pure drug) + inactive substances: starch or sugar / grease or cocoa butter / water or alcohol

manufacturing process = tablets, capsules, dusting powder, creams and ointments, rectal suppositories, spray, drops, injections, inhalation aerosol

Most frequently drugs are taken by mouth and swallowed. Oral administration is not only painless, convenient, safe, and economical but also the only practical method for the self-administration of most drugs by patients. Only a small number of drugs that are destroyed by gastric acid and digestive enzymes (e.g., insulin, immunologic preparations) or are poorly absorbed from the gut (e.g., most types of penicillin, streptomycin) cannot be administered orally. In addition, the oral route is contraindicated in emergency situations (because of a delayed drug action), when the patient is unconscious (hazard of aspiration), and when the patient is vomiting or has swallowing difficulties.

Tablets and capsules

Drugs to be taken by mouth are usually formulated as tablets and capsules and less frequently as powders, granules, or liquid preparations. In the past, pills coated with sugar or chocolate were the most common oral dosage form, and because of their popularity, any solid dosage form (except for powders and granules) is still called a "pill" by most laypersons.

Tablets come in many shapes, but most frequently they are round with flat or convex faces. They vary in size, and many are scored so that they may be easily broken into two or four parts to allow flexible dosing. Some tablets are coated with gelatin, sugar, or chocolate in order to protect the active ingredients in the core, to mask unpleasant taste, or to improve the appearance. Other tablets are coated with a thin layer of cellulose derivative or resin, which protects the drug (e.g., erythromycin) from destruction by the gastric juices or prevents gastric irritation by the drug (e.g., aspirin). Coated tablets must not be crushed; however, uncoated tablets may be crushed for easy swallowing.

A number of different types of tablets have been developed for special application:

1. Sublingual tablets (e.g., nitroglycerin) are designed to dissolve rapidly under the tongue.

2. Chewable tablets (e.g., antacids, vitamins) are especially designed to be administered to young children and geriatric patients who cannot swallow tablets easily.

3. Lozenges (e.g., Dequadin) are intended to be sucked so that they can be slowly dissolved, releasing the active agent, usually an antiseptic or local anesthetic.

4. Effervescent tablets (e.g., Alka-Seltzer) are formulated to produce bubbles of carbon dioxide (CO_2) gas due to the reaction of citric acid with sodium bicarbonate or some other effervescent combination when the tablet is placed in water.

Some tablets have been given fancy names by drug manufacturers to underscore a particular shape (e.g., caplets) or a prolonged action (e.g., durules). Tylenol caplets are basically tablets shaped as capsules; they

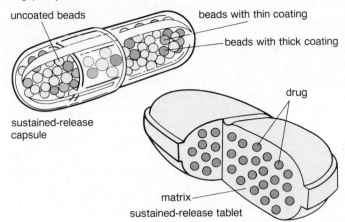

uncoated beads

beads with thin coating

beads with thick coating

drug

sustained-release capsule

matrix

sustained-release tablet

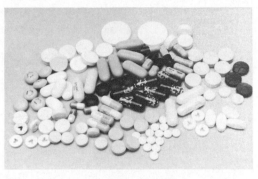

Pills come in many shapes and sizes. The capsule and tablet in the diagram show dosage forms that release the drug over a prolonged period of time.

were developed in response to the public's concern about the safety of Extra Strength Tylenol capsules, some of which were laced with cyanide (for reasons that may never be uncovered) in a major and widely publicized drug-tampering scandal in the U.S. in 1982 in which seven victims died. Most pharmaceutical companies have not discontinued manufacturing drugs in a capsule form.

Capsules are cylindrical containers made of gelatin and filled with a powdered drug, which is more rapidly absorbed than a tablet once the capsule has been dissolved in the gut. Some capsules (*e.g.,* Contac capsules) contain hundreds of beads or pellets, some uncoated and others coated with wax or other material that dissolves at different times depending upon the thickness of the coating. Such sustained-release capsules provide prolonged action of a drug.

Tablets and capsules are frequently marked with letters, words, symbols, and numbers. This, together with the color of tablets and capsules, helps to identify the manufacturer and, more important, to identify the product and the dosage in case of emergency.

Suppositories

In some situations medications are administered rectally in order to avoid irritation of the gastrointestinal tract by some drugs (*e.g.,* antirheumatics), achieve a prolonged overnight action of other drugs (*e.g.,* antiasthmatics), or obtain local effects (*e.g.,* to relieve pain and itching caused by hemorrhoids). Drugs for insertion into the rectum are mixed with cocoa butter or glycerinated gelatin and molded into conical or bullet-shaped forms.

Once inserted into the rectum, the suppository melts and releases the active agent, which either acts locally or is absorbed into the bloodstream and exerts systemic action. Many drugs are better utilized when they are given rectally and retained deeply enough to be past the muscular range for a specified amount of time; however, this route of administration has never gained popularity, especially in the Western societies.

In addition to rectal suppositories, there are also ovoid or globular suppositories for insertion into the vagina. They are used only for the treatment of local inflammatory conditions of the female genital organs.

Aerosols

Aerosols are suspensions of fine particles of liquid or solid therapeutic agents in air or inert gases. Physically they resemble such familiar household and cosmetic aerosol products as air fresheners and hair sprays. Medical aerosols are dispensed from metal containers in which a solution or suspension of one or more drugs is packed under the pressure of a compressed or liquefied gas such as freon, which delivers the propellant force. A mist or fine dust is produced when the medication is forcefully expelled through an exceedingly small valve orifice by the vapor pressure of the propellant when it comes into contact with the warm air at atmospheric pressure. To facilitate the transfer of the medication into the tracheobronchial tree, the container is fitted with an oral or nasal adapter. With the adapter correctly placed and the aerosol dispenser held vertically, the valve is actuated by finger pressure on the base of the container. For potent drugs such as some antiasthmatic agents, the valve includes a metering device that delivers a measured dose.

Aerosols are used mainly for relieving the spasm or controlling inflammatory conditions of the respiratory tracts (*e.g.,* asthma, chronic bronchitis). When they are inhaled, the active agents such as bronchodilators or corticosteroids are delivered directly to the site of action so that high therapeutic concentrations can be achieved in the mucosa and smooth muscles of the respiratory tract while systemic concentrations can be lower, thus minimizing or avoiding side effects.

Injections

Injections are sterile solutions of drugs (usually in water) intended for subcutaneous, intramuscular, and intravenous administration. Injectable medications come in small volumes (usually less than 30 ml), which are

427

administered rapidly, and in large volumes (usually 500 ml or more), which are allowed to drip slowly into the circulatory system over a period of hours. Small-volume injections are dispensed in single-dose containers (ampules) and multiple-dose containers (vials), whereas large-volume injections are available in glass bottles and plastic bags. Drugs that are unstable in aqueous solution are placed in the vial or ampule as dry solids, and a suitable solvent must be added just prior to administration.

Drugs given by injection usually provide rapid and reliable therapeutic effects because they do not have to pass through many biologic membranes or survive various hazards. Injected drugs either enter directly into the systemic circulation (if they are administered intravenously) or are absorbed from a depot made at the site of a subcutaneous or intramuscular injection. Those patients who are impressed by injections—i.e, consider them a more dramatic or effective method— may also benefit more psychologically (placebo effect) from drugs taken as "shots" rather than as "pills." Injections, however, require an aseptic technique and are frequently painful, more expensive, and not suitable for self-administration by patients. One exception is insulin, which many diabetic patients must inject subcutaneously to themselves on a daily basis.

New and experimental dosage forms

Drug manufacturers are constantly looking for new drugs as well as trying to develop better dosage forms. The traditional dosage forms have to be administered frequently (usually three or four times a day) and in large doses to achieve and maintain a sufficiently high concentration of drug in the blood. Frequent administration is quite often a nuisance to those patients who have to take drugs for a prolonged or lifelong period of time (e.g., patients with asthma or hypertension), while large doses in some cases cause various adverse effects.

Newer dosage forms include adhesive skin patches, disks worn under the eyelid, rods inserted into the uterine cavity, and tablets consisting of an inert matrix (made of wax or plastic) that contains the active agent in a network of pores resembling those in a sponge. Such dosage forms release the active agent more or less continuously over a prolonged period of time so that they require less frequent administration.

For example, a skin patch containing nitroglycerin provides a therapeutic effect for as long as 24 hours, quite long compared with the very short action (usually less than 30 minutes) of a sublingual tablet. A disk containing pilocarpine (which lowers intraocular pressure) can provide continuous slow delivery of the drug for up to seven days. In skin patches as well as ocular disks, the drug is suspended in a liquid vehicle and diffuses at a slow rate through a microporous, rate-controlling membrane. An antihypertensive drug in a matrix preparation leaches out at a slow rate and thus can be taken once a day, while the same drug in a traditional tablet form has to be taken three times a day. New dosage forms, owing to a lower dosage and more efficient delivery of drug, also reduce the number and severity of adverse effects.

In recent years drug manufacturers have been trying to develop "smart" drugs or dosage forms that would deliver the active agent predominantly to the organ or tissue affected by disease in order to maximize therapeutic effects and reduce toxicity. Targeting of drugs to external organs or tissues (e.g., nose, eye, ear, skin) has been done with topical preparations (e.g., ointment, drops, spray) for many years. Also, the delivery of the active agent to the tracheobronchial system was relatively easily achieved with aerosol preparations. However, a real challenge is to target drugs to internal organs or tissues that can be reached only through the blood.

In order to deliver a drug to a specific organ or tissue, it is necessary to combine it with a substance that is selectively taken up by that organ or tissue. Recently, very promising results have been achieved through the combination of drugs with liposomes, antibodies, albumin, dextran, and red blood cells; however, such dosage forms are still experimental. When drugs are incorporated into liposomes (i.e., vesicles made of lipid bilayer resembling natural cell membrane), they are "ingested" by cells of the liver and spleen and also by cancer cells. When antibodies tagged with a drug are injected into the patient's bloodstream, they stick to a specific type of cells and expose them to a high level of drug while other cells receive a very small amount of drug. Targeting of drugs is particularly important in cancer chemotherapy, which employs very toxic agents that destroy both the cancer cells and other normal body cells. In laboratories worldwide, physicians, pharmacologists, chemists, and bioengineers will continue their search for powerful, new, and better ways to "sharpshoot" the body's ills.

Hands at Risk

by Tom D. Naughton

Anthropologists believe that civilization became possible only when the forerunners of modern humans stood up on their hind legs and began to use their hands to manipulate the environment around them. Starting fires, using stones as tools, and drawing symbols that would become written language—all these seeds of civilization required the use of hands. Modern humans rely even more heavily on their hands. The vast majority of all tasks, whether in the workplace or at home, involve pushing, pulling, gripping, or holding with the hands. Humans depend on their hands not just to manipulate the environment but to experience it as well; the fingers contain some of the densest concentrations of nerves in the body. For this reason, an inability to use the hands can lead to great physical and psychological frustration.

Despite people's dependence on their hands, however, the very act of using them—or overusing them—can lead to conditions known as repetitive motion injuries or cumulative trauma disorders. Four of the ailments that can impair the use of the hands are tendinitis, tenosynovitis, carpal tunnel syndrome, and de Quervain's disease.

Tendinitis and tenosynovitis

It is common to hear tendinitis and tenosynovitis talked about interchangeably because they often occur together and both involve the workings of the tendons, the fibrous tissues that connect bones to the muscles that move them. However, the two ailments are not exactly the same. Tendinitis involves inflammation of the tendons themselves, whereas tenosynovitis involves inflammation of the tendon sheaths.

Tendon, or synovial, sheaths, are found in the body wherever tendons must bend around a joint or glide over each other—for example, in the fingers, thumbs, and wrists. Tendons and sheaths operate like a rope-and-pulley system to reduce friction; the sheaths remain fixed and excrete a lubricating fluid (synovia) as the tendons glide through them. Despite this lubricating system, too much repetitive motion can create friction and begin to cause wear on the sheaths. As the sheaths become irritated, the blood supply to them is increased, leading to inflammation and swelling. The swollen sheaths begin to impinge on the tendons that must glide through them and, as a result, moving the affected joints becomes difficult and painful. This condition is known as tenosynovitis.

One particular form of tenosynovitis, known as "trigger finger," occurs in people who regularly use a tool such as an electric drill that presses into a particular part of a finger. The tendon sheath under the compressed area of the finger will swell, or the tendon will develop a swollen, fluid-filled nodule that is too thick to pass smoothly through the sheath. Moving the finger thus becomes very difficult; in some cases the nodule will make a clicking sound as it is pulled through the sheath. Unfortunately, when a single finger is affected in this way, it can impair the functioning of the entire hand. All the fingers work together as a unit; if one is held back, so are the others. If tenosynovitis is allowed to progress, the resulting pain can spread into the forearm, causing the muscles to stiffen and eventually atrophy, or become wasted.

Treating tendinitis is a matter of relieving the swelling of a tendon; for tenosynovitis it is a matter of relieving the swelling within the sheath. In mild cases rest and anti-inflammatory drugs are sufficient to reduce swelling. In more severe cases a surgeon must relieve the pressure by making an incision in the sheath. Although this procedure leaves a portion of the tendon with no sheath, the side effects are usually minimal. The tendon may protrude slightly during movement, but it is held in place by the skin covering the finger.

Carpal tunnel syndrome

The carpal tunnel is a channel in the wrist. It is surrounded on all sides by connective tissue. On the palm side of the hand, the tunnel is enclosed by a tough, fi-

429

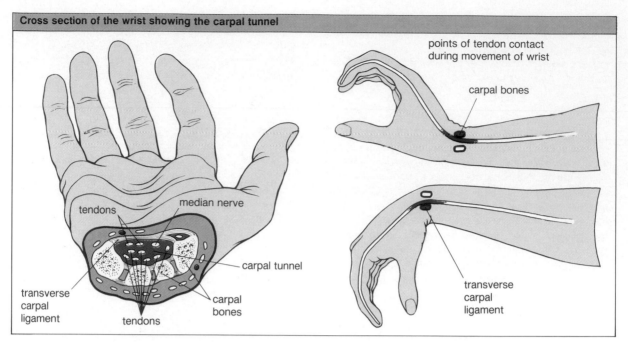

Cross section of the wrist showing the carpal tunnel

points of tendon contact during movement of wrist

carpal bones

carpal bones

tendons

median nerve

carpal tunnel

transverse carpal ligament

carpal bones

tendons

transverse carpal ligament

The carpal tunnel is a channel in the wrist that encases tendons, blood vessels, and the median nerve. If the wrist is used in an awkward position, with the tendons pulled over the transverse carpal ligament (right, bottom) or the carpal bones (right, top), friction causes swelling of the tendons or sheaths.

brous tissue known as the transverse carpal ligament. The other sides are enclosed by the carpal (wrist) bones. Nine tendons, several blood vessels, and the median nerve all pass from the forearm into the hand through this small tunnel, leaving little room to spare. Any swelling inside the carpal tunnel can cause compression of the tendons and the median nerve, leading to the condition known as carpal tunnel syndrome.

The median nerve controls movement of the thumb muscles and supplies sensation to the thumb, index finger, middle finger, and half of the ring finger. If this nerve is compressed in the carpal tunnel, the fibers that supply sensation are the first to be affected, leading to a numbness that is often described as feeling as if one is wearing a glove over the thumb and affected fingers. This numbness often first manifests itself at night, when the hands naturally tend to swell. As carpal tunnel syndrome progresses, it causes pain, loss of control, and atrophy of the thumb muscles.

There are many causes of carpal tunnel syndrome. Arthritis or injury can cause swelling within the tunnel. Pregnant women whose bodies are retaining fluids and women who take birth control pills may also suffer from carpal tunnel syndrome; in fact, any drug that causes the body to retain fluids can lead to swelling within the carpal tunnel. However, the most common cause of the condition is tenosynovitis. As the sheaths surrounding the tendons that pass through the tunnel become swollen, they can, in turn, compress the median nerve.

When carpal tunnel syndrome is caused by a temporary condition, such as an injury or pregnancy, the preferred treatment is simply to wait for the swelling to subside. Other mild cases may be treated with rest and anti-inflammatory drugs. Sometimes the forearm and hand are splinted to keep the wrist from bending and further irritating the tendons. Severe cases must be treated surgically. The surgeon opens the tunnel by making an incision in the transverse carpal ligament. Once the tunnel has been opened, the numbness slowly subsides. In advanced cases, however, it may take a year or more for full functioning of the hand to return, and in some cases a full recovery is never achieved.

De Quervain's disease

De Quervain's disease, named for the Swiss surgeon Fritz de Quervain, who first described the ailment in 1895, is very similar to carpal tunnel syndrome, but only the thumb is affected. Two of the tendons that raise the thumb pass through a small tunnel formed by ligaments. This tunnel is located on the wrist at the base of the thumb. Repetitive use of the thumb can cause tenosynovitis within these two tendon sheaths; the resulting swelling can squeeze the tendons within the ligament-bound tunnel and make movement of the thumb difficult.

The first symptom of de Quervain's disease is pain on the thumb side of the wrist. A locking or catching sensation may also be present, and the base of the thumb may feel tender to the touch. As with carpal tunnel syndrome, the preferred treatment is rest and anti-inflammatory drugs. If this does not correct the problem, a surgeon will free the tendons by making an incision in the sheath of ligament that covers them.

Common causes

Although pregnancy or arthritis can lead to swelling in the hands, most cumulative trauma disorders—a classification that includes all of the conditions described above—are caused by repetitive exertions. Because the majority of people in the Western world spend more time at work than at any other activity, a large proportion of these disorders can be traced to occupations that involve nearly constant use of the hands. Typists or word-processor operators may develop tenosynovitis because their fingers are continuously pecking away at a keyboard. Factory workers who turn screws all day or perform other repetitive hand-intensive movements may experience swelling of the wrists. Musicians are also commonly afflicted with tendinitis or carpal tunnel syndrome. In recent years supermarket cashiers have been known to develop carpal tunnel syndrome from spending all day sweeping grocery items over the computerized scanner that automatically reads prices.

Sports and leisure activities can also lead to cumulative trauma disorders of the hand and wrist. Bowling, golf, tennis, and racquetball have all been known to cause tendinitis or tenosynovitis among enthusiasts and professionals alike. Even bicyclists have experienced wrist problems because they rest their upper-body weight upon their hands. In recent years doctors have reported a new condition they sometimes call "Space Invaders wrist": tendinitis suffered by overly enthusiastic players of video games.

In short; any forceful, repetitive hand motion can lead to these cumulative trauma disorders. The effects are worse, however, if the motion is performed while the hand is being held in an awkward position. For example, when the hand is used while the wrist is bent, the tendons are forced to operate while bent over the carpal bones or transverse carpal ligament; the additional friction caused by this position can quickly result in irritation of the synovial sheaths or the tendons themselves.

A pinching movement—holding an object between the fingers and thumb—can also place harmful stress on the hands. Compared with a gripping position, with the fingers curled around an object, a pinching position requires the muscles to work up to five times harder to produce the same force. (This is simply demonstrated by holding a book in one hand between the thumb and fingers while holding another book in the other hand by curling the fingers under it. The hand that is pinching the book will tire much more quickly than the hand that is gripping the book.)

Prevention

In recent years an entire science has been developed for the adaptation of working environments so that they do not place undue strains on the body: ergonomics, sometimes called human factors engineering. Ergonomics engineers have found that the least traumatic operating position for the hands and wrists is the same position that they are in when the arms are dangled loosely at the sides of the body. In this position the palms face neither up nor down, the wrist

Occupations that involve repetitive motions can lead to a variety of chronic injuries known as cumulative trauma disorders. The repetitive use of poorly designed tools, which may press into a finger or cause the wrist to be held in a bent position, results in such disorders as "trigger finger" and carpal tunnel syndrome.

(Left) Barbara Van Cleve—Click/Chicago; (right) April A. Oswald

is straight, and the forearms are not rotated either forward or backward.

Using this principle, manufacturers have designed many tools with a bend in the handle; this allows people to use them without bending the wrist. Tools with sharp, hard edges that dig into the hand or wrist can irritate the tendons or sheaths and cause tendinitis; ergonomic tools are now being designed to avoid these stresses. A short-handled screwdriver, for example, leaves the user little choice but to grip the tool in such a way that the end of the handle digs into one spot on the flesh of the palm. A screwdriver with a long handle allows the user to grip the tool with the entire palm, thus dispersing the stress.

In other cases engineers have been able to redesign work areas so that workers are able to avoid bending their wrists. A machine, for example, may come with a height-adjustment mechanism so that each employee who operates it can do so at a height that does not require bending the wrists up or down. In the office setting, adjustable work stations allow workers to operate computer keyboards without bending their wrists; wrist pads are also used to help keep the wrists in a straight position. Similarly, typists who have been experiencing wrist pain may find that the solution is as simple as adjusting the height of their chairs so that they are typing with straight wrists.

While engineers and other professionals undertake the tasks of reducing or eliminating cumulative trauma from the workplace, individuals must take responsibility for the care of their hands in off-the-job activities. One way to avoid tendinitis or tenosynovitis is to choose well-designed tools. Consumers should look for screwdrivers that do not have sharp, hard edges on the handles; plastic or rubber padding on the handles will help reduce stress on the hands. It is also wise to choose tools with long handles that extend beyond the palm instead of digging into it. Auto mechanics can do their hands a favor by not using their palms to pound parts into place.

No matter what kind of tools are used, awkward positions can still place stress on the hands. People performing any repetitive task with their hands should check to see if the wrist is bent. If it is, they should stop and see if there is another way to perform the same action while keeping the wrist straight.

Keeping the hands warm can also help reduce the stresses on them. Cold decreases sensory feedback in the hands, which in turn reduces dexterity and makes a task more difficult. Anyone who has tried to change a flat tire on a freezing-cold day knows how difficult it can be to operate tools with cold hands. However, gloves should be used with caution. Some gloves interfere with the motions of the fingers and thus increase the strength needed for a task. In some cases gloves can be modified according to the task; fingerless gloves, for example, keep most of the hand warm but do not interfere with the ability of the fingers to move freely. Keeping the entire body warm also indirectly warms the hands; if the body is cold, blood moves away from the extremities and toward the trunk. If the trunk is kept warm, blood continues to circulate freely to the hands to warm them.

Hands deserve a break

Hands are meant to be used, and fear of cumulative trauma injuries should not prevent people from performing necessary tasks, engaging in sports, or playing a favorite musical instrument. The key is to avoid overworking the hands by giving them a rest now and then. It is not a good idea, for example, to play a difficult musical passage for hours on end; nor it is wise to pull weeds all day without taking several rest breaks. Rest may not necessarily mean sitting still; often simply moving on to another type of activity that uses the hands in a different position will provide the necessary relief.

If the hands do occasionally become sore or numb, there is no reason to panic. Not every case of numbness indicates the beginning of tenosynovitis or carpal tunnel syndrome. However, anyone who begins to experience recurring numbness or soreness should seek medical attention right away. The sooner a cumulative trauma disorder is treated, the better the chance that the hand can be restored to full functioning.

Problem Pregnancies
by Bruce D. Shephard, M.D.

High-risk pregnancies are those in which there is an increased chance of a medical complication for either the mother or the baby. Fetal complications may include miscarriage, stillbirth, birth defects, preterm birth, growth problems, and fetal distress (asphyxia). Maternal complications include obstetrical complications such as hemorrhage, as well as medical conditions such as diabetes and high blood pressure, each of which may either arise or worsen during pregnancy. Roughly one-fifth of the pregnancies in the U.S. are considered high risk, and these account for 80% of poor pregnancy outcomes. Overall, maternal problems are fewer and tend to be less dangerous than those of the fetus.

Early identification of problem pregnancies is now considered vital in the continuing process of lowering perinatal and maternal mortality, the primary statistical indexes for measuring pregnancy outcome. Perinatal mortality, as calculated by the U.S. National Centers for Health Statistics, is derived by adding the number of fetal deaths (stillbirths) after 20 weeks of pregnancy and the number of infant deaths in the first month of life per 1,000 births. In the U.S. perinatal mortality fell 50% over 25 years, to a rate of 14.5 births per 1,000 in the early 1980s (according to the most current available statistics). Maternal mortality likewise has declined substantially in the past three decades, from a rate of 83 per 100,000 live births in 1950 to less than 10 per 100,000 in the 1980s. Although there has been a trend toward overall improvement in pregnancy outcomes, uneven patterns of risks exist for different segments of the population; *e.g.,* among nonwhites the maternal mortality rate is triple and the frequency of low-birth-weight infants is double that of whites. Such discrepancies may reflect social and economic factors—*e.g.,* lack of prenatal care, nutritional deficiencies, or unavailability of medical services.

Identifying risk factors

While a precise definition of high-risk pregnancy is difficult—risks vary from one patient population to another and depend on the criteria used—in general, if even one recognized risk factor is present, the pregnancy is considered high risk. Some types of risk factors are readily identifiable in the woman's medical history. Anemia and high blood pressure are examples of obvious medical conditions, but just as important may be a past history of pregnancy complications (certain specific birth defects, stillbirth, or preterm labor). A woman with a known history of premature labor, for example, has a 25 to 50% chance of having premature labor recur in a subsequent pregnancy. A family history of an inherited condition such as diabetes, certain kidney disorders, or hemophilia also indicates risk.

Overall, about 15% of pregnant women can be identified as high risk at some point during pregnancy. An additional 5% are identified as high risk for the first time during labor. These two groups account for about 80% of poor pregnancy outcomes. Thus, risk assessment must be a continuing process because complications may occur even in apparently low-risk pregnancies. In an effort to refine risk assessment, various quantitative scoring systems have been developed that assign a point value corresponding to degree of risk.

Diagnosing high-risk pregnancy—common tests

Ultrasound (sonography). Ultrasound, a technique that uses sound waves to assess the fetus, placenta, and amniotic fluid, has become one of the most valuable tools in evaluating high-risk pregnancies. Ultrasound is used in the early weeks to confirm pregnancy, evaluate possible miscarriage, and identify ectopic, or tubal, pregnancies (those occurring outside the uterus). In mid pregnancy (15 to 25 weeks), the technique is used to search for certain suspected birth defects, identify twins, evaluate placental location, and pinpoint gestational age (establish the pregnancy's duration and thus estimate a due date). In late pregnancy ultrasound can be used to measure fetal growth and to assess the amount of amniotic fluid, which may be decreased in the presence of early or chronic fetal distress. Ultrasound has also been used recently in high-risk pregnancies to obtain a "biophysical profile" of the fetus—a kind of super sonogram that quantitatively assesses several factors, including fetal movement, heart rate, and breathing patterns and amniotic fluid volume. A fetal "profile score" is thereby established and indicates whether the physician should deliver the baby immediately or postpone delivery and perform further tests. Although there is no reliable evidence that ultrasound causes any harm to the developing human fetus, the procedure is usually performed only when the physician has reason to suspect a potential problem.

Amniocentesis. Amniocentesis is a procedure for removing a small amount of amniotic fluid (the "waters" that surround the baby) through a hollow needle inserted through the mother's abdomen into the uterine cavity. In early pregnancy the test is used to identify suspected birth defects and chromosomal abnormalities such as Down syndrome. Amniocentesis is often recommended for women over the age of 35, women with a history of inherited birth defects or three or more miscarriages, or women who have chromosomal abnormalities. In late pregnancy amniocentesis is usually performed to assess fetal maturity; *i.e.,* to confirm that the baby's lungs are sufficiently developed to function normally after delivery.

Alpha-fetoprotein level. In this test a sample of blood is drawn from the mother at about the 17th week of pregnancy so that the level of α-fetoprotein in the maternal circulation can be measured. Increased concentrations of this substance are an indication of neural tube defects (NTDs), a group of birth defects that includes spina bifida ("open spine") and anencephaly (failure of brain development). The test is most strongly indicated for couples with a family history of such birth defects, for which the recurrence risk may be as high as 5%. Even among low-risk couples this relatively inexpensive test has become widely used to screen for NTDs.

Nonstress and stress testing. The nonstress test (NST), one of the safest and most widely used tests for assessing problem pregnancies, is a form of fetal monitoring often performed in the physician's office. The test evaluates the fetus by measuring changes in fetal heart rate (normally a slight acceleration) during either a uterine contraction or a fetal movement. In a negative (normal) test, the baby shows at least two accelerations coinciding with fetal movement during the testing period. A normal NST almost always means the fetus is in healthy condition. An abnormal, or nonreactive, test indicates the need to go one step further and perform an oxytocin challenge test (OCT).

The OCT, also called a contraction stress test, evaluates the fetal heart rate during uterine contractions produced by an injection of the drug oxytocin. In a negative (normal) test the fetal heart rate usually does not change during contractions. A negative OCT usu-

ally means that the pregnancy can be safely continued for another week, while a positive test indicates the need for prompt delivery, often by cesarean section. The OCT is often performed in the hospital because there are slight risks involving the use of oxytocin, which can cause fetal distress if not given in proper dosage. NSTs and OCTs are often performed on a weekly basis in the last three months of high-risk pregnancies.

Some specific high-risk conditions

Diabetes. Two forms of diabetes may complicate pregnancy: diabetes first discovered during pregnancy, called gestational diabetes, and preexisting diabetes. Gestational diabetes, the more common and milder form, refers to slightly elevated blood sugar (glucose) levels usually detected after the pregnant patient drinks a sugar solution (glucose tolerance test). This form of diabetes, found in 1 to 3% of pregnant women in the U.S., seldom produces symptoms. It is more common among women who are obese or over 35. Although it tends to subside within six weeks of delivery, approximately half of the women with gestational diabetes ultimately will develop permanent diabetes. Preexisting diabetes includes both insulin-dependent diabetes and so-called adult onset diabetes, which can be controlled by oral medication or by diet alone. While pregnancy risks are higher for women with preexisting diabetes, especially those requiring insulin, perinatal mortality in this group has dropped from 10% in the 1960s to below 3% at most U.S. medical centers in the 1980s.

Preexisting diabetes may cause a variety of fetal complications, among them higher rates of birth defects (including NTDs), stillbirth, premature labor, traumatic delivery (due to large fetal size), or various metabolic problems, such as low blood sugar, during the newborn period. Maternal complications include high blood pressure and increased difficulty in controlling blood sugar levels, which may lead to problems involving the kidneys, the eyes, or other organs. The risks to the fetus in cases of gestational diabetes are only slightly higher than in normal pregnancies. They include difficult delivery due to large fetal size and, rarely, stillbirths. The primary maternal risk is the persistence of the diabetes after delivery.

Blood sugar testing has replaced less accurate urine testing following a diagnosis of diabetes. Home glucose monitoring of the blood, via a device called a glucometer, has become routine for patients on insulin. Screening for α-fetoprotein levels and a sonogram at 16 to 20 weeks are used to evaluate the possibility of birth defects in cases of maternal diabetes. Subsequent sonography may be performed to check fetal growth. Periodic nonstress testing after 28 weeks is often performed, and some physicians have their patients with diabetes keep a record of daily fetal movements ("kick counts").

The pregnant woman with diabetes needs a diet of 2,200–2,400 calories per day, with 20% of the calories derived from protein, 35% from fats, and 45% from carbohydrates. Snacks between meals help to minimize blood sugar fluctuations. Some patients with gestational diabetes require insulin, and pregnant women who are insulin dependent usually need an increase in their insulin dosage. Oral diabetic medications are contraindicated in pregnancy because they have been associated with birth defects and are less effective than insulin. In prior years planned early delivery was customary, but today delivery is usually delayed until term in well-controlled women with diabetes but no other complications. Because of larger than normal fetal size, cesarean section rates are significantly increased among insulin-dependent women and slightly increased among patients with gestational diabetes.

High blood pressure. Pregnancy-induced hypertension (PIH)—formerly known as toxemia—refers to high blood pressure that first develops during pregnancy. PIH usually develops after the 24th week. It is more common among first-time mothers, nonwhites, and teenagers. Chronic, or essential, hypertension refers to a form of high blood pressure that exists prior to pregnancy and is more common among women over the age of 30. Nearly 10% of pregnancies are complicated by high blood pressure, the cause of which has been linked to both genetic factors and inadequate nutrition. Uncomplicated high blood pressure in pregnancy may be symptomless or may begin with swelling of the hands and feet along with a weight gain of 2.3 kg (five pounds) or more in one week due to fluid retention. Later symptoms may include headaches and visual disturbances such as blurred vision.

Moderate to severe high blood pressure may disrupt the flow of blood through the placenta, reducing the baby's supply of oxygen and nutrients. This may result in a fetal condition known as intrauterine growth retardation. The growth-retarded fetus characteristically appears scrawny at birth and has cracked, peeling skin. These babies have eight to ten times the perinatal mortality of other infants and must be watched closely for signs of fetal distress before and during labor and for a variety of medical complications after birth. Maternal complications of high blood pressure, while less frequent than fetal problems, can be serious; they include seizures, damage to the kidneys and liver, stroke, and heart attack.

Nonstress tests and ultrasound are performed if fetal growth problems are suspected in the third trimester. Some physicians request that patients keep daily records of the baby's movements. Special blood and urine tests may be obtained to evaluate the mother's liver and kidney function.

Treatment consists of delivery as soon as the baby's lungs are mature. Amniocentesis is often performed as early as 34 weeks to test for fetal lung maturity, which occurs earlier in hypertensive pregnancies. Until delivery, increased bed rest or decreased physical activity or both are helpful. In more severe cases the pregnant woman may be hospitalized, and blood-pressure-lowering drugs may be required. Preterm delivery, sometimes by cesarean section, may be necessary if complications such as fetal distress or fetal growth problems develop. Salt restriction and diuretics ("water pills") are no longer used to treat pregnancy-induced hypertension.

Advanced maternal age. Advanced maternal age is usually defined as age 35 or older. Between 1970 and 1979 the percentage of U.S. women starting childbearing in their early thirties increased 66%. With more and more couples delaying childbearing, age has become a more frequently identified high-risk factor. Fortunately, even in the later reproductive years, a healthy outcome for mother and baby can be expected more than 95% of the time.

Medical risk for the mother gradually increases with age from about the age of 30. The risk of pregnancy-related death, for example, increases from 11 per 100,000 for women in their late twenties to 46 per 100,000 for women in their late thirties. Complications such as high blood pressure, diabetes, and placenta previa (abnormal placental location causing bleeding) are at least twice as frequent in women over 35 compared with those in their twenties. Fetal complications associated with maternal age include an increased risk of miscarriage and a slightly increased risk of premature birth. The most feared fetal complication among older mothers is the birth of a baby with a chromosomal defect such as Down syndrome. The incidence of Down syndrome rises from less than one per 1,000 live births before age 30 to one per 100 by age 40. Compared with women in their twenties, women over 35 have a severalfold greater risk of having a child with a birth defect due to a chromosomal abnormality.

For pregnant women over 35, amniocentesis for chromosome evaluation is usually recommended at approximately the 16th week of pregnancy. Some physicians use nonstress tests in the last few weeks of pregnancy or if the pregnancy goes past the expected due date. Many physicians advise increasing bed rest for their older pregnant patients and possibly reducing or stopping work in the last few weeks of pregnancy. There is a somewhat higher rate of cesarean births among women over the age of 35 since the incidence of fetal distress is slightly increased.

Multiple pregnancy. Twins occur in one out of about 90 pregnancies and triplets in one out of every 9,000. The actual number of women who are pregnant with more than one fetus has been increasing slightly owing to the widespread use of fertility drugs, which stimulate ovulation (egg release). Maternal problems in multiple pregnancy may include anemia, high blood pressure, gestational diabetes, and polyhydramnios (excessive amniotic fluid collection, sometimes causing shortness of breath in the mother). These complications cause twin pregnancies to be among those with the highest risk. Fetal complications may include prematurity, growth problems, birth defects, and abnormal positions (such as breech), all of which occur with increased frequency when there is more than one fetus.

Twins are usually diagnosed by ultrasound, which is also subsequently used to screen for birth defects and monitor fetal growth. Mothers with twins must be watched closely for preterm labor, although no specific test is available. (The use of home monitoring devices for detecting premature labor is experimental.) Periodic nonstress testing is also helpful in evaluating fetal condition and growth.

The role of strict bed rest is controversial in twin pregnancy, but it is advised to varying degrees by many physicians. Cesarean section is performed more frequently with twins, often because of the abnormal position of the babies at the time of delivery or labor that fails to progress normally.

Preterm labor. Preterm, or premature, labor complicates about 7% of pregnancies and is the leading cause of infant mortality in the newborn period. This condition is associated with a number of other known risk factors, such as twin pregnancy, high blood pressure, bleeding in late pregnancy, and a history of premature labor or multiple miscarriages. Preterm labor is also more common among the poor and among nonwhite populations.

Prematurity exposes the newborn to respiratory and other organ system complications. Risks are directly proportionate to the degree of prematurity. Maternal complications may be related to underlying causes of prematurity, such as twins, and to the increased likelihood of cesarean delivery, which is a major surgical procedure that carries all the risks associated with any surgery.

No specific tests are available, so diagnosis depends on early recognition of labor symptoms (*e.g.,* cramping, backache, increasing pelvic pressure) and the identification and treatment of underlying risk factors such as high blood pressure. Frequent pelvic examinations are helpful in patients at risk for preterm labor because the cervix may begin to dilate before symptoms are present. Ultrasound is used to assess the degree of prematurity of the fetus at the onset of preterm labor. Home monitoring systems, which are still experimental, may be appropriate for some patients at high risk for this complication. The mainstay of treatment continues to be bed rest, usually in combination with the use of labor-inhibiting drugs. These are often very effective in delaying labor a few weeks, if not postponing it until term.

Congenital herpes. Genital herpesvirus infection, a common sexually transmitted disease, can cause serious neurological damage or even death to the new-

born who contracts the herpesvirus by direct contact at the time of vaginal delivery. Fortunately, neonatal, or congenital, herpes is rare (only about 100 cases are reported each year in the U.S.). Maternal symptoms of herpes outbreaks, painful sores in and around the genital area, are not more frequent or more severe during pregnancy.

Women with a history of herpes episodes or exposure to the virus are often tested weekly in the last four to five weeks of pregnancy, as the disease can be present in the cervix without causing symptoms. The test, a laboratory culture of the virus from maternal cervical secretions, is obtained in the same way as a pap smear. Results are available within a few days. If the woman has an active infection or has had a recent outbreak or recent positive herpes culture, a cesarean section is usually performed. This approach almost always prevents neonatal herpes. The drug acyclovir (Zovirax), which effectively reduces symptoms in nonpregnant individuals, has not been approved for use during pregnancy.

Prenatal care

Regular prenatal care is of value for all pregnant women since some conditions (*e.g.,* high blood pressure, gestational diabetes, and urinary infections) typically produce no symptoms initially. Women with identified risk factors usually need more frequent prenatal visits and diagnostic tests during their pregnancies. Some high-risk pregnancies may require hospitalization, but many problems can be dealt with by reducing the woman's level of activity at work or at home and by increased bed rest. Fetal testing is usually reassuring, but if complications develop, early delivery either by inducing labor or by cesarean delivery is sometimes medically indicated. Although the number of cesarean births has risen dramatically in recent years, those performed because of high-risk conditions such as maternal high blood pressure, twin pregnancy, breech presentation, and fetal distress appear to be among the most clearly necessary.

High-risk pregnancies often require consultation with a perinatologist, a physician who specializes in treating complications of pregnancy, labor, and delivery. Many others may become involved, including a geneticist (a specialist in genetically transmitted disorders), a neonatologist (a specialist in the care of the newborn), an endocrinologist (a specialist in diabetic pregnancies), and a family pediatrician or an internist. The work of this health "team" is coordinated by the obstetrician. In some cases it also may be advisable to plan for delivery at a medical center equipped to deal with special high-risk situations; the facility should have a neonatal intensive care unit and a full-time neonatologist. These options should be discussed with the obstetrician early in the course of a high-risk pregnancy.

Progressive Resistance Exercise

by Tom D. Naughton

In the days before the movie *Pumping Iron* brought weight lifting out of dingy clubs and conferred an aura of glamour to the activity, weight lifters were often considered freaks. Even many athletes avoided barbells; it was not unusual for swimming and baseball coaches to forbid their athletes to lift weights for fear that they would become muscle-bound and graceless. But the health craze that began with running eventually had fitness enthusiasts trying out all kinds of exercises, and training with weights began to grow in popularity. Sports equipment manufacturers quickly responded with sleek, padded machines that look much less forbidding than cast-iron barbells. Health clubs sprang up, offering everything from heavy-duty body-building programs to half-hour Nautilus routines designed primarily to improve strength and muscle tone.

Today an estimated seven million Americans—men and women—work out with weights regularly, and with good reason; most people find that after only six weeks of regular training, their muscles are firmer and stronger, their bodies are trimmer, and their energy level has risen. Nevertheless, few people who work out understand exactly how straining against a weight causes a muscle to grow and become stronger.

How weight training works

When a muscle is forced to work harder than usual—whether by lifting weights or lifting bales of hay—the proteins that form muscle fibers begin to pull apart. Muscle tissue is actually broken down. This is the reason that engaging in hard physical work can leave muscles feeling weak and sore. The body then acts to regenerate the damaged muscle tissue. For reasons that doctors and physiologists do not understand fully, the body regenerates fibers that are bigger and stronger than those destroyed. When this process is repeated over time, the muscles become noticeably larger and stronger. When the male hormone testosterone is present in the body in a sufficiently large amount, the damaged muscle not only produces larger fibers, it begins producing a greater number of fibers as well. For this reason, males who are in their teens and early twenties—a time when their bodies are producing high levels of testosterone—make the largest gains in muscle mass from weight lifting.

Even for healthy young athletes, the body needs about 48 hours to regenerate the proteins within muscles. That is why experts advise against working out the same groups of muscles every day. People who continue to strain their muscles again and again without giving them time to recover fully can actually slow down their progress. Those who want to work out every day usually alternate their routines, exercising the lower body one day and the upper body the next.

It is important to realize that even though working out with weights yields a firmer, more attractive, and stronger body, weight training alone is not sufficient for becoming physically fit. The single most important element of fitness is cardiovascular endurance—the ability of the heart, lungs, and blood vessels to oxygenate the blood and carry it to the cells. To reach a healthy level of cardiovascular fitness, a person must engage in exercise that is aerobic, or oxygen-consuming. During long, sustained periods of exertion, the muscles must use oxygen to convert carbohydrates and fats into usable energy. Running, cycling, swimming, rowing, and other forms of aerobic exercise place increased demands on the body's ability to deliver oxygen to the cells. The body responds by developing a stronger heart muscle and greater lung capacity, eventually leading to increased aerobic fitness.

Weight training, however, is anaerobic, or non-oxygen-consuming, exercise. The relatively short bursts of strength required to lift a weight several times generally consume only the energy already stored in the muscles themselves. Weight training therefore does not place significantly increased demands on the body's ability to deliver oxygen. Some manufacturers of weight-training machines, such as the most widely used Nautilus system (comprising some 20 pieces of

Progressive resistance exercise, whether performed with free weights or with machines, produces a firmer, stronger, more attractive body. The woman at right is doing leg extensions—straightening her leg against the resistance offered by the machine.

equipment, each of which exercises a specific group of muscles), claim that if several of their machines are used in succession without rest periods—a practice known as circuit training—the heart and lungs will get an aerobic workout. However, most people who use these machines do so at health clubs, and they find they are rarely able to complete an entire routine without having to wait for at least a couple of machines while others use them. The aerobic benefits are lost during these waiting periods.

Choosing a progressive resistance program

A good all-around fitness program should include aerobic exercise for cardiovascular endurance, resistance training for muscle tone, and stretching for flexibility. Aerobic and stretching exercises can be performed with little or no equipment, but resistance training involves either free weights or some type of machine. There are advantages and disadvantages to both.

Machines are safer for novices. The weights on machines are usually held in a stack safely away from the lifter's limbs; there is little danger of dropping the weights on the body. Most machines are used to perform only one or two exercises; they are therefore easy to learn. Using a machine can make for a quicker workout because changing the amount of weight lifted is as easy as moving a pin from one slot to another in a weight stack. However, machines take up a great

Ordinary weight training is an anaerobic form of exercise. However, combining aerobic movements with weight-lifting routines can provide an excellent all-around workout with both aerobic and anaerobic benefits.

Most authorities now agree that progressive resistance exercise is safe for prepubescent children as long as they avoid power lifting—that is, lifting the maximum weight possible. To avoid accidents, youngsters should not work out without supervision.

deal of room and are usually very expensive, so they may not be feasible for the home gym. For example, a Nautilus system, with 20 pieces of equipment, costs many thousands of dollars.

Free weights, barbells and dumbbells, are relatively inexpensive. Small weight sets and a basic weight bench may cost as little as $100. Free weights are flexible—a barbell can be used for numerous exercises—and they take up much less room than machines. One can accomplish the same kind of fitness possible with the sophisticated health-club machines at home with free weights. However, more training and guidance is necessary for learning how to use the latter. There is more potential for injury with free weights as well, because they can be accidentally dropped on the body. A man lying on a bench and lifting a barbell over his chest, for example, needs a "spotter" present to lift the weight away from the chest if he cannot complete the exercise.

Serious weight trainers, those who aim for large gains in strength and muscle size, say that both free weights and machines are necessary. Squats—doing knee bends with weights on shoulders—cannot be performed with a machine, they claim, while leg extensions—straightening the leg against a weight's resistance—cannot be done with free weights. For people who simply want to improve their muscle tone and strength, a routine using either machines or free weights will probably be sufficient. In either case, it is important to find out how to exercise correctly. Most health clubs have professional instructors on staff to teach novices, and numerous books are available describing how to incorporate weight training into a fitness program.

The home alternative

Many people who want to work with weights find health clubs crowded, costly, or inconvenient. As a result, they may decide to buy equipment and work out at home. Sports equipment manufacturers, with an eye on this growing market, have scaled down some of their health-club machines to fit into the corner of a room at home.

Consumers who choose this alternative need to make sure they buy equipment that will give them a full workout. Some machines may be designed for only a few exercises. Other machines may not have enough weight on them to provide resistance for the strong muscles of the legs. Consumers who are investing in home weight machines definitely need to shop around, ask a lot of questions, and try several different models before they buy.

Working out at home usually means working out without supervision. It is especially important for those who exercise at home to observe safety precautions. According to the U.S. Consumer Product Safety Commission, the number of injuries associated with home exercise equipment has doubled since 1980.

The first precaution is to buy sturdy equipment; cheap equipment can break during use and cause serious injuries. Consumers should inspect machines carefully before buying them. The machine should be made of heavy tubular steel with heavy bolts instead of thin screws. Cables should be made of steel. Machines should carry the label of Underwriters Laboratories or another recognized testing laboratory.

Barbell sets should be purchased with care as well. Consumers should look for a sturdy bar and collars that will hold the weights firmly in place. If a collar loosens while in use, the weights on that side of the barbell may slide off. The sudden imbalance can cause the user to drop the weights on his or her body.

The next precaution is to start using the equipment or weight set slowly. Too many people who work out at home, where there are no instructors to insist that they begin with light weights, immediately try to lift the maximum amount possible. The result can be strained muscles and torn tendons—or broken toes from dropped weights.

Even though machines are generally safe for the people using them, home fitness buffs need to keep an eye on curious youngsters. A toddler may stick a finger into a moving weight stack or cable-and-pulley assembly.

Of course, the machines or weights themselves do not have to cause injury for exercise to be dangerous. People who are seriously out of shape or have heart trouble can suffer a heart attack if they overexert themselves. A sedentary person may have a weak heart without realizing it. Anyone preparing to embark on a strenuous exercise program, be it resistance training or jogging, should first see a physician for a complete physical.

Pumping iron—for almost everyone

Not long ago weight training was still considered an all-male activity. Women would not benefit from weight training, many experts said, because they lack the testosterone necessary for increasing muscle mass. At the same time, many women avoided weight training for exactly the opposite reason; they were afraid weights would give them bulky, masculine-looking physiques. In fact, women can benefit greatly from weight training. A well-planned routine can improve a woman's muscle tone and help to burn off fat. Women who train with weights actually find themselves developing a shape that is more, not less, attractive. Like men, women find that having a well-toned body seems to give them more energy. Finally, research into the causes of osteoporosis, a bone disease associated with aging, indicates that weight-bearing exercises can help strengthen bones and prevent them from thinning. As a result of these findings, the weight-machine rooms in health clubs today are likely to be used regularly by as many women as men.

Because women lack the high testosterone level of men, and because they have fewer muscle fibers to begin with, very few women find themselves "bulking up" from their weight training. However, women have begun to compete with each other in body-building contests. These women work very hard to increase their muscle mass; even so, they do not develop anywhere near the bulk of male body builders.

Prepubescent children also used to be steered away from weight training. Many doctors believed that resistance exercises would not benefit immature boys because, like women, they lack high levels of testosterone. However, recent studies have shown that weight training benefits young children in much the same manner that it benefits women—with gains in strength but few gains in bulk.

In the past, doctors were also afraid that lifting weights might damage an adolescent's growing bones. Studies of the effects of weight training on adolescents, however, have demonstrated that supervised routines do not harm the bones. This does not mean that adolescents can heft weights around with as much vigor as older weight lifters do. Doctors are still strongly opposed to their participating in power lifting—trying to lift the maximum weight possible. While mature athletes can withstand the strain of lifting as much as possible in one repetition, young bones are not ready to exert this kind of force. Pediatricians say that growing adolescents who participate in resistance training should be restricted to performing many repetitions with light weights. They should never be allowed to exert themselves to the point of pain.

Unfortunately, many of the people using barbell sets in their basements are unsupervised adolescents. Parents should not allow boys (or girls) to lift weights without supervision. Both parents and children should become familiar with proper weight-training techniques to prevent injuries from using the weights incorrectly. Even if a young person is working out in a school-sponsored program, parents would still be wise to ask the coach about his or her methods. The coach should be qualified to instruct growing children in weight training and should not allow them to exercise on their own. Furthermore, any weight-training programs for youngsters should be part of a comprehensive athletic program designed to increase motor skills and improve overall level of fitness.

Given these precautions, pediatricians are now generally in favor of resistance training for prepubescent athletes. Rather than causing injuries, weight training may prevent other sports injuries among adolescents by strengthening the body so it can withstand competition. Pediatricians also point out that adolescents who develop good weight-training habits early while using light weights are less likely to hurt themselves when they mature and can lift much more weight.

As weight-training techniques have developed and sports medicine has advanced, many of the fears surrounding weight training have been laid to rest. Coaches in nearly all sports have found that, combined with stretching and flexibility programs, weight training can improve athletes' strength and endurance without diminishing their grace and quickness. People who do not participate in any particular sport find that they simply enjoy the way weight training makes them look and feel. In short, barring any major physical problems, weight training can benefit just about anyone.

Pacemakers for the Heart
by Marc K. Effron, M.D.

Implantable cardiac pacemakers have developed over the past three decades from relatively simple devices with limited battery life to highly refined and long-lasting units that can mimic the physiological responsiveness of the heart's own natural pacemaker to the body's circulatory needs. Thanks to advances in technology, the capabilities and dependability of cardiac pacemakers have increased substantially, and their implantation has become increasingly common. Approximately 500,000 patients in the United States have received cardiac pacemakers, and about 150,000 new devices are implanted each year. Accordingly, interest has widened among physicians and nonphysicians in learning about these lifesaving electronic prostheses.

The cardiac conduction system

A need for artificial cardiac pacing arises in patients with disorders of the conduction system of the heart. The normal cardiac conduction system is composed of specialized nervelike tissue that conducts electrical stimuli from the natural pacemaker site to the chambers of cardiac muscle, affecting muscular contraction of the chambers. The primary natural pacemaker is the sinoatrial node. This small focus of specialized tissue is located at the top of the heart near the junction of the right atrium and superior vena cava. The cells of the sinoatrial node depolarize spontaneously in a rhythmic fashion and send stimuli at nearly regular intervals down the conduction system. Stimuli first travel through the atria; contraction of the right and left atria thus precedes contraction of the right and left ventricles. The impulse is then briefly delayed in the atrioventricular node, situated at the junction of the atria and ventricles. This delay, usually lasting only 160 milliseconds, permits the atria to assist with ventricular filling prior to the forceful ventricular contraction. Below the atrioventricular node, the impulse rapidly travels in sequence to certain anatomical areas of the heart—from the bundle of His, dividing into the right and left bundle branches, to the Purkinje fibers and, finally, the cardiac muscle cells.

This system of conduction enables the regular beating of the heart. In most people a cardiac rate of 60–100 beats per minute carries on the normal circulatory work of the heart. However, if the electrical conduction is interrupted, the rate may be slowed to as low as 30 beats per minute, and in some people the heart actually stops.

Conduction system disease

Conduction system disease most commonly develops in patients older than age 60 and in patients with coronary artery disease. Other, less common causes include degeneration of the cardiac valves adjacent to the conduction pathways, infiltrative heart disorders, and inflammatory or infective heart conditions. The majority of patients with conduction system disease are advanced in years and display a localized degeneration of the sinoatrial node or conduction tissue below the atrioventricular node. Fibrosis and destruction of conduction system tissue may be demonstrated microscopically, but the actual cause of the degenerative process is often unknown.

Bradycardia is the term for a disturbance of the heart rhythm that leads to slowing of the heart rate. Sick sinus syndrome results from dysfunction of the sinoatrial node as manifested by a sustained slow heart rate or intermittent pauses of the heartbeat. Spells of light-headedness, profound weakness, episodic loss of consciousness, or death may result. Complete heart block (or complete atrioventricular block) results from interruption of the conduction system below the site of the sinoatrial node. Most commonly, the block is below the atrioventricular node at the bundle of His or the right and left bundle branches. The sinoatrial node continues to send impulses to the atria, but the stimuli do not reach the ventricles and the circulation ceases. Clinical manifestations may be similar to those of the sick sinus syndrome, although precipitous collapse is more likely with complete heart block.

A tendency toward severe sinus node dysfunction

441

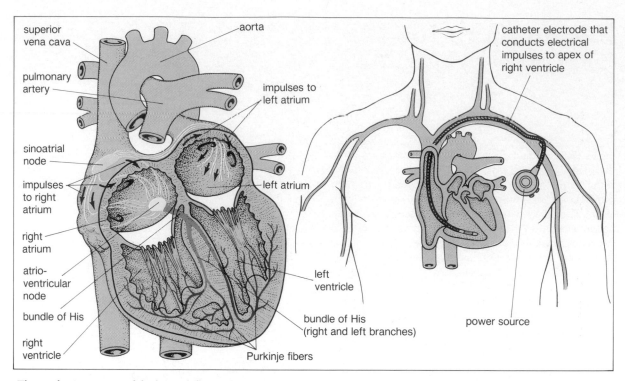

The conduction system of the heart (left) enables its regular beating. The sinoatrial node in the wall of the right atrium, in setting the basic rhythm, functions as the heart's natural "pacemaker." When this conduction system fails to function properly, a surgically implanted artificial pacemaker (right) can take over the pacing.

or sustained complete heart block may be evident to a physician when the electrocardiographic recordings are reviewed. The physician can often recommend implantation of an artificial pacemaker prior to the appearance of truly life-threatening bradycardia.

Pacemaker implantation

Implantation of pacemakers has become a reliable and safe procedure. Most pacing systems consist of a pulse generator, the power source that contains the battery and circuitry, and an endocardial pacemaker lead, a coated wire that conducts the electrical stimulus from the generator to the cardiac muscle. Surgical implantation is usually performed under local anesthesia. The patient may be alert or slightly sedated. A "pocket" for the generator is surgically formed below the skin and over the surface of the pectoralis muscles of the upper chest wall. The pacemaker lead is introduced into the subclavian vein beneath the clavicle (collarbone) and positioned, with fluoroscopic guidance, to the apex of the right ventricle. The lead tip contacts the inner surface of the heart chamber (endocardium). The effectiveness and stability of the lead position are verified by electrical testing. The lead is then connected to the pulse generator, which is inserted into the subcutaneous pocket. Following implantation, the patient's heart rhythm is usually closely observed in the hospital for one or two days.

Serious complications of the implantation procedure, although rare, include perforation of the heart and hemorrhage into the thoracic cavity surrounding the lungs. Less severe, but also rare, complications are pneumothorax (from lung perforation), extensive bleeding at the pulse generator pocket, and infection. Dislodgement of the lead may occur following implantation, requiring surgical repositioning.

Single-chamber pacing

Most implantable pacemakers are single-chamber devices. A single endocardial lead is positioned to the apex of the right ventricle. Although single-chamber ventricular pacing does not reproduce the natural sequential contraction of the atria and ventricles, isolated pacing of the large and more important ventricular chambers reestablishes the circulation.

The earliest pacemakers paced the heart in a fixed-rate mode. These pacemakers continuously delivered impulses at a specified rate even if an internal heart rhythm reappeared intermittently. This fixed-rate pacing led to constant depletion of the battery as well as a risk of inducing abnormal, rapid heart rhythms by firing an artificial stimulus soon after an endogenous stimulus. Demand pacing was then developed and emerged as the preferred pacing modality. Circuitry in the pulse generator could detect or sense internal electrical activity in the ventricular chamber. If the internal (endogenous) conduction system functioned intermittently, the artificial system would withhold stimuli during these periods—the implanted pacemaker thus paced on the basis of need, or on demand.

The majority of modern pacing systems are single-chamber ventricular devices that function in a demand mode. This type of pacemaker functions particularly well for older patients who do not require a major augmentation of cardiac output with extremes of physical exertion. Patients with chronic atrial fibrillation, in whom the atria do not perform with an organized muscular contraction, may also be served optimally by a single-chamber ventricular device. Occasional patients with sinus node dysfunction but an intact conduction system below the sinoatrial node may benefit from single-chamber atrial pacing. Synchrony of atrial and ventricular actions can then be maintained.

Dual-chamber pacing

Dual-chamber pacing has evolved during the last decade and has played a major role in recently applied pacemaker technology. Leads are positioned to both the right atrium and the right ventricle. The pulse generator can sense intrinsic electrical activity in both chambers as well as pace both chambers. The dual-chamber pacemaker may thus respond to endogenous increases of sinoatrial node rate, such as occurs during exercise, by pacing the ventricles sequentially after each atrial depolarization period. The system can maintain atrioventricular synchrony by monitoring both atrial and ventricular activity and pacing either or both chambers on demand. Sequential pacing of both chambers augments the cardiac output at rest and during exercise. It is particularly useful for patients with weakened ventricular function.

Programmability and telemetry

Virtually all pacemakers now being implanted are programmable. A hand-held programming device is applied to the chest surface overlying the pulse generator. The pacemaker rate and electrical output can be reset by means of a coded electromagnetic signal. Programmability permits adjustments of rate and energy output of the pacemaker system without the need for surgical manipulations. Failure of a pacing system at standardized pulse widths and sensitivity settings can be corrected by reprogramming. The rate may be adjusted in accordance with the physiological needs of the patient. Battery life may be prolonged by minimizing the electrical output required for the achievement of chamber stimulation. Programmability has also been extended to other features of the modern pacemaker. Sensitivity of the inhibitory circuit and the time delay prior to the onset of pacing can be adjusted. Dual-chamber systems can be set to function in single-chamber or dual-chamber modes, and the time delay between atrial and ventricular activation can also be adjusted.

Telemetry is the transmission of pacemaker information from the pulse generator to the programming device. The programmer thus functions also as a receiver. The clinician is able to assess with precision the currently programmed settings of the pacemaker. Recent pacemakers provide telemetric communication of battery supply, lead resistance, and a record of pacemaker utilization in the demand mode.

Pacing in response to vigorous exercise

Single-chamber demand pacemakers provide backup pacing when the native impulses drop below a designated rate. There is no augmentation of this preset

An early silicone rubber pacemaker (left) could pace the heart only at a fixed rate. Among the most recent developments is a titanium rate-responsive device (right), housing a sensor that reacts automatically to the body's needs—increasing heart rate to as high as 150 beats per minute in response to exercise and decreasing the rate to as low as 60 beats when the body is at rest.

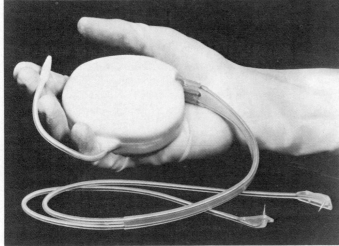
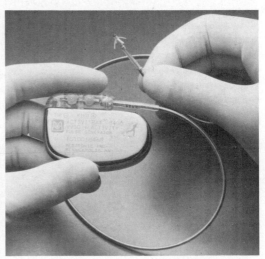

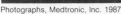
Photographs, Medtronic, Inc. 1987

backup rate in the presence of physical exercise. A dual-chamber system can increase the ventricular rate only by responding to an increase in the internal activity of the sinoatrial node. If there is a lack of increased sinoatrial node activity in response to physiological needs, known as chronotropic incompetence, then even a dual-chamber system is caused to pace at an inappropriately low rate.

The problem of chronotropic incompetence can be surmounted by the use of a rate-responsive, activity-dependent pacemaker. This recently developed device contains what is known as a piezoelectrode within the pulse generator casing. This pressure-sensitive component detects body movement and enables the pacemaker to respond to increases in the physical activity by acceleration of the pacing rate. The system is designed to increase the pacing rate briskly at the initiation of exercise and to slow the rate gradually as exercise is completed. The maximum rate, the activity threshold for rate response, and the briskness of rate acceleration are all programmable features.

Clinical studies have shown a significant enhancement of cardiac output during exercise in patients with rate-responsive pacemakers. This augmentation of cardiac function can be achieved in a ventricular pacing system without the complexities of a dual-chamber system and without reliance upon a normally functioning sinoatrial node.

Pacemaker follow-up

After the initial in-hospital observation following pacemaker implantation, a series of weekly or biweekly visits may be recommended during the next one to two months. The clinician examines the incision at the implantation site and evaluates the function of the pacemaker by electrocardiography. The programming device may be utilized during this period to establish reliable and energy-efficient pacemaker settings.

The battery life of pacemakers generally ranges from six to ten or more years, depending upon the type of pacemaker, the frequency of pacing activity, the pacing rate, and the amount of energy used for each stimulus. Battery energy level is monitored every three months by measurement of the stimulus pulse width and pacing rate, which are designed to change as the battery is depleted of charge. Newer telemetry systems can also transmit a more direct measurement of battery status.

Long-term observation is additionally needed for monitoring for pacemaker malfunction. The pulse generator may malfunction, or the endocardial lead may deteriorate and lose the ability to conduct impulses effectively. Certain types of generators and leads have been shown to have an unacceptably high failure rate. Patients with these particular devices must be notified and either kept under close surveillance or advised to undergo replacement of their pacemaking systems.

Pacemakers for rapid heart rate

Whereas conventional pacemakers treat bradycardia, highly specialized pacemaker devices can detect and terminate tachycardia, or rapid heart rates. Pathological tachycardias can be life-threatening, as the human heart does not function well at abruptly fast rates or at rates above 200 beats per minute. Tachyarrhythmias are usually amenable to therapy with medications. Yet, when such treatment is either ineffective or associated with intolerable side effects, an antitachycardia pacemaker device provides a critical function. These devices are capable of sensing an abnormal rapid heart rhythm and can be programmed to terminate the rhythm with a rapid burst of interruptive stimuli or by specially timed competitive beats. Such devices are applicable to a rare group of patients with medically refractory heart rhythm problems.

Shocking the heart to prevent sudden death

Another specialized application of pacemaker technology is the automatic cardioverter-defibrillator. Ventricular tachycardia is a highly dangerous rhythm disturbance that may not always be suppressible by drug therapy. Ventricular fibrillation is a form of cardiac arrest and is fatal unless a corrective electrical shock is applied to restart the rhythmic beating of the heart. Patients with recurring attacks of ventricular tachycardia or ventricular fibrillation may be treated by implantation of an automatic cardioverter-defibrillator. Studies have shown that 30 to 60% of people with these disturbances die annually of sudden cardiac arrest. This device both detects the arrhythmia and delivers a high-energy shock to correct the heart rhythm. The higher risks, developmental status, and inconvenience of this device restrict its use to cases of life-threatening ventricular arrhythmias. Recent follow-up studies of patients who received the defibrillator showed that fewer than 2% died in the first year after the devices were implanted.

New frontiers in cardiac pacing

Implantable cardiac pacemakers have become increasingly sophisticated and versatile, with programmable features and sensing capabilities that permit approximation of normal circulatory physiology in many patients. It is hoped and expected that future pacing systems will continue to approach truly physiological modulation of cardiac output by sensing physical activity, nervous system stimulation, respiratory rate, blood acid-base balance, and other metabolic indicators of the body's need for a changing circulation.

Common Drugs:
Psychiatric Side Effects
by Todd Wilk Estroff, M.D.

Ellie was 67 years old. For about five years she had been experiencing such severe mood swings that she had been hospitalized two to three times each year. The symptoms were convincing and classical. A diagnosis of manic-depressive illness seemed certain—that is, until during one of her later hospitalizations, a new psychiatrist asked her which medications she was taking. Her response left him aghast. She was on high blood pressure medications, heart medications, and massive doses of thyroid supplements in addition to psychiatric medications used to treat manic-depressive illness. Specialists were consulted to confirm his impression that she was not medically ill and did not need most of the nonpsychiatric medications she was taking. This information was very useful because it changed her diagnosis to that of a medication-induced psychiatric illness. The situation was explained to the patient and members of her family. Her medications were carefully and systematically discontinued while she was examined frequently. Over a period of weeks she improved remarkably and stabilized on only two medications. She has not suffered extremes of mood or needed hospitalization since.

At 76 years old Sam had lived a happy and productive life until one day his friends and family noticed that he was getting apathetic and forgetful. This continued to progress over the next week as he became more absentminded and depressed and started to neglect his appearance. He became so "senile" that the family started to look for a nursing home—convinced that the time had come when he would no longer be lucid or able to care for himself at home. Luckily, before they institutionalized him they took him to his physician, who examined him carefully. The doctor discovered that Sam was wearing a small, round, skin-colored patch behind his left ear. It was a time-release transdermal scopolamine patch that he had been given to prevent motion sickness during a recent bus trip he had taken. The doctor removed the patch, and Sam's "senility" disappeared in a few days and he resumed his productive life at home.

Bizarre behavior, panic, depression, and even psychosis can be caused by medications used to treat medical illness. Unfortunately, when these symptoms occur, they are often undetected. Frequently the result is the incorrect diagnosis that the problem is purely psychiatric. As a direct consequence of this error, the patient is treated for the wrong disorder and does not improve.

Hundreds of newer advanced medications are available today that were not in use 50 years ago. In fact, the vast majority of modern pharmaceuticals were developed during the past three decades. In addition, it is possible today to use higher doses of these newer medications because technological advances and relatively recently developed laboratory tests permit doctors to monitor drug levels in the blood more closely. These developments represent major advances in all specialities of medicine. Although the new drugs and higher dosage levels are effective and useful, they are bringing with them more unwanted and unforeseen psychiatric side effects than were seen in the past.

Misinterpreted symptoms

The symptoms caused by medications can run the entire psychiatric spectrum from mild anxiety to severe psychosis requiring hospitalization. The most frequent of all are depression, confusion, and forgetfulness (called "organicity"). Many physicians mistakenly believe that organicity is necessary for proof of the existence of a medication-induced psychiatric disorder, but elation, personality changes, panic anxiety, sleeplessness, impotence, sedation, and even auditory and visual hallucinations have all been reported in patients who did not show any sign of organicity or senile memory loss. All the symptoms can be severe. Most physicians feel that if there is even a suspicion that these symptoms are occurring as a result of drugs the patient is taking, the offending medications should be discontinued.

Which drugs cause psychiatric effects?

A wide variety of drugs can cause unwanted side effects. The worst offenders include antihypertensive, cardiovascular, anticonvulsant, anticancer, and gastrointestinal drugs, pain relievers (of the nonsteroidal anti-inflammatory and narcotic classes), anesthetics, antibiotics, and antihistamines, as well as drugs of abuse and psychiatric medications. Selected medications are listed in the table on page 447. These drugs are among those most likely to cause psychiatric side effects. Because new preparations are entering the market almost daily, the list is necessarily incomplete.

Mechanism unknown

The mechanism or mechanisms that produce these side effects are unclear; they are undoubtedly com-

445

plex and produced by a variety of different processes. It would appear that the so-called blood-brain barrier plays an important role. The blood-brain barrier is a not yet fully understood mechanism whereby the cells lining the cerebral capillaries generally act in a discriminatory fashion that prevents many, but not all, substances that circulate in the bloodstream from passing into the brain; many chemicals in the brain, likewise, are unable to diffuse outward into the general circulation. Thus, the blood-brain barrier is a vital defense that usually keeps the brain stable while the body's blood chemistry is subject to significant fluctuations. The very young can develop psychiatric symptoms from drugs because their blood-brain barriers are not fully developed.

In adults some medications more easily penetrate the brain by crossing the blood-brain barrier, while others cannot cross as easily. Obviously those medications that are able to cross into the brain can alter its chemical balance and are much more likely to have psychiatric side effects. Psychiatric medications are designed to do exactly this and are among the most likely to cause unwanted psychobehavioral effects.

The ability to traverse the blood-brain barrier is also important when a medication is suspected of causing psychobehavioral symptoms and the treating physician wants to stop the medication. If the patient must continue to be medicated in order to be kept comfortable or for preservation of life, an alternate medication must be substituted that will produce essentially the same therapeutic effects. The substitute medication chosen will most likely be selected from the group that does not cross the blood-brain barrier.

Who is at risk?

The health, age, and brain function of the individual receiving a medication are major factors in the development of these side effects. Young healthy individuals taking a minimal amount of a single medication for a limited amount of time are least likely to be affected. Their brain reserve capacity allows them to function normally and withstand outside stress.

As people age, however, arteriosclerosis, strokes, poor nutrition, and severe or chronic illness can decrease that reserve. The elderly are able to live normal lives as long as nothing upsets the delicate balance of brain functioning. When medications are added to their progressively declining systems, the limited reserve can be overloaded and thus upset, causing brain malfunction in the form of psychiatric symptoms, which may at first be subtle and therefore overlooked.

In addition, as an individual ages, a variety of physical illnesses can develop that require long-term treatment with combinations of various medications that can interact with each other. Medication combinations can produce powerful synergistic effects that would not result if single medications were used.

Individuals who are very ill are also more susceptible because their livers and kidneys may not metabolize and detoxify drugs properly. Medications can quickly build up to toxic levels, impairing a variety of brain functions.

Toxic levels can also result when patients do not take their medications as directed. Some patients take their medication only when they feel ill. Then they often take more medication than was prescribed, in the mistaken belief that the additional medicine will make up for missed doses. Other patients may forget that they have already taken their medicine and unintentionally take an extra dose, subsequently developing toxic blood levels.

Patients with a preexisting vulnerability to developing a psychiatric illness also have a much greater chance of developing psychiatric symptoms when a new medication or combination of medications is added to their treatment. Some patients have already experienced noticeable psychiatric symptoms such as depression or psychosis and should be warned that a medication could reactivate that illness. Other patients carry the vulnerability toward psychiatric illness but never develop psychiatric symptoms until they take certain medications. These individuals would not be aware of psychiatric symptoms that could be activated by a particular drug therapy.

Patients unwarned

Unfortunately, patients are not usually warned by their physicians about these possible adverse reactions. Psychiatric side effects of nonpsychiatric medications can often be very subtle. Mild confusion and forgetfulness, fleeting panic, and depression are often misdiagnosed by treating physicians as being purely psychiatric and are not correctly attributed to the medications prescribed. The result is that the patients have not been warned, and the side effects are not detected by physicians until they have progressed to severe stages. Even when a psychiatrist is consulted, the correct diagnosis depends upon how informed that particular psychiatrist is about such effects.

Danger of misdiagnosis

The real danger of misdiagnosing medication-induced psychiatric disorders is that the patient may be incorrectly declared hopeless or untreatable psychiatrically. This can lead to the prescribing of more medications that make symptoms more severe or even to the administration of shock treatments (electroconvulsive therapy), which can lead to even worse symptoms and more confusion. Worse still, some patients may be incorrectly labeled as senile or as having Alzheimer's disease and placed permanently in a nursing home or other institution. The tragedy is that simply stopping the offending drug will often reverse the process and restore the patient to normal functioning.

Physical illness medications

brand name	generic name	drug class	possible side effects
Aldomet	methyldopa	antihypertensive	nightmares, depression, hallucinations, paranoia, amnesia
Aralen	chloroquine	antimalarial	confusion, delusions, hallucinations
Artane	trihexyphenidyl	antiparkinsonism	confusion, agitation, disturbed behavior
Atabrine	quinacrine	antimalarial	anxiety, hallucinations, delirium
Benadryl	diphenhydramine	antihistamine (H_1 blocker)	confusion, restlessness, excitation, nervousness, irritability, euphoria
Catapres	clonidine	antihypertensive	delirium, hallucinations, depression
Clinoril	sulindac	nonsteroidal anti-inflammatory	paranoia, rage, personality change
Crystodigin	digitoxin	cardiovascular	depression, restlessness, confusion, disorientation, delirium
Dilantin	phenytoin	anticonvulsant	confusion, delirium
Elspar	asparaginase	anticancer	confusion, depression, paranoia, agitation, hallucinations
Fluothane	halothane	general anesthetic	depression
Fluorouracil	fluorouracil	anticancer	euphoria, disorientation, confusion
Fungizone	amphotericin B	antifungal antibiotic	delirium
Inderal, Inderide	propranolol	antihypertensive	depression, confusion, nightmares, paranoia, hallucinations, delusions, mania, hyperactivity
Indocin, Indo-Lemmon	indomethacin	nonsteroidal anti-inflammatory	depression, confusion, hallucinations, anxiety, hostility, paranoia
INH, Rifamate	isoniazid	antituberculosis	depression, agitation, auditory and visual hallucinations, paranoia
Klonopin	clonazepam	anticonvulsant	confusion, depression, forgetfulness, hallucinations, hysteria, psychosis
Lanoxin	digoxin	cardiovascular	psychosis
Matulane	procarbazine	anticancer	mania
Methotrexate and others	methotrexate	anticancer	confusion, irritability, dementia
Mysoline	primidone	anticonvulsant	irritability, emotional disturbances
Norpace	disopyramide	cardiovascular	agitation, depression, paranoia, hallucinations, panic
Oncovin	vincristine	anticancer	hallucinations
Parlodel	bromocriptine	antiparkinsonism	mania, delusions, hallucinations, paranoia, aggressive behavior, sudden relapse of schizophrenia, depression, anxiety
Pfizerpen, Bicillin, and others	penicillin G procaine	antibiotic	terror, hallucinations, delusions, disorientation, agitation, confusion, bizarre behavior, seizures, incoherence
Pronestyl	procainamide	cardiovascular	depression, paranoia, hallucinations, agitation
Seromycin	cycloserine	antituberculosis	confusion, anxiety, depression, disorientation, hallucinations, paranoia, aggression, hyperirritability, loss of memory, character changes
Serpasil, Diupres	reserpine	antihypertensive	depression, nervousness, nightmares
Sinemet	carbidopa-levodopa	antiparkinsonism	confusion, nightmares, hallucinations, delusions, agitation, anxiety, euphoria
Sudafed, Actifed	pseudoephedrine	antiasthma/allergy	hallucinations, paranoia
Tagamet	cimetidine	gastrointestinal antihistamine (H_2 blocker)	hallucinations, paranoia, confusion, bizarre behavior, delirium, disorientation, depression
Talwin	pentazocine	narcotic pain reliever	nightmares, hallucinations, disorientation, panic, paranoia, depression
Tegretol	carbamazepine	anticonvulsant	confusion, hallucinations, depression
Transderm Scop	scopolamine	anti-motion sickness	disorientation, confusion, hallucinations, memory disturbances
various	barbiturates	anticonvulsant/ sedative-hypnotic	excitement, hyperactivity, hallucinations, depression
various	ephedrine	antiasthma/allergy	hallucinations, paranoia
various	atropine	antiparkinsonism	confusion, memory loss, disorientation, delirium, depersonalization, hallucinations, fear, paranoia, agitation, bizarre behavior
various	aminophylline	antiasthma/allergy	nervousness, agitation
various	T_3, T_4	thyroid hormone	mania, depression, hallucinations, paranoia
Xylocaine, Dalcaine	lidocaine	anesthetic	disorientation, hallucinations, paranoia
Zantac	ranitidine	gastrointestinal antihistamine (H_2 blocker)	confusion, disorientation, aggression, depression
Zarontin	ethosuximide	anticonvulsant	euphoria, irritability, hyperactivity

Managing the side effects

Physicians in all specialities should always maintain a high index of suspicion that these reactions can occur in patients who are elderly, chronically ill, or taking multiple medications or have had a previous psychiatric illness. Whenever a patient is suspected of having a psychiatric reaction to a medication, a complete psychiatric evaluation is in order. Of course, one of the first and most important questions asked is which medications the patient is taking. Any medications suspected of producing such a reaction should be discontinued as rapidly and as safely as possible. Next, it is critical to make sure that the patient does not have any physical illness that could cause the psychiatric symptoms all by itself (*e.g.,* disseminated lupus erythematosus, respiratory insufficiency, or inadequately treated congestive heart failure).

Since it is hard to prove that a psychiatric side effect is occurring, any suspicions should be acted upon. Substitute medications should be used only if absolutely necessary to keep the patient comfortable or from becoming more seriously ill. If no substitute can be found and the original medication is deemed necessary, its use should be continued but at the minimal effective dosage.

Many patients will experience a complete remission once the offending medication has been removed or decreased. Other patients will experience a partial improvement, but some psychiatric symptoms can remain. After an appropriate period of time has passed (usually one or two months), it may be necessary to gingerly add appropriate psychiatric medications to treat the remaining symptoms.

If a patient suspects that one of these reactions is occurring, it is important to tell the treating physician. Often, however, friends and family notice the subtle changes first. A patient who notices these changes should discuss the matter with the doctor in a calm manner. If the doctor disagrees or refuses to adjust the medications or heed such concerns on the patient's part, the patient must ask for a second opinion from a board-certified psychiatrist, preferably one who has a background in internal medicine and is knowledgeable about the various drugs that can cause unwanted psychiatric side effects.

In some instances, when specific medications are suspected to be causing a reaction, the physician may choose to measure that drug's level in the patient's blood. Blood-level monitoring of medications is a relatively new advance in medicine that can provide rapid, accurate diagnosis of drug-induced psychiatric disorders that occur with the toxic buildup of a medication. Toxic buildup can be due to inadvertent overdosage or to the affected individual's abnormally slow metabolism of the drug. It is critical, however, that the levels be measured at the correct time after the last dose. This time period can vary widely according to the individual metabolic characteristics of the medication being assayed. Idiosyncratic readings, however, are not uncommon. The serum concentration may appear to be in the toxic range when there are no toxic effects, or the drug may not be detectable in the measured serum when, in fact, it is producing unwanted effects.

Proof: difficult to establish

If the patient recovers normal functioning when the medication is discontinued, it does not *prove* that the suspected offending drugs actually caused the psychiatric side effects. Often, however, physicians are asked to prove that this was the case. Some people just want to know for interest's sake, but others are interested in initiating a malpractice suit.

Blood levels of the medication that are in the toxic range while the symptoms are present are highly suggestive that the medication is causing the symptoms. Proof of a causal relationship, however, requires that the offending drug be restarted and that the same side effects recur and again disappear when it is stopped. This proof is called an on/off/on/off, or ABAB, design. Most patients do not want proof badly enough to take the chance that their symptoms will recur. Most physicians believe that it is unethical to attempt such a proof, especially if the patient has recovered. Remarkably few of the patients who do take the medication again have the same symptoms develop for a second time. Other factors that may have had a profound influence when the patient first took the medicine may not be present the second time; thus, the result would be different side effects or none at all.

Inevitable price of better treatments

It is important to emphasize that these problems are part of the price people have to pay for the prodigious advances in medicine that have been made in the past 30–50 years. They can occur among the patients of the best and most careful physicians and rarely occur because of negligence or malpractice. However, many doctors are still not fully aware of these side effects; therefore, concerned friends and family can help spot the early stages of these reactions and make both patient and treating physician aware of the possible existence of a problem. The importance of a careful, thoughtful psychiatric evaluation to making the correct diagnosis cannot be overemphasized. Before a diagnosis is made, an evaluation that includes examination of all pertinent medical, neurological, endocrinologic, neuroendocrinologic, psychiatric, and toxicological problems that might contribute to the problem should be made. Once the proper diagnosis has been made, the corrective treatment generally is relatively straightforward.

In the Swim
by Beverlee A. Burke

Swimming is one of the most popular sports the world over. In spite of all the attention given runners, cyclists, and aerobic dancers, according to recent polls it is the single most popular fitness activity in the United States. A 1985 survey by the National Sporting Goods Association found that 73.3 million Americans over the age of seven had swum during the previous year.

Swimming draws athletes who want to maintain conditioning during off-season months, athletes who have been injured and want to stay active during recovery and rehabilitation, triathletes—participants in a sport that combines swimming with running and cycling—and a wide range of people of all ages interested in building fitness through a sport with low injury rates and high rewards.

Many benefits

A regular swimming program can increase cardiorespiratory fitness, which is the measure of how efficiently the heart and lungs can supply oxygen to working muscles. Because of the resistance water presents, swimming can also increase muscle strength, although it will not produce bulky, defined muscles like those some weight lifters strive to develop.

Many people find they lose excess weight when they begin a swimming program. Swimming compares favorably with other exercises in terms of burning calories; swimming the crawl at the moderate rate of 1.61 km (one mile) per hour uses about the same number of calories as jogging at 8.05 km (five miles) per hour.

Most fitness swimmers also report psychological and emotional benefits. Their sessions in the pool bring them a sense of peace; some even refer to their swims as "meditation." Although such subjective judgments cannot be accurately measured, swimming, like running, induces the release of endorphins, narcotic-like chemicals produced by the brain in response to strenuous exercise. Endorphins are presumed to be responsible for the phenomenon known as "runner's high," a feeling of euphoria many runners experience during and after a long workout, and probably account for similar feelings among swimmers.

The swimming environment itself may contribute to this feeling of calm produced by the exertion. The water supports the body and provides what some trainers refer to as a "massage effect"—that is, a gentle, soothing pressure against the skin. A swimmer does not have to cope with the distractions and dangers of running outside—dogs and traffic, rough surfaces, inclement weather, exhaust fumes, other runners, etc.

Because water supports the body and reduces gravity's stress on the joints and muscles, swimming is often recommended for older people, the disabled, and those with degenerative diseases or joint pain. It has also become a popular prescription for people recovering from heart attacks.

Swimming offers special rewards for women. Their relatively higher percentage of body fat—a hindrance in many other sports—increases their buoyancy in water, insulates them against the cold, and provides additional energy over long distances. The support of the water makes swimming ideal during pregnancy, when a woman's added weight and changing center of gravity may lead to discomfort during land exercises.

A good swimming program can benefit anyone of any age and any level of physical fitness, however. Even infants and toddlers are now being acclimatized to the water environment in special classes with their parents. While children under the age of four cannot usually coordinate their movements well enough to really swim, once someone has learned to swim, he or she has learned a fitness skill that can be pursued well past the age when most other sports have become too difficult or tiring. In addition, since the intensity of swimming can be regulated by the swimmer, even the most unfit people can begin a swimming program at their own level and gradually increase their training to achieve health and well-being.

Learning to swim

The major drawback to swimming is that it requires a certain amount of skill and practice. Although the splashing beginner may be putting out more effort than the smooth-stroking Masters swimmer, the beginner's less efficient stroke will quickly become tiring, often before he or she has exercised long enough to get a real workout. A beginner should therefore take lessons so that he or she can swim continuously for at least 20 minutes without getting winded.

Those who are returning to the water after many years—having learned to swim in youth—may also need to seek instruction. Stroke mechanics have taken on more importance over the past 20 years, particularly as coaches (through high-speed underwater photography) have learned more about how elite swimmers actually perform. Better stroking technique can reduce the chance of injuries while increasing the efficiency of a swimmer's workout.

The crawl (also known as the Australian crawl or the freestyle) has changed radically. Formerly instructors taught a paddlewheel-style stroke—elbow stiff, arm traveling straight through the water, a straight-arm recovery. Current theory favors a bent elbow throughout the stroke, a keyhole or S-shaped pull through the water under the body, and a recovery featuring a high, flexed elbow. This increases speed and minimizes stress on the shoulder muscles and ligaments. The backstroke has also changed to include a bent-arm pull, although the recovery is still with the straight arm. The arm movements of the breaststroke have stayed basically the same, but most breaststrokers have abandoned the "frog" kick in favor of the whip kick, in which the feet describe circles while the upper parts of the legs stay close together.

Swimmers at any level can benefit from lessons. An instructor can not only help improve stroke technique but also suggest workout routines. However, if swimmers know their fitness goals and are familiar with some basic outlines for fitness swimming, they can set up their own workouts to meet those goals.

Swimming gear

The equipment needed is minimal: a suit, goggles, and a cap. Some swimmers also use such training aids as kickboards, etc., during a workout (*see* below).

Most fitness swimmers wear racing suits made of nylon or nylon blends, which dry quickly and keep their color and shape. The suit should fit snugly to reduce resistance in the water but should not bind around the arms, legs, or back or be uncomfortably tight.

Goggles protect the eyes from chlorine and provide clearer vision. Many different styles and tints are available; darker tints are generally recommended for those who swim in outdoor pools. People with poor vision can order goggles with prescription lenses. While some swimmers wear contact lenses under their goggles, most optometrists do not recommend this; hard lenses may float off the eye and get lost if the goggles start to leak, and soft lenses may absorb harmful chemicals from the water.

A cap (required for female swimmers at some pools) cuts down on chlorine damage to hair and reduces loss of body heat through the head—a major consideration when swimming in cool water. Caps also keep water out of the ears and prevent hair from flowing across the eyes or into the mouth during inhalation while the swimmer is doing the crawl. Male swimmers, too, especially with longer hairstyles, often wear caps for the above reasons.

Setting up a personal fitness program

The American College of Sports Medicine (ACSM) has established the following parameters for healthy adults who want to set up a fitness program to develop and maintain cardiorespiratory fitness and make favorable changes in body composition:
- mode of exercise: continuous and rhythmic, using large muscle groups
- frequency of exercise: three to five times a week
- intensity of exercise: 60–90% maximum heart rate
- duration of exercise: 15–60 minutes' continuous activity

Swimming qualifies as a rhythmic exercise. It uses the muscles of the arms and shoulder, the back, and, to a lesser degree, the legs. Three times a week is a good schedule for a beginning swimmer. This stresses the body sufficiently while still giving muscles enough time between workouts to recover from the stress, thus achieving adaptation response, which strengthens the body. A more advanced swimmer may want to increase the number of workouts.

In order to judge the intensity of exercise, a person must first determine his or her maximum heart rate. The most precise way to do this is to have an exercise stress test, in which the subject works (usually by walking on a treadmill that becomes steeper and steeper) until exhaustion. This test can be dangerous for persons with undiagnosed heart troubles and must be administered under careful clinical conditions.

A simpler way is for the subject to subtract his or her age from 220. This number is the maximum heart rate. Multiplying it by 0.6 yields the minimum heart rate to achieve fitness; by 0.8, the maximum the person should try for in a workout. For instance, the range a 40-year-old man should aim for would be $220 - 40 = 180 \times 0.6 = 108$ (minimum); $180 \times 0.8 = 144$ (maximum). To ensure that the exercise is within this target zone, a swimmer should take the pulse during rest intervals and at the end of the workout. If the pulse exceeds the maximum, he or she is working too hard; if it does not reach the minimum, the intensity must be increased.

Easier still is a technique favored by many swimming coaches: the perceived exertion scale. By rating their feelings about how hard they are working on a numerical scale from six (very very light exertion) to 20 (very very hard exertion), test subjects consistently performed at approximately 60 to 80% of maximum when they rated their exertion as 12 to 15.

While the ACSM recommends 15 minutes as the minimum time for a workout, it takes a few minutes in the water to raise heartbeat to the training range. Most swimmers plan on a minimum workout of 20 minutes to allow for this.

Swimmers who want to improve cardiorespiratory fitness should plan medium-intensity, long workouts. Known to swimmers as "long steady distance" (LSD), these are workouts at 60 to 70% of maximum heart rate lasting 40 minutes to an hour. LSD workouts also build strength. However, long relaxed workouts like these can sometimes encourage sloppy form.

In order to lose weight a person must exercise three days a week for at least 20 to 30 minutes at 80 to 85% of maximum heart rate. Increasing the frequency to four days a week and the duration to 40 to 50 minutes while decreasing the intensity to 60 to 75% of maximum heart rate will also induce weight loss. For people who undertake a swimming program chiefly for the sake of weight loss, some swimming coaches advise swimming as much as an hour per session, six days a week.

Working out in the pool

Every workout should begin with poolside exercises—slow stretches that warm up the muscles and prepare them for exertion. Swimmers should avoid ballistic stretches, where the body bounces at full extension, because they can injure muscles and joints. For the same reason, swimmers should not help each other stretch. Having another person extend a limb or joint could cause injury.

The warmup should continue in the pool with several lengths of slow and easy swimming. This accustoms the muscles to specific movements required by swimming and also gives the body a chance to adjust to the water temperature. Beginning a vigorous workout without a warmup can increase the chance of injury. It can also lead to muscle soreness the next day.

The main sets are the part of the swim that provides training benefits. Most swimmers divide this part of the swim into a set number of lengths at the pace that will maintain their heart rates in the target range. Pauses between sets should be brief so that the heart rate does not drop below the target zone.

Varying the stroke within a workout can add interest as well as give the swimmer a more complete workout. Each stroke calls on a specific set of muscles; by interspersing a few lengths of breaststroke among the longer sets of freestyle, a swimmer can round out the muscle motions used throughout the workout.

Swimmers can vary their workouts in other ways as well. Among the most popular is *fartlek,* a Swedish word meaning "speed play." It simply means swimming at varying speeds—two lengths at a slow pace, six at the swimmer's fastest pace, then two at a moderate pace.

Various training aids can also add variety to workouts. Pull buoys are two plastic foam cylinders held together with a cord or strap. The swimmer holds them between the legs and swims without kicking, thereby providing all the propulsion with the arms.

Swimmers also use paddles that come in various sizes. They are attached to the hand with rubber tubing over the wrist and fingers. By increasing the area of resistance encountered in the water, they increase the work of the arms and shoulders. Swimmers often work out with paddles to correct poor stroke form.

Kickboards give the legs an all-out workout. The swimmer holds on to these thin slabs of plastic foam and kicks the length of the pool. Fins also intensify the work done by the legs while promoting flexibility in the ankles.

Cooling down after a workout is important. It gives the heart a chance to return slowly to its normal pace and keeps circulation up to return the waste products of exercise from the muscles to the liver for processing and disposal. Swimming a few very slow laps or just walking around in the shallow end of the pool for a few minutes are two methods of cooling down.

Although swimming exercises most of the muscle groups, it favors upper body development. In fact, as much as 80% of a swimmer's power comes from arm movements. Many coaches advise combining a swimming program with another endurance activity, such as jogging or cycling, that will give legs as vigorous a workout. Coaches also often encourage swimmers to augment the strength training with land exercises such as free-weight workouts or weight-machine sessions. Any swimmer can improve stroke strength by performing the strokes on land with hand and ankle weights.

Aquatic exercise: another kind of workout

In spite of the appeal of water, many people are afraid of it or simply never learned how to swim. To give these people the benefits of exercise in water,

The "aqua jog," performed in chest-deep water, takes advantage of the body's buoyancy and resistance in water. It gives the benefits of aerobic exercise without the usual sweat and strain. Such aquatic exercises are well suited for pregnant women, obese people, and those with joint problems or recovering from injuries.

Ariel Skelley

recreational specialists and sports physiologists are exploring the field of aquatic exercise, a variety of movements performed in waist- to chest-deep water.

Aquatic exercise differs from hydrotherapy, which is medically supervised and specifically designed to promote recovery from injury or illness. By taking advantage of the buoyancy of bodies in water, as well as the resistance the medium offers, aquatic exercise is designed to increase general levels of fitness. It is often recommended for older people who have joint difficulties and for the physically handicapped, but its supporters claim it can be beneficial to everyone. Aquatic exercises are well-suited for pregnant women or the obese, who may have trouble with land exercise programs.

An aquatic exercise workout is similar to an aerobic dance workout. It combines vigorous, rhythmic movement (running in place, bobbing, or dancing) for cardiorespiratory training effect with stretching, twisting, or calisthenics to develop muscle strength and flexibility. Many YMCAs, YWCAs, municipal pools, and private clubs offer aquatic exercise classes under a variety of names; there are also many books available with suggested programs.

Because aquatic exercise is a relatively new field, little research has yet been done to determine its risks and value. The caloric expenditure is probably similar to that of swimming at a slow to moderate pace. Few injuries have been reported to date. One preliminary study concluded that those who would benefit most from aquatic exercise are people with minimal levels of aerobic fitness.

Low-injury exercise

While swimmers as a group have fewer injuries than most other exercise enthusiasts, the sport is not risk-free. The most common problem may be eye and skin irritation from the chlorine used to reduce bacteria levels in the water. A pair of goggles that fits snugly around the eyes protects them from chlorine exposure, and eye drops will relieve redness and itching. Thoroughly showering with a mild soap after swimming will remove chlorine from the skin; lotion will help replace oils lost in the water.

Some swimmers find they develop sinus difficulties. Nose clips will keep water out of the nasal passages. Breathing out gently through the mouth and nose, instead of through the nose alone, may also prevent sinus trouble.

Swimmers can prevent ear infections by wearing plugs, although the plugs themselves may injure the ear. A thorough drying of the ears after showering can minimize outer ear infections. A few drops of rubbing alcohol or commercial ear drops can help dry the ears; a hair dryer on the lowest heat setting held 13–15 cm (5–6 in) away from the ear and moved in a circle will work, too.

Swallowing water may cause nausea but is rarely serious if the pool is maintained at the right temperature and chlorine level. In rare cases an improperly maintained pool may harbor *Giardia lamblia,* an intestinal bacteria. If swallowed in large quantities, it can cause gastrointestinal upset that can be severe.

The repetitive motion of swimming can sometimes lead to injuries, although few fitness swimmers train for long enough distances to injure themselves. Shoulder complaints are common among freestyle swimmers but usually respond to a few days' rest. Breaststroker's knee sometimes occurs as a result of the whip-kick. Both of these are most often due to starting the stroke with too much power instead of letting force develop over the course of the stroke. Correcting the stroke defect will usually prevent recurrence.

Training in water that is too cold can lead to painful muscle cramps; water that is too warm, on the other hand, can lead to fatigue. For safe, comfortable swimming most pools are maintained at 25.5°–25.7° C (78°–82° F).

Swimmers who choose an outdoor pool should be aware of the possibility of sunburn. Avoiding the pool during peak sun hours (10 AM to 2 PM) and wearing a water-resistant sunscreen offer some protection.

Diving accidents, while few, can lead to serious injuries or even death. In crowded lap pools there is also the possibility of landing on another swimmer. Entering the deep end cautiously from the edge of the pool, from either a seated or a standing position, or climbing down a ladder will prevent these accidents.

Few drownings occur at recreational pools that have lifeguards on duty; no one should ever swim alone or if there is no lifeguard present. Also, swimming within an hour of eating will not cause a fatal cramp, although a heavy meal or a lot of very cold liquid can cause discomfort. Since swimmers, like any other athletes, are susceptible to dehydration during their workouts, however, they should be sure to drink some water before and after a swim. Taking a break during a long swim—more than 45 minutes—to drink more water is advisable.

Making a challenge of it

In the U.S. swimmers over age 25 with the urge to compete can register with a Masters swimming program and attend meets either as independent entrants or as members of a Masters team. Masters competitions are divided into events by length (ranging from 45 to 1,510 m [50 to 1,650 yd]), stroke (crawl, backstroke, breaststroke, and butterfly), age (five-year ranges), and sex. The age and sex divisions allow Masters swimmers to compete with others of roughly the same abilities. Information on Masters swimming is available from local teams or Y's or from U.S. Masters Swimming, 5 Piggott Lane, Avon, CT 06001.

What's Lurking in Your Kitchen?
by Beverlee A. Burke

The varied diet enjoyed by people in many industrialized nations is sustained year round, thanks to modern food processing and transportation. Fresh foods once available only seasonally or regionally are no longer so restricted, and commercially processed foods can be relied upon to be safe for consumption. In the U.S. current food-preservation technology, teamed with stringent quality control and regular inspections, has reduced the incidence of foodborne diseases to a very low level.

Relatively few cases of foodborne illness are caused by contamination during commercial food processing. More often, food-preparation and serving methods in restaurants or institutional kitchens are responsible. However, approximately one-third of the cases reported to the U.S. Centers for Disease Control are traced to improper food storage or handling in the home. By recognizing and preventing the conditions that lead to food contamination and spoilage, consumers can ensure that the foods they buy will stay fresh and wholesome from the time of purchase through preparation and serving.

What makes food spoil?

Microbes (microorganisms) are everywhere. They live in the air, soil, and water, in the digestive tracts of humans and animals, on their skin, and in their noses. Microbial contamination is the major villain in food spoilage and foodborne disease. However, not all microbes are pathogenic (disease-causing). Some are harmless, and others, such as the lactobacillus added to milk to make yogurt, are actually helpful. Others—for example, some molds and yeasts—cause spoilage but not illness. Still others are not harmful themselves

but, under certain conditions, produce toxins as they grow and multiply.

While it would be nearly impossible for consumers to remove all microorganisms from their kitchens, it is possible to prevent their spread and to keep those that cause spoilage and disease from multiplying. All microbes need food and water to grow. Beyond that, their needs vary. Some are aerobic; they require oxygen to live. Others are anaerobic and multiply in the absence of oxygen. Some are thermophilic—that is, they require warm temperatures; others are psychrophilic (cryophilic), thriving at lower temperatures. Some cannot survive in very acid or very alkaline environments. Changing these conditions—for instance, by boiling— may destroy most bacteria, but some bacteria may survive. Refrigerating or freezing only slows down bacterial reproduction. Once favorable conditions have been restored, they will continue to multiply.

Molds

Molds are the most common microbes that cause food spoilage. Mold is a type of many-celled fungal growth. The part that is visible on food—the fuzzy or cottony mat—is the reproductive, or spore-forming, portion. Beneath the surface are long filaments of vegetative cells, invisible without a microscope. By the time mold is visible on food surfaces, thousands of these long filaments have spread deep within the food. Even if only one spot of mold is visible, the vegetative cells probably have already contaminated the rest of the food. And if conditions are favorable for mold growth, the food may also be contaminated with disease-causing bacteria.

Molds require moisture and air for growth. They like

453

warmth, although they can survive and reproduce at refrigerator temperatures. They favor carbohydrates and high-acid foods. Soft fruits and vegetables with high moisture content, typical leftovers, and bakery or dairy products are most susceptible to mold invasion.

Most molds will not cause illness if eaten, but only laboratory analysis can confirm whether a mold is harmful. However, as molds grow, they produce metabolic products, or metabolites, that change the taste and texture of the host food, making it less appetizing and possibly even reducing its nutritional value. Some of the mold metabolites are, in fact, poisonous mycotoxins. For example, aflatoxin is produced by the mold *Aspergillus flavus* when it grows on high-carbohydrate foods such as grain or peanuts. Because of the possible presence of such mycotoxins, moldy food should be thrown away. The exceptions to this rule are cheese and hard salami, foods with a low moisture content that retards mold growth. A small moldy area on these foods can be cut away—along with a generous 2.5-cm (one-inch) margin all around and under the mold—and the food will still be wholesome.

Yeasts

Yeasts are another type of fungus. Some yeasts are anaerobic (*i.e.,* they thrive in the absence of oxygen); these are the fermentative yeasts that make bread rise and produce alcohol, vinegar, and soy sauce. Other yeasts are aerobic (oxygen-requiring); they impart flavor and color to aged cheeses. While yeasts are welcome in some foods, in others they can cause spoilage.

Yeasts favor foods containing sugar, although they can grow on nearly any food. They can survive high sugar and salt concentrations that would kill most bacteria. They are sensitive, however, to temperature extremes; few grow at refrigerator temperatures or can survive heat over 49° C (120° F).

Because they grow as single cells, yeasts are rarely visible in contaminated food. Large concentrations in liquids may settle to the bottom or make the liquid cloudy, or they may form a scum on top. On solid food they may form a light-colored slime. Yeasts are not pathogens, but they make foods less palatable; *e.g.,* fermentation in fruit juice. Their presence may indicate that the food has been contaminated by bacteria. Their activity can also alter food chemically to make it more favorable to pathogenic bacteria.

Bacteria

Thousands of types of bacteria can cause food spoilage. Most are active at temperatures of 4.4°–60° C (40°–140° F), although some are psychrophilic (thrive at a relatively low temperature) or thermophilic (grow at a high temperature). For growth they require a good deal of moisture; because salt and sugar can reduce available water, foods high in either are rarely contaminated. Most bacteria prefer a neutral pH, so high acidity or alkalinity will inhibit their growth. Some are aerobic, while others are anaerobic. Bacteria are amazingly prolific; under optimal conditions certain types can double in number every 20 minutes.

Of the many types of bacteria, only about 100 are pathogenic. Although most cause only limited gastrointestinal illness, some can be very serious or even fatal, especially to the very young and the very old. People who have recently taken antibiotics are also susceptible because the medication kills normally occurring bacteria in the body, leaving disease-causing organisms free to establish themselves.

Pathogenic bacteria cause illness in humans in two ways: intoxication, in which the bacteria produce a toxin (poison) that causes illness when ingested; and infection, in which the bacteria themselves attack the digestive system. In order to produce symptoms, bacterial activity must reach a critical level where either enough live pathogens are present to cause infection or the population has produced sufficient toxins to cause intoxication. The critical level varies. Mere traces of *Clostridium botulinum* can cause a serious disease, while larger populations of other *Clostridium* species must be present for illness to be triggered. Pathogens do not necessarily signal their presence in foods by changing the color, flavor, or texture of the food.

Major causes of food poisoning

Salmonella. Infection with various species of the genus *Salmonella* accounts for about half of the reported cases of food poisoning in the U.S. There are more than 1,700 strains of salmonella bacteria. They live in the intestinal tracts of many animals and can contaminate meat and poultry during the slaughtering process. Salmonellae are also found in eggs, fish, and milk and in foods made with any of these. Salmonellae multiply rapidly at room temperature. Cold temperatures—under 4.4° C (40° F)—will not kill them but will inhibit their growth. Heating contaminated food to 66° C (150° F) or higher will kill them.

Symptoms of salmonella infection, or salmonellosis, begin 12 to 48 hours after a person has eaten food containing large numbers of the bacteria. Salmonellosis causes headache, nausea, diarrhea, vomiting, abdominal cramps, and fever. The infection usually clears up in two to seven days.

Staphylococcus aureus. About a quarter of reported foodborne illnesses in the U.S. are caused by the bacterium *Staphylococcus aureus.* Staph bacteria occur on the skin and in the nose; infected cuts or boils usually carry staph organisms. When the bacteria are transferred to food—by a cook, for example—they produce an enterotoxin (*i.e.,* a toxin that causes gastrointestinal symptoms), which then causes intoxication. *S. aureus* flourishes at room temperature on high-protein foods, such as meats, eggs, or foods contain-

Food storage timetable

food	refrigerator	pantry	freezer	special instructions
fruit, fresh apples, pears berries, cherries grapes melons citrus fruits	 1–3 weeks 1–2 days 3–5 days 1 week 3 weeks		12 months	most last longer and taste better when refrigerated; in general, should not be washed before storage
fruit, canned	opened, 1 week*	unopened, 12 months		
milk	5 days		1 month	most dairy products are wholesome for use for a week after package date, but poor storage by processor or at grocery store can reduce this time
cottage cheese	9–10 days		(freezing not recommended)	
cheese, hard, aged, or wax-coated	opened, 3–4 weeks		unopened, 6–8 weeks	
butter	1–2 weeks		6–9 months	
eggs, in shell	2–3 weeks			
whites only	3 days		12 months	freeze separated eggs only
yolks	3 days		12 months	
vegetables, fresh (e.g., green beans, corn, peas)	1–7 days			
head lettuce	unwashed, 5–7 days; washed and drained, 3–5 days			
vegetables, canned	opened, 3 days*	unopened, 12 months		
vegetable oil	opened, 1–3 months	unopened, 6 months		all except olive oil should be refrigerated after opening
beef, ground	1–2 days		3–4 months	
beef, roast	3–5 days		6–12 months	
whole chicken or turkey	1–2 days		12 months	
fish, lean (e.g., cod, haddock, sole)	1–2 days		6 months	
bacon	7 days		1 month	
luncheon meats	opened, 3–5 days unopened, 2 weeks		unopened, 1–2 months	
catsup	opened, 1 month	unopened, 12 months		
mayonnaise	opened, 3 months	unopened, 2–3 months		
peanut butter	opened, 2–3 months	unopened, 6–9 months		
salad dressings	opened, 3 months	unopened, 10–12 months		
jams and jellies	opened, 12 months	unopened, 12 months		
sugar, granulated		2 years		keep in tightly closed container
flour, white or whole wheat		8 months		refrigerate in warm weather; keep in tightly closed container
breakfast cereal		unopened, 12 months; opened, 3 months		

*to prevent discoloration or alteration of taste, all canned foods should be transferred to plastic or glass containers before being refrigerated

From *The Safe Food Book*, U.S.D.A. Home and Garden Bulletin no. 241

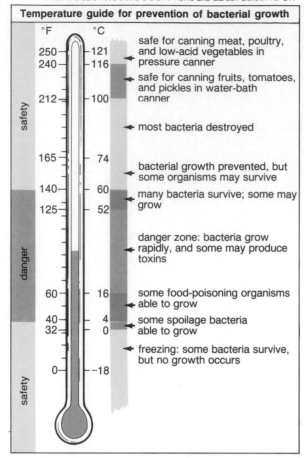

Temperature guide for prevention of bacterial growth

°F / °C

250 / 121 — safe for canning meat, poultry, and low-acid vegetables in pressure canner
240 / 116 — safe for canning fruits, tomatoes, and pickles in water-bath canner
212 / 100
— most bacteria destroyed
165 / 74
— bacterial growth prevented, but some organisms may survive
140 / 60 — many bacteria survive; some may grow
125 / 52
— danger zone: bacteria grow rapidly, and some may produce toxins
60 / 16 — some food-poisoning organisms able to grow
40 / 4 — some spoilage bacteria able to grow
32 / 0
— freezing: some bacteria survive, but no growth occurs
0 / –18

safety / danger / safety

ing milk products. Although heating will destroy the bacteria, the toxin is resistant to high temperatures. Staph intoxication causes diarrhea, vomiting, nausea, abdominal cramps, and general malaise within one to eight hours after ingestion of the toxin. Symptoms last 24 to 48 hours.

Clostridium perfringens. In about 10% of reported cases of foodborne illness, *Clostridium perfringens* is the cause. *C. perfringens* bacteria are widespread in soil and are found in the intestines of humans and animals. *C. perfringens* is anaerobic and grows only in foods high in protein. It is most often found in soups and stews, where boiling can drive out oxygen and leftovers tend to cool slowly, creating ideal conditions for the bacteria to multiply.

In its growing state, *C. perfringens* can cause infection, but it is easily destroyed by heat. *C. perfringens* produces spores, however, that are able to survive conditions that kill the growing bacteria. The spores become active at temperatures between 21° and 49° C (70° and 120° F) and start to produce toxins, leading to food intoxication. *C. perfringens* infection or intoxication causes relatively mild symptoms of abdominal pain, gas, diarrhea, and nausea. These symptoms appear within 8 to 22 hours after ingestion and usually

last a day or less. Because of its mildness, *C. perfringens* poisoning is often dismissed as "stomach flu" and thus is probably greatly underreported.

Clostridium botulinum. A fourth pathogen that deserves careful attention is *Clostridium botulinum,* which causes the deadly form of food poisoning known as botulism. Relatively few cases occur, but botulism can be fatal if not promptly and correctly treated. Botulin spores are common in soil and in the air and can be ingested without harm by adults. Infants, however, can develop botulism from eating the spores. The spores can be killed by very high temperatures, but some may survive and produce toxins if the food is not processed properly. Botulism is almost always associated with improperly canned low-acid foods, such as green beans, corn, meat, and fish. Canning creates the anaerobic atmosphere that allows the spores to reactivate and produce their deadly toxin.

Botulism causes neurological symptoms: double vision, difficulty in swallowing and talking, and progressive respiratory paralysis. Symptoms usually begin 8 to 36 hours after a person has eaten tainted food. Victims should get immediate medical attention, as untreated botulism can be fatal.

Campylobacter jejuni. Several other pathogens have been identified only recently. One is *Campylobacter jejuni,* associated with raw milk and meat and contaminated water supplies. It causes both infection and intoxication. It grows at cooler temperatures in the absence of oxygen. Both the bacteria and the toxin can be destroyed by thorough heating. *C. jejuni* causes symptoms similar to those of salmonellosis, but the onset is later—between three and five days after the ingestion of contaminated food.

Listeria monocytogenes. This is another recently identified pathogen. Although common in soil, water, and air and on animals and people, *L. monocytogenes* is most often associated with milk and milk products. Thorough cooking will destroy the bacteria, although some may survive the pasteurization process. Listeriosis most severely affects those people whose resistance has already been compromised: pregnant women, newborns, and the chronically ill. It generally causes flulike symptoms but can lead to meningitis, a potentially fatal inflammation of the membranes surrounding the spinal cord.

Viruses and parasites

Foods can also be infected with viruses, such as the ones that cause viral gastroenteritis or infectious hepatitis (hepatitis A). These viruses live in the human intestine. Viral contamination can occur directly, owing to poor hygienic practices by a food preparer, or indirectly, when human sewage is used as fertilizer or when shellfish beds are contaminated with sewage. Viral gastroenteritis causes severe diarrhea, nausea, and vomiting 24 hours after eating and may persist for

Cooking meat and poultry

meat and poultry cooked throughout to these temperatures are generally safe to eat (not applicable to microwave cooking)

	degrees Celsius	degrees Fahrenheit
fresh beef		
rare	60*	140*
medium	71	160
well done	77	170
ground beef	77	170
fresh veal	77	170
fresh lamb		
medium	77	170
well done	82	180
fresh pork	77	170
poultry		
chicken	82–85	180–185
turkey	82–85	180–185
stuffing (inside or outside of bird)	74	165
cured pork		
ham, raw (cook before eating)	77	170
ham, fully cooked (heat before serving)	60	140
game		
deer	71–77	160–170
duck, goose	82–85	180–185

*some food-poisoning organisms may survive in rare beef

weeks. Hepatitis causes fatigue and jaundice; if left untreated, it can produce liver damage that may even lead to death.

Single-celled protozoan parasites such as members of the genuses *Giardia* and *Amoeba* also live in the human intestinal tract and can contaminate food by the same route as the viruses. The diseases they cause are known respectively as giardiasis and amebiasis. These illnesses are generally characterized by diarrhea, abdominal pain, and loss of weight.

Another parasitic illness is trichinosis, which results from infestation with the tiny roundworm *Trichinella spiralis*. The source of the disease is inadequately cooked pork containing the larvae of the parasite. Meat from wild game may also transmit the disease. Trichinosis symptoms appear within 12 to 24 hours. They include gastrointestinal upset, fever, muscle pain, and swelling around the eyes.

Precautions

Preventing foodborne illness and spoilage is actually quite simple. The task of the individual cook and consumer is to minimize exposure to microbes and to make the kitchen environment hostile to them.

Shopping and storage. The process of prevention begins at the store. Shoppers should not purchase dented or bulging cans or packages that are soiled or torn. Foods susceptible to mold should be carefully inspected and rejected if there are signs of contamination. Perishables, meats, poultry, and frozen foods should be picked up last so they stay cool. All groceries should be taken home and stored properly as soon as possible.

Prepackaged foods generally include manufacturers' storage instructions, which should be followed carefully. Some packages also include a "sell by" or "best if used by" date; after this time the food may still be wholesome, but flavor and nutritional quality may decline. Outdated foods should probably be disposed of.

In the home, keeping stored foods covered protects them from contamination by airborne microbes. So does regular cleaning of storage areas and containers. Cool, dry storage protects foods from microbial growth. Dry foods, such as pasta, beans, and flour, should never be stored near water pipes, where condensation could dampen them. Nor should they be kept near such heat-producing appliances as stoves, refrigerators, or dishwashers.

Temperature control during storage, preparation, and serving will minimize growth of harmful microbes in perishables. The rules are simple: hot foods must be kept hot (over 60° C [140° F]) and cold foods cold (under 4.4° C [40° F]). Foods should never be held between these temperatures for more than two hours—the time it takes most microbes to establish themselves and start to multiply.

Refrigerators should be checked with a reliable thermometer to ensure that they are maintaining temperatures below 4.4° C (40° F). Freezers should be at −17.8° C (0° F). Food that is being marinated should be kept in the refrigerator. Even though most marinades are acidic, this factor only slows the development of some pathogens; it does not kill them. All of the ingredients to be used in salads, casseroles, and other high-moisture dishes should be chilled before mixing to retard microbial growth.

Salmonella bacteria are often found in fresh poultry. Frequent washing of hands, utensils, and cutting boards prevents cross-contamination of other foods.

April A. Oswald

Handling and cooking. To minimize contamination, cooks should handle food as little as possible during preparation. Frequent washing of hands, utensils, and work surfaces during food preparation prevents cross-contamination, a common cause of bacterial disease. A typical cross-contamination scenario is as follows: A cook cuts up a raw chicken that carries salmonella bacteria. The bacteria in the chicken will be destroyed when it is cooked; however, some bacteria remain on the knife and cutting board. Any food the cook subsequently prepares with those utensils will be contaminated unless the cook thoroughly washes the knife, the board, and his or her hands.

Using the same spoon to taste and stir, or to stir several different dishes, can also cross-contaminate foods. Wooden cutting boards and utensils may harbor microbes in tiny surface cracks; they should be thoroughly washed in hot, soapy water after each use and regularly sanitized in a mild solution of water and chlorine bleach. Kitchen linens, storage containers, and refrigerators can also be sources of cross-contamination and should be kept clean.

Meats and poultry should be cooked thoroughly so that internal temperatures reach a safe level. The standing times recommended by microwave manufacturers should be closely observed so that cooking is complete. Partially cooking meat one day and finishing it the next is not wise; this can encourage bacterial growth.

Reheating. Cooked foods not eaten should be cooled quickly. Leftovers should be covered and placed in the refrigerator immediately. Large batches of soups, stews, sauces, or casseroles should be cooled in an ice bath—*i.e.,* the container is placed in a sink filled with ice or ice water—or divided up into small containers before refrigeration. Otherwise the internal temperature can stay in the danger zone long enough for the food to become contaminated, even in the refrigerator. When leftovers are going to be eaten, they should be reheated thoroughly so that any surviving contaminants will be destroyed.

Dealing with frozen foods. Frozen food should always be defrosted in the refrigerator—never at room temperature. To speed defrosting, the food can be sealed in a watertight plastic bag and thawed under cold running water, or it can be thawed in a microwave oven according to the manufacturer's instructions.

When preparing frozen food directly from the freezer, cooks should remember to allow extra time for thorough heating—usually about one and one-half times as long as the cooking time recommended for thawed foods. Frozen food that thaws partially owing to freezer failure can safely be refrozen if there are still ice crystals in the product itself. Thawed foods without ice crystals can be cooked and refrozen, but any defrosted foods that look or smell suspicious should be discarded.

Home-canned foods. Anyone who cans meat or produce at home should follow processing instructions exactly to prevent the possibility of botulism. Home-canned or commercially processed foods should be discarded without being tasted if the seal is broken, the can is bulging, the food looks or smells bad, or the container spurts liquid when opened. Home-canned low-acid foods (meats, poultry, fish, and most vegetables) should be brought to a rapid boil before they are tasted; this will sometimes bring out bad odors that are an indication of botulism. If the product does not smell bad, it should be covered and boiled for an additional 20 minutes to kill any botulinum toxins that still may be present.

Helpful resources

In the United States the following federal agencies monitor the processing and packaging of foods and can be contacted for information or to report negligence: the Food and Drug Administration (FDA); the Environmental Protection Agency (EPA); and the U.S. Department of Agriculture (USDA), specifically the branch known as the Food Safety and Inspection Service (FSIS). For consumers who have specific questions about meat and poultry, the FSIS maintains a toll-free telephone number: 1-800-535-4555.

How Healthy Is Day Care?
by Vincent A. Fulginiti, M.D.

In societies in which most children are reared at home and contact is limited to a few other children (siblings and neighbors) and only a few adults (parents, relatives, neighbors, and perhaps babysitters), youngsters are slowly exposed to infectious agents and gradually build up immune defenses against such agents. Entry into kindergarten or first grade marks the child's first true group contact. Along with such contact comes the first exposure to many infectious agents and the first opportunity to experience epidemic spread of contagious diseases. The postponement of major exposure until the ages of five to seven years allows for immunity to amass, with each subsequent exposure broadening the child's defenses. As a result, these children run little risk of serious disease in early infancy and later develop only relatively mild to moderate disease after repeated exposure to certain agents. In addition, for most children exposure to the epidemic contagious agents comes at a time when their bodies are capable of handling such challenges.

Today, however, as a result of the growing acceptance of day care for infants and older preschoolers, group contact and first exposure to infectious disease comes at a much earlier age, often to a larger variety of organisms, and in much more massive amounts than occurred when first exposure was at ages five to seven. Also, as a consequence of this earlier exposure, the modes of transmission of infectious agents have changed. The respiratory route and direct contact were once the principal means of transmission of an infection from one child to another. Today diseases of the gastrointestinal tract have assumed greater importance because of day-care attendance by infants in diapers along with older children who may not be completely toilet trained. Furthermore, transmission of disease by the fecal-oral route has been added to the respiratory and direct-contact modes. Thus, not only do the diseases that can be acquired differ today but the mass of exposure has also been increased substantially.

Common diseases in the day-care setting

Common respiratory diseases are the illnesses most frequently contracted in a day-care population. A multitude of viruses and bacteria cause these infections. In addition, many infections that manifest themselves elsewhere in the body are acquired by the respiratory route—inhalation of infectious particles sneezed, coughed, or otherwise deposited into the environment. Recent evidence suggests that many of these infectious agents are carried on the hands and that transmission also occurs by means of physical contact with a contaminated person; in fact, for many of the viral infections this mode of transmission may be the predominant one. Because of the ages of the infants and children in day care today, many of these are "first contact" infections—that is, they represent the first encounter the child has had with that particular agent of disease. In addition, because of the prolonged nature of contact in the day-care setting, any individual child may be exposed to a large "dose" of the infectious agent. The resulting illness may be more severe than one acquired in more fleeting contact and may affect not only the nose and throat but also the deeper passages of the respiratory tract. The common cold is still the most frequent manifestation of respiratory infection, but young infants may develop otitis media (middle ear infection), caused by the transfer of the infectious agent from the nose into the ear cavity, bronchitis (inflammation of the larger air tubes), bronchiolitis (inflammation of the smaller air tubules and air sacs), and pneumonia (infection of the lung itself). Respiratory syncytial virus, or RSV, a major source of respiratory throat infection in children under age two, is also known to be transmitted in the day-care setting. Older children may have encountered these agents previously and in smaller doses and thus be reinfected or come down with a milder disease because of partial immunity.

Infections that are spread by the respiratory route and are manifest elsewhere in the body, but that may

459

also include involvement of the respiratory tract, are *Hemophilus influenzae,* type B, or HIB (not to be confused with viral influenza), which may develop into a serious form of meningitis; measles; mumps; German measles (rubella); and meningococcal infections. The disease-causing agents gain entry via the respiratory tract and then spread, usually through the bloodstream, to other organs, where the damage is done.

Gastrointestinal infections and infections transmitted by secretions of the gastrointestinal tract but manifest elsewhere are the second most common forms of disease acquired in the day-care setting. Viruses, bacteria, and parasites can be transmitted in this way. The presence of infants who have not yet developed bowel control, the need for regular changing of diapers, and the lack of hygienic practice among the children and the staff contribute to potential contamination of the environment and of the hands of the caretakers, which can lead to transmission of the agent from child to child, from child to adult, and from adult to child. It is not surprising that such diseases occur with greater frequency among populations in day-care centers that are large and busy, that include children not yet toilet trained, and in which infants and children stay for prolonged periods during the day.

The most common gastrointestinal illnesses encountered in this setting are rotavirus diarrhea (especially common in infants), bacterial dysenteric diseases (shigella and salmonella), other viral and bacterial disorders associated with vomiting and diarrhea, and parasitic infections such as cryptosporidiosus. Among the agents transmitted by the gastrointestinal route but manifest elsewhere are the viruses that cause infectious hepatitis (hepatitis A) and polio. (The latter is not a major threat today, but even the virus in the vaccine can be transmitted in this way.)

There are other possible modes of transmission among infants and older preschoolers: direct contact with infected skin sores; eye-to-eye spread; and biting, scratching, and other injuries. Although less common than respiratory or gastrointestinal transmission in a given setting, these modes may become important at a given time. For example, an epidemic form of adenovirus conjunctivitis, an infection of the eye, can spread rapidly in a small population.

Assessing the risks of day care

From the standpoint of exposure to infection, just how risky is it for infants and children to attend day-care facilities? This is a complex question, one that cannot be answered with a formula applicable to all children, in all settings, and at all times. That children acquire infectious diseases in day-care settings is an established fact. Whether acquisition of such infections is "bad" or "good" depends in part on one's point of view and in part on the actual experience of the particular child. Most children who acquire infections in group settings experience mild to moderate illness, acquire permanent or semipermanent immunity, and are healthier for the experience. However, some acquire severe infections that they might not have experienced had they not been in the day-care setting.

The size and composition of the group are important factors that influence risk to the individual child. Among small groups of children, risk is minimal to slight; among large groups of children, especially groups in which infants and older children come into contact, the risks are higher. The duration of contact is another factor for consideration. Children put in day-care facilities for short periods during the day have a lower risk of infection than do youngsters who are in day care for long periods on a continuous, all-day basis. There

The size and composition of the day-care group are important factors that influence the risk of infection to the individual child. A large group, like the one shown here, which includes infants and toddlers along with older children, poses a greater risk than does a smaller, more homogeneous one.

are also individual factors in assessing risk. Children with underlying increased susceptibility to infection as a result of impaired immune responsiveness or a pre-existing disorder that may be complicated by infection (for example, a heart condition) are at higher risk than their peers. Given all of these different circumstances, it is difficult for the physician or public health official to state with any certainty what is the "average" frequency of particular infections or the "average" risk to the individual child. No simple formula can predict the risk of acquisition of infection, nor can statistical data provide a sure estimate of the likelihood of exposure to severe infection.

Also to be taken into consideration when assessing risk are the character, training, number, and behavior of the adult staff at a given day-care center and the parent population of the children. For example, if careful health screening is not performed by operators of the day-care center, attendants could be employed who are themselves ill; such attendants may serve as vectors for transmission of disease to the children. Further, unless hygienic practices are carefully taught and practiced by the staff, the risk of disease transmission rises. If the center is a large one, with many attendants who have multiple contacts with all of the youngsters, and either of the factors mentioned above is also present, then the risk can be quite high. On the other hand, there are advantages to having a large staff—adequate numbers of staff can reduce risk of disease by providing more supervision of the children and promoting better hygiene. In addition, the physical facility in and of itself can contribute to risk. If diaper changing is conducted in an area where children play or if it takes place close to food-preparation areas, gastrointestinal organisms are likely to spread more easily than if diapering is restricted to an area set aside for that function.

Risks by type of disease

All studies to date have either suggested or proved (although findings vary widely) that, in general, respiratory infections are increased among day-care attendees. Older children have lower rates of infection than do younger children and infants. Some studies comparing day-care populations with home-reared children of comparable ages have shown increased rates for serious respiratory infections, including increased rates for hospitalization, among the day-care attendees. Most studies, however, have not shown an increased rate for the most serious respiratory infections. The best conducted studies thus far have shown no increase in more virulent pathogens among day-care attendees than among home-reared children. One significant finding has been the increased frequency of middle ear infection in children who attend day-care centers. According to these studies, not only was this condition more common but a larger number of children were

noted to have recurrent episodes. The risk for the day-care population has been estimated at two to three times that of children reared at home. Small, family-run day-care groups have an intermediate risk, falling somewhere between the numbers seen in larger centers and the cases reported in home rearing.

With respect to gastrointestinal illnesses, studies indicate that day-care attendees do experience outbreaks of diarrheal disease, irrespective of the size of the facility, the socioeconomic makeup of the group, and other factors. Whether such outbreaks result in a greater number of diarrheal episodes for day-care attendees, in contrast to children reared at home, cannot be judged accurately since comparable data are lacking. Existing information, however, suggests that day-care attendees do experience more frequent diarrheal episodes. What is clear is that attack rates for both children and attendants who work in centers are very high when outbreaks occur. The major causes of diarrhea in day care are the parasite *Giardia lamblia,* the bacterium *Shigella sonnei,* and the rotaviruses. Infection with these agents is not as likely to be observed in home settings; thus, the risk of acquiring serious gastrointestinal infection must be judged to be higher for children in day care.

Hepatitis A, or infectious hepatitis, is a special problem. The virus responsible for this disease is transmitted by the fecal-oral route. There is clear evidence that day-care centers are often the focus of miniepidemics of hepatitis A and can account for the spread of the disease into the community at large. The problem is that infants and children show few if any symptoms or signs of hepatitis; it is only when the infection is transmitted to adults that symptomatic disease occurs. Epidemics of hepatitis A occur most frequently in centers with children under two years of age, and their occurrence is directly related to lack of bowel control in children in this age group and the resulting need for children's diapers to be changed on the premises. Other factors that have been shown to be related to high rates of hepatitis A incidence are size of the center (especially if there are 50 or more children) and the number of hours the facility is open (longer hours being associated with higher rates). Proprietary centers (*i.e.,* those run for profit) may have increased incidence, at least according to one study.

Diseases spread by the respiratory route but manifest elsewhere in the body may also occur in miniepidemic form among day-care attendees. However, there are marked differences in disease rates, with some centers reporting episodes of meningitis subsequent to cases of HIB, for example, and others having few or no secondary cases, despite the occurrence of illness in one attendee. Experts disagree in their interpretations of such disparate findings. On one hand, many authorities feel that all day-care attendees are at greater risk for meningitis caused by HIB. Others cite the inconsistent findings from study to study and doubt that the risk is substantial. There is also some controversy over the question of increased risk to children at home from a sibling who attends a day-care center where cases of meningitis have occurred. Most, but not all, of the evidence suggests that these children do face a substantial increase in risk. At this time it simply is not clear whether the demonstrated increased risk of meningitis in day-care attendees or their siblings at home that has been documented in some settings can be generalized to include all settings and all siblings.

Measles, pertussis (whooping cough), and other contagious diseases pose a potential threat to any group of children gathered together for prolonged periods of time. Some epidemics have been reported in day-care centers, but the number is small, relative to the incidence of the other diseases discussed above, and mass immunization has tended to blunt the occurrence of outbreaks of these diseases.

In contrast, cytomegalovirus (CMV) infections pose a potential threat that could assume serious proportions. CMV infection is common and is often asymptomatic among healthy children and adults. For prolonged periods after recovery, the virus can be found in various bodily secretions but especially in urine and in throat secretions. The true threat of cytomegalovirus is to the previously uninfected pregnant woman. In such a case the virus may be transmitted from the mother to the fetus at a critical stage of development, causing a serious congenital infection. Fetal infection may also occur without obvious harm to the infant, but the virus can linger, causing later developmental or neurological difficulties. CMV has been shown to be transmitted among day-care attendees and attendants, as well as among their household contacts. The rate of transmission of CMV in day-care centers may be two to three times that among home-reared children.

Precaution and prevention: the parents' role

Clearly there are certain measures that can reduce the risk of infection to individual children, to the group, and to the community at large. Parents play an important part in the process.

Any day-care center should be evaluated by every parent who intends to use it. There are a number of steps involved in this evaluation. Before enrolling a child in a day-care facility, parents should:
- identify the owner of the center
- investigate community regulations covering day-care centers and determine whether the facility is licensed or approved under those regulations
- inspect the premises for cleanliness; food service areas (if any) should be separated from other areas
- inquire about the screening procedures (health and otherwise) used for potential employees
- ask if medical consultation is available to the staff

- ask whether all employees have undergone special day-care training
- determine the limitations on attendance of a child who has a potentially infectious illness
- ask if physical exams are required for attendees
- find out what procedures are used for notifying parents in case of illness or accident and for handling children who are injured or ill
- learn of the provisions for isolating children who become ill while at the center

Parents can play an active part in decreasing the risk of exposure by not taking to the day-care center children who are ill with respiratory, febrile, or gastrointestinal illnesses. Sometimes the temptation to do so is great, since staying at home with the sick child may involve loss of time from work and possibly loss of salary. Some communities have resolved this issue by establishing "sick children" day-care facilities, where youngsters with relatively minor illness can be tended. It is also the parents' responsibility to ensure that their child is up-to-date on all required immunizations and health care checkups. All day-care attendees should be immunized as is appropriate for their age, and attendance by children who do not have proof of immunization should be prohibited. The specific requirements differ in various states and municipalities.

Some special considerations should be borne in mind when parents are assessing the adequacy of a given day-care facility. Since hand washing is the single most important consideration in preventing the transmission of most of the infectious agents discussed here, the presence of an adequate number of sinks in good working order and their regular use by the attendants are paramount. The physical facility should be spacious enough to accommodate the number of attendees and should have clear separation of diapering, food service, and other areas. This requirement may seem obvious, but many day-care facilities are run in buildings not originally designed for the purpose and therefore are not optimally arranged for child care needs.

Community responsibilities

Community evaluation and regulation of day-care facilities depend largely on local circumstances. Physicians in the community should be active in ensuring that local health authorities have a role in regulating and inspecting day-care facilities. This may require legislation in some communities, development of regulations under enabling legislation in others, and simply active enforcement of established regulations in yet other settings. Controversy may occur when the cost of day care is increased in order to comply with safety and health regulations, but these standards should not be compromised at the cost of increasing risks to the children.

Say "Cheese": Today's Cosmetic Dentistry

by Richard J. Simonsen, D.D.S.

The smile plays an important role in social interaction, and because contemporary society tends to emphasize certain uniform standards as to what is considered attractive, the person with stained, missing, or crooked teeth may be less likely to smile broadly in a natural and relaxed way than someone who has "beautiful" teeth. Dentists have for many years been able to place caps over irregularly shaped stained teeth, giving them a "perfect" appearance. This appearance, however, is sometimes too perfect—many film stars have obviously fake smiles. The challenge therefore for the dentist today is to improve a person's appearance without making it look false.

The advantages of bonding

"Cosmetic" dentistry began with the discovery by Michael Buonocore in the 1950s of a technique for etching tooth enamel. The so-called acid etch technique is now used in many areas of dentistry, particularly in preventive and cosmetic procedures. The most common process associated with acid etching is bonding. Bonding simply refers to the sticking together of two surfaces, as when plastics are bonded to tooth enamel. The dentist prepares an enamel surface for bonding by applying a weak solution of phosphoric acid. This produces a microscopically roughened ("etched") surface onto which a free-flowing liquid plastic resin can be applied, much as nail polish is applied to fingernails. The plastic hardens chemically after a short time or is "cured" by activation with a visible light. Once the first coating of the material has hardened in the microscopic pores of the enamel, more resin material can be added on top of it to change the shape of teeth, repair cavities, or attach veneers or bridges. In order for bonding to be successful, the teeth must have sufficient enamel to allow the dentist to bond materials to them. For the repair of teeth that have large cavities or extensive destruction of enamel, bonding is not a practical technique.

From the patient's point of view, a major benefit of bonding is that the dentist needs to remove little or none of the existing tooth enamel. (In a few bonding procedures it is necessary to remove a thin layer of enamel in order to provide the best anchor for the bonded material.) Conventional procedures that do not use bonding require that extensive amounts of tooth structure be cut down so the cap can be attached over the remaining tooth structure.

There are other advantages to bonding. One is that the bonding resin can be matched to the tooth color. Another is that bonding need not extend beneath the gum tissue. For aesthetic purposes it has been common when capping teeth to place the metal edges of a cap underneath the gum tissue. This can irritate the gum and cause subsequent gum disease. Further, bonded material has a much smaller propensity for allowing leakage of saliva and food acids between the material and the tooth. Thus, the chance of developing additional cavities, as often results from leaking at the edges of fillings, is less.

The first extensive use of bonding was in pit and fissure sealing. This technique involves cleaning and conditioning the cavity-prone surfaces of the teeth and subsequently applying a thin resinous material that coats the teeth and prevents cavities. The most cavity-prone surfaces in the mouth are the biting surfaces of the back teeth, which usually become decayed prior to the teenage years. Application of a pit and fissure

463

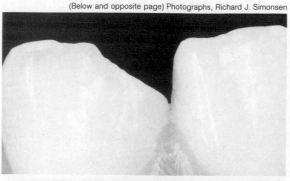

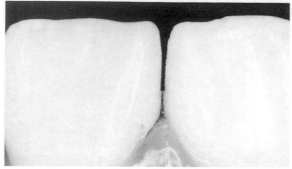

The angled fracture of the front tooth (shown at top) was repaired with bonding and a composite resin; the method preserved the remaining natural tooth enamel.

sealant has been shown to be extremely effective in protecting these cavity-prone areas.

Repairing injured teeth

Bonding has also been extremely beneficial in the repair of broken or fractured teeth. Injuries to the teeth frequently occur as a result of sports activities, car or biking accidents, or falls. Fractured teeth can be painful at times and are also unsightly. To correct the damage the dentist smooths the fractured area, prepares the enamel for bonding, and carefully applies one of the plastic tooth-colored materials to the area. The injured person can go home with a repair that looks as good as the original tooth. It is also possible to bond broken pieces of natural tooth structure back into place after injury. The success of these repairs depends to a large extent upon the type of material chosen and the difficulties encountered in color matching. Many of the plastic resin materials developed over the years have proved to be quite color stable, and a repair may be expected to last a minimum of 3 to 5 years, perhaps as long as 10 to 15 or more. If the material needs to be replaced, further destruction of tooth enamel is not necessary.

Replacing missing teeth

Bonding has also been useful in developing alternative means of replacing missing teeth. The conventional procedure for replacing a missing tooth involves grinding down the adjacent healthy teeth into small stubs so that caps may be applied over them. The false tooth that replaces the missing tooth is secured to these caps. A technique developed at the University of Maryland and called the "Maryland bridge" consists of bonding an etched metal framework to the inside (tongue side) surfaces of the adjacent teeth. The false tooth is attached to this bonded metal, and the healthy teeth remain intact. The procedure eliminates not only the grinding down of healthy teeth but also the irritation to the surrounding gum tissues caused by the edges of caps. This type of tooth replacement has been extremely successful, and although its longevity is not yet possible to predict, its potential should be for a minimum of five years and probably much longer.

Changing shape and color

The use of bonding and other techniques to change the shape or color of healthy teeth has gained popularity in recent years. By skillful application of resin materials called composite resins, a dentist can close the space between front teeth by simply building up the edges of the teeth to make them slightly larger. A fairly common staining is the yellow-gray-brown discoloration that results from the use of tetracycline antibiotics during the tooth-forming years, either by the mother in the last half of pregnancy or the child up to age eight. Stained or malformed teeth can be covered with a plastic resin, or other material such as porcelain, to alter an individual's appearance significantly.

Treating discoloration by using materials such as porcelain for veneering is a recent development in dentistry. Whereas the tooth would previously have been cut down to a peg and a cap of porcelain made to cover it, now the dentist can effectively attach a thin, custom-made piece of porcelain (shaped much like a false fingernail) onto the outer surface of the tooth. This usually requires the removal of some enamel; otherwise the veneer would significantly increase the thickness of the tooth, which is usually undesirable. The technique of porcelain veneering, combined with the acid etch technique, was developed initially in 1982. The long-term durability of such a recent procedure cannot be determined, but veneers have proved successful thus far. Dentists predict that the porcelain veneer will last for many years, on the basis of the proven durability of similar procedures that have been in use for some time (*e.g.,* the application of a composite resin onto the front surfaces of the tooth). The process can be repeated, too, if necessary, with little or no effect on the remaining tooth structure.

Another conservative procedure for the improvement of tooth color is bleaching. Bleaching can be done either to the "live" (or vital) tooth or to one on which root canal treatment has been performed (such a tooth is called nonvital). Vital bleaching is generally more successful in situations where the teeth are

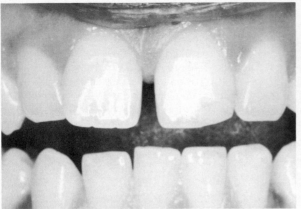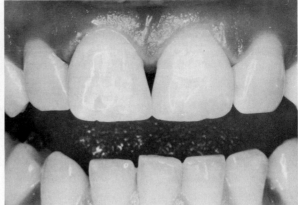

For a more uniform smile, gaps between teeth can be closed by bonding techniques. Coats of a resin material are used to build up the teeth for the desired appearance. Dentists can reshape crooked teeth similarly.

somewhat yellower than normal but is generally less successful in cases of tetracycline staining. Bleaching may require from one to six treatments, the duration of each treatment depending on the nature of the stain and the number of teeth involved. If successful, bleaching is usually permanent and does not usually result in any deleterious effect to the teeth. Nonvital bleaching (*i.e.*, done after root canal therapy) is also generally quite successful. However, bleaching a nonvital tooth can contribute to an increased brittleness, which may make the tooth more susceptible to fracture.

Filling cavities

There are some individuals who are allergic to the mercury contained in silver fillings who can benefit from the use of alternative filling materials. However, there is little evidence at this time to support routine replacement of all silver amalgam fillings based on suspicion of systemic harm. The benefits of using a bonded resin for routine filling are aesthetic improvement and the minimizing of leakage, which causes

cavities at the edges of fillings. (The most cavity-susceptible areas in a person's mouth have usually been filled by adulthood, and a majority of the cavities that develop later in life occur at the edges of old fillings.) Development of so-called posterior composite resins has progressed very rapidly in the past ten years, and there are now several viable alternatives to the conventional silver amalgam materials. The major benefit of the posterior composite resins is that a greater amount of tooth structure is saved in cutting down the teeth and removing the decay prior to filling. The major disadvantage is that the materials presently available are not as durable as silver amalgam.

Cost considerations

Bleaching is probably the least expensive of the procedures discussed above since it involves much less time than do the others. Stains from tea, coffee, or tobacco generally do not call for this kind of treatment, as they are usually surface stains that can be easily removed by proper cleaning. Stains do not usually

Teeth stained as a result of the drug tetracycline (below left) need not be ground down and capped for a brighter smile. Here thin porcelain veneers are attached to the teeth surfaces. "Acid etching" beforehand helped prepare the teeth for a secure bond.

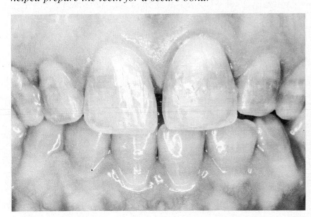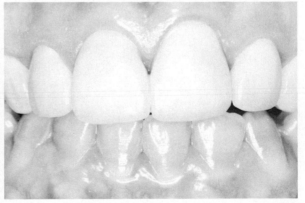

adhere to clean tooth surfaces, and it should thus be possible for an individual to keep his or her teeth stain-free with regular oral hygiene—brushing and flossing properly and consistently.

The use of pit and fissure sealant is certainly a cost-effective measure. It is much more expensive to repair the cavities that would occur in untreated teeth than it is to seal them and prevent the cavities from forming. Other procedures, such as posterior composite resin fillings, may require a higher fee for the patient because they take a little more time for the dentist to complete than do conventional fillings.

While it was thought that many of the bonding procedures would eventually lead to lower dental costs, bonded restorations require considerably more attention to detail in preparation of the teeth than was originally thought, and the cost savings are less than expected. For example, it was once believed that the Maryland bridge or porcelain veneers could easily be attached to the teeth with no prior removal of enamel. It is now known that these techniques are far more successful if very careful—although minimal—removal of the surface enamel is carried out prior to the bonding of a bridge or a veneer. Thus, it takes approximately as long for a dentist to skillfully prepare a central incisor (i.e., one of the two "front" teeth) for a porcelain veneer as it would to cover the tooth with a full porcelain cap. It is difficult to give general rules as to how many visits a bonding procedure will take. Some dentists may choose to do little or no preparatory tooth cutting and begin the bonding itself almost immediately. Others might require considerable time, e.g., working with laboratories to ensure that the bonding is well-suited to the individual patient—providing the best possible cosmetic correction; therefore, several appointments might be necessary.

In general, bonded plastic resin surfaces are quite durable, although improvement in materials is a continuing aspect of dental research. Of course, no filling of any sort is better than a healthy natural tooth, and eventually any foreign material that is added to the human body will tend to break down and have to be replaced or repaired. Exactly how long deterioration will take is not possible to predict, and individual situations vary widely. Covering a tooth with a cap of an extremely durable material such as gold is unlikely to weaken the tooth in terms of fracture potential, but it does predispose the tooth, directly and indirectly, to earlier than normal loss. Porcelain is actually more susceptible to fracture. In most bonding procedures, however, the bond between tooth and material is extremely strong, even stronger than the material that is being bonded to the tooth. Thus, it is unlikely that a bonded filling is going to be any weaker than the tooth itself unless the material being bonded is inherently weak.

Healthy smiles

A key health benefit of the new aesthetic procedures that involve less tooth reduction is that dentists work on the outer enamel surface rather than cutting into the more susceptible dentin, which is connected directly to the pulp (nerve and blood supply) of the tooth. Any time the dentin is involved, there is some risk of irritating the pulp, perhaps even to the extent that root canal treatment will be required at some later time. All of these factors can affect the long-term viability of the tooth. Thus, procedures that minimize the destruction of natural tooth material must be regarded as highly desirable. Additionally, procedures that do not penetrate enamel can frequently be carried out without an anesthetic.

Cosmetic dentistry has rapidly gained popularity in the United States in the past decade. Surprisingly, it is not uncommon to see people from other Western nations with quite poor teeth, and statistics indicate that there are high percentages of individuals who have lost all their teeth, even in industrialized countries such as the United Kingdom. However, the techniques described here certainly have vast applications for people around the world. In particular, techniques that save money (such as pit and fissure sealing and other minimal uses of composite resin) will probably become more common, and the concept of saving tooth structure by means of more conservative dentistry is likely to spread. Because of the new materials and techniques being developed today, the dental patient of tomorrow will have a happier smile with fewer cavities and less pain.

Estrogen Replacement Therapy
by Edward C. Hill, M.D.

The production of sex hormones by the body is one of the most intricate and fascinating aspects of human physiology. The human female is essentially the only female animal that outlives her reproductive period. A woman in the United States today, with a current life expectancy of 78 years, spends more than one-third of her life in the postmenopausal state. The menopause—*i.e.,* cessation of menstruation—is a direct result of a steady decline in ovarian function and the loss of estrogen production.

Estrogen replacement therapy (ERT), the administration of supplemental estrogen to replace the hormone that is no longer being produced by the body, has been used since the 1940s. ERT became a subject of controversy during the mid-1970s, when a number of studies demonstrated an association between estrogen supplementation and the development of cancer of the uterine lining. Recently, however, with new estrogen formulations and improved methods of administration, estrogen replacement therapy has been thoroughly reevaluated and reconsidered.

Menstruation and menopause

At birth a woman's ovaries contain approximately one million eggs, or ova, each enclosed in a tiny cystlike follicle. By puberty the number has been reduced by about half. During adolescence a number of follicles begin to grow and develop, producing the female hormone estrogen in the process. The bloodstream carries estrogen throughout the body. Each menstrual cycle uses up a number of follicles so that by the time a woman reaches the age of 40, some 350 cycles later, relatively few follicles remain. These, being comparatively old, are less responsive to the hormonal stimuli that activate them. Thus, ovarian senescence, with cessation of ovulation and steady decline in estrogen secretion, is a gradual process occurring over a period of several years; this is the period called the climacteric.

The menopause, or the complete cessation of menstrual function, ensues when estrogen levels fall below the threshold that will support the endometrium, the highly vascularized mucous membrane lining of the uterine cavity. The usual age of the physiological menopause is 46 to 52 years. An artificial menopause may occur prior to that time—*e.g.,* as a result of radiation therapy to the pelvic organs or surgical removal of the ovaries.

Estrogen and the menstrual cycle

Estrogen and progesterone are the dominant hormones of the ovary, but they are not produced in significant amounts until puberty. Then, under the influence of increasing amounts of follicle-stimulating hormone coming to the ovary from the pituitary gland, the amount of estrogen, principally in the form of estradiol, increases. Also produced are the weaker forms of naturally occurring estrogens, estrone and estriol.

Specific target organs containing cells with estrogen receptors are affected by this increased hormone production. The mammary ducts grow, resulting in enlargement of the breasts. The mucous membrane that lines the vagina thickens. The glandular surface tissue of the cervix begins to secrete larger amounts of clear mucus with a low viscosity, designed to facilitate the migration of sperm through the cervix. Estrogen is a powerful growth stimulus for the endometrium. With the gradual establishment of regular ovulatory function, a process that takes three to five years from the first menstrual period, progesterone is also produced by the ovary during the second half of the menstrual cycle. This hormone has a modifying effect on estrogenic stimulation, halting the growth of the endometrium and causing the cells to undergo secretory changes in preparation for the reception of a fertilized egg. Following ovulation and for about 12 days thereafter, both hormones, estrogen and progesterone, are secreted in gradually increasing amounts. In the absence of pregnancy, the production of these hormones by the ovary rapidly declines, and the endometrium is shed in the process of menstruation. During the menstrual years this process repeats itself about every 28 days.

Other effects of estrogen on the body

Estrogen influences the temperature-regulating center in the brain in such a way as to lower the basal body

467

temperature. Progesterone has the opposite effect. Thus, a daily recording of the basal temperature will show the approximate time of ovulation in any menstrual cycle. By some obscure means not yet fully understood, the vasomotor centers in the brain, which regulate the constriction and dilation of the blood vessels, are also affected. In addition, estrogen exerts a bone-building influence. It does this either by acting as an antagonist (*i.e.,* opposing force) to parathyroid hormone, which stimulates bone breakdown, or by enhancing the action of calcitonin, a potent inhibitor of bone resorption.

Estrogen production at puberty produces the wider pelvis and hips characteristic of the adult female body. It helps maintain not only the mucous membrane of the vagina but those of the vulva, bladder, and urethra as well. The levels of blood cholesterol and low-density lipoproteins, LDL, the fats most strongly implicated in the development of atherosclerosis, are lowered under the influence of estrogen, while high-density lipoproteins, or HDL, considered protective against atherosclerosis, are increased by the activity of estrogen. The male hormone testosterone, on the other hand, has the opposite effect; it increases the blood level of LDL and decreases the level of HDL. The influence of estrogen on LDL and HLD accounts in part for the relatively low incidence of coronary heart disease in premenopausal women. Following the menopause, however, the female incidence of heart disease approaches that of males. Estrogen also enhances the clotting ability of the blood.

The physical toll of menopause

The majority of women reaching menopausal age experience episodic hot flashes (or flushes) and night sweats. Probably the result of an instability in the heat-regulating center in the brain, these are true physiological disturbances. Hot flashes occurring frequently during the night may disturb sleep, and chronic sleep deprivation, in turn, can cause fatigue, anxiety, and loss of concentration and memory.

In the postmenopausal years the breasts become smaller and less firm. There may be thinning of scalp hair and an increase in facial hair because of the in-

The newest method of delivering estrogen is transdermally; i.e., via absorption through the skin from a hormone-impregnated skin patch about the size of a silver dollar.

AP/Wide World

fluence of androgenic (masculinizing) hormone, which has become relatively unopposed by estrogen. The skin becomes thinner, drier, and less elastic. Vulvar and vaginal mucous membranes became pale, thin, dry, and more prone to infection and inflammation. As a result of these changes, some women find that intercourse becomes painful.

In the majority of postmenopausal women there is a steady loss of calcium from the bones, resulting in an increased risk of vertebral, wrist, and hip fractures. Osteoporosis, loss of bone mass, is one of the most important health hazards facing the woman over 50 years of age. As the bones become more porous, the skeleton is no longer able to support the body weight. Caucasian women are at greater risk of osteoporosis than are women of other races. Weight is also a factor. The thin Caucasian woman is particularly at risk, especially if she has a history of cigarette smoking or alcohol abuse. The overweight woman, on the other hand, has internal sources of estrogen that are lacking in her thinner counterpart.

After the ovaries lose the ability to make estrogen, other sources of the hormone become critical. One such source is the adrenal gland, which produces the androgen known as androstenedione. Although levels of this hormone gradually fall with age, some is converted in the body fat cells to the form of estrogen called estrone. Furthermore, over time this conversion occurs with increasing efficiency. Overweight and markedly obese women are better equipped to perform this conversion than are women of normal weight. Moreover, there is also a positive correlation between obesity and serum estradiol levels; both forms of estrogen are more abundant in overweight postmenopausal women than in women of average weight. Although heavier women are at lower risk for severe estrogen deficiency and associated conditions, including osteoporosis, they are more likely than average-weight women of the same age to develop endometrial and breast cancer.

Natural and synthetic estrogens

Chemists experimenting with follicular fluid from the ovaries of rats first identified estrogen in the form of estrone in 1923. Subsequently, larger amounts of this substance were found in the urine of pregnant women. By 1929 a pure, crystalline form of estrone had been recovered. Within the following decade all three forms of human estrogen—estrone, estradiol, and estriol—had been identified.

Beginning in the 1930s these naturally occurring hormones—called steroidal hormones because they are derived from the natural fatty substance (chemically a steroidal alcohol) cholesterol—became the main source of estrogen for ERT. They were not widely used, however, because of the difficulty and expense of production and because they could be administered only by injection. It was not until a group of chemists in England discovered that certain nonsteroidal chemicals, stilbene and its derivatives, had a weakly estrogenic effect when injected into laboratory animals and subsequently succeeded in markedly enhancing this effect through chemical manipulation that ERT came into its own. The resultant product, diethylstilbestrol (DES), proved to be a very potent and cheap estrogen. Furthermore, it was effective when taken by mouth because, unlike naturally occurring steroidal hormones, this synthetic estrogen was not chemically altered— and thus rendered inactive—in the liver. The decade of the 1940s ushered in the widespread medical use of DES and other synthetic nonsteroidal estrogens.

It should be noted that DES was used extensively not only in postmenopausal women but in younger pregnant women as well, on the basis of a 1948 clinical study showing it to be effective in the prevention of spontaneous abortion. However, a controlled clinical investigation conducted several years later failed to demonstrate the efficacy of DES in preventing loss of pregnancy. By that time several million women had taken the drug to prevent miscarriage. Subsequently, in 1971 an epidemiological study demonstrated an association of DES with the development of an unusual type of vaginal cancer in the female offspring of woman who had taken the drug during pregnancy. Additional investigation also revealed maternal use of DES to be related to certain congenital abnormalities in the reproductive organs. Soon afterward the U.S. Food and Drug Administration (FDA) prohibited its use by pregnant women.

At the same time, advances in technology enabled the pharmaceutical industry to produce increasing quantities of the naturally occurring steroidal estrogens derived from the urine of horses. When conjugated (chemically combined) with sodium sulfate, these equine estrogens were not rendered inactive in the liver when taken orally.

As opposed to naturally occurring estrogens, synthetic estrogens may be either steroidal or nonsteroidal. Laboratory alterations of the estradiol molecule have increased its estrogenic potency and enhanced its oral activity. Most nonsteroidal preparations available today are related to diethylstilbestrol.

How estrogens are administered

A great variety of estrogens, steroidal and nonsteroidal, natural and synthetic, are available. They can be given by mouth, by injection, by vaginal application, or by absorption through the skin.

Natural and synthetic hormones are effective when they are given by injection, but the discomfort and the need to return to the physician's office or the clinic for continued therapy are disadvantages. These drawbacks can be partially offset by the use of preparations that are long acting, but it is impossible to withdraw the injected, circulating hormone from the body if it becomes necessary to stop the treatment. Because a number of orally effective preparations are now available, there is little need, except in patients who have intestinal absorption problems, to give estrogens by injection.

The effectiveness of naturally occurring estrogens given by mouth is low because they are carried by the intestinal blood circulation to the liver, where they are partially inactivated. Conjugation of natural hormones, combining them with other chemical compounds, is a method of enhancing oral activity. Conjugated estrogens are currently the most widely prescribed estrogen preparation in the U.S. Still another preparation, ethinyl estradiol, is a chemically modified natural hormone. All of the oral preparations, once absorbed into the bloodstream from the intestine, are carried directly to the liver, where they undergo some degree of breakdown before reaching the general circulation and the target organs. Therefore, relatively larger amounts must be used for a satisfactory effect.

Sublingual administration (absorption under the tongue) or transdermal (through the vaginal mucosa or skin) bypasses the liver. The sublingual method has not received much attention, but vaginal preparations in the form of creams and suppositories are available. They are not very popular because of inconvenience and messiness.

The newest product on the U.S. market, approved by the FDA in 1986, uses the transdermal route by means of an estradiol-containing skin patch changed twice weekly. The patch, which is about the size of a silver dollar, is affixed to the abdomen in much the same way as an adhesive bandage. Blood levels of estradiol delivered by this method are comparable to those achieved by oral administration, with about $1/20$ of the dose. Skin irritation at the site of application is the most frequent side effect, occurring in about one out of six patients. It is best managed by changing the location of the patch with each application. Approximately one patient in 50 must discontinue use of the patch because of skin problems.

Who needs estrogen replacement therapy?

Not every postmenopausal woman suffers from estrogen deficiency so severe that supplementation is warranted. The woman who can benefit most from ERT is the patient who is either naturally or artificially postmenopausal and who suffers from the hot flashes, sweating, and related symptoms of menopausal syndrome, shows physical manifestations of estrogen deficiency such as atrophic vaginitis, vulvitis, or cystitis (*i.e.*, thinning and drying of the mucous membranes), or is at high risk for the development of postmenopausal osteoporosis. Since the underlying cause of all of these conditions is estrogen deficiency, ERT is the logical treatment.

Side effects, risks, and contraindications

As with any potent medication, there are side effects and risks associated with ERT. These are related to the known physiological and possibly pathological effects of estrogen. A certain degree of fluid retention is not uncommon in women undergoing ERT. This may aggravate existing high blood pressure or cardiac failure. The increased coagulability of the blood calls for caution in the use of estrogens in patients with a history of blood clots. Breast tenderness experienced as a result of ERT is related to stimulation of the mammary ductal tissues, but there is no evidence that the incidence of breast cancer increases in postmenopausal women who are taking estrogens.

Nausea may be a side effect of oral administration of estrogens, but it does not occur as frequently with the low doses used in ERT as it does with contraceptive pill formulations. (The amount of estrogen administered in ERT is considerably less than that contained in the most commonly used oral contraceptives.)

At one time it was thought that estrogen administration increased a woman's risk of gallstone formation, but a closer look at the data revealed that obesity is a much more critical factor in this process. It is unlikely that ERT in a woman of normal weight increases this gallstone risk.

Vaginal bleeding may occur as a result of proliferation of the endometrium, or it may be due to malignant disease. Overstimulation, or unusual responsiveness, of the endometrium to estrogen may result in an abnormal buildup of tissue, a condition known as endometrial hyperplasia. In a small number of women, this condition may set the stage for the subsequent development of endometrial cancer. During the 1970s many studies demonstrated an increased risk of endometrial cancer in women who were undergoing ERT, prompting many physicians to stop prescribing estrogens. However, recent evidence shows that endometrial cancer may be prevented during ERT—and perhaps even reduced below the incidence in the general population—by combining the estrogen with a progestin, a synthetic form of progesterone. This lowered cancer rate was first demonstrated in a study of women who had taken oral contraceptives containing a combination of estrogen and progestin over a span of several years. Subsequently it was also found to be the case in postmenopausal women who were given a cyclical dosage of estrogen and progestin, stopping both agents for five to seven days at the end of each dosage cycle to allow any endometrial tissue that had built up in response to the hormones to be shed in a menstruation-like process. However, if a woman on ERT experiences any "out-of-phase" or unexpected bleeding, an endometrial biopsy to check for possible malignancy is indicated. In most instances this procedure can be performed in the physician's office.

The absolute contraindications to ERT are primarily the estrogen-dependent endometrial and breast cancers (*i.e.,* those in which tumor tissue is known to contain receptors for estrogen or those in which receptor status is in doubt). Even these, at times, however, must be considered relative risks. The quality of life without ERT must be weighed against the risk of stimulating a possible residual malignancy. By the same token, there are benign but potentially dangerous conditions that may be aggravated by estrogen administration—fibroid tumors of the uterus, severe diabetes with marked arteriosclerosis, essential hypertension, cardiac failure, deep venous thrombosis, severe liver disease, and sickle-cell anemia. Depending upon the response, estrogen administration may have to be markedly curtailed or even discontinued in women with these conditions.

A fringe benefit of ERT for postmenopausal women lies in its protective effect against cardiovascular disease. In six studies during the past decade, all but one demonstrated that women receiving estrogen replacement, when compared with matched controls, have a reduced risk of developing or dying of coronary heart disease. This protection probably stems from the demonstrated ability of estrogens to alter favorably the blood lipid levels and lipoprotein constituents. However, it is not yet known whether this benefit will hold up when ERT is combined with progestin therapy. Synthetic progestins lower the HDL level and elevate the level of LDL, just the opposite of the effect observed with estrogen administration. There is some promise in a new preparation of micronized natural progesterone, which has been reported as showing no tendency to decrease HDL. Careful epidemiological studies are needed for the question to be answered, but these will not be forthcoming for a number of years. In the meantime, some authorities recommend that progestins not be added to ERT in women who have undergone hysterectomy.

Weighing risks and benefits

Estrogen replacement therapy is highly effective in relieving the symptoms and signs of the menopausal syndrome and has recently been shown to prevent or reverse the steady loss of bone that ultimately affects the majority of women. There are risks involved, but these can be minimized.

In general, the benefits of ERT far outweigh the risks. The enlightened physician has the knowledge to balance the benefits against the risks in specific medical circumstances and owes it to the patient to engage in a full and frank discussion of these. Together they can make an informed decision on whether estrogen replacement therapy should be initiated and, if so, what form it should take. Once begun, unless there are contraindicating circumstances, estrogen therapy should be continued indefinitely.

Littlest Swimmers

by Marcia J. Opp

Before they can walk or talk, many babies and toddlers start taking swimming lessons at their neighborhood pools. In the last ten years, organized swimming programs for preschoolers have become so popular that hundreds of thousands of young children and their parents now are participating in them. Parents and swim instructors believe that the lessons provide a fun and meaningful parent-child activity, familiarize the little ones with water so they do not grow up afraid of swimming, and serve as a safeguard against water accidents.

However, many physicians warn that swimming lessons produce more risks than benefits for children under the age of three, especially if the classes force children to go underwater. Medical authorities contend that the child's health, even life, is at risk because of the increased susceptibility to eye, ear, bacterial, and respiratory infections and water intoxication if the child swallows too much water when submerged.

Forced infant and toddler submersion has drawn the strong disapproval of the American Academy of Pediatrics, the largest organization of physicians who treat children, and of the Young Men's Christian Association (YMCA), the largest owner and operator of pools in the world. In the United States the Council for National Cooperation in Aquatics (CNCA), an educational organization composed of 37 national organizations, including the Young Women's Christian Association (YWCA) of the USA, the Red Cross, and the Boy Scouts and Girl Scouts of America, had objected to the submersion of infants but recently has revised its stand to some extent.

Many swim instructors promote submersion as part of their programs, citing parental pressure in favor of it and claiming that physicians' warnings of health risks are overblown. Even though debate continues on mandatory submersion, there is near universal agreement that classes should not make claims that they are "drownproofing" children or helping them become "water safe." These terms, popular in the past, have virtually been abandoned by all programs because of the recognition that no toddler can be considered water safe or drownproofed. For one thing, according to water safety authorities, children this age are not able to remember water safety rules and apply them in an emergency. Moreover, the CNCA's guidelines for children under the age of three explain that children have not developed adequate physical skills for being around the water—a beach, a pool, or a lake—without supervision by an adult.

Nevertheless, because parents see their wee ones "swim" or paddle a few strokes, they easily can develop a false sense of security that the children can handle themselves in an emergency. This misplaced confidence can mean that they do not watch their children as carefully as they ought to when they are near the water. Medical and aquatics policymakers, therefore, agree that any water program that makes parents confident of their children's "swim" skills at this age does a real disservice. Programs, instead, should promise self-confidence, water adjustment, and better communications skills.

Submersion

The YMCA's "safest and latest methods of aquatics instruction and water safety for young children and their parents" do not include forced submersion, although instructors at some local Y's may teach it. Instructors who favor submersion typically tell the accompanying adults to face their children as they hold them in the water. On the count of three, the adults blow into the children's faces. The puff of air is supposed to trigger a submersion reflex that stimulates the babies or toddlers to close their eyes, take a breath, and hold it during the few seconds they are underwater. The teacher may also tell the adults to blow into the children's faces to "ready" them before they jump or are whisked into the pool and then underwater.

The "breath-holding" reflex does not guarantee that youngsters will not swallow large amounts of water. It is even possible for a tiny child to swallow up to half a liter (a pint) of water. Therefore, many persons involved in swim programs recommend delaying submersion until children can understand and control their breathing and swallowing when they are underwater. In most programs that promote submersion, children go underwater only a few times (fewer than six sub-

Swimming classes for infants that include forced submersion are popular among many parents who desire to give their babies a head start in the water, but the practice is controversial and may pose serious health hazards.

mersions per lesson) for only one to five seconds each time.

When young children are dropped from a height into the water, they can suffer adverse physical and psychological effects. Water can be forced into their noses, ears, and sinuses, and obviously it can scare them. Any kind of force, compulsion, punishment, or threat can be traumatizing. The notion that submerging children repeatedly will teach them to hold their breath in self-defense is both irresponsible and dangerous. Moreover, authorities warn that psychological trauma can have long-term ramifications, which are ignored by proponents of this technique.

The most extreme result of swallowing too much water is that it can result in hyponatremia, or water intoxication, especially in infants under a year old. This potentially dangerous condition causes an alteration of the essential balance of body chemicals, resulting in diluted body sodium, which can lead to swelling of the brain with seizures and other severe effects. Physicians have reported the following less serious symptoms—lethargy, vomiting, crying, and weakness. An extreme case can cause death.

Factors that can contribute to the severity of water intoxication are the child's age and size, the amount of water swallowed, the number of submersions, the length of time in the water, and the child's degree of fatigue. Symptoms may occur within minutes after the pool activity or develop slowly over several hours. While severe hyponatremia incidents are rare, several have been reported in medical journals and newspapers in the last few years. The incidence of milder cases involving irritability or lethargy is much higher. Frequently, parents will not make the association of these milder symptoms with the child's underwater activity.

Infections

The medical profession recently has become concerned about transmission in swimming pools of giardiasis, an intestinal parasitic infection that can cause severe diarrhea. This parasite can pose a serious health hazard because it is not effectively eradicated by chlorine in the pool, and there is no simple test for detecting its presence in a pool. The *Giardia lamblia* parasite develops in the intestinal tract. If an infected child's stool is released into the pool, the infection can be spread when another child swallows bits of the fecal material along with pool water.

The infection has been identified in pools used by many children who are not toilet trained. To prevent the potential spread of the *Giardia* parasite, some pool-maintenance experts recommend frequent emptying of any pools that are used regularly by large numbers of non-toilet-trained children. Requiring children to wear plastic pants with tight-fitting legs over their diapers and prohibiting their participation in classes if they have any signs of diarrhea are more practical methods of prevention.

Youngsters are more likely to contract other infections—bacterial, parasitic, or viral—from the air or from contact with infected individuals than directly from chlorine-treated pool water. Even so, most pool rules stipulate that children (and adults) must stay away from pools if they have colds, rashes, fevers, or other communicable diseases.

Another problem is that many children who go underwater experience excessive ear infections because their eustachian tubes are underdeveloped. Also, skin rashes and red, sore eyes can occur in children who are sensitive to chlorine.

Children under the age of three are the most vulnerable to all of the problems described above. Many of these ill-health effects can be avoided if children do not go underwater until they are older; at three years or older, their immune systems have become more mature and their bodies are more developed. The YMCA guidelines advise that to minimize the infection risk, children wait until they are three or older to begin a swimming program.

Drowning

Drowning is perhaps the most common danger of early toddler water training. This is especially true in

Many parents enroll in water-enrichment classes with their infants and toddlers at local Y's and other neighborhood pools in order to share an enjoyable and meaningful activity. In the pool it is important for the adults to convey assurance and a happy attitude to their little ones.

programs that require or encourage submersion of the toddler's head below the water. In a recent study on water safety issues by Stephen Langendorfer (of the Kent [Ohio] State University Motor Development Center) and Diane Hicks-Hughes (of the State University of New York at Cortland), some 63 of 134 swim program operators reported that a child in their programs had experienced a "water emergency." Some 65% of the "water emergencies" involved "sudden, unexpected immersion" of infant students; 17%, "near drowning"; and 5% (four actual cases), "drowning deaths." Those who conducted the study believe that "even a single drowning death is tragic and one too many for programs which claim to improve water safety in young children." While the survey indicated that 69% of the emergencies occurred outside the actual instruction period, some 25% of the emergencies did occur during infant swim classes.

Many program directors assert that submerging young children and making them comfortable around the water will reduce their risks of drowning. However, their claim cannot be verified; there are no well-documented studies supporting the theory that swim programs reduce the incidence of drowning. Safety experts advise that a reduction in drownings is more likely to occur if parents or responsible caretakers watch the children at all times, put life jackets on the children if they are on a boat, and install fencing around home pools.

In the U.S. an estimated 600 children up to the age of four drowned in accidents in 1985, according to the latest statistics from the National Safety Council. While some drowned in lakes, rivers, and pools, many drowned in or around their homes—and in some unexpected ways. For instance, children have drowned in water in toilets, bathtubs, diaper pails, small wading pools, and sinks.

The right time to begin

The debate concerning when and how swimming experiences for youngsters should begin has been widely waged in the media and by various medical and swimming professionals—all of whom relate their individual experiences and opinions. Well-designed research studies with statistics would assist parents and physicians in determining whether children were ready for classes and whether a particular program's teaching methods were sound. But these are unfortunately lacking.

Two barometers currently used to assess a child's readiness for water programs are age and motor development. Some child development specialists recommend 12 to 18 months, or when a child begins to walk, as a good age for beginning some type of program. Most pediatricians caution that infants who are not holding up their heads are too young because they face a higher risk of accidental submersion.

Some swim instructors have asserted that there are one-year-olds who may be able to benefit from a pool experience. At that age many can mimic a dog paddle and do a "backstroke" and float if they have had sufficient water experience. By age three children who have been in a pool regularly usually can move around on their own in the water.

Current motor development research suggests that motor skills (including swimming) are acquired in gradual, developmentally ordered sequences. While no known teaching or behavioral techniques can override the stages, some well-founded techniques can accelerate the rate of acquisition of the sequence levels.

Starting children at very young ages does not necessarily mean that they will swim early and continue an accelerated pace of swimming achievement. Learning how to swim depends on physical maturity as well as the ability to think. Children must be able to want to propel themselves in the water and then have the physical strength to do it.

Instructors have found that children who start lessons at the age of five may "catch up" and even surpass youngsters who started at age two or three. On the other hand, children who start a program early and enjoy the experience with their parents often have more self-confidence in the water and more desire to engage in water activities as they grow older.

Some water experience programs, especially ones promoting submersion, require that parents obtain the written consent of their child's physician before beginning. The best programs inform parents in advance of health problems their child might encounter.

Recommendations and guidelines

Before enrolling a child in a water enrichment or swim instruction program, concerned parents may want to find out whether their chosen program follows these general (and condensed) guidelines developed by the YMCA. Not all local Y branches adhere to the guidelines.

1. Any water experience/orientation program requires the in-water participation of a parent, guardian, or other adult.
2. The participating parent or adult assumes responsibility for monitoring the child's health before, during, and after participation in such a program.
3. All state and local government laws and regulations applicable to the program setting, including those pertaining to water purity and sanitation, must be followed carefully.
4. In order to ensure a minimum or no loss of body wastes, the appropriate clothing must be worn. (Among the recommendations are tight-fitting plastic pants.)
5. For indoor pools, the recommended water temperature is 29.4° C (85° F), with the air temperature higher than the water temperature.
6. Forced submersion or dropping of the child from a height is strictly prohibited.
7. No young children, particularly those who are preschool aged, can ever be considered "water safe."
8. For participation in the program, the infant must have achieved head control.
9. The maximum time for water classes is 30 minutes per session.

10. Programs for children under the age of three should be conducted only by certified aquatic personnel with training in child development.

The American Academy of Pediatrics has also issued a policy statement, the major points of which are as follows:

1. A parent who enrolls an infant in a water adjustment program should understand and accept the risks.
2. To reduce these risks, the program should follow the national YMCA guidelines, which include: prohibiting total submersion, maintaining an appropriate water temperature, and providing measures to control fecal contamination.
3. The swimming experience of each infant should be on a one-to-one basis with a parent or responsible adult. Organized group swimming instruction should be reserved for children more than three years of age.
4. Instruction should take place in properly maintained pools by qualified instructors familiar with infant cardiopulmonary resuscitation techniques.
5. Infants with known medical problems should receive their physicians' approval before participation.

A typical session

Water enrichment classes for children as young as three months range in size from private, one-on-one lessons with an instructor to groups of ten children with their parents or other responsible adults. The accompanying adult does not need to be a good swimmer to hold the child, walk around in the water, and carry out the instructor's suggestions. But the adult does need to convey assurance in the water and a happy attitude.

The first few sessions of an enrichment program typically are devoted to making the children feel comfortable in the water. Games and toys play a big role. To entice reluctant youngsters into the water, instructors may give them toys to throw into the water from the side. Then the children and their trusted adult companions slip into the water to retrieve them. When children are exposed to the water at a young age, they tend to adapt quickly and happily. Any crying or whining usually is due to the water's being too cold or to submersion. By the age of two, many children who have been in a pool regularly will cry when they are taken *out* because they are having such a good time that they do not want to stop.

Plastic Surgery of the Breast
by Robert M. Goldwyn, M.D.

In recent years a variety of factors have been responsible for the increasing demand for plastic surgery of the breast. Among them are new, improved, and safer techniques; greater respect for the psychological needs of the individual; women's increasing willingness to articulate their feelings about their bodies and to acknowledge their dissatisfactions and remedy them; wider acceptance by the public of procedures that aim to improve the quality of life and not just its length; more exposure of the body because of current clothing styles and sexual mores; technical progress that has produced relatively inert materials, such as silicone, for implantation into the body; and greater recognition by the medical profession of the benefits of immediate reconstruction following mastectomy.

Plastic surgery of the breast falls into five general categories: (1) operations for breasts that are too large (mammary hypertrophy); (2) operations for breasts that are too small (mammary hypoplasia); (3) operations for breasts that are asymmetrical; (4) operations for breasts that are not in the desired position (mammary ptosis); and (5) operations for breasts that have been removed or deformed from trauma (burns) or surgery (mastectomy).

All these conditions and their associated procedures require a thoughtful consultation with a plastic surgeon before reconstructive surgery is undertaken. The physician will want to know not only the patient's problem but also her motivations and expectations. Is the patient realistic in what she anticipates the operation will produce in terms of an anatomic outcome or a social change? If not, that individual is a poor candidate for the operation. The plastic surgeon must take a thorough history with emphasis on past medical health, possibly including other operations and family history, with attention to breast cancer.

The patient must determine whether she likes and trusts the surgeon. Since most plastic and reconstructive surgery of the breast is elective, she has time to get other opinions if she so desires.

Some plastic surgeons show photographs and even videotapes of other patients to convey information regarding the nature of the procedure and its likely result. Other plastic surgeons do not attempt to represent outcome with pictures because they believe that it may be putting themselves at risk legally if the patient alleges that she was promised explicitly or implicitly the same result as that depicted.

Reduction mammoplasty
Patients with excessively large breasts can be any age, but most typically the patient is an adolescent or a young woman whose weighty, pendulous breasts cause embarrassment along with pain in the shoulders, the neck, and the back; a rash under the breasts; and difficulty in buying clothes and relating comfortably to the opposite sex. A woman who is encumbered with very large breasts may resent being looked upon as a "sexual object." Some women try to hide their large breasts by walking with their shoulders slumped, wearing voluminous clothes, buying very expensive and tight bras, avoiding athletics, not going to the beach, not dating, or terminating relationships because of fear of exposing their breasts. Some patients gain considerable weight not only because they are depressed by their appearance but also as a means of making their body larger so that their breasts will not look so huge by comparison.

The plastic surgeon may want the prospective patient who is 35 or older to have mammograms preoperatively in order to rule out the presence of a suspicious lesion that might be difficult to detect clinically within such a large breast. If such a lesion is found, a biopsy procedure before reduction surgery is wise.

Possible complications. The patient contemplating reduction mammoplasty must understand that complications are possible. The worst complication for any patient is death, but for a healthy individual such an outcome is extremely rare; it would most likely occur as a result of an unusual event during anesthesia or, postoperatively, from a pulmonary embolus. Another

Breast reduction

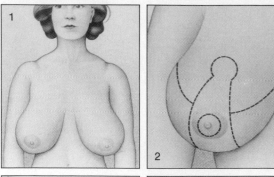

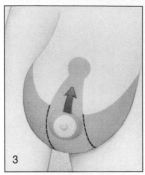

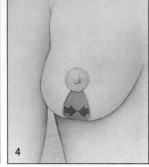

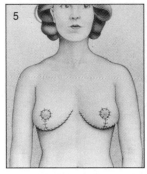

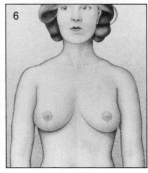

*(1) Oversized heavy breasts are pictured before surgery;
(2) incisions are made to define the area of excision
and the new location for the nipple; (3) tissue, fat, and
skin in the shaded area are removed, and the nipple is
raised; (4) skin that was formerly above the nipple is lowered
and brought together to reshape the breast; (5) sutures
close the incisions, leaving some inevitable permanent
scarring; (6) well-contoured breasts are pictured after
reduction mammoplasty.*

possible complication of reduction mammoplasty is
wound infection; the incidence of wound infection is
about 5%. Excessive bleeding immediately after an
operation is more unusual, so the patient is usually
asked not to take any aspirin or aspirin-containing
medicine for at least ten days prior to the procedure
because aspirin can interfere with blood clotting.

The most common undesirable sequela—but one
that is unavoidable—is scarring. Scars are usually
around the areola—the pigmented ring around the

nipple—radially from a six o'clock position on the areola to the fold under the breast and along that fold.
Although scars become less noticeable with time, they
never disappear. Unsightly scarring, however, is not
common and is usually the result of the particular
way the individual patient heals or the outcome of an
infection of or separation of the wound that can result
from too tight a closure. No surgeon can guarantee
to any patient the final result of wound healing; many
factors are beyond human control.

The ability of the patient to nurse a baby after
reduction mammoplasty is decreased. However, the
majority can do so if the underlying tissue of the nipple
and areola have been left intact.

Reduction mammoplasty does not cause cancer,
but the scarring produced by the procedure may make
subsequent clinical and radiological examination more
difficult. Self-examination is also harder since the patient may confuse a scar with a potentially cancerous
mass. It is imperative therefore that every patient who
has mammoplasty be followed closely by her regular
physician, who would be more likely to note a significant change. Any persistent lump must be biopsied to
rule out cancer.

Reduction mammoplasty alters sensation to the nipple and areola, usually only temporarily but occasionally permanently. Even among those with permanent
loss of sensation, satisfaction with the procedure remains high. These women state that during physical
intimacy their loss of sensation is compensated for by
their improved self-image, which allows them to feel
more relaxed.

The most serious technical mishap is the inadvertent
interruption of blood supply to the nipple and areola
resulting in loss of viability and subsequent slough
(tissue death), partial or total, of the nipple-areola complex. This complication is most likely to occur in older
patients with extremely large breasts. The overall incidence of nipple-areola necrosis is 4%. Procedures are
available, however, for reconstruction of the nipple-
areola, as is commonly done following reconstruction
of the breast after mastectomy.

The operation and outcome. In the past, reduction
mammoplasty was usually performed by cutting away
excess skin and breast and grafting the nipple and areola to a new location that was higher and aesthetically
more pleasing. Reduction mammoplasty today is generally done by leaving the nipple and areola attached
to underlying tissue. Through incisions, which usually
do not show when a brassiere is worn, excess skin,
fat, and breast are removed, an overly large areola
can be decreased in proportion, and the entire nipple-
areola is moved upward.

The operation is almost always done under general
anesthesia during hospitalization lasting two or three
days. The patient goes home with dressings, which
she changes daily for the next two weeks. Sutures

Illustrations by William Graham for the American Society of Plastic and Reconstructive Surgeons

Breast augmentation

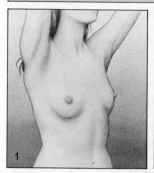

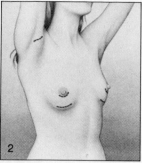

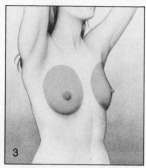

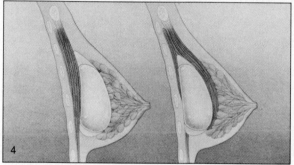

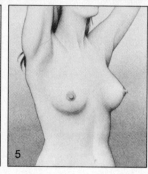

(1) Underdeveloped breasts are pictured before augmentation surgery; (2) incisions are made where the breast meets the chest and under the areola or in the armpit; (3) a retractor is used in the shaded areas to form a pocket for an implant; (4) cross sections of the breast show the location of the implant either in a pocket under the breast tissue (left) or under the chest muscle (right); (5) after surgery, the fuller breasts are natural in tone and contour.

will have been removed by the 14th day. The patient must avoid heavy lifting and stretching for three or four weeks, but she may return to work in two weeks. Pain after the first 36 hours is well tolerated and easily managed by minimal medication.

Most patients who have had a reduction mammoplasty are extremely happy with their results. Secondary procedures to improve the outcome are usually unnecessary. Occasionally minor asymmetry may need a correction by the removal of additional tissue—a procedure that can be done easily under local anesthesia on an outpatient basis.

Most insurance policies cover hospitalization and part or all of the surgeon's fee if the operation has been undertaken for breasts that are large. Some policies stipulate the number of grams that must be removed from each breast to merit coverage. In the United States surgical fees generally vary from $3,000 to $8,000, depending upon the specific nature of the patient's problem.

Augmentation mammoplasty

Many women are extremely self-conscious and embarrassed by the small size of their breasts, which is usually either the result of insufficient pubertal development or due to changes after pregnancy and nursing. Feelings of inadequacy because of small breasts can persist despite high personal, intellectual, and professional achievement and even with loving, supportive family and friends. Many husbands, in fact, say that they are not as concerned about their wives' breast

size; they love their spouses just the way they are.

Occasionally a patient may seek augmentation mammoplasty less for herself than to please somebody else, possibly as a means of keeping a marriage together. She might think that having larger breasts will make her more attractive to an uninterested and perhaps unfaithful husband. In such an instance the patient is not a good candidate for the operation. Rather, she and her husband should seek family counseling.

Before augmentation surgery the doctor will likely inquire whether the patient has a family history of breast cancer or whether she has ever had a breast biopsy. A woman over the age of 34 should have a mammogram before the operation.

The correction of mammary hypoplasia is by the insertion of an implant. The surgeon may show the patient the actual implant and then explain that there are various incisions that can be used for inserting it: through the armpit, through the fold under the breast, or through the areola—the last two being the most common. Preferences differ among surgeons and patients.

Possible complications. Scarring after augmentation mammoplasty is generally minimal, no matter what incision is used. Unexpected bleeding within 24 hours after the operation occurs in 5% of patients. The incidence of infection is less than 2%. Decreased or altered sensation of the nipple and areola is also possible, but permanent numbness is infrequent. The most common unwanted result of augmentation mammoplasty is abnormal firmness characterized by excessive

477

scar formation around the implant, which is, of course, a foreign body. Such firmness, the cause of which is unknown, occurs in approximately 30% of patients and is unpredictable; it may happen unilaterally or bilaterally and is not related to how the patient scars in other areas of her body. If the firmness is severe, another operation with division of the constricting scar may be helpful, but in some patients scarring may recur. Occasionally the surgeon may be successful in manually compressing an excessively firm breast in his office, alleviating the need for another operation. Too often, however, firmness returns after compression.

The operation and outcome. The operation is usually done on an outpatient basis under local anesthesia with intravenous sedation. The implant, which is silicone gel or saline or a combination of both, is placed under the breast tissue itself or under the muscle (pectoral)—the latter, a location chosen to decrease the possibility of firmness. (Silicone injections should never be used in the breast. They are always hazardous and, in many U.S. states, illegal.)

The patient will have some pain during the first 18 hours after the procedure—enough to require oral medication. In an attempt to reduce scar formation and resultant firmness, many surgeons ask the patient to discard her bulky dressings after 48 hours and to begin massaging her breasts. Oral vitamin E has also been used to decrease scarring, but its efficacy has not been proved. By four weeks after an operation, most patients have recovered sufficiently to engage in vigorous athletics.

Subsequent examination of the breast for lesions or other abnormalities in most cases is not difficult, particularly if the patient's family doctor, internist, or gynecologist has had previous patients who have undergone this procedure. Mammograms may be hard to read, however, because of the presence of the implant.

Patient satisfaction following this operation is extremely high, even among patients who have abnormal firmness. The operation satisfies their principal desire for larger breasts. They feel more freedom in their daily lives; no longer must they wear padded bras or experience anxiety about physical intimacy.

The costs for augmentation mammoplasty have to be borne by the patient. Surgical fees range from $2,000 to $4,000.

Operations to correct breast asymmetry

Some women have asymmetrical breast development. Typically, one breast is small or absent and the other is normal or abnormally large. Patients are usually seen in their adolescence, but some seek surgical correction for the first time after many years of marriage. In general, the treatment of breast asymmetry involves an augmentation mammoplasty on one side or a reduction mammoplasty or correction of ptosis (sagging)

on the other. The patient usually knows whether she wants an overly large breast reduced to match a relatively normal breast or the smaller breast enlarged to resemble the opposite breast. Many patients give a history of not telling even their mothers about their problem because they are ashamed of what they consider their deformity.

Even the most careful surgery rarely achieves precise matching of the breasts. Nevertheless, almost all patients will immediately feel normal because they are rid of what in their minds was a grotesque feature. Insurance coverage and surgical costs vary widely, depending on patients' individual conditions and on the extent of surgery needed.

Operations to correct sagging breasts

Sagging, or ptosis, of the breasts may be familial. Some women develop this condition early in life; others later, after marriage, childbirth, and nursing. Almost all dislike seeing themselves as looking elderly. The surgeon must assess whether the patient's problem is due only to the downward displacement of the breast or, in addition, to a lack of tissue. In the latter situation the patient will need an augmentation as well as a correction of ptosis.

For breast ptosis alone the surgical procedure involves resecting excess skin. The patient will have scars; they are permanent although not usually conspicuous. Many patients have the misconception that surgery for ptosis is scarless. Another mistaken idea is that the surgical correction of ptosis will be permanent. Unfortunately, time and gravity cause recurrence to some degree.

Most operations for ptosis are done on an outpatient basis, under local anesthesia with intravenous medication. Most commonly an incision is made around the areola, vertical to the fold under the breast, and along the fold. Redundant skin is discarded as the nipple and areola are raised to a higher location.

The patient usually has little pain afterward. Sutures are removed in 10 to 14 days. The patient returns to work in a week or sooner but is told to refrain from athletics for at least three weeks. Most surgeons advise women who have undergone this procedure to wear brassieres most of the day in order to lessen the effect of gravity. Since this operation is considered purely cosmetic, there is no insurance coverage. Surgical fees vary from $2,000 to $5,000, depending upon the problem. If an augmentation is also done, the surgical fee is correspondingly greater and the recovery longer.

Reconstruction after mastectomy

Rebuilding the breast after mastectomy is more accepted today than it was five years ago. It has been estimated that of the approximately 90,000 women yearly in the United States who have mastectomies, about 10,000 will have breast reconstruction. The trend now is to reconstruct the breast at the same time as mastectomy—so-called immediate reconstruction. The decision about the advisability and timing of reconstruction must be made not just by the plastic surgeon but by an informed patient in consultation with all her doctors: the surgeon who removes the breast, the oncologist, and possibly the radiotherapist.

Another consideration in reconstructing one breast is the opposite breast. If the opposite breast is very large, reduction may be necessary for symmetry to be achieved. Occasionally the general surgeon who performs the mastectomy may have advised the patient to have the opposite removed as prophylaxis against future cancer if it shows evidence of worrisome precancerous changes. Reconstruction of both breasts then may be necessary.

The two principal types of reconstruction are by means of an implant (prosthesis) or by the addition of tissue (a flap) of skin and muscle, of skin alone, or of a combination of both. The crucial determinant in choosing the appropriate method is whether the patient has enough tissue to accommodate an implant (silicone gel or saline or both) or whether she needs more tissue, which a flap provides. In the latter case either the implant will not be necessary or, if needed, it will be adequately covered without being too tight.

Each of the procedures for postmastectomy reconstruction has its own proponents. The choice of procedure depends upon the patient's needs and preferences and the surgeon's judgment.

Implant method. Recently, as a means of obtaining a more natural, looser breast with an implant, the use of an expander as a first step has become more frequent. An expander is a flat silicone device that is placed beneath the chest muscle and is gradually filled with saline over a period of two weeks, then left for one to two months in this overly expanded state, finally to be replaced with a permanent implant of silicone alone or silicone-saline. The stretched skin thereby allows a larger implant with less likelihood of abnormal firmness. An advantage of an implant (with or without an expander) is the avoidance of the additional scars that are associated with using a flap. The disadvantages are that the patient who has an expander must make repeated visits to the surgeon for the expansion process, and during this time she must accommodate an oversized breast until the expander has been replaced with a permanent prosthesis; thus, she undergoes still another operation. Finally, even though an expander has been used, the reconstructed breast with the implant may still not be soft.

If an infection occurs and an implant has been used to rebuild the breast, the implant will likely have to be removed. If it remains and the infection can be successfully treated with antibiotics, excessive firmness is almost a certainty.

Illustrations by William Graham for the
American Society of Plastic and Reconstructive Surgeons

Breast reconstruction

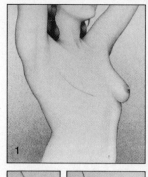
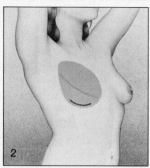

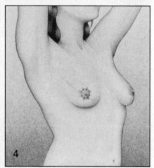

(1) Before reconstruction surgery a patient is shown with postmastectomy scar; (2) skin and muscle in the shoulder area are lifted to form a pocket for the insertion of an implant; (3) cross sections show the location of the implant under the chest muscle; (4) the reconstructed breast is shown with resultant scar. When breast skin is thin, a supporting flap of skin and muscle may be taken from the back area or from the lower abdomen.

The flap method. The alternative to an implant, which involves reconstruction of the breast by means of a flap of skin and muscle, entails a longer procedure, hospitalization, and recovery. The procedure utilizes skin taken from either the back (latissimus dorsi), the abdomen (rectus abdominis), or, less commonly, a distal location such as the buttocks. In general, the rectus abdominis flap gives enough tissue, obviating the need for an implant. For smaller breasts, the latissimus dorsi serves very well without an implant. With either the latissimus dorsi or the rectus abdominis flap, an implant can be used to make the breast larger if necessary. Transplanting a large amount of tissue from the buttocks to make a breast requires microsurgery, is a long procedure and the most difficult technically, and has a failure rate of 5%.

Using a latissimus dorsi flap produces tightness in the back, which usually relents after several months. Permanent, significant disability of the shoulder or back is rare. Since the rectus abdominis flap utilizes part of the abdominal musculature, some abdominal weakness may result—particularly noticeable during such exercises as sit-ups. However, function for most daily activities is usually unimpaired. If the flap has been taken from a location low in the abdomen and it was not possible to close the underlying tissues tightly, an abdominal bulge and a hernia may result.

Because the flap method requires that skin be taken from another part of the body, additional scarring is involved. Some patients favor a scar on the back to one on the abdomen. Other patients prefer to have tissue removed from the abdomen and thereby obtain the added benefit of flattening the abdomen. However, occasionally the abdominal flap method is not possible because previous abdominal or gynecologic surgery has interrupted the blood supply that nourishes the rectus abdominis flap.

The chief advantage of either the rectus abdominis flap or latissimus dorsi flap without an implant is that the breast will always be soft. Furthermore, the patient's own tissue is used to rebuild her breast. Should an infection occur, the flap-reconstructed breast will survive.

The patient must understand that with any flap there is a possibility for necrosis (death) of the flap tissue because of insufficient blood supply. The latter, however, occurs less than 5% of the time.

The nipple and areola. Making a new nipple and areola is usually done two or three months after reconstructing the breast. This interval allows the breast to assume its permanent position, thereby facilitating proper location of the nipple and areola. Many techniques exist for reconstructing these parts of the breast. The most common today is using the tissue in the flap or, in the absence of a flap, the tissue above the implant for the nipple. The areola is well simulated by a skin graft from the area of the thigh near the groin. Some surgeons achieve the appearance of a nipple and areola by tattoo, but this method fails to give projection to the nipple.

Nipple and areola reconstruction can be done under general or local anesthesia with intravenous medication, either on an outpatient basis or with overnight hospitalization. The patient must not go back to work for about ten days, however, so that the nipple and graft can heal properly, and she must be careful to avoid friction that could dislodge the graft.

Most insurance policies cover the hospital costs of nipple and areola reconstruction as well as part or all of the surgeon's overall reconstruction fee, which may range from $1,500 to $3,000.

Surgical correction of male breasts

The condition of enlarged breasts in males, generally in adolescents or postadolescents, is called gynecomastia. These patients complain of extreme embarrassment because their breasts look like a woman's. Commonly, they avoid going to beaches and going shirtless. Their families as well as their doctors may tell them that with time and exercise their problem will disappear. Indeed, it may, but it does not in all cases. The cause of gynecomastia in most patients is not known; one infrequent cause is an endocrine disorder. Another possible cause is the taking of certain medications, such as cimetidine for duodenal ulcer, diazepam (Valium) for anxiety, tricyclic derivatives for depression, amiodarone for cardiac conditions, and reserpine for hypertension. There is also evidence that in some cases marijuana also can produce gynecomastia, though the mechanism is still unknown. In these latter situations surgery is not necessary if the medication or drug is discontinued. In older men hormonal changes that occur with aging may produce breast enlargement; so may enlargement occur with estrogen administration for prostatic carcinoma.

For most males the surgical result is excellent and complications unlikely. The most common complication of the correction of gynecomastia is excessive bleeding. If this occurs, the patient may have to undergo another immediate operation to stop the bleeding. Rarely, however, is a transfusion necessary. Sensation in the nipple and areola is commonly reduced after an operation to correct gynecomastia. The patient should be informed of this possibility prior to the procedure. If too much tissue is removed, a displeasing concavity may result. Unfortunately, such a postoperative deformity is hard to revise.

Correction of gynecomastia is usually done under general anesthesia either on an outpatient basis or during hospitalization of two days. Incisions are made just inside the areola, from the three o'clock to the nine o'clock position, so that the eventual scar will be almost imperceptible. Through this incision breast tissue and fat can be removed either by surgical scissors alone or with suction.

Pain is minimal after operation, and the patient returns to work after ten days or sooner. In the case of gynecomastia, most insurance policies do not defray the cost of either the hospitalization or the surgeon's fee, which varies from $1,500 to $5,000.

Finding a plastic surgeon

The successful outcome of plastic surgery of the breast depends to a large measure on the competence of the surgeon as well as the cooperation of the patient. Considerable training is required for becoming a board-certified or board-eligible plastic surgeon. Any patient seeking a consultation with a plastic surgeon should obtain the proper advice and direction from a physician or surgeon who is well acquainted with that plastic surgeon's work. In the United States the American Society of Plastic and Reconstructive Surgeons provides a referral service. Prospective patients may obtain a listing of plastic surgeons in their area by calling a toll-free exchange. (Check with the operator for the number.)

Contributors to the World of Medicine

Edward L. Applebaum, M.D.
Ear, Nose, and Throat Disorders
Francis L. Lederer Professor and Head, Department of Otolaryngology–Head and Neck Surgery, University of Illinois College of Medicine, Chicago

Felicity Barringer
Special Report *Chernobyl Aftermath: Soviet Life in the Wake of Disaster*
Correspondent, Moscow Bureau, the *New York Times*

Arthur E. Baue, M.D.
Surgery
Vice-President for the Medical Center and Professor of Surgery, St. Louis University, St. Louis, Mo.

Douglas C. Benson
Sports Medicine
Managing Editor, *The Physician and Sportsmedicine,* Minneapolis, Minn.

Joyce Bermel
Medical Ethics
Free-lance writer, New Rochelle, N.Y.; former Managing Editor, *Hastings Center Report,* the Hastings Center, Hastings-on-Hudson, N.Y.

Elizabeth B. Connell, M.D.
Sexual and Reproductive Health and **Special Report** *Foreboding Trends in Health Care*
Professor, Gynecology and Obstetrics, Emory University School of Medicine, Atlanta, Ga.

William J. Cromie
Cancer
Knight Science Journalism Fellow, Massachusetts Institute of Technology, Cambridge, Mass.; Executive Director, Council for the Advancement of Science Writing

Richard D. deShazo, M.D.
Immunology (coauthor)
Professor of Medicine and Pediatrics, Department of Medicine, Tulane University School of Medicine, New Orleans, La.

Stephen E. Epstein, M.D.
Heart and Blood Vessels (coauthor)
Chief, Cardiology Branch, National Heart, Lung, and Blood Institute, National Institutes of Health, Bethesda, Md.

Sherman C. Feinstein, M.D.
Eating Disorders (coauthor)
Director, Child Psychiatry Research, Psychosomatic and Psychiatric Institute, Michael Reese Hospital and Medical Center, Chicago; Clinical Professor of Psychiatry, Pritzker School of Medicine, University of Chicago

Arthur L. Frank, M.D., Ph.D.
Environmental and Occupational Health
Professor and Chairman, Department of Preventive Medicine and Environmental Health, University of Kentucky College of Medicine, Lexington

Pierluigi Gambetti, M.D.
Special Report *Fatal Insomnia: A Medical Mystery* (coauthor)
Director, Division of Neuropathology, Institute of Pathology, Case Western Reserve University, Cleveland, Ohio

Richard M. Glass, M.D.
Mental Health and Illness
Associate Professor of Psychiatry, Pritzker School of Medicine, University of Chicago

Mark S. Gold, M.D.
Drug Abuse
Director of Research, Fair Oaks Hospital, Summit, N.J., and Fair Oaks Hospital at Boca/Delray, Delray Beach, Fla.

Jan Hudis
Genetics and **Special Report** *A Controversy in Genetics*
Science Information Editor, March of Dimes Birth Defects
Foundation, White Plains, N.Y.

Raphael Jewelewicz, M.D.
Special Report *Choosing a Child's Sex: Possibilities and
Problems*
Associate Professor of Obstetrics and Gynecology,
Columbia University College of Physicians and Surgeons,
New York City

Robert J. Joynt, M.D., Ph.D.
Neurology
Dean and Vice Provost for Health Affairs, University of
Rochester School of Medicine and Dentistry, Rochester,
N.Y.

Mike C. Korologos
Special Report *Technology's Wonders: New Generations
of Artificial Body Parts*
Free-lance writer, Salt Lake City, Utah

Nathan W. Levin, M.D.
Kidney Disease
Head, Division of Nephrology and Hypertension, Henry
Ford Hospital, Detroit; Clinical Professor of Internal
Medicine, University of Michigan, Ann Arbor

Robert Lindsay, M.B.Ch.B., Ph.D.
Osteoporosis
Director, Regional Bone Center, Helen Hayes Hospital,
West Haverstraw, N.Y.; Professor of Clinical Medicine,
Columbia University College of Physicians and Surgeons,
New York City

Jean D. Lockhart, M.D.
Adolescent Health and *Pediatrics*
Director, Maternal, Child, and Adolescent Health, Ameri-
can Academy of Pediatrics, Elk Grove Village, Ill.

Elio Lugaresi, M.D.
Special Report *Fatal Insomnia: A Medical Mystery* (co-
author)
Director, Neurology Clinic, University of Bologna, Italy

Edward F. Miller
Smoking
Executive Director, American Lung Association of Maine,
Augusta

Pasquale Montagna, M.D.
Special Report *Fatal Insomnia: A Medical Mystery* (co-
author)
Research Fellow, Neurology Clinic, University of Bologna,
Italy

Jane E. Morgan, Ph.D.
Immunology (coauthor)
Department of Medicine, Tulane University School of
Medicine, New Orleans, La.

Ray Moseley
Special Report *Chernobyl Aftermath: Ill Wind over Europe*
London correspondent, *Chicago Tribune*

Tom D. Naughton
Accidents and Safety
Free-lance health and science writer, Chicago

Ralph Pelligra, M.D.
Special Report *Fitness at Zero G*
Medical Services Officer, National Aeronautics and Space
Administration, Ames Research Center, Moffett Field,
Calif.

Arshed A. Quyyumi, M.D.
Heart and Blood Vessels (coauthor)
Associate, Cardiology Branch, National Institutes of
Health, National Heart, Lung, and Blood Institute,
Bethesda, Md.

David B. Reuben, M.D.
Aging
Assistant Professor, Department of Community Health, Brown University Program in Medicine; Associate Physician, Division of General Internal Medicine, Rhode Island Hospital, Providence

R. Bradley Sack, M.D., Sc.D.
Infectious Diseases
Professor of International Health and Director, Division of Geographic Medicine, Johns Hopkins University School of Hygiene and Public Health, Baltimore, Md.

Christopher D. Saudek, M.D.
Diabetes
Director, Johns Hopkins Diabetes Center; Associate Professor of Medicine, Johns Hopkins University School of Medicine, Baltimore, Md.

James C. Sheinin, M.D.
Special Report *Hyperprolactinemia: Increasingly Recognized Hormonal Disorder*
Attending Physician, Division of Endocrinology and Metabolism, Department of Medicine, Michael Reese Hospital and Medical Center, Chicago; Clinical Associate Professor, Pritzker School of Medicine, University of Chicago

Joanne M. Silberner
Awards and Prizes
Health Editor, *U.S. News and World Report,* Washington, D.C.

Arthur D. Sorosky, M.D.
Eating Disorders (coauthor)
Associate Clinical Professor of Psychiatry, University of California at Los Angeles

Alan D. Tice, M.D.
AIDS
Private Practice, Infectious Diseases; Clinical Assistant Professor, University of Washington, Tacoma

George O. Waring III, M.D.
Special Report *Reshaping the Eye for Better Vision*
Professor of Ophthalmology, Emory University School of Medicine, Atlanta, Ga.

Myron Winick, M.D.
Special Report *Limiting Cholesterol: How Early to Begin?*
R. R. Williams Professor of Nutrition; Professor of Pediatrics; Director, Institute of Human Nutrition; and Director, Center for Nutrition, Genetics, and Human Development, Columbia University College of Physicians and Surgeons, New York City

Contributors to the Health Information Update

Beverlee A. Burke
In the Swim and *What's Lurking in Your Kitchen?*
Free-lance health and science writer, Chicago

Paul Cutler, M.D.
Chest Pain
Honorary Clinical Professor of Medicine, Jefferson Medical College, Philadelphia

Marc K. Effron, M.D.
Pacemakers for the Heart
Staff Cardiologist, Specialty Medical Clinic and Scripps Memorial Hospitals Cardiovascular Institute; Clinical Instructor, University of California at San Diego School of Medicine, La Jolla

Todd Wilk Estroff, M.D.
Common Drugs: Psychiatric Side Effects
Medical Director, Gulf Coast Hospital, Fort Walton Beach, Fla.

Vincent A. Fulginiti, M.D.
How Healthy Is Day Care?
Vice Dean and Professor of Pediatrics, College of Medicine, University of Arizona, Tucson

Robert M. Goldwyn, M.D.
Plastic Surgery of the Breast
Clinical Professor of Surgery, Harvard University Medical School; Senior Surgeon and Head, Division of Plastic Surgery, Beth Israel Hospital; Senior Surgeon, Brigham and Women's Hospital, Boston

Edward C. Hill, M.D.
Estrogen Replacement Therapy
Professor, Obstetrics and Gynecology, School of Medicine, University of California at San Francisco

Alan E. Kazdin, Ph.D.
Behavior Therapy
Professor of Psychiatry and Psychology, Western Psychiatric Institute, School of Medicine, University of Pittsburgh, Pa.

Tom D. Naughton
Hazards of the High-Tech Kitchen; Hands at Risk; and *Progressive Resistance Exercise*
Free-lance health and science writer, Chicago

Marcia J. Opp
Littlest Swimmers
Free-lance health and science writer, Chicago

Reed E. Pyeritz, M.D., Ph.D.
Marfan Syndrome
Associate Professor, Medicine and Pediatrics, and Director, Medical Genetics Clinic, Johns Hopkins University School of Medicine, Baltimore, Md.

Bruce D. Shephard, M.D.
Problem Pregnancies
Clinical Associate Professor, Department of Obstetrics and Gynecology, University of South Florida College of Medicine, Tampa

Richard J. Simonsen, D.D.S.
Say "Cheese": Today's Cosmetic Dentistry
Chairman, Department of General Dentistry, College of Dentistry, University of Tennessee, Memphis

Joseph Wartak, M.D.
Delivering the Right Dosage
Associate Professor, Department of Surgery, Faculty of Medicine, University of Alberta, Edmonton

Myron Winick, M.D.
Breakfast: How Important Is It?
R. R. Williams Professor of Nutrition; Professor of Pediatrics; Director, Institute of Human Nutrition; and Director, Center for Nutrition, Genetics, and Human Development, Columbia University College of Physicians and Surgeons, New York City

Title cartoons by John Everds

Index

This is a three-year cumulative index. Index entries to *World of Medicine* articles in this and previous editions of the *Medical and Health Annual* are set in boldface type, *e.g.* **Alcoholism.** Entries to other subjects are set in lightface type, *e.g.,* amniocentesis. Additional information on any of these subjects is identified with a subheading and indented under the entry heading. The numbers following headings and subheadings indicate the year (boldface) of the edition and the page number (lightface) on which the information appears. The abbreviation "*il.*" indicates an illustration.

> **Alcoholism 87**–280; **86**–184
> fetal alcohol syndrome **88**–359
> polydrug abuse **87**–310
> Soviet campaign (special report) **87**–277
> testing **88**–346
> *see also* Drug Abuse
> astigmatism
> contact lens correction **87**–485
> surgery (special report) **88**–401

All entry headings are alphabetized word by word. Hyphenated words and words separated by dashes or slashes are treated as two words. When one word differs from another only by the presence of additional characters at the end, the shorter precedes the longer. In inverted names, the words following the comma are considered only after the preceding part of the name has been alphabetized. Names beginning with "Mc" and "Mac" are alphabetized as "Mac"; "St." is alphabetized as "Saint." Examples:

> Lake
> Lake, Simon
> Lake Charles
> Lakeland

N ow there's a way to identify all your fine books with flair and style. As part of our continuing service to you, Britannica Home Library Service, Inc. is proud to be able to offer you the fine quality item shown on the next page.

B ooklovers will love the heavy-duty personalized embosser. Now you can personalize all your fine books with the mark of distinction, just the way all the fine libraries of the world do.

T o order this item, please type or print your name, address and zip code on a plain sheet of paper. (Note special instructions for ordering the embosser). Please send a check or money order only (your money will be refunded in full if you are not delighted) for the full amount of purchase, including postage and handling, to:

Britannica Home Library Service, Inc.
Attn: Yearbook Department
Post Office Box 6137
Chicago, Illinois 60680

(Please make remittance payable to: Britannica Home Library Service, Inc.)

IN THE BRITANNICA TRADITION OF QUALITY...

PERSONAL EMBOSSER

A mark of distinction for your fine books. A book embosser just like the ones used in libraries. The 1½″ seal imprints "Library of _____" (with the name of your choice) and up to three centered initials. Please type or print clearly BOTH full name (up to 26 letters including spaces between names) and up to three initials.
Please allow six weeks for delivery.

Just $20.00

plus $2.00 shipping and handling

This offer available only in the United States.
Illinois residents please add sales tax

 Britannica Home Library Service, Inc.